TRANS HISTORY

FROM ANCIENT TIMES TO THE PRESENT DAY

TRANS HISTORY

FROM ANCIENT TIMES TO THE PRESENT DAY

a graphic novel by
ALEX L. COMBS
&
ANDREW EAKETT

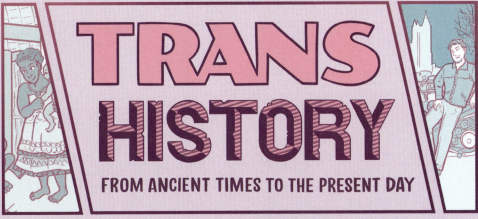

CANDLEWICK PRESS

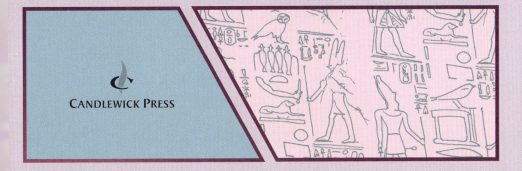

CONTENTS

PREFACE vi

INTRODUCTION TO TRANS HISTORY 1

CHAPTER 1
A Long, Long Time Ago: The Ancient World 9

CHAPTER 2
Europeans Behaving Badly: From the Old World
to the "New" World 51

CHAPTER 3
Sex and Gender Under the Microscope: Sexology 93

CHAPTER 4
Progress and Backlash: Trans in the USA 155

CHAPTER 5
The Present Moment: Community Voices 259

ACKNOWLEDGMENTS 355

SOURCE NOTES 358

INDEX 371

PREFACE

Dear readers,

Thanks for picking up *Trans History: From Ancient Times to the Present Day*!

We hope this book will accomplish three things:

1. Help dispel the myth that trans people are a "new thing."
2. Demonstrate that what it means to be trans varies greatly among trans people.
3. Empower trans people by helping them learn about trans history.

We're nerds who are excited about trans history and want to share what we know! Over the years it took to research, write, and illustrate this book, it has become clear to us how urgently this information is needed. As the spread of misinformation about trans people continues to accelerate, there have been an unprecedented number of anti-trans laws introduced and passed in the US.

We are not accredited historians. So, when writing this book we stuck to the most well-known and documented research, finding primary sources whenever possible, and checking our understanding of the information with historians and other experts.

The first two chapters give examples of people whose lives provide evidence that trans people have existed much longer than most people realize. We're not trying to prove that any of these historical figures would have identified as trans, but their lives are relevant to trans history. Chapter three primarily focuses on the emergence of sexology and the roots of trans medicalization in Europe. Chapter four brings us to the current medical model of transness, as well as the beginnings of political activism by trans people in the US and media representations of trans people. The final chapter shares a variety of trans and GNC people's perspectives presented in their own words.

This book is written from a specific viewpoint—that of two trans white-passing Americans raised in the US. Therefore, we wanted to avoid attempting to explain identities with which we're not personally familiar. Instead, when talking about other identities, we focused on how culturally dominant Western biases have been imposed on them. Our goal here is to share information while holding white people accountable and without perpetuating harmful stereotypes.

One beautiful thing about trans history, and the larger history of gender diversity on Earth, is that it's so vast and enormous it could never fit in one book. We hope that this comic will be a jumping-off point for further exploration!

CONTENT WARNING

Being trans ourselves, studying and writing about this history has been rewarding but difficult. The history covered in this book involves a lot of disturbing and anti-trans viewpoints, as well as violence against a variety of people who didn't conform to prevailing norms. Violence is not visually depicted in this comic (except for a skirmish in which the trans person has the upper hand), but there is a lot of discussion of it. The book also includes discussion of abuse, suicide, racism, anti-Semitism, ableism, misogyny, homophobia, and violence against intersex people.

QUOTATIONS

Direct quotations from primary sources are used whenever possible and are indicated with quotation marks. You can find more info about these quotations in the notes at the end of the book. The only section that doesn't follow this rule is the "Community Voices" chapter, because it consists only of the words of the interviewees. A longer list of the sources we used is available as a downloadable PDF on the book's website: alexlcombs.com/transhistory.

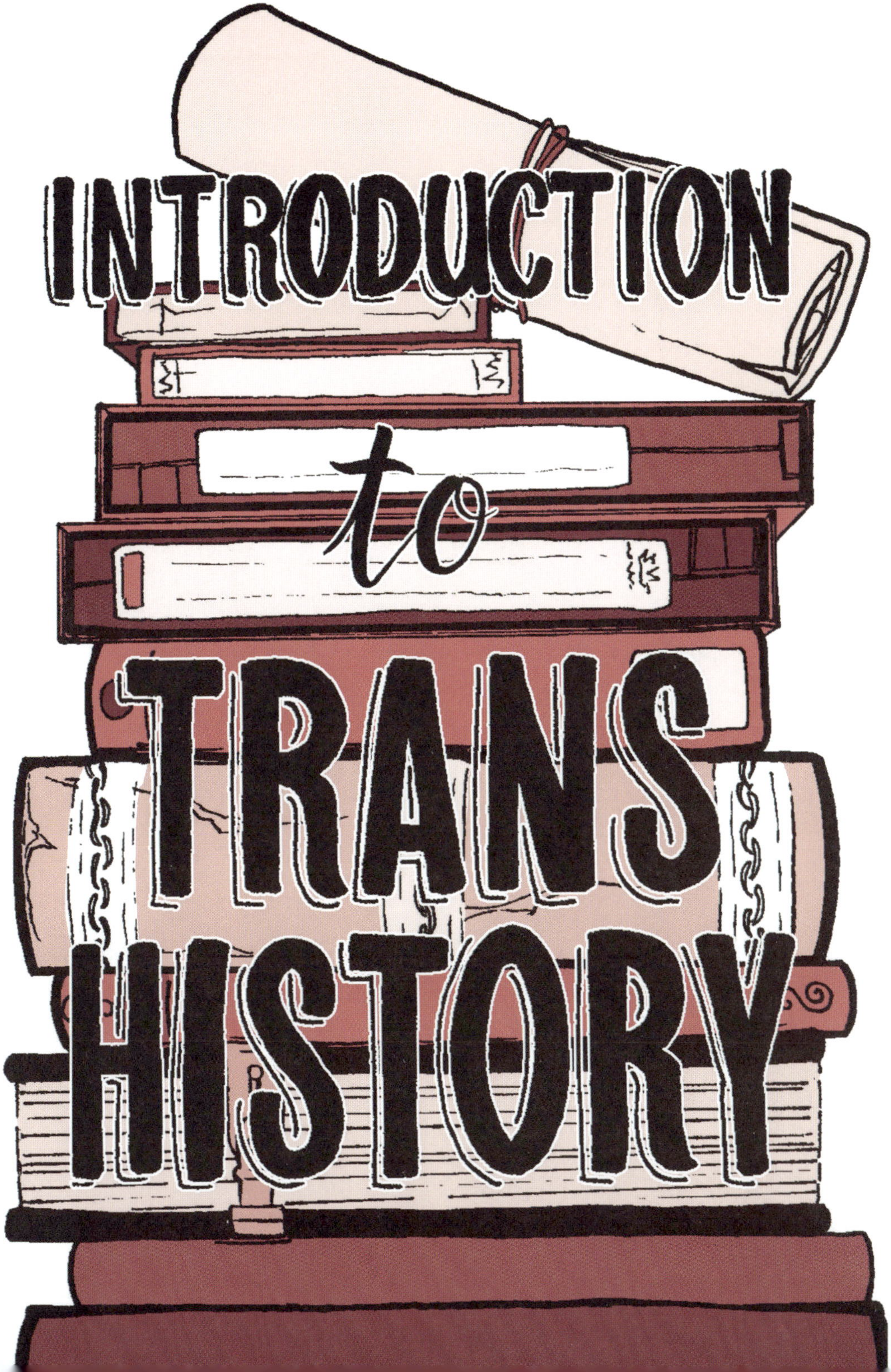
INTRODUCTION
to
TRANS
HISTORY

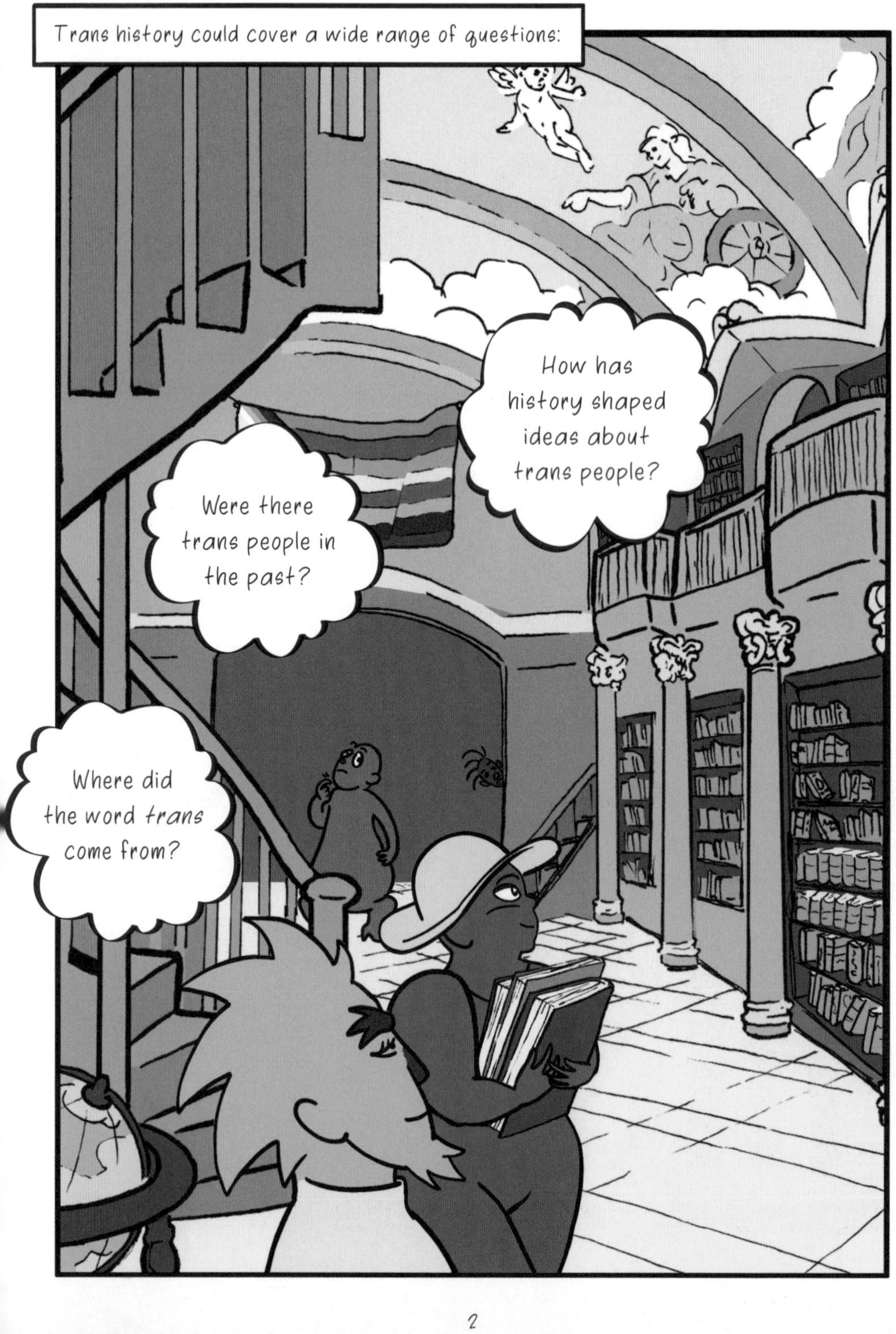
Trans history could cover a wide range of questions:
How has history shaped ideas about trans people?
Were there trans people in the past?
Where did the word *trans* come from?

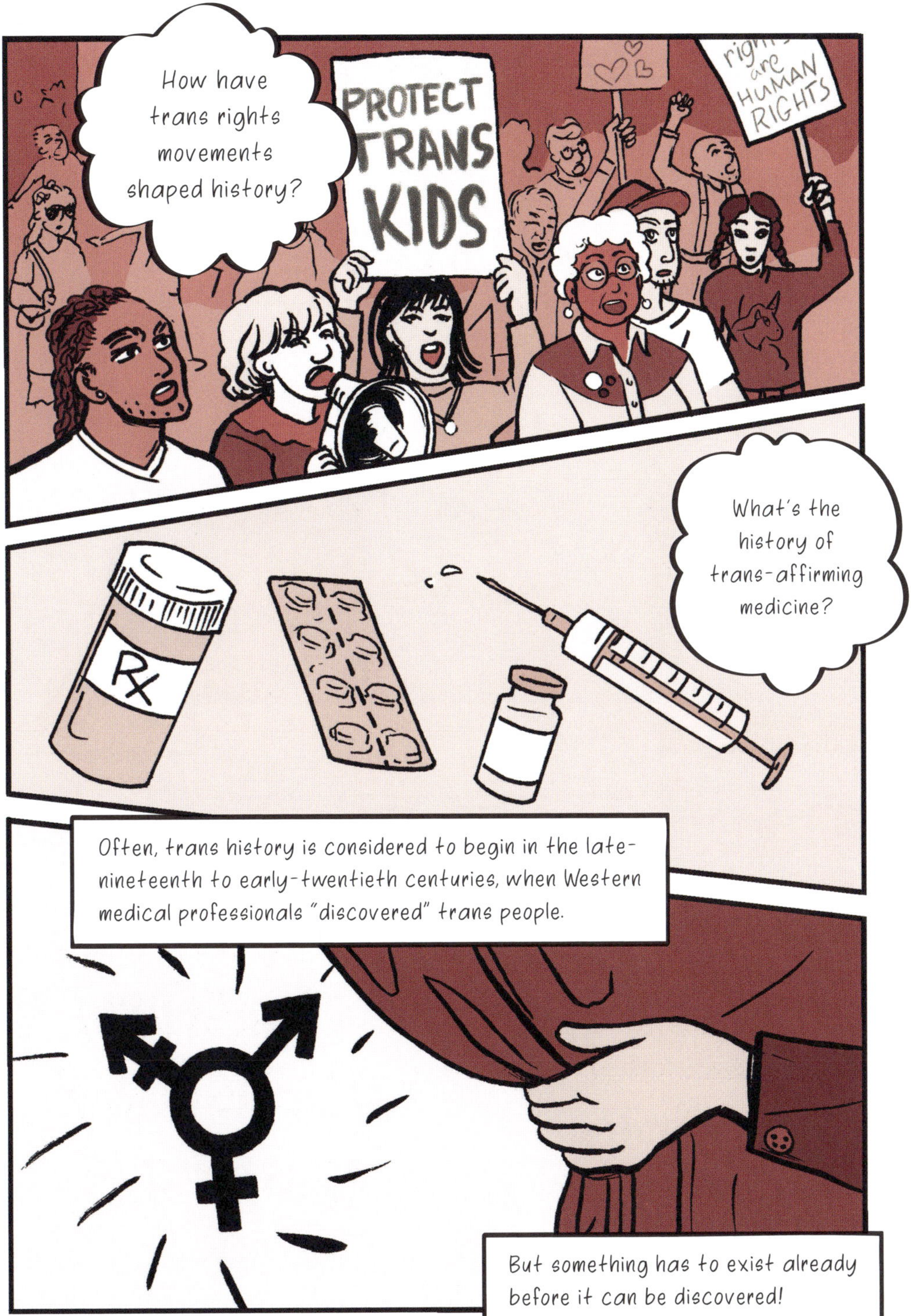
How have trans rights movements shaped history?
PROTECT TRANS KIDS
are HUMAN RIGHTS
What's the history of trans-affirming medicine?
Rx
Often, trans history is considered to begin in the late-nineteenth to early-twentieth centuries, when Western medical professionals "discovered" trans people.
But something has to exist already before it can be discovered!

What does TRANS mean?

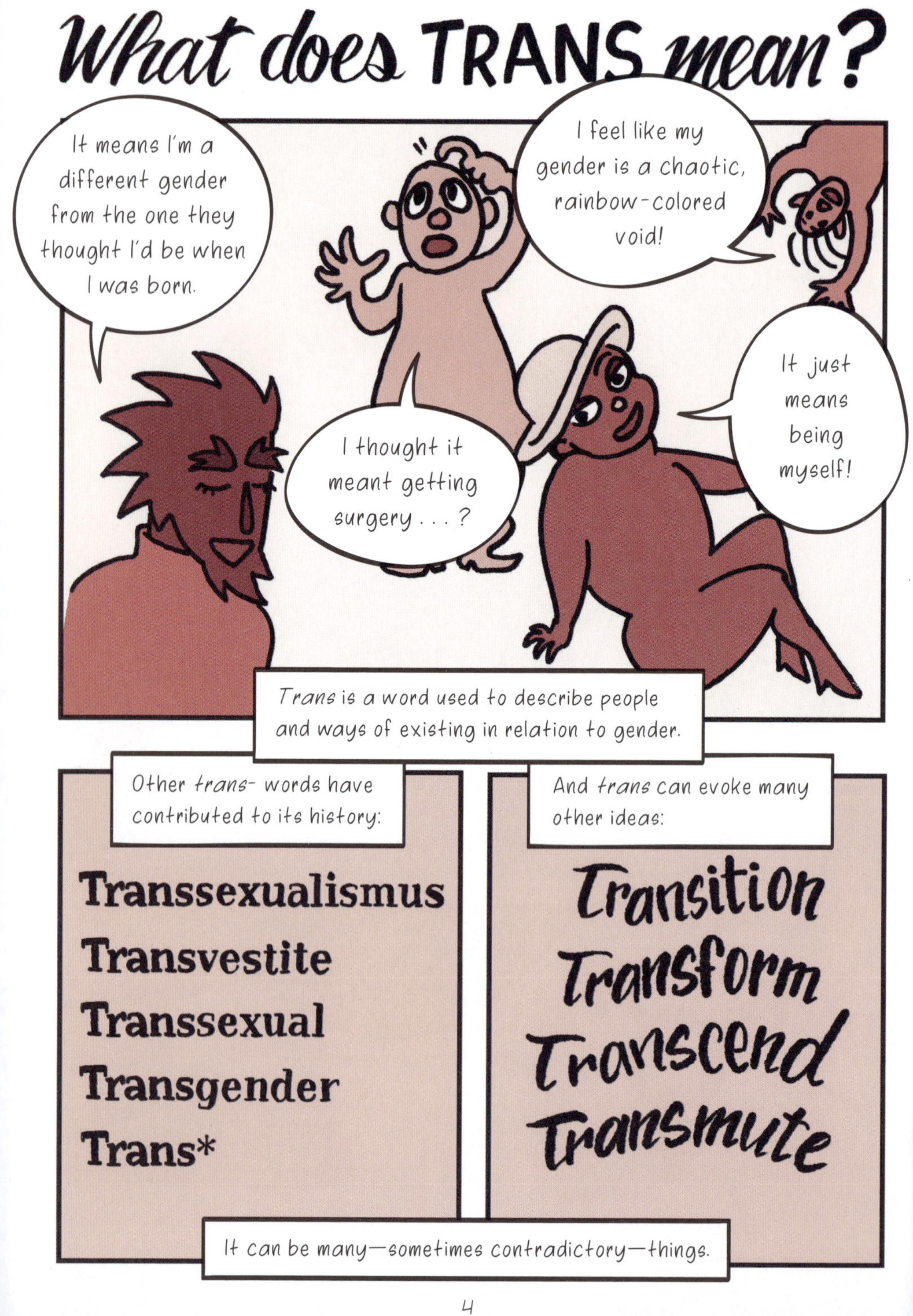
It means I'm a different gender from the one they thought I'd be when I was born.
I feel like my gender is a chaotic, rainbow-colored void!
I thought it meant getting surgery . . . ?
It just means being myself!
Trans is a word used to describe people and ways of existing in relation to gender.
Other *trans-* words have contributed to its history:
Transsexualismus
Transvestite
Transsexual
Transgender
Trans*
And *trans* can evoke many other ideas:
Transition
Transform
Transcend
Transmute
It can be many—sometimes contradictory—things.

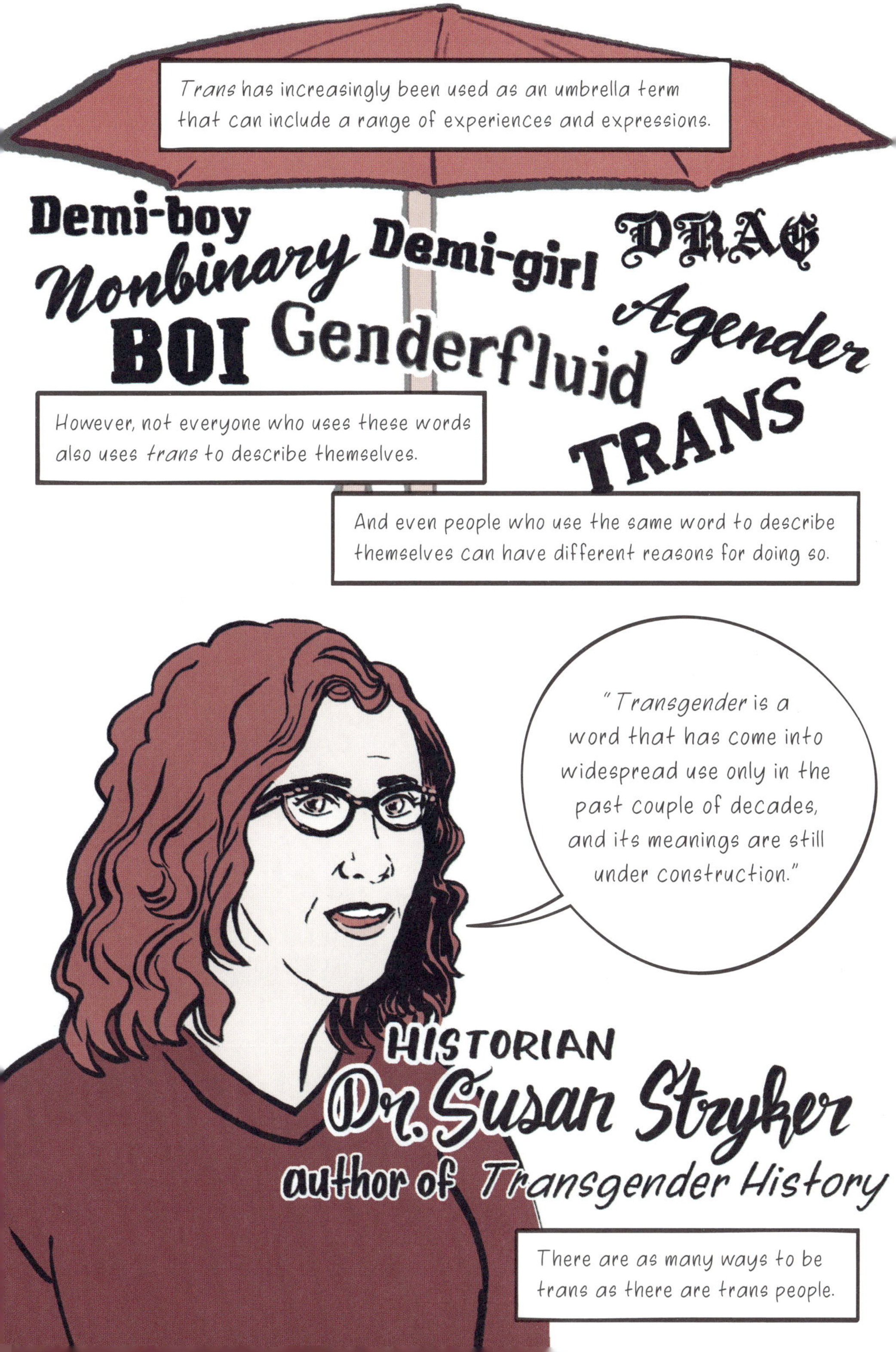
Trans has increasingly been used as an umbrella term that can include a range of experiences and expressions.
Demi-boy
Nonbinary
Demi-girl
DRAG
BOI
Genderfluid
Agender
TRANS
However, not everyone who uses these words also uses *trans* to describe themselves.
And even people who use the same word to describe themselves can have different reasons for doing so.
"*Transgender* is a word that has come into widespread use only in the past couple of decades, and its meanings are still under construction."
HISTORIAN
Dr. Susan Stryker
author of *Transgender History*
There are as many ways to be trans as there are trans people.

People often point to identities from cultures outside their own in order to show that trans people exist everywhere, but they are not exactly the same thing as trans, or as one another.

Besides trans, there are many other examples of culturally specific gender identities used by people living today, and they have unique and evolving histories that could fill entire books of their own.

Quariwarmi ANDES REGION in SOUTH AMERICA

Tchinda Cape Verde

Fa'afafine and Fa'afatama SAMOA

Two-Spirit TURTLE ISLAND

Dilbaa and Nádleehi DINÉ (NORTH AMERICA)

Muxe SOUTHERN MEXICO

Winkte LAKOTA (NORTH AMERICA)

Baté CROW (NORTH AMERICA)

Hijra INDIA and PAKISTAN

Khawaja Sara PAKISTAN

Māhū HAWAII

Vakasalewalewa FIJI

Leiti TONGA

Omeggid GUNA YALA

Travesti SOUTH AMERICAN and LATIN AMERICAN COUNTRIES

跨兒 Kuà er HONG KONG

Phuying THAILAND

X-gender JAPAN

Burrnesha ALBANIA

Although many people from these communities also identify as trans, there are many who intentionally don't.

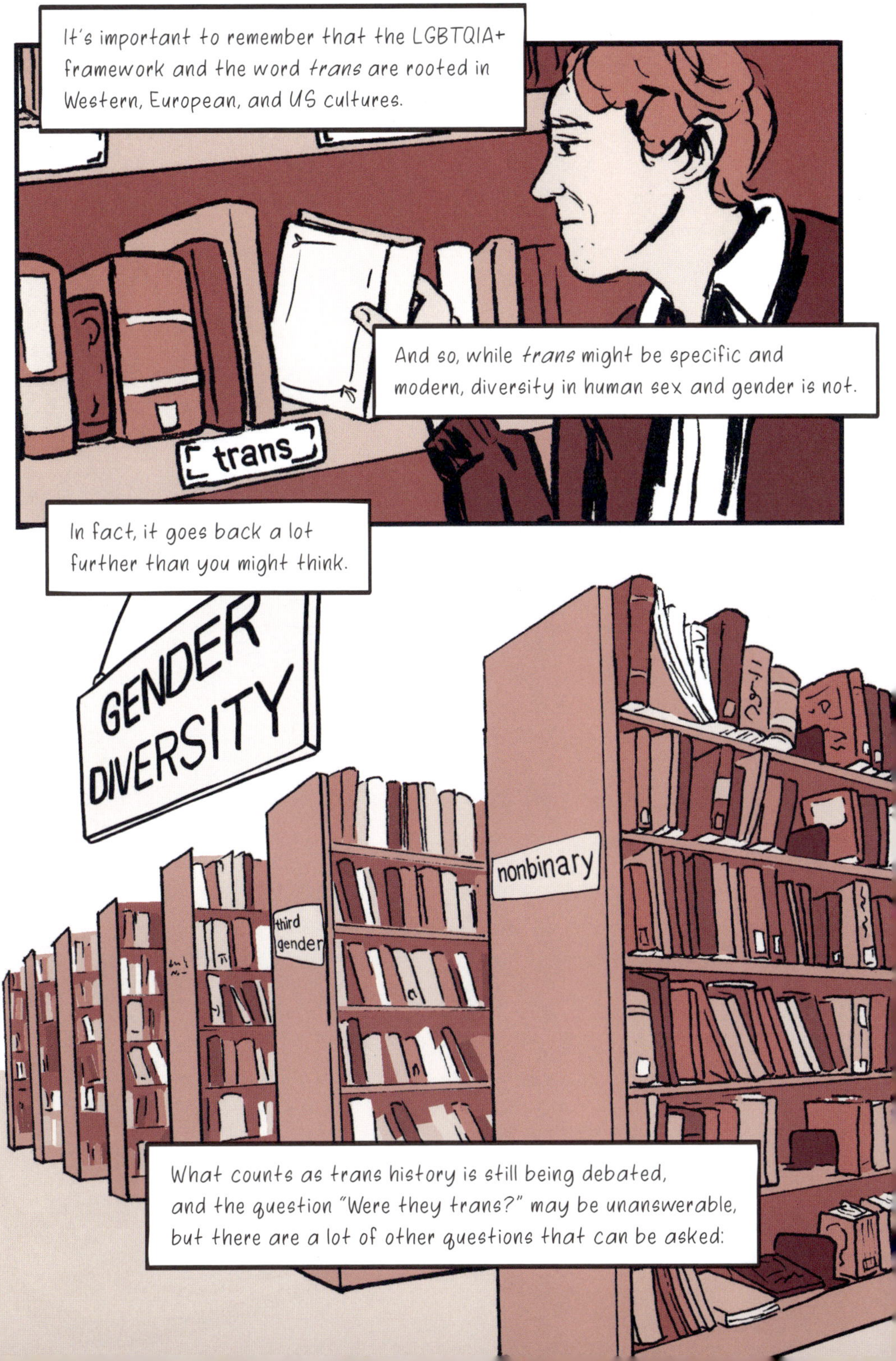
It's important to remember that the LGBTQIA+ framework and the word trans are rooted in Western, European, and US cultures.
trans
And so, while trans might be specific and modern, diversity in human sex and gender is not.
In fact, it goes back a lot further than you might think.
GENDER DIVERSITY
third gender
nonbinary
What counts as trans history is still being debated, and the question "Were they trans?" may be unanswerable, but there are a lot of other questions that can be asked:

Why do we care whether historical figures were trans or not?

How do these individuals' lives reflect or resist contemporary trans narratives?

Do these stories challenge any common assumptions about the timelessness of gender roles?

How has this history shaped the lives of trans and gender-nonconforming people?

Does learning about the people in this book open any possibilities for self-understanding?

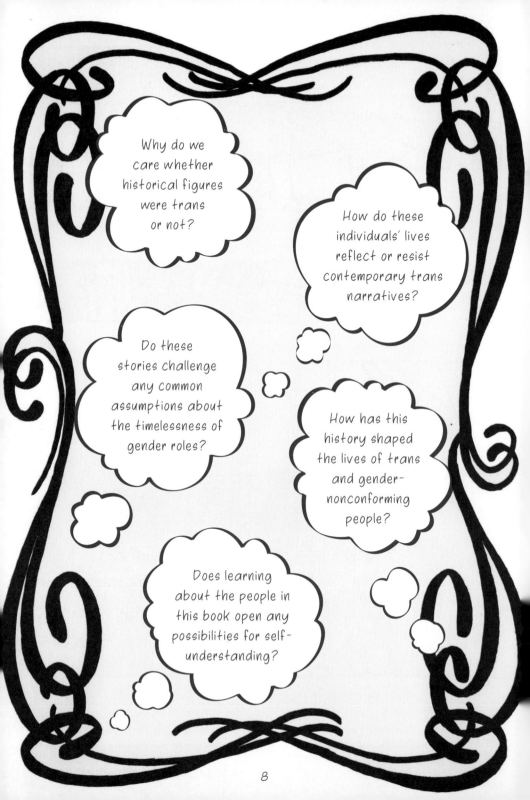

1

A Long, Long Time Ago: The Ancient World

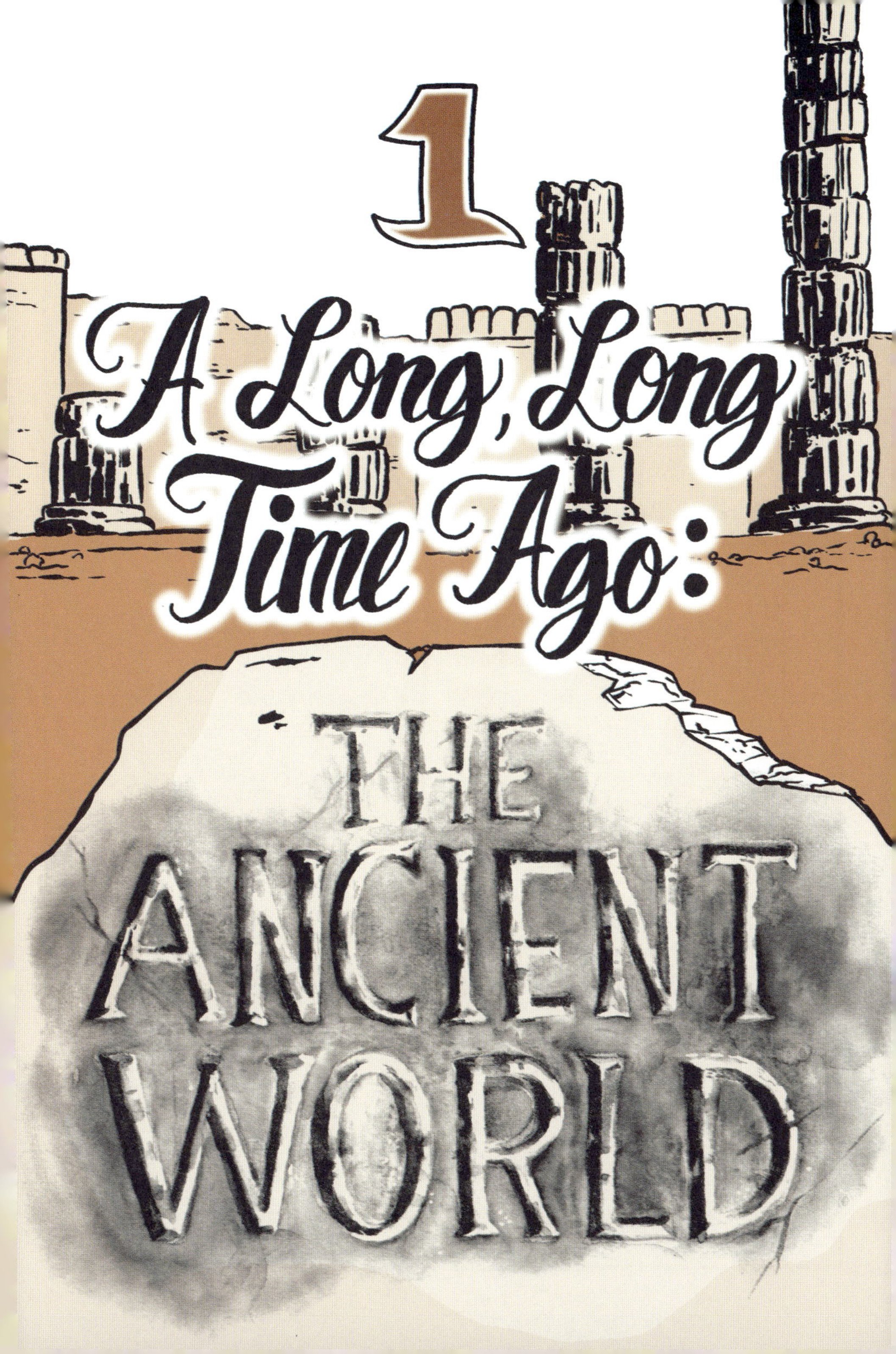

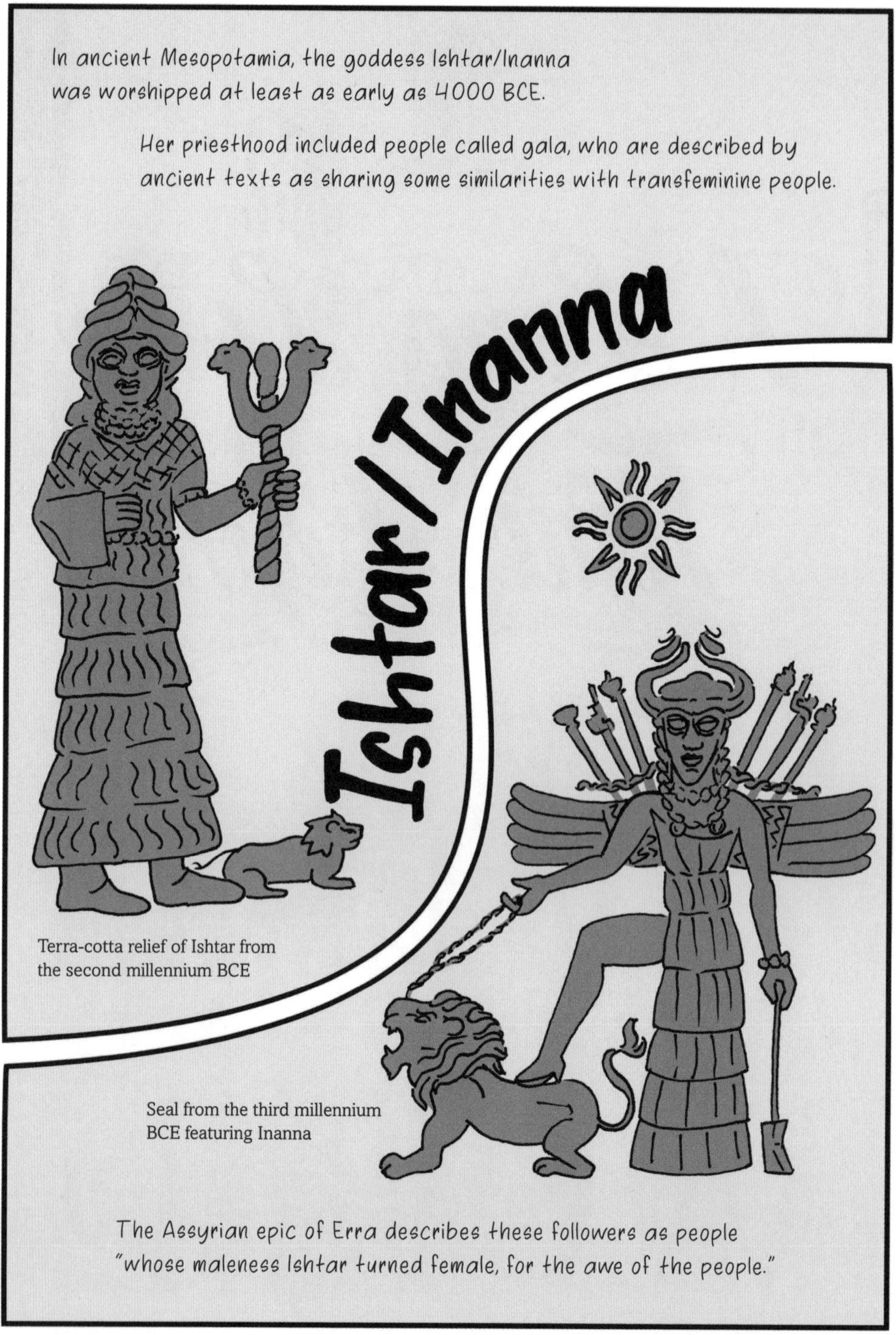
In ancient Mesopotamia, the goddess Ishtar/Inanna was worshipped at least as early as 4000 BCE.
Her priesthood included people called gala, who are described by ancient texts as sharing some similarities with transfeminine people.
Ishtar/Inanna
The Assyrian epic of Erra describes these followers as people "whose maleness Ishtar turned female, for the awe of the people."

Terra-cotta relief of Ishtar from the second millennium BCE

Seal from the third millennium BCE featuring Inanna

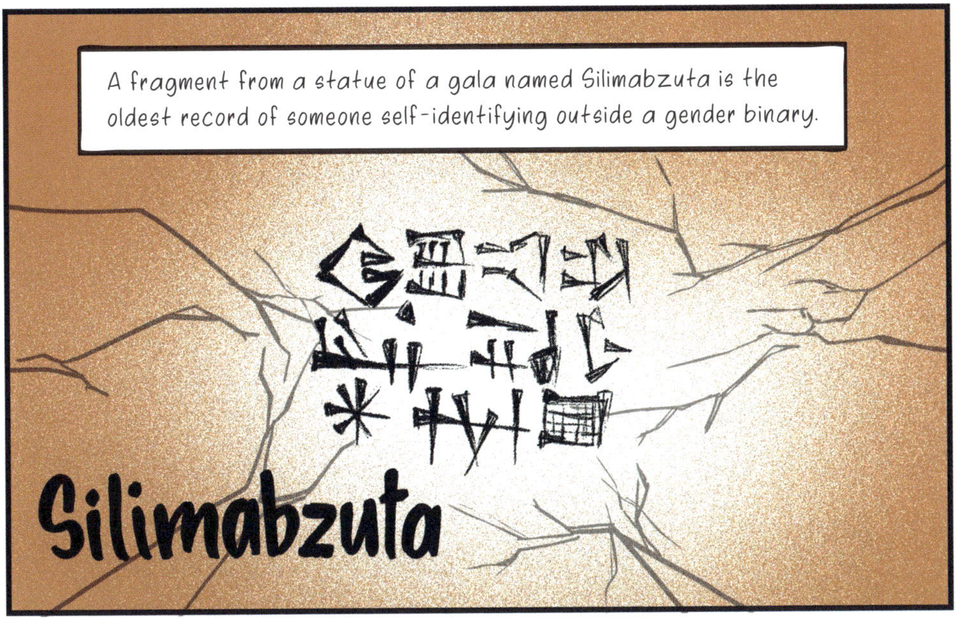
A fragment from a statue of a gala named Silimabzuta is the oldest record of someone self-identifying outside a gender binary.
Silimabzuta

Cuneiform from the third millennium BCE found in a temple to Inanna, courtesy of Cheryl Morgan

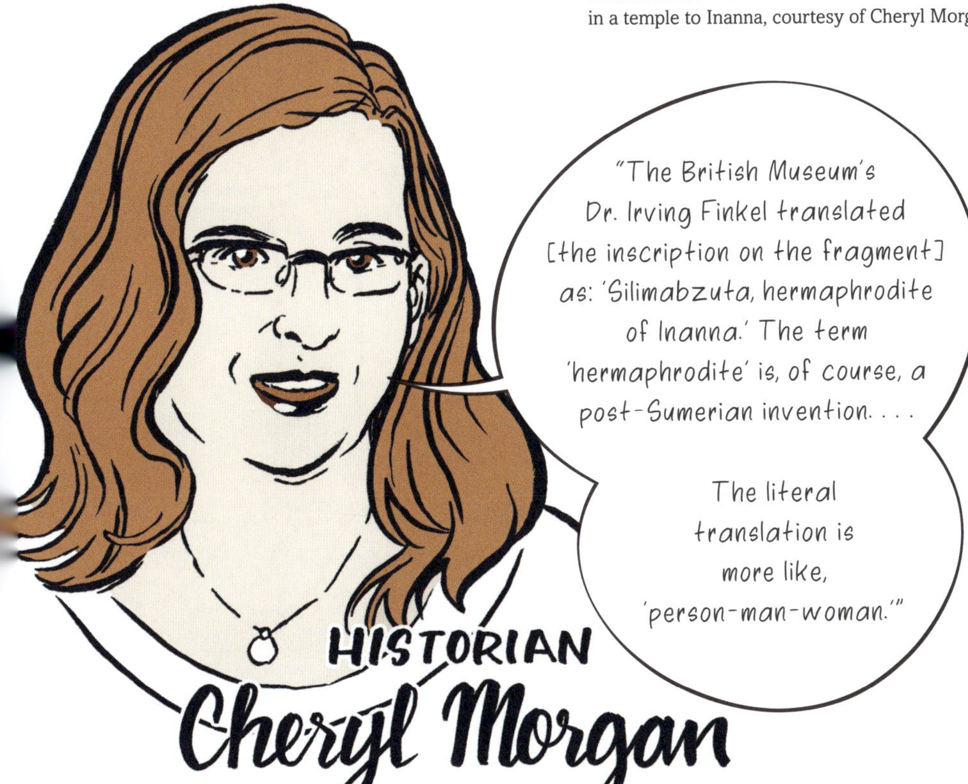
"The British Museum's Dr. Irving Finkel translated [the inscription on the fragment] as: 'Silimabzuta, hermaphrodite of Inanna.' The term 'hermaphrodite' is, of course, a post-Sumerian invention. . . .
The literal translation is more like, 'person-man-woman.'"
HISTORIAN
Cheryl Morgan

The rest of Silimabzuta's statue has been destroyed, but it's speculated to have looked something like another one that was found in the same temple . . .

that of a singer named Ur-Nanshe, who may also have been a gala.

Ur-Nanshe

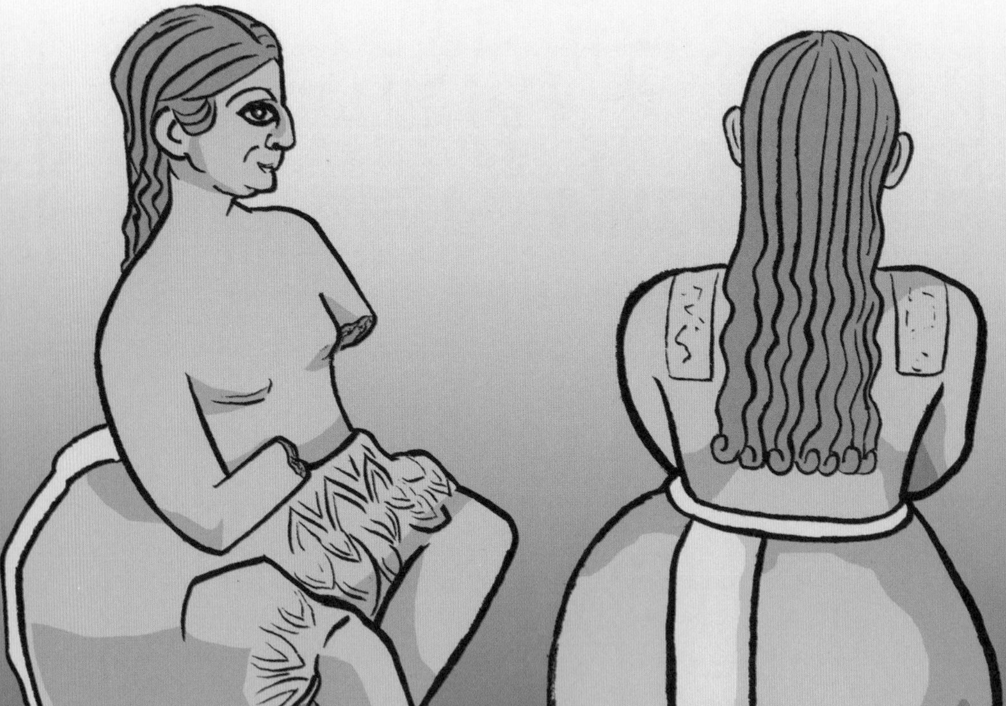

The masculine name of Ur-Nanshe, accompanied by the appearance of breast buds, has led researchers to speculate that Ur-Nanshe may have been a gala who had their testicles removed.

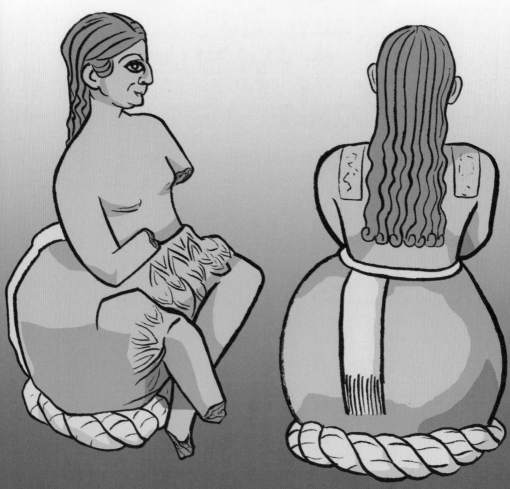

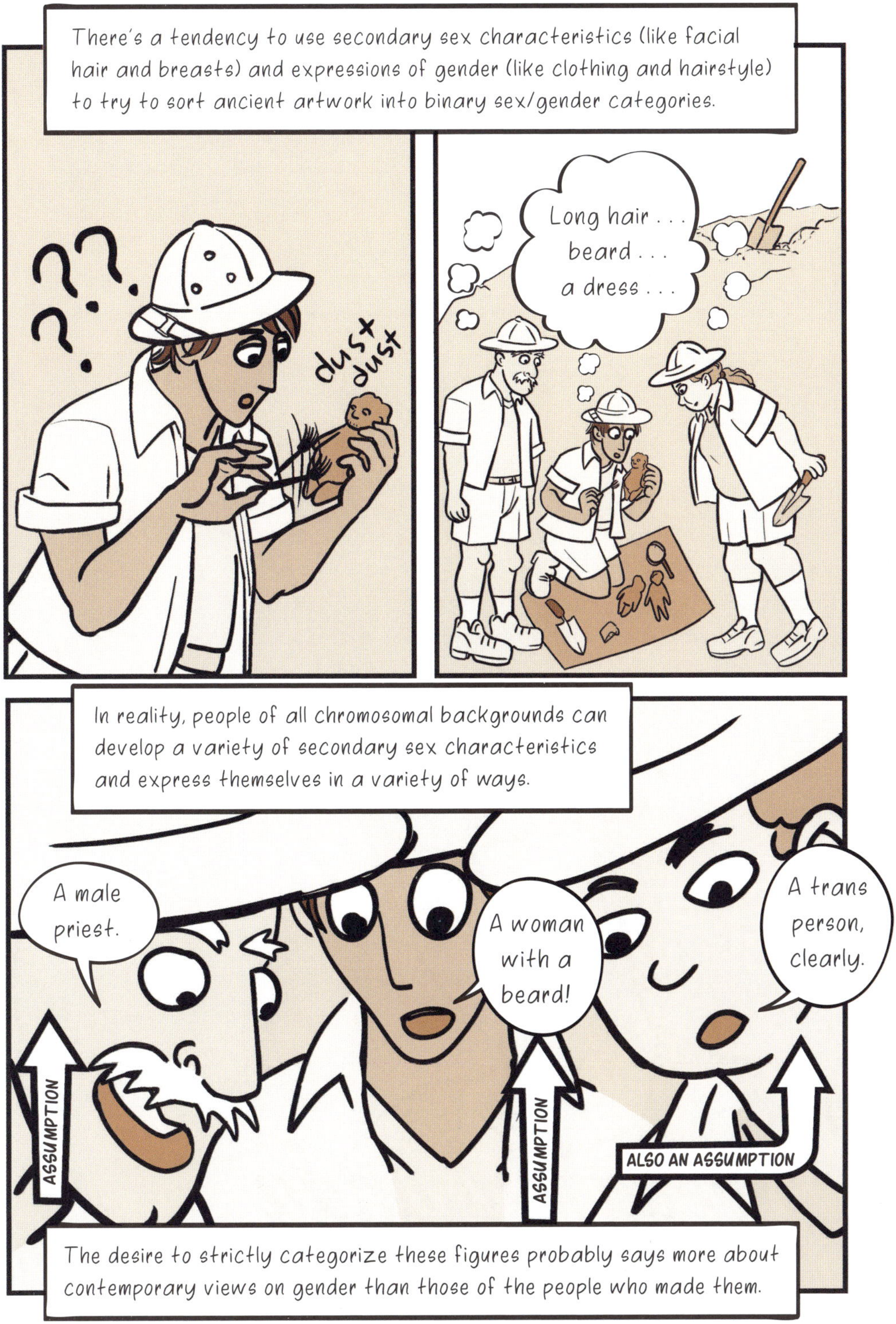
There's a tendency to use secondary sex characteristics (like facial hair and breasts) and expressions of gender (like clothing and hairstyle) to try to sort ancient artwork into binary sex/gender categories.
???
dust dust
Long hair . . . beard . . . a dress . . .
In reality, people of all chromosomal backgrounds can develop a variety of secondary sex characteristics and express themselves in a variety of ways.
A male priest.
A woman with a beard!
A trans person, clearly.
ASSUMPTION
ASSUMPTION
ALSO AN ASSUMPTION
The desire to strictly categorize these figures probably says more about contemporary views on gender than those of the people who made them.

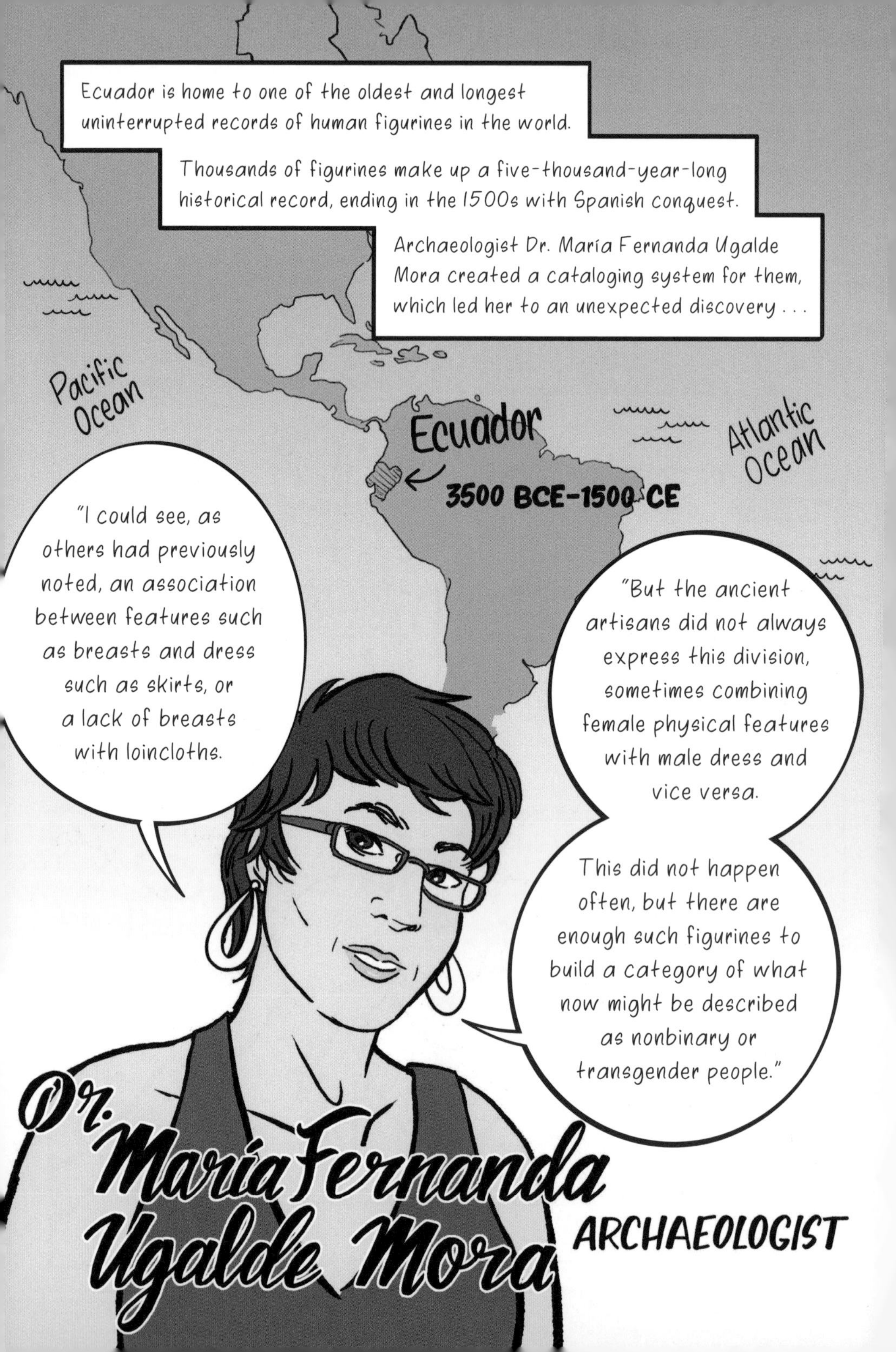

Ecuador is home to one of the oldest and longest uninterrupted records of human figurines in the world.
Thousands of figurines make up a five-thousand-year-long historical record, ending in the 1500s with Spanish conquest.
Archaeologist Dr. María Fernanda Ugalde Mora created a cataloging system for them, which led her to an unexpected discovery . . .
Pacific Ocean
Ecuador
3500 BCE–1500 CE
Atlantic Ocean
"I could see, as others had previously noted, an association between features such as breasts and dress such as skirts, or a lack of breasts with loincloths.
"But the ancient artisans did not always express this division, sometimes combining female physical features with male dress and vice versa.
This did not happen often, but there are enough such figurines to build a category of what now might be described as nonbinary or transgender people."
Dr. María Fernanda Ugalde Mora
ARCHAEOLOGIST

As opposed to being archetypal, the figures are thought to represent actual individual people.

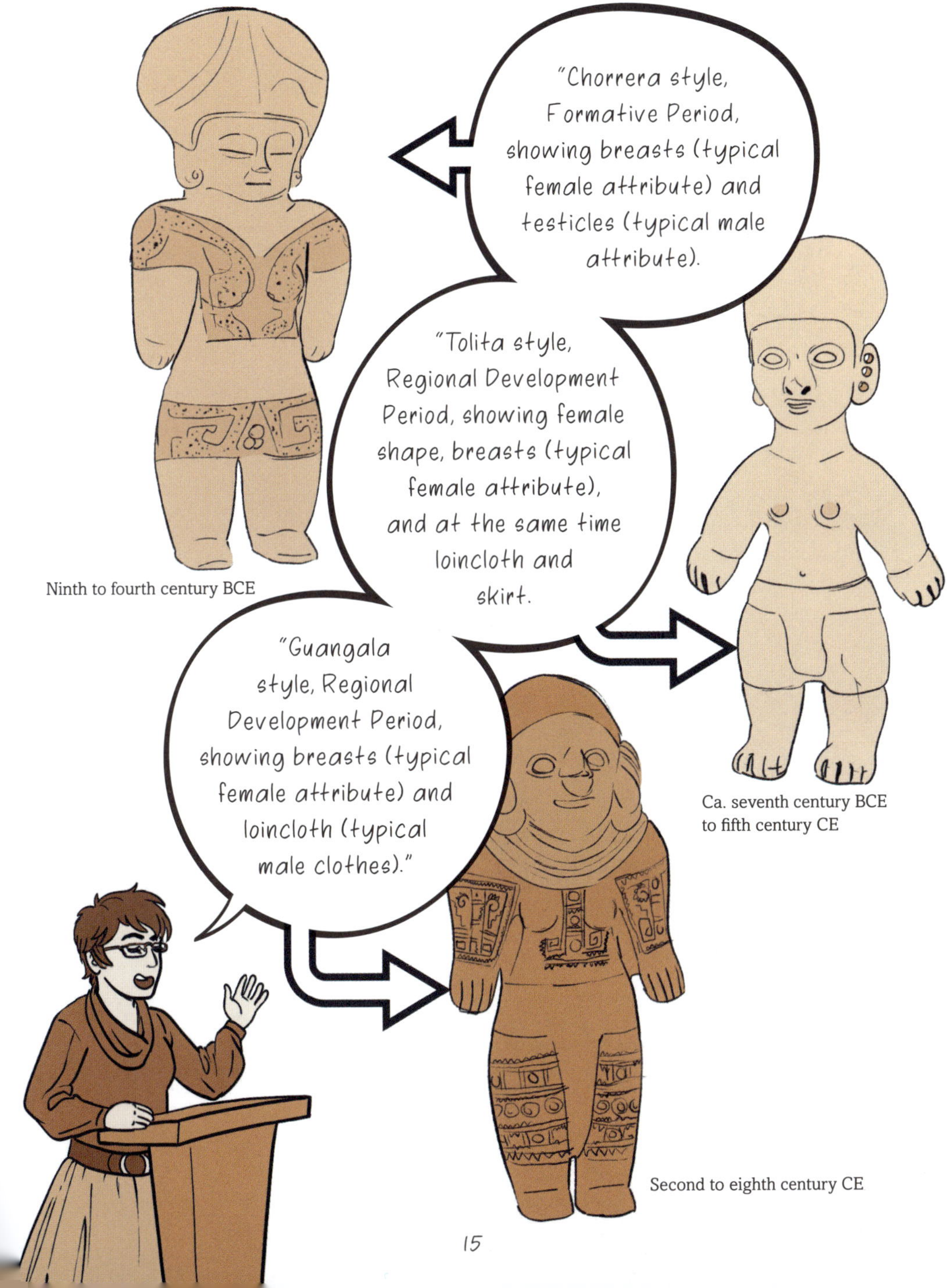
"Chorrera style, Formative Period, showing breasts (typical female attribute) and testicles (typical male attribute).
"Tolita style, Regional Development Period, showing female shape, breasts (typical female attribute), and at the same time loincloth and skirt.
"Guangala style, Regional Development Period, showing breasts (typical female attribute) and loincloth (typical male clothes)."
Ninth to fourth century BCE
Ca. seventh century BCE to fifth century CE
Second to eighth century CE

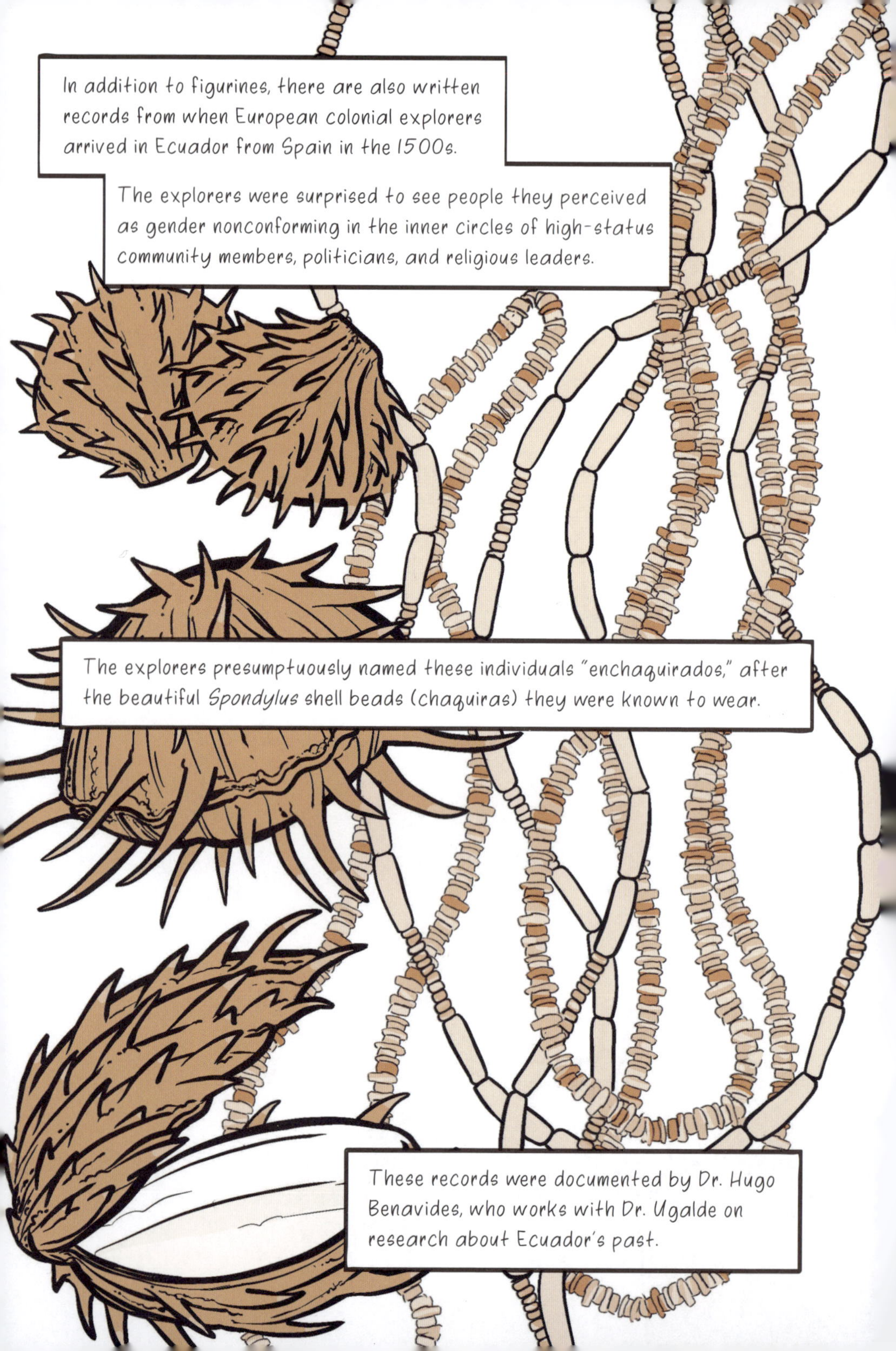
In addition to figurines, there are also written records from when European colonial explorers arrived in Ecuador from Spain in the 1500s.
The explorers were surprised to see people they perceived as gender nonconforming in the inner circles of high-status community members, politicians, and religious leaders.
The explorers presumptuously named these individuals "enchaquirados," after the beautiful *Spondylus* shell beads (chaquiras) they were known to wear.
These records were documented by Dr. Hugo Benavides, who works with Dr. Ugalde on research about Ecuador's past.

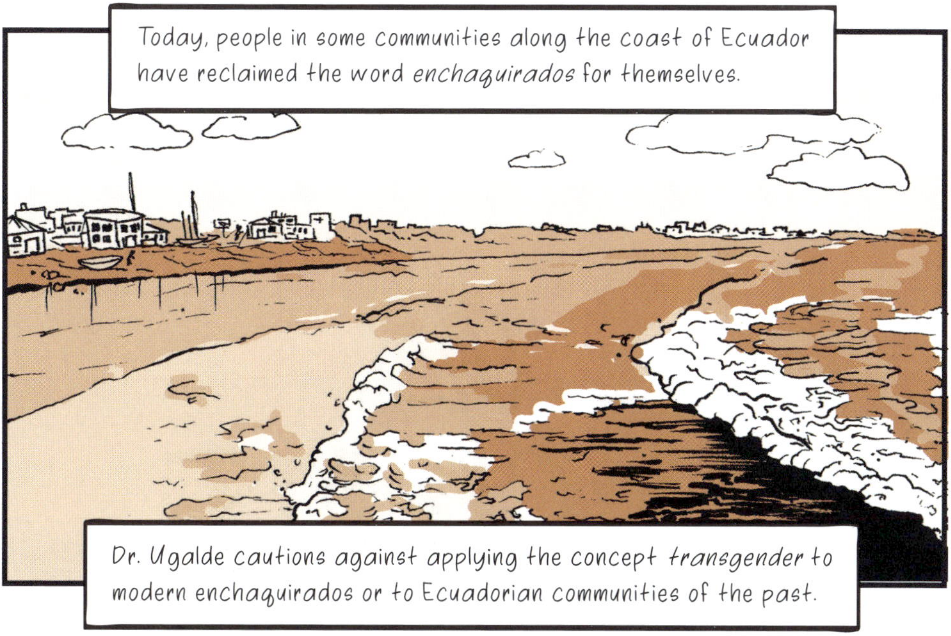
Today, people in some communities along the coast of Ecuador have reclaimed the word *enchaquirados* for themselves.
Dr. Ugalde cautions against applying the concept *transgender* to modern enchaquirados or to Ecuadorian communities of the past.

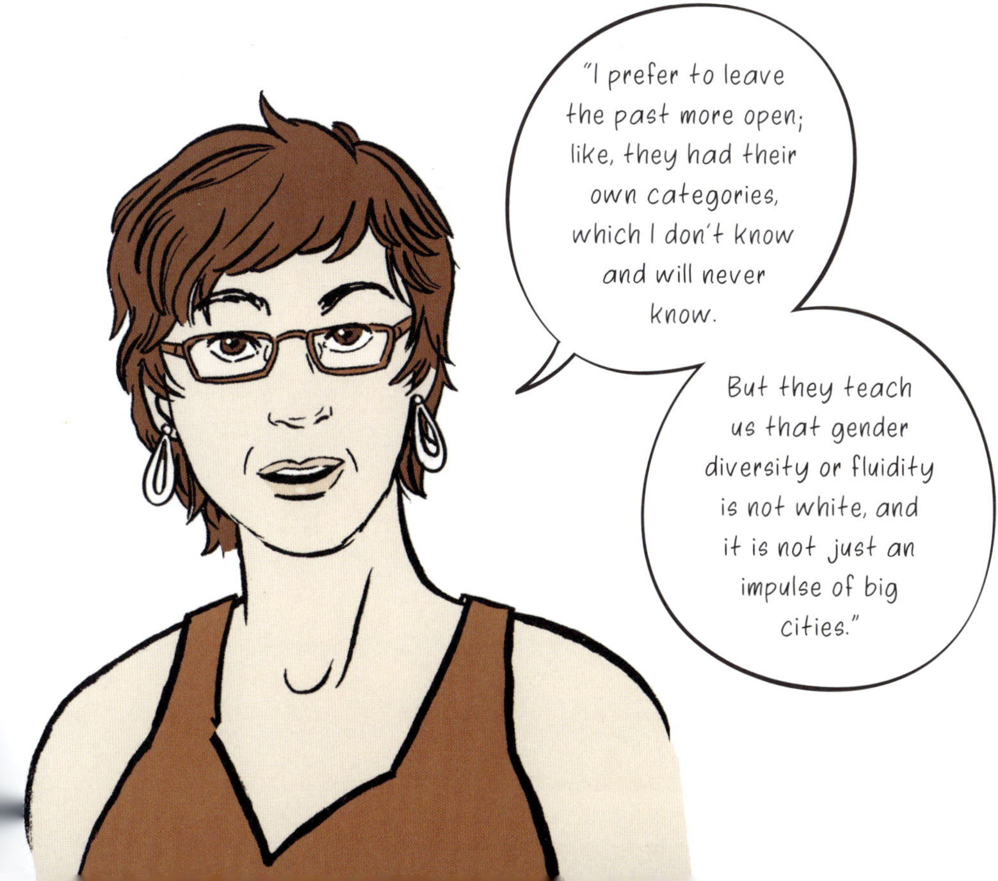
"I prefer to leave the past more open; like, they had their own categories, which I don't know and will never know.
But they teach us that gender diversity or fluidity is not white, and it is not just an impulse of big cities."

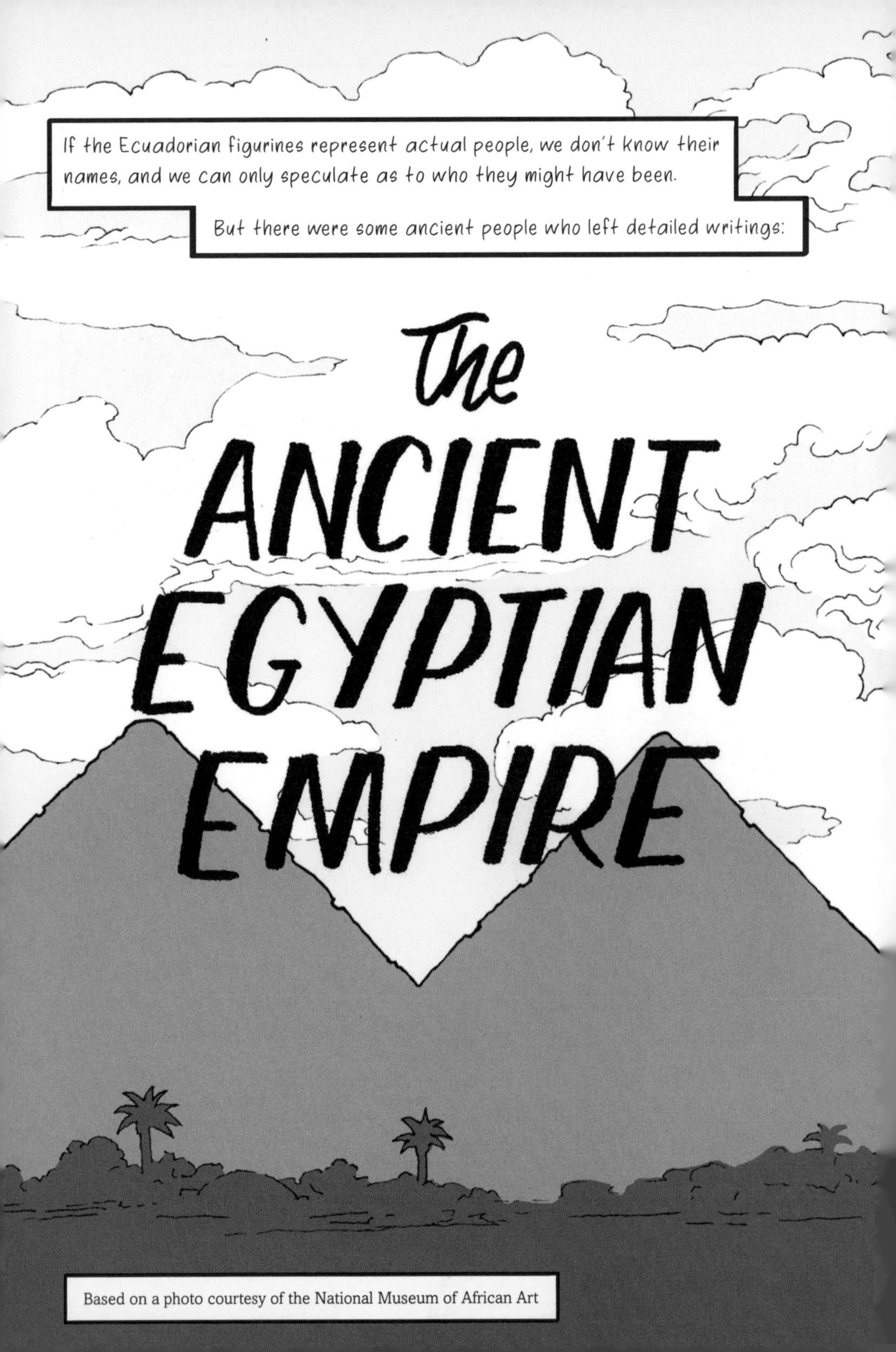
If the Ecuadorian figurines represent actual people, we don't know their names, and we can only speculate as to who they might have been.
But there were some ancient people who left detailed writings:
The ANCIENT EGYPTIAN EMPIRE
Based on a photo courtesy of the National Museum of African Art

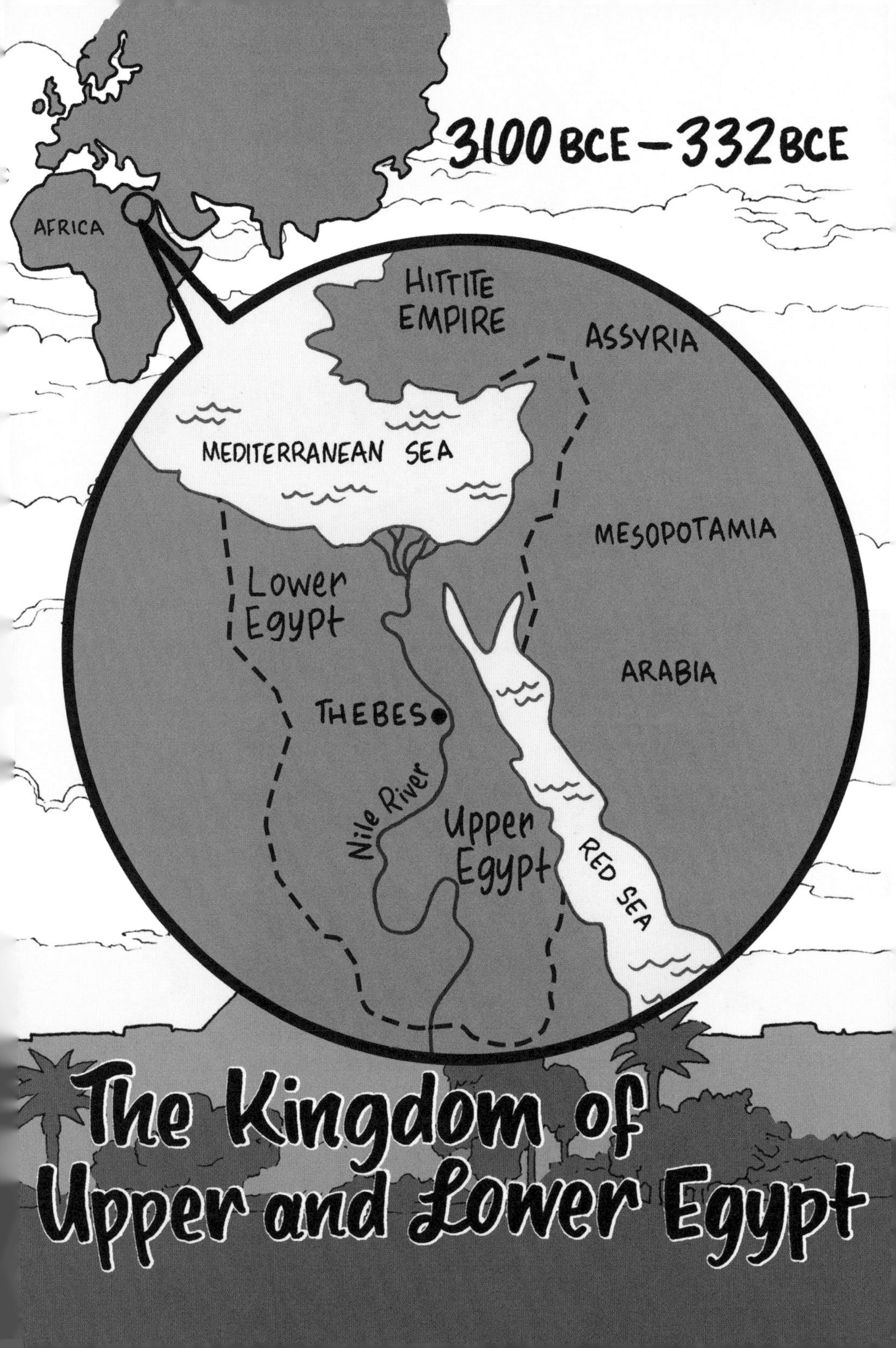
3100 BCE – 332 BCE
AFRICA
HITTITE EMPIRE
ASSYRIA
MEDITERRANEAN SEA
MESOPOTAMIA
Lower Egypt
ARABIA
THEBES
Nile River
Upper Egypt
RED SEA
The Kingdom of Upper and Lower Egypt

When archaeologists first learned about an ancient Egyptian pharaoh named Hatshepsut, they uncovered a story about a person who was raised to be a queen but instead became a king.

Pharaoh Maatkare Hatshepsut

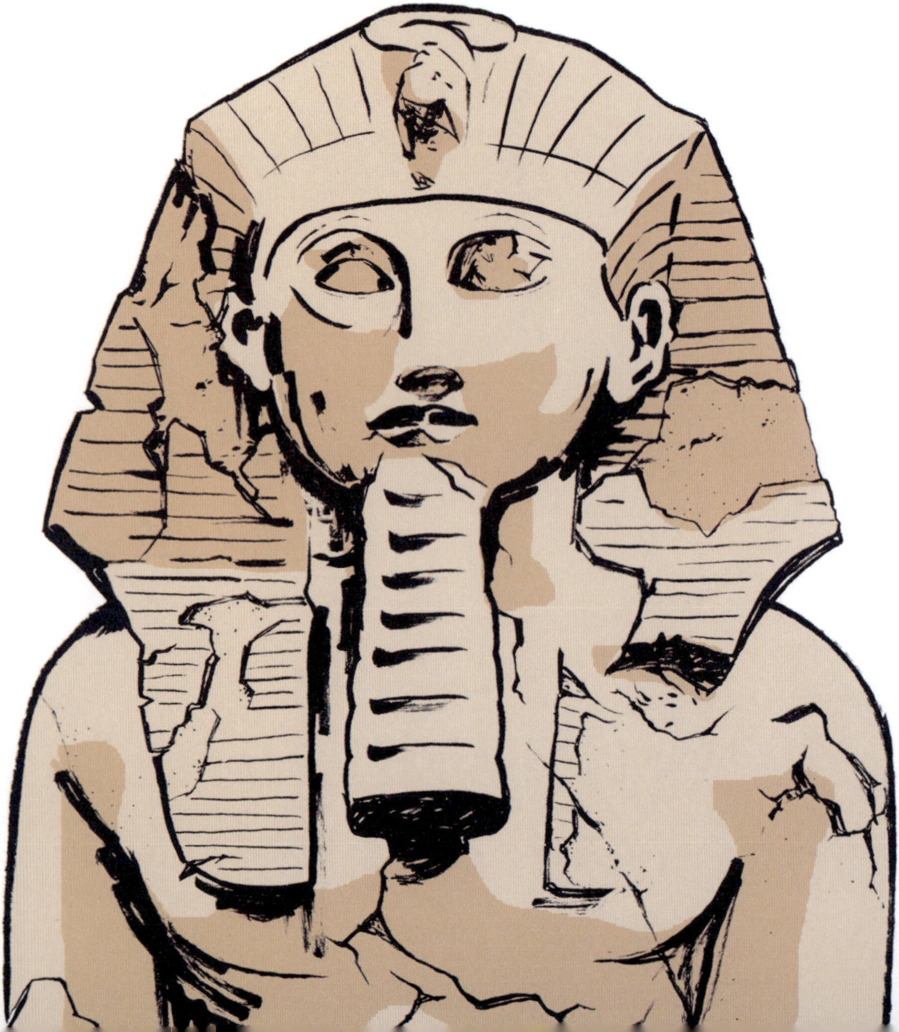

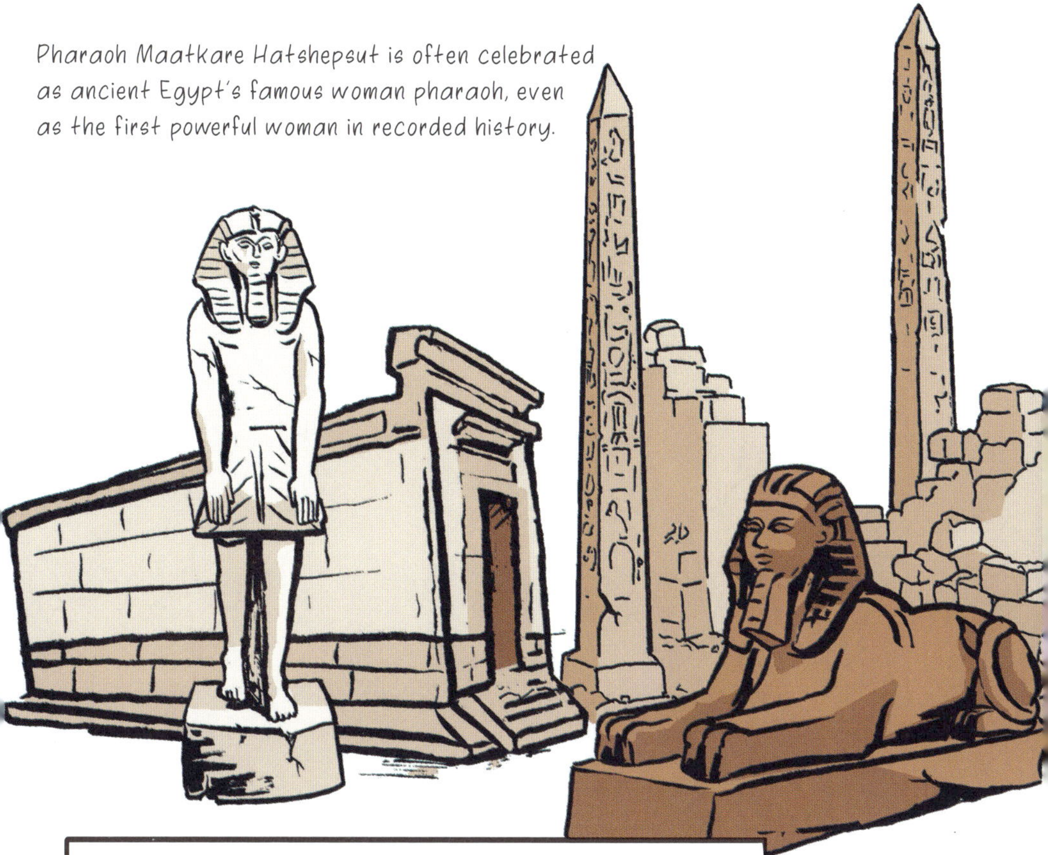
Pharaoh Maatkare Hatshepsut is often celebrated as ancient Egypt's famous woman pharaoh, even as the first powerful woman in recorded history.

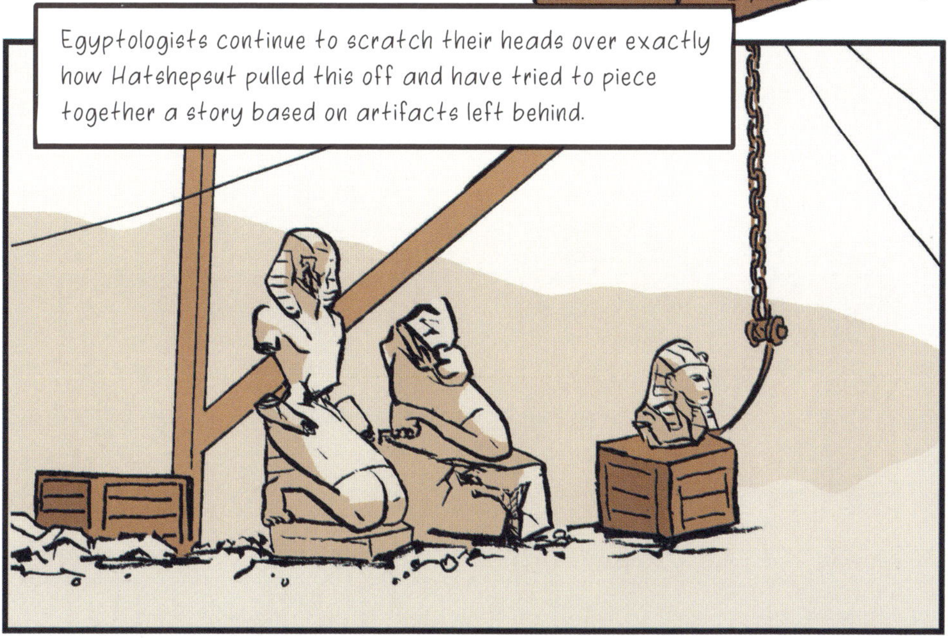
Egyptologists continue to scratch their heads over exactly how Hatshepsut pulled this off and have tried to piece together a story based on artifacts left behind.

The statues depicted in this section are based on those housed in the Metropolitan Museum of Art and are from the mid-1400s BCE (about 3,500 years ago).

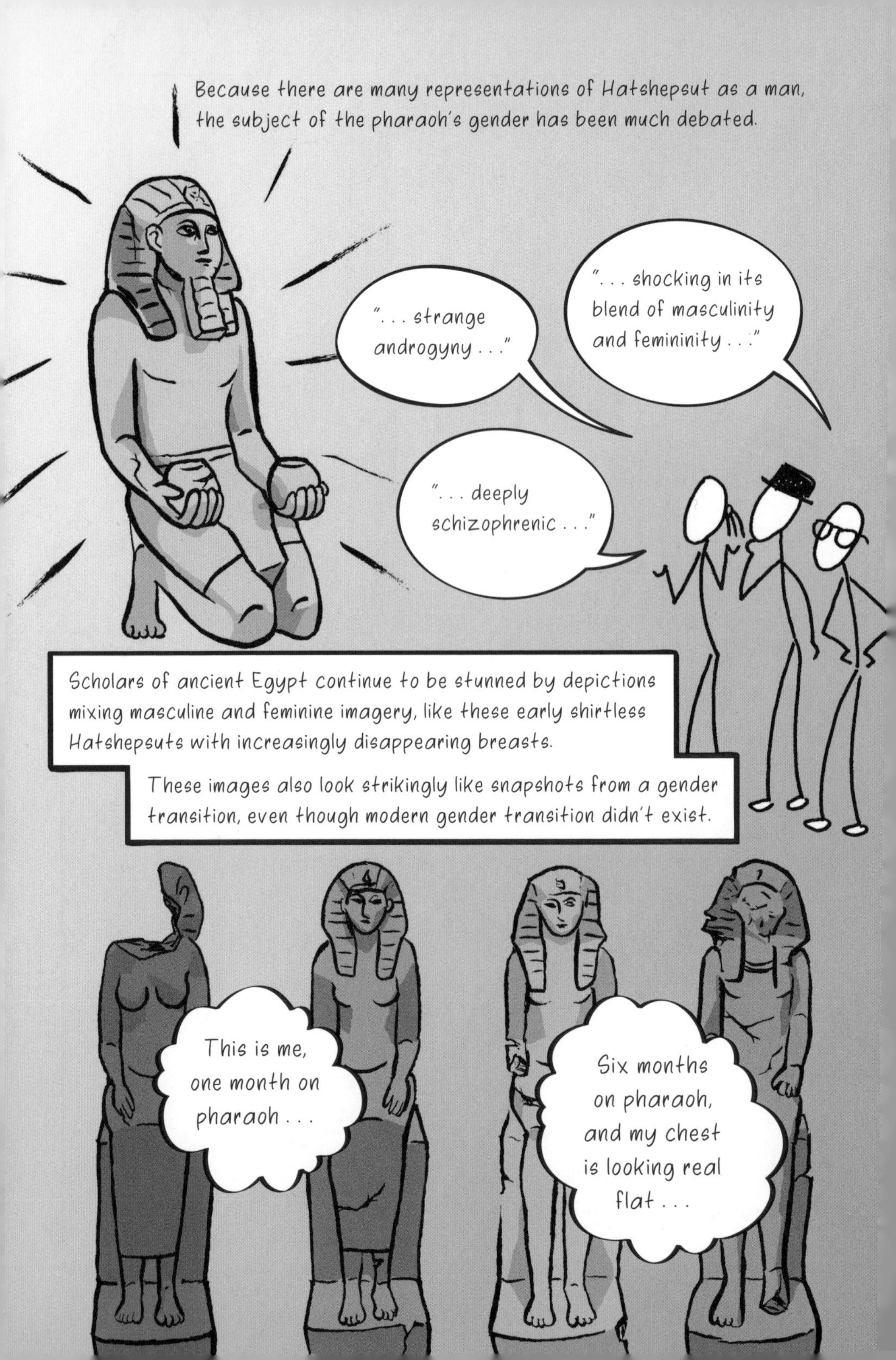
Because there are many representations of Hatshepsut as a man, the subject of the pharaoh's gender has been much debated.
". . . strange androgyny . . ."
". . . shocking in its blend of masculinity and femininity . . ."
". . . deeply schizophrenic . . ."
Scholars of ancient Egypt continue to be stunned by depictions mixing masculine and feminine imagery, like these early shirtless Hatshepsuts with increasingly disappearing breasts.
These images also look strikingly like snapshots from a gender transition, even though modern gender transition didn't exist.
This is me, one month on pharaoh . . .
Six months on pharaoh, and my chest is looking real flat . . .

> After Hatshepsut became pharaoh, official images were more consistent with other representations of men, but they still occasionally incorporated feminine traits, and feminine designations were usually used in writing.

NAME: The Living Horus: Mighty-of-Kas
Two Ladies: Flourishing-in-years
Gold-Horus: Divine-of-diadems
King of Upper and Lower Egypt: Maatkare
Daughter of Re: Hatshepsut Khenemet-Amun

LIVED: 1507 to 1458 BCE (almost 50 years)
GENDER: Pharaoh
BLOOD TYPE: ?
LIKES: Monumental structures
DISLIKES: Toothaches

> Hatshepsut's five throne names also incorporated both masculine and feminine meanings; Maatkare was used most often on monuments.

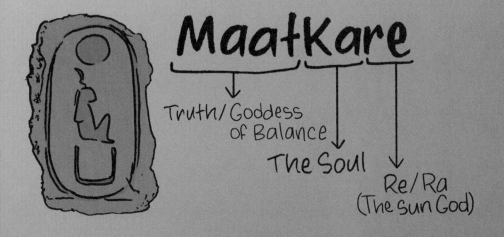

Maatkare
- Maat → Truth/Goddess of Balance
- Ka → The Soul
- Re → Re/Ra (The Sun God)

Since pharaoh was considered a male role, Hatshepsut's representations as a man have often been interpreted as a kind of public relations campaign in a bid for the throne.

And the mixing of gendered traits has sometimes been explained as Hatshepsut clinging to femininity or resisting becoming fully masculine.

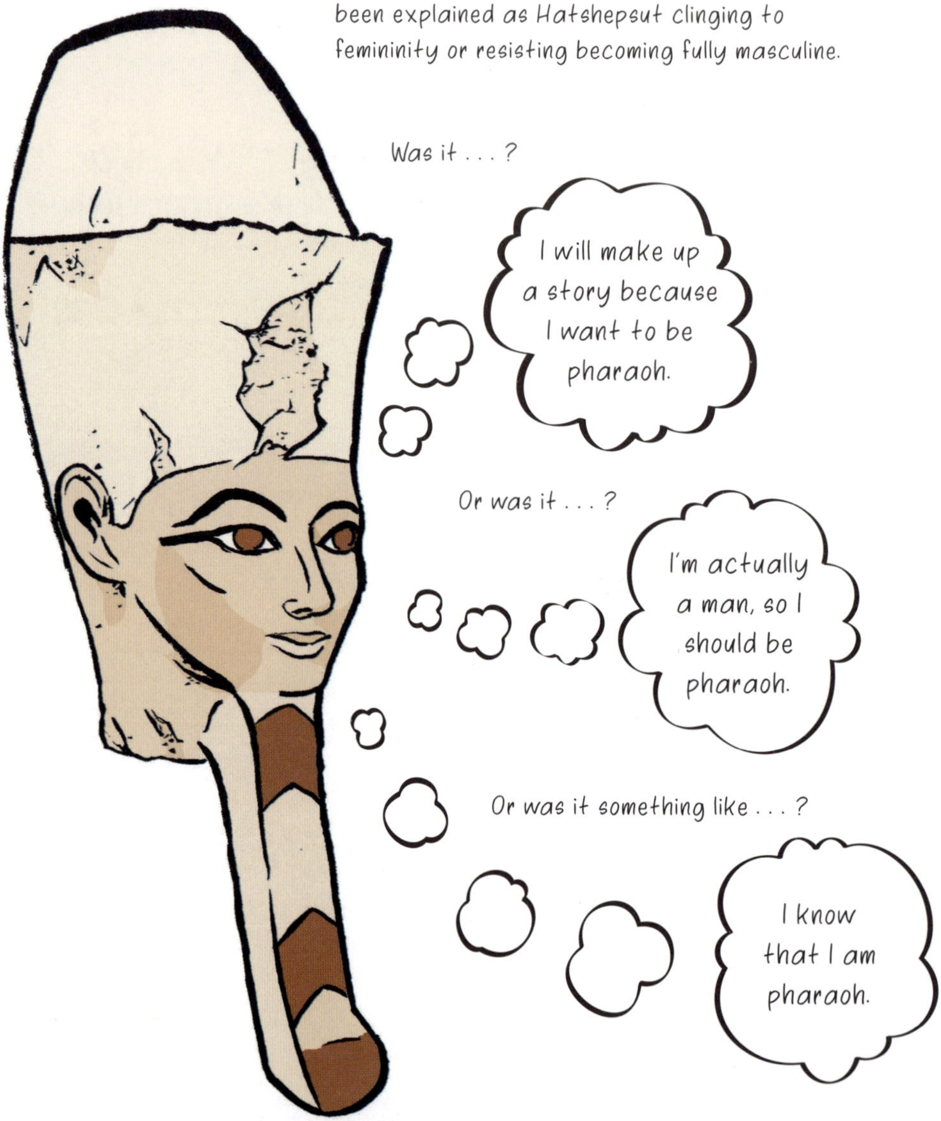

Was it . . . ?
I will make up a story because I want to be pharaoh.
Or was it . . . ?
I'm actually a man, so I should be pharaoh.
Or was it something like . . . ?
I know that I am pharaoh.

But it's also possible that occupying the masculine role of the pharaoh could have been an alignment of Hatshepsut's gendered feelings and/or presentation instead of being at odds with them.

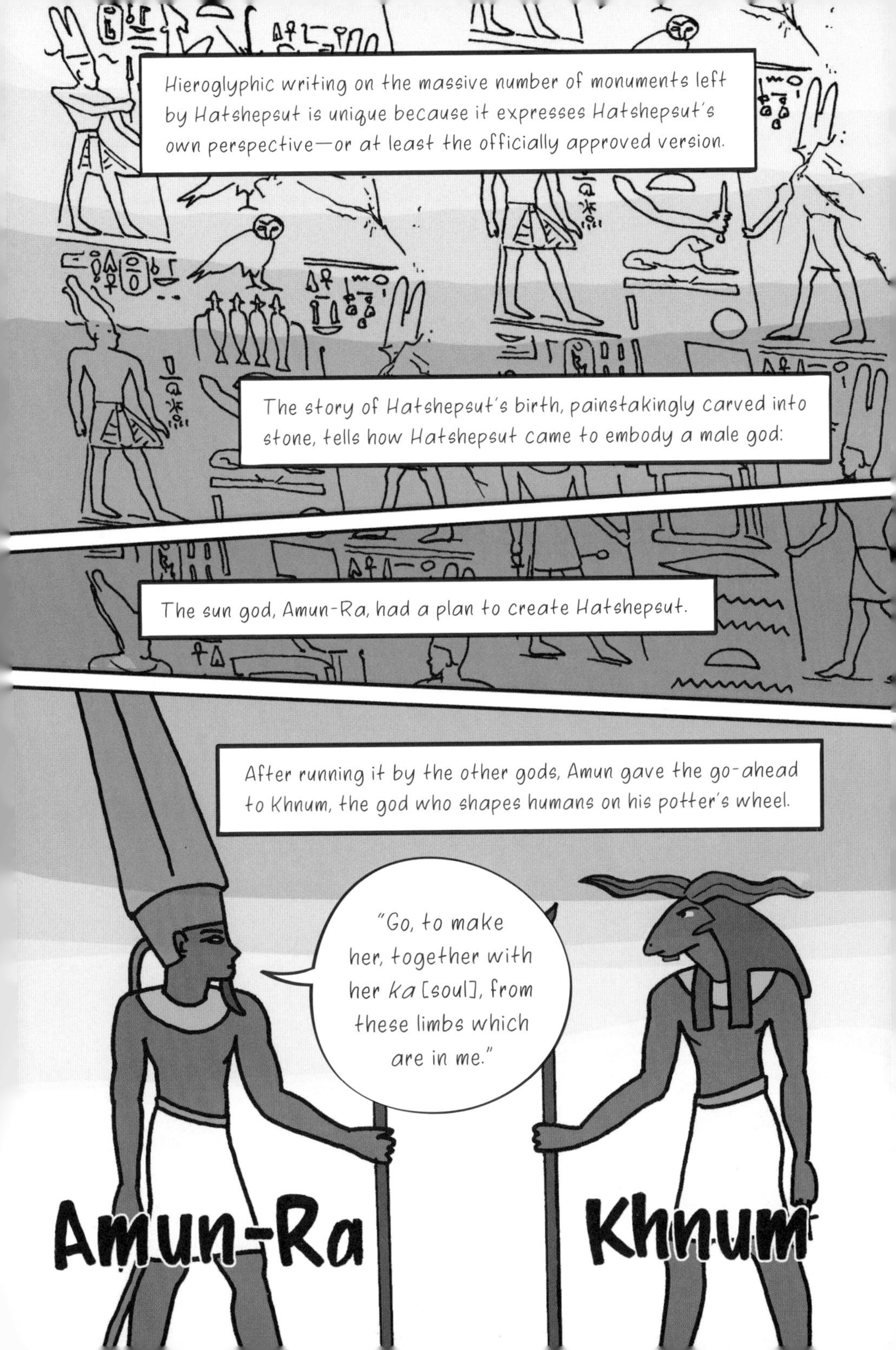
Hieroglyphic writing on the massive number of monuments left by Hatshepsut is unique because it expresses Hatshepsut's own perspective—or at least the officially approved version.
The story of Hatshepsut's birth, painstakingly carved into stone, tells how Hatshepsut came to embody a male god:
The sun god, Amun-Ra, had a plan to create Hatshepsut.
After running it by the other gods, Amun gave the go-ahead to Khnum, the god who shapes humans on his potter's wheel.
"Go, to make her, together with her *ka* [soul], from these limbs which are in me."
Amun-Ra
Khnum

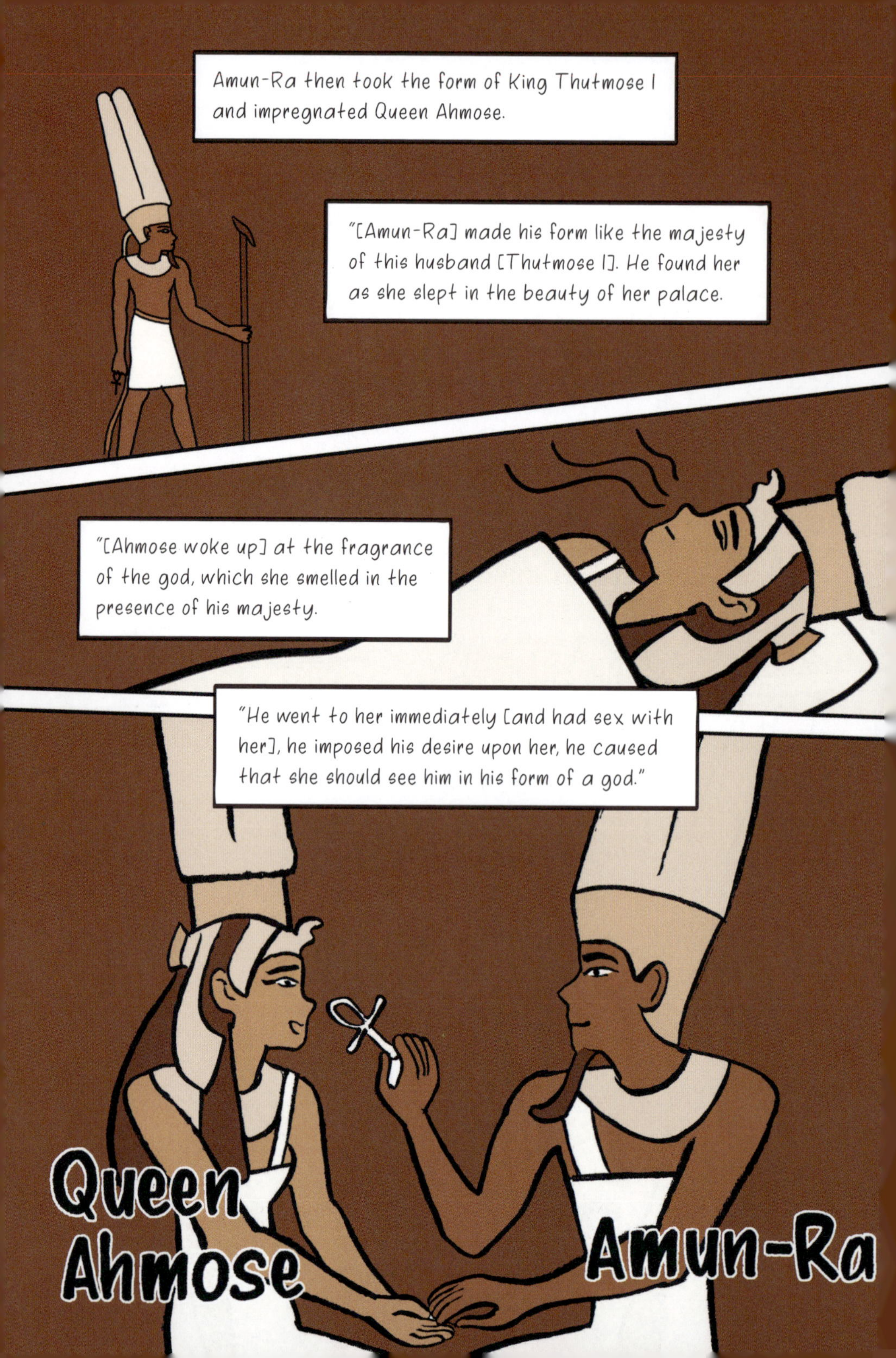
Amun-Ra then took the form of King Thutmose I and impregnated Queen Ahmose.
"[Amun-Ra] made his form like the majesty of this husband [Thutmose I]. He found her as she slept in the beauty of her palace.
"[Ahmose woke up] at the fragrance of the god, which she smelled in the presence of his majesty.
"He went to her immediately [and had sex with her], he imposed his desire upon her, he caused that she should see him in his form of a god."
Queen Ahmose
Amun-Ra

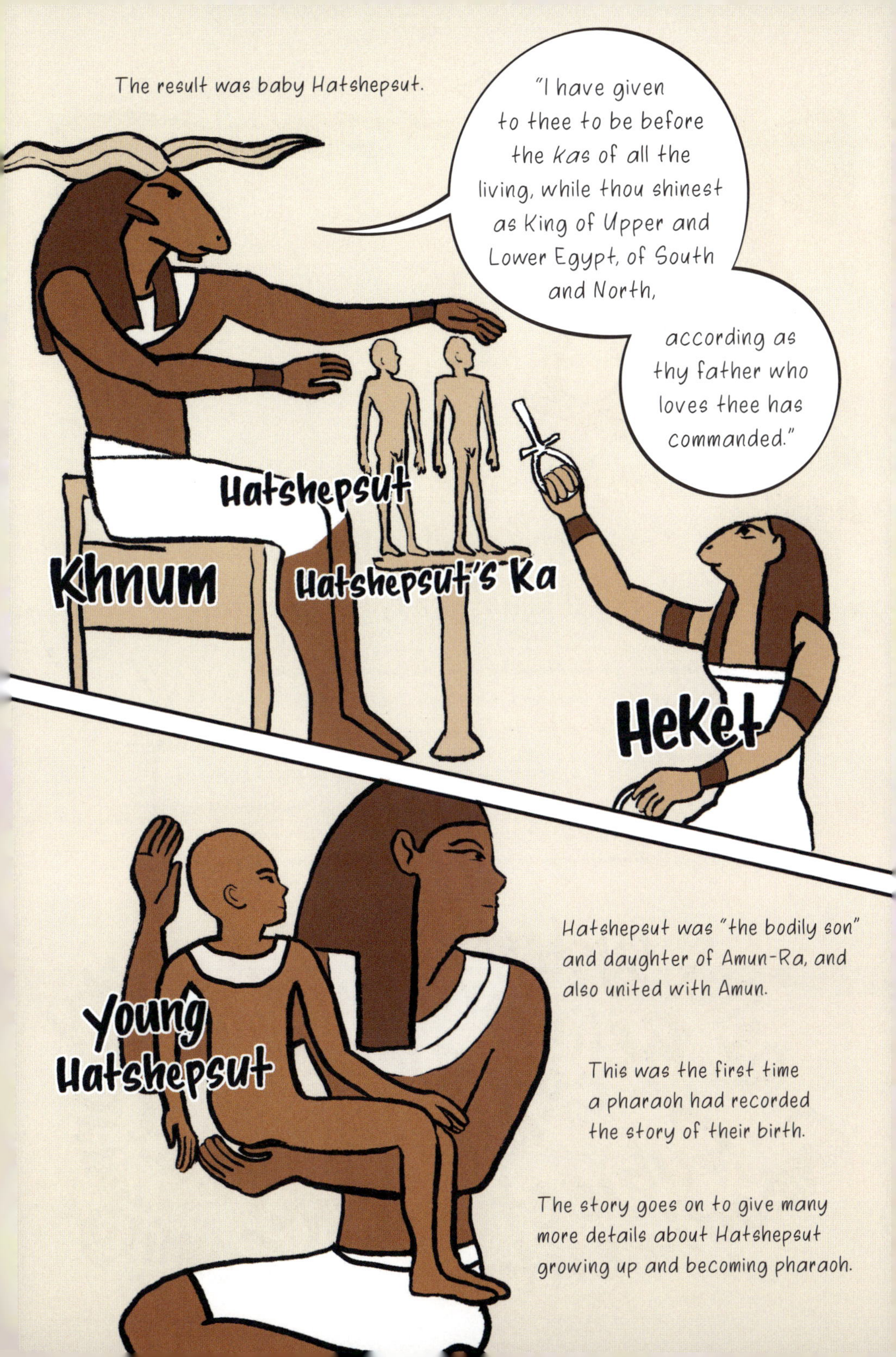
The result was baby Hatshepsut.
"I have given to thee to be before the *kas* of all the living, while thou shinest as King of Upper and Lower Egypt, of South and North,
according as thy father who loves thee has commanded."
Hatshepsut
Khnum
Hatshepsut's Ka
Heket
Young Hatshepsut
Hatshepsut was "the bodily son" and daughter of Amun-Ra, and also united with Amun.
This was the first time a pharaoh had recorded the story of their birth.
The story goes on to give many more details about Hatshepsut growing up and becoming pharaoh.

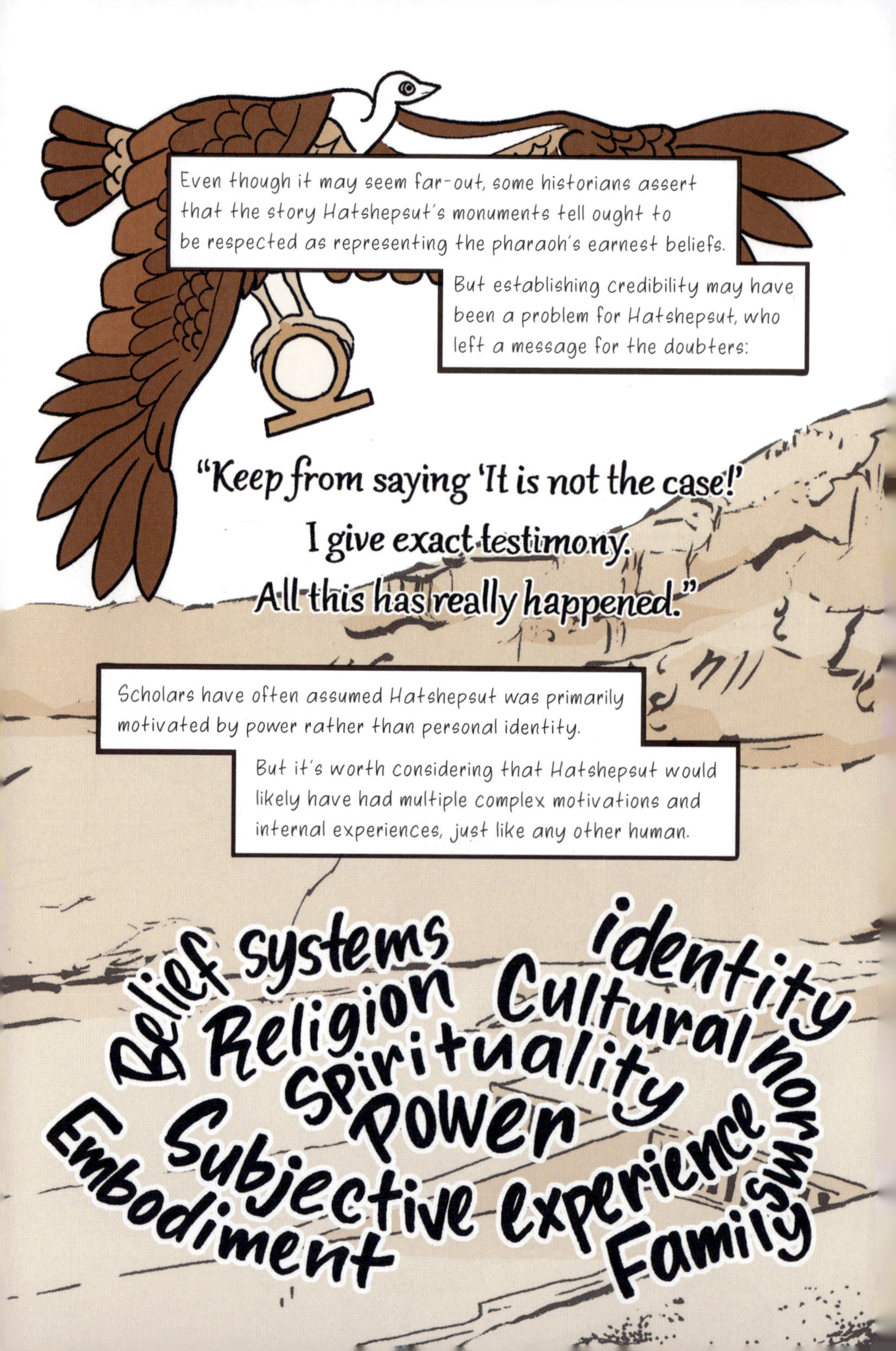
Even though it may seem far-out, some historians assert that the story Hatshepsut's monuments tell ought to be respected as representing the pharaoh's earnest beliefs.
But establishing credibility may have been a problem for Hatshepsut, who left a message for the doubters:
"Keep from saying 'It is not the case!' I give exact testimony. All this has really happened."
Scholars have often assumed Hatshepsut was primarily motivated by power rather than personal identity.
But it's worth considering that Hatshepsut would likely have had multiple complex motivations and internal experiences, just like any other human.
Belief systems
identity
Religion
Cultural norms
Spirituality
Power
Subjective
experience
Embodiment
Family

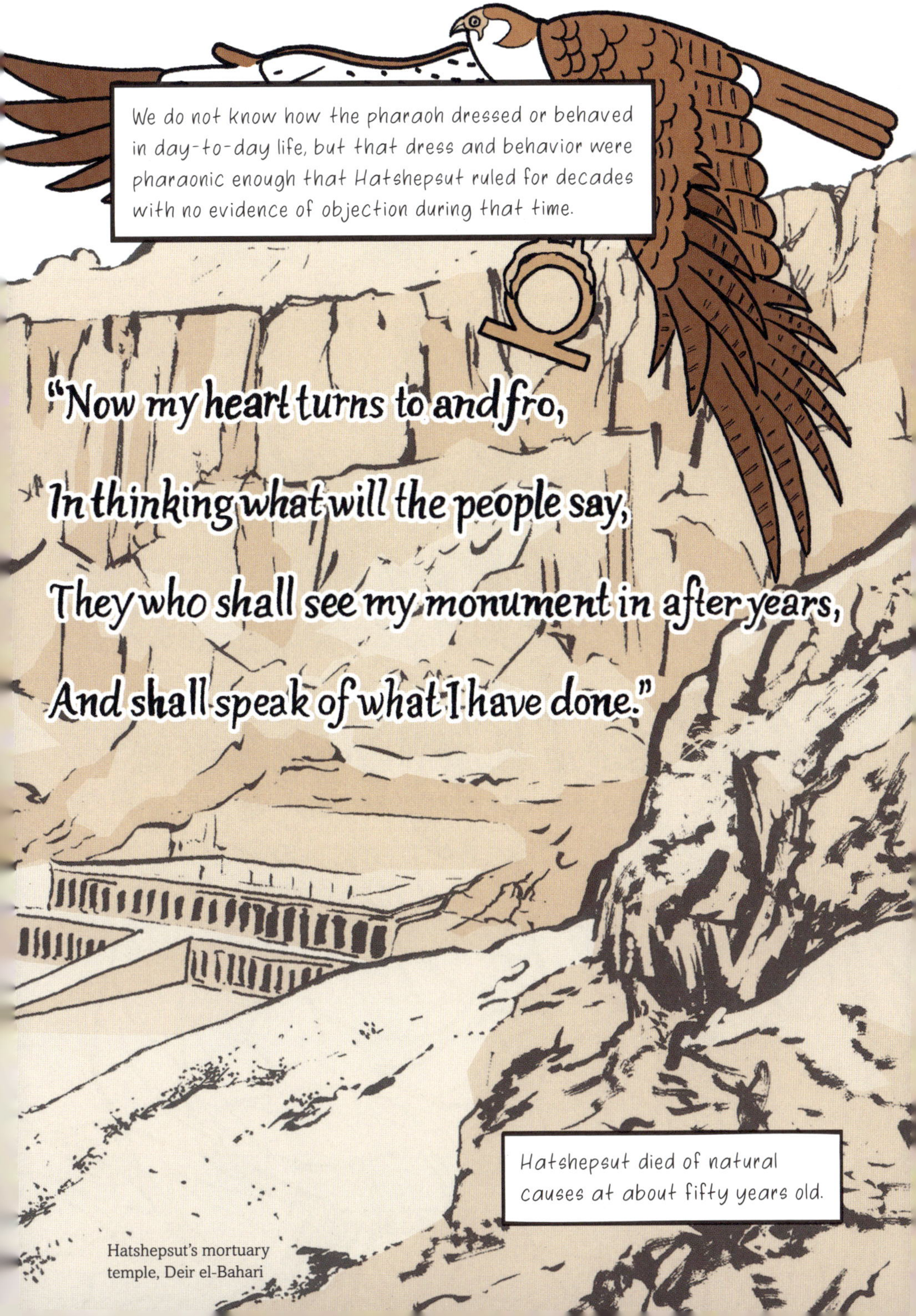
We do not know how the pharaoh dressed or behaved in day-to-day life, but that dress and behavior were pharaonic enough that Hatshepsut ruled for decades with no evidence of objection during that time.
"Now my heart turns to and fro,
In thinking what will the people say,
They who shall see my monument in after years,
And shall speak of what I have done."
Hatshepsut died of natural causes at about fifty years old.

Hatshepsut's mortuary temple, Deir el-Bahari

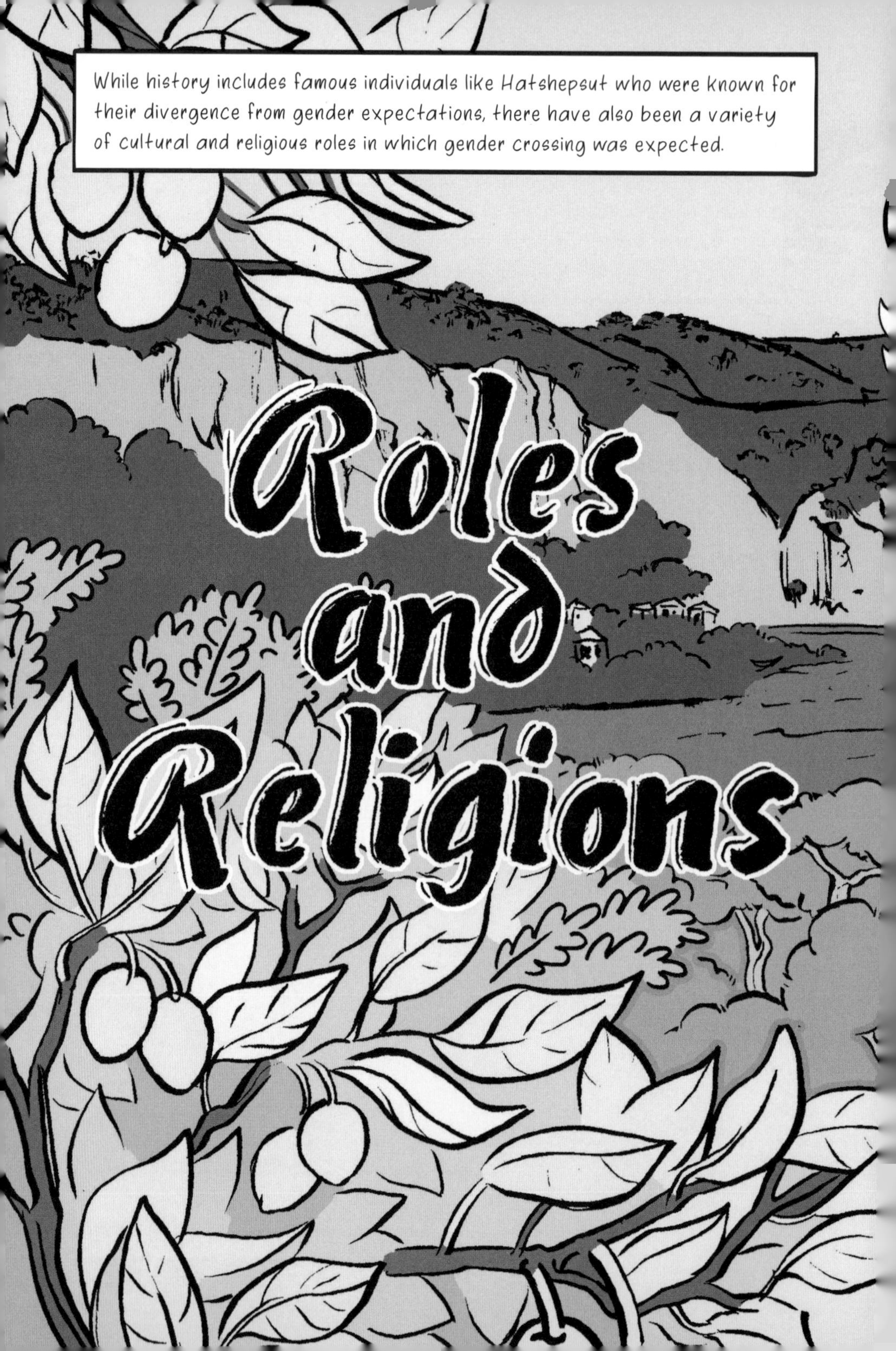
While history includes famous individuals like Hatshepsut who were known for their divergence from gender expectations, there have also been a variety of cultural and religious roles in which gender crossing was expected.
Roles and Religions

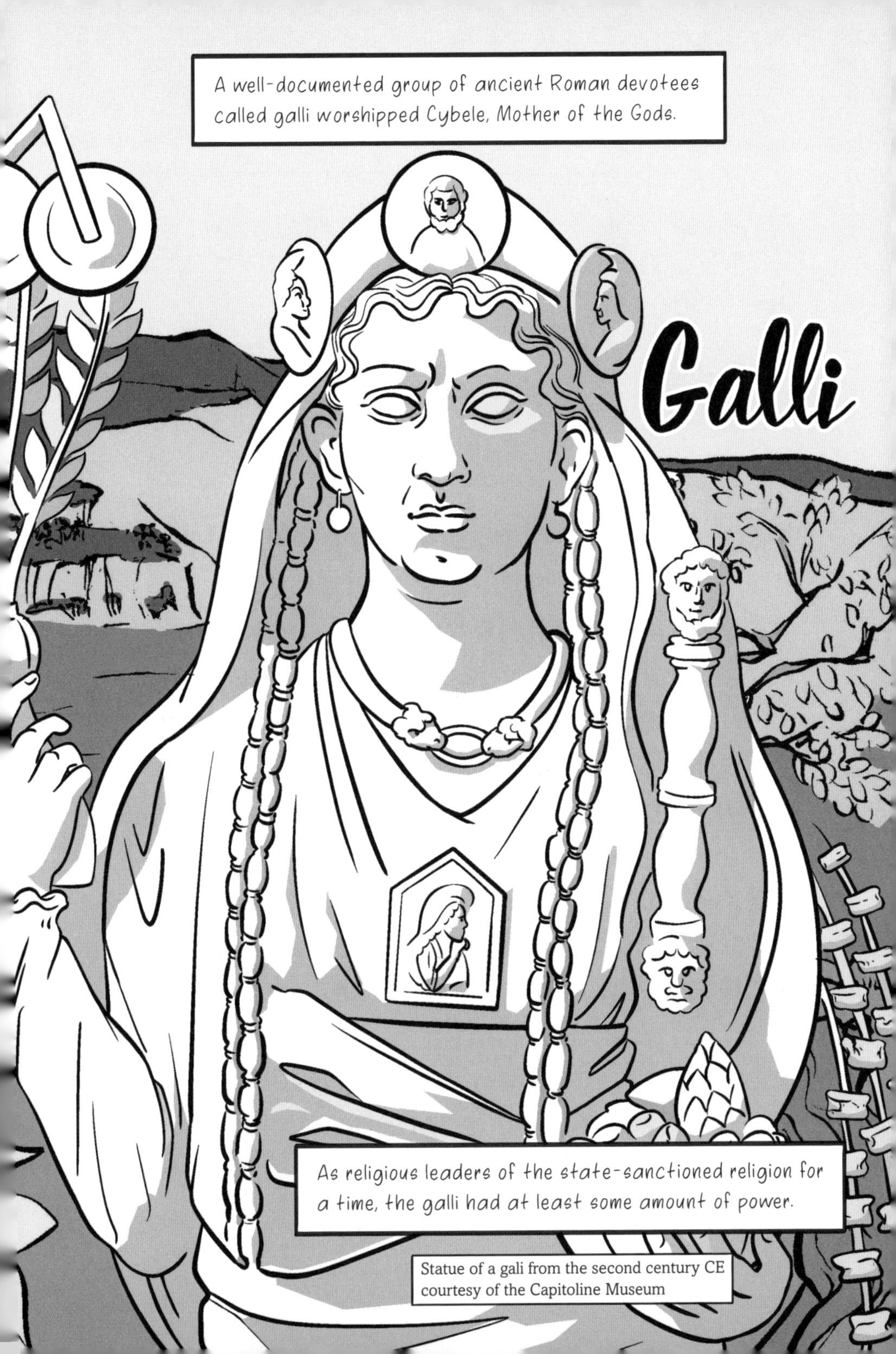
A well-documented group of ancient Roman devotees called galli worshipped Cybele, Mother of the Gods.
Galli
As religious leaders of the state-sanctioned religion for a time, the galli had at least some amount of power.
Statue of a gali from the second century CE courtesy of the Capitoline Museum

They were regarded by the Roman mainstream as effeminate men, who were alternately accepted and condemned depending on who was in charge.

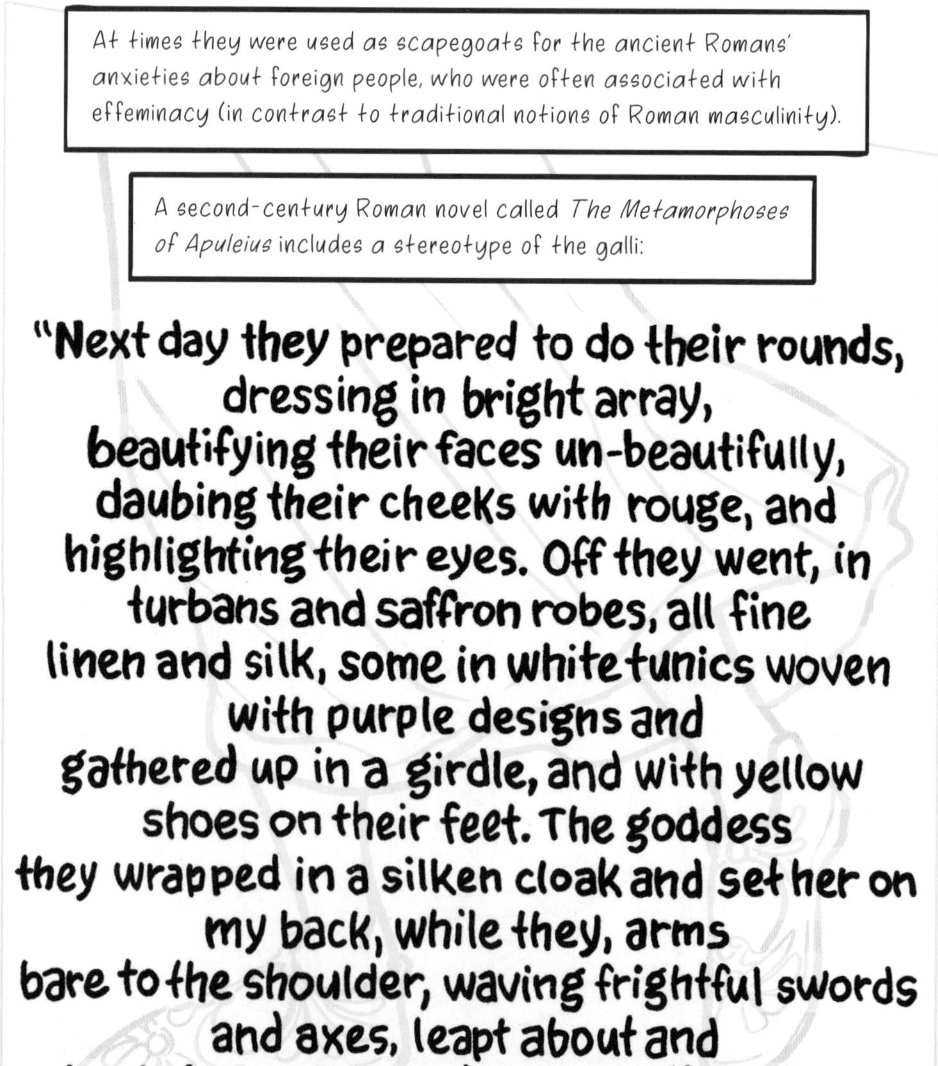
At times they were used as scapegoats for the ancient Romans' anxieties about foreign people, who were often associated with effeminacy (in contrast to traditional notions of Roman masculinity).
A second-century Roman novel called *The Metamorphoses of Apuleius* includes a stereotype of the galli:
"Next day they prepared to do their rounds, dressing in bright array, beautifying their faces un-beautifully, daubing their cheeks with rouge, and highlighting their eyes. Off they went, in turbans and saffron robes, all fine linen and silk, some in white tunics woven with purple designs and gathered up in a girdle, and with yellow shoes on their feet. The goddess they wrapped in a silken cloak and set her on my back, while they, arms bare to the shoulder, waving frightful swords and axes, leapt about and chanted, in a frenzied dance to the stirring wail of the flute."

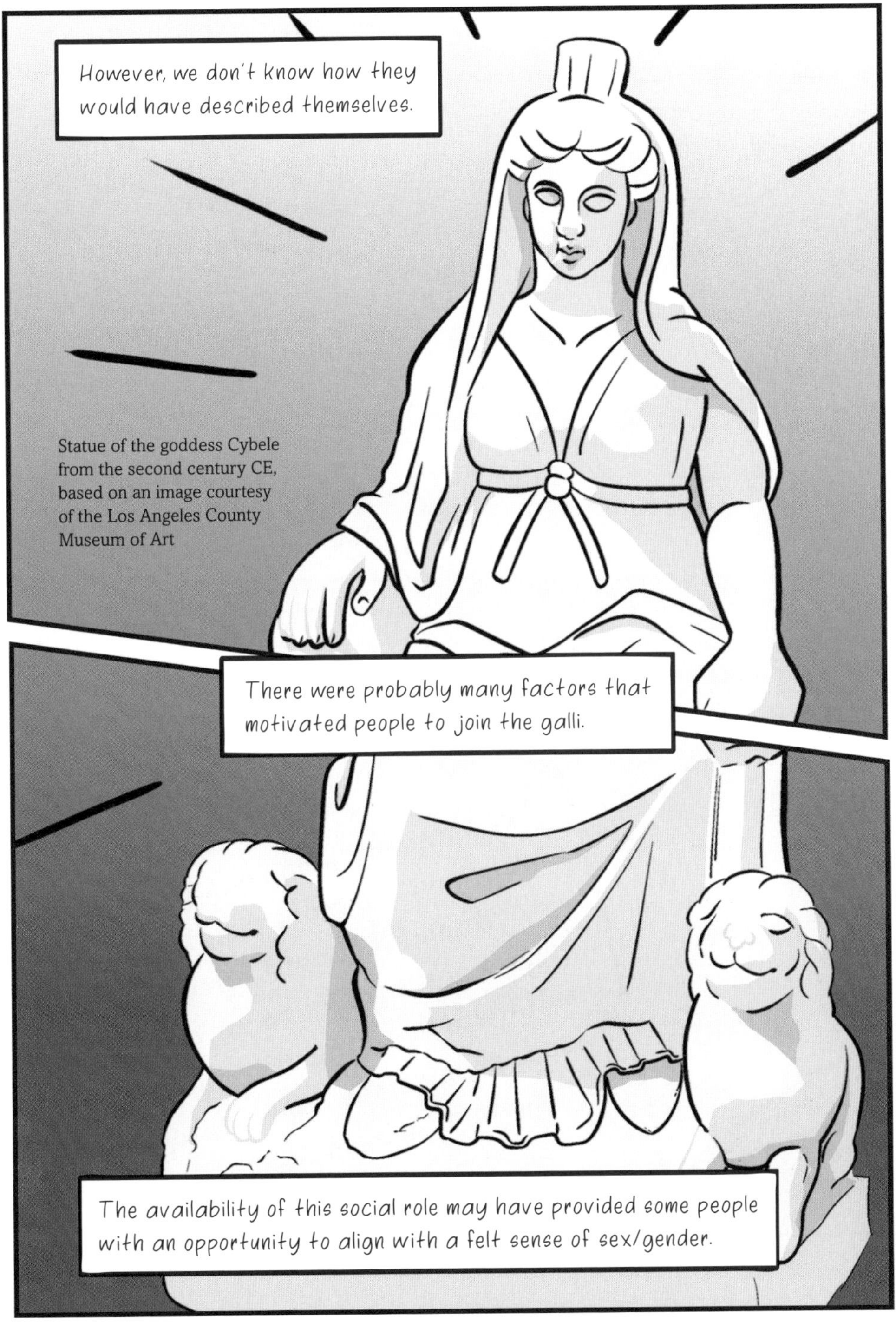
However, we don't know how they would have described themselves.
There were probably many factors that motivated people to join the galli.
The availability of this social role may have provided some people with an opportunity to align with a felt sense of sex/gender.
Statue of the goddess Cybele from the second century CE, based on an image courtesy of the Los Angeles County Museum of Art

Ornate castration clamps found in the river Thames are thought to have been used as part of the galli's initiation.

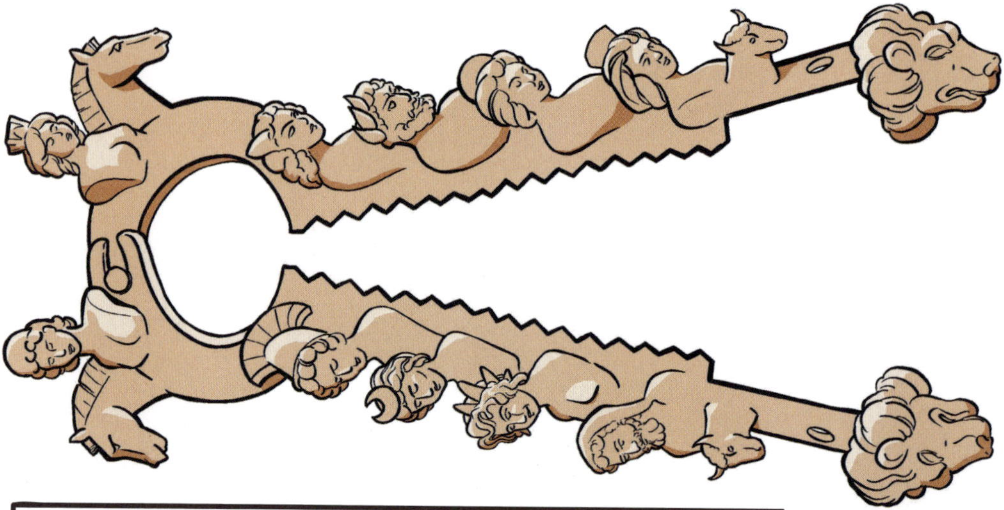

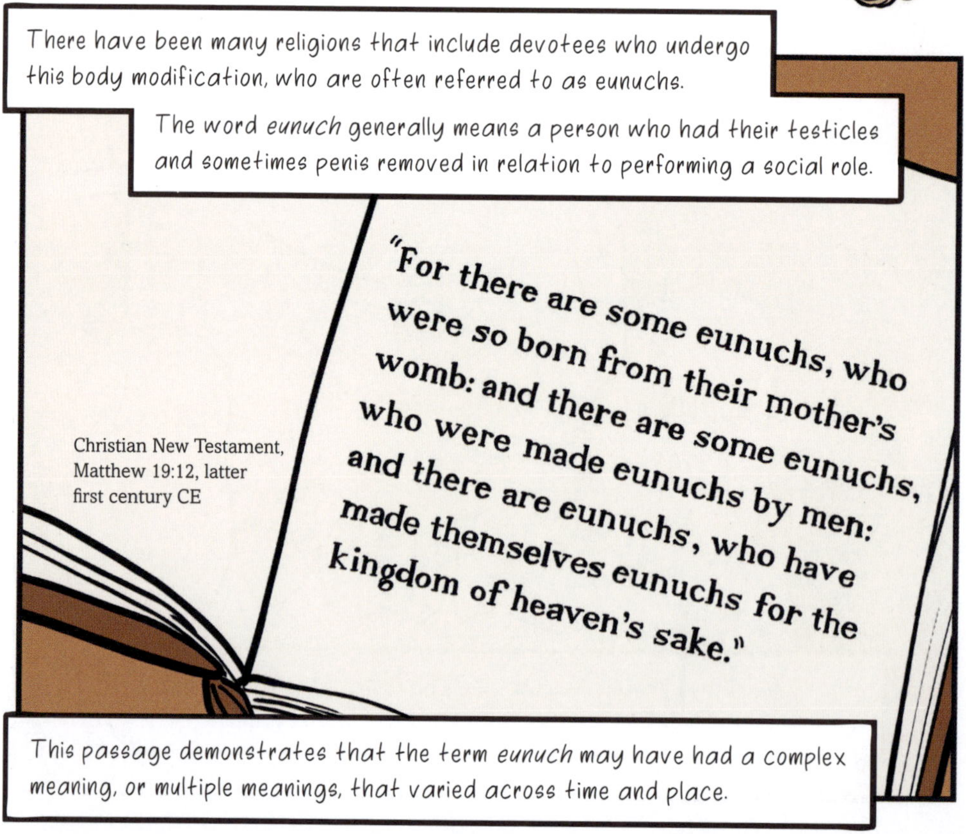
There have been many religions that include devotees who undergo this body modification, who are often referred to as eunuchs.
The word *eunuch* generally means a person who had their testicles and sometimes penis removed in relation to performing a social role.
"For there are some eunuchs, who were so born from their mother's womb: and there are some eunuchs, who were made eunuchs by men: and there are eunuchs, who have made themselves eunuchs for the kingdom of heaven's sake."
Christian New Testament, Matthew 19:12, latter first century CE
This passage demonstrates that the term *eunuch* may have had a complex meaning, or multiple meanings, that varied across time and place.

For example, as Dr. Howard Chiang explains, eunuchs working in Chinese imperial courts did not necessarily have cross-gender feelings:

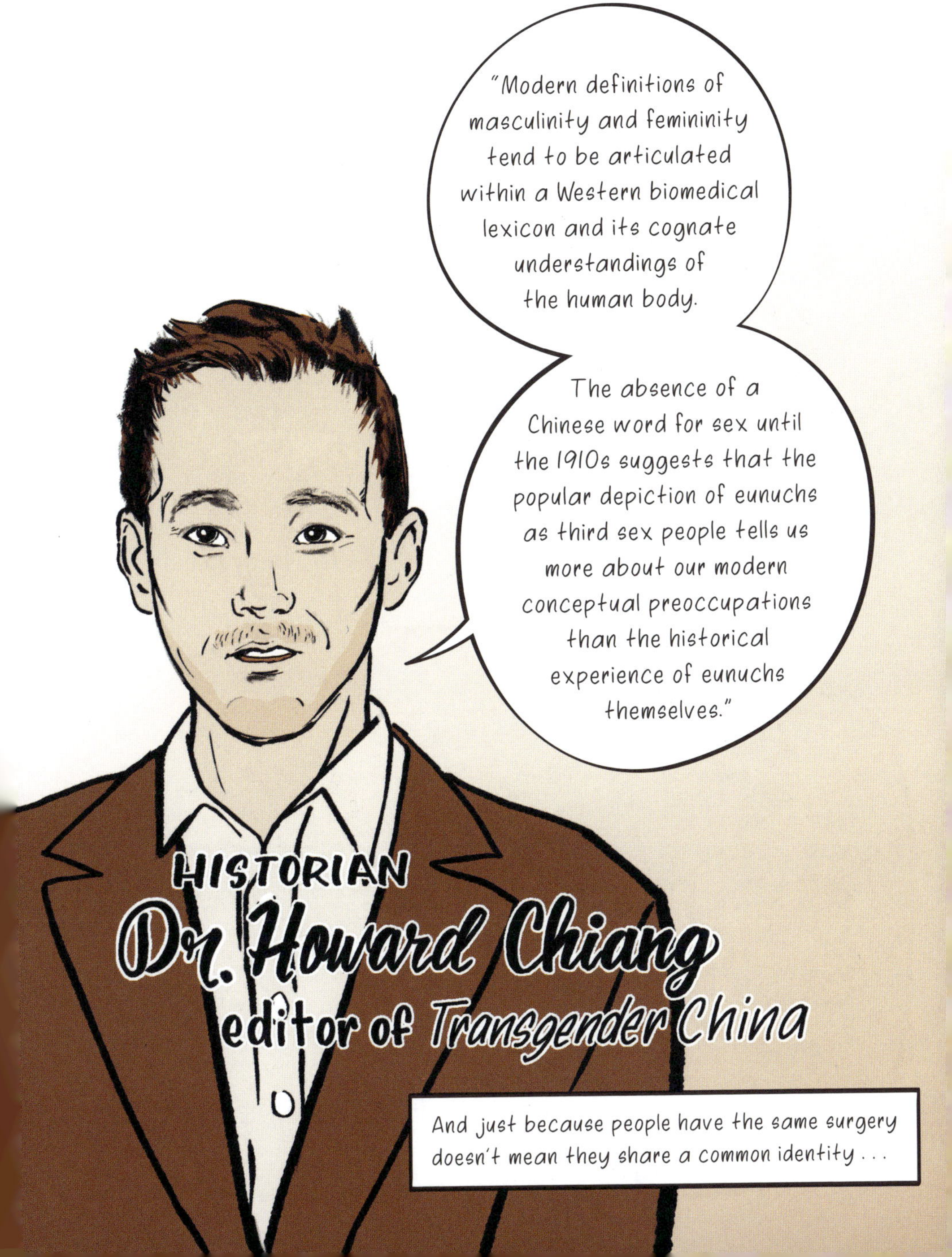
"Modern definitions of masculinity and femininity tend to be articulated within a Western biomedical lexicon and its cognate understandings of the human body.
The absence of a Chinese word for sex until the 1910s suggests that the popular depiction of eunuchs as third sex people tells us more about our modern conceptual preoccupations than the historical experience of eunuchs themselves."
HISTORIAN
Dr. Howard Chiang
editor of Transgender China
And just because people have the same surgery doesn't mean they share a common identity . . .

Having undergone specific body modifications doesn't necessarily mean someone was trans.

However, since body modification is a major desire of many modern trans people, it's often one of the few clues that someone from history might have had a trans-similar experience.

ANCIENT ROME

Third Century CE

Britain
EURASIA
BLACK SEA
ATLANTIC OCEAN
Rome (capital)
Macedonia
Anatolia
Emesa
Hispania
Italy
Cyprus
Syria Palestina
Sicily
Crete
MEDITERRANEAN SEA
Arabia
Nile River
RED SEA
Egypt
AFRICA

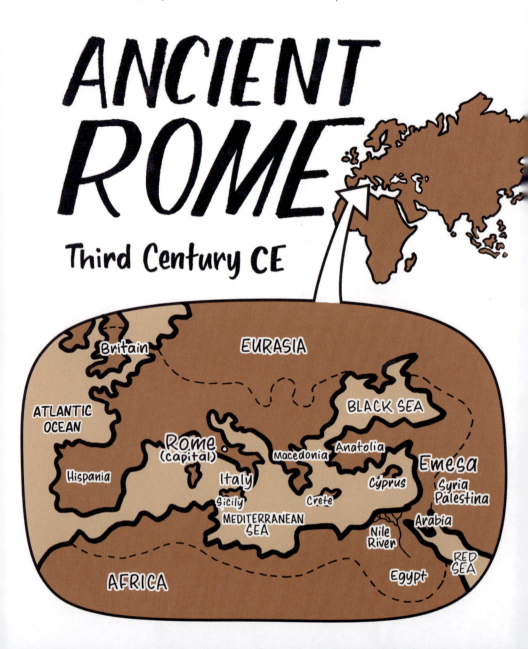

Elagabalus

The emperor Elagabalus of ancient Rome has been an inspiration for many literary and artistic works over the past couple thousand years.

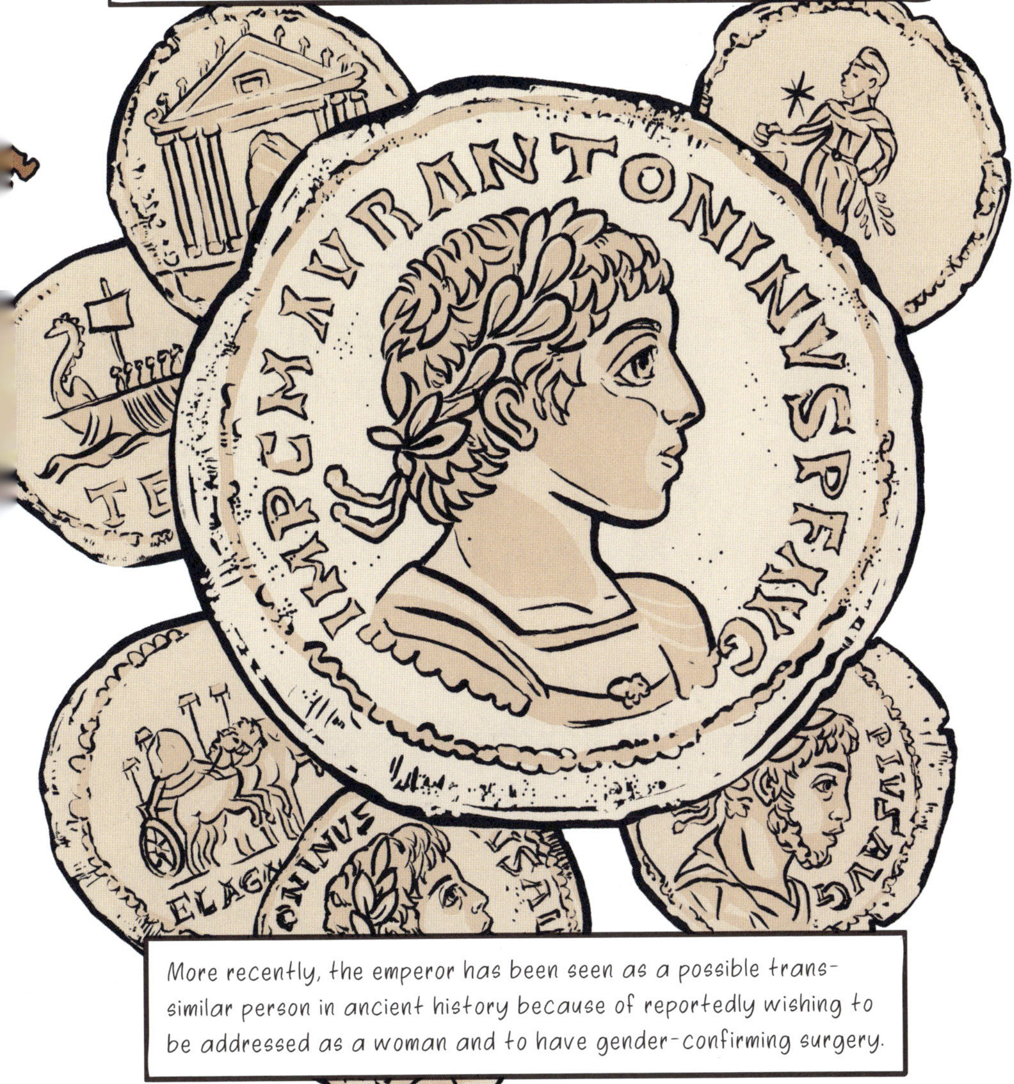

IMPCMAVRANTONINVSPFAVG
TE
ELAGA
ONINVS
PIVS AVG

More recently, the emperor has been seen as a possible trans-similar person in ancient history because of reportedly wishing to be addressed as a woman and to have gender-confirming surgery.

Official coins from the rule of Elagabalus

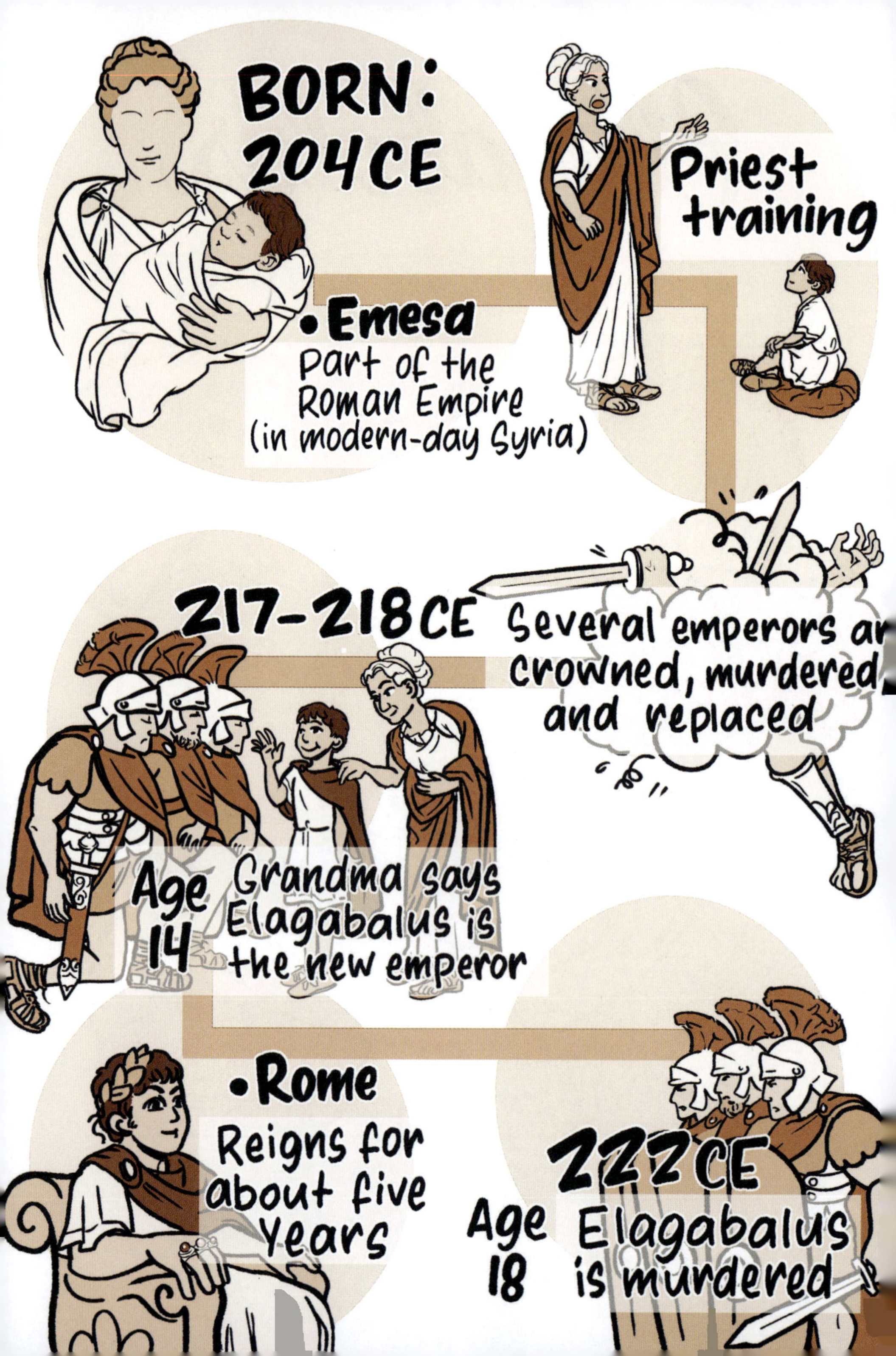
BORN: 204CE
•Emesa
Part of the Roman Empire (in modern-day Syria)
Priest training
217-218CE
Several emperors ar crowned, murdered, and replaced
Age 14
Grandma says Elagabalus is the new emperor
•Rome
Reigns for about five years
222CE
Age 18
Elagabalus is murdered

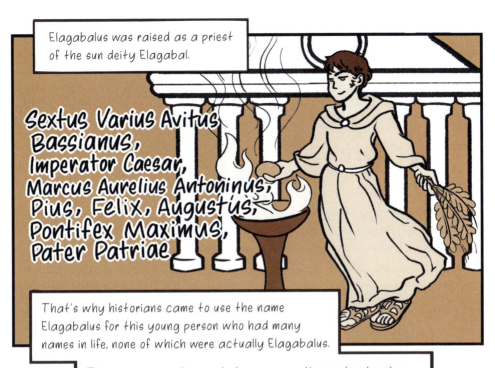

Elagabalus was raised as a priest of the sun deity Elagabal.

Sextus Varius Avitus Bassianus, Imperator Caesar, Marcus Aurelius Antoninus, Pius, Felix, Augustus, Pontifex Maximus, Pater Patriae

That's why historians came to use the name Elagabalus for this young person who had many names in life, none of which were actually Elagabalus.

The emperor was known to be a very enthusiastic devotee and placed the god Elagabal, represented by a black meteorite called a baetyl, at the top of the Roman Pantheon.

Baetyl →

Elagabalus's practice of a religion from the East (which was considered foreign) was blamed for increasing discontent among Roman soldiers and elites. That, along with her gender presentation, may have contributed to her eventual assassination.

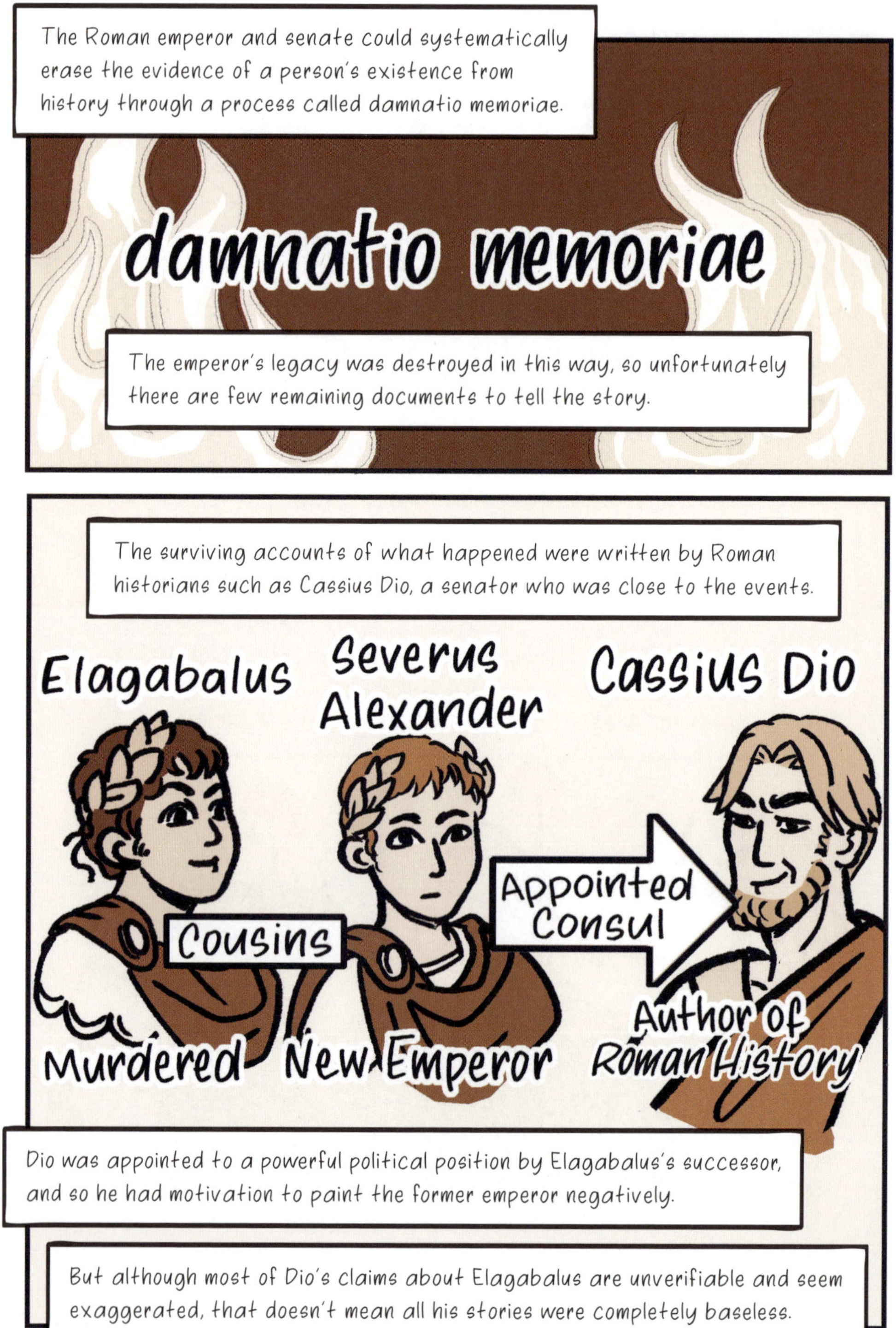
The Roman emperor and senate could systematically erase the evidence of a person's existence from history through a process called damnatio memoriae.
damnatio memoriae
The emperor's legacy was destroyed in this way, so unfortunately there are few remaining documents to tell the story.
The surviving accounts of what happened were written by Roman historians such as Cassius Dio, a senator who was close to the events.
Elagabalus
Severus Alexander
Cassius Dio
Cousins
Appointed Consul
Murdered
New Emperor
Author of Roman History
Dio was appointed to a powerful political position by Elagabalus's successor, and so he had motivation to paint the former emperor negatively.
But although most of Dio's claims about Elagabalus are unverifiable and seem exaggerated, that doesn't mean all his stories were completely baseless.

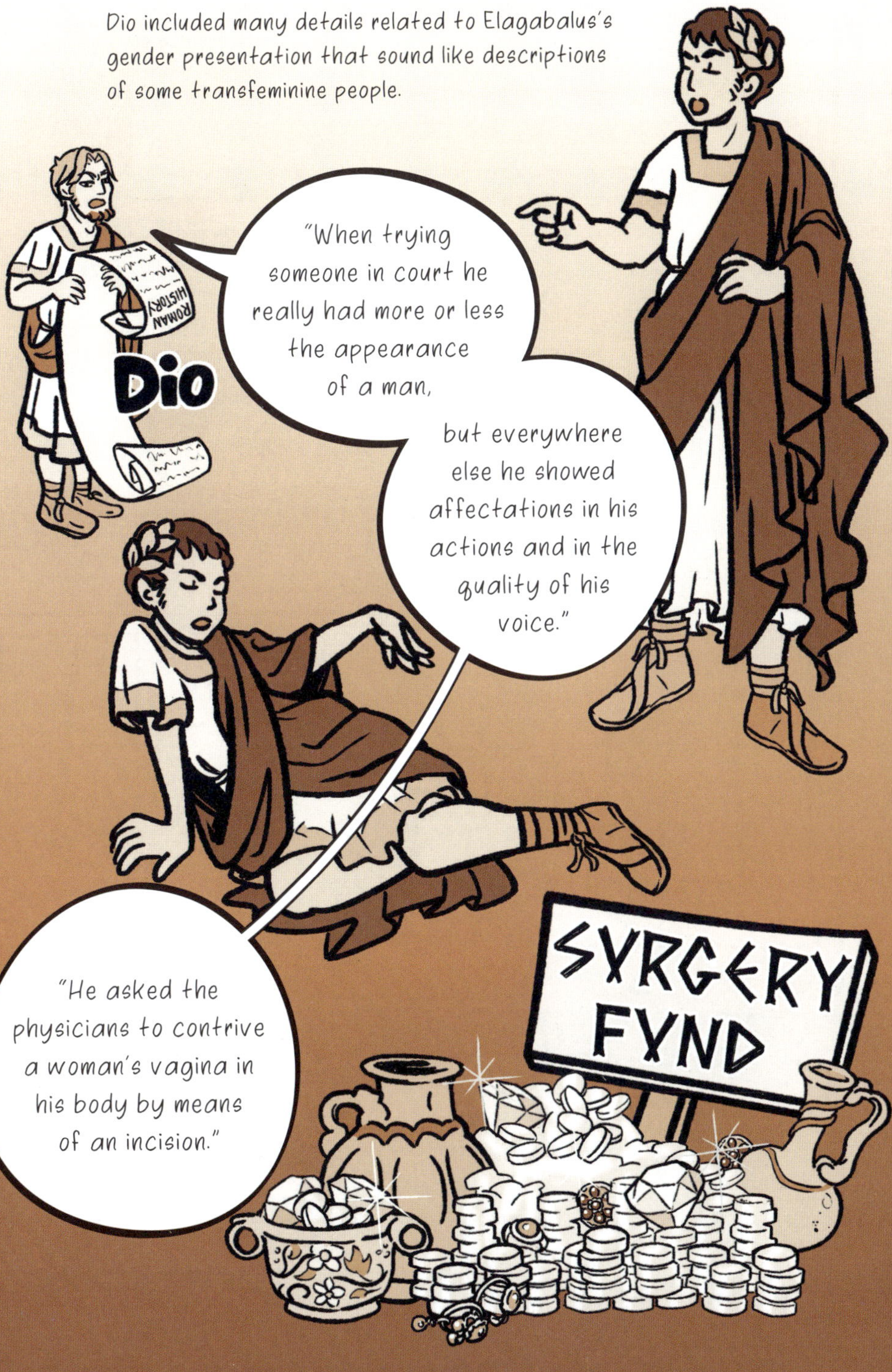
Dio included many details related to Elagabalus's gender presentation that sound like descriptions of some transfeminine people.
ROMAN HISTORY
Dio
"When trying someone in court he really had more or less the appearance of a man,
but everywhere else he showed affectations in his actions and in the quality of his voice."
"He asked the physicians to contrive a woman's vagina in his body by means of an incision."
SVRGERY FVND

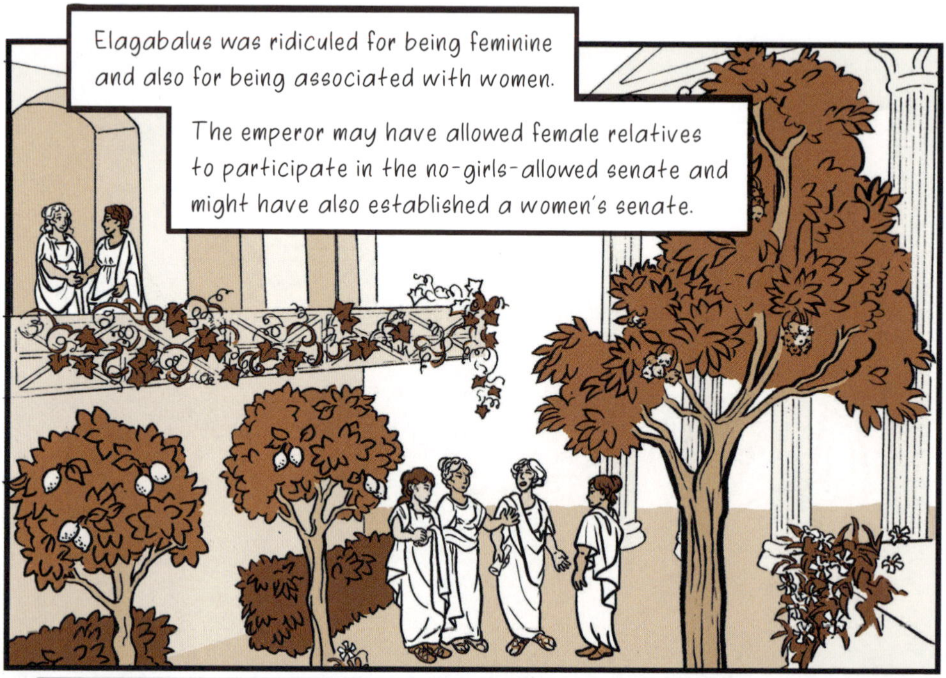
Elagabalus was ridiculed for being feminine and also for being associated with women.
The emperor may have allowed female relatives to participate in the no-girls-allowed senate and might have also established a women's senate.

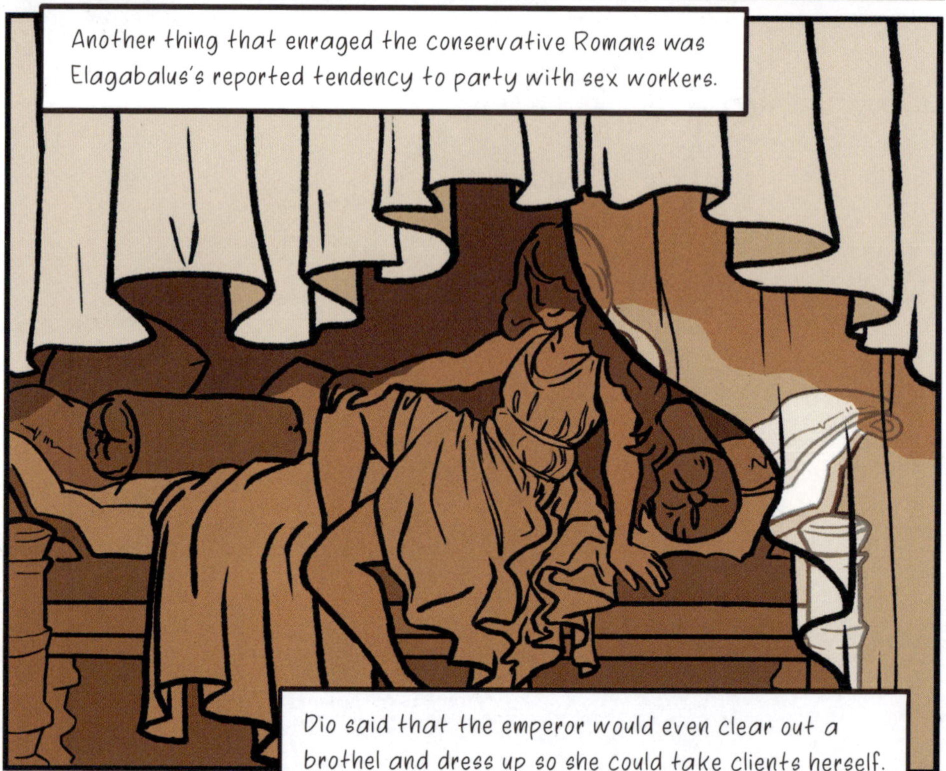
Another thing that enraged the conservative Romans was Elagabalus's reported tendency to party with sex workers.
Dio said that the emperor would even clear out a brothel and dress up so she could take clients herself.

Dio's descriptions of Elagabalus's religious practices are somewhat outlandish:

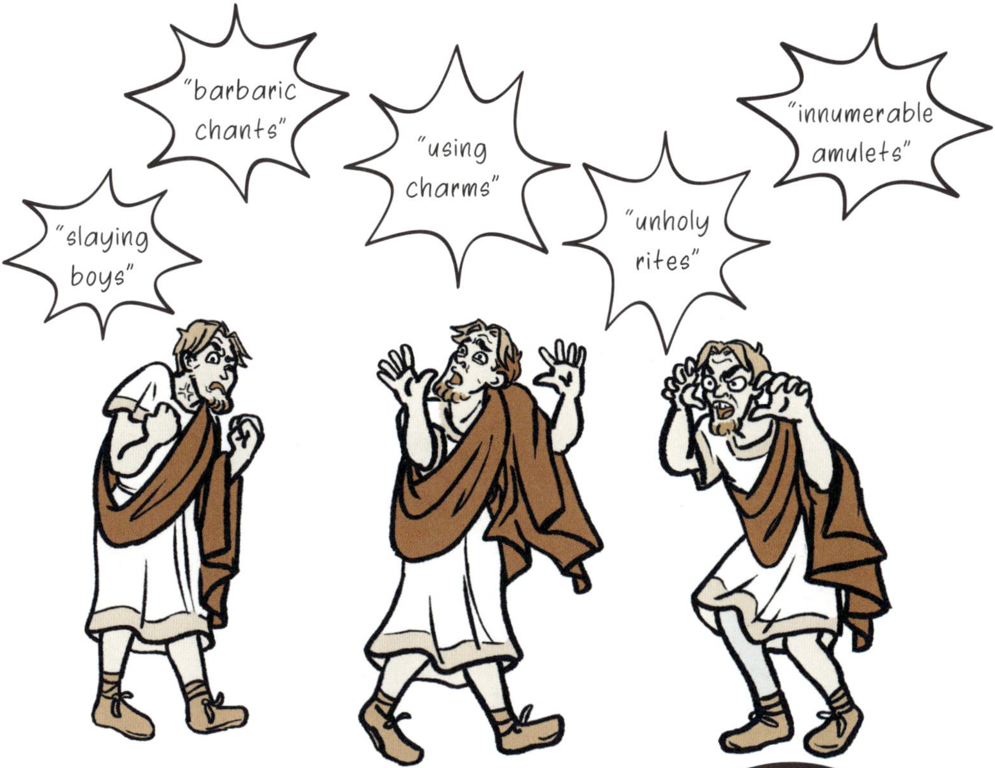
"slaying boys"
"barbaric chants"
"using charms"
"unholy rites"
"innumerable amulets"

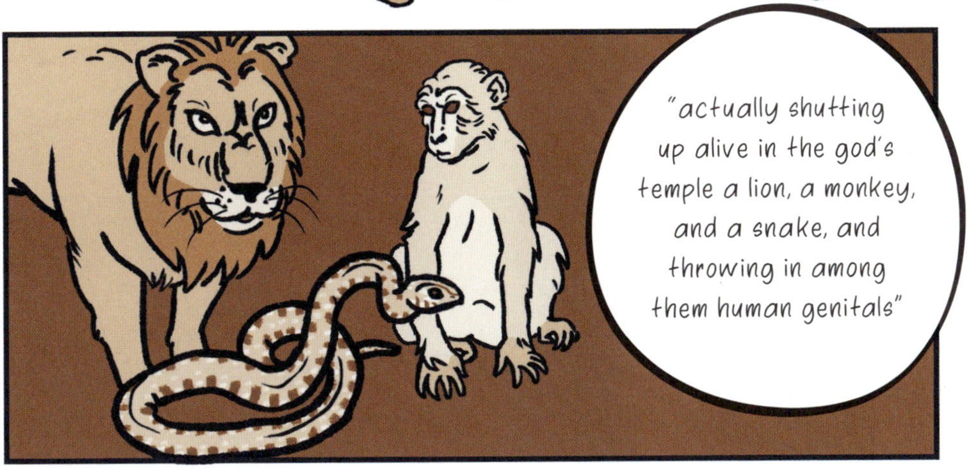
"actually shutting up alive in the god's temple a lion, a monkey, and a snake, and throwing in among them human genitals"

Sacrificing animals like sheep and cows was common in Roman religion, but what actually transpired during Elagabalus's rituals is unverifiable.

Elagabalus is also rumored to have had a scandalous love life, even for a Roman emperor!

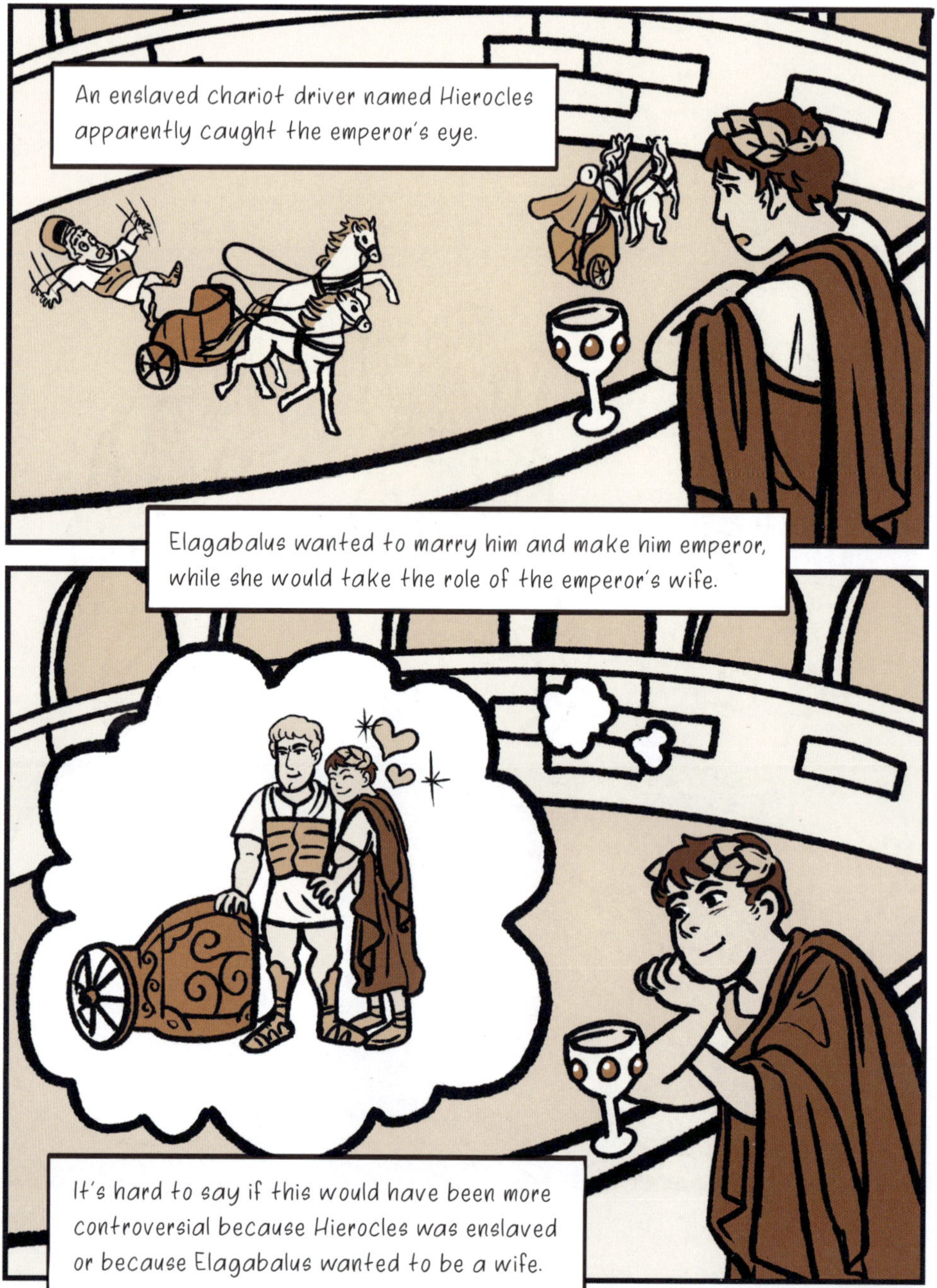
An enslaved chariot driver named Hierocles apparently caught the emperor's eye.
Elagabalus wanted to marry him and make him emperor, while she would take the role of the emperor's wife.
It's hard to say if this would have been more controversial because Hierocles was enslaved or because Elagabalus wanted to be a wife.

Elagabalus did get married several times, at one point to a Vestal Virgin named Aquilia Severa, which was particularly taboo in traditional Roman religion.

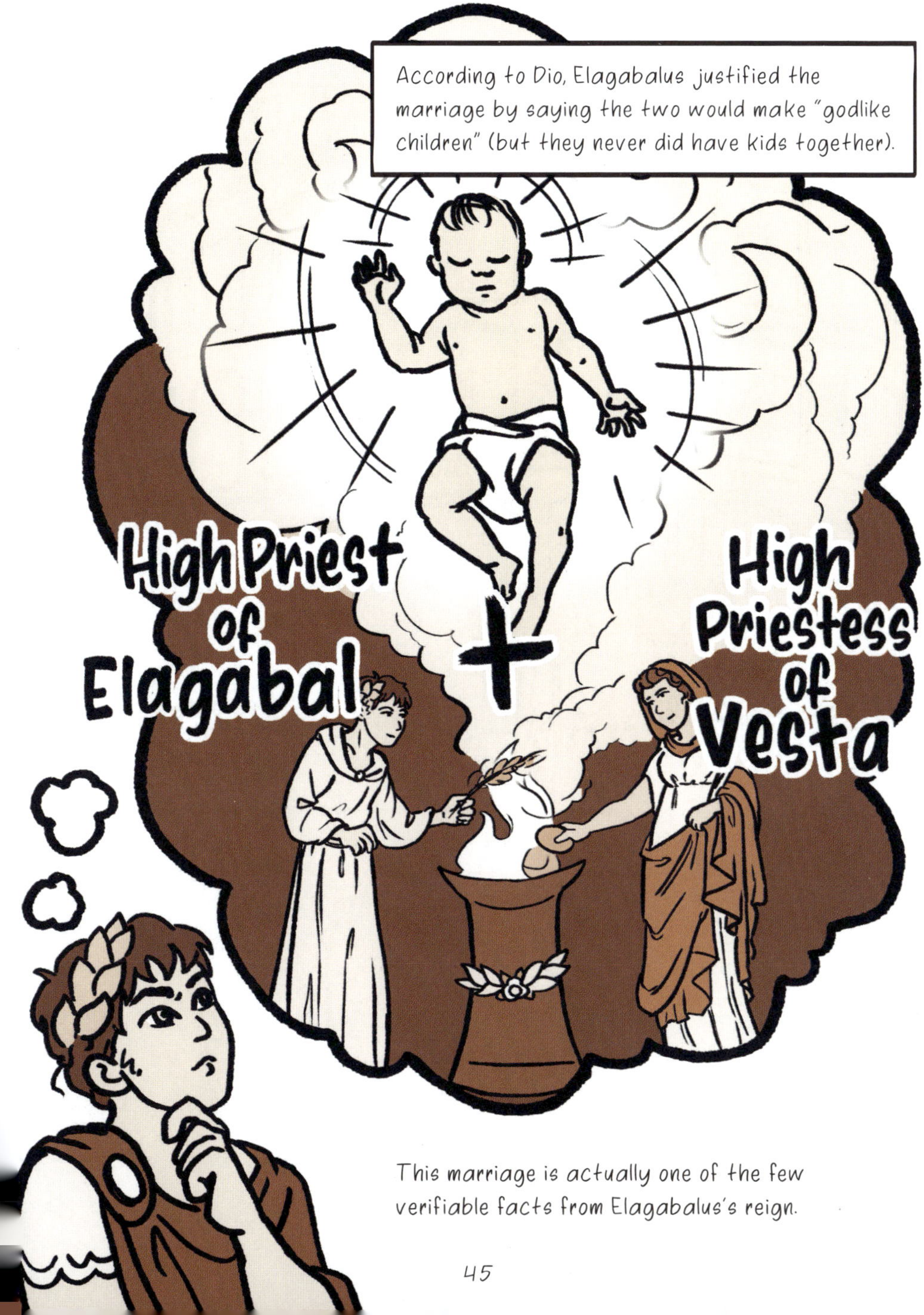
According to Dio, Elagabalus justified the marriage by saying the two would make "godlike children" (but they never did have kids together).
High Priest of Elagabal
+
High Priestess of Vesta

This marriage is actually one of the few verifiable facts from Elagabalus's reign.

But it wasn't all scandal:

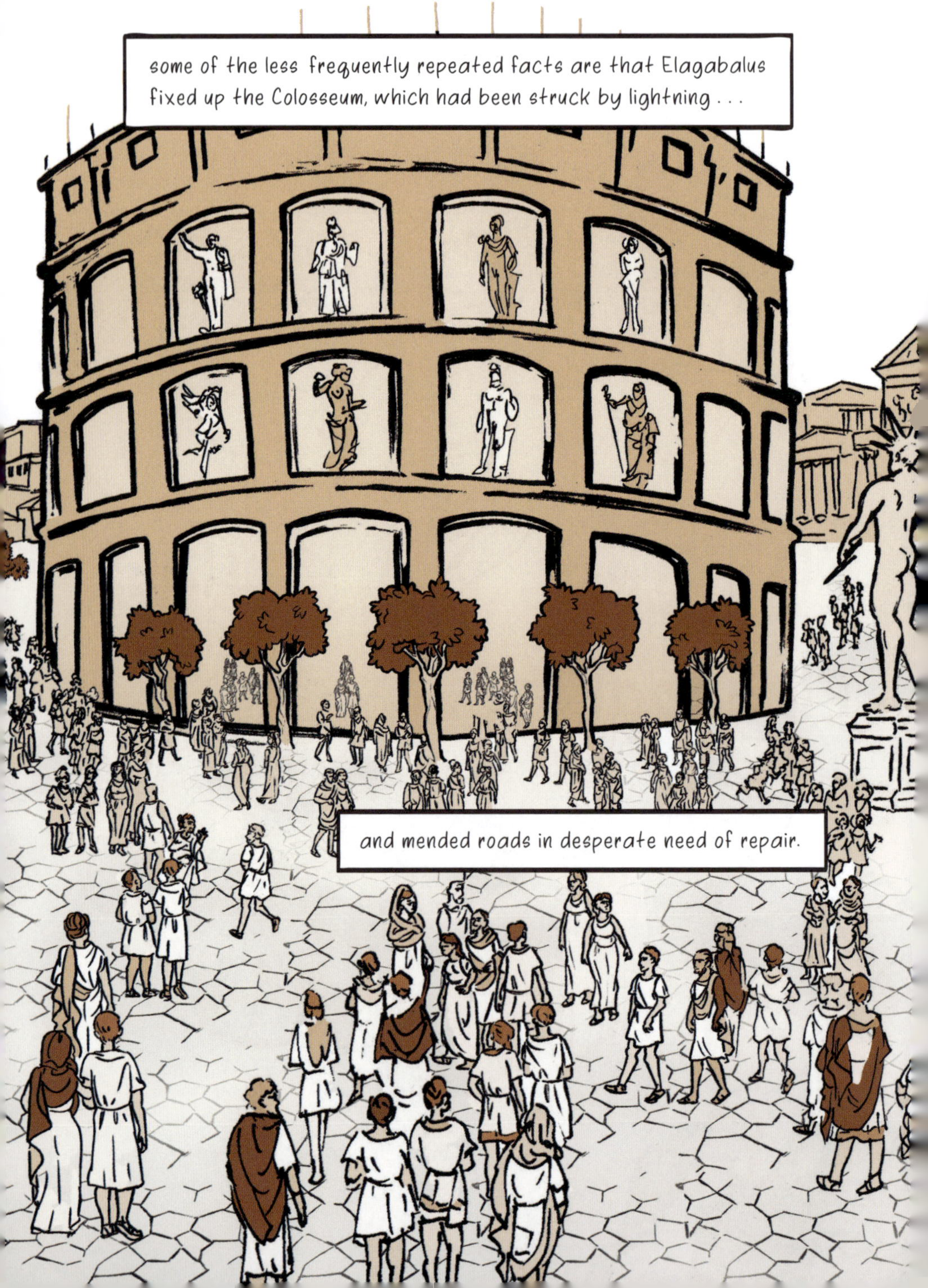
some of the less frequently repeated facts are that Elagabalus fixed up the Colosseum, which had been struck by lightning . . .
and mended roads in desperate need of repair.

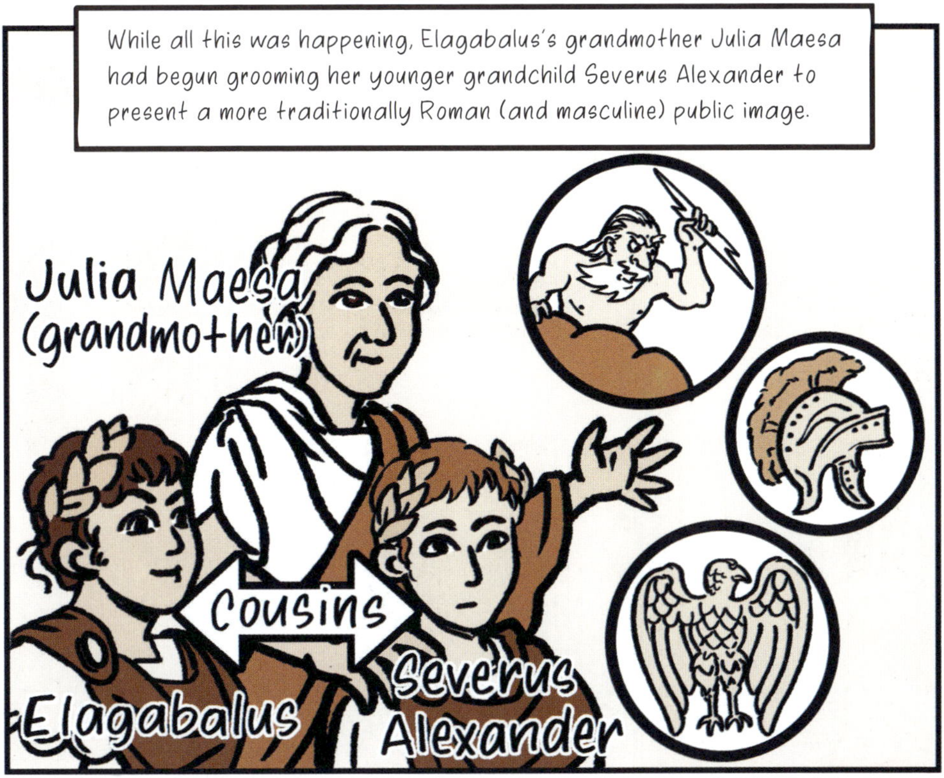
While all this was happening, Elagabalus's grandmother Julia Maesa had begun grooming her younger grandchild Severus Alexander to present a more traditionally Roman (and masculine) public image.
Julia Maesa (grandmother)
Cousins
Elagabalus
Severus Alexander

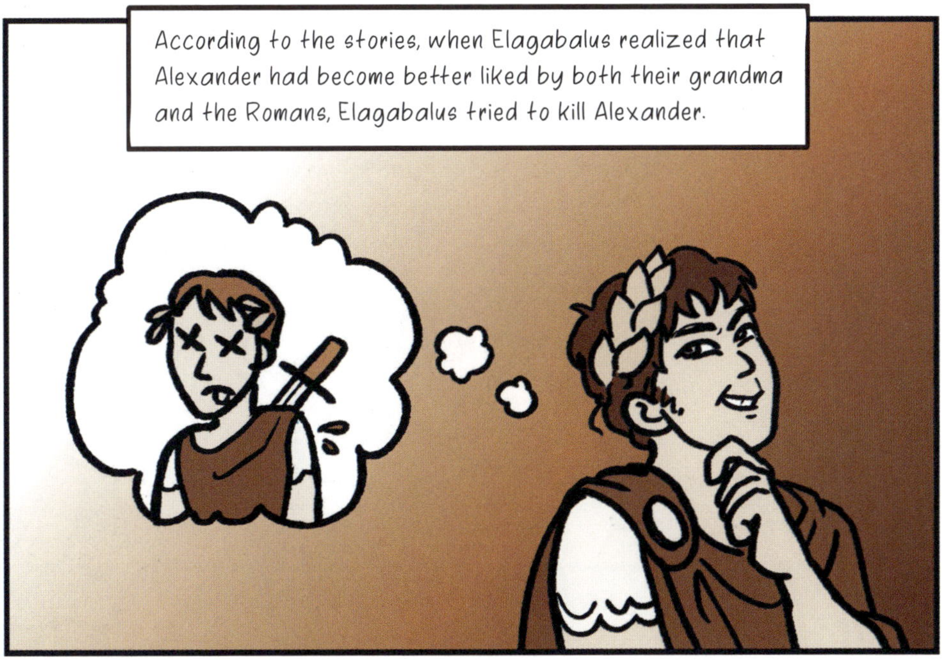
According to the stories, when Elagabalus realized that Alexander had become better liked by both their grandma and the Romans, Elagabalus tried to kill Alexander.

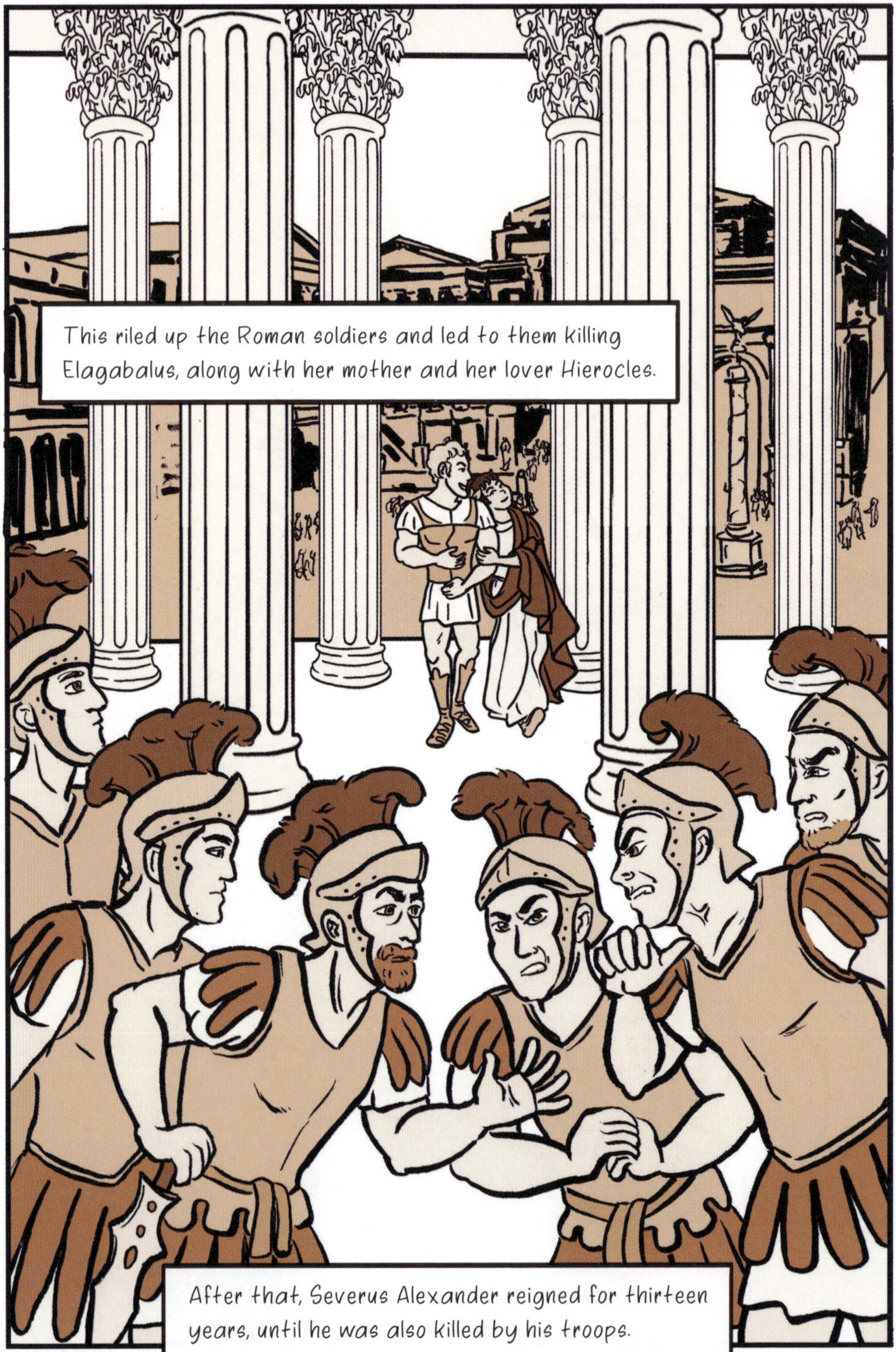
This riled up the Roman soldiers and led to them killing Elagabalus, along with her mother and her lover Hierocles.
After that, Severus Alexander reigned for thirteen years, until he was also killed by his troops.

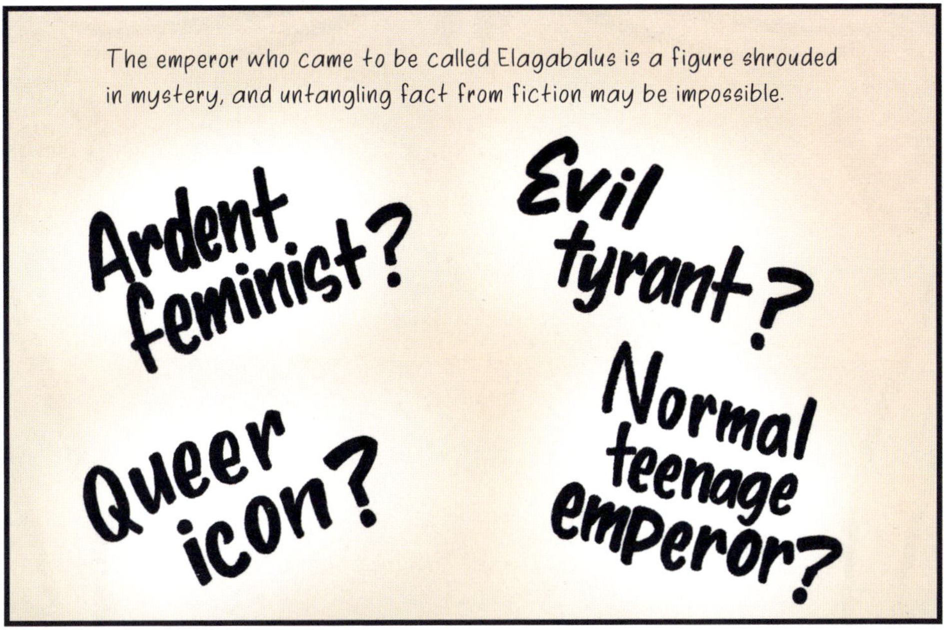
The emperor who came to be called Elagabalus is a figure shrouded in mystery, and untangling fact from fiction may be impossible.
Ardent feminist?
Evil tyrant?
Queer icon?
Normal teenage emperor?

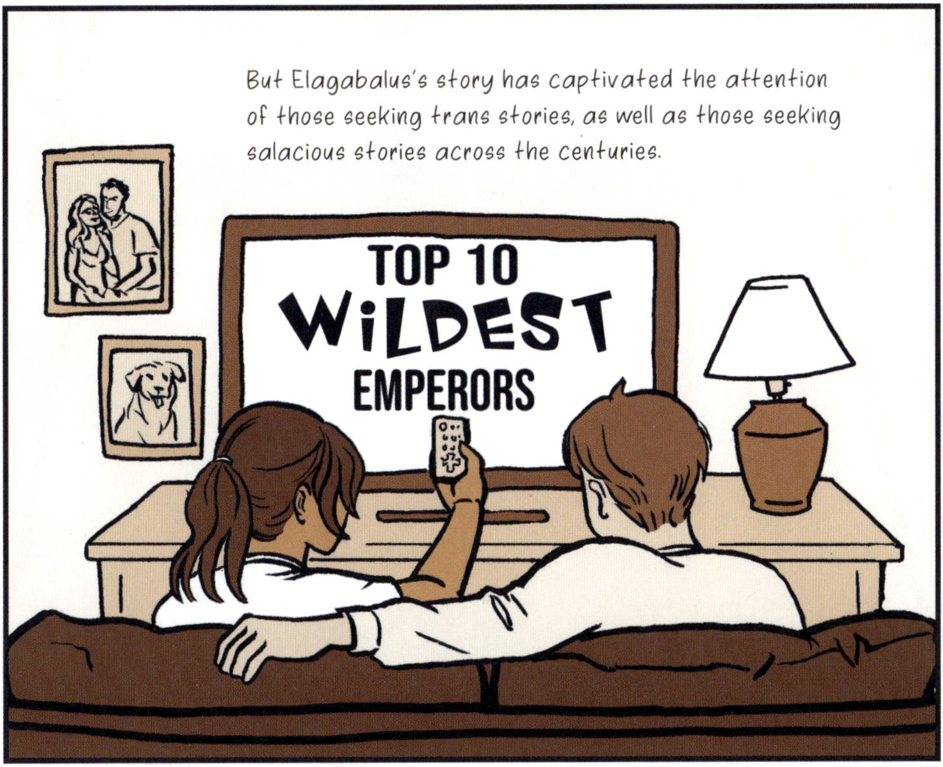
But Elagabalus's story has captivated the attention of those seeking trans stories, as well as those seeking salacious stories across the centuries.
TOP 10 WiLDEST EMPERORS

Why do certain stories from history get repeated over and over, while others are not remembered at all?

Who is telling the story?

Why?

Who is the audience?

What does the story reveal about the point of view of whoever recorded it?

What were the motivations for recording it?

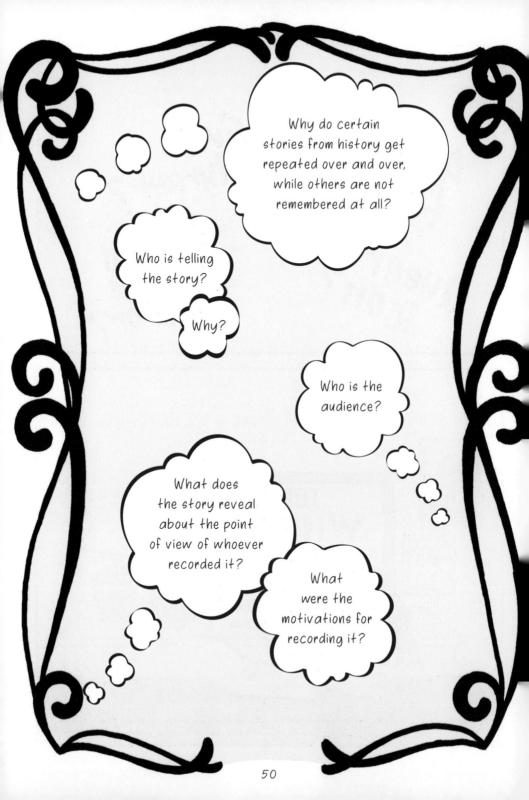

2

Europeans Behaving Badly: From the OLD WORLD to the "NEW" WORLD

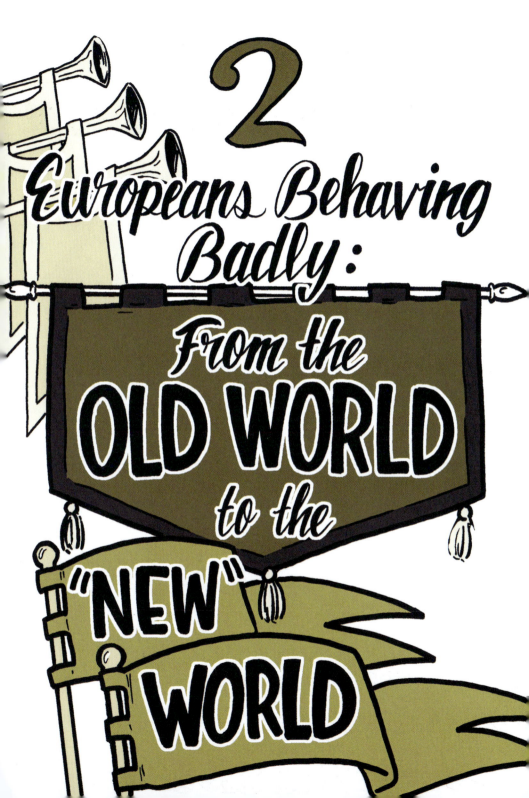

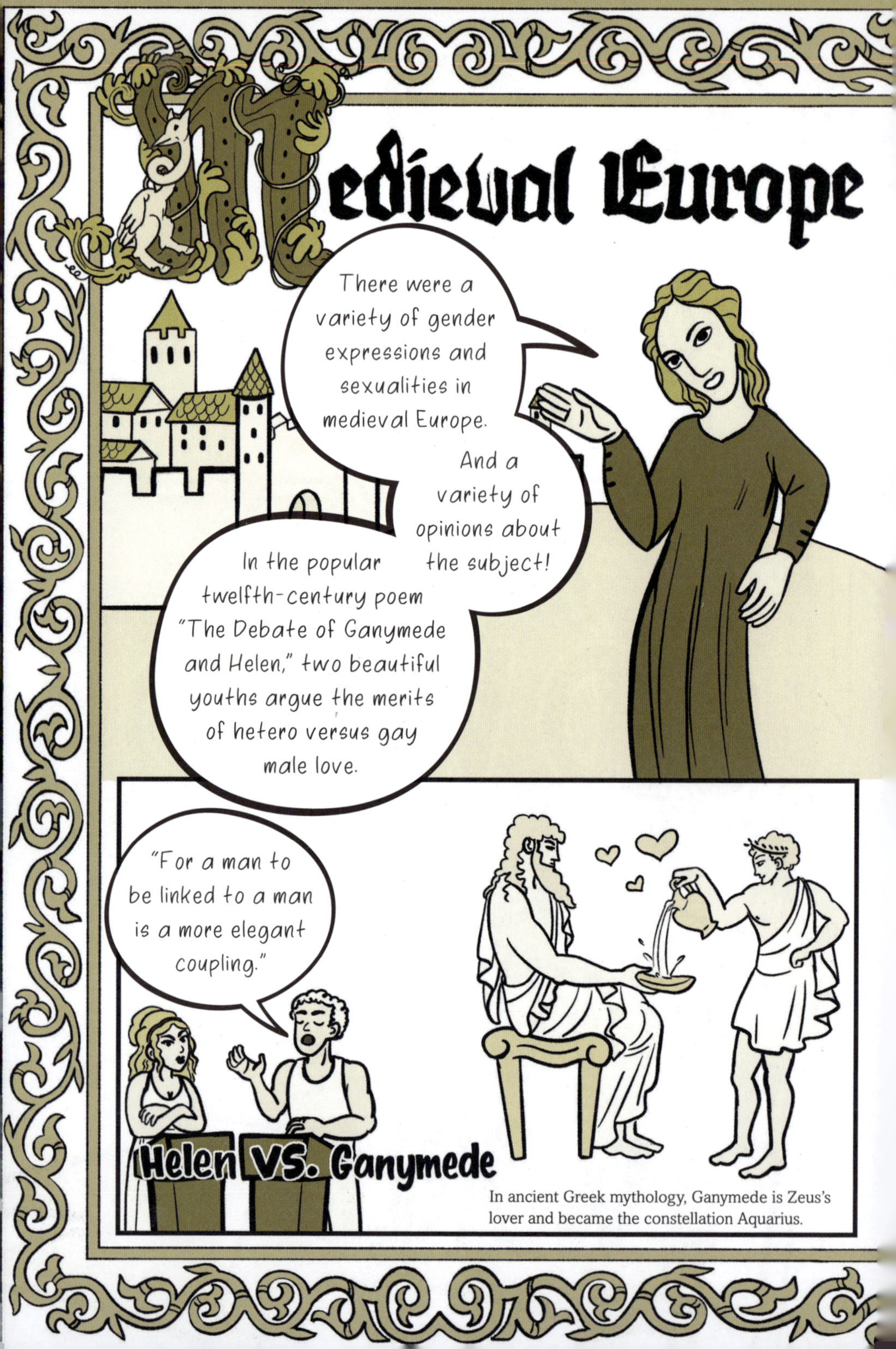
Medieval Europe
There were a variety of gender expressions and sexualities in medieval Europe.
And a variety of opinions about the subject!
In the popular twelfth-century poem "The Debate of Ganymede and Helen," two beautiful youths argue the merits of hetero versus gay male love.
"For a man to be linked to a man is a more elegant coupling."
Helen VS. Ganymede

In ancient Greek mythology, Ganymede is Zeus's lover and became the constellation Aquarius.

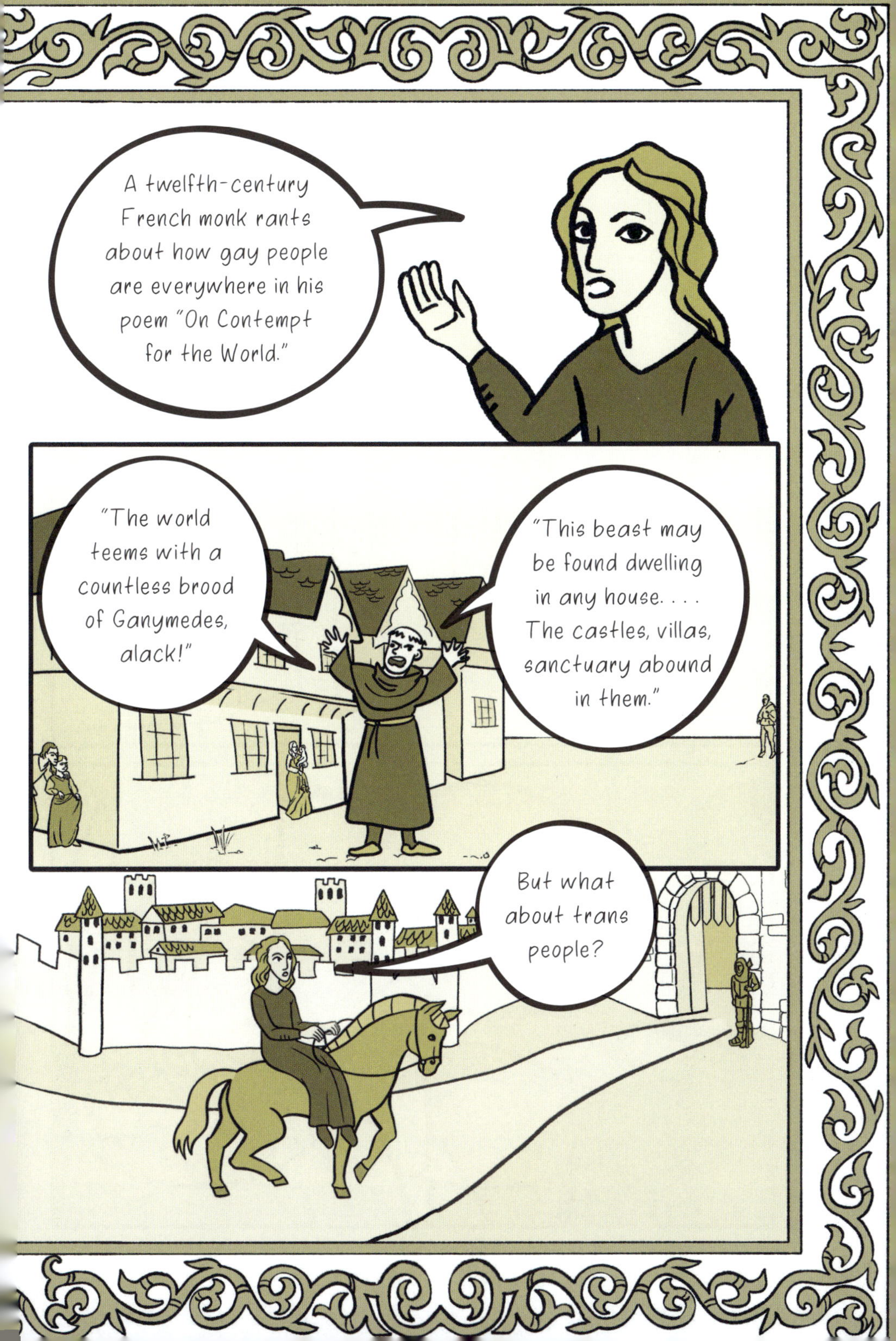
A twelfth-century French monk rants about how gay people are everywhere in his poem "On Contempt for the World."
"The world teems with a countless brood of Ganymedes, alack!"
"This beast may be found dwelling in any house. . . . The castles, villas, sanctuary abound in them."
But what about trans people?

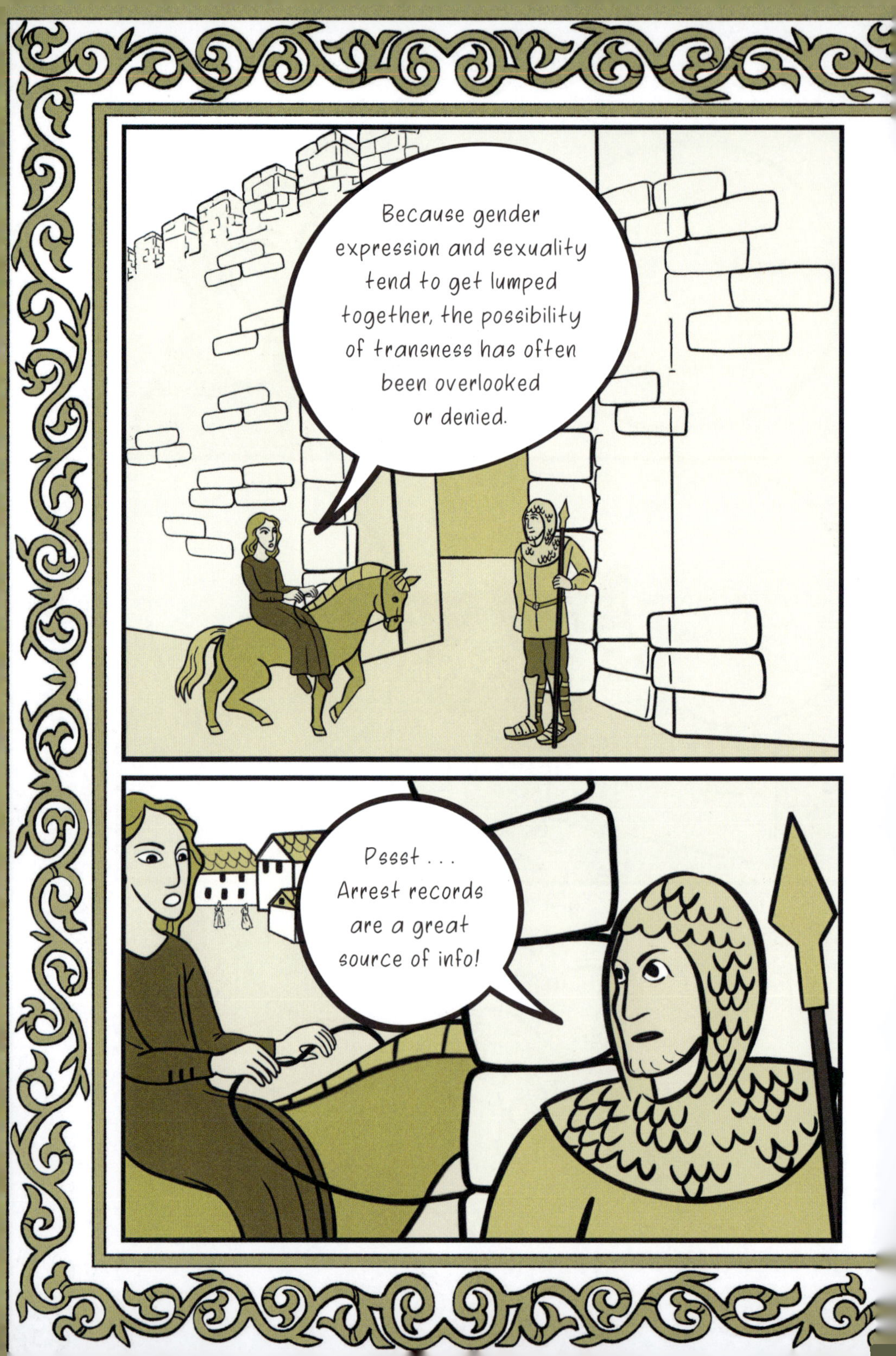
Because gender expression and sexuality tend to get lumped together, the possibility of transness has often been overlooked or denied.
Pssst . . . Arrest records are a great source of info!

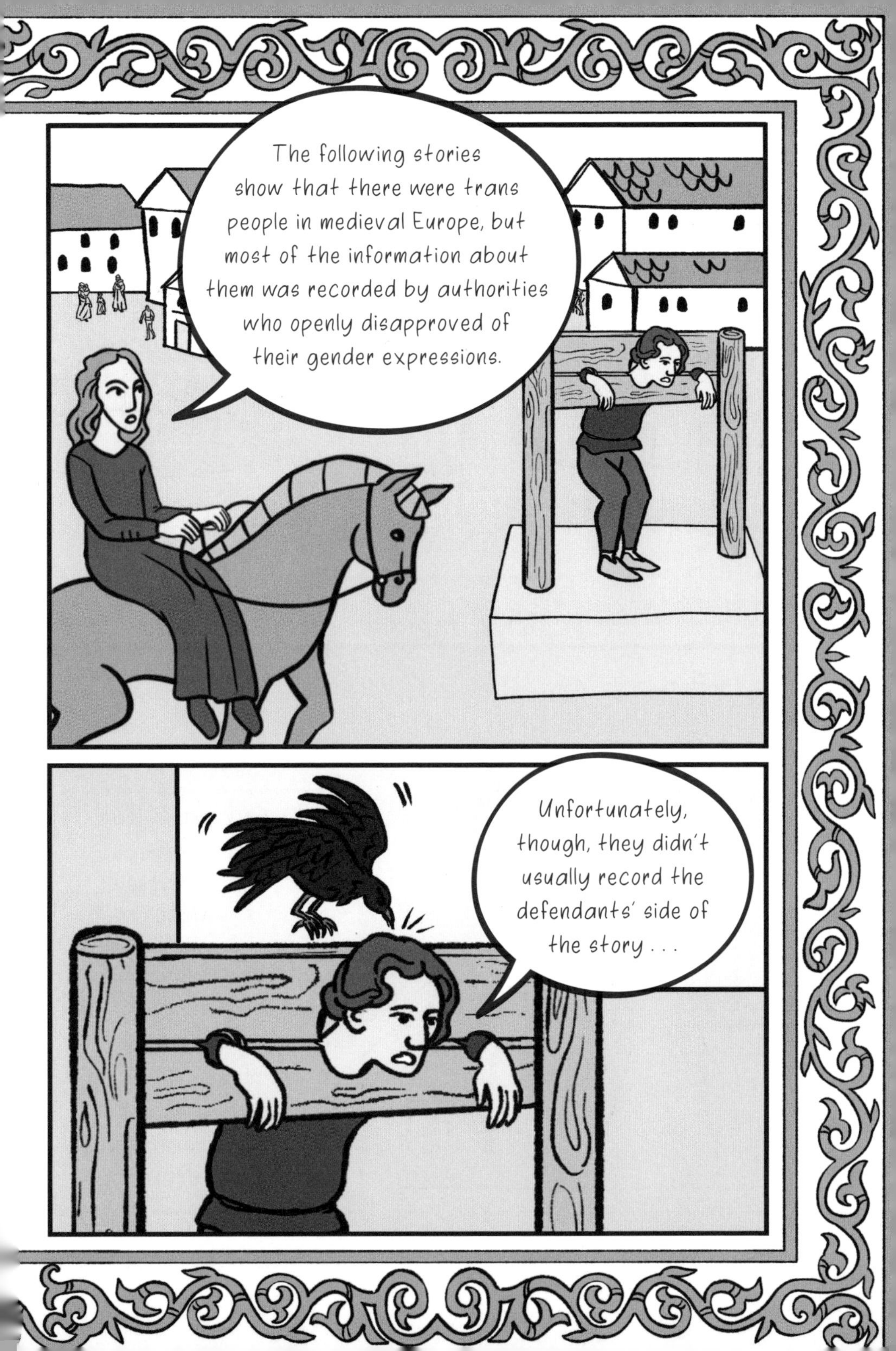
The following stories show that there were trans people in medieval Europe, but most of the information about them was recorded by authorities who openly disapproved of their gender expressions.
Unfortunately, though, they didn't usually record the defendants' side of the story . . .

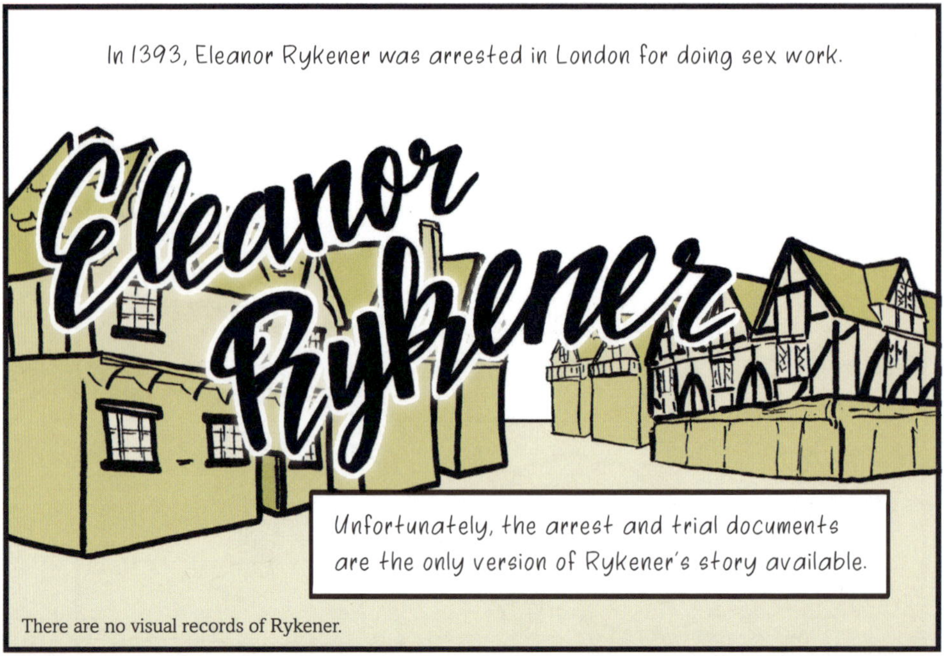
In 1393, Eleanor Rykener was arrested in London for doing sex work.
Eleanor Rykener
Unfortunately, the arrest and trial documents are the only version of Rykener's story available.
There are no visual records of Rykener.

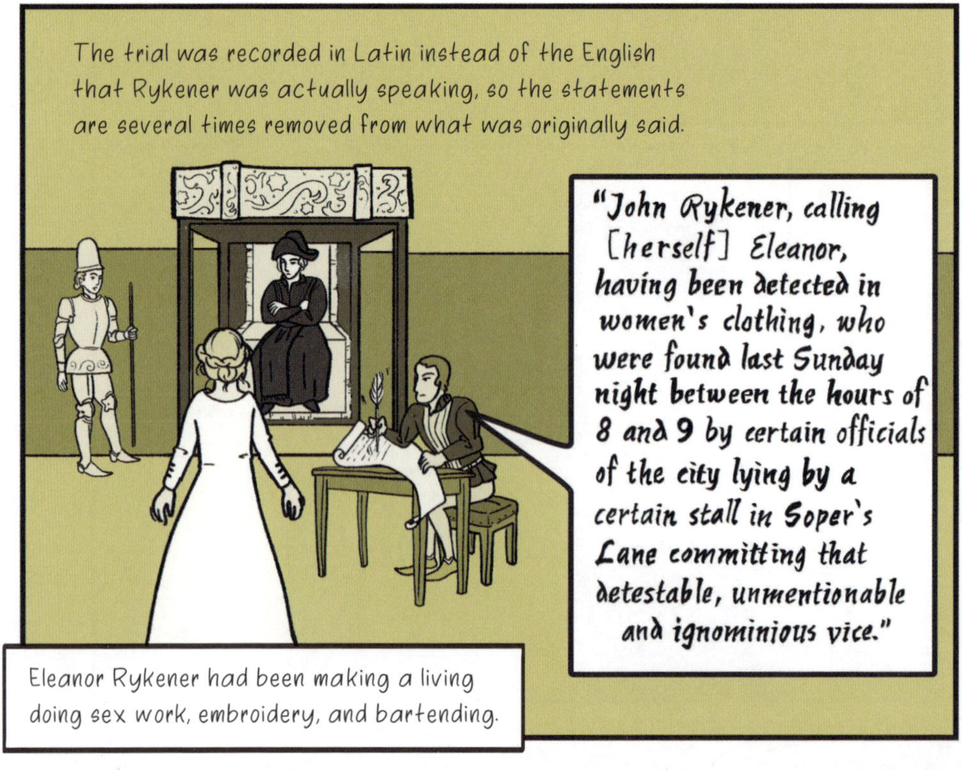
The trial was recorded in Latin instead of the English that Rykener was actually speaking, so the statements are several times removed from what was originally said.
"John Rykener, calling [herself] Eleanor, having been detected in women's clothing, who were found last Sunday night between the hours of 8 and 9 by certain officials of the city lying by a certain stall in Soper's Lane committing that detestable, unmentionable and ignominious vice."
Eleanor Rykener had been making a living doing sex work, embroidery, and bartending.

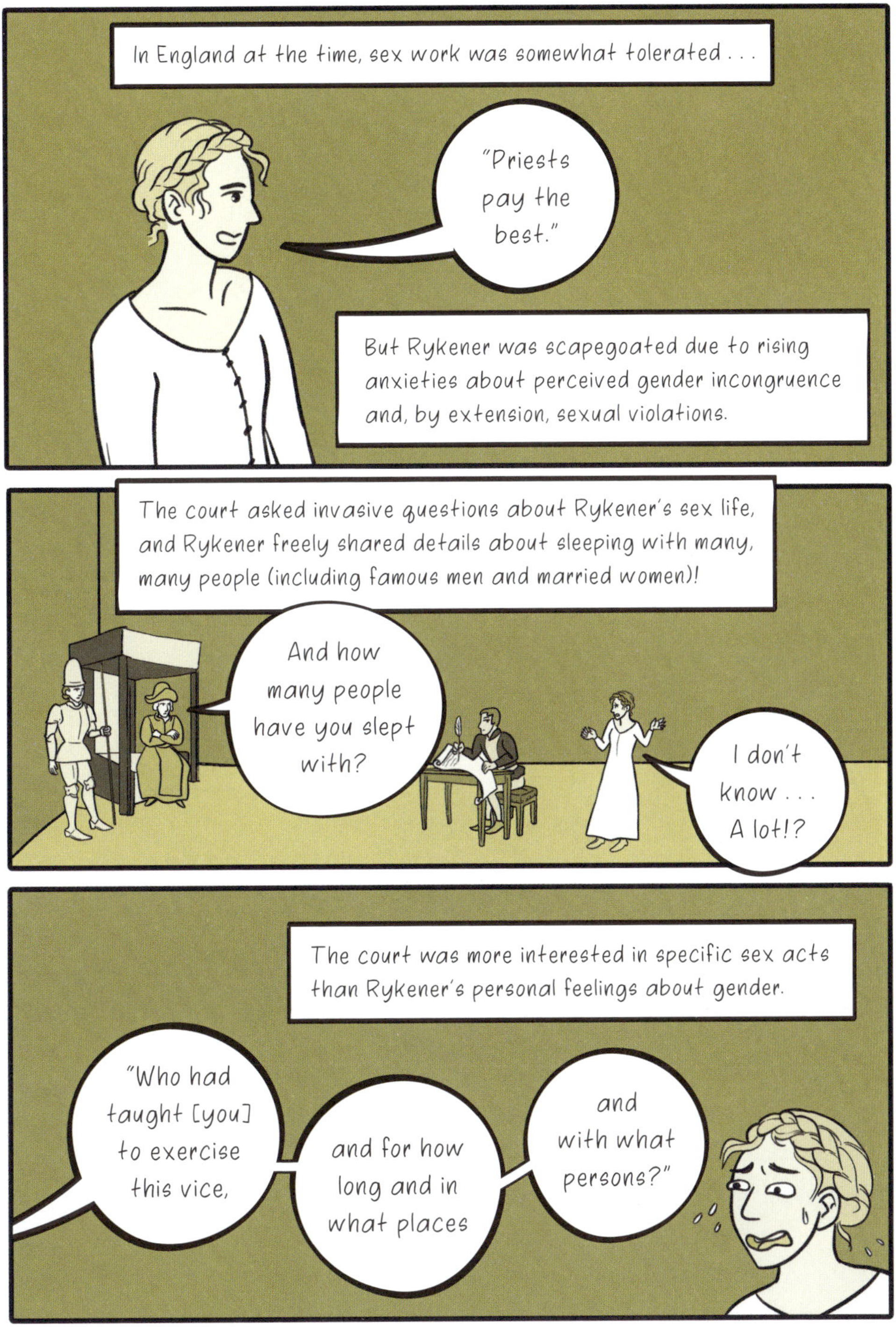
In England at the time, sex work was somewhat tolerated . . .
"Priests pay the best."
But Rykener was scapegoated due to rising anxieties about perceived gender incongruence and, by extension, sexual violations.
The court asked invasive questions about Rykener's sex life, and Rykener freely shared details about sleeping with many, many people (including famous men and married women)!
And how many people have you slept with?
I don't know . . . A lot!?
The court was more interested in specific sex acts than Rykener's personal feelings about gender.
"Who had taught [you] to exercise this vice,
and for how long and in what places
and with what persons?"

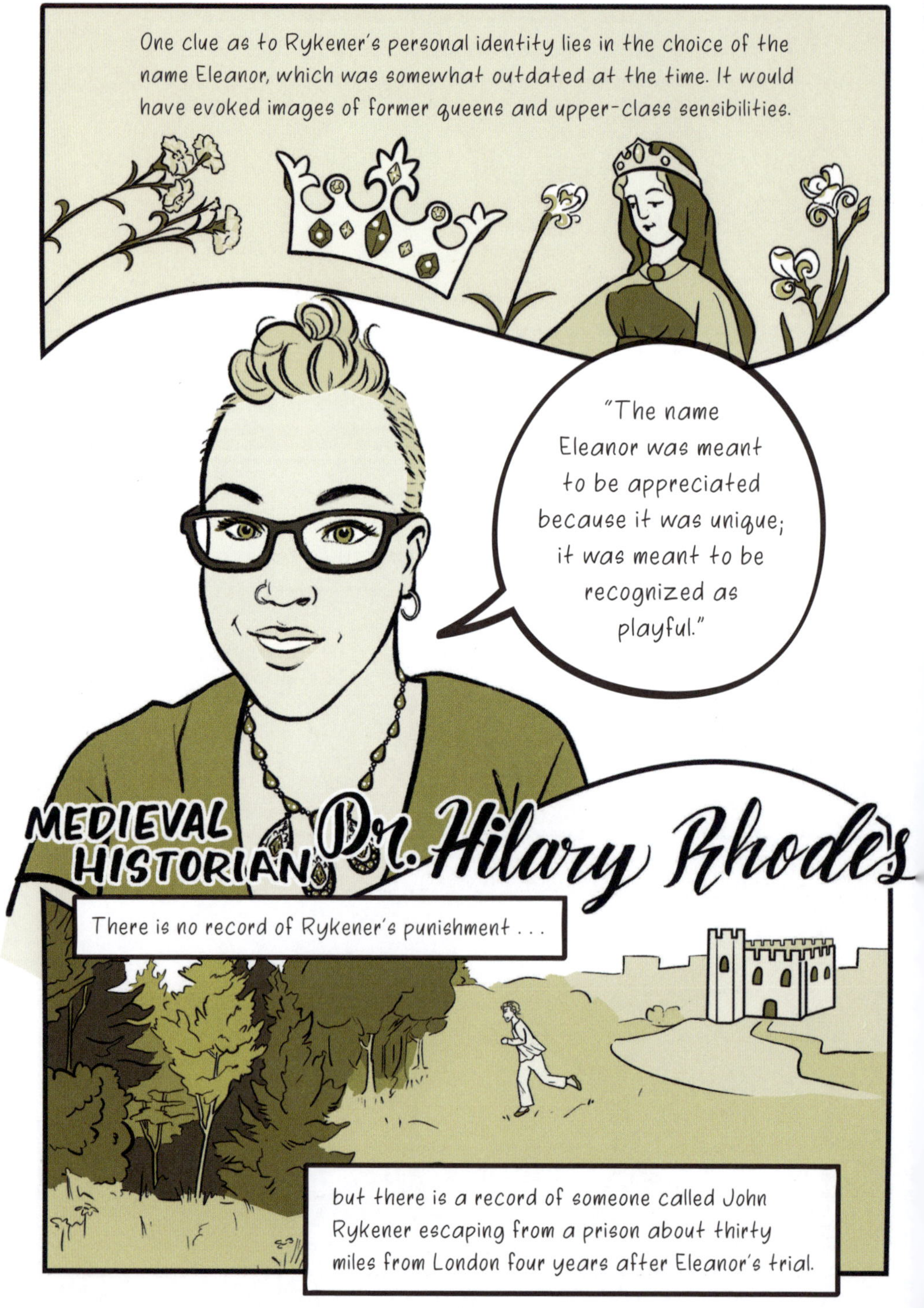
One clue as to Rykener's personal identity lies in the choice of the name Eleanor, which was somewhat outdated at the time. It would have evoked images of former queens and upper-class sensibilities.
"The name Eleanor was meant to be appreciated because it was unique; it was meant to be recognized as playful."
MEDIEVAL HISTORIAN Dr. Hilary Rhodes
There is no record of Rykener's punishment . . .
but there is a record of someone called John Rykener escaping from a prison about thirty miles from London four years after Eleanor's trial.

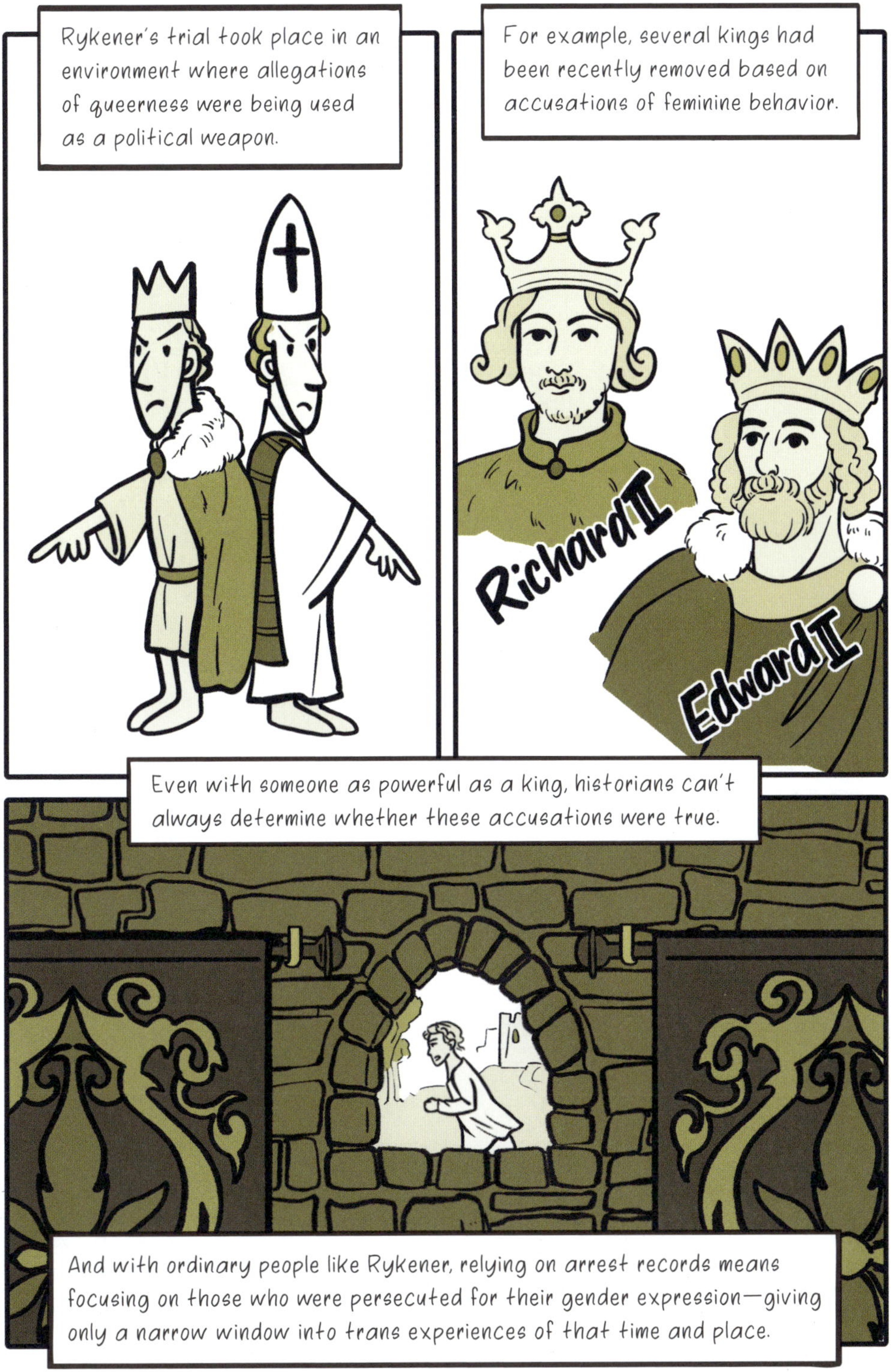
Rykener's trial took place in an environment where allegations of queerness were being used as a political weapon.
For example, several kings had been recently removed based on accusations of feminine behavior.
Richard II
Edward II
Even with someone as powerful as a king, historians can't always determine whether these accusations were true.
And with ordinary people like Rykener, relying on arrest records means focusing on those who were persecuted for their gender expression—giving only a narrow window into trans experiences of that time and place.

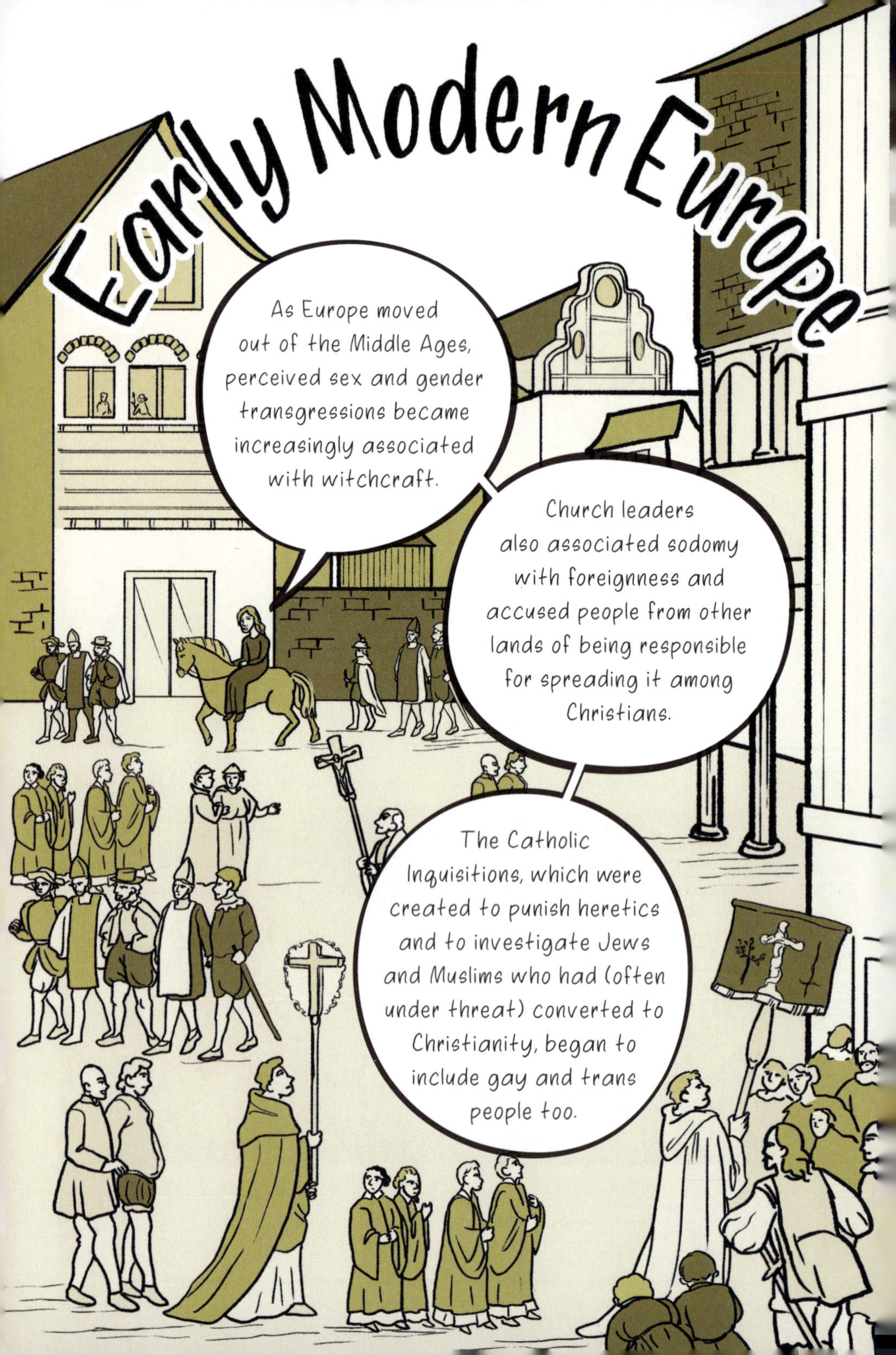
Early Modern Europe
As Europe moved out of the Middle Ages, perceived sex and gender transgressions became increasingly associated with witchcraft.
Church leaders also associated sodomy with foreignness and accused people from other lands of being responsible for spreading it among Christians.
The Catholic Inquisitions, which were created to punish heretics and to investigate Jews and Muslims who had (often under threat) converted to Christianity, began to include gay and trans people too.

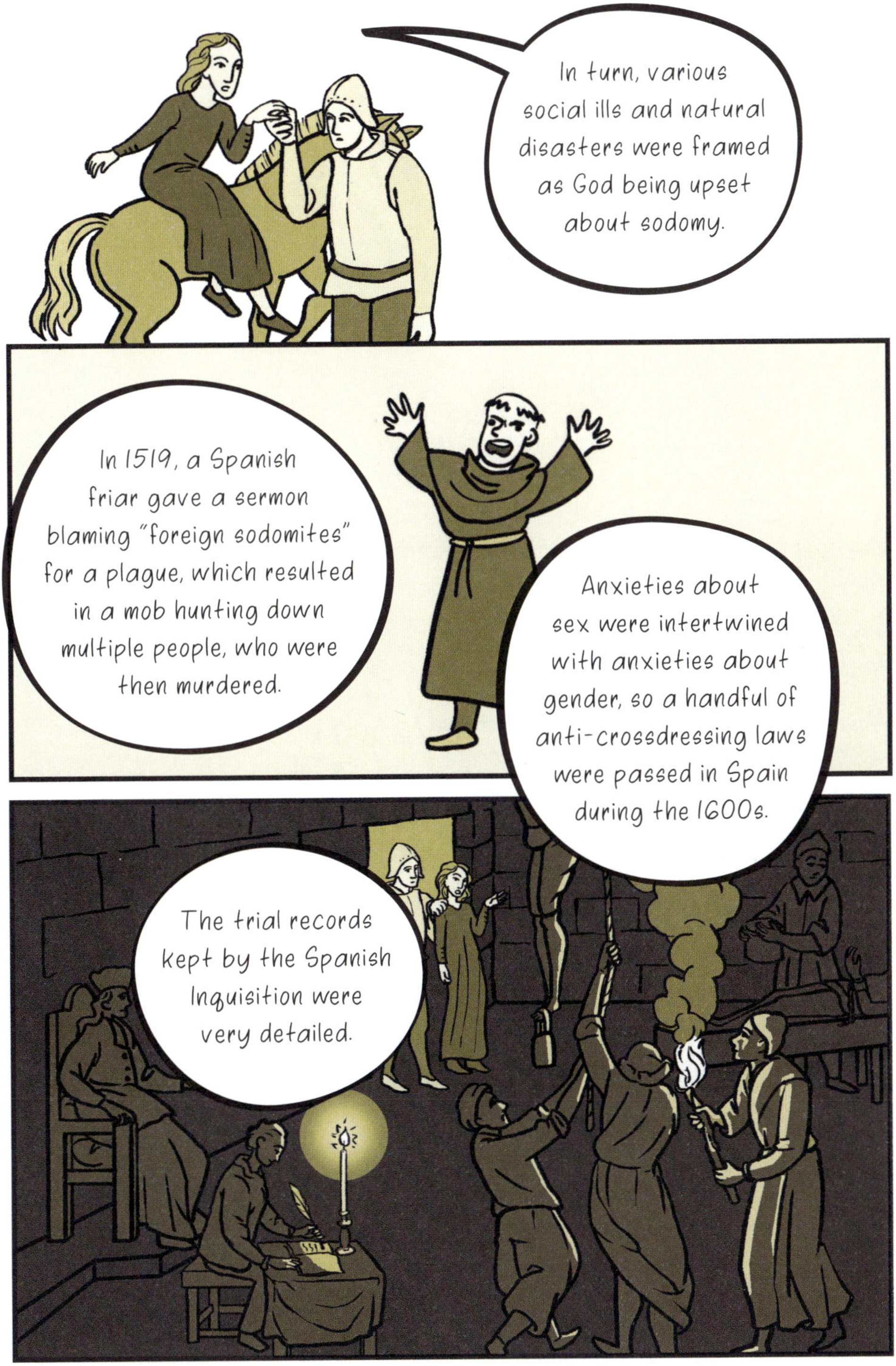
In turn, various social ills and natural disasters were framed as God being upset about sodomy.
In 1519, a Spanish friar gave a sermon blaming "foreign sodomites" for a plague, which resulted in a mob hunting down multiple people, who were then murdered.
Anxieties about sex were intertwined with anxieties about gender, so a handful of anti-crossdressing laws were passed in Spain during the 1600s.
The trial records kept by the Spanish Inquisition were very detailed.

In 1587, Eleno de Céspedes was arrested and accused of making a deal with the devil and pretending to be a man.

Eleno de Céspedes

There are no visual records of Céspedes.

Born in Spain around 1545 to a Spanish farmer father and an enslaved North African mother, Céspedes was enslaved at birth, yet he grew up to be a self-educated medical professional.

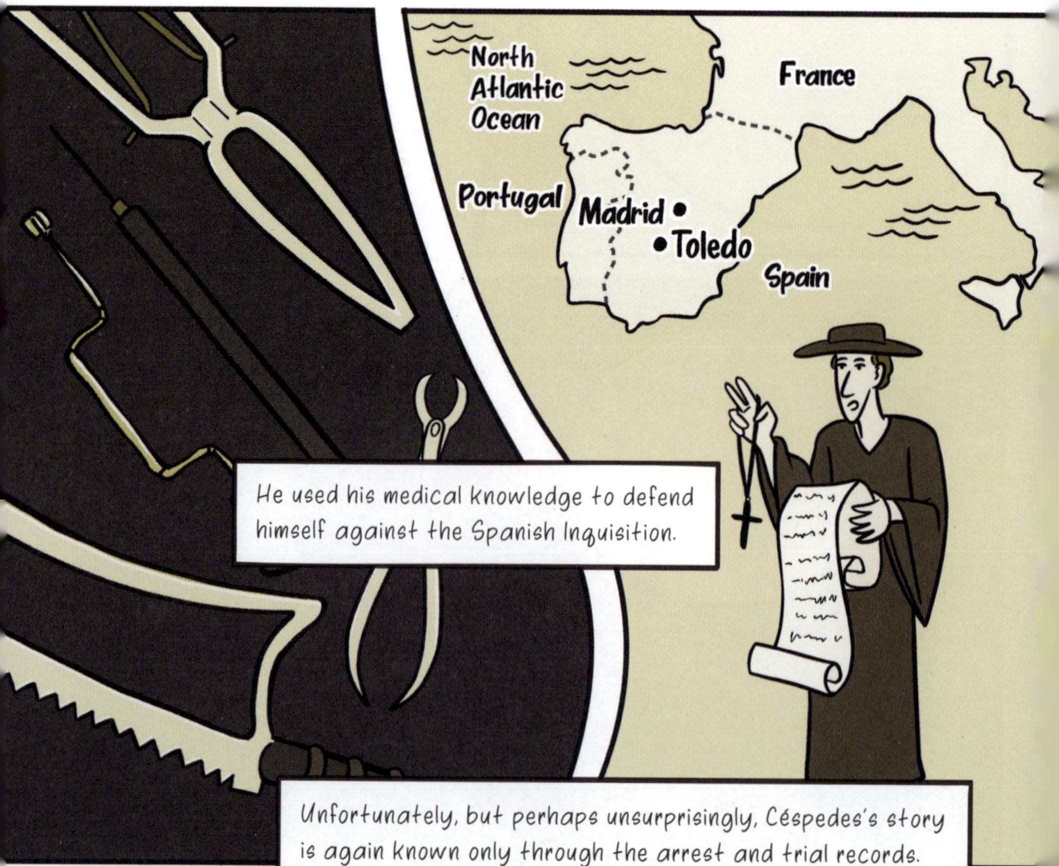
North Atlantic Ocean
France
Portugal
Madrid
Toledo
Spain
He used his medical knowledge to defend himself against the Spanish Inquisition.
Unfortunately, but perhaps unsurprisingly, Céspedes's story is again known only through the arrest and trial records.

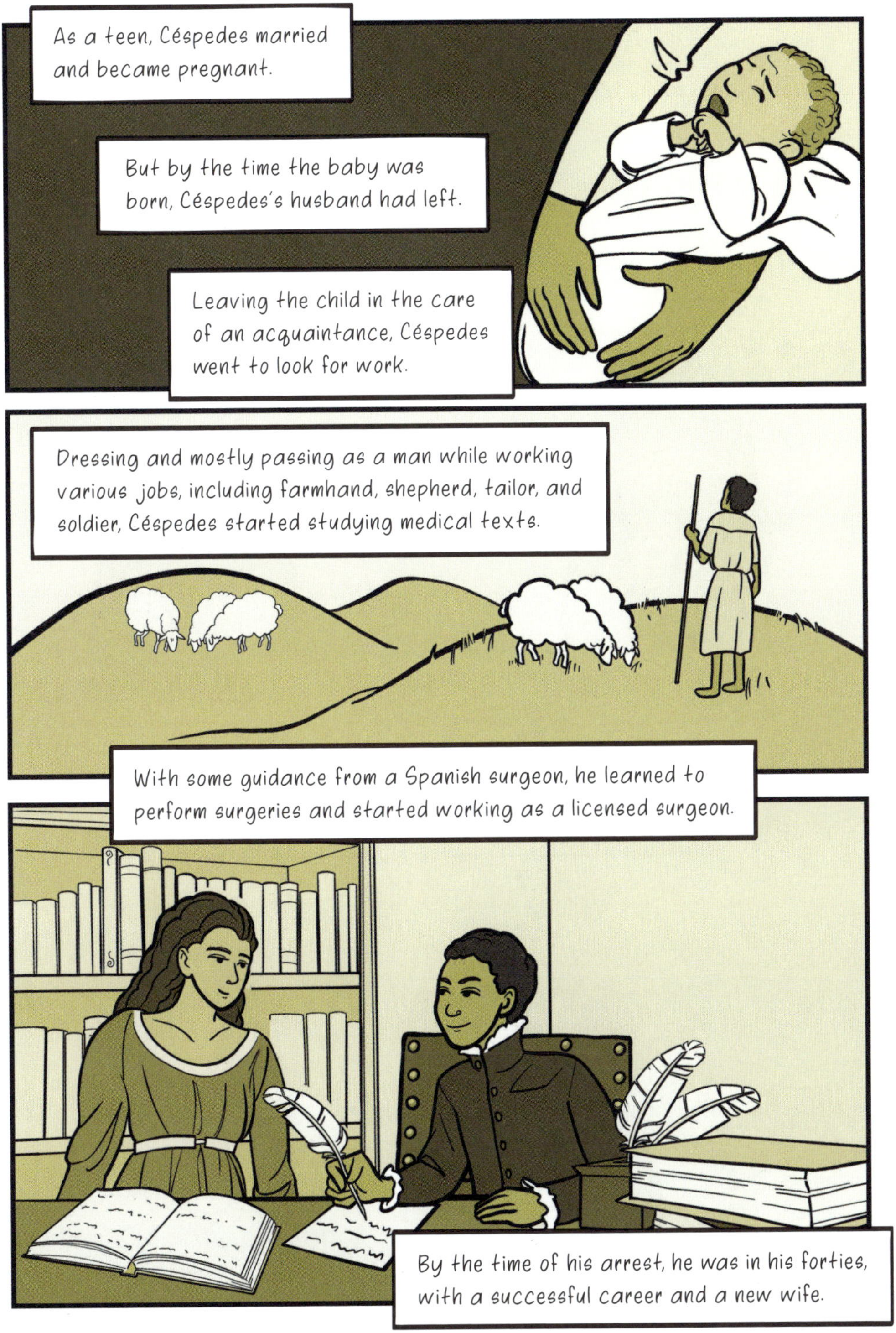
As a teen, Céspedes married and became pregnant.
But by the time the baby was born, Céspedes's husband had left.
Leaving the child in the care of an acquaintance, Céspedes went to look for work.
Dressing and mostly passing as a man while working various jobs, including farmhand, shepherd, tailor, and soldier, Céspedes started studying medical texts.
With some guidance from a Spanish surgeon, he learned to perform surgeries and started working as a licensed surgeon.
By the time of his arrest, he was in his forties, with a successful career and a new wife.

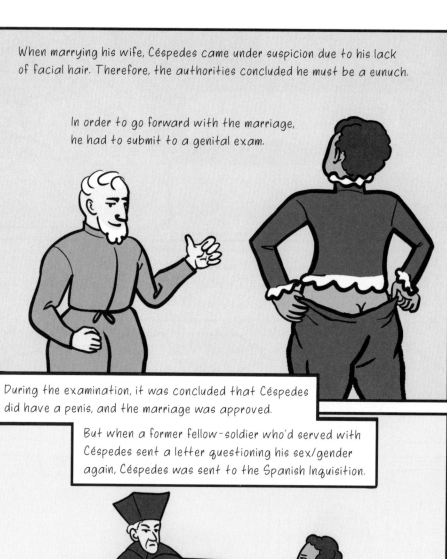

When marrying his wife, Céspedes came under suspicion due to his lack of facial hair. Therefore, the authorities concluded he must be a eunuch.

In order to go forward with the marriage, he had to submit to a genital exam.

During the examination, it was concluded that Céspedes did have a penis, and the marriage was approved.

But when a former fellow-soldier who'd served with Céspedes sent a letter questioning his sex/gender again, Céspedes was sent to the Spanish Inquisition.

The Inquisition would later claim that the penis seen during the pre-marriage exam must have been the result of witchcraft.

But Céspedes explained his situation differently:

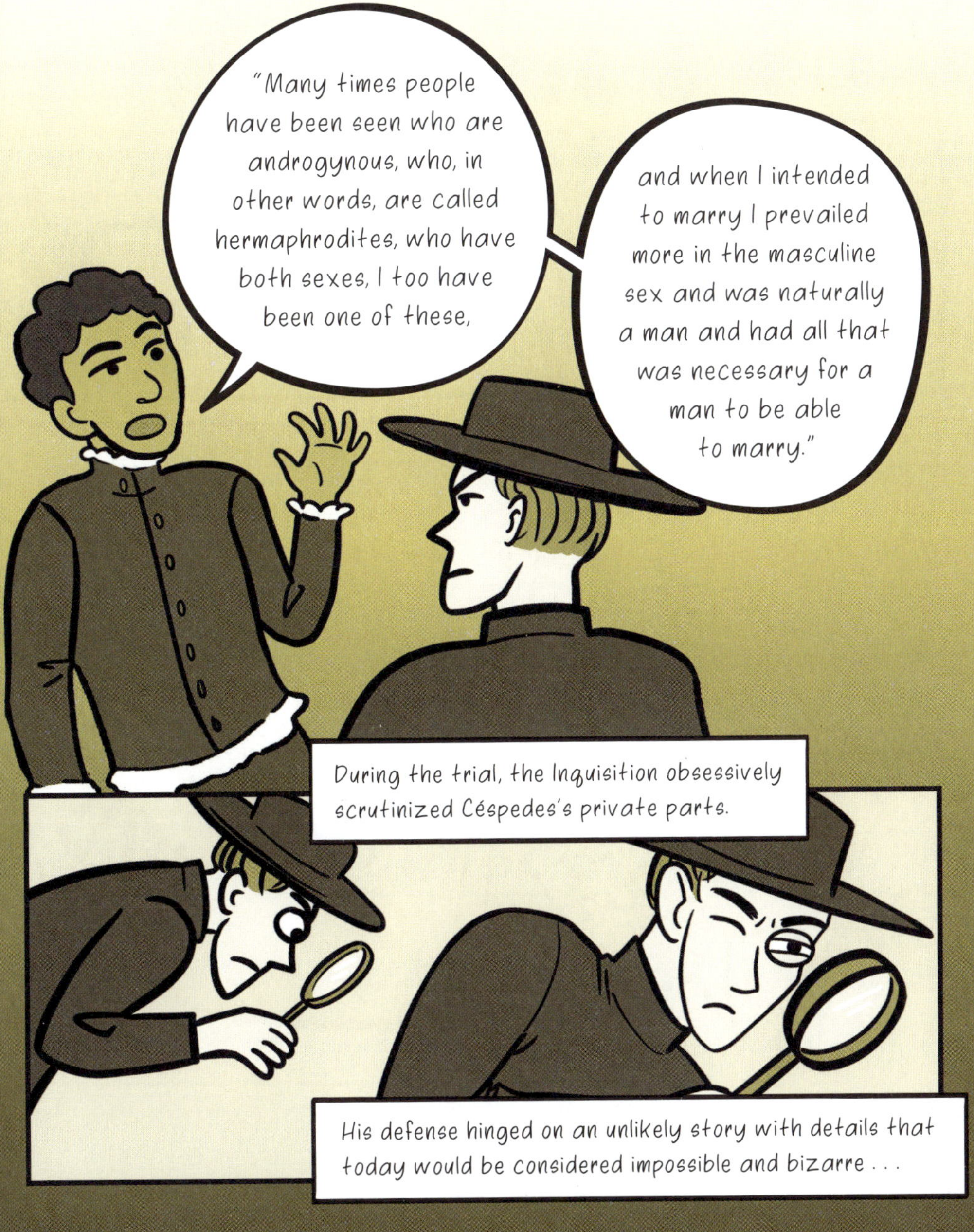
"Many times people have been seen who are androgynous, who, in other words, are called hermaphrodites, who have both sexes, I too have been one of these,
and when I intended to marry I prevailed more in the masculine sex and was naturally a man and had all that was necessary for a man to be able to marry."
During the trial, the Inquisition obsessively scrutinized Céspedes's private parts.
His defense hinged on an unlikely story with details that today would be considered impossible and bizarre . . .

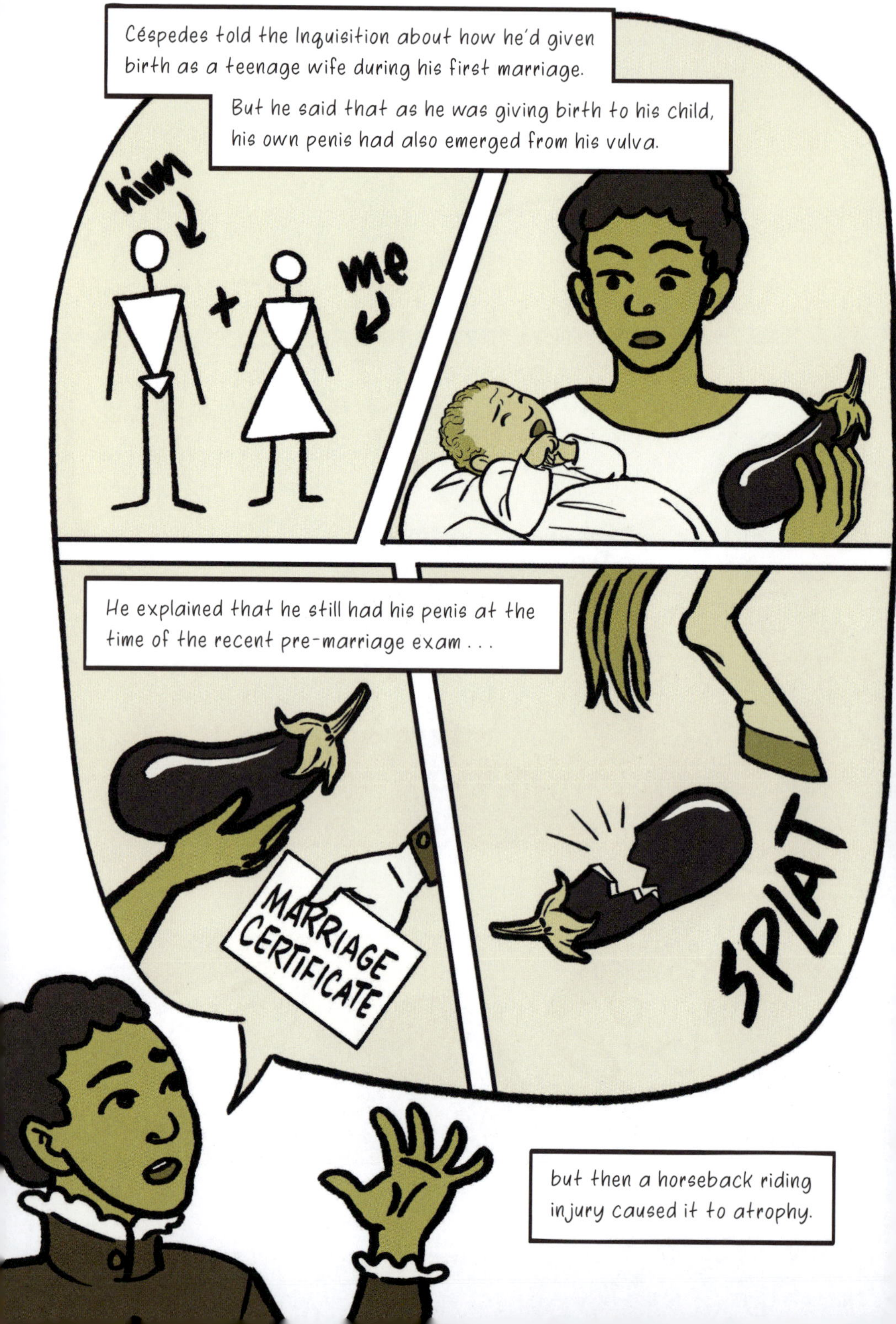
Céspedes told the Inquisition about how he'd given birth as a teenage wife during his first marriage.
But he said that as he was giving birth to his child, his own penis had also emerged from his vulva.
him
me
He explained that he still had his penis at the time of the recent pre-marriage exam . . .
MARRIAGE CERTIFICATE
SPLAT
but then a horseback riding injury caused it to atrophy.

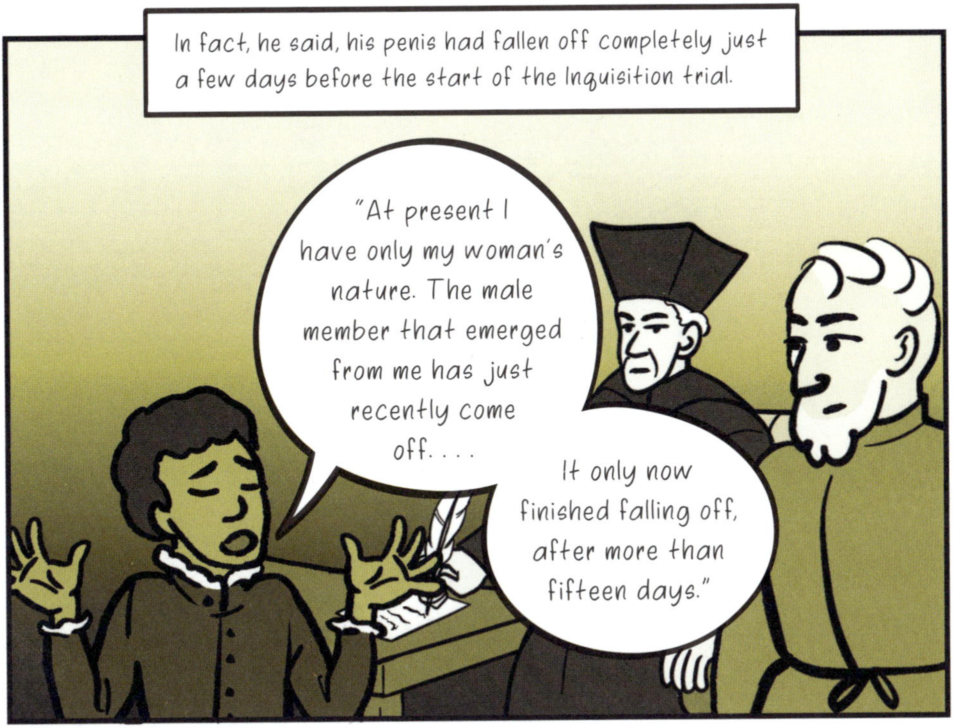
In fact, he said, his penis had fallen off completely just a few days before the start of the Inquisition trial.
"At present I have only my woman's nature. The male member that emerged from me has just recently come off. . . .
It only now finished falling off, after more than fifteen days."

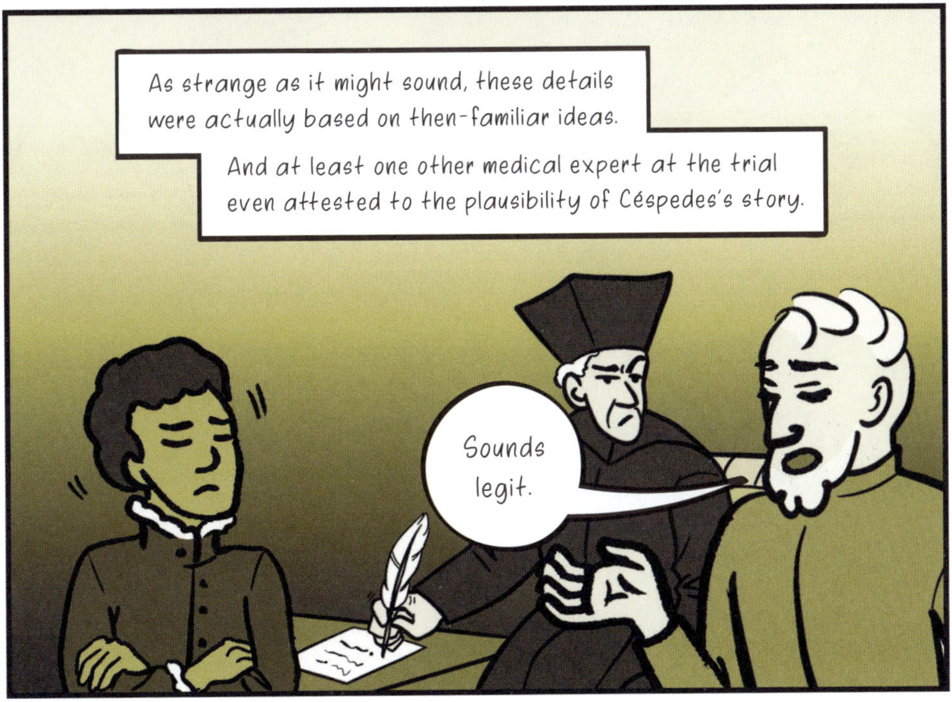
As strange as it might sound, these details were actually based on then-familiar ideas.
And at least one other medical expert at the trial even attested to the plausibility of Céspedes's story.
Sounds legit.

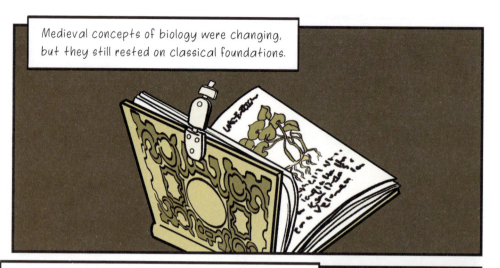

Medieval concepts of biology were changing, but they still rested on classical foundations.

Several famous Greek and Roman philosophers were cited during the trial in support of Céspedes's defense.

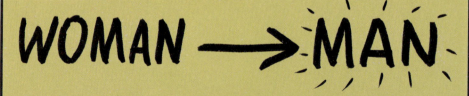

It was thought that men and women existed on a scale, with their reproductive anatomy being inverted versions of each other.

WOMAN ⟶ MAN

A spontaneous sex change was considered theoretically possible, but really only going in one direction—from woman to man.

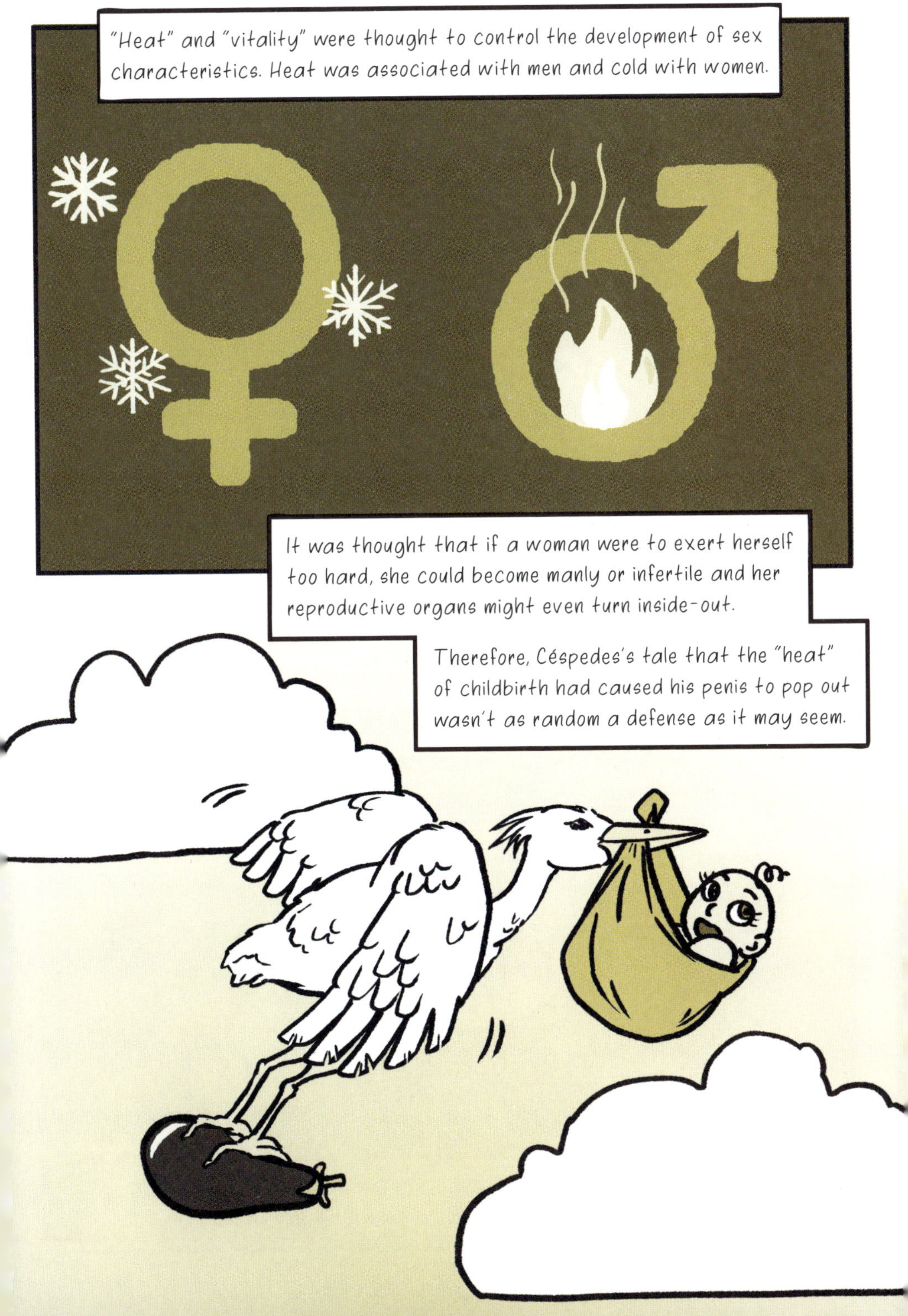
"Heat" and "vitality" were thought to control the development of sex characteristics. Heat was associated with men and cold with women.
It was thought that if a woman were to exert herself too hard, she could become manly or infertile and her reproductive organs might even turn inside-out.
Therefore, Céspedes's tale that the "heat" of childbirth had caused his penis to pop out wasn't as random a defense as it may seem.

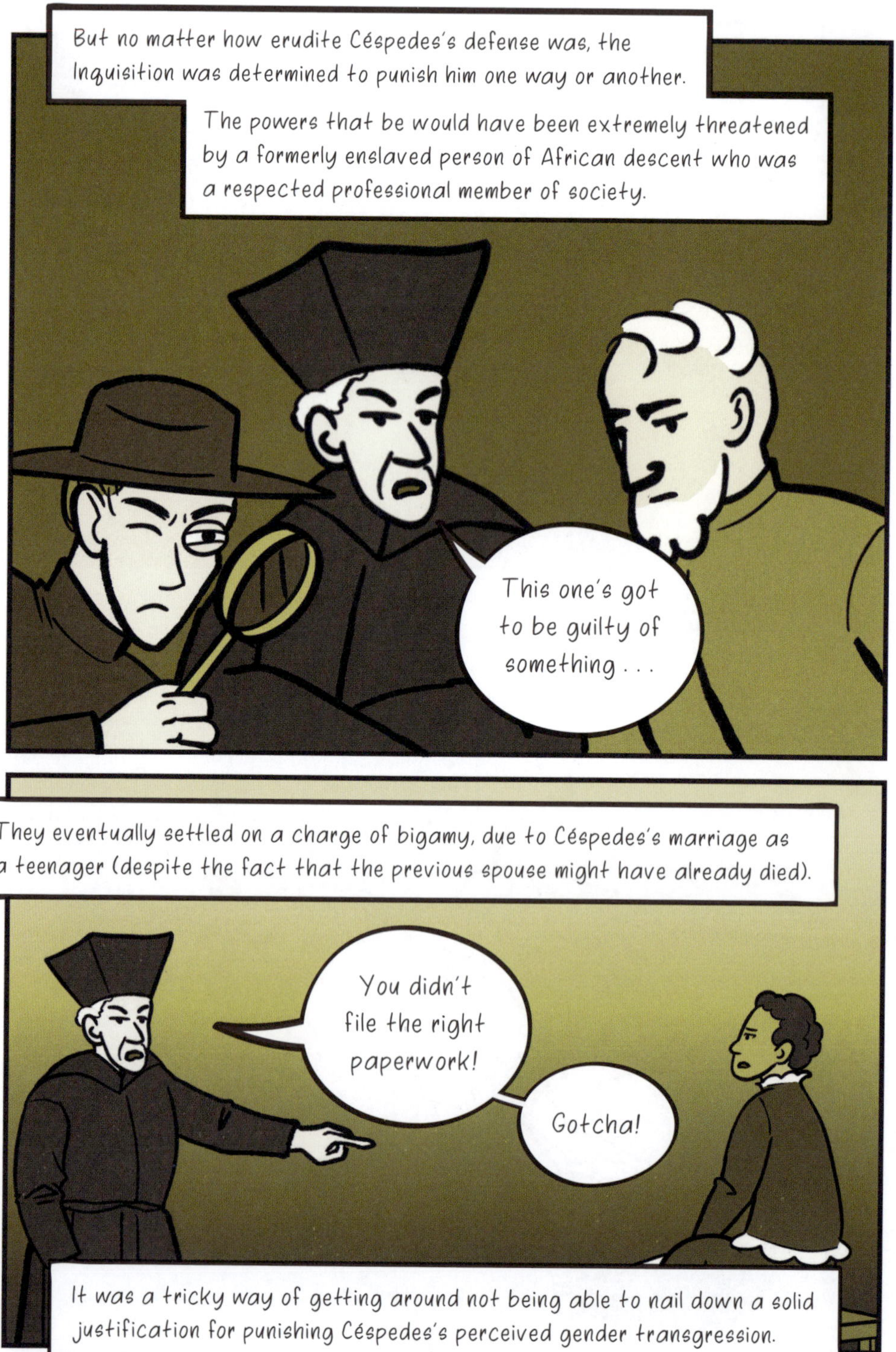
But no matter how erudite Céspedes's defense was, the Inquisition was determined to punish him one way or another.
The powers that be would have been extremely threatened by a formerly enslaved person of African descent who was a respected professional member of society.
This one's got to be guilty of something . . .
They eventually settled on a charge of bigamy, due to Céspedes's marriage as a teenager (despite the fact that the previous spouse might have already died).
You didn't file the right paperwork!
Gotcha!
It was a tricky way of getting around not being able to nail down a solid justification for punishing Céspedes's perceived gender transgression.

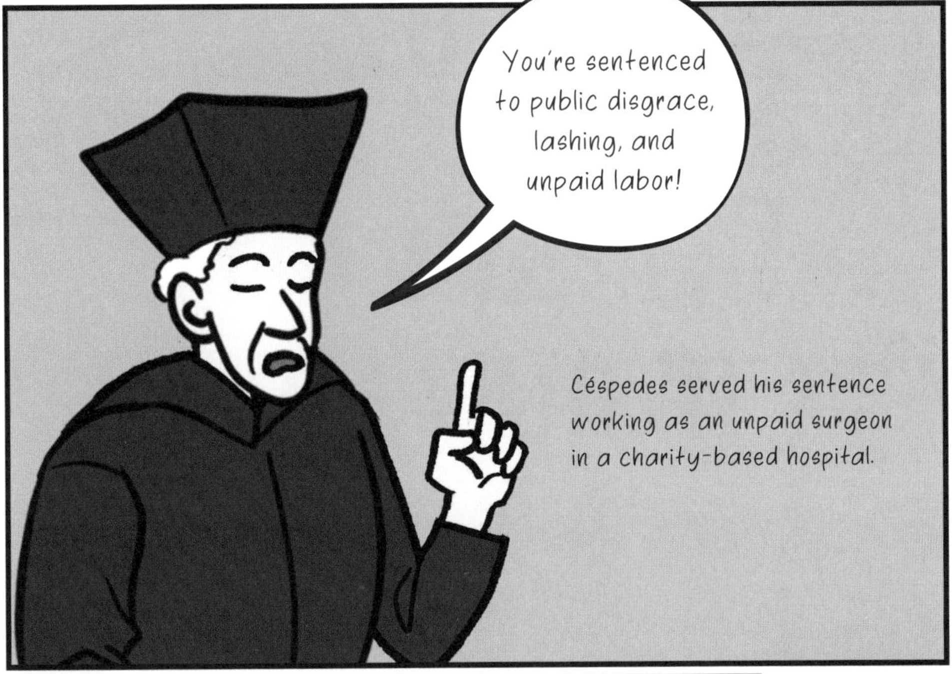
You're sentenced to public disgrace, lashing, and unpaid labor!
Céspedes served his sentence working as an unpaid surgeon in a charity-based hospital.

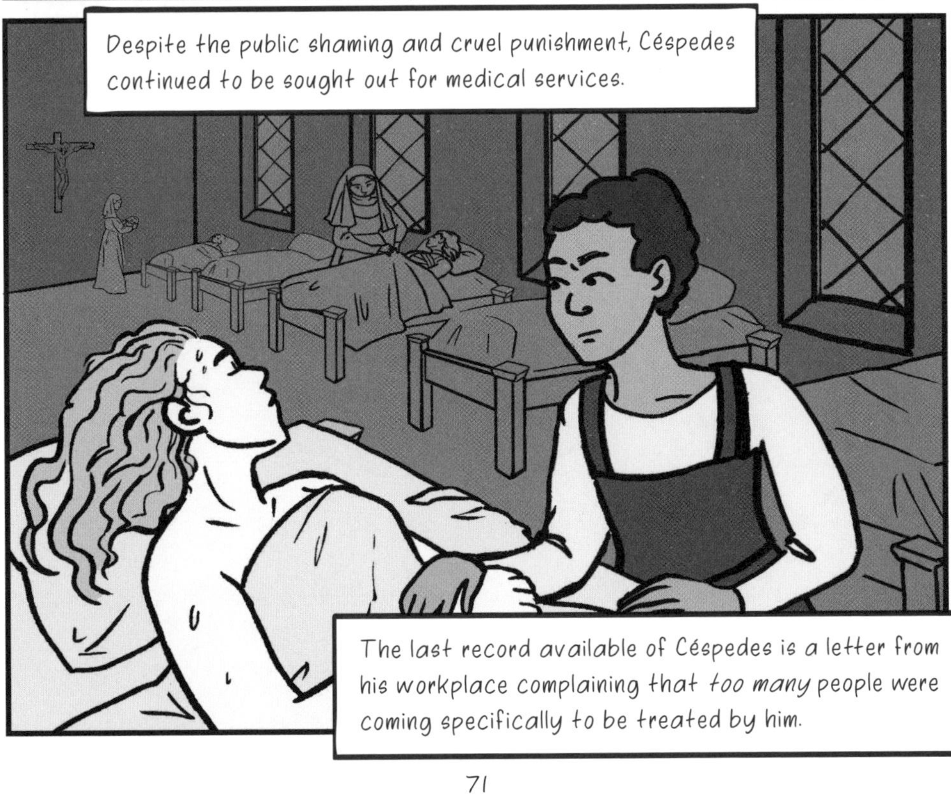
Despite the public shaming and cruel punishment, Céspedes continued to be sought out for medical services.
The last record available of Céspedes is a letter from his workplace complaining that *too many* people were coming specifically to be treated by him.

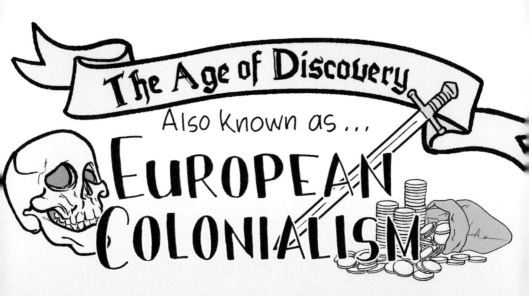

The Age of Discovery

Also Known as . . .

European Colonialism

Modern Western colonialism began in the late 1400s.

Netherlands
France
Belgium
England
Portugal
Italy
Spain
Germany

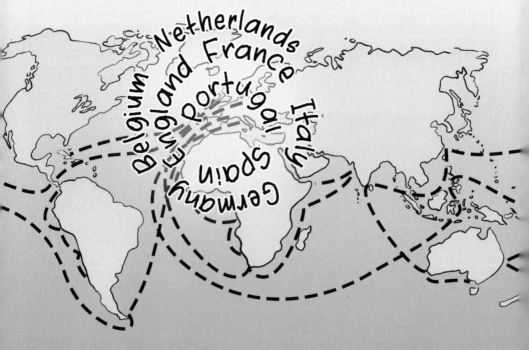

Starting with Portugal and Spain, western European countries figured out sea routes to the Americas, the Pacific Islands, and around the southern coast of Africa to Asia and Australia.

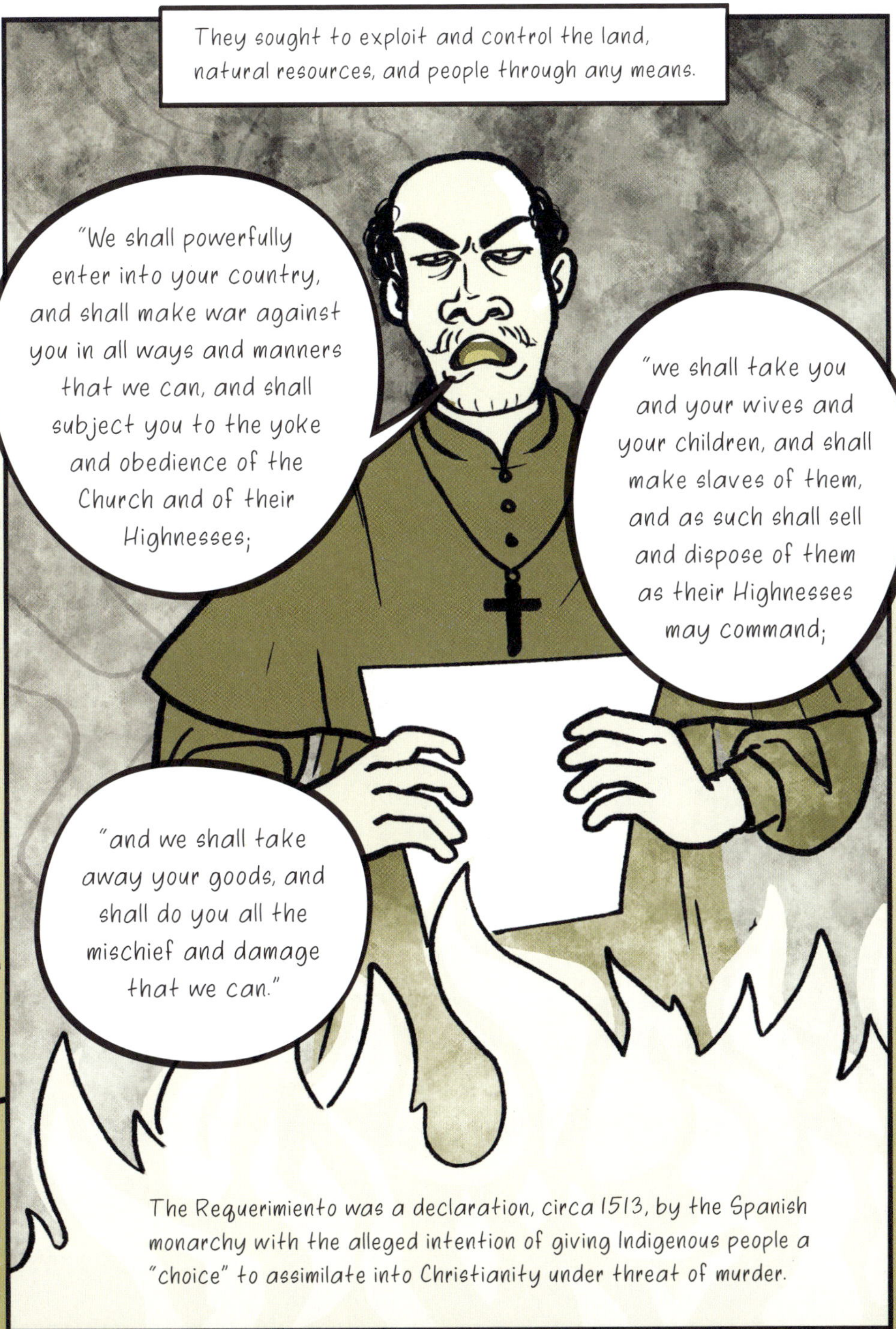
They sought to exploit and control the land, natural resources, and people through any means.
"We shall powerfully enter into your country, and shall make war against you in all ways and manners that we can, and shall subject you to the yoke and obedience of the Church and of their Highnesses;
"we shall take you and your wives and your children, and shall make slaves of them, and as such shall sell and dispose of them as their Highnesses may command;
"and we shall take away your goods, and shall do you all the mischief and damage that we can."
The Requerimiento was a declaration, circa 1513, by the Spanish monarchy with the alleged intention of giving Indigenous people a "choice" to assimilate into Christianity under threat of murder.

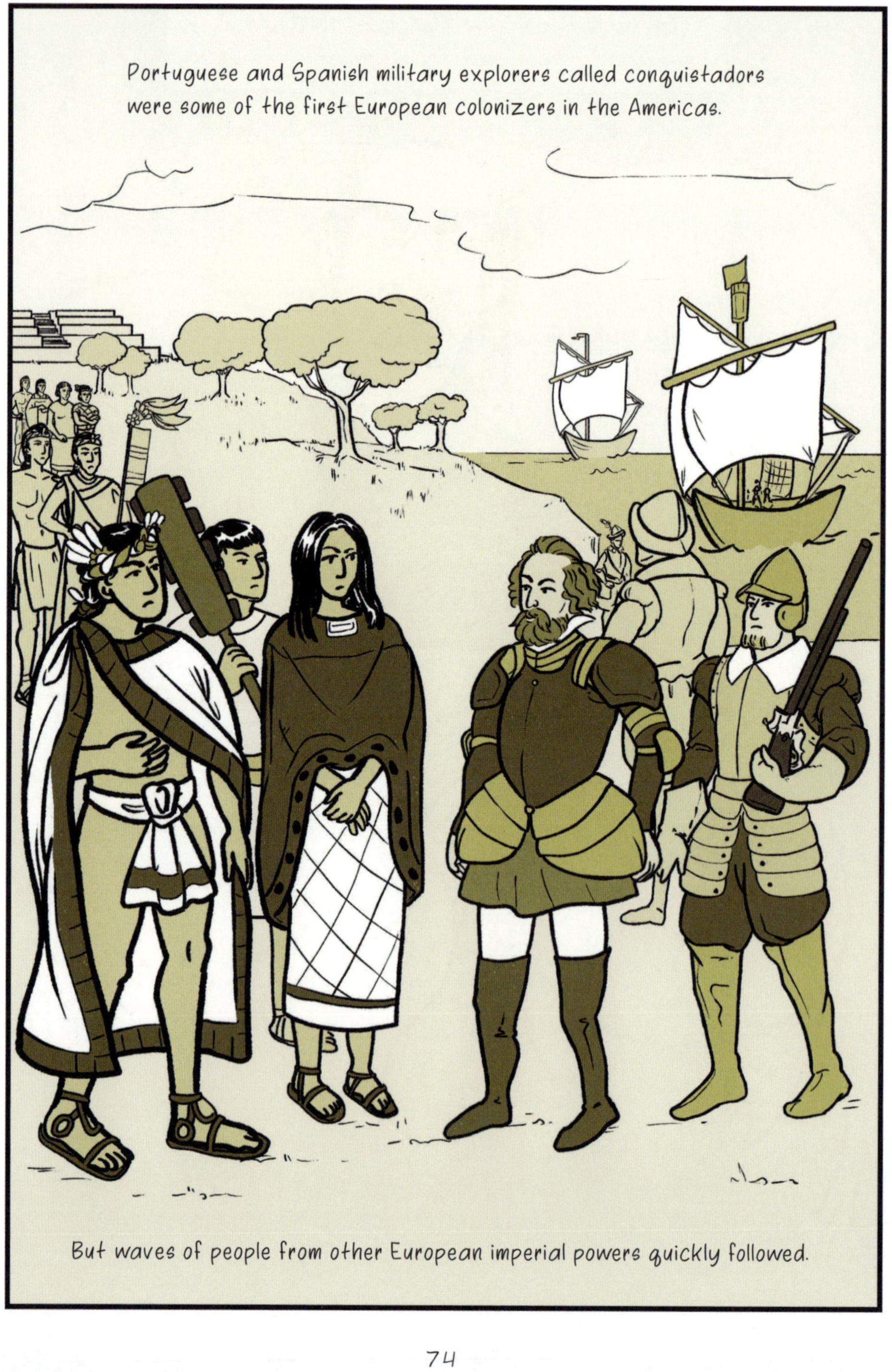
Portuguese and Spanish military explorers called conquistadors were some of the first European colonizers in the Americas.
But waves of people from other European imperial powers quickly followed.

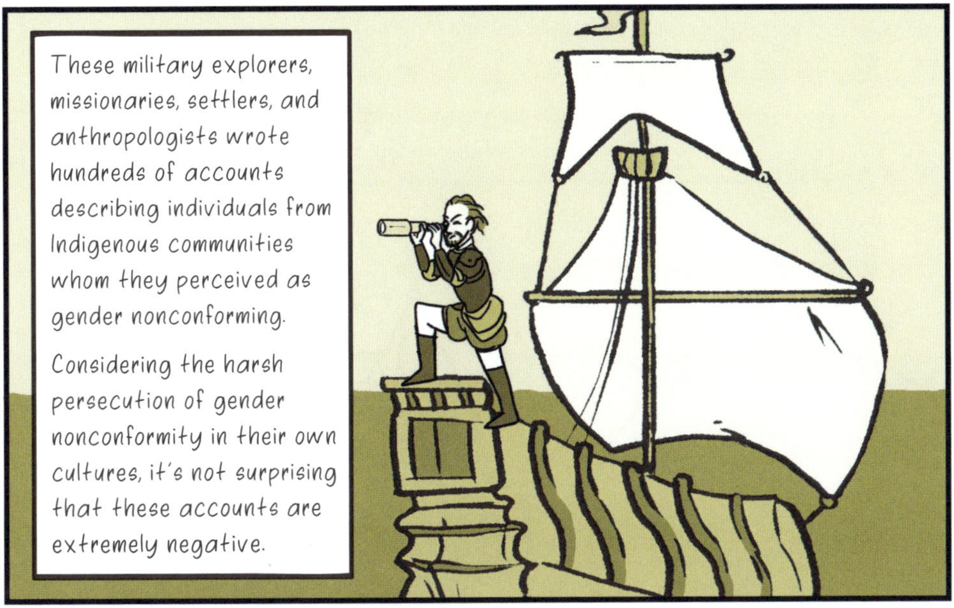
These military explorers, missionaries, settlers, and anthropologists wrote hundreds of accounts describing individuals from Indigenous communities whom they perceived as gender nonconforming.
Considering the harsh persecution of gender nonconformity in their own cultures, it's not surprising that these accounts are extremely negative.

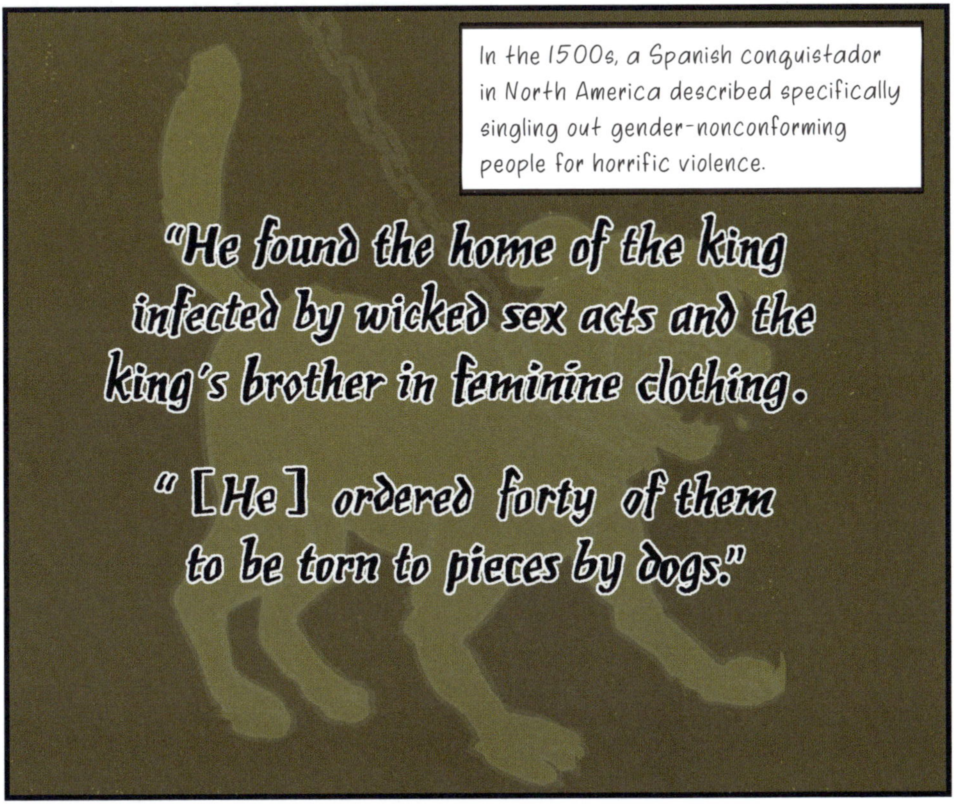
In the 1500s, a Spanish conquistador in North America described specifically singling out gender-nonconforming people for horrific violence.
"He found the home of the king infected by wicked sex acts and the king's brother in feminine clothing.
"[He] ordered forty of them to be torn to pieces by dogs."

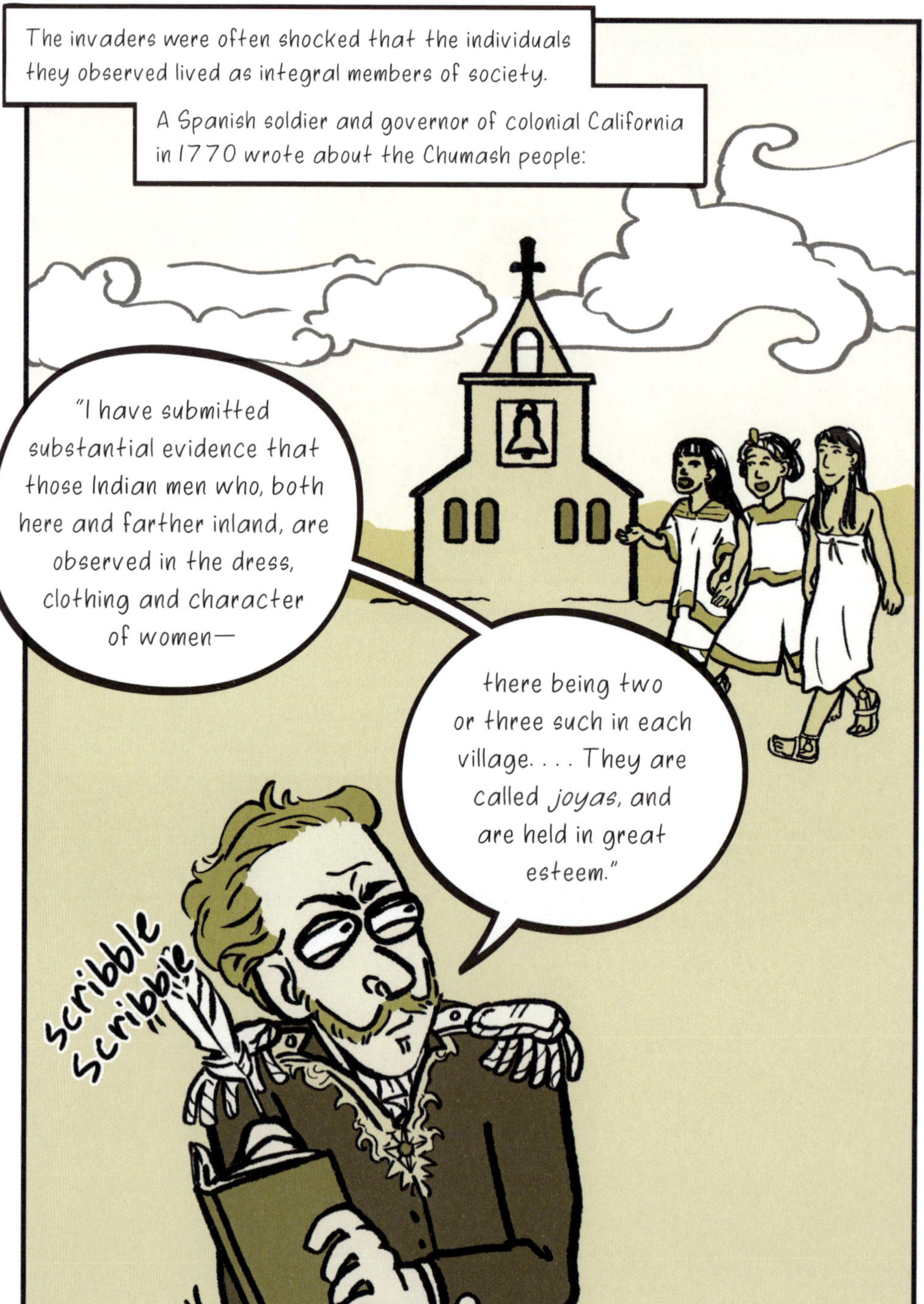

The invaders were often shocked that the individuals they observed lived as integral members of society.
A Spanish soldier and governor of colonial California in 1770 wrote about the Chumash people:
"I have submitted substantial evidence that those Indian men who, both here and farther inland, are observed in the dress, clothing and character of women—
there being two or three such in each village. . . . They are called *joyas*, and are held in great esteem."
scribble scribble

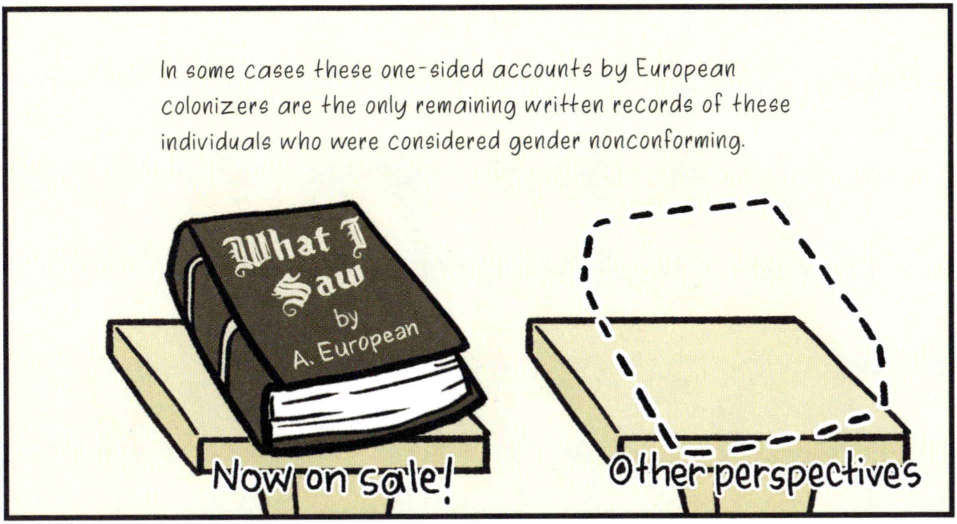
In some cases these one-sided accounts by European colonizers are the only remaining written records of these individuals who were considered gender nonconforming.
What I Saw by A. European
Now on sale!
Other perspectives

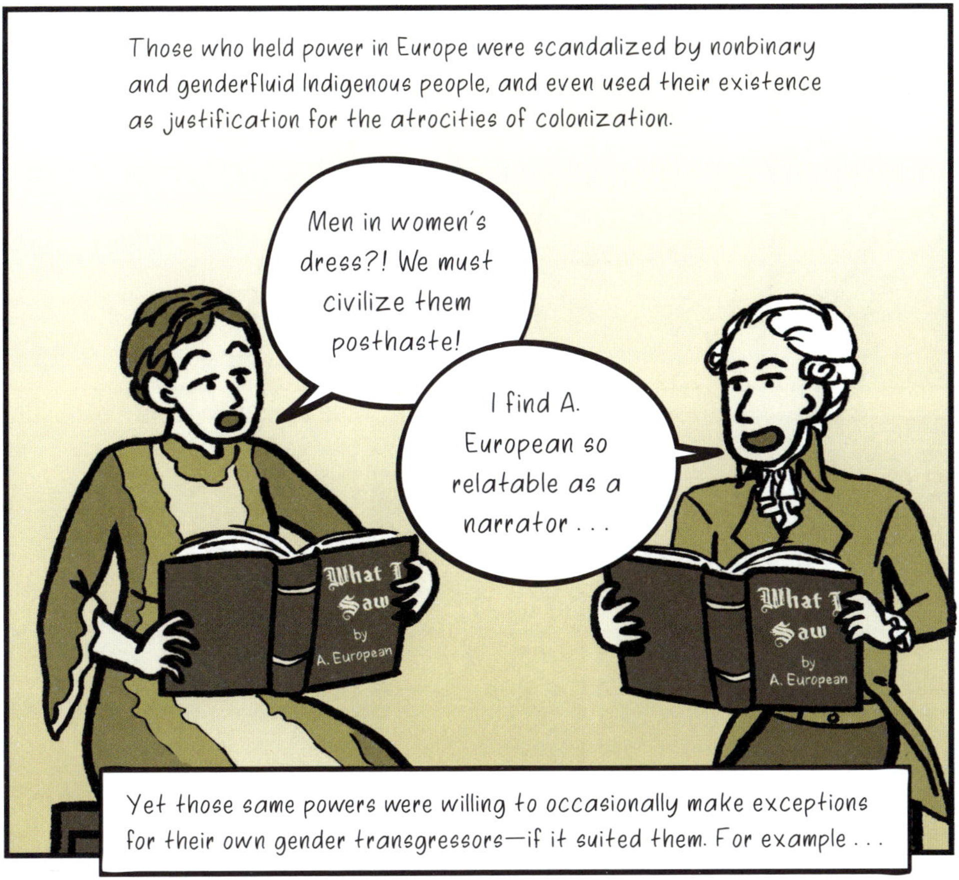
Those who held power in Europe were scandalized by nonbinary and genderfluid Indigenous people, and even used their existence as justification for the atrocities of colonization.
Men in women's dress?! We must civilize them posthaste!
I find A. European so relatable as a narrator . . .
What I Saw by A. European
What I Saw by A. European
Yet those same powers were willing to occasionally make exceptions for their own gender transgressors—if it suited them. For example . . .

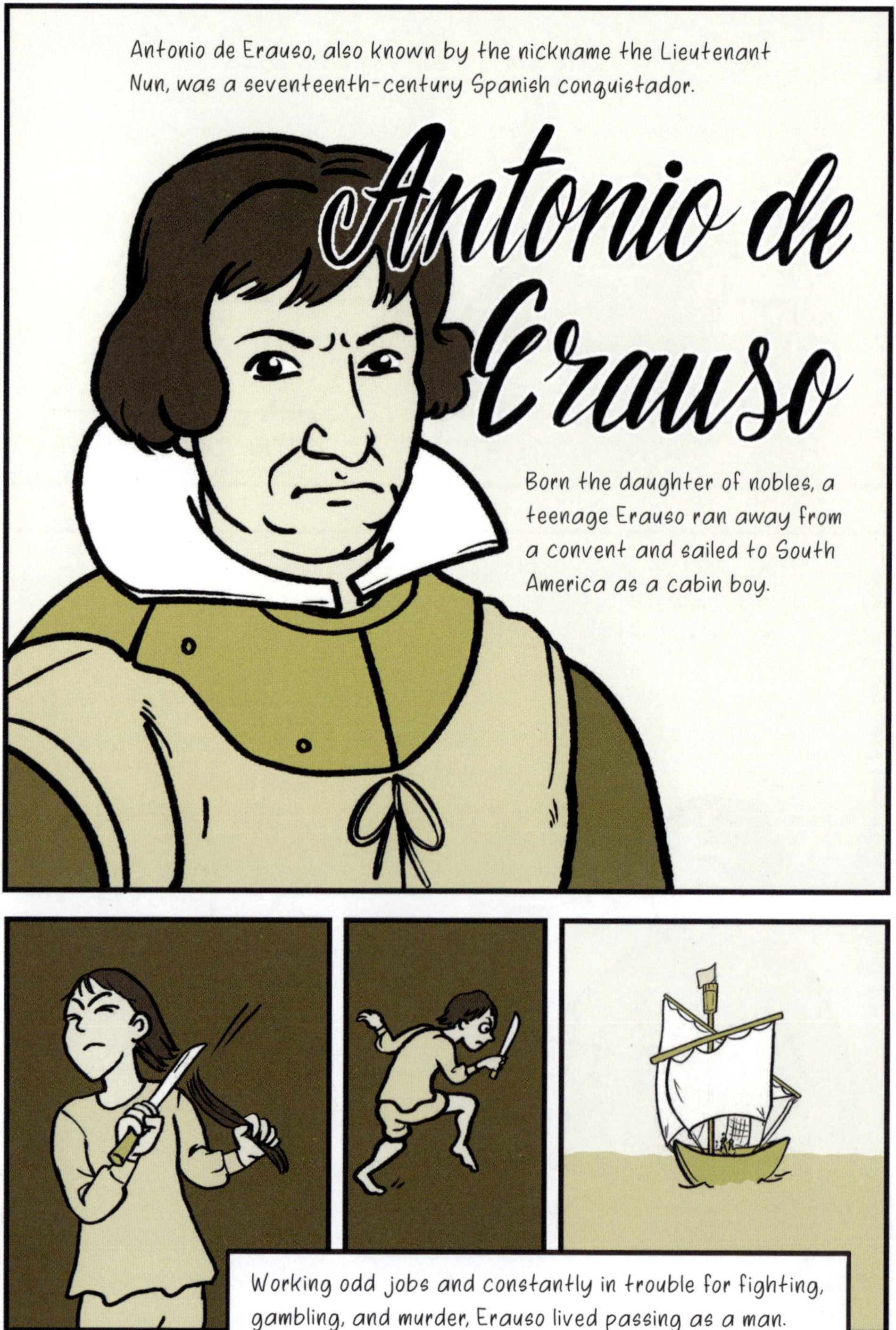

Antonio de Erauso, also known by the nickname the Lieutenant Nun, was a seventeenth-century Spanish conquistador.
Antonio de Erauso
Born the daughter of nobles, a teenage Erauso ran away from a convent and sailed to South America as a cabin boy.
Working odd jobs and constantly in trouble for fighting, gambling, and murder, Erauso lived passing as a man.

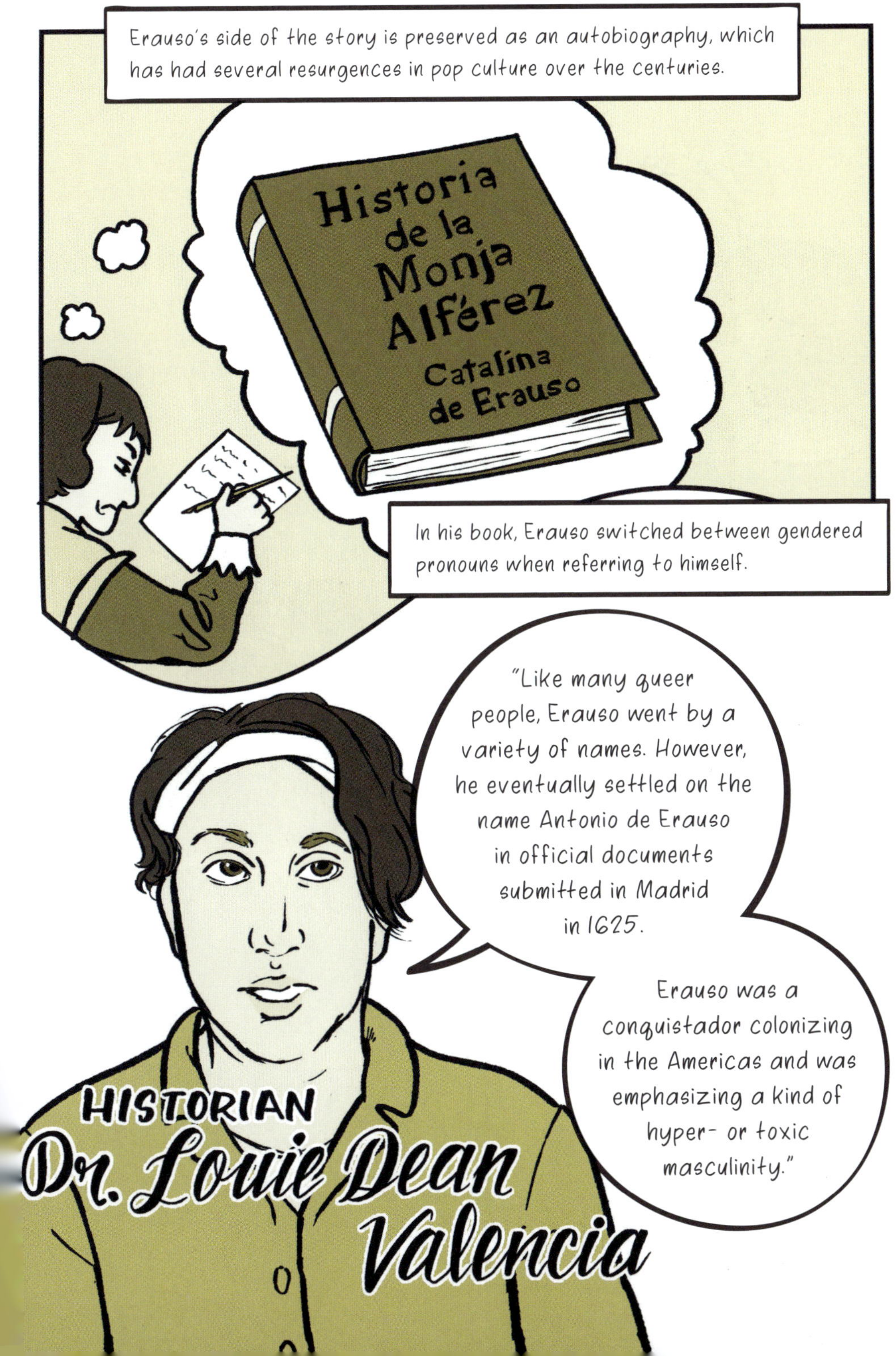
Erauso's side of the story is preserved as an autobiography, which has had several resurgences in pop culture over the centuries.
Historia de la Monja Alférez Catalina de Erauso
In his book, Erauso switched between gendered pronouns when referring to himself.
"Like many queer people, Erauso went by a variety of names. However, he eventually settled on the name Antonio de Erauso in official documents submitted in Madrid in 1625.
Erauso was a conquistador colonizing in the Americas and was emphasizing a kind of hyper- or toxic masculinity."
HISTORIAN Dr. Louie Dean Valencia

Erauso really went all out with the tough-guy thing . . .

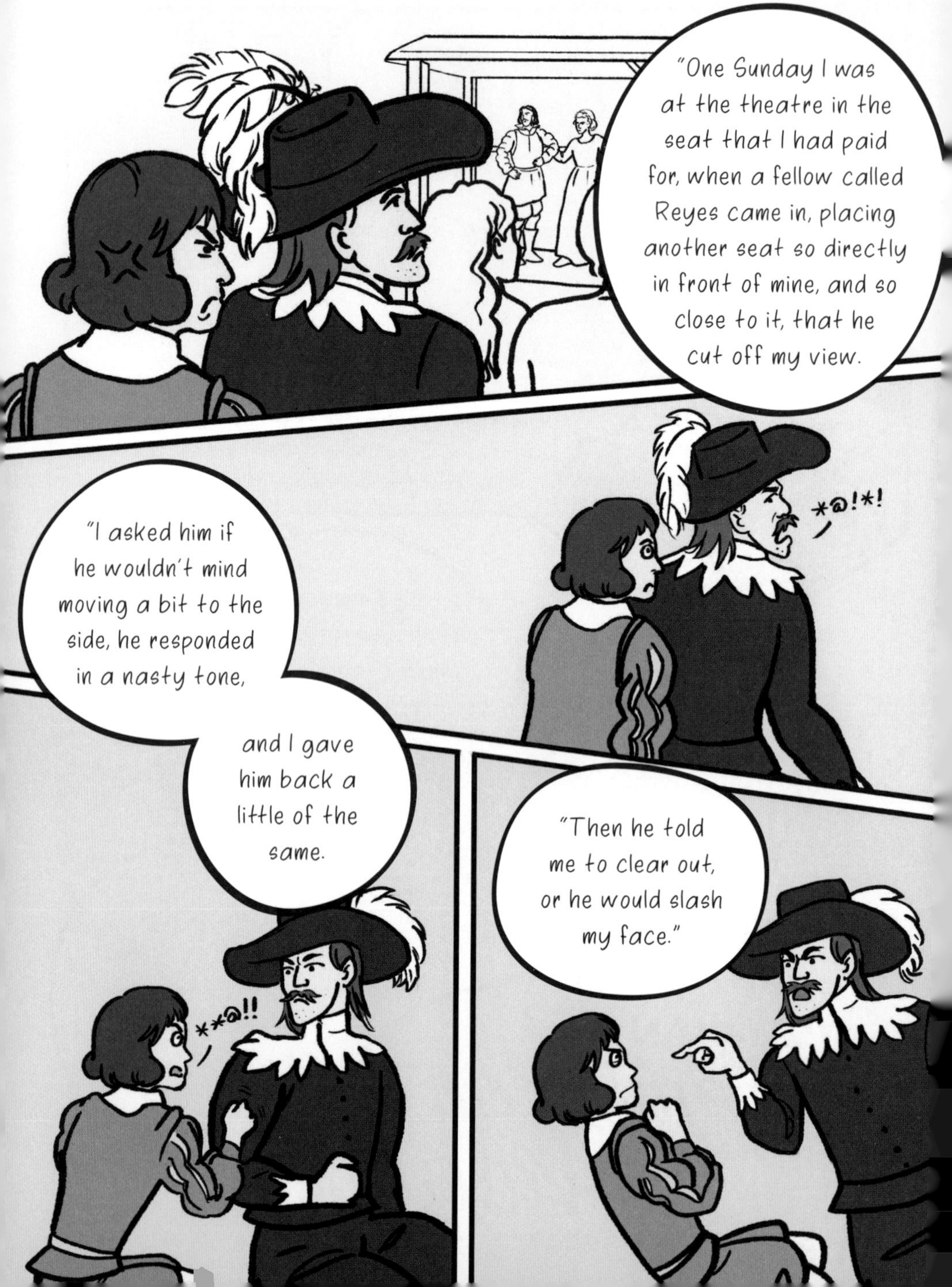
"One Sunday I was at the theatre in the seat that I had paid for, when a fellow called Reyes came in, placing another seat so directly in front of mine, and so close to it, that he cut off my view.
"I asked him if he wouldn't mind moving a bit to the side, he responded in a nasty tone,
@!!
and I gave him back a little of the same.
**@!!
"Then he told me to clear out, or he would slash my face."

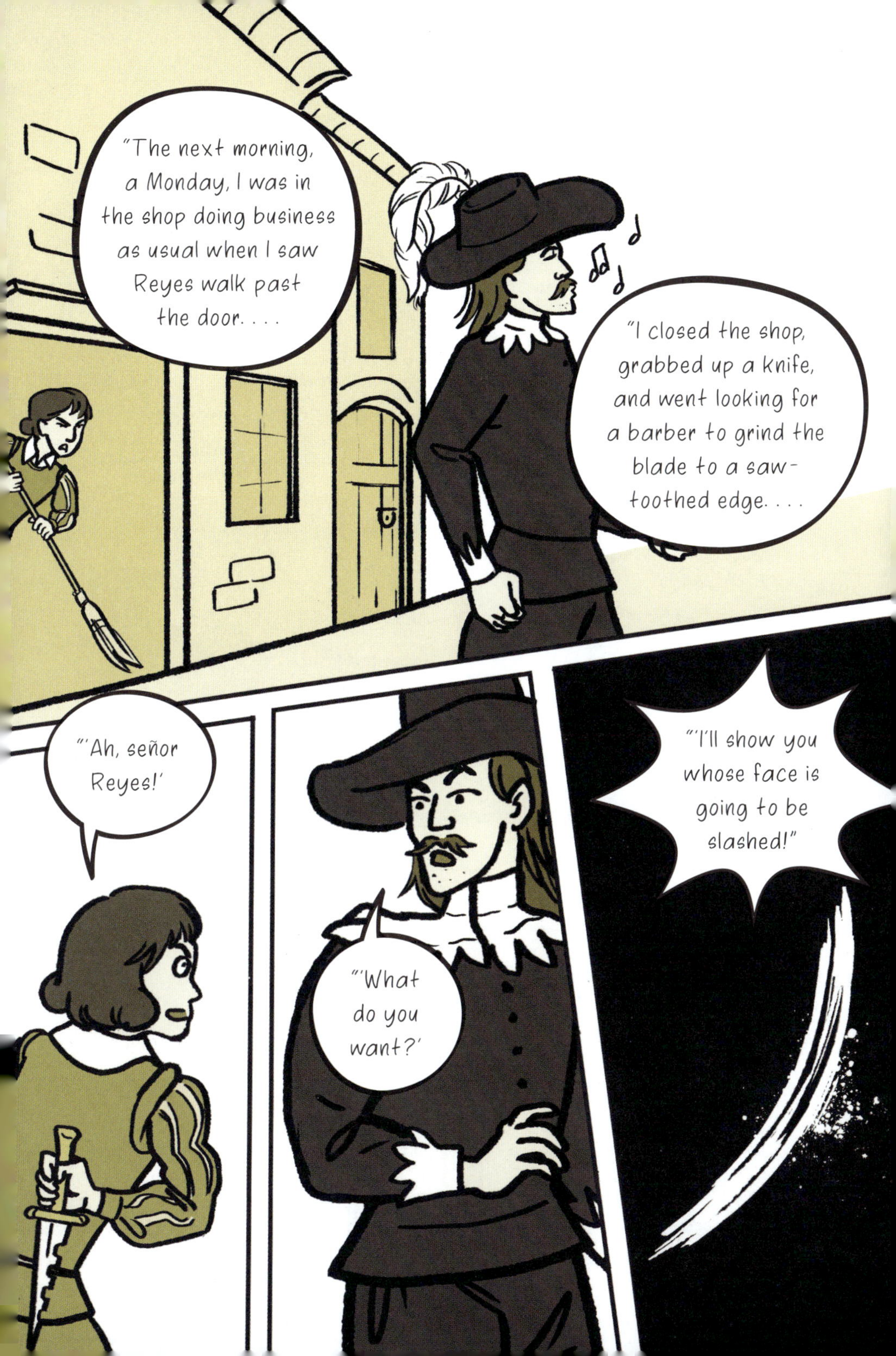
"The next morning, a Monday, I was in the shop doing business as usual when I saw Reyes walk past the door. . . .
"I closed the shop, grabbed up a knife, and went looking for a barber to grind the blade to a saw-toothed edge. . . .
"'Ah, señor Reyes!'
"'What do you want?'
"'I'll show you whose face is going to be slashed!"

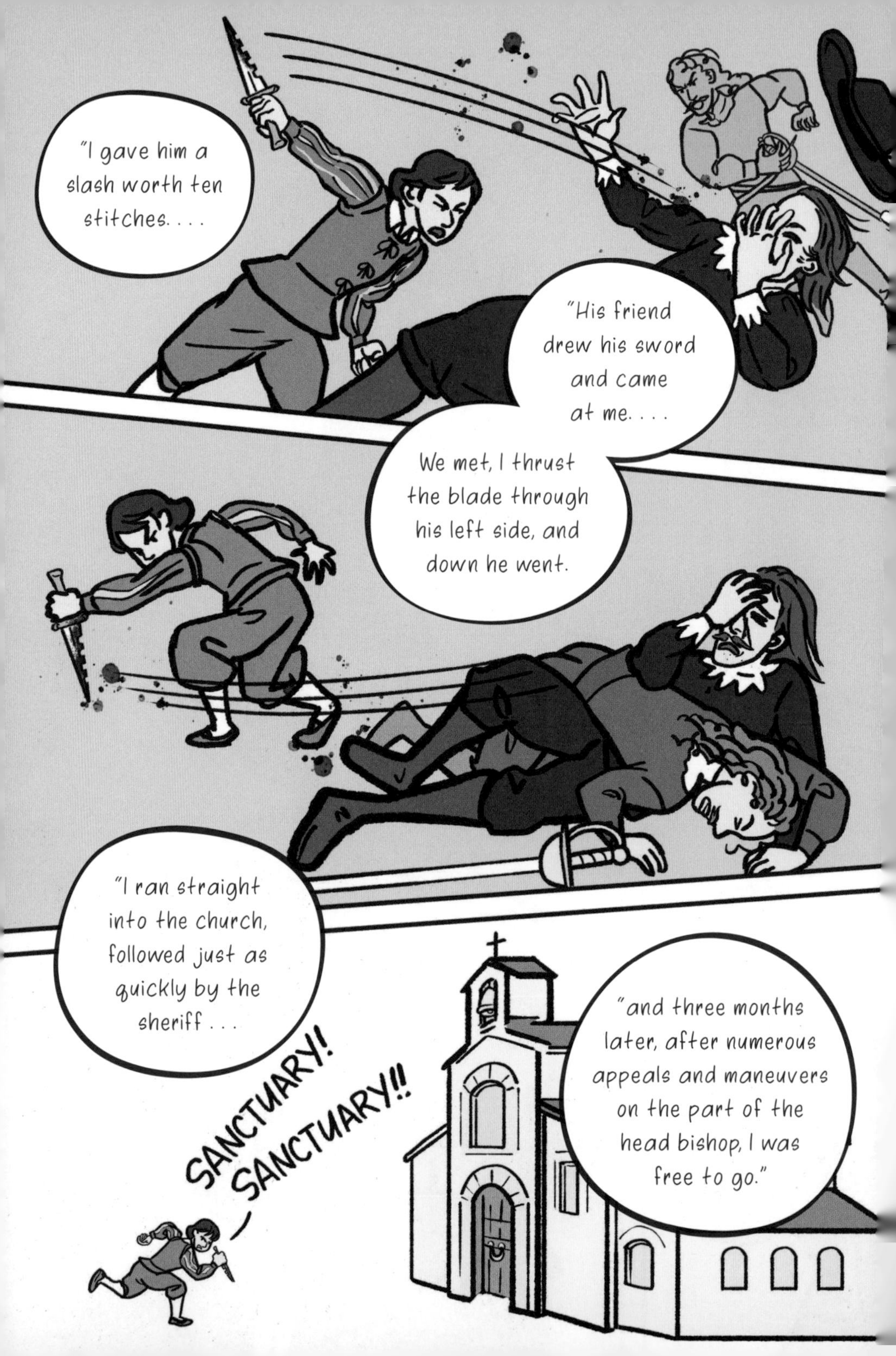
"I gave him a slash worth ten stitches. . . .
"His friend drew his sword and came at me. . . .
We met, I thrust the blade through his left side, and down he went.
"I ran straight into the church, followed just as quickly by the sheriff . . .
SANCTUARY! SANCTUARY!!
"and three months later, after numerous appeals and maneuvers on the part of the head bishop, I was free to go."

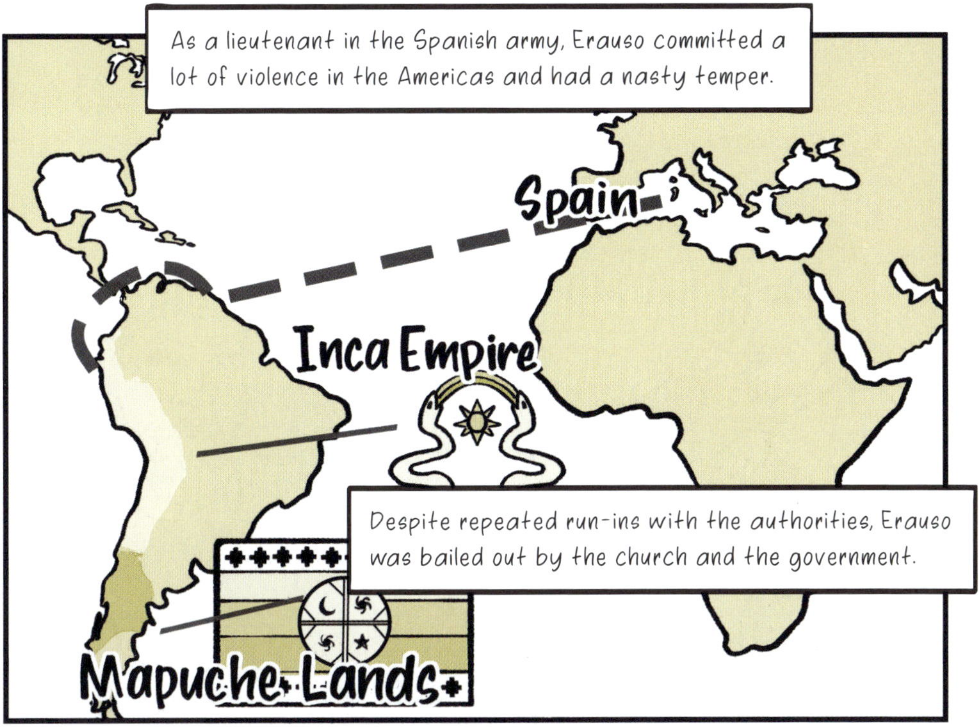
As a lieutenant in the Spanish army, Erauso committed a lot of violence in the Americas and had a nasty temper.
Spain
Inca Empire
Mapuche Lands
Despite repeated run-ins with the authorities, Erauso was bailed out by the church and the government.

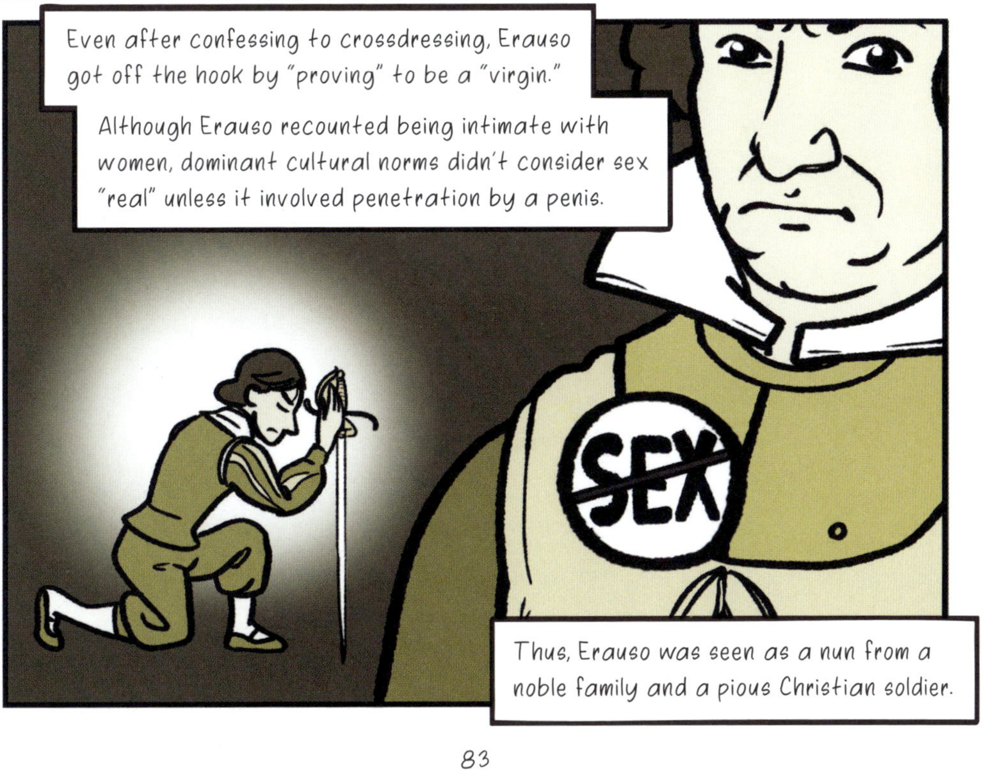
Even after confessing to crossdressing, Erauso got off the hook by "proving" to be a "virgin."
Although Erauso recounted being intimate with women, dominant cultural norms didn't consider sex "real" unless it involved penetration by a penis.
SEX
Thus, Erauso was seen as a nun from a noble family and a pious Christian soldier.

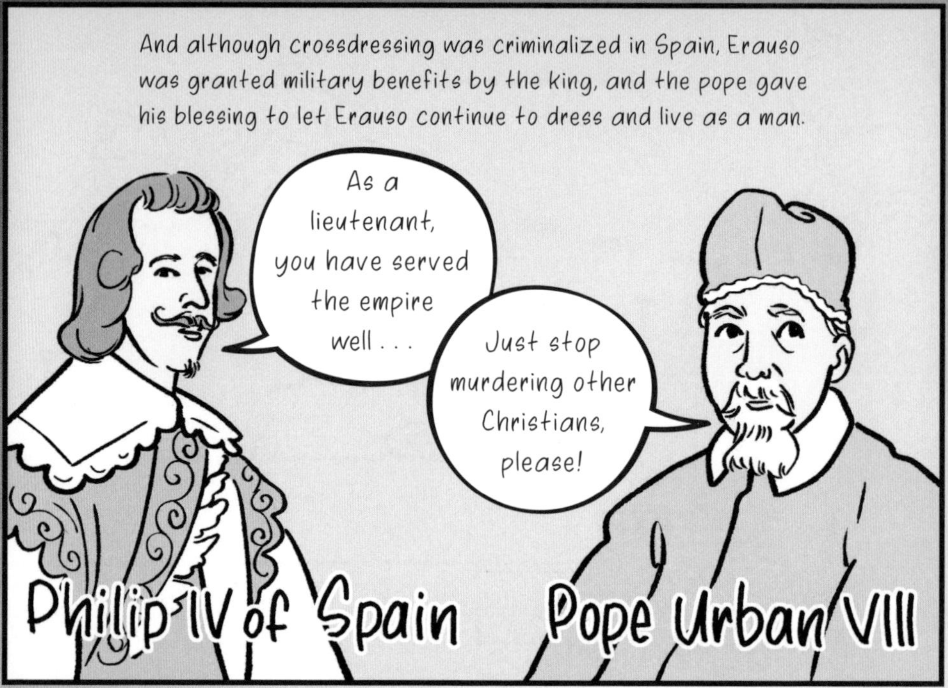
And although crossdressing was criminalized in Spain, Erauso was granted military benefits by the king, and the pope gave his blessing to let Erauso continue to dress and live as a man.
As a lieutenant, you have served the empire well . . .
Just stop murdering other Christians, please!
Philip IV of Spain
Pope Urban VIII

In fact, after being outed, Erauso became a bit of a celebrity . . .

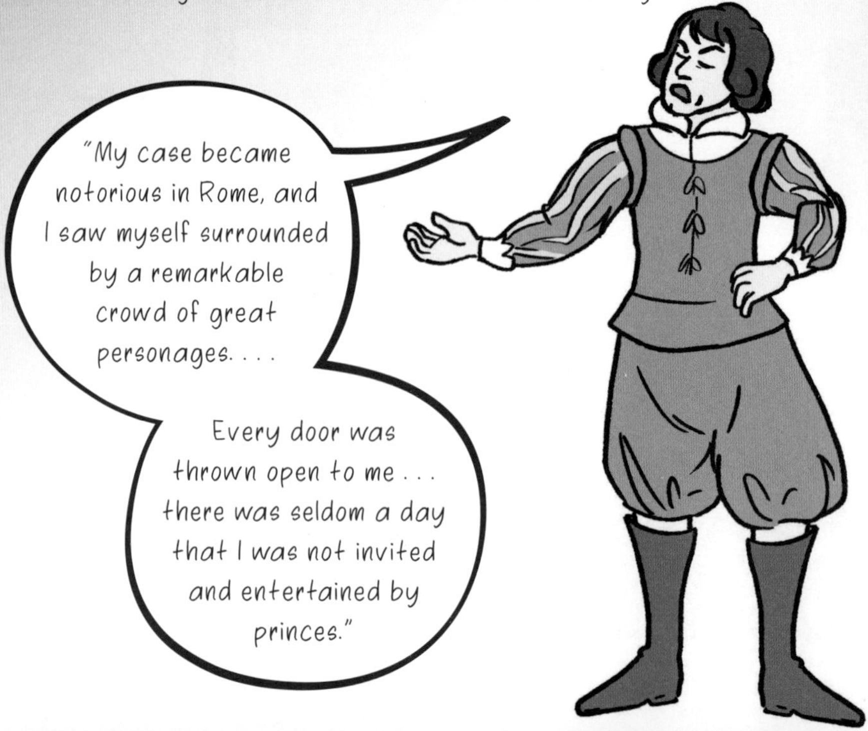
"My case became notorious in Rome, and I saw myself surrounded by a remarkable crowd of great personages. . . .
Every door was thrown open to me . . . there was seldom a day that I was not invited and entertained by princes."

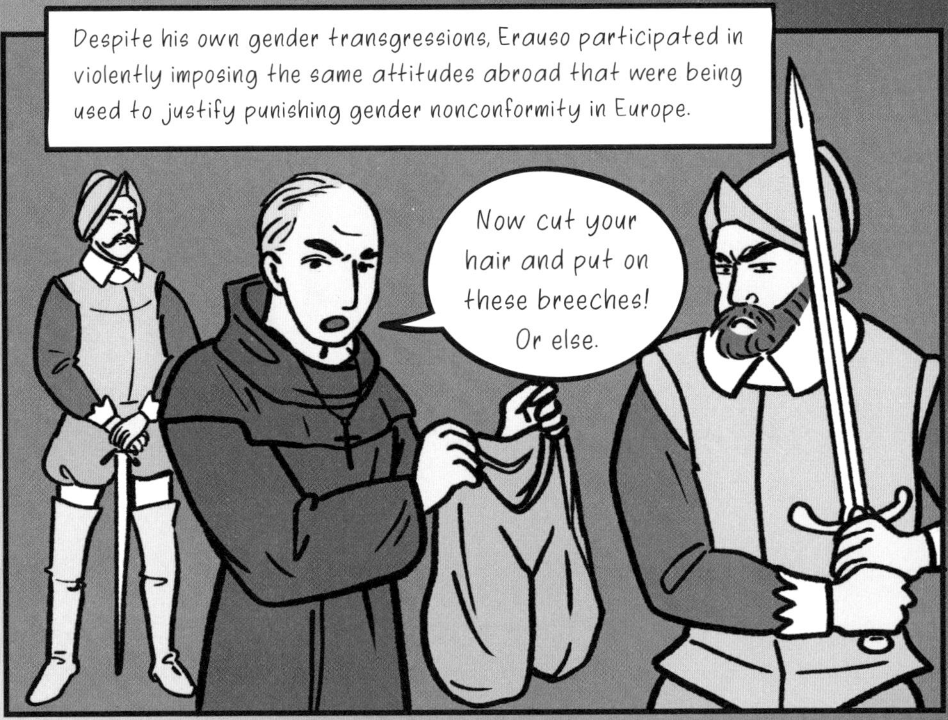
Despite his own gender transgressions, Erauso participated in violently imposing the same attitudes abroad that were being used to justify punishing gender nonconformity in Europe.
Now cut your hair and put on these breeches! Or else.

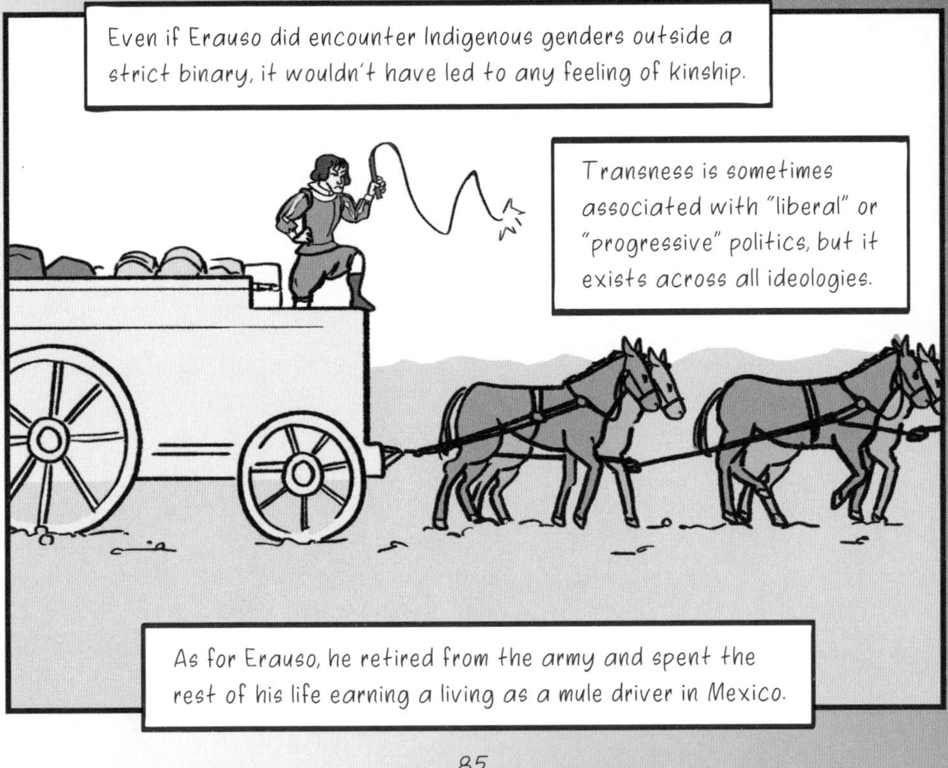
Even if Erauso did encounter Indigenous genders outside a strict binary, it wouldn't have led to any feeling of kinship.
Transness is sometimes associated with "liberal" or "progressive" politics, but it exists across all ideologies.
As for Erauso, he retired from the army and spent the rest of his life earning a living as a mule driver in Mexico.

In 1776, European invaders established the United States in the "New World." But of course it wasn't new to the hundreds of Indigenous tribes already living there.

THE AMERICAS

With the Indian Removal Act of 1830, thousands of Indigenous Americans were violently relocated, and many of them died.

Over the next fifty years, the US government forced them into reservations and cheated them out of even more land, which was then sold to white people.

ILLINOIS
MISSOURI
KENTUCKY
TENNESSEE
ARKANSAS
OMA
MISSISSIPPI
ALABAMA

MILLIONS OF ACRES
IOWA AND NEBRASKA
LANDS
FOR SALE ON 10 YEARS CREDIT
AT 6 PER CT. INTEREST AND LOW PRICES.

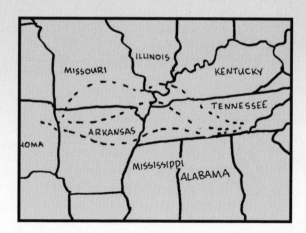

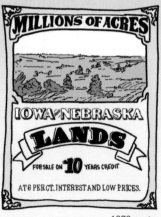

1872 poster

In 1845, a popular political columnist used the term "manifest destiny" to describe the idea that the white colonists had a divine right to take over the land of North America from coast to coast:

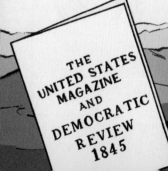

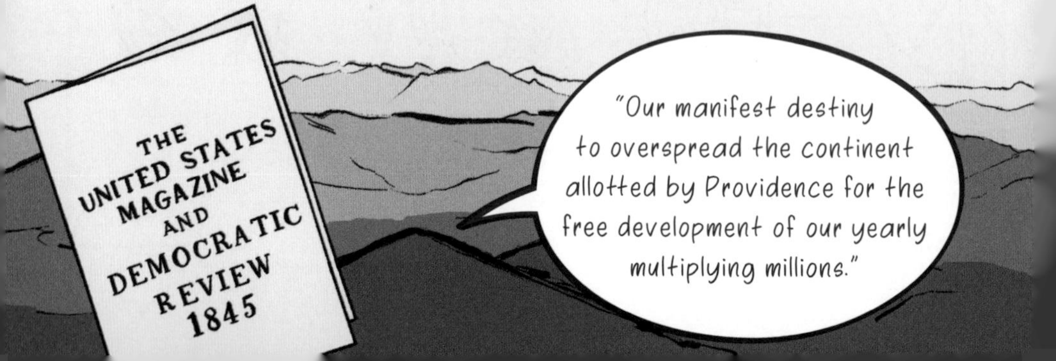

THE UNITED STATES MAGAZINE AND DEMOCRATIC REVIEW 1845
"Our manifest destiny to overspread the continent allotted by Providence for the free development of our yearly multiplying millions."

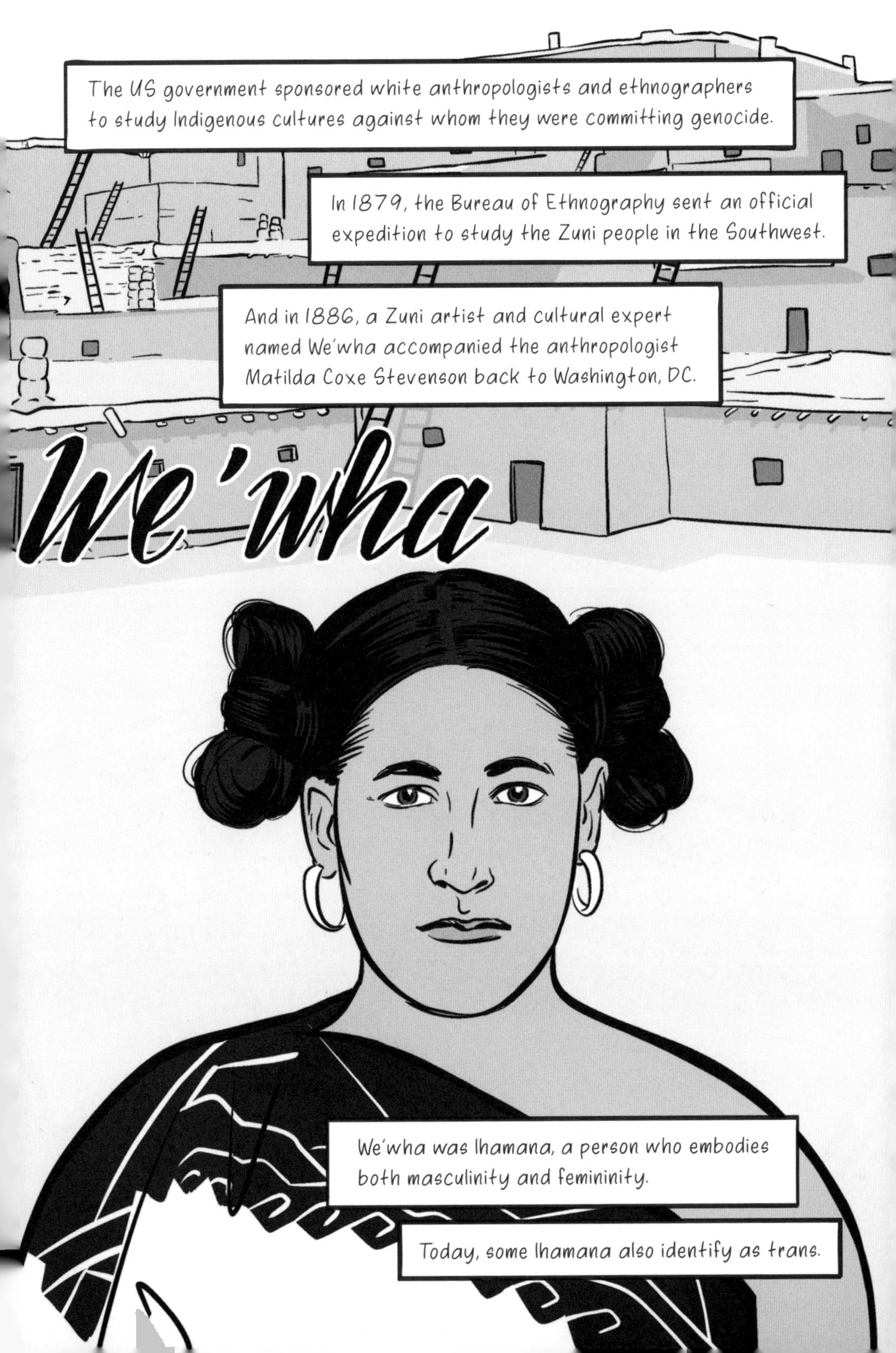
The US government sponsored white anthropologists and ethnographers to study Indigenous cultures against whom they were committing genocide.
In 1879, the Bureau of Ethnography sent an official expedition to study the Zuni people in the Southwest.
And in 1886, a Zuni artist and cultural expert named We'wha accompanied the anthropologist Matilda Coxe Stevenson back to Washington, DC.
We'wha
We'wha was lhamana, a person who embodies both masculinity and femininity.
Today, some lhamana also identify as trans.

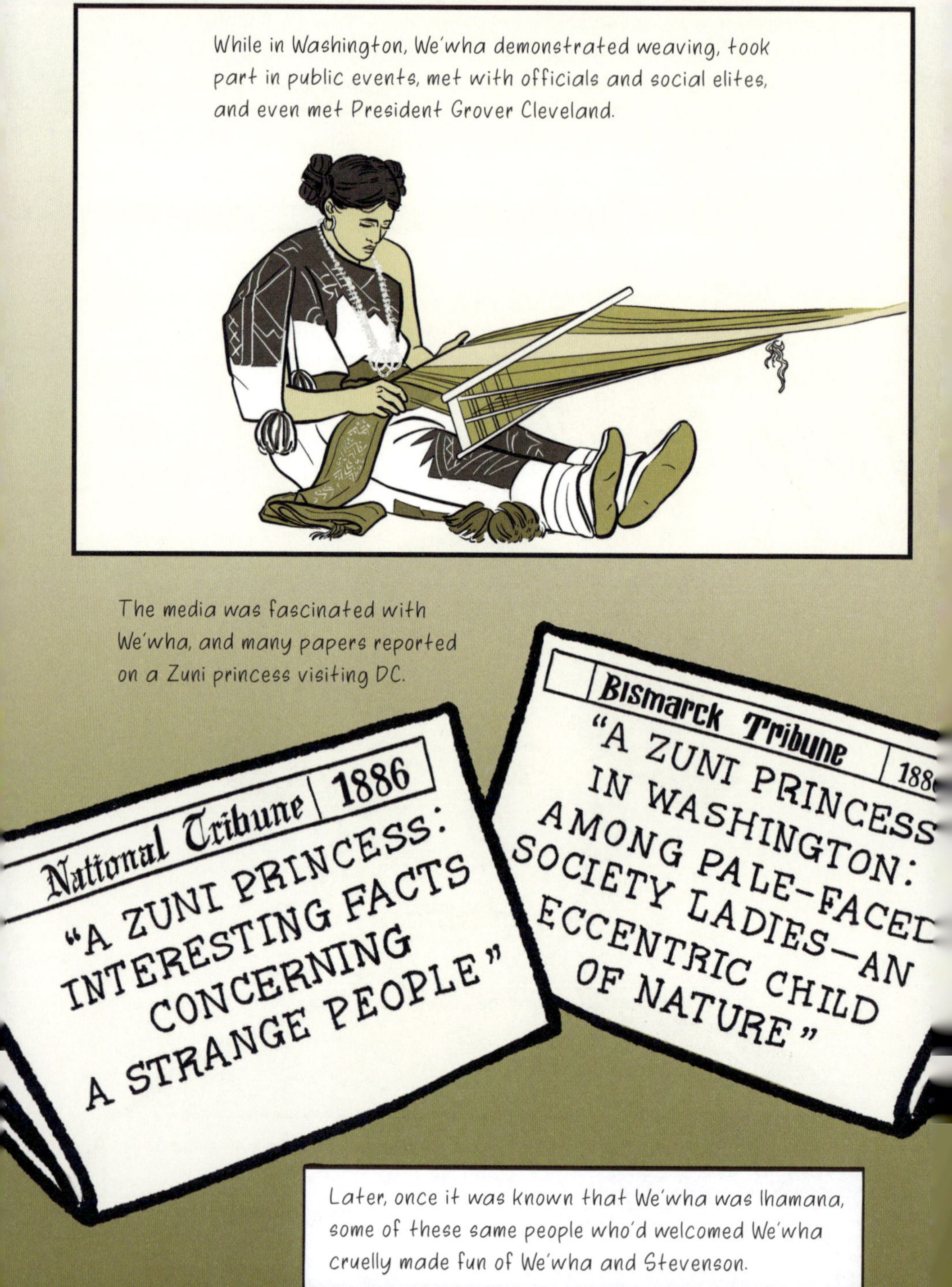

While in Washington, We'wha demonstrated weaving, took part in public events, met with officials and social elites, and even met President Grover Cleveland.
The media was fascinated with We'wha, and many papers reported on a Zuni princess visiting DC.
National Tribune 1886
"A ZUNI PRINCESS: INTERESTING FACTS CONCERNING A STRANGE PEOPLE"
Bismarck Tribune
"A ZUNI PRINCESS IN WASHINGTON: AMONG PALE-FACED SOCIETY LADIES—AN ECCENTRIC CHILD OF NATURE"
Later, once it was known that We'wha was lhamana, some of these same people who'd welcomed We'wha cruelly made fun of We'wha and Stevenson.

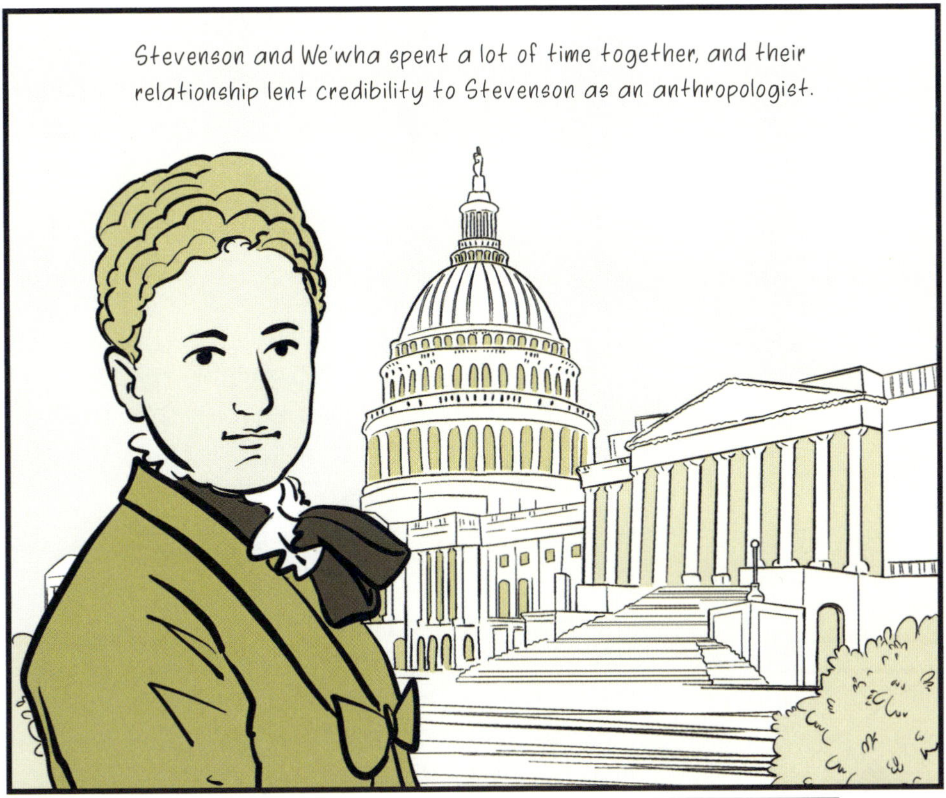
Stevenson and We'wha spent a lot of time together, and their relationship lent credibility to Stevenson as an anthropologist.

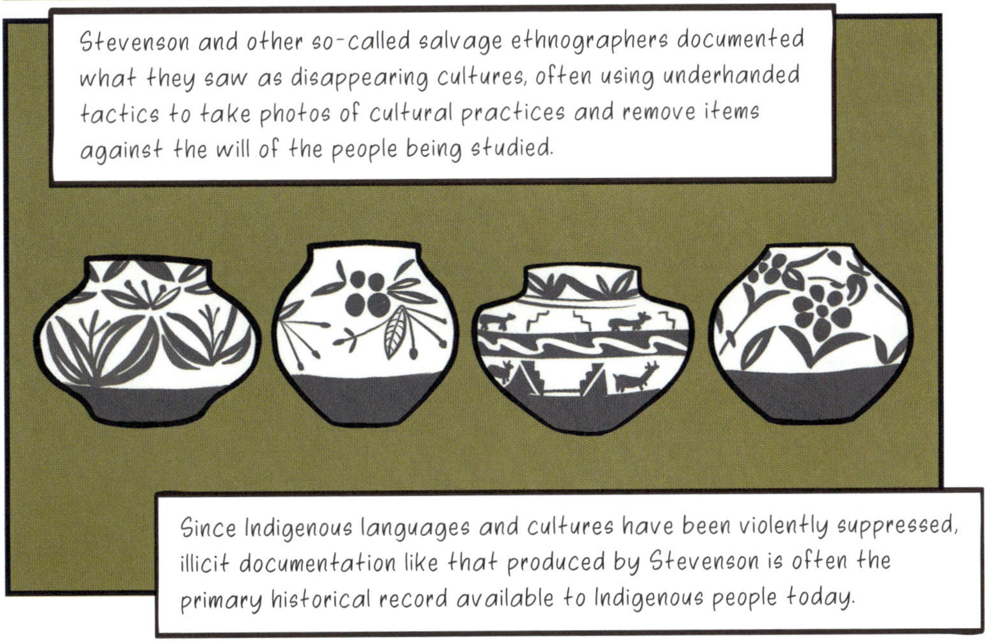
Stevenson and other so-called salvage ethnographers documented what they saw as disappearing cultures, often using underhanded tactics to take photos of cultural practices and remove items against the will of the people being studied.
Since Indigenous languages and cultures have been violently suppressed, illicit documentation like that produced by Stevenson is often the primary historical record available to Indigenous people today.

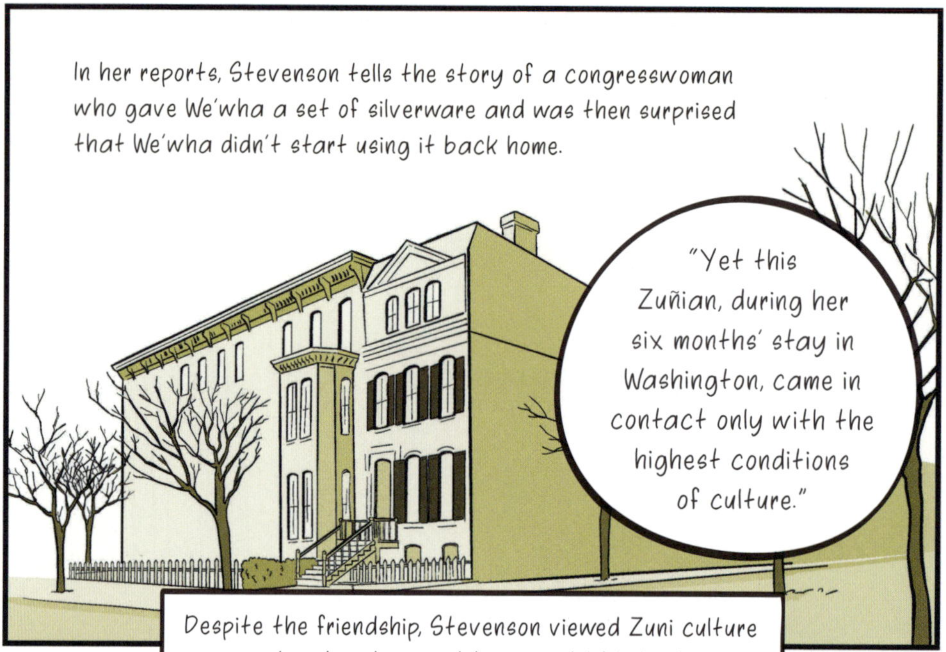
In her reports, Stevenson tells the story of a congresswoman who gave We'wha a set of silverware and was then surprised that We'wha didn't start using it back home.
"Yet this Zuñian, during her six months' stay in Washington, came in contact only with the highest conditions of culture."
Despite the friendship, Stevenson viewed Zuni culture as uncivilized and seemed to expect We'wha to convert to white/Euro-American cultural practices.

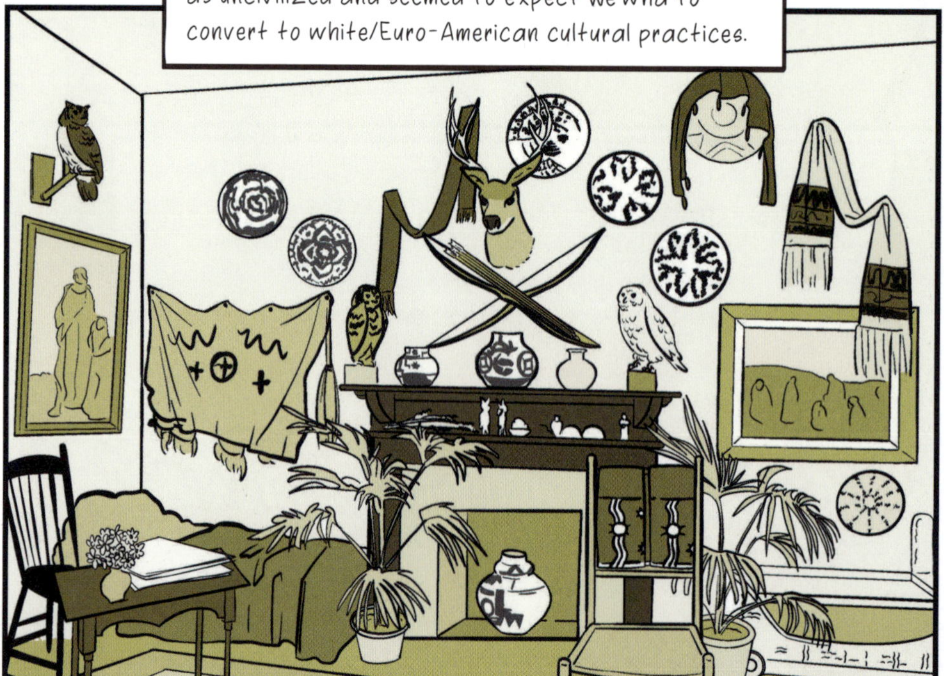

Based on photos of Stevenson's house, courtesy of the National Anthropological Archives

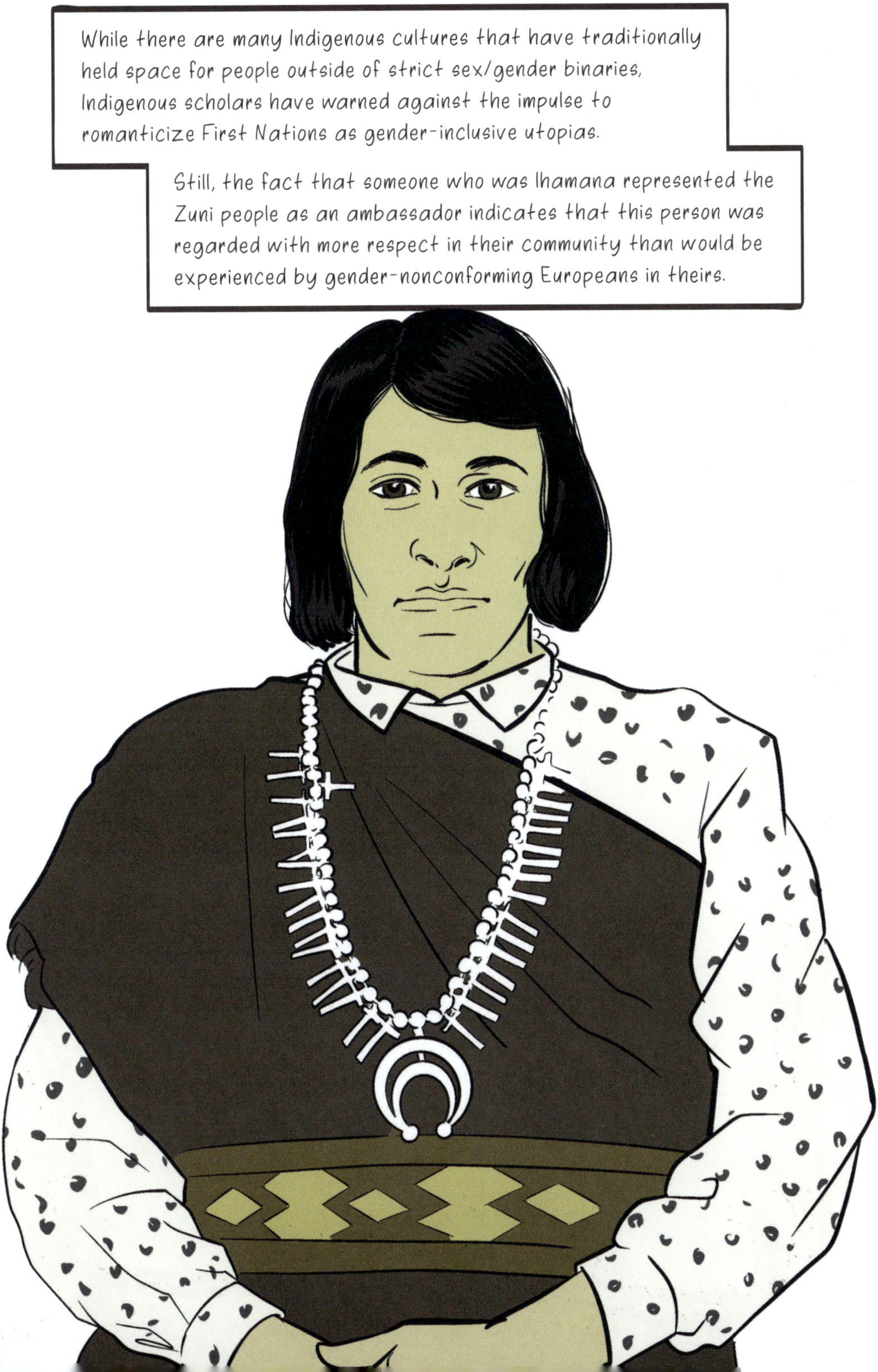
While there are many Indigenous cultures that have traditionally held space for people outside of strict sex/gender binaries, Indigenous scholars have warned against the impulse to romanticize First Nations as gender-inclusive utopias.
Still, the fact that someone who was lhamana represented the Zuni people as an ambassador indicates that this person was regarded with more respect in their community than would be experienced by gender-nonconforming Europeans in theirs.

What might gender diversity look like around the world if it hadn't been subjected to colonialism?

How did colonial-era European subjects navigate their own culture's gender norms?

In what ways did gender-nonconforming Europeans disrupt some gender norms while upholding others?

How are sex and gender expressions used to justify oppression?

Why are some people given more freedom to transgress gender norms while others are given less?

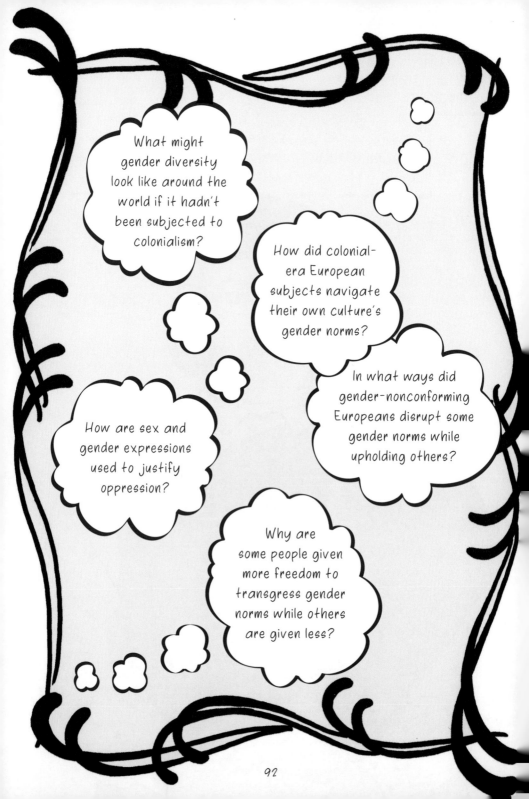

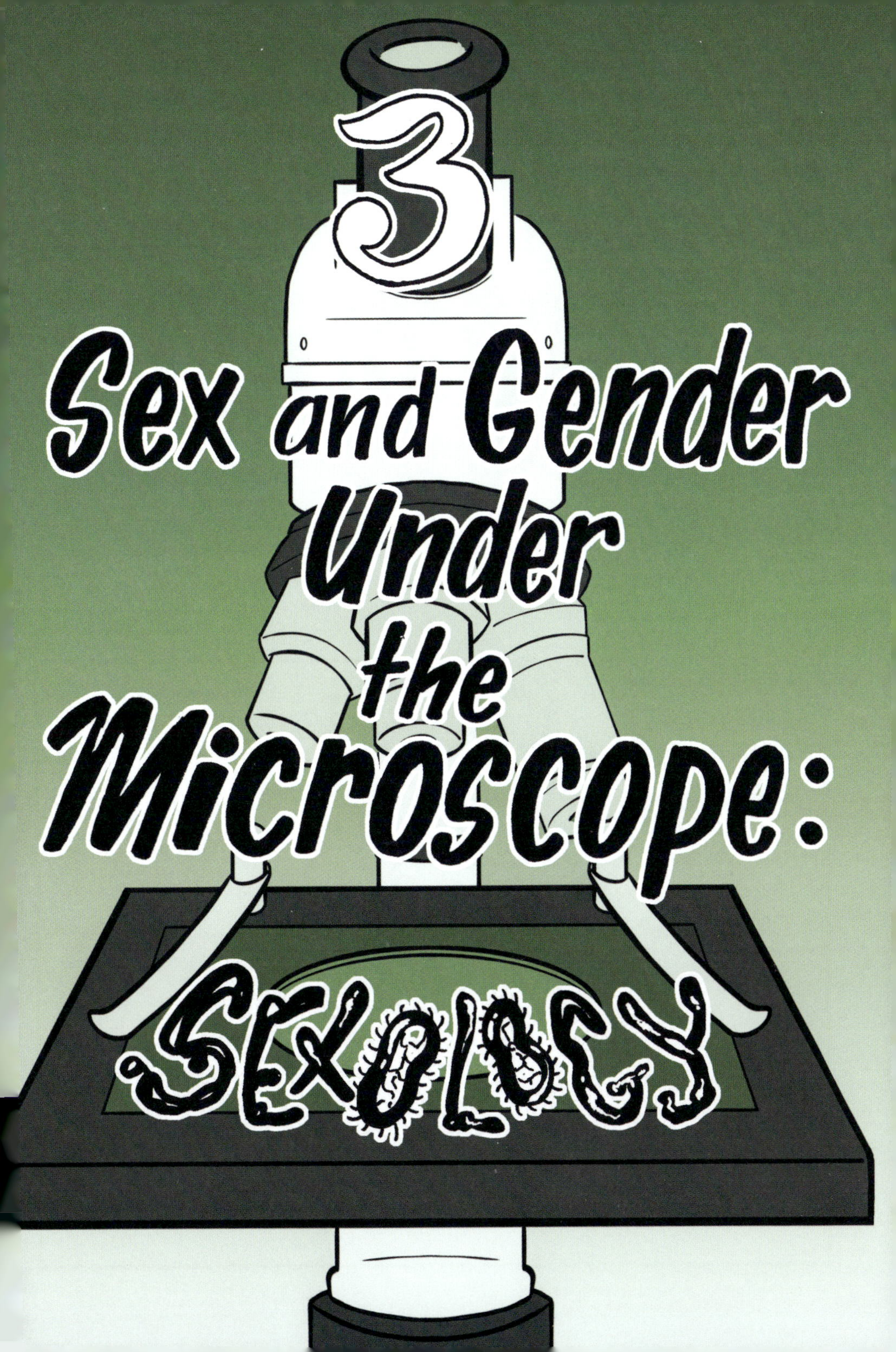
3
Sex and Gender Under the Microscope:
SEXOLOGY

Making It Official: Codifying Sex

As scientific ideas changed in Europe during the nineteenth century, they were used—as new ideas often are—in the service of reigning power structures.

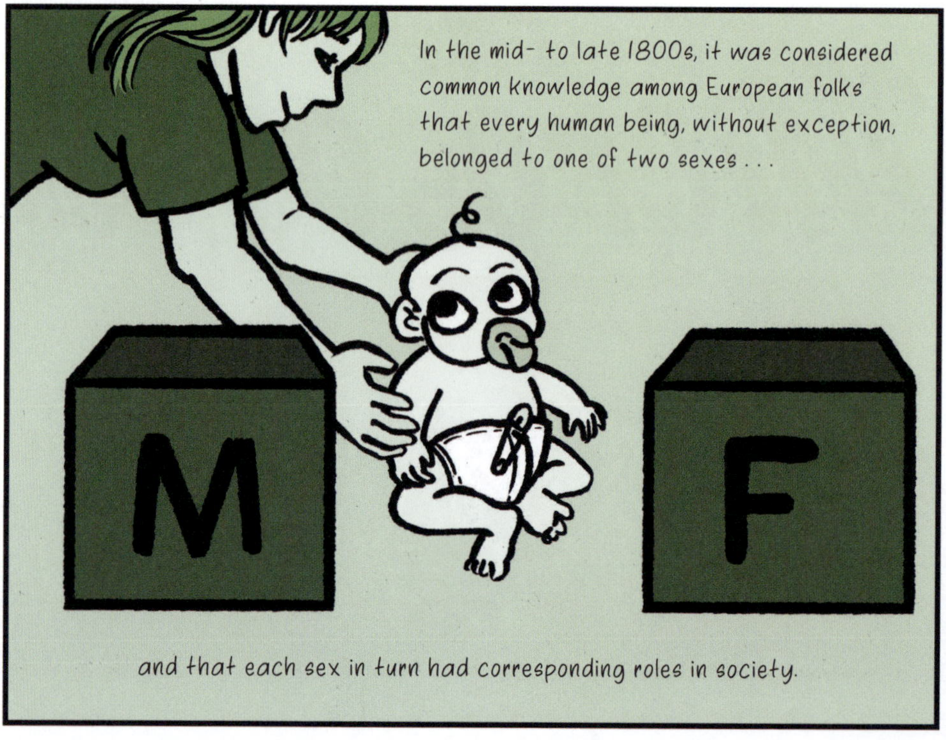
In the mid- to late 1800s, it was considered common knowledge among European folks that every human being, without exception, belonged to one of two sexes . . .
M
F
and that each sex in turn had corresponding roles in society.

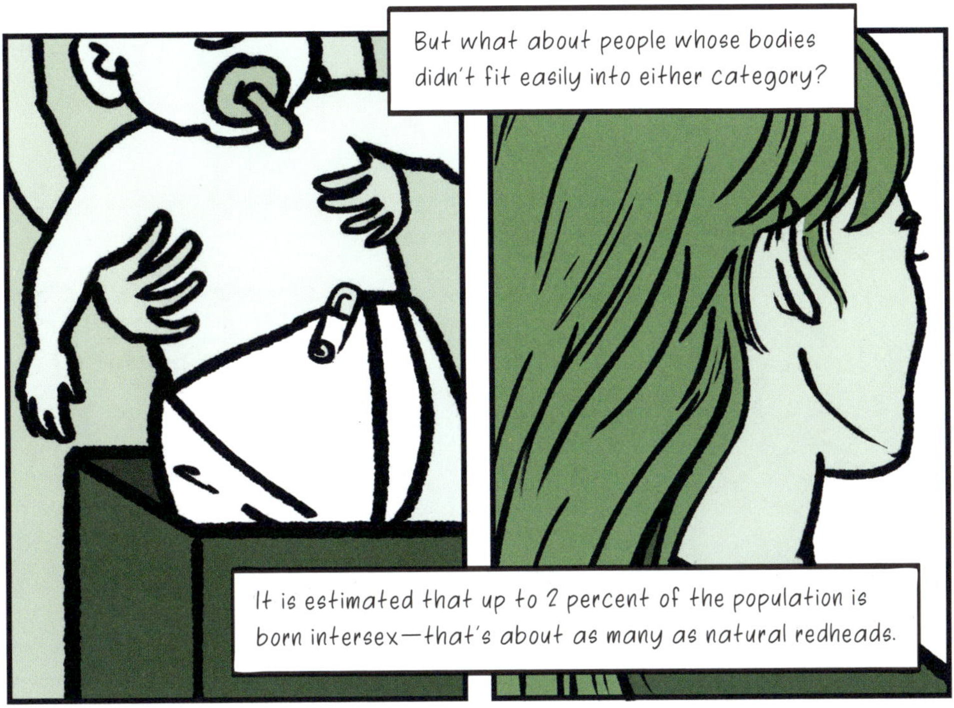
But what about people whose bodies didn't fit easily into either category?
It is estimated that up to 2 percent of the population is born intersex—that's about as many as natural redheads.

Sexologists were people who, during the nineteenth century, were trying to turn the study of sex and gender into a legitimate field of scientific inquiry.

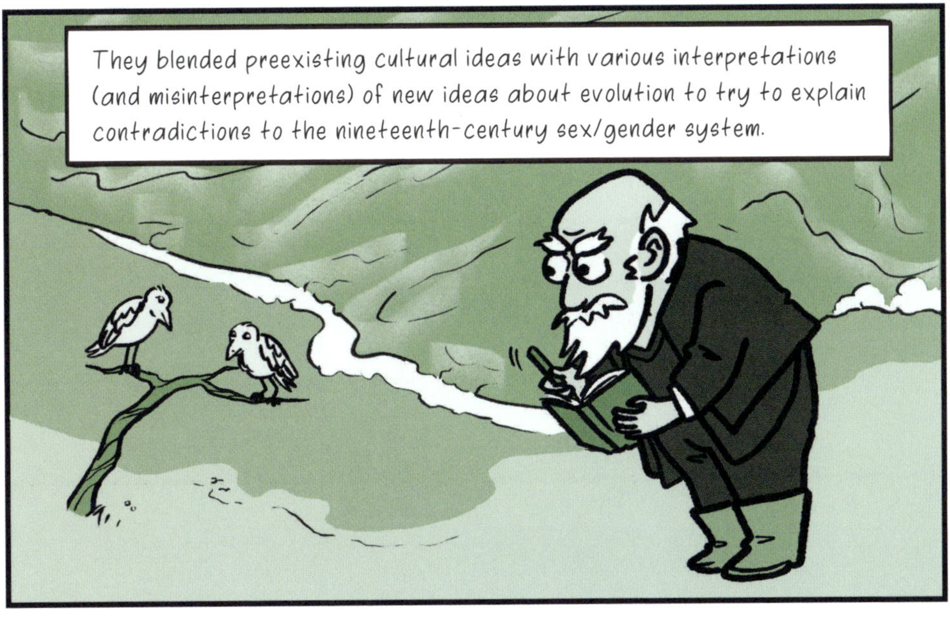
They blended preexisting cultural ideas with various interpretations (and misinterpretations) of new ideas about evolution to try to explain contradictions to the nineteenth-century sex/gender system.

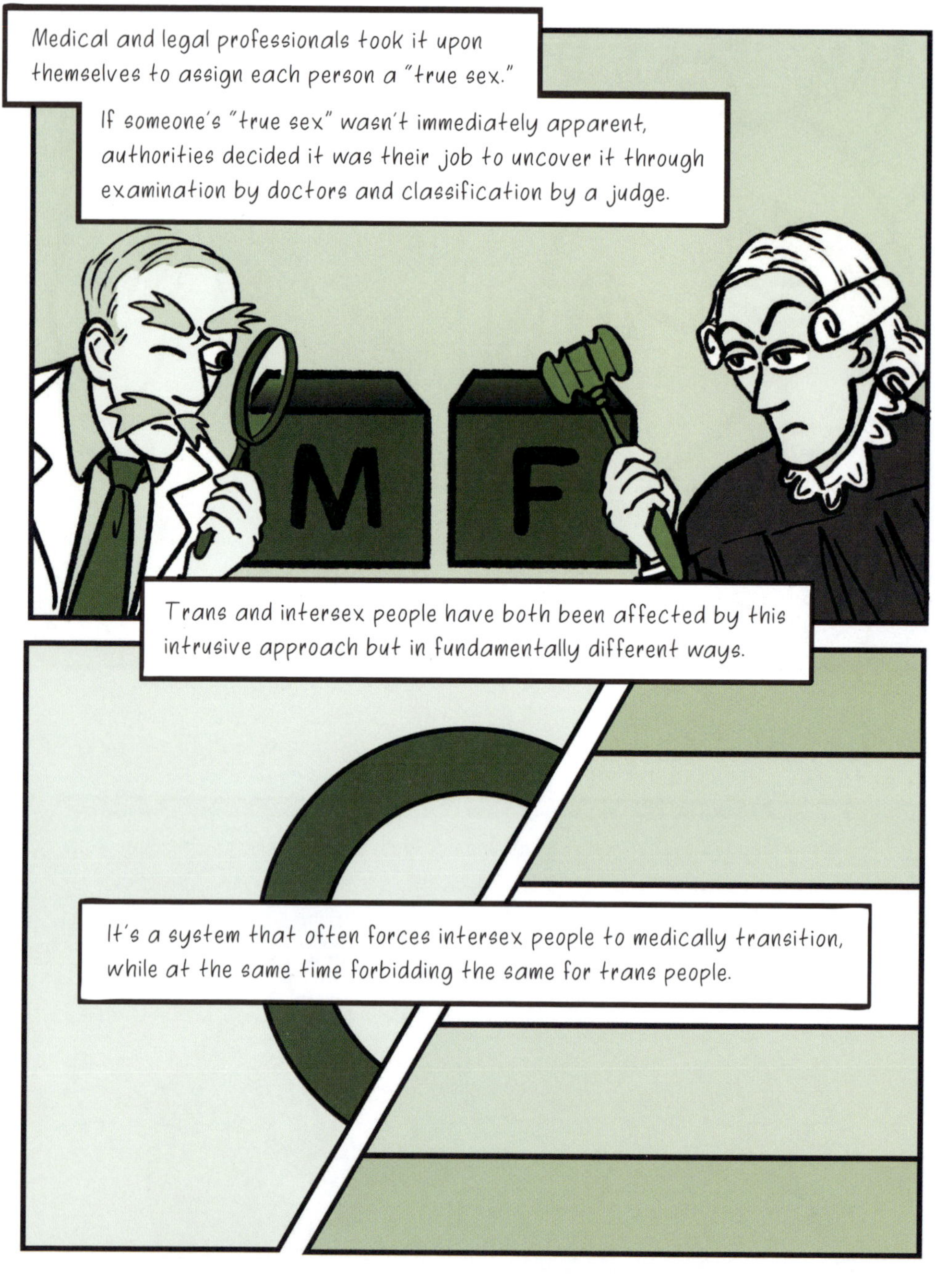
Medical and legal professionals took it upon themselves to assign each person a "true sex."
If someone's "true sex" wasn't immediately apparent, authorities decided it was their job to uncover it through examination by doctors and classification by a judge.
M
F
Trans and intersex people have both been affected by this intrusive approach but in fundamentally different ways.
It's a system that often forces intersex people to medically transition, while at the same time forbidding the same for trans people.

A memoir from the mid-1800s provides an account of the unfair burden placed on people born with sex characteristics outside the binary . . .

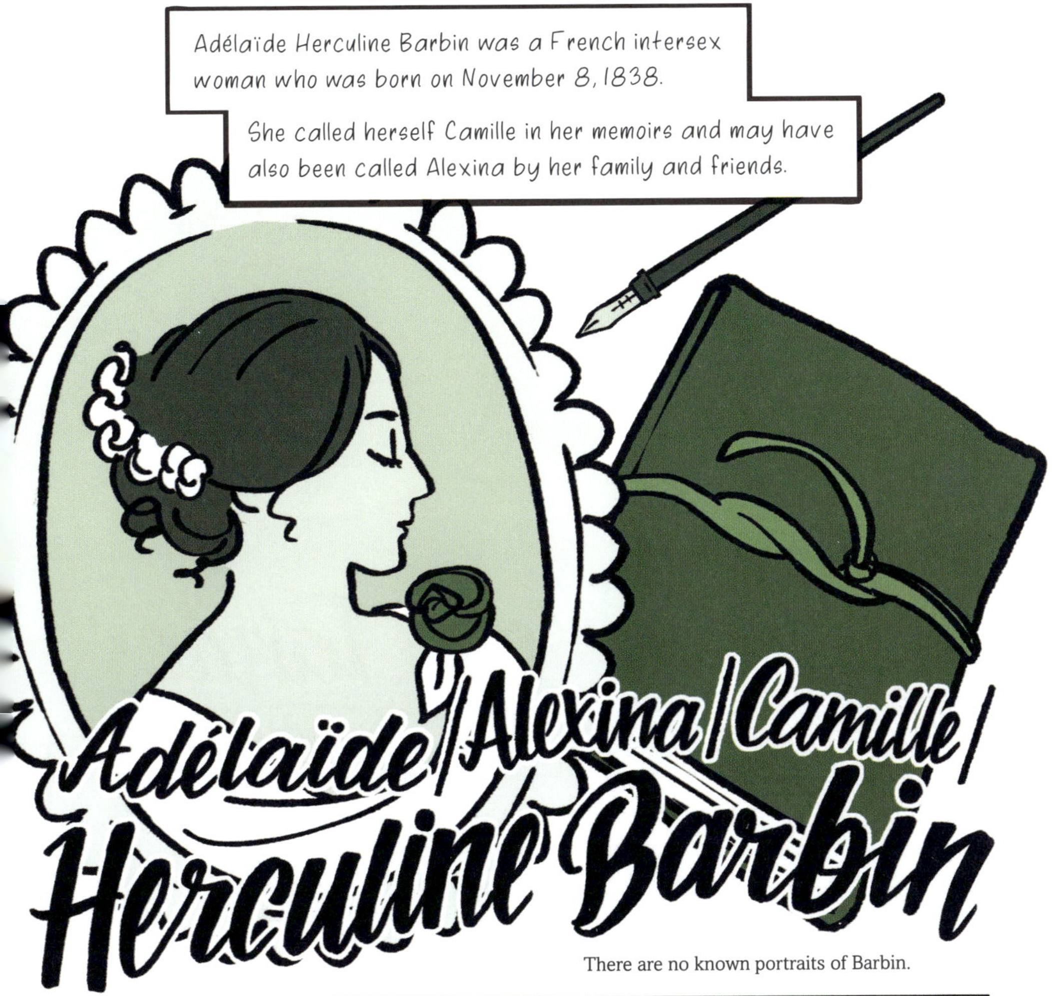
Adélaïde Herculine Barbin was a French intersex woman who was born on November 8, 1838.
She called herself Camille in her memoirs and may have also been called Alexina by her family and friends.
Adélaïde/Alexina/Camille/
Herculine Barbin

There are no known portraits of Barbin.

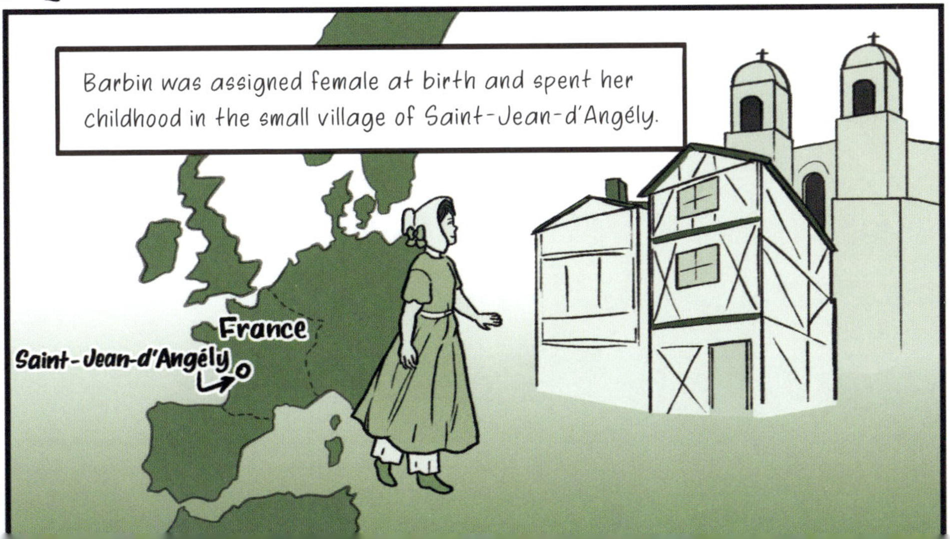
Barbin was assigned female at birth and spent her childhood in the small village of Saint-Jean-d'Angély.
France
Saint-Jean-d'Angély

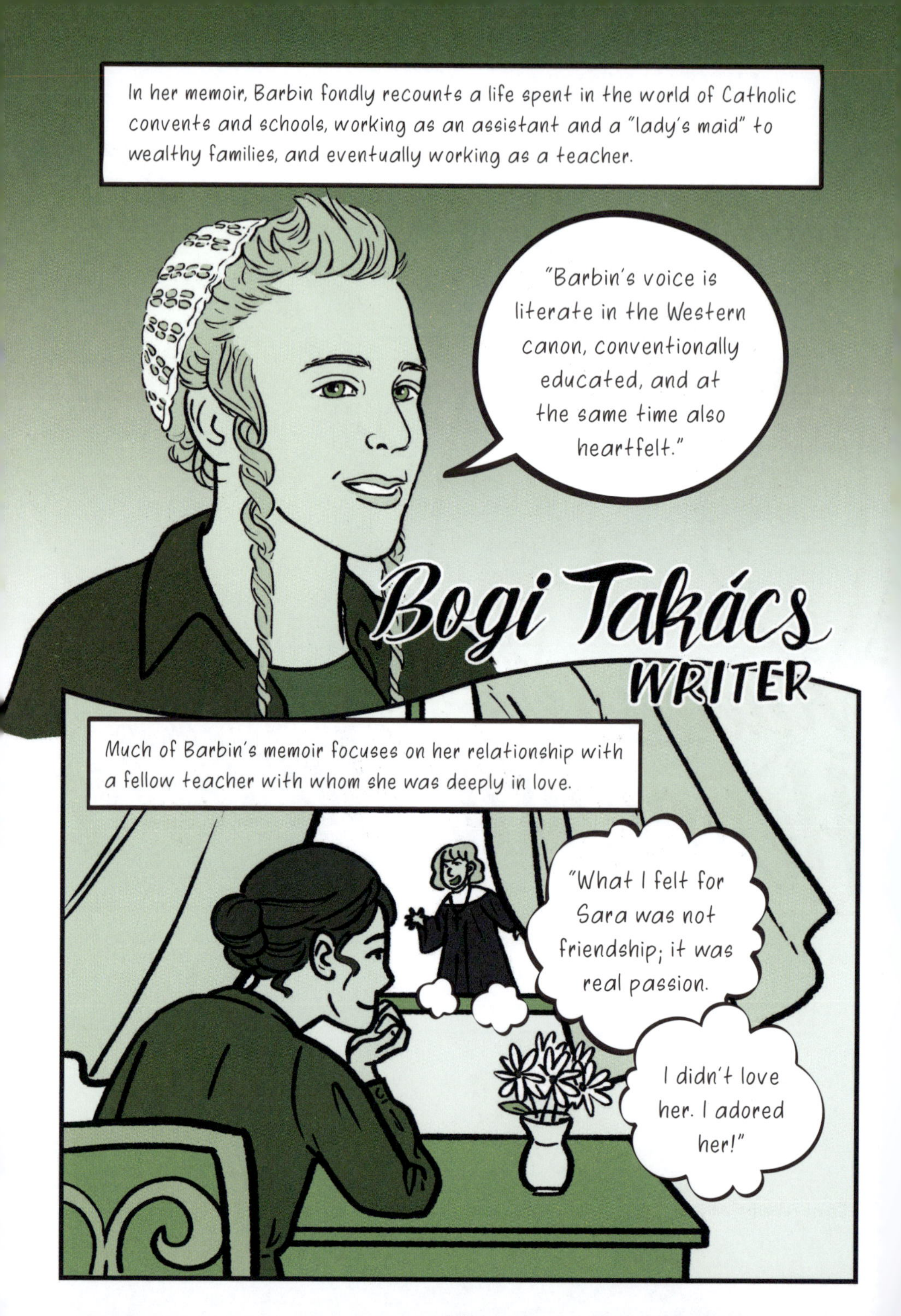
In her memoir, Barbin fondly recounts a life spent in the world of Catholic convents and schools, working as an assistant and a "lady's maid" to wealthy families, and eventually working as a teacher.
"Barbin's voice is literate in the Western canon, conventionally educated, and at the same time also heartfelt."
Bogi Takács
WRITER
Much of Barbin's memoir focuses on her relationship with a fellow teacher with whom she was deeply in love.
"What I felt for Sara was not friendship; it was real passion.
I didn't love her. I adored her!"

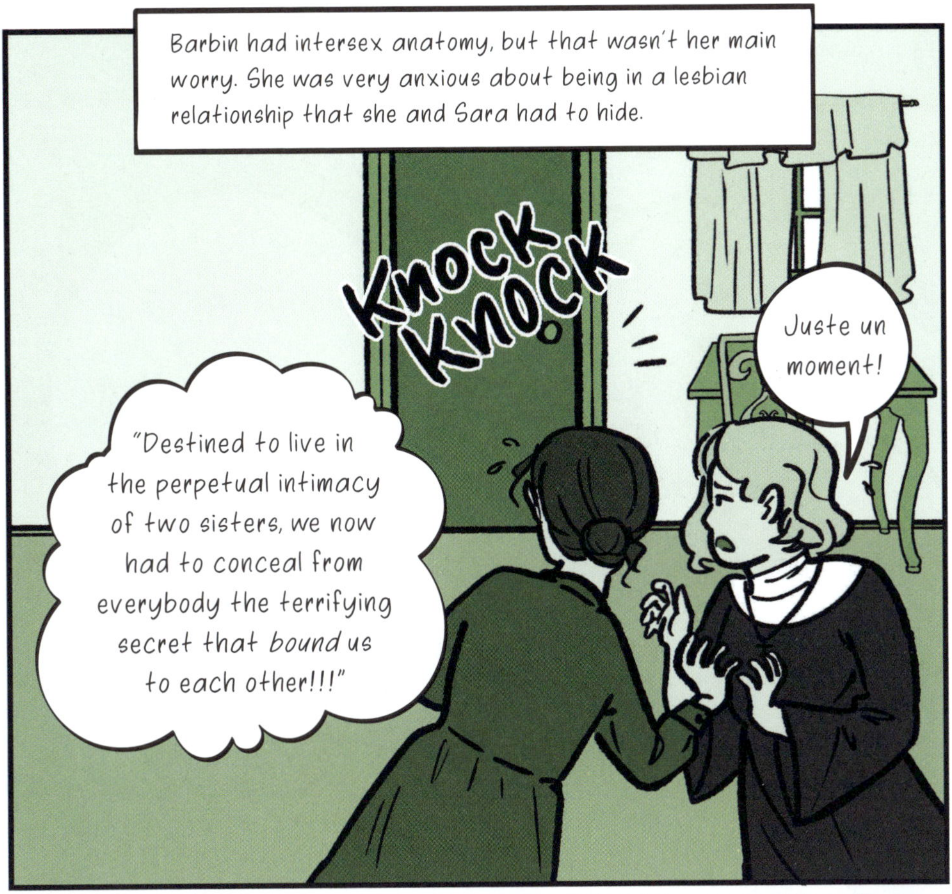
Barbin had intersex anatomy, but that wasn't her main worry. She was very anxious about being in a lesbian relationship that she and Sara had to hide.
KNOCK KNOCK
Juste un moment!
"Destined to live in the perpetual intimacy of two sisters, we now had to conceal from everybody the terrifying secret that *bound* us to each other!!!"

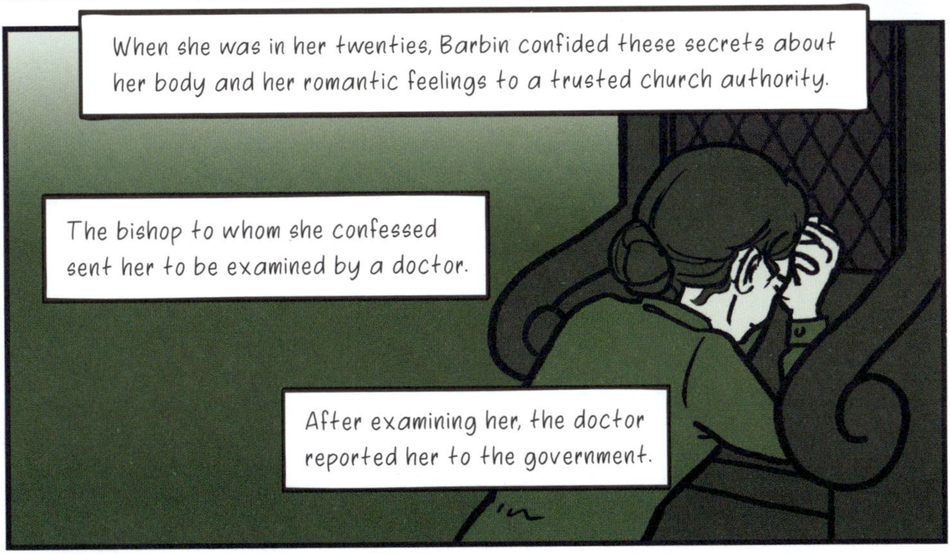
When she was in her twenties, Barbin confided these secrets about her body and her romantic feelings to a trusted church authority.
The bishop to whom she confessed sent her to be examined by a doctor.
After examining her, the doctor reported her to the government.

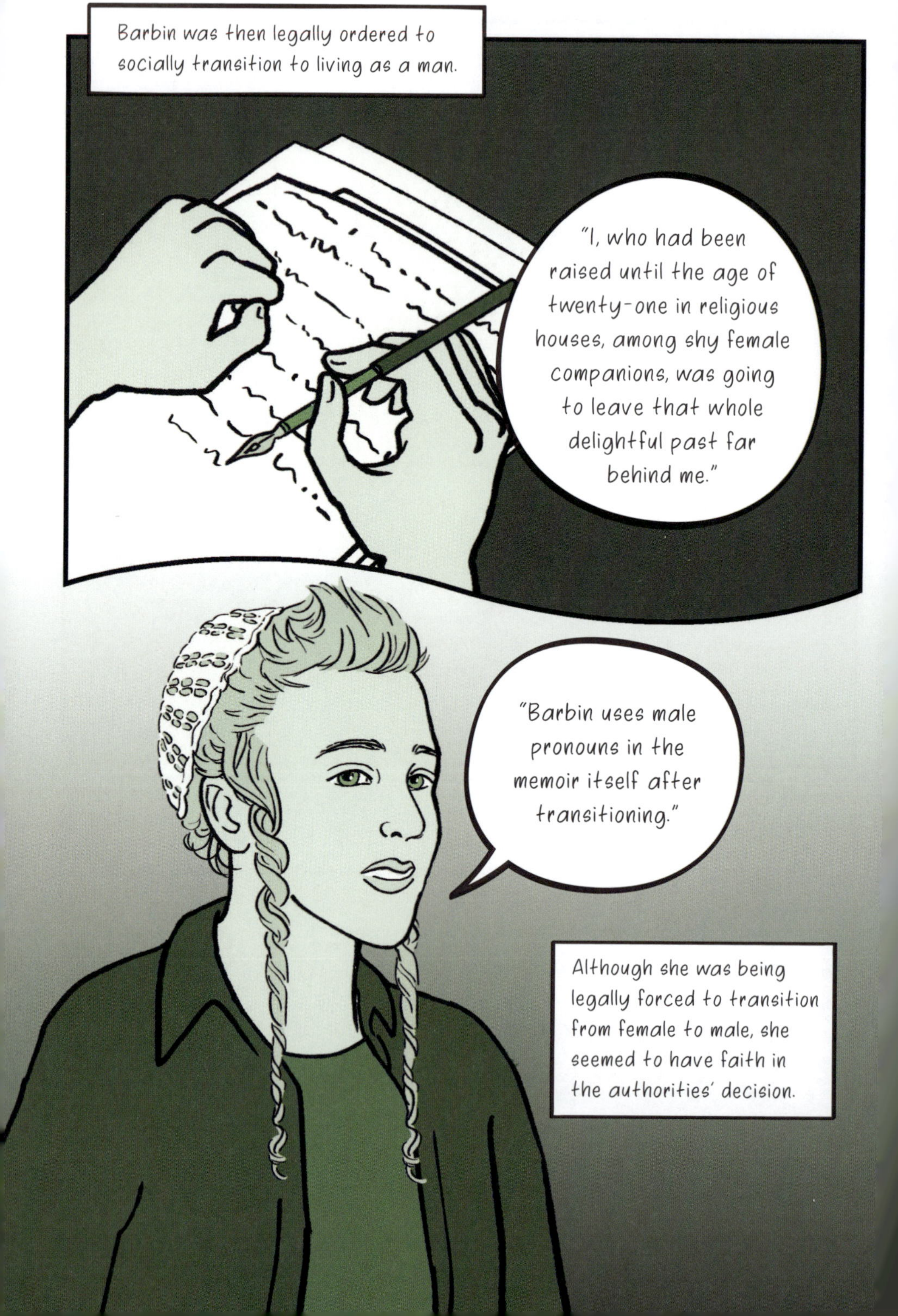
Barbin was then legally ordered to socially transition to living as a man.
"I, who had been raised until the age of twenty-one in religious houses, among shy female companions, was going to leave that whole delightful past far behind me."
"Barbin uses male pronouns in the memoir itself after transitioning."
Although she was being legally forced to transition from female to male, she seemed to have faith in the authorities' decision.

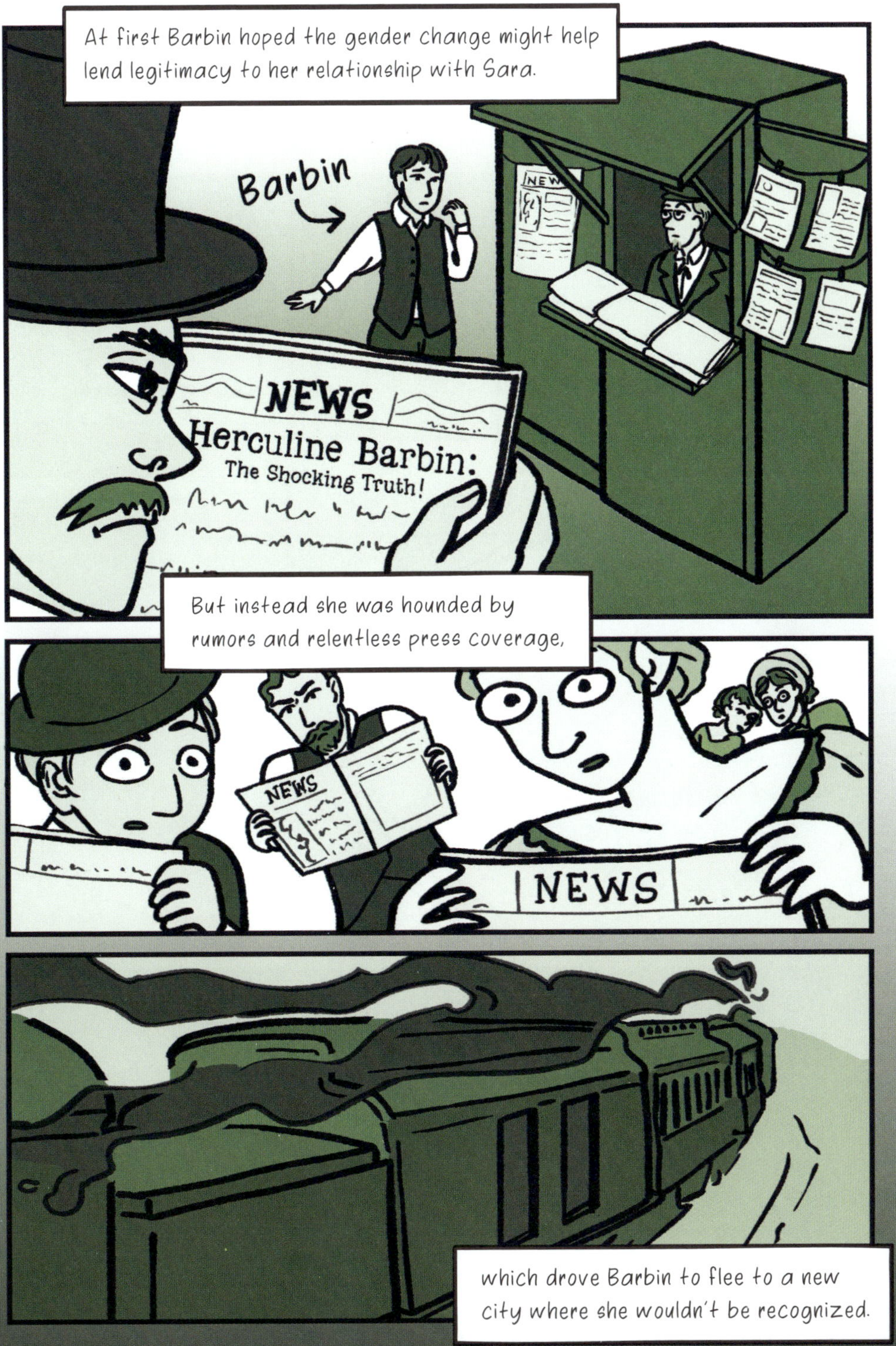
At first Barbin hoped the gender change might help lend legitimacy to her relationship with Sara.
Barbin
NEWS
Herculine Barbin: The Shocking Truth!
But instead she was hounded by rumors and relentless press coverage,
NEWS
NEWS
which drove Barbin to flee to a new city where she wouldn't be recognized.

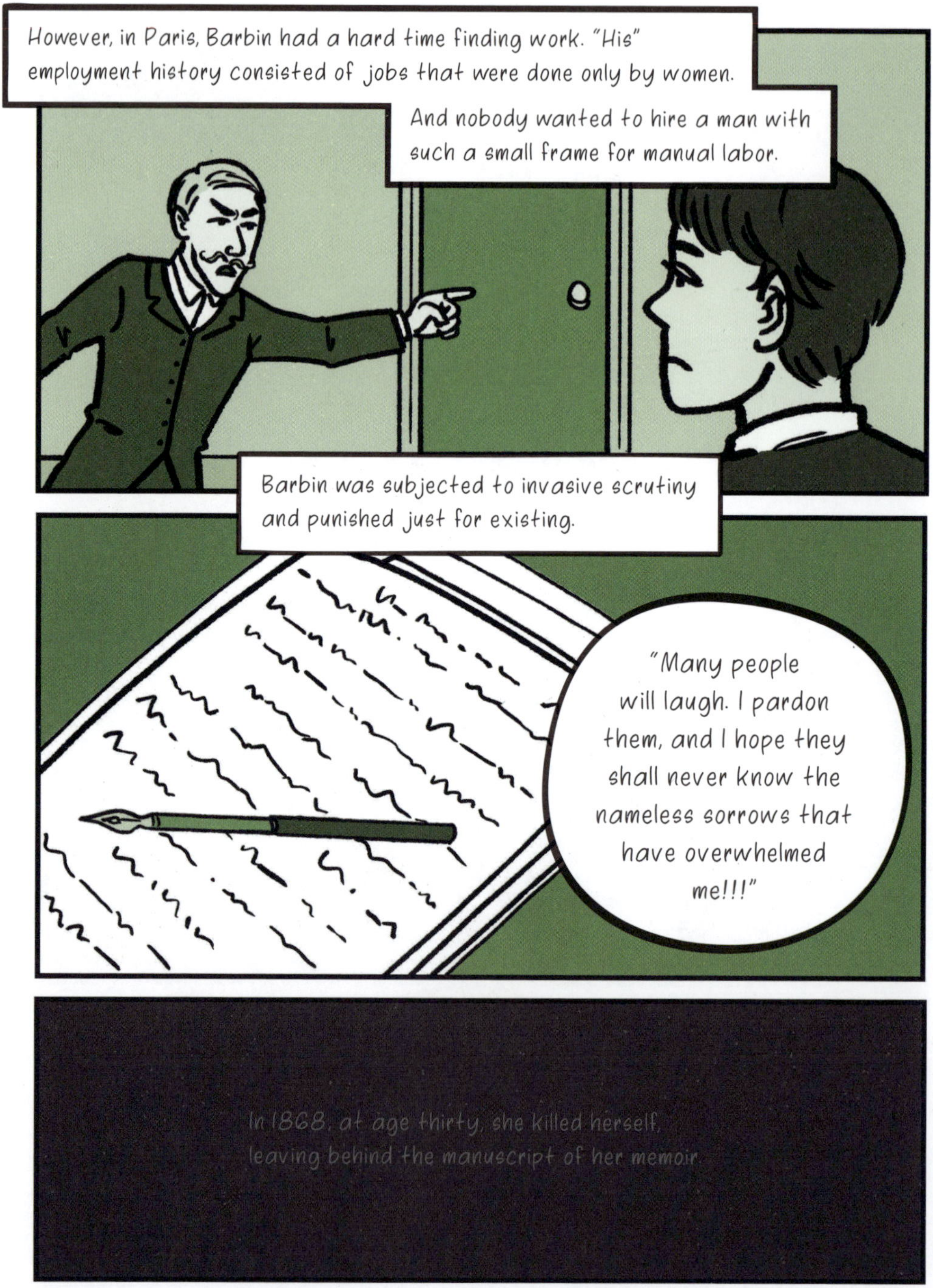

However, in Paris, Barbin had a hard time finding work. "His" employment history consisted of jobs that were done only by women.
And nobody wanted to hire a man with such a small frame for manual labor.
Barbin was subjected to invasive scrutiny and punished just for existing.
"Many people will laugh. I pardon them, and I hope they shall never know the nameless sorrows that have overwhelmed me!!!"
In 1868, at age thirty, she killed herself, leaving behind the manuscript of her memoir.

Intersex Day of Remembrance is held on November 8, Barbin's birthday.

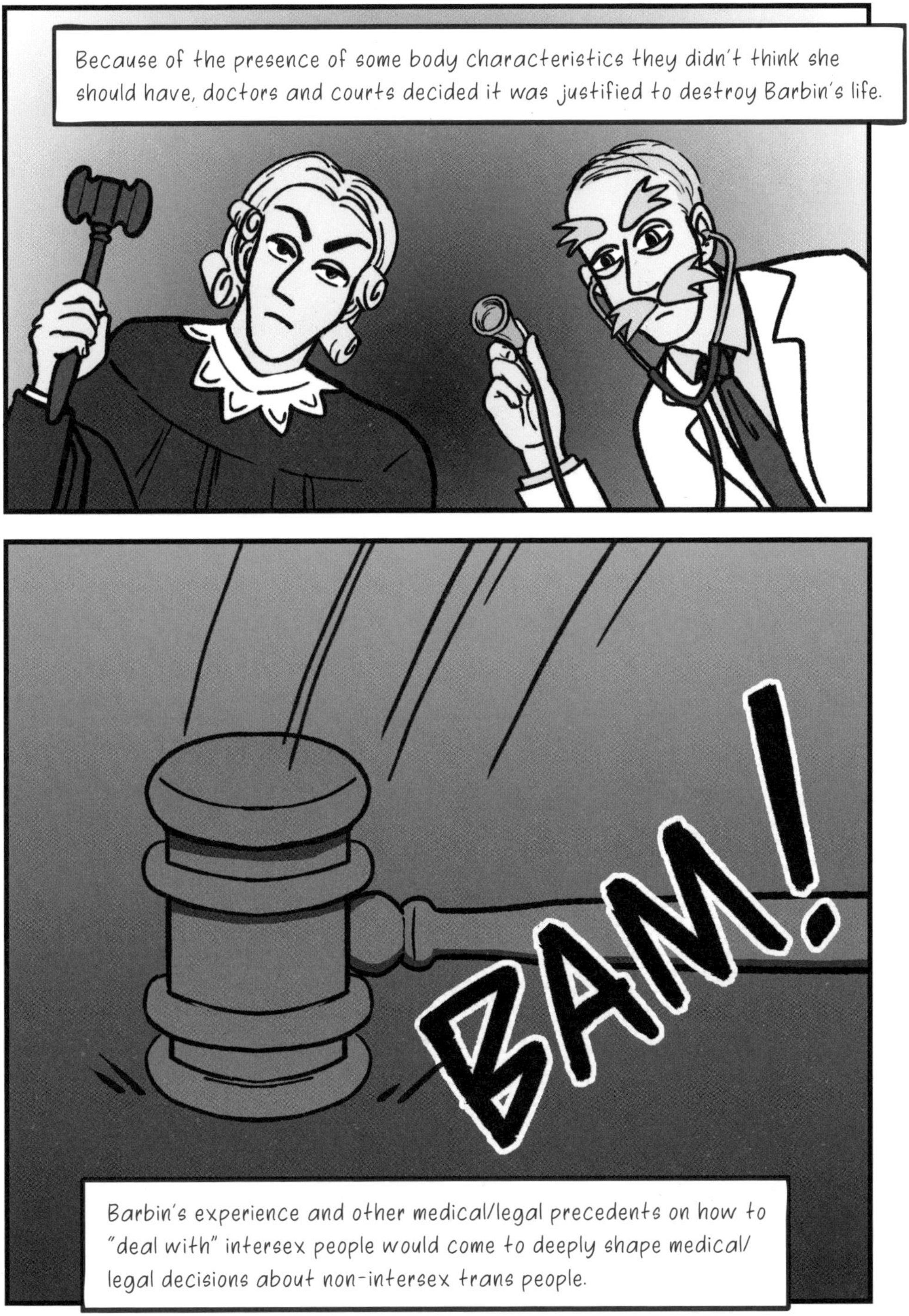
Because of the presence of some body characteristics they didn't think she should have, doctors and courts decided it was justified to destroy Barbin's life.
BAM!
Barbin's experience and other medical/legal precedents on how to "deal with" intersex people would come to deeply shape medical/legal decisions about non-intersex trans people.

Scientists of Sex

The nineteenth century was a time of great scientific development in Europe. Professionals in newly emerging scientific fields were going hog-wild coming up with new terms and categories for objects and phenomena within their respective fields. As their name implies, sexologists focused on sex and gender categories.

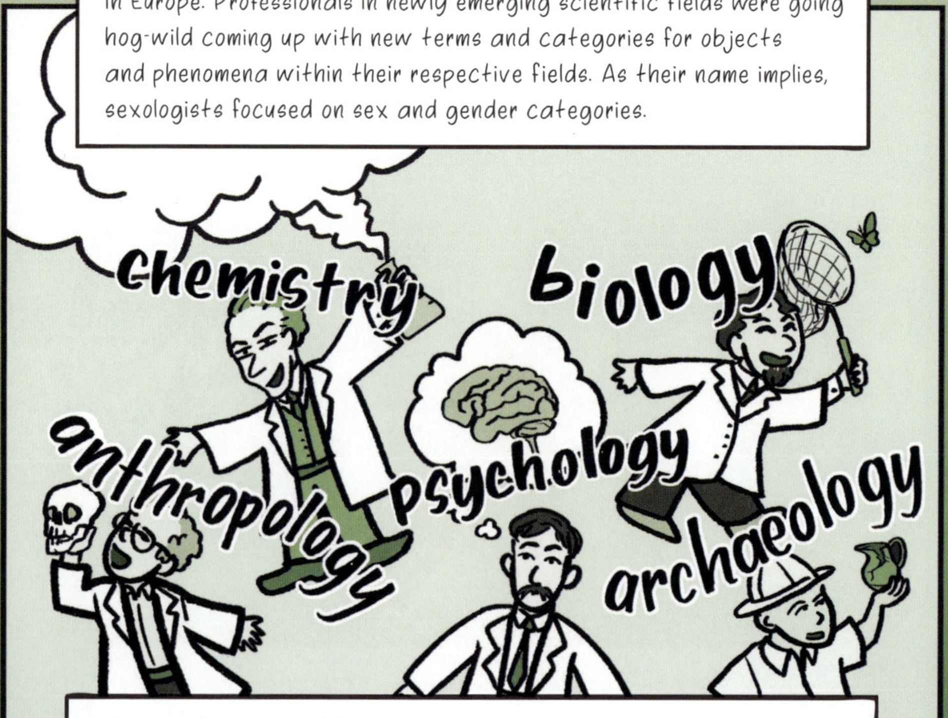
chemistry
biology
anthropology
psychology
archaeology

These professionals often used intersex people as a starting point when it came to thinking about gay, lesbian, queer, and trans people.

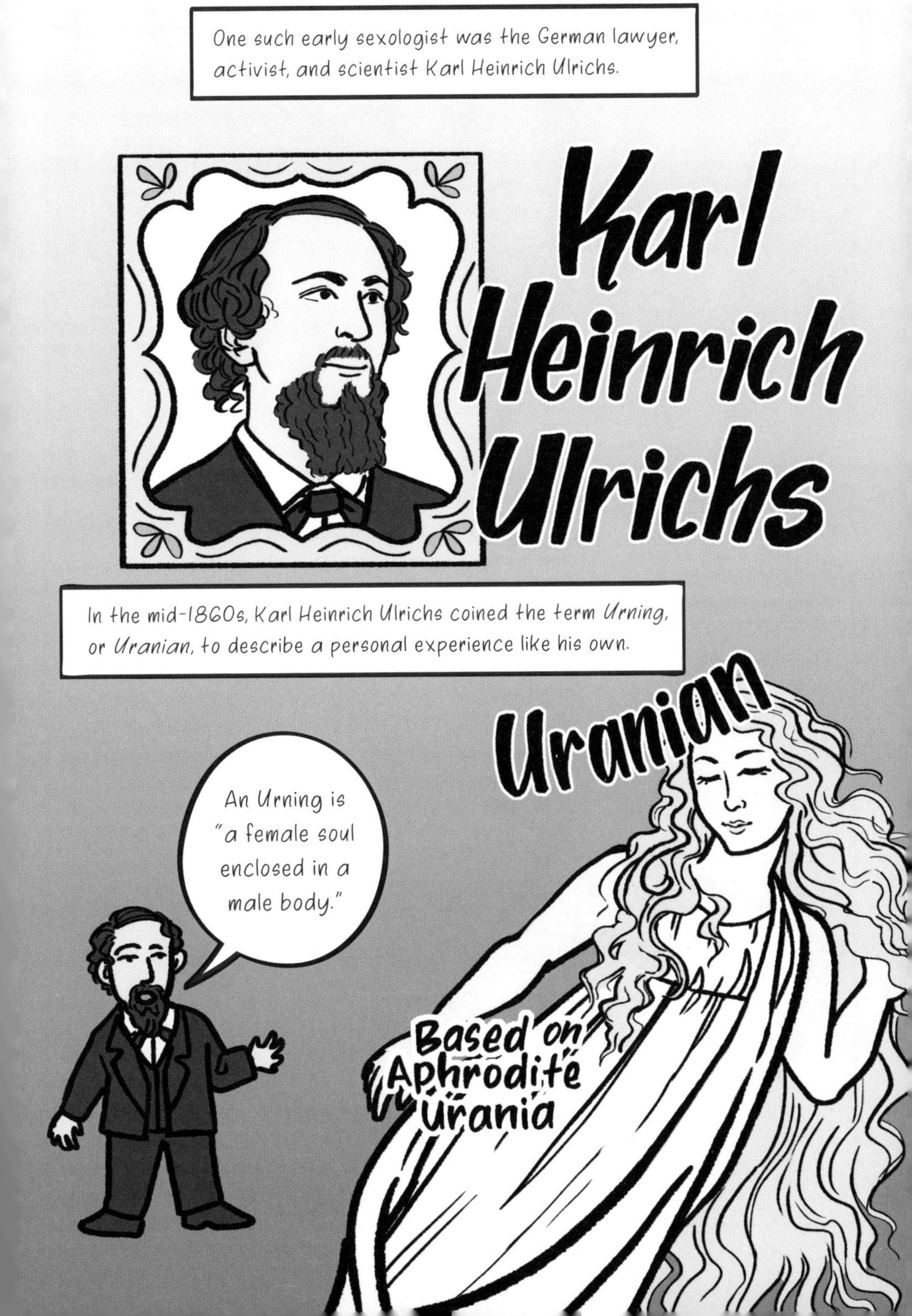

One such early sexologist was the German lawyer, activist, and scientist Karl Heinrich Ulrichs.
Karl Heinrich Ulrichs
In the mid-1860s, Karl Heinrich Ulrichs coined the term *Urning*, or *Uranian*, to describe a personal experience like his own.
Uranian
An *Urning* is "a female soul enclosed in a male body."
Based on Aphrodite Urania

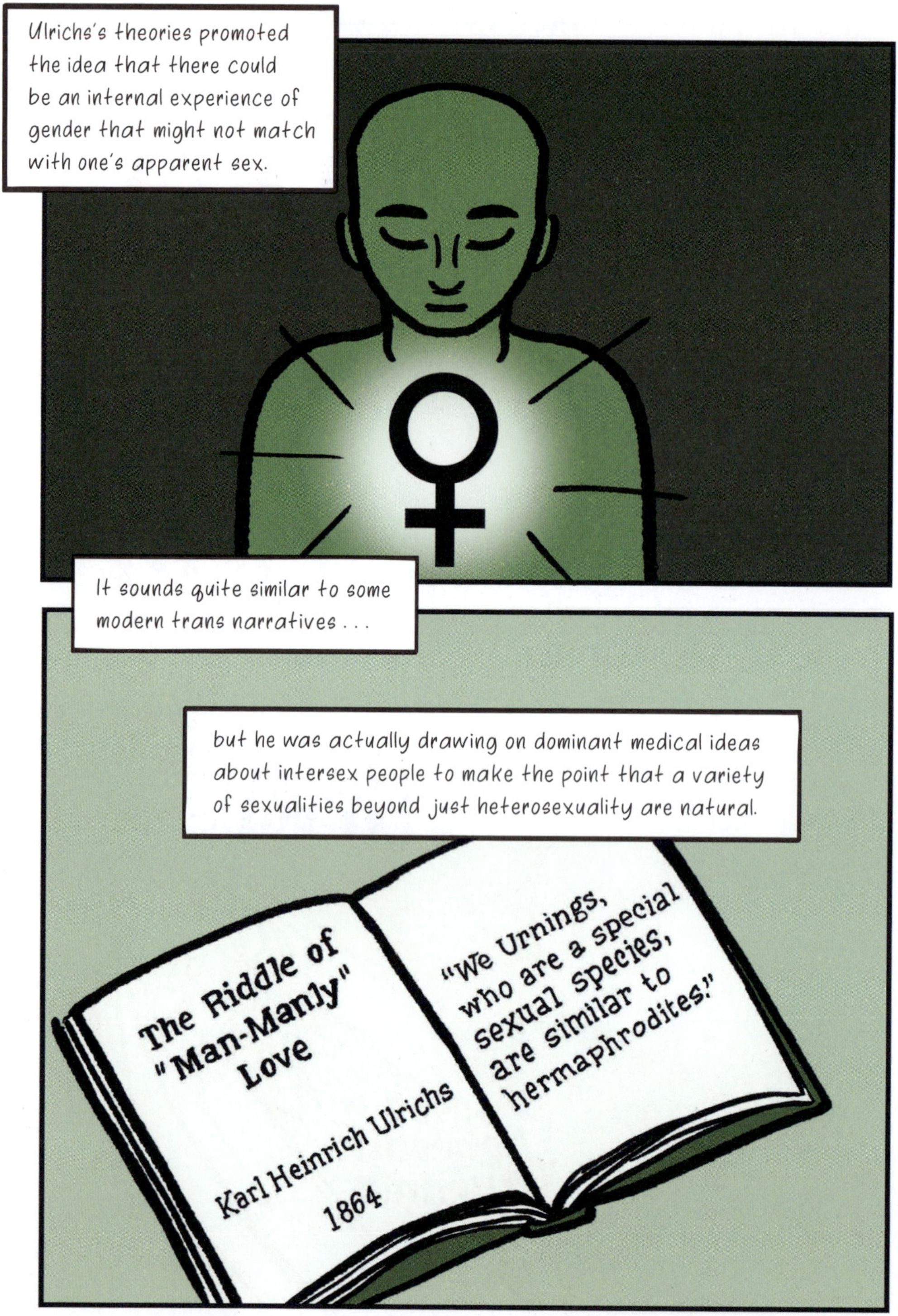
Ulrichs's theories promoted the idea that there could be an internal experience of gender that might not match with one's apparent sex.
It sounds quite similar to some modern trans narratives . . .
but he was actually drawing on dominant medical ideas about intersex people to make the point that a variety of sexualities beyond just heterosexuality are natural.
The Riddle of "Man-Manly" Love
Karl Heinrich Ulrichs
1864
"We Urnings, who are a special sexual species, are similar to hermaphrodites."

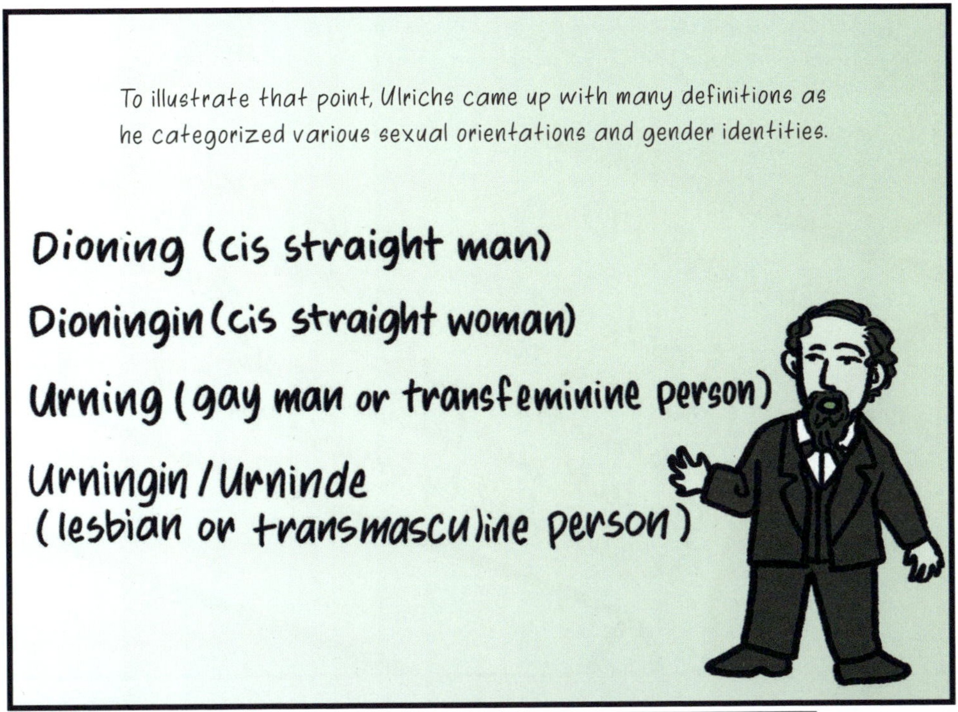
To illustrate that point, Ulrichs came up with many definitions as he categorized various sexual orientations and gender identities.
Dioning (cis straight man)
Dioningin (cis straight woman)
Urning (gay man or transfeminine person)
Urningin / Urninde (lesbian or transmasculine person)

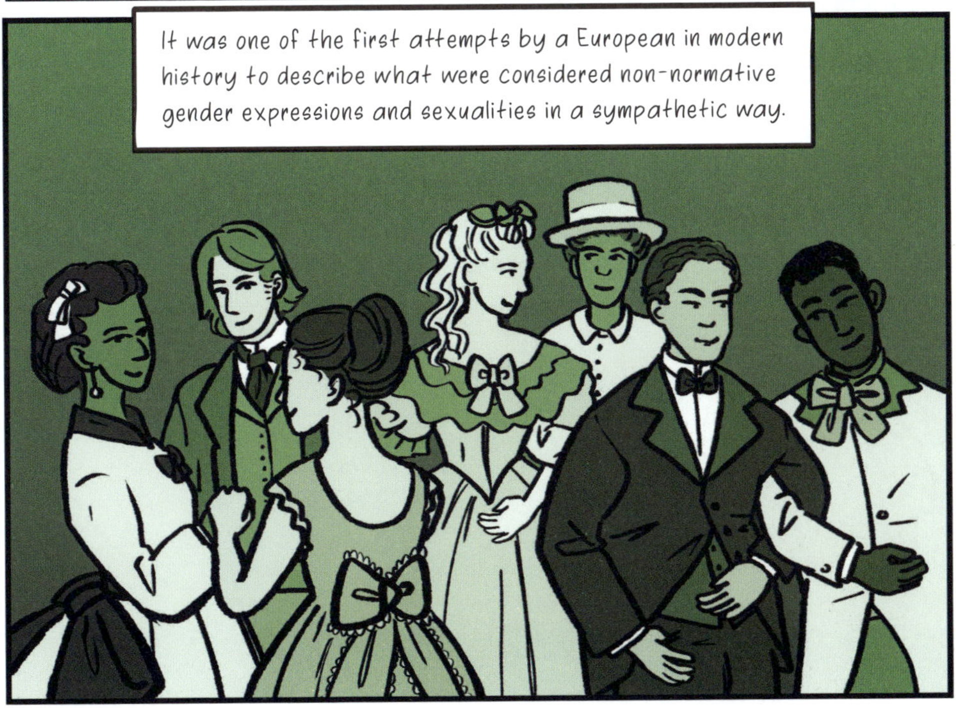
It was one of the first attempts by a European in modern history to describe what were considered non-normative gender expressions and sexualities in a sympathetic way.

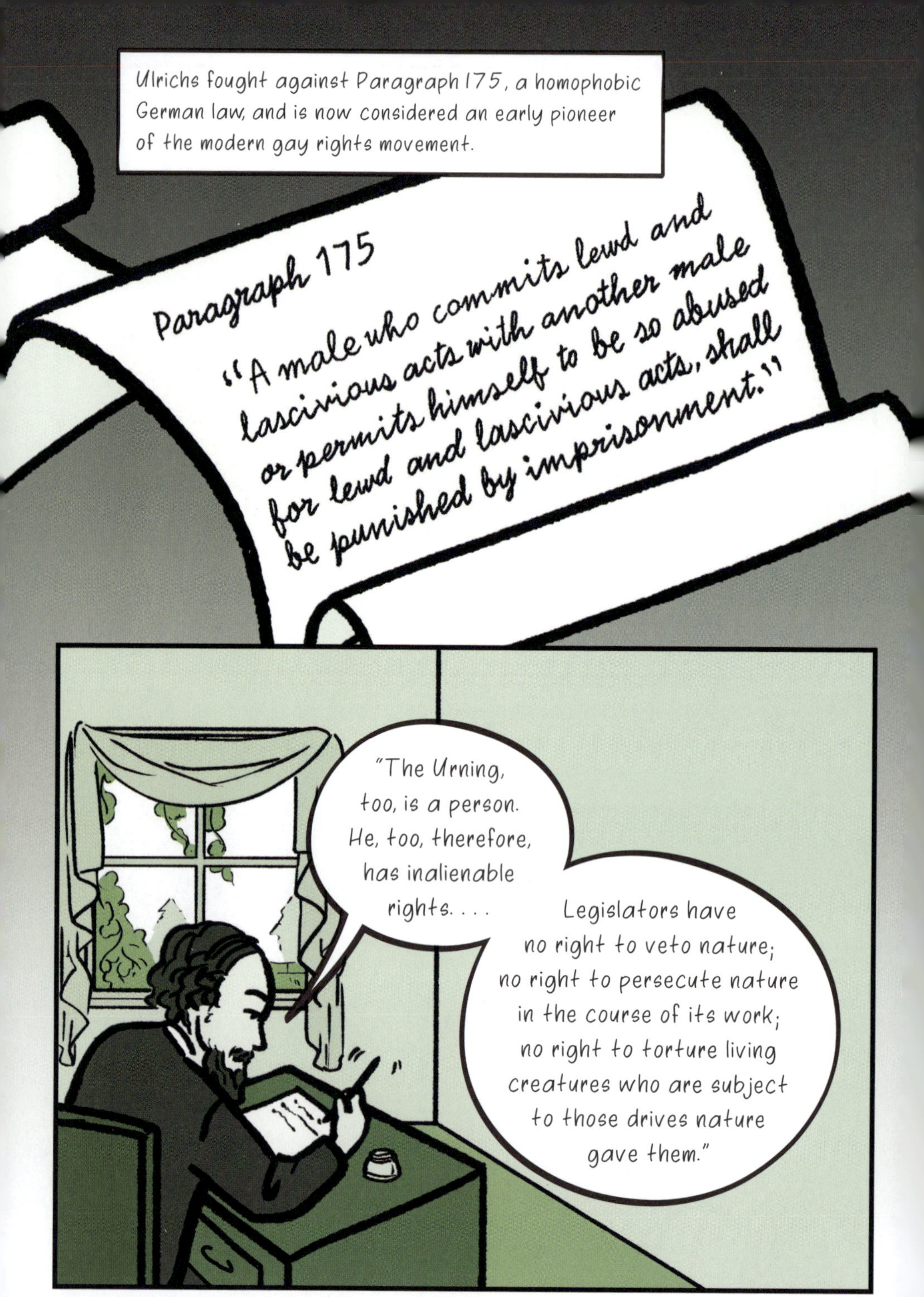
Ulrichs fought against Paragraph 175, a homophobic German law, and is now considered an early pioneer of the modern gay rights movement.
Paragraph 175
"A male who commits lewd and lascivious acts with another male or permits himself to be so abused for lewd and lascivious acts, shall be punished by imprisonment."
"The Urning, too, is a person. He, too, therefore, has inalienable rights. . . .
Legislators have no right to veto nature; no right to persecute nature in the course of its work; no right to torture living creatures who are subject to those drives nature gave them."

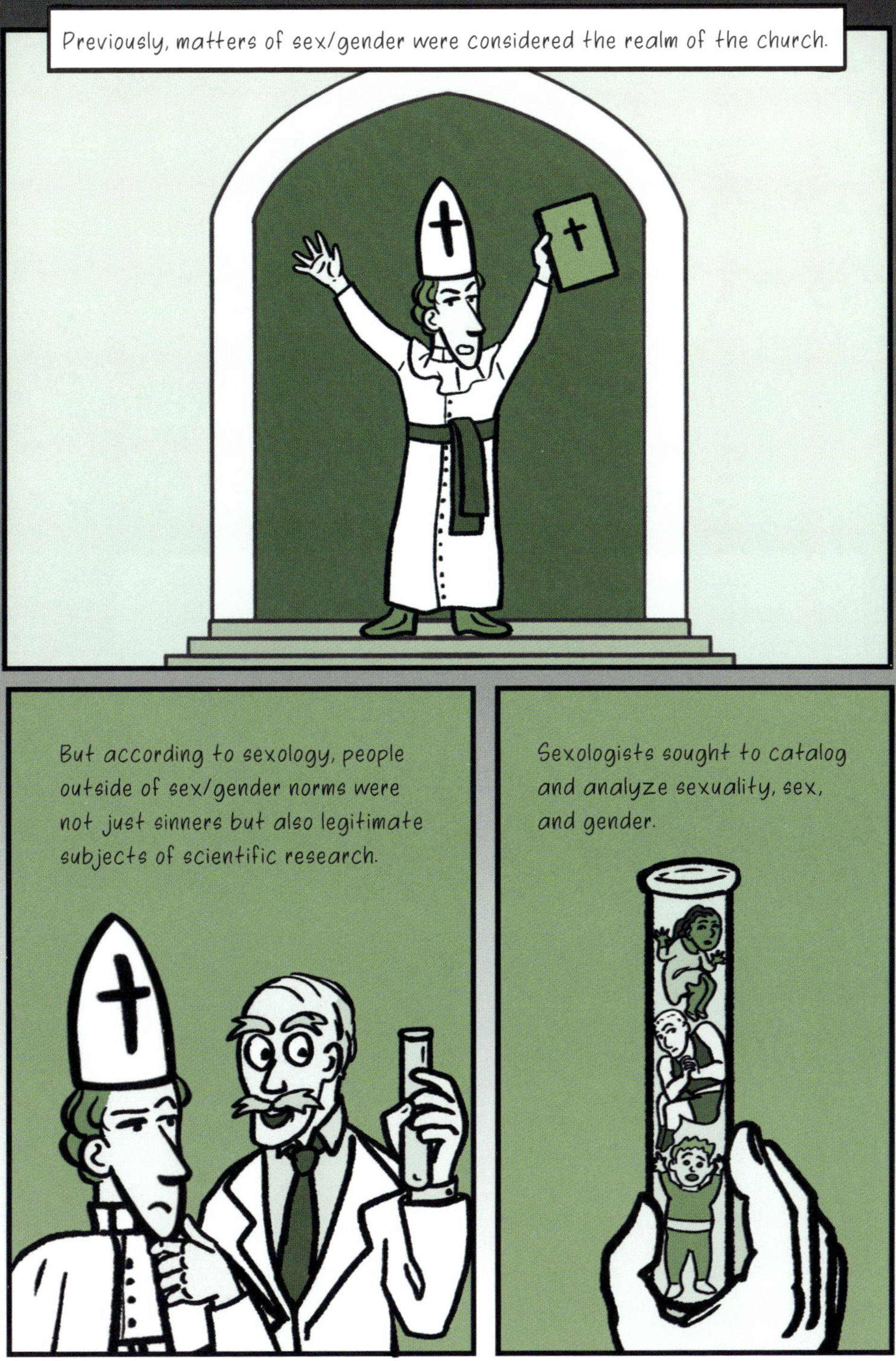
Previously, matters of sex/gender were considered the realm of the church.
But according to sexology, people outside of sex/gender norms were not just sinners but also legitimate subjects of scientific research.
Sexologists sought to catalog and analyze sexuality, sex, and gender.

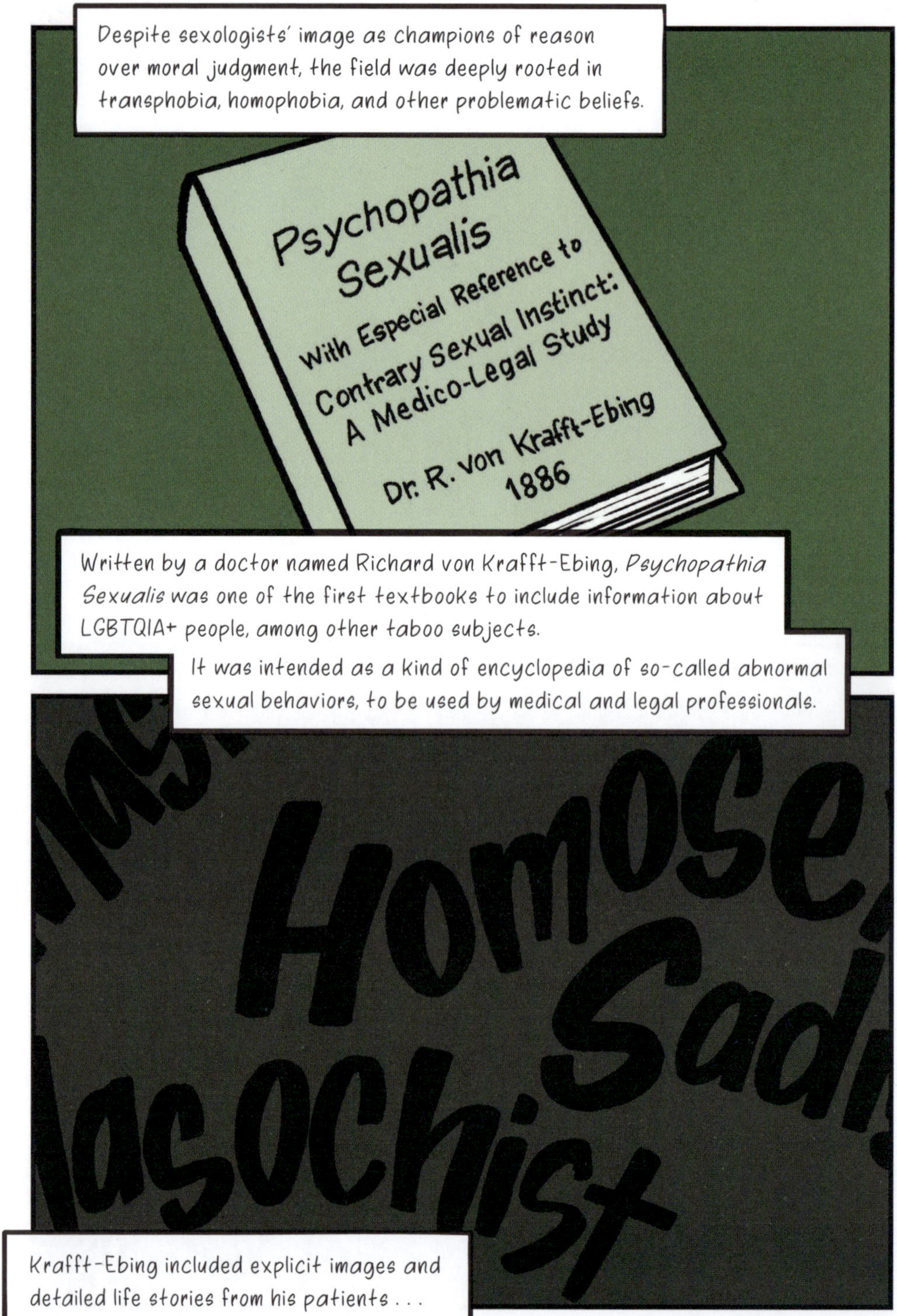
Despite sexologists' image as champions of reason over moral judgment, the field was deeply rooted in transphobia, homophobia, and other problematic beliefs.
Psychopathia Sexualis
With Especial Reference to Contrary Sexual Instinct: A Medico-Legal Study
Dr. R. von Krafft-Ebing
1886
Written by a doctor named Richard von Krafft-Ebing, *Psychopathia Sexualis* was one of the first textbooks to include information about LGBTQIA+ people, among other taboo subjects.
It was intended as a kind of encyclopedia of so-called abnormal sexual behaviors, to be used by medical and legal professionals.
Krafft-Ebing included explicit images and detailed life stories from his patients . . .

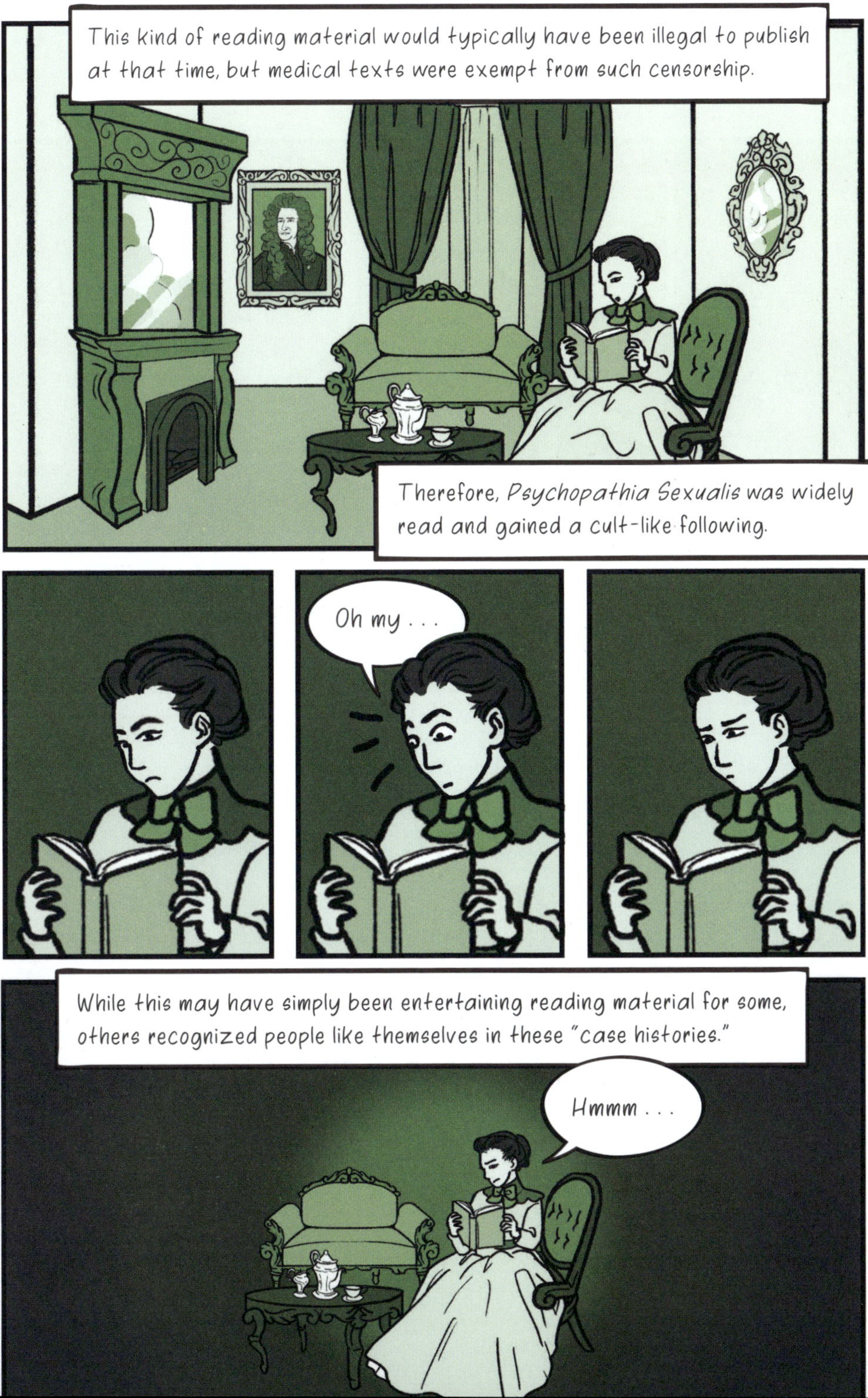
This kind of reading material would typically have been illegal to publish at that time, but medical texts were exempt from such censorship.
Therefore, *Psychopathia Sexualis* was widely read and gained a cult-like following.
Oh my . . .
While this may have simply been entertaining reading material for some, others recognized people like themselves in these "case histories."
Hmmm . . .

People with "sexual problems" started seeking the advice of sexologists, who were seen as psychologists, medical experts, and scholars rolled into one.

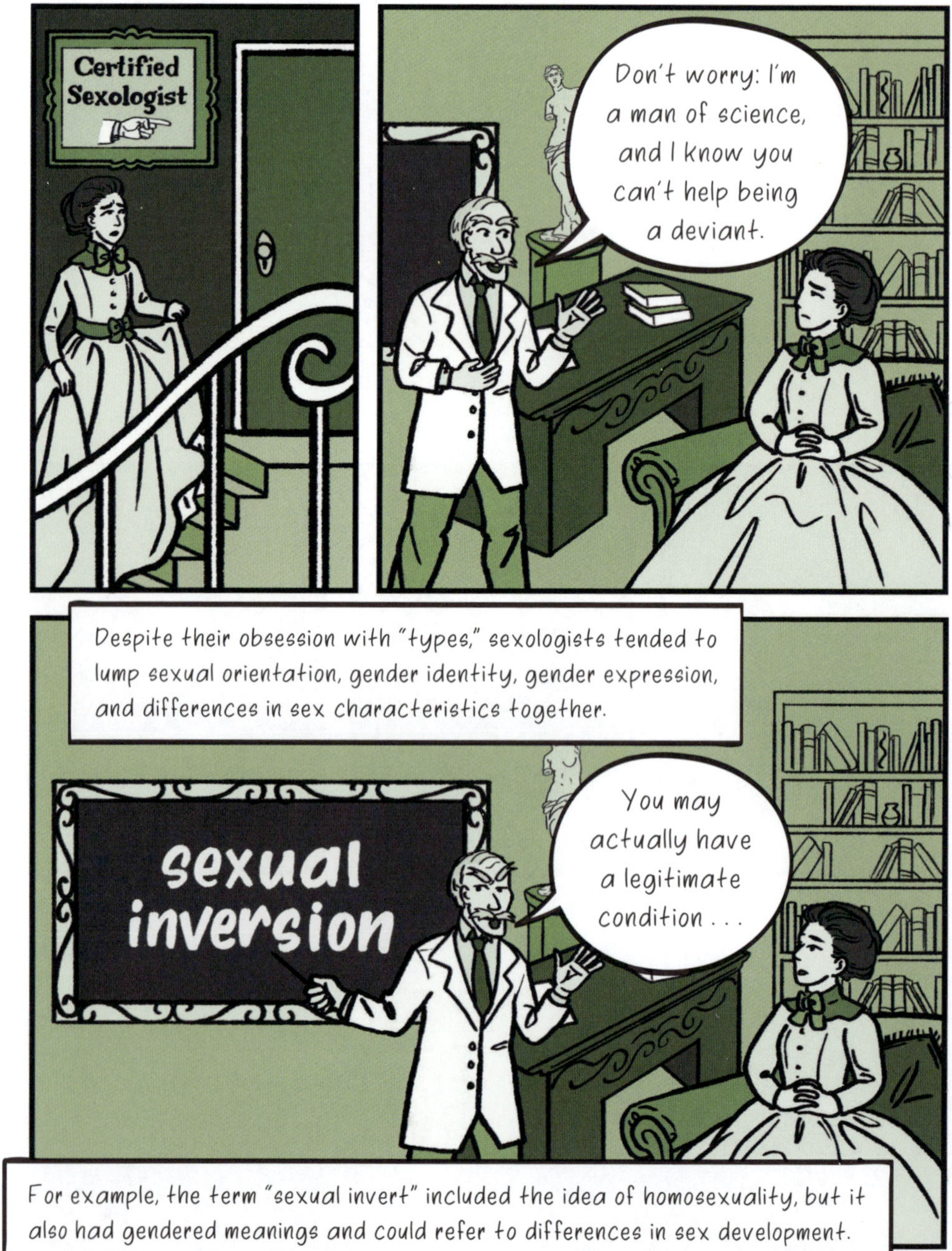
Certified Sexologist
Don't worry: I'm a man of science, and I know you can't help being a deviant.
Despite their obsession with "types," sexologists tended to lump sexual orientation, gender identity, gender expression, and differences in sex characteristics together.
sexual inversion
You may actually have a legitimate condition . . .
For example, the term "sexual invert" included the idea of homosexuality, but it also had gendered meanings and could refer to differences in sex development.

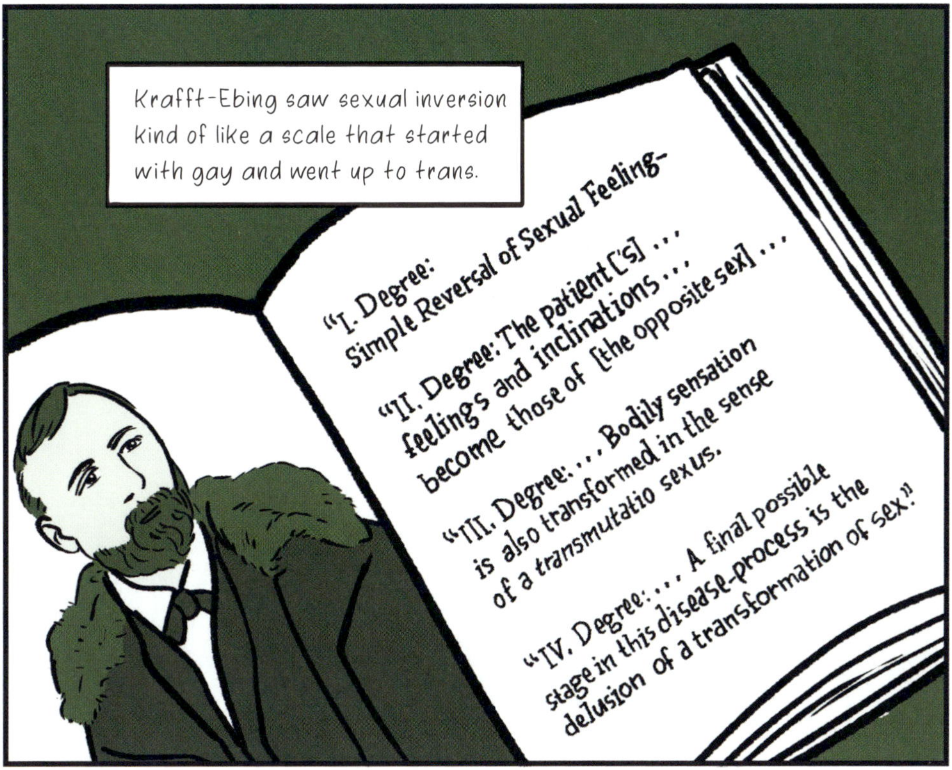
Krafft-Ebing saw sexual inversion kind of like a scale that started with gay and went up to trans.
"I. Degree: Simple Reversal of Sexual Feeling-
"II. Degree: The patient['s] ... feelings and inclinations ... become those of [the opposite sex] ...
"III. Degree: ... Bodily sensation is also transformed in the sense of a *transmutatio sexus*.
"IV. Degree: ... A final possible stage in this disease-process is the delusion of a transformation of sex."

This framework may be considered offensive today, but it provided some people with personal validation and a basis on which to argue for rights.

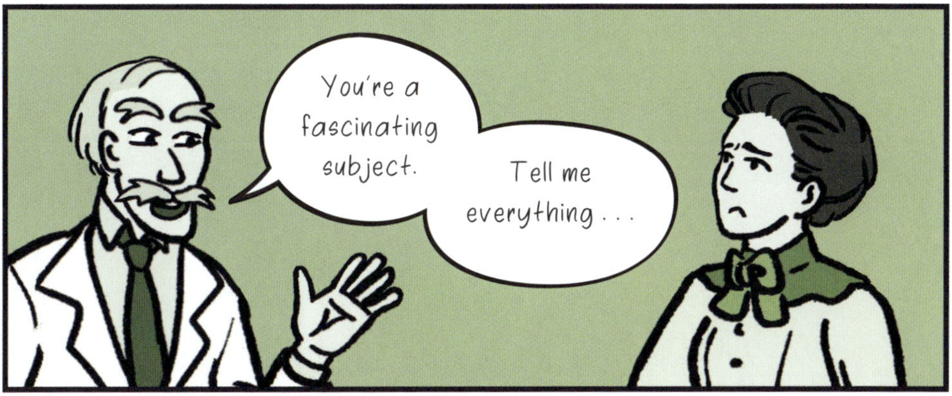
You're a fascinating subject.
Tell me everything . . .

Although he believed sexuality outside of reproductive sex was "perverse," Krafft-Ebing opposed Paragraph 175 because he thought it was unjust.

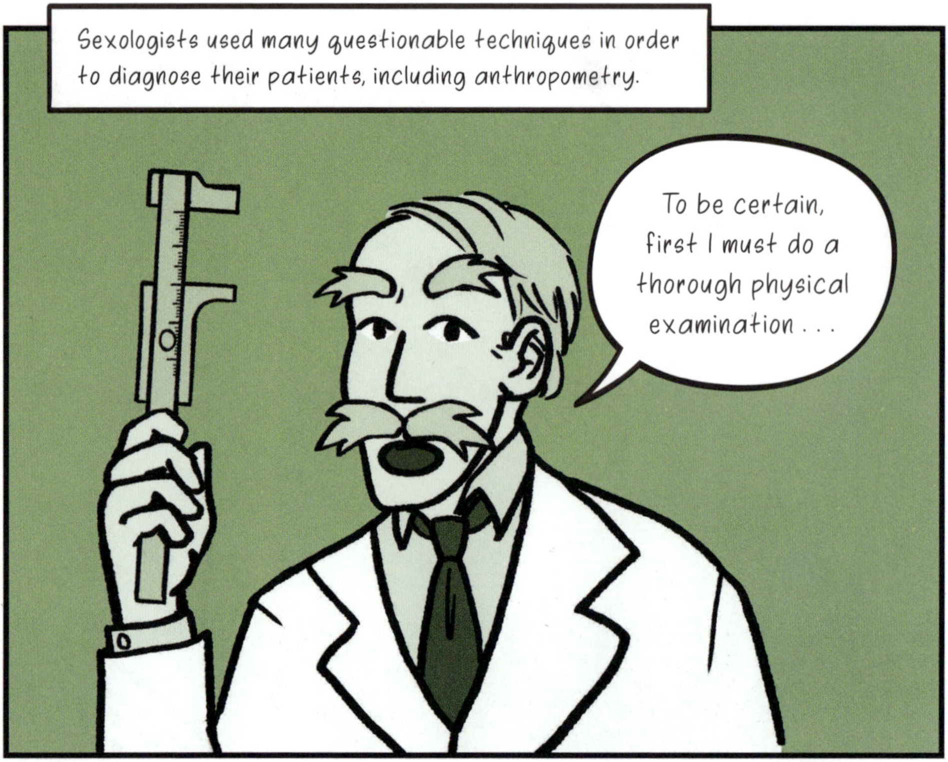
Sexologists used many questionable techniques in order to diagnose their patients, including anthropometry.
To be certain, first I must do a thorough physical examination . . .

Anthropometry is a pseudoscience that measures parts of people's bodies in an attempt to sort them into meaningful categories.

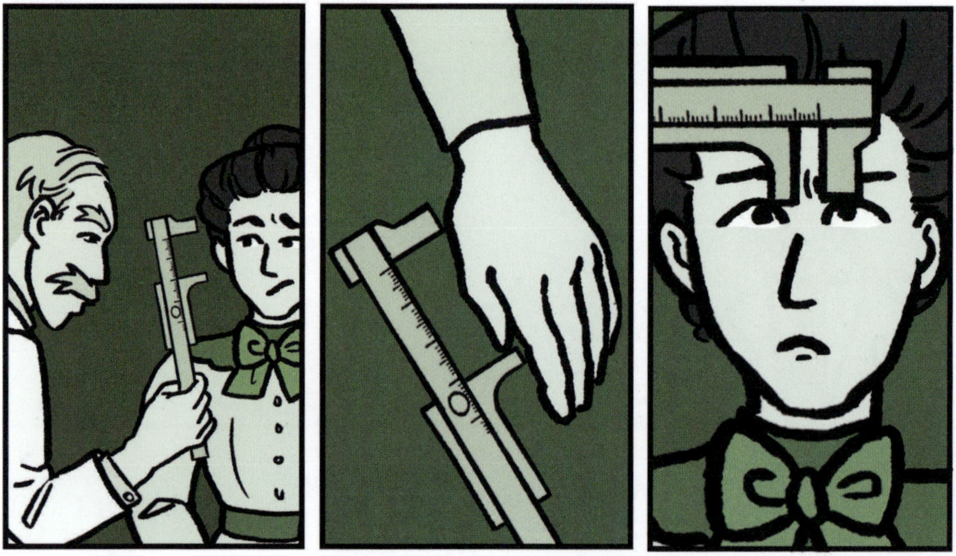

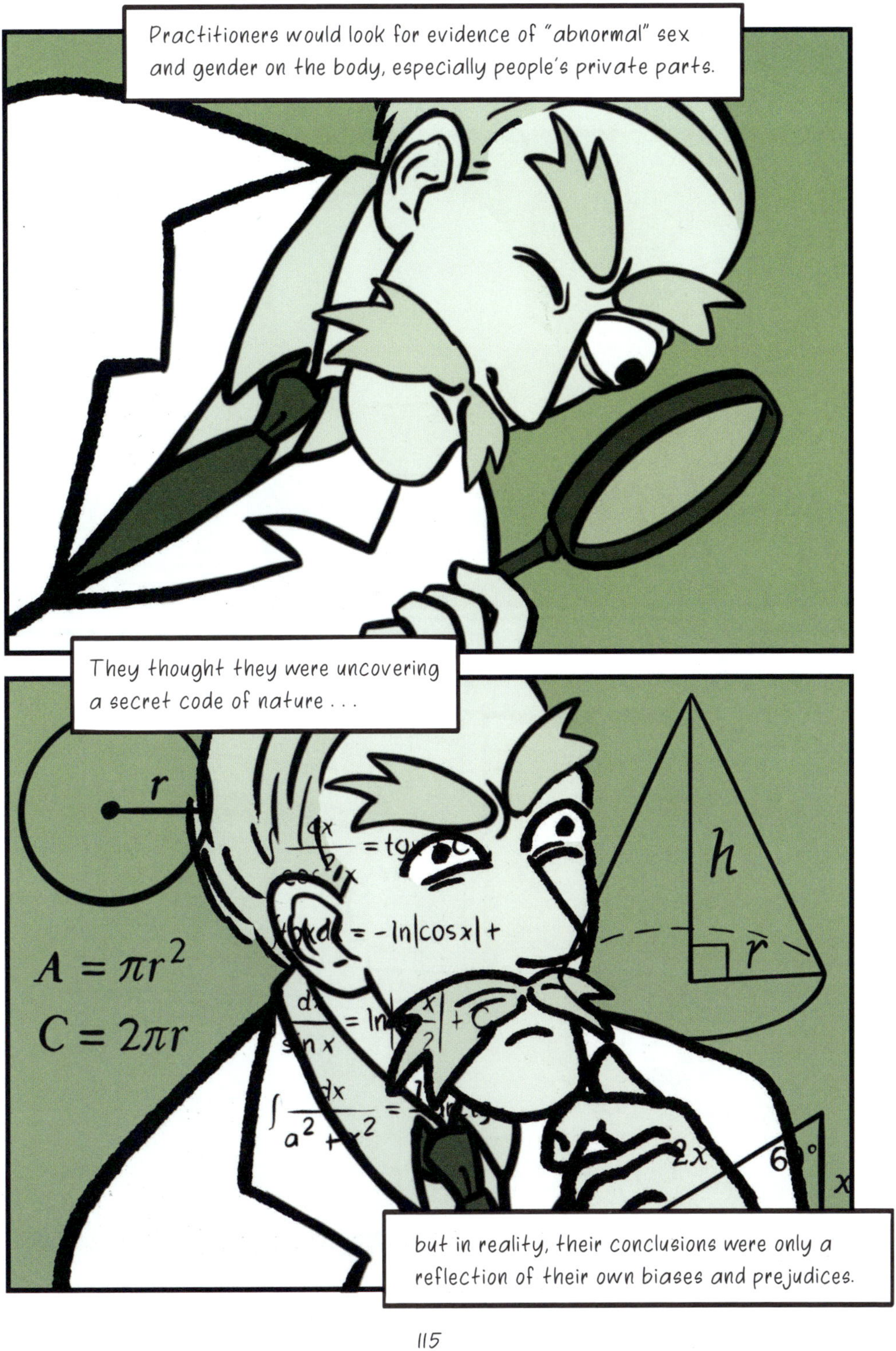
Practitioners would look for evidence of "abnormal" sex and gender on the body, especially people's private parts.
They thought they were uncovering a secret code of nature . . .
r
A = πr²
C = 2πr
h
r
but in reality, their conclusions were only a reflection of their own biases and prejudices.

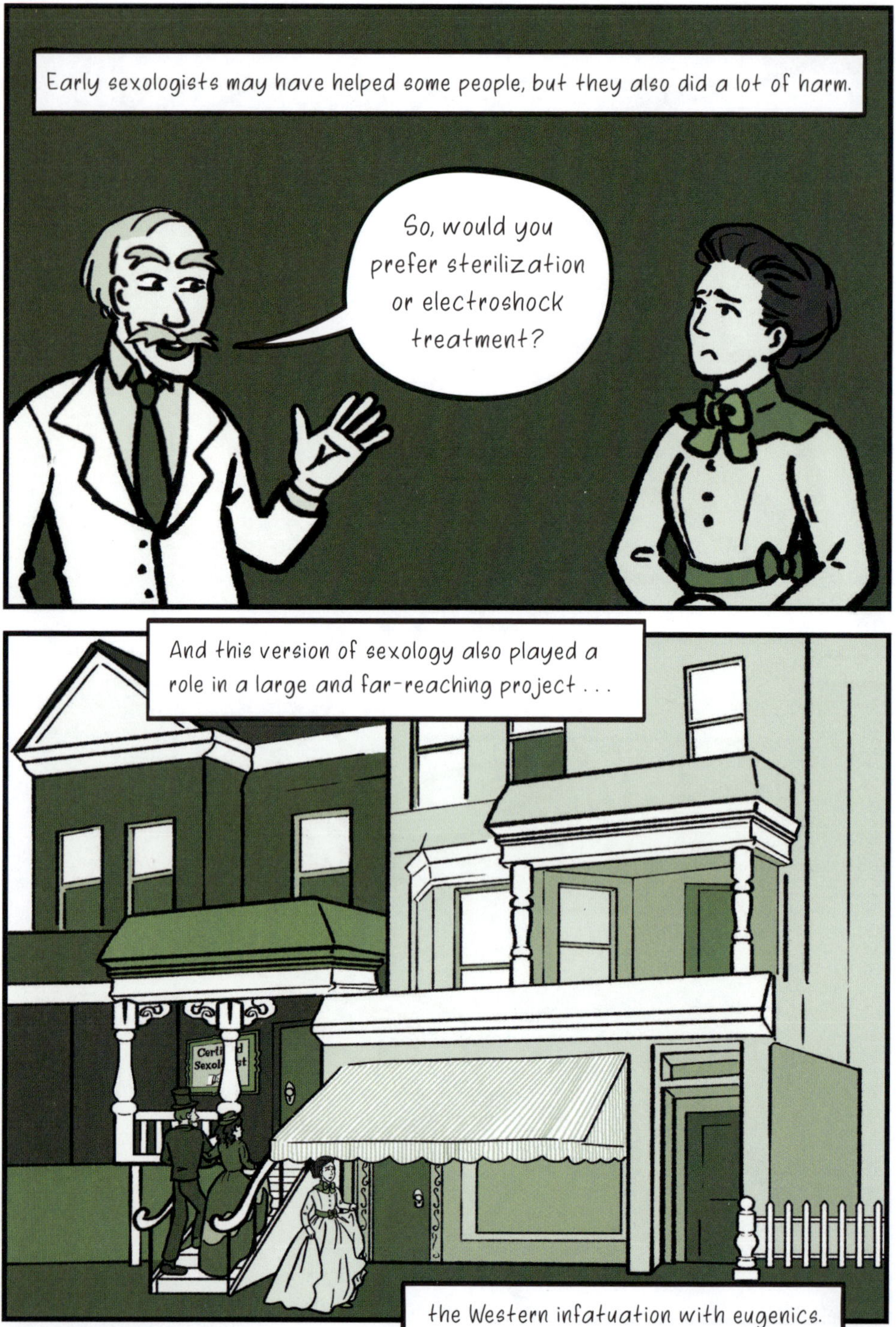
Early sexologists may have helped some people, but they also did a lot of harm.
So, would you prefer sterilization or electroshock treatment?
And this version of sexology also played a role in a large and far-reaching project . . .
the Western infatuation with eugenics.

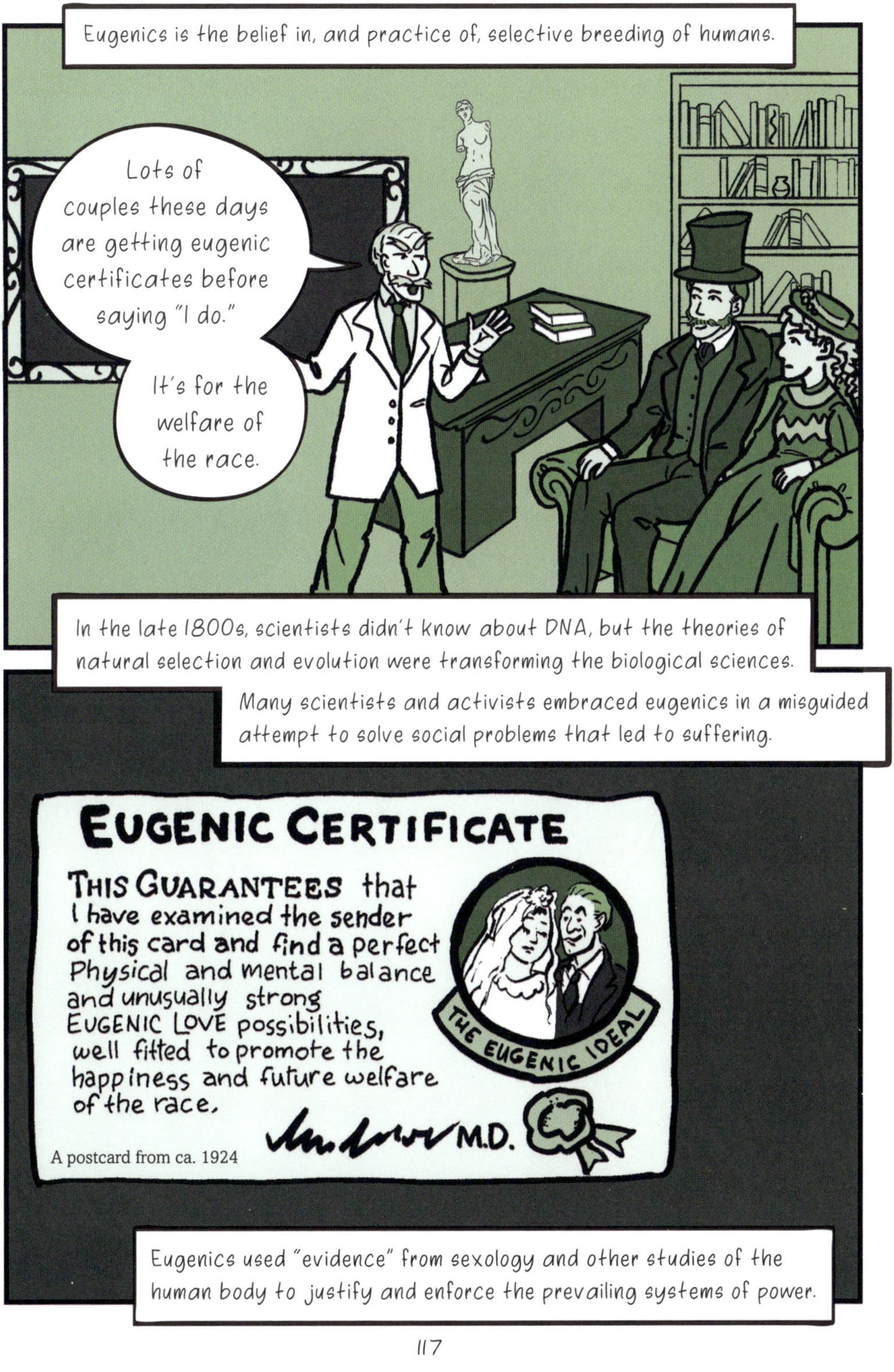
Eugenics is the belief in, and practice of, selective breeding of humans.
Lots of couples these days are getting eugenic certificates before saying "I do."
It's for the welfare of the race.
In the late 1800s, scientists didn't know about DNA, but the theories of natural selection and evolution were transforming the biological sciences.
Many scientists and activists embraced eugenics in a misguided attempt to solve social problems that led to suffering.
EUGENIC CERTIFICATE
THIS GUARANTEES that I have examined the sender of this card and find a perfect Physical and mental balance and unusually strong EUGENIC LOVE possibilities, well fitted to promote the happiness and future welfare of the race.
M.D.
THE EUGENIC IDEAL
Eugenics used "evidence" from sexology and other studies of the human body to justify and enforce the prevailing systems of power.

A postcard from ca. 1924

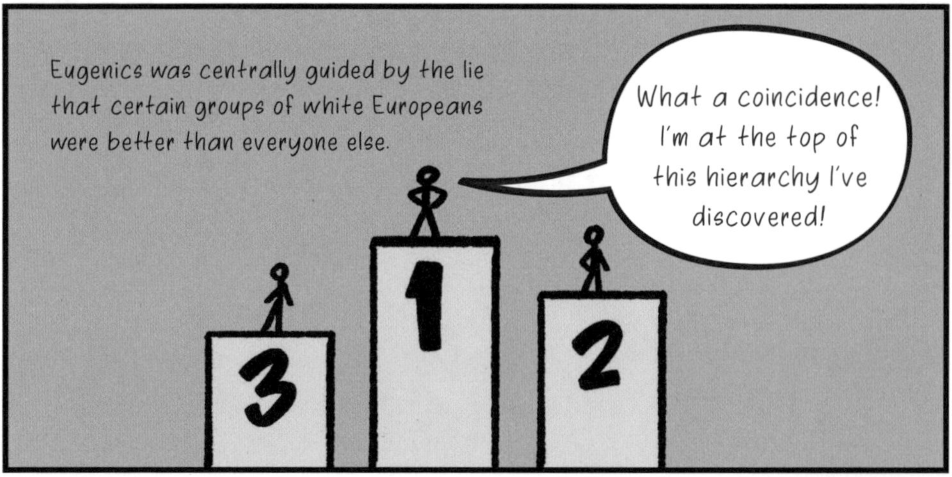

Eugenics was centrally guided by the lie that certain groups of white Europeans were better than everyone else.
What a coincidence! I'm at the top of this hierarchy I've discovered!
1
2
3

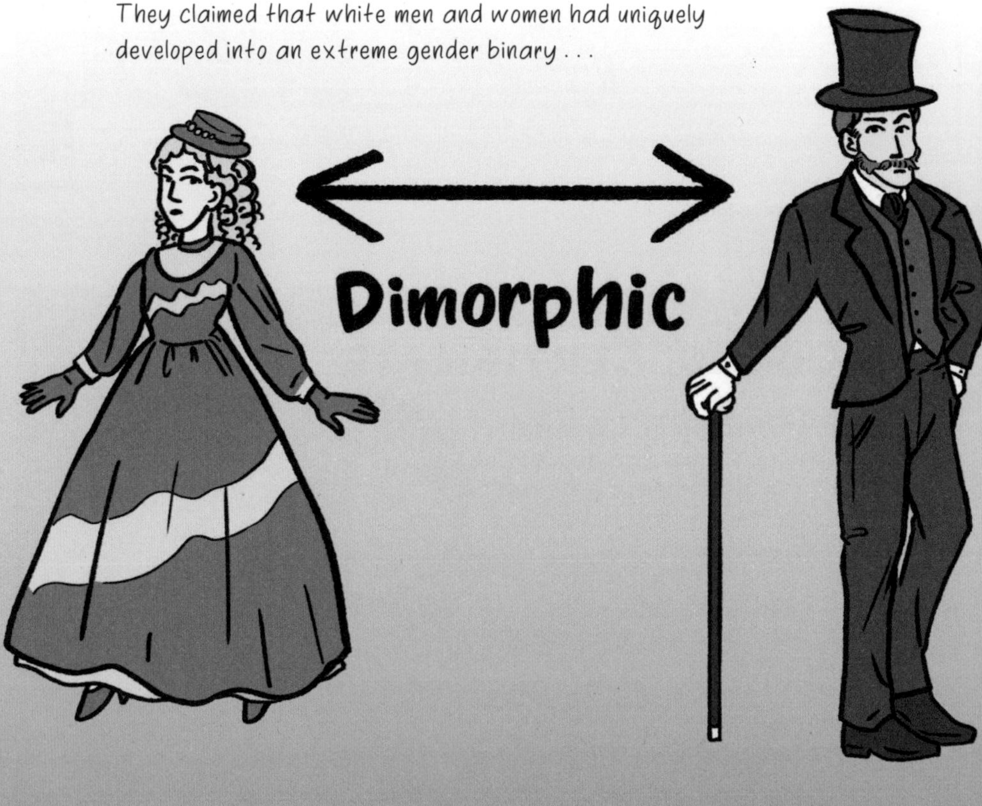

They claimed that white men and women had uniquely developed into an extreme gender binary . . .
Dimorphic

the idea being that "highly evolved" men and women are supposed to be physically and socially specialized and very different from each other.

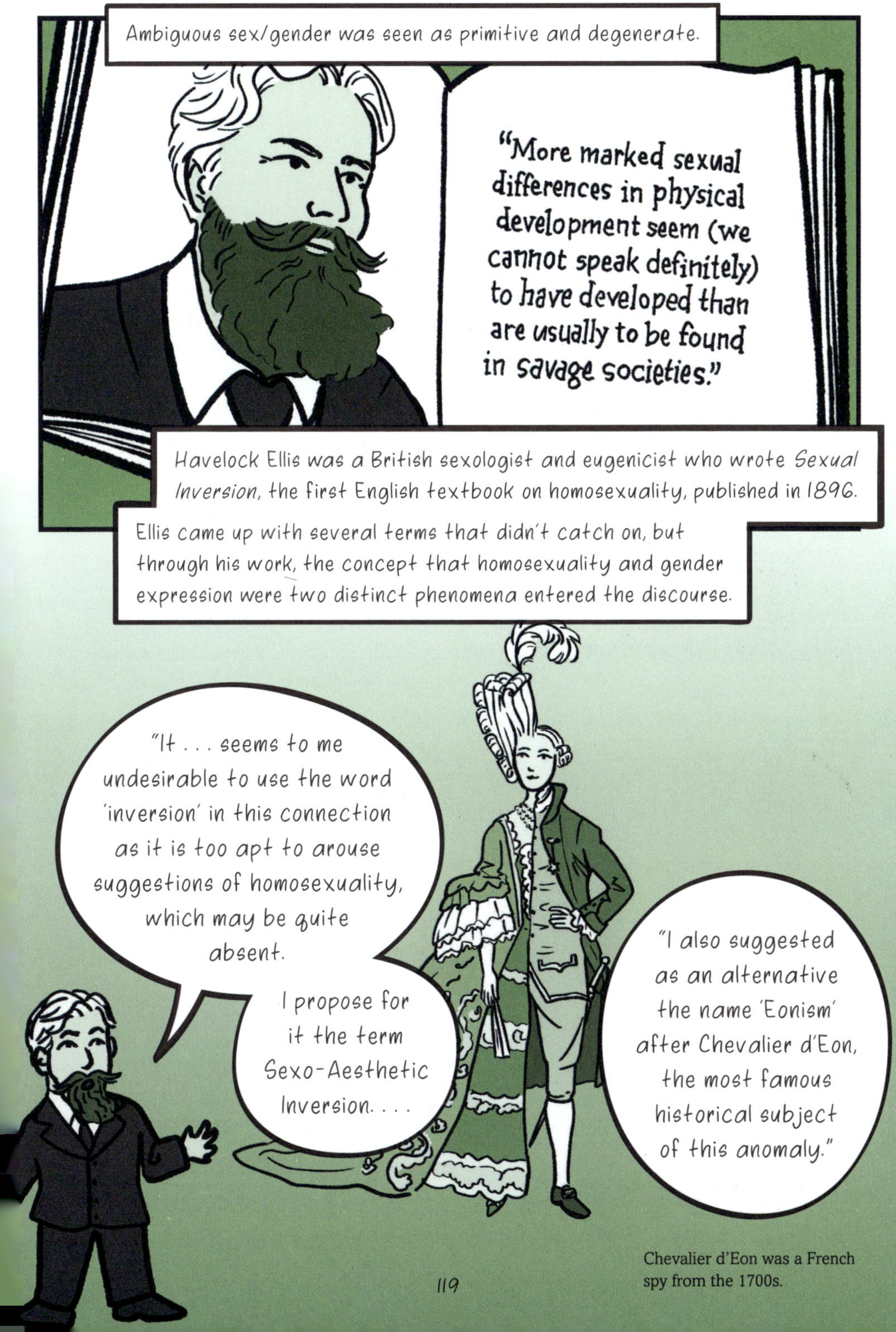

Ambiguous sex/gender was seen as primitive and degenerate.
"More marked sexual differences in physical development seem (we cannot speak definitely) to have developed than are usually to be found in savage societies."
Havelock Ellis was a British sexologist and eugenicist who wrote *Sexual Inversion*, the first English textbook on homosexuality, published in 1896.
Ellis came up with several terms that didn't catch on, but through his work, the concept that homosexuality and gender expression were two distinct phenomena entered the discourse.
"It . . . seems to me undesirable to use the word 'inversion' in this connection as it is too apt to arouse suggestions of homosexuality, which may be quite absent.
I propose for it the term Sexo-Aesthetic Inversion. . . .
"I also suggested as an alternative the name 'Eonism' after Chevalier d'Eon, the most famous historical subject of this anomaly."

Chevalier d'Eon was a French spy from the 1700s.

One particular sexologist of this period has been closely associated with trans history:

Magnus Hirschfeld

Images of Hirschfeld and the Institute for Sexual Science are based on photos courtesy of the Magnus Hirschfeld Society

In the early twentieth century, Hirschfeld coined the word *transvestite*, as well as *transsexualismus*, a term that referred to internal experiences.

transvestite
"One disadvantage of the term is that it describes only the external side, while the internal is limitless."

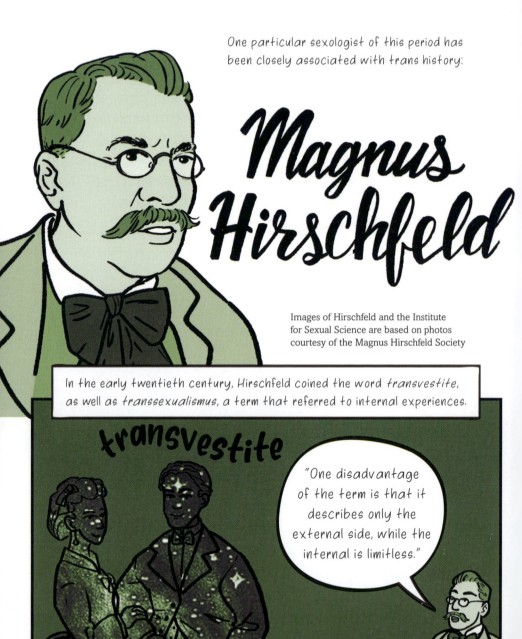

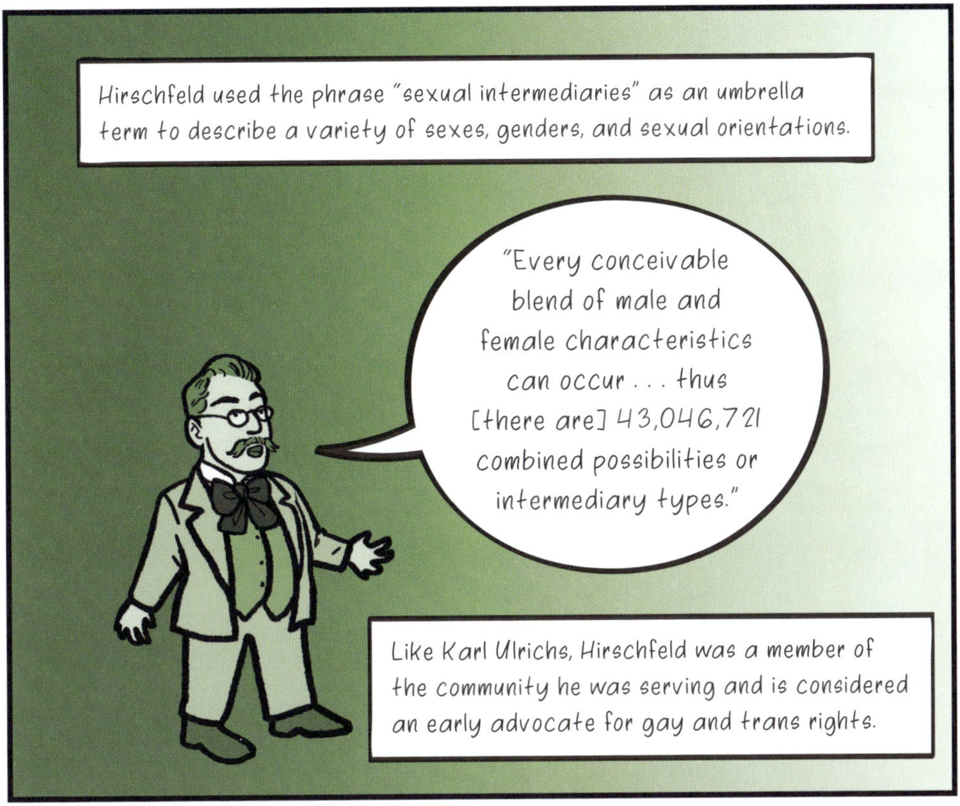
Hirschfeld used the phrase "sexual intermediaries" as an umbrella term to describe a variety of sexes, genders, and sexual orientations.
"Every conceivable blend of male and female characteristics can occur . . . thus [there are] 43,046,721 combined possibilities or intermediary types."
Like Karl Ulrichs, Hirschfeld was a member of the community he was serving and is considered an early advocate for gay and trans rights.

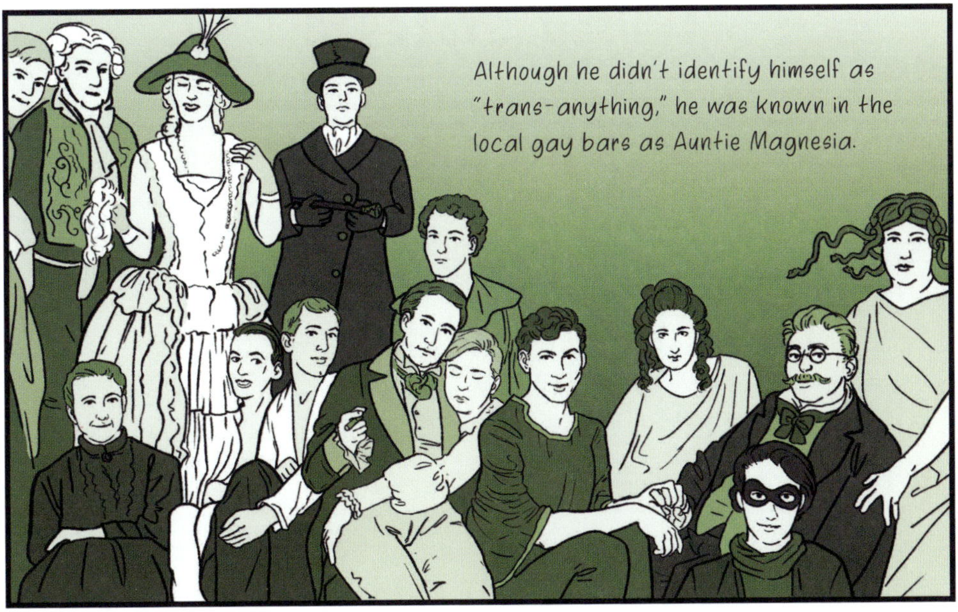
Although he didn't identify himself as "trans-anything," he was known in the local gay bars as Auntie Magnesia.

Based on a photo of a holiday party at Hirschfeld's Institute for Sexual Science

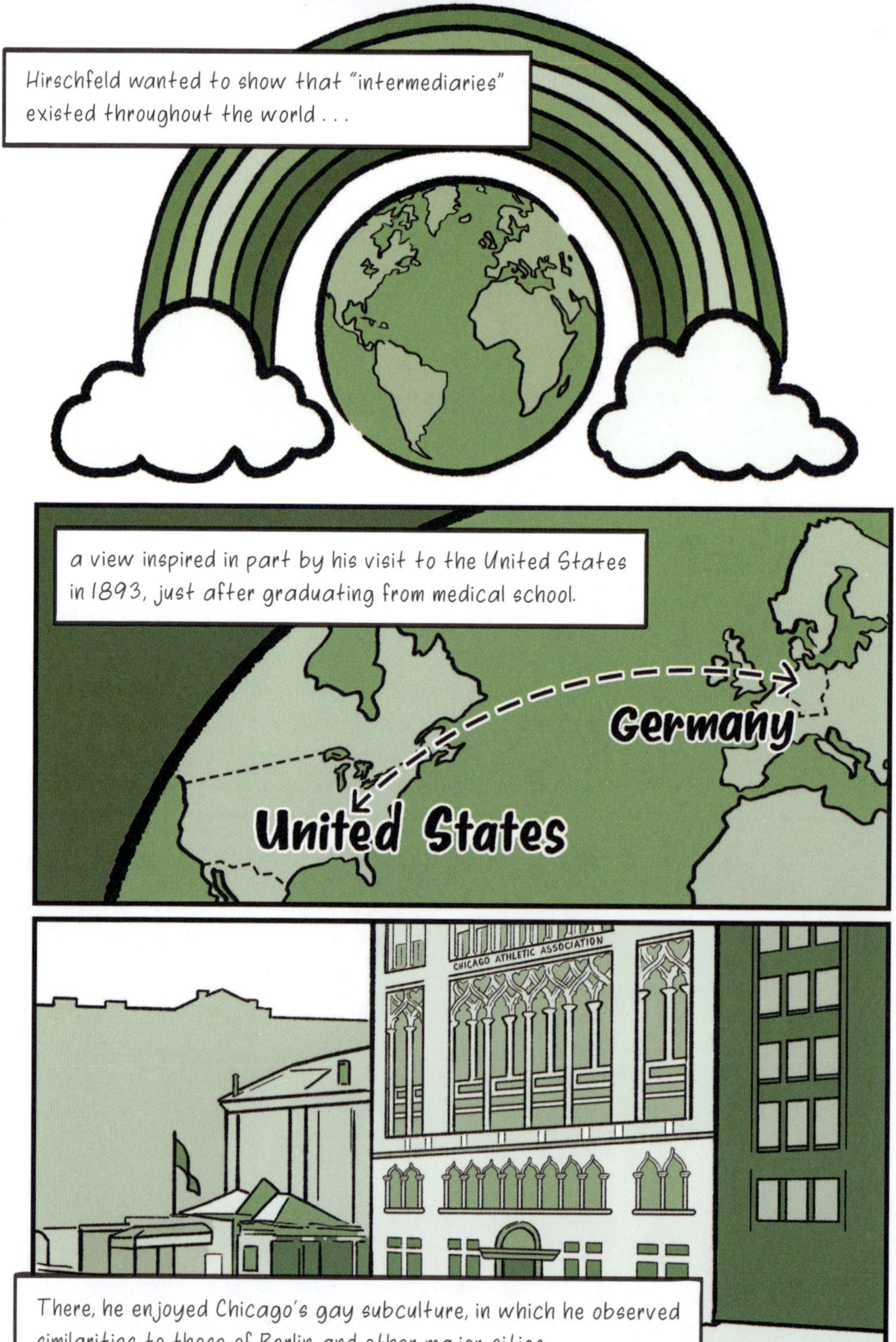
Hirschfeld wanted to show that "intermediaries" existed throughout the world . . .
a view inspired in part by his visit to the United States in 1893, just after graduating from medical school.
Germany
United States
CHICAGO ATHLETIC ASSOCIATION
There, he enjoyed Chicago's gay subculture, in which he observed similarities to those of Berlin and other major cities.

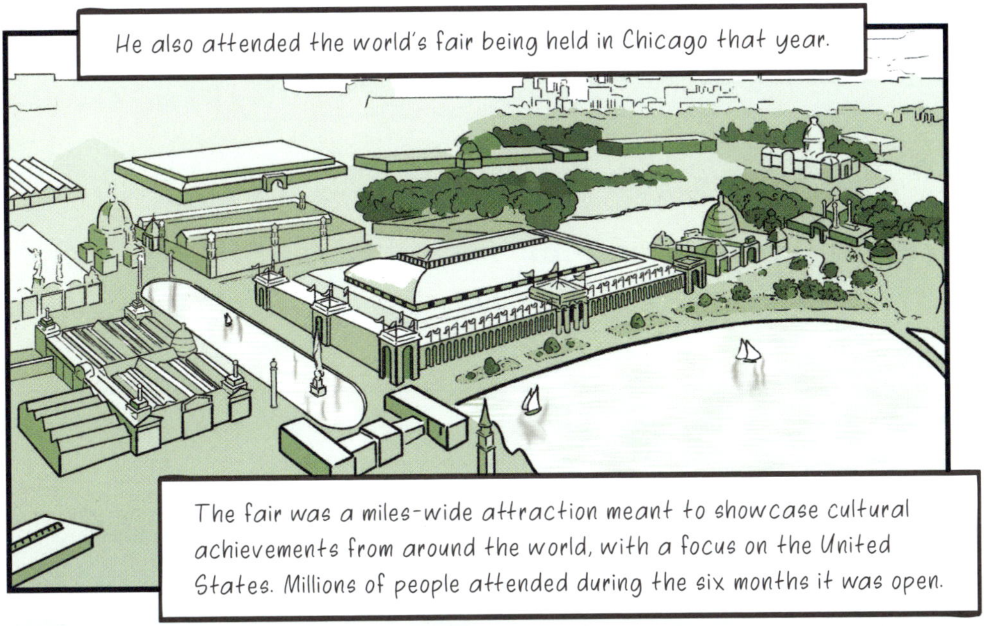
He also attended the world's fair being held in Chicago that year.
The fair was a miles-wide attraction meant to showcase cultural achievements from around the world, with a focus on the United States. Millions of people attended during the six months it was open.

It was a massive display of colonial power . . .

**This year's theme:
celebrating Christopher Columbus's
arrival in the Americas!**

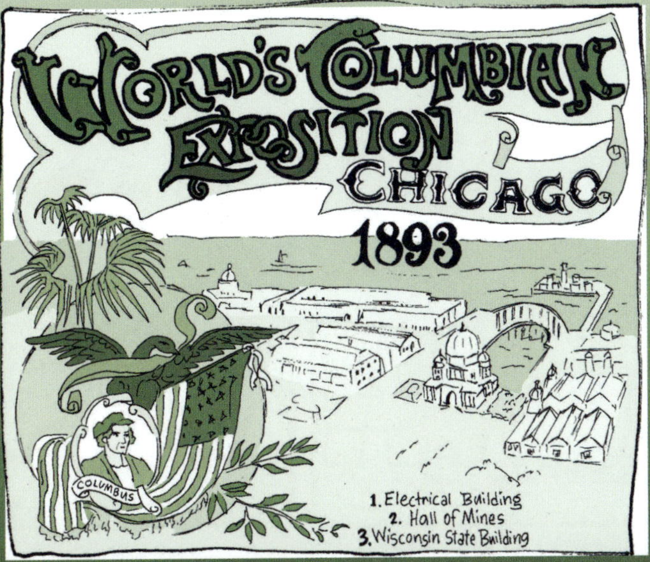
WORLD'S COLUMBIAN EXPOSITION
CHICAGO
1893
COLUMBUS
1. Electrical Building
2. Hall of Mines
3. Wisconsin State Building

Based on an ad for the fair

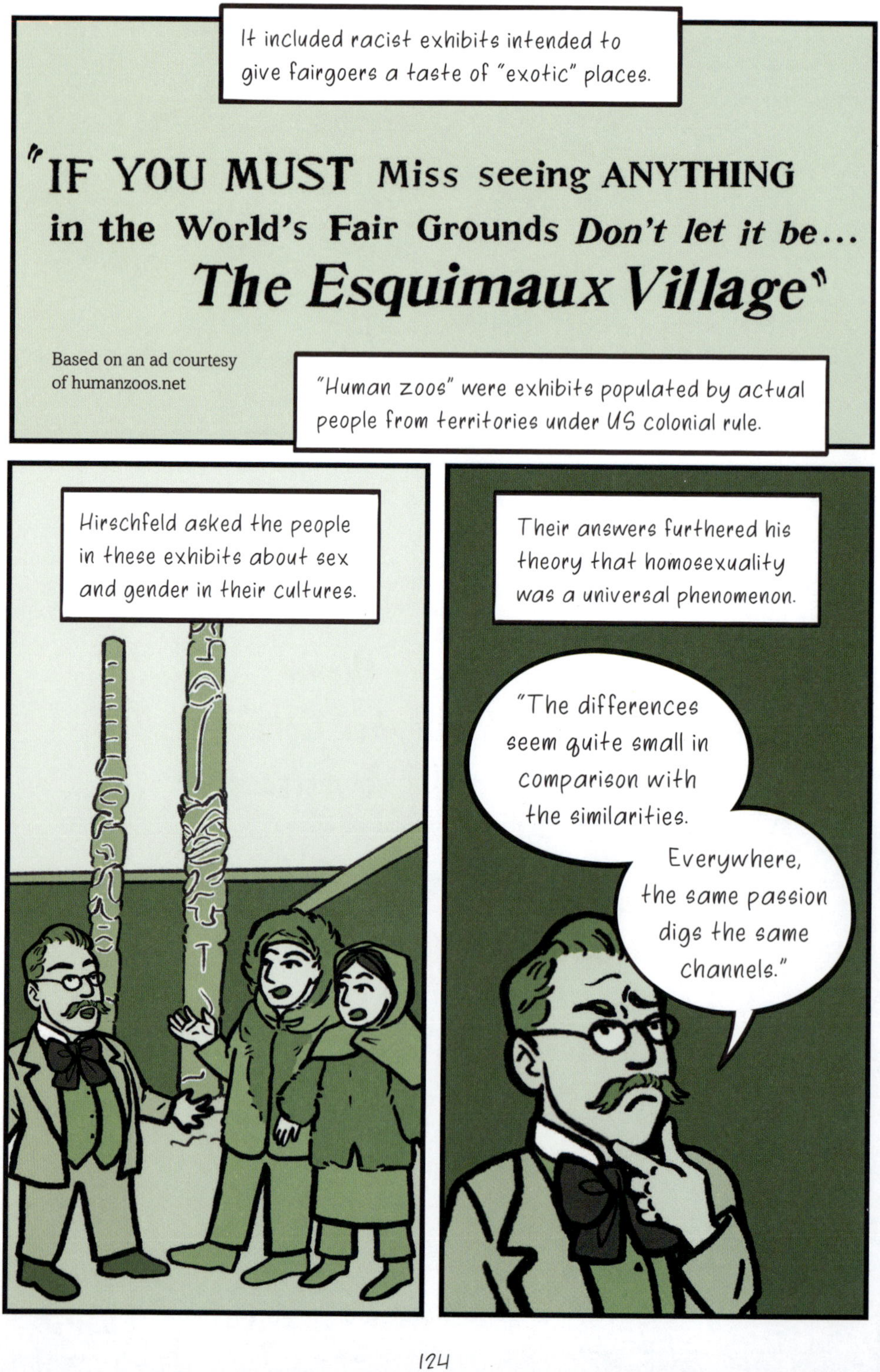
It included racist exhibits intended to give fairgoers a taste of "exotic" places.
"IF YOU MUST Miss seeing ANYTHING in the World's Fair Grounds Don't let it be... The Esquimaux Village"
Based on an ad courtesy of humanzoos.net
"Human zoos" were exhibits populated by actual people from territories under US colonial rule.
Hirschfeld asked the people in these exhibits about sex and gender in their cultures.
Their answers furthered his theory that homosexuality was a universal phenomenon.
"The differences seem quite small in comparison with the similarities.
Everywhere, the same passion digs the same channels."

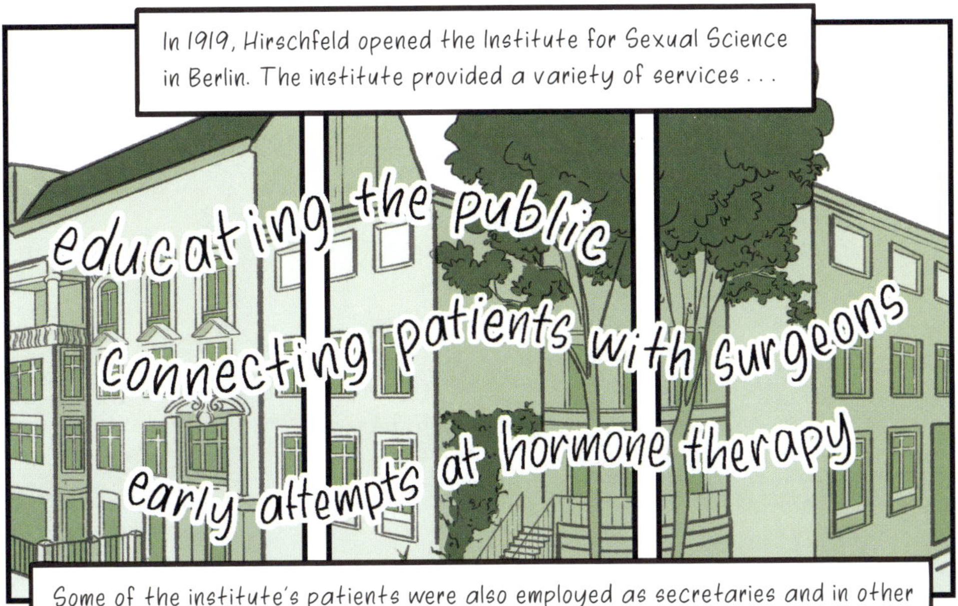
In 1919, Hirschfeld opened the Institute for Sexual Science in Berlin. The institute provided a variety of services . . .
educating the public
connecting patients with surgeons
early attempts at hormone therapy

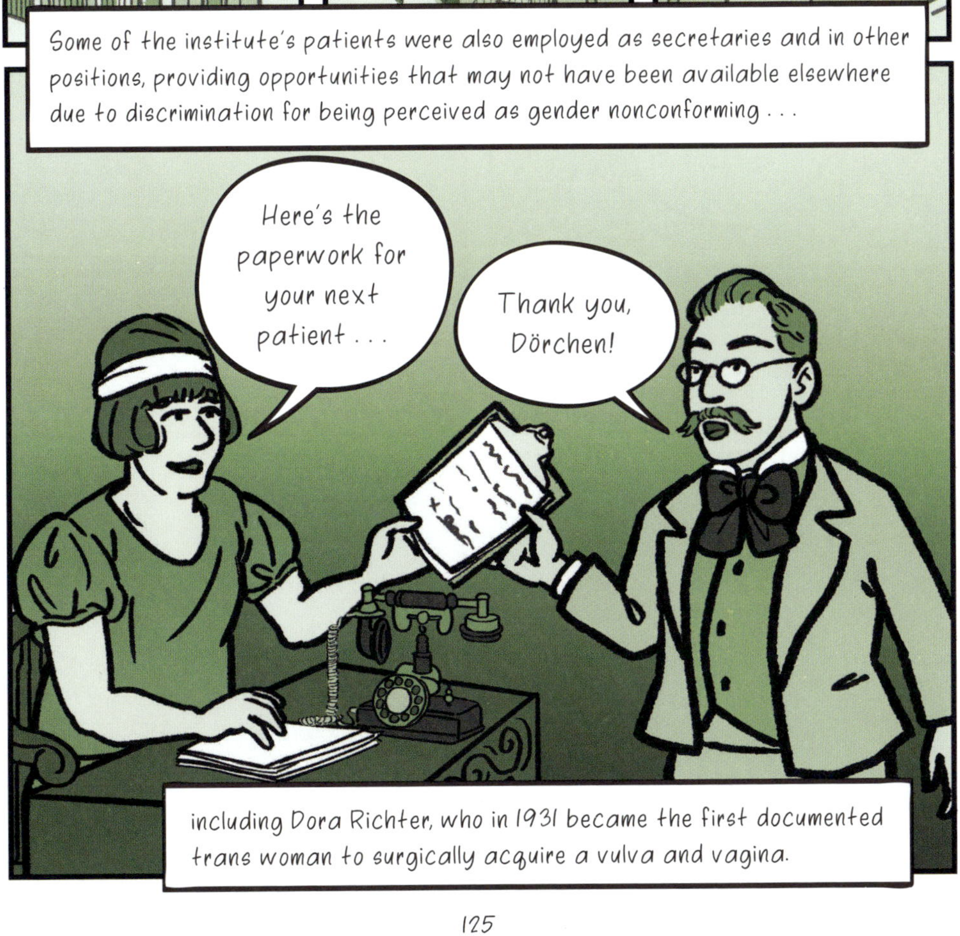
Some of the institute's patients were also employed as secretaries and in other positions, providing opportunities that may not have been available elsewhere due to discrimination for being perceived as gender nonconforming . . .
Here's the paperwork for your next patient . . .
Thank you, Dörchen!
including Dora Richter, who in 1931 became the first documented trans woman to surgically acquire a vulva and vagina.

At the time, there was a thriving gay scene in Berlin, and Hirschfeld advocated for his local community through his work.

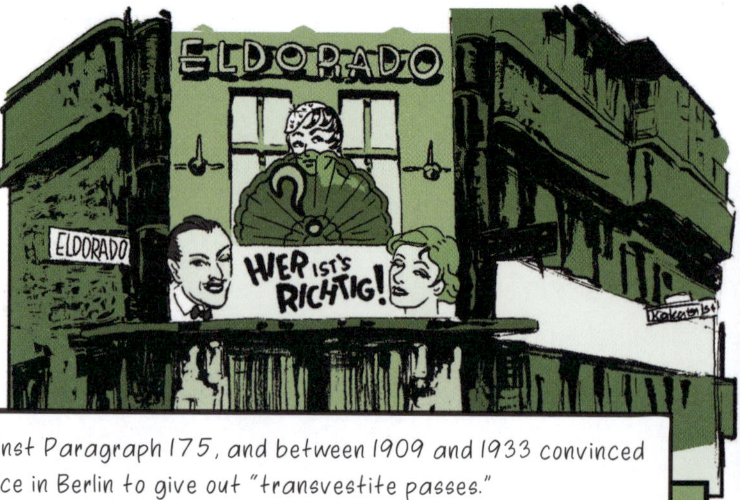
ELDORADO
ELDORADO
HIER ist's RICHTIG!

Berlin's famous "transvestite club," Eldorado, courtesy of the German Federal Archives

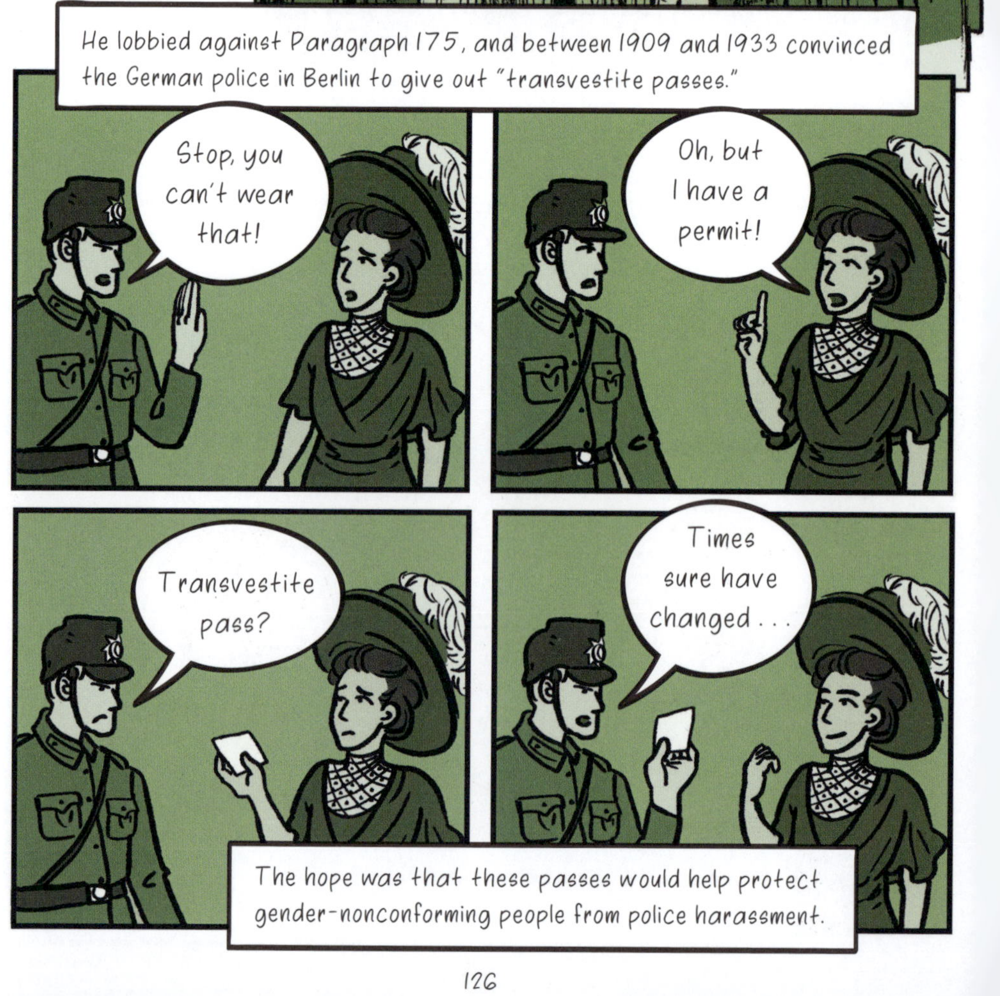
He lobbied against Paragraph 175, and between 1909 and 1933 convinced the German police in Berlin to give out "transvestite passes."
Stop, you can't wear that!
Oh, but I have a permit!
Transvestite pass?
Times sure have changed . . .
The hope was that these passes would help protect gender-nonconforming people from police harassment.

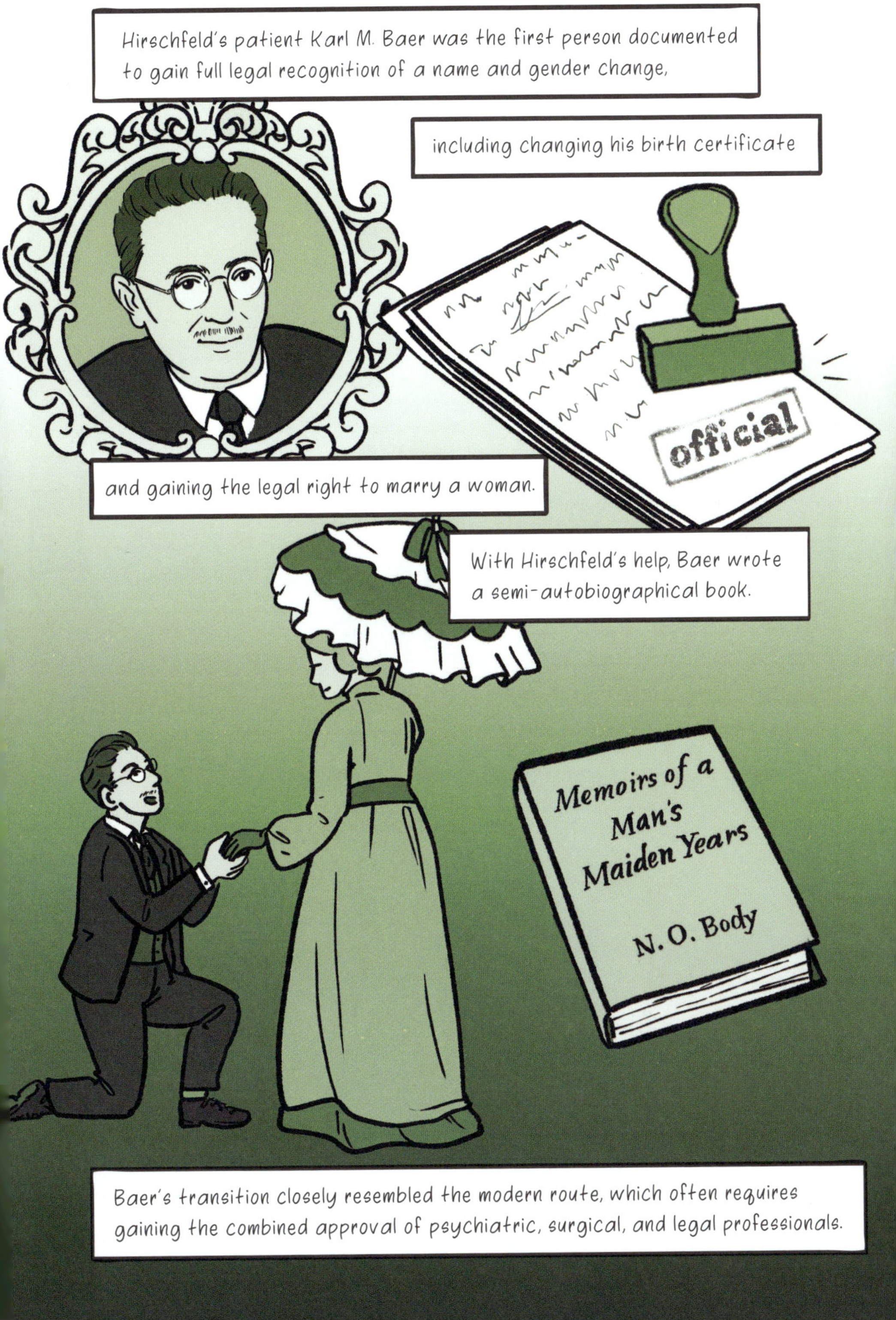
Hirschfeld's patient Karl M. Baer was the first person documented to gain full legal recognition of a name and gender change,
including changing his birth certificate
official
and gaining the legal right to marry a woman.
With Hirschfeld's help, Baer wrote a semi-autobiographical book.
Memoirs of a Man's Maiden Years
N. O. Body
Baer's transition closely resembled the modern route, which often requires gaining the combined approval of psychiatric, surgical, and legal professionals.

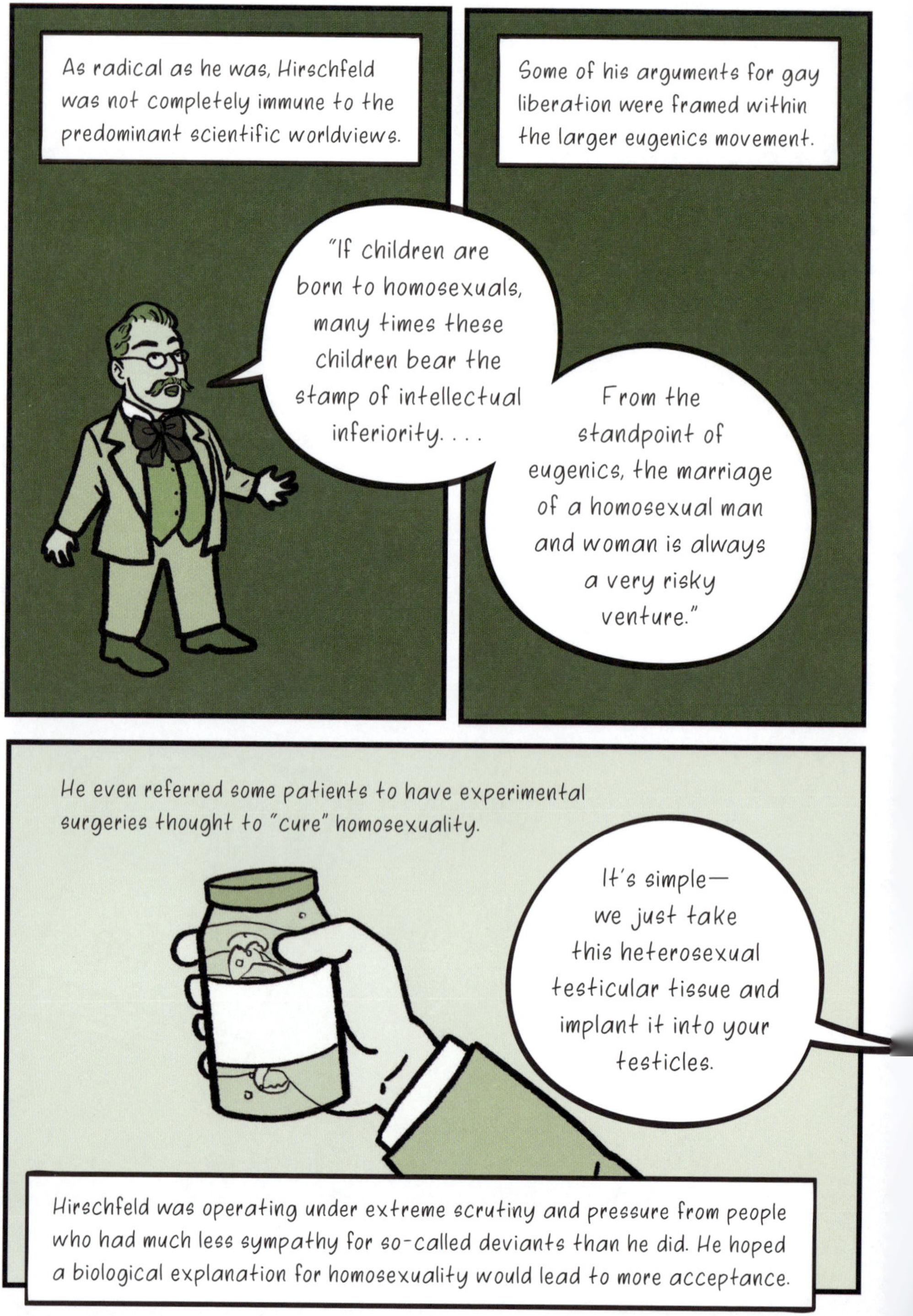

As radical as he was, Hirschfeld was not completely immune to the predominant scientific worldviews.
Some of his arguments for gay liberation were framed within the larger eugenics movement.
"If children are born to homosexuals, many times these children bear the stamp of intellectual inferiority. . . .
From the standpoint of eugenics, the marriage of a homosexual man and woman is always a very risky venture."
He even referred some patients to have experimental surgeries thought to "cure" homosexuality.
It's simple— we just take this heterosexual testicular tissue and implant it into your testicles.
Hirschfeld was operating under extreme scrutiny and pressure from people who had much less sympathy for so-called deviants than he did. He hoped a biological explanation for homosexuality would lead to more acceptance.

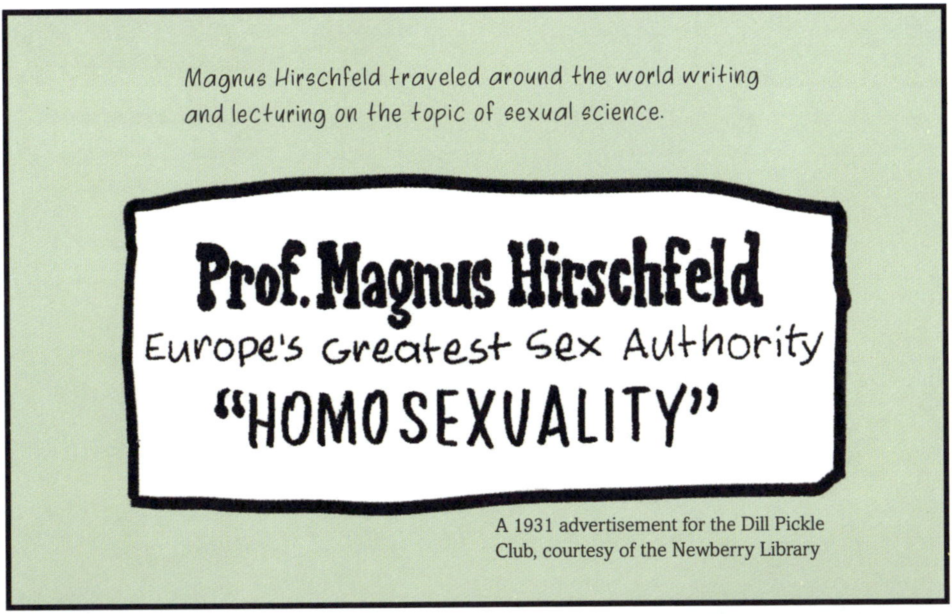
Magnus Hirschfeld traveled around the world writing and lecturing on the topic of sexual science.
Prof. Magnus Hirschfeld
Europe's Greatest Sex Authority
"HOMOSEXUALITY"

A 1931 advertisement for the Dill Pickle Club, courtesy of the Newberry Library

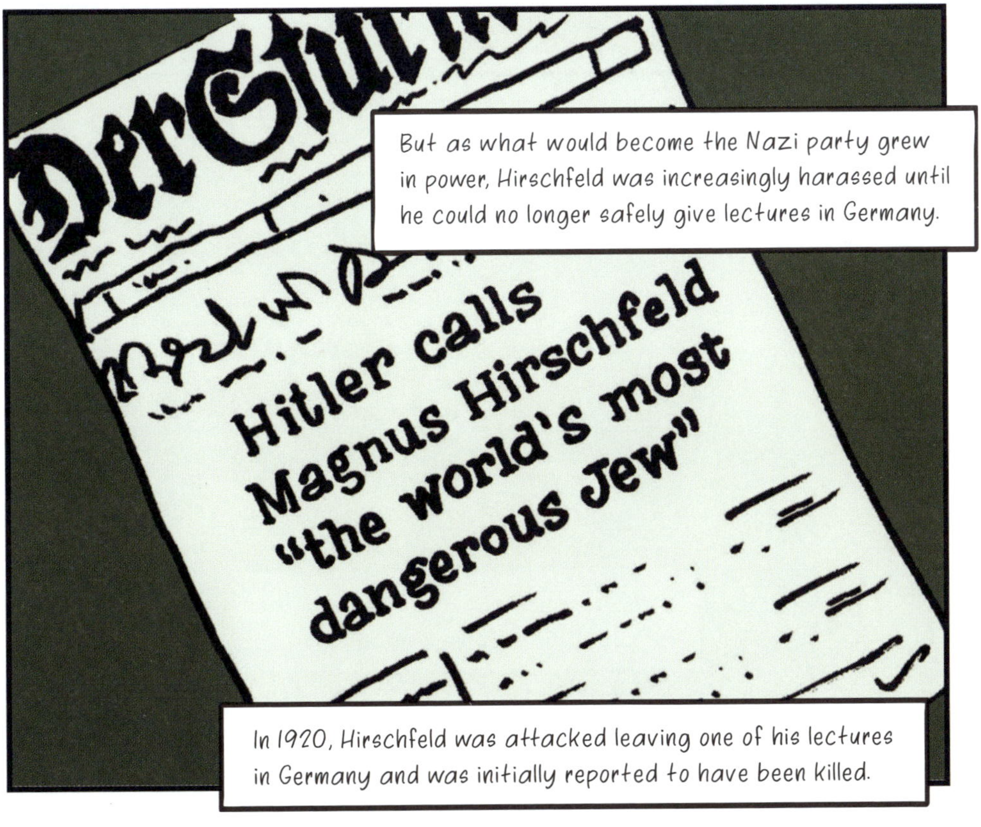
But as what would become the Nazi party grew in power, Hirschfeld was increasingly harassed until he could no longer safely give lectures in Germany.
Hitler calls Magnus Hirschfeld "the world's most dangerous Jew"
In 1920, Hirschfeld was attacked leaving one of his lectures in Germany and was initially reported to have been killed.

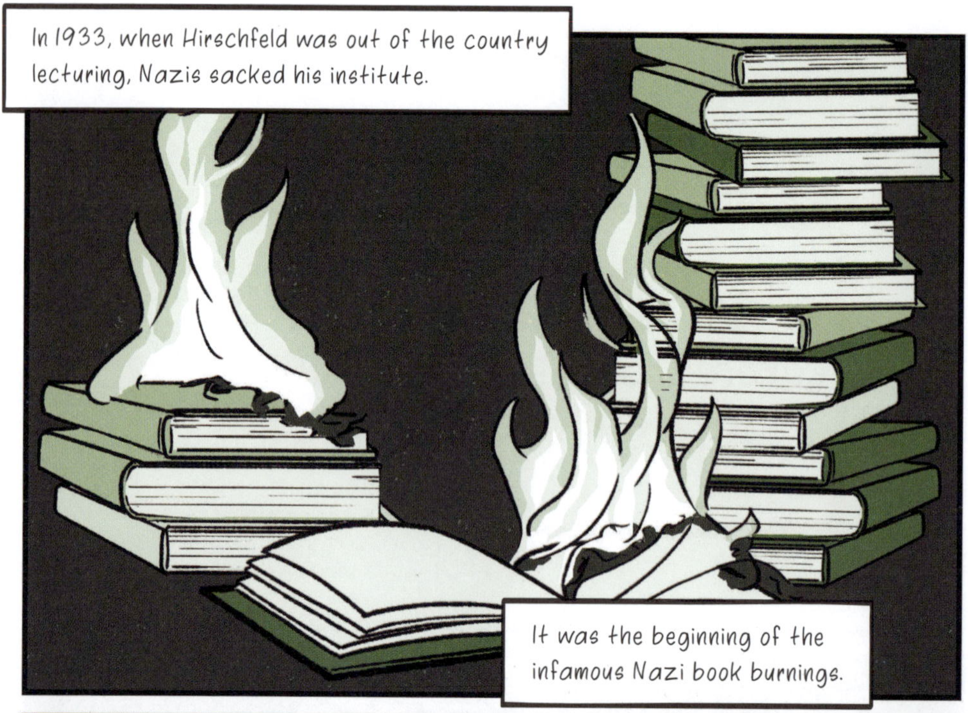
In 1933, when Hirschfeld was out of the country lecturing, Nazis sacked his institute.
It was the beginning of the infamous Nazi book burnings.

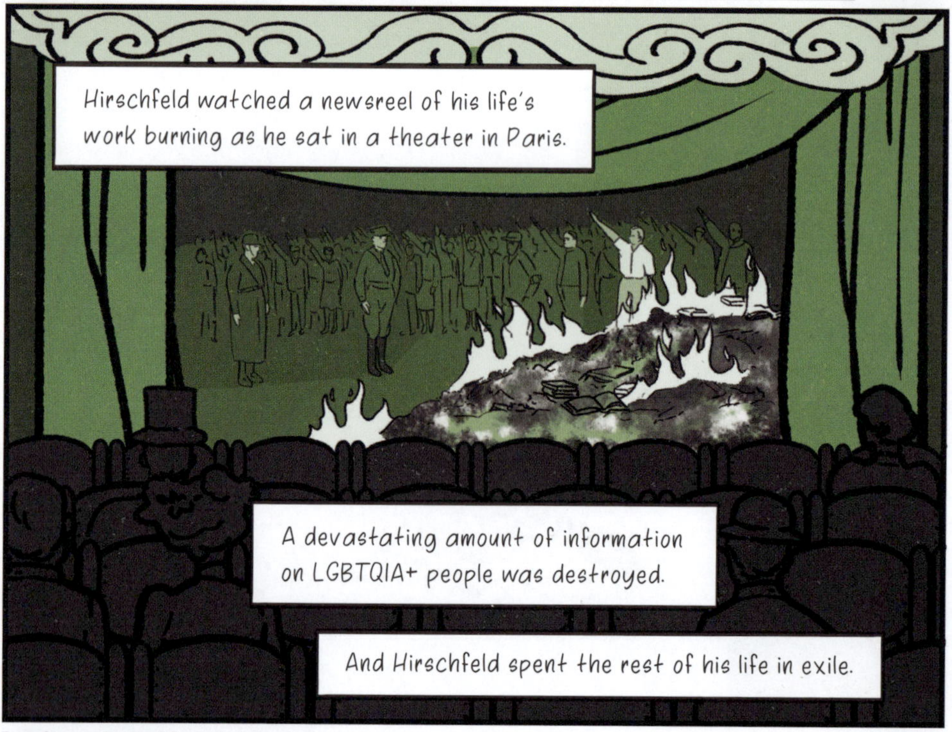
Hirschfeld watched a newsreel of his life's work burning as he sat in a theater in Paris.
A devastating amount of information on LGBTQIA+ people was destroyed.
And Hirschfeld spent the rest of his life in exile.

Based on a photo of the actual event

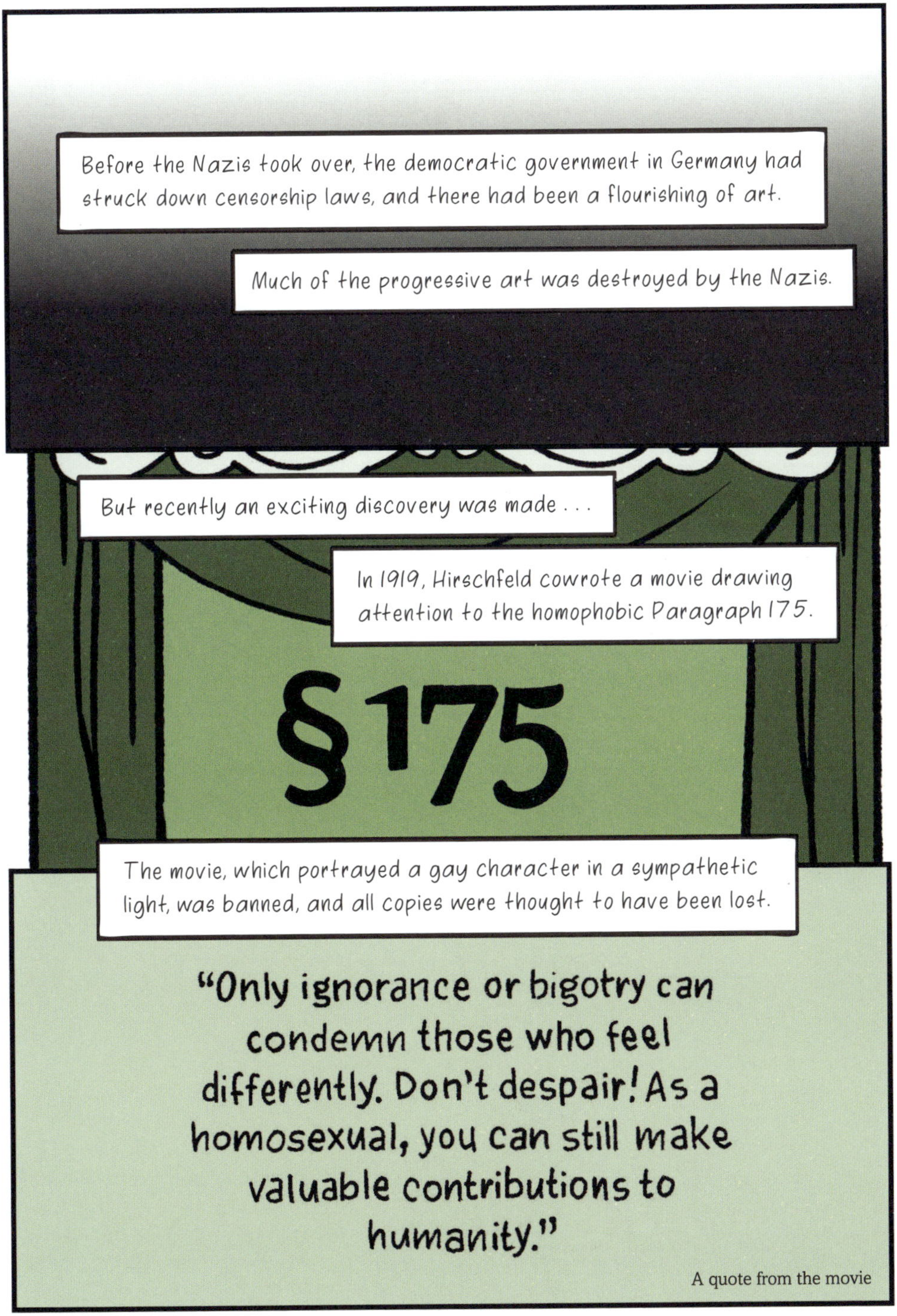
Before the Nazis took over, the democratic government in Germany had struck down censorship laws, and there had been a flourishing of art.
Much of the progressive art was destroyed by the Nazis.
But recently an exciting discovery was made . . .
In 1919, Hirschfeld cowrote a movie drawing attention to the homophobic Paragraph 175.
§175
The movie, which portrayed a gay character in a sympathetic light, was banned, and all copies were thought to have been lost.
"Only ignorance or bigotry can condemn those who feel differently. Don't despair! As a homosexual, you can still make valuable contributions to humanity."
A quote from the movie

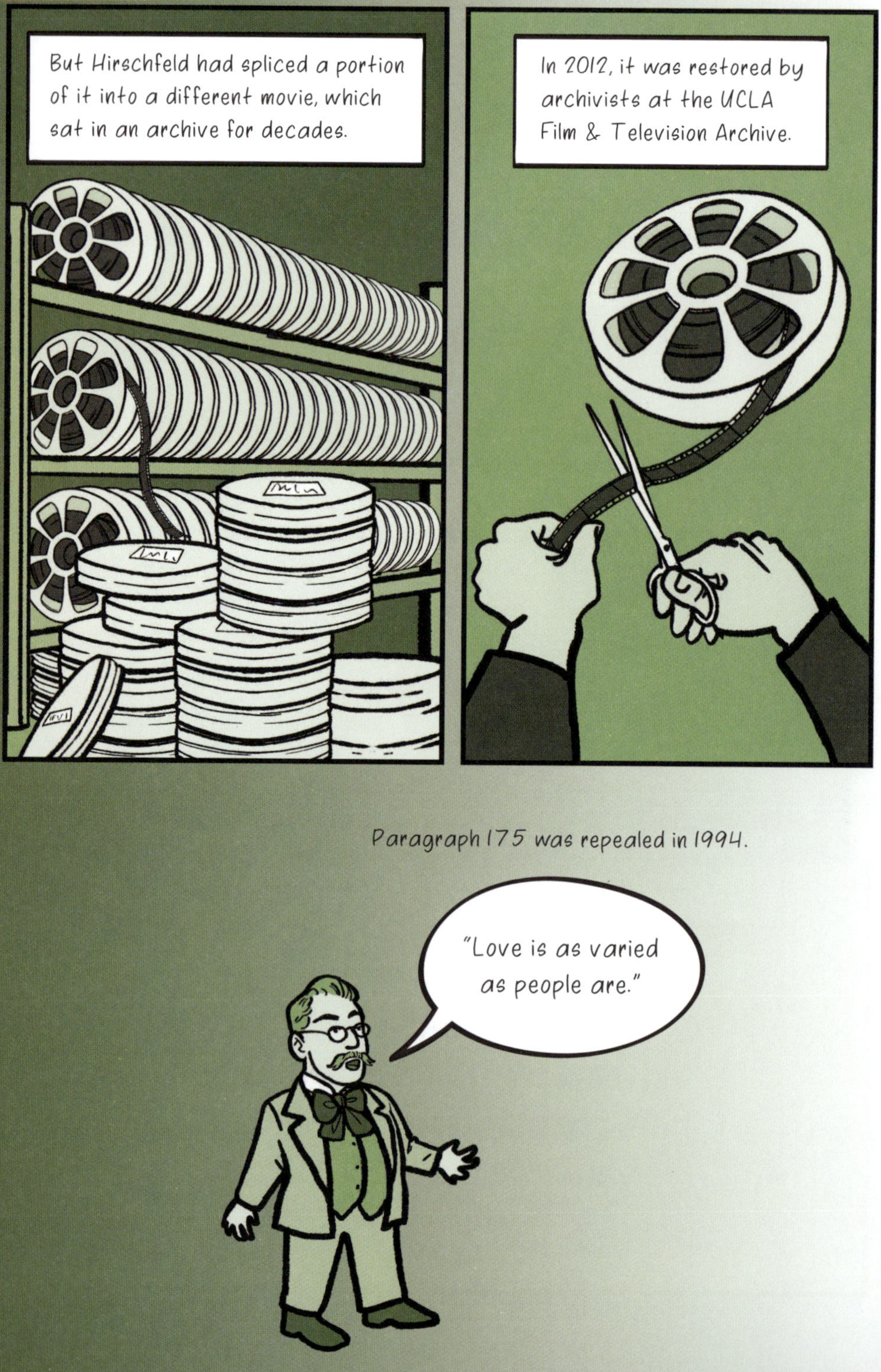

But Hirschfeld had spliced a portion of it into a different movie, which sat in an archive for decades.
In 2012, it was restored by archivists at the UCLA Film & Television Archive.
Paragraph 175 was repealed in 1994.
"Love is as varied as people are."

One of Hirschfeld's more famous patients was Lili Elbe, whose story inspired several contemporary fictionalizations.

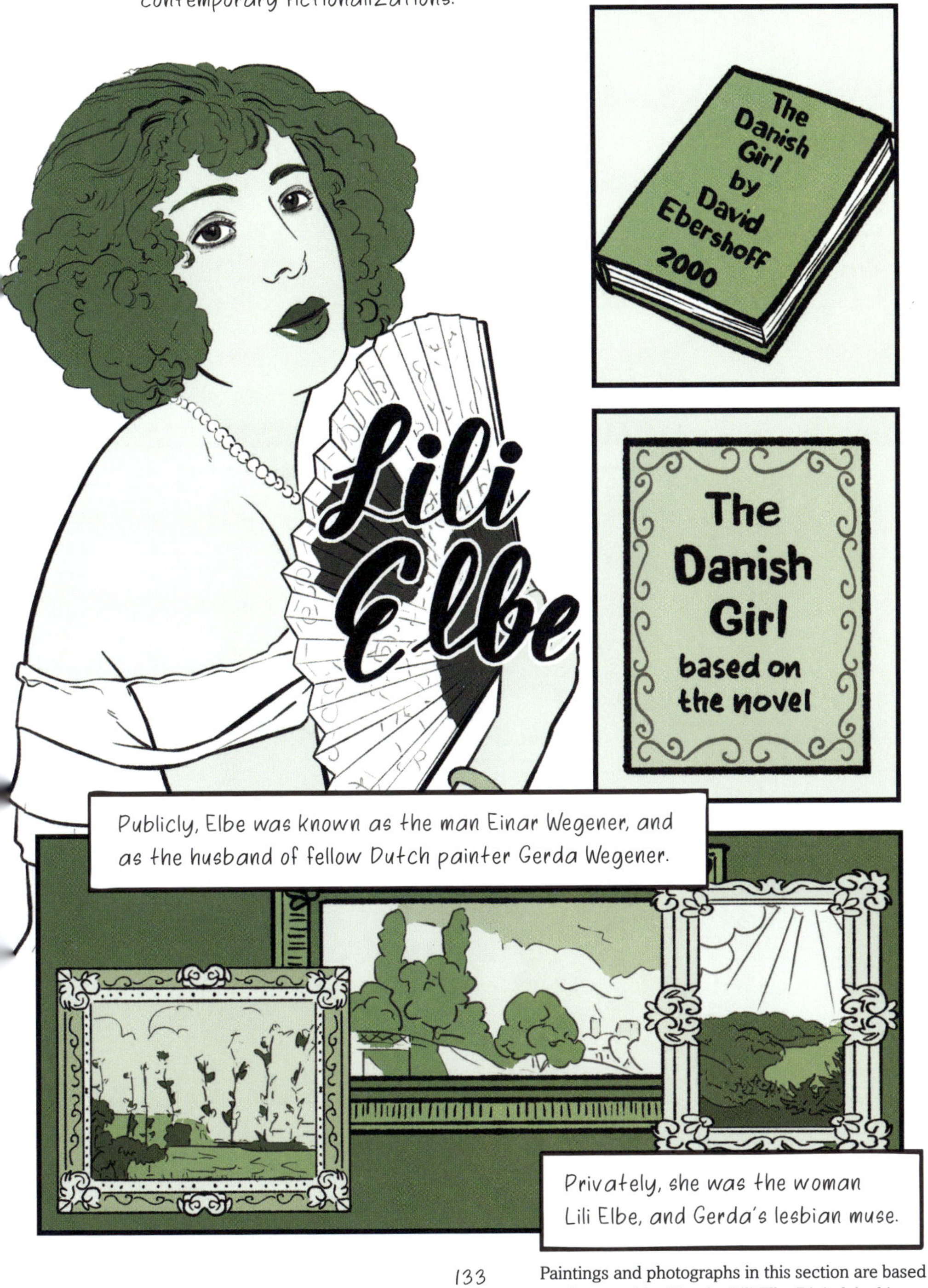
The Danish Girl by David Ebershoff 2000
Lili Elbe
The Danish Girl based on the novel
Publicly, Elbe was known as the man Einar Wegener, and as the husband of fellow Dutch painter Gerda Wegener.
Privately, she was the woman Lili Elbe, and Gerda's lesbian muse.

Paintings and photographs in this section are based on those archived by the Lili Elbe Digital Archive

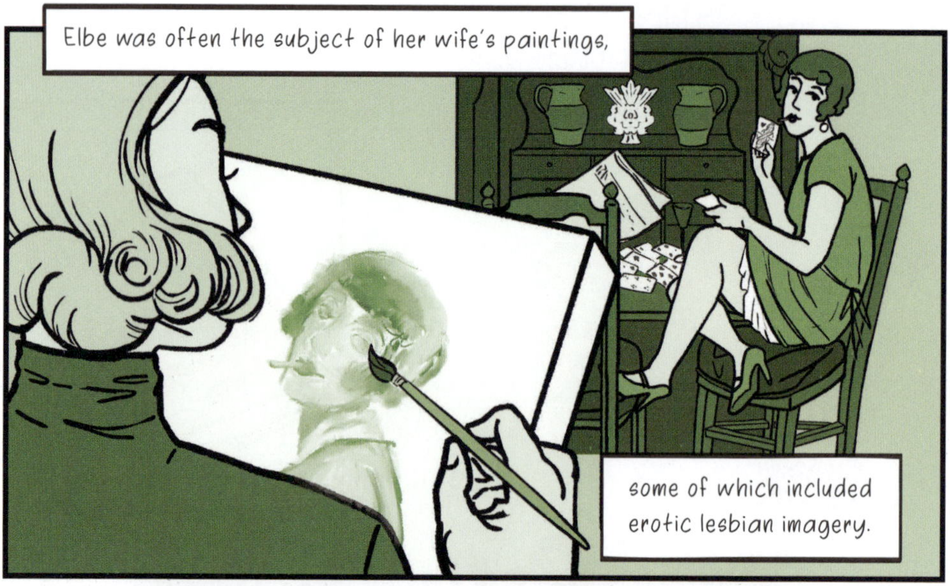
Elbe was often the subject of her wife's paintings,
some of which included erotic lesbian imagery.

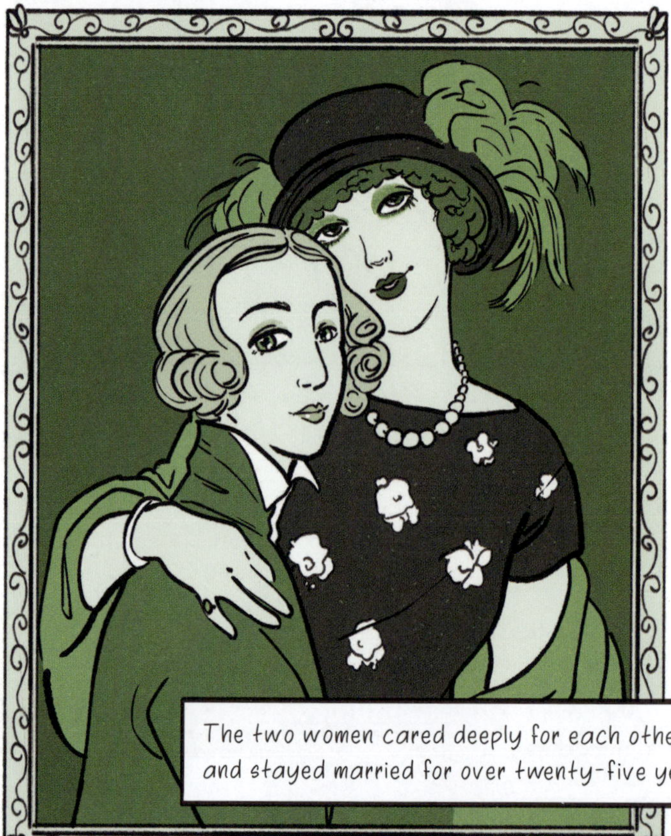
The two women cared deeply for each other and stayed married for over twenty-five years.

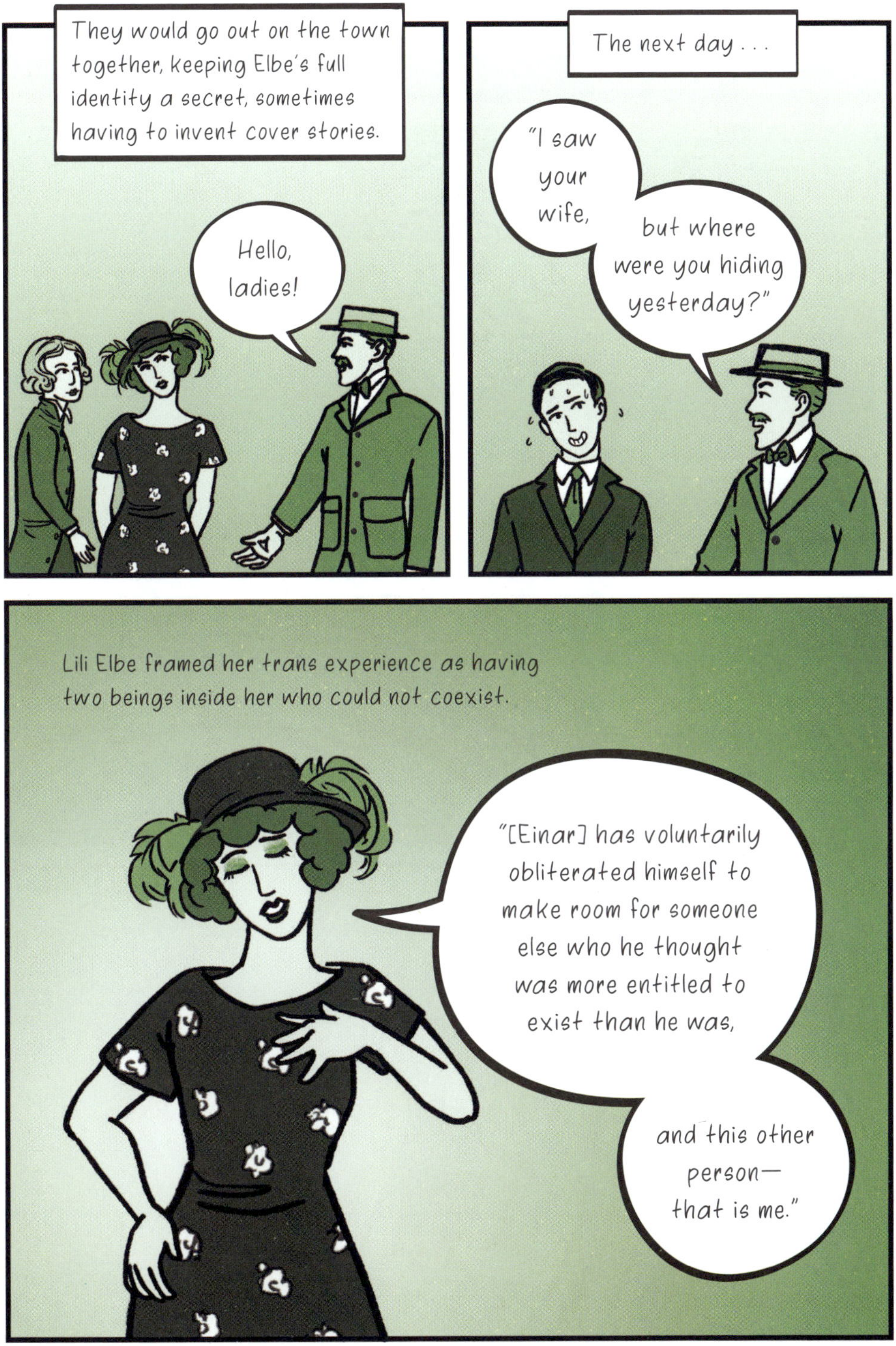
They would go out on the town together, keeping Elbe's full identity a secret, sometimes having to invent cover stories.
Hello, ladies!
The next day . . .
"I saw your wife,
but where were you hiding yesterday?"
Lili Elbe framed her trans experience as having two beings inside her who could not coexist.
"[Einar] has voluntarily obliterated himself to make room for someone else who he thought was more entitled to exist than he was,
and this other person— that is me."

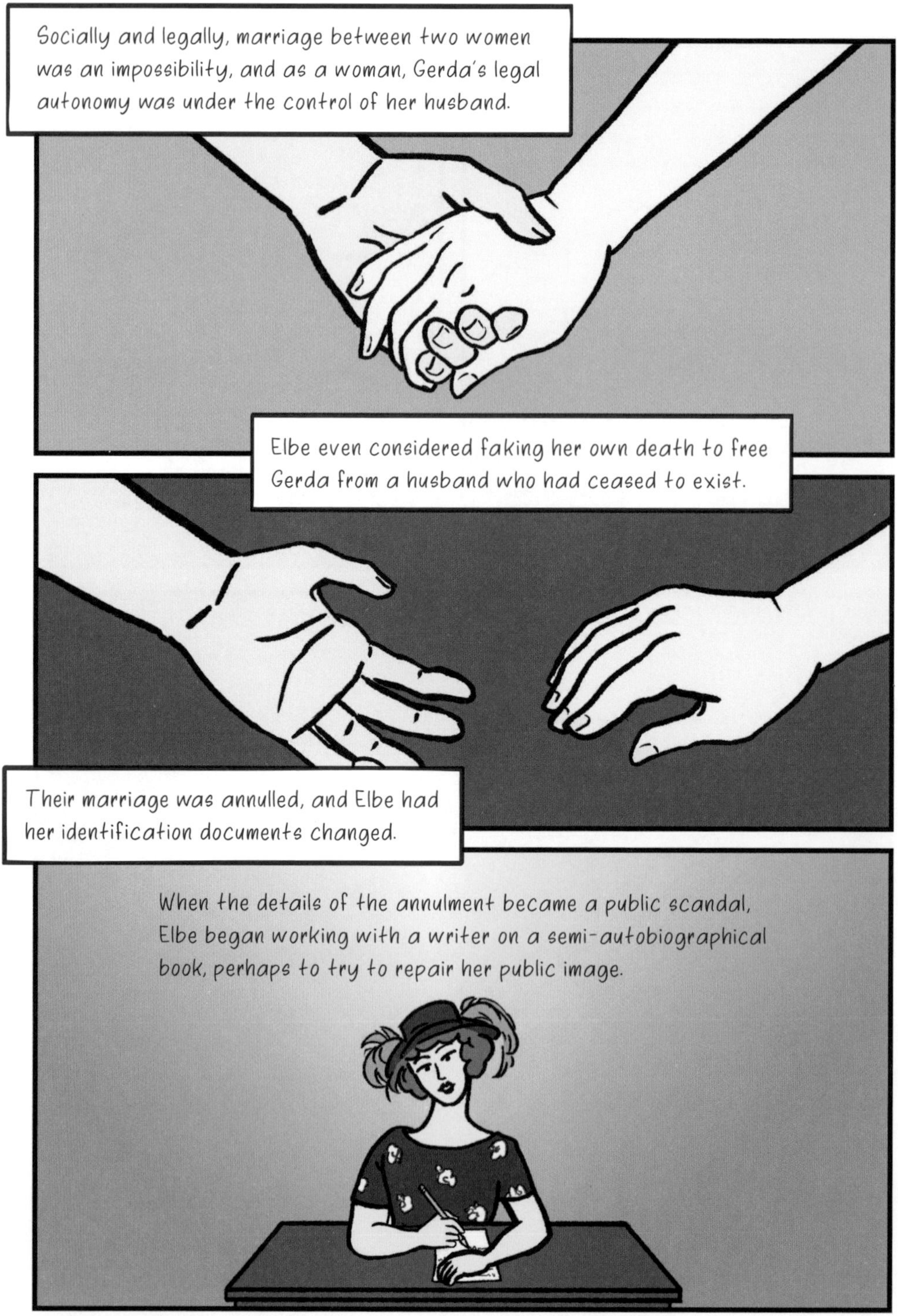
Socially and legally, marriage between two women was an impossibility, and as a woman, Gerda's legal autonomy was under the control of her husband.
Elbe even considered faking her own death to free Gerda from a husband who had ceased to exist.
Their marriage was annulled, and Elbe had her identification documents changed.
When the details of the annulment became a public scandal, Elbe began working with a writer on a semi-autobiographical book, perhaps to try to repair her public image.

According to the autobiography, Lili Elbe deeply longed to be able to bear children.
In 1931, a surgeon named Kurt Warnekros performed an operation on Elbe that she described as a uterus transplant.
However, historians have questioned if this is really what happened, since human organ transplant techniques wouldn't be viable for another couple of decades.
Doctors like Warnekros were pioneers, but also mad scientists who wanted to gain fame in their respective fields.
"Excellent French doctors that she had approached had not been able to help her . . . and as I had the greatest compassion for the unhappy person, I deferred to their wish."
The welfare of their patients was not necessarily their top priority.

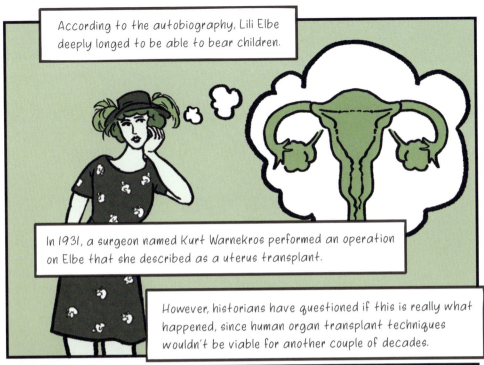

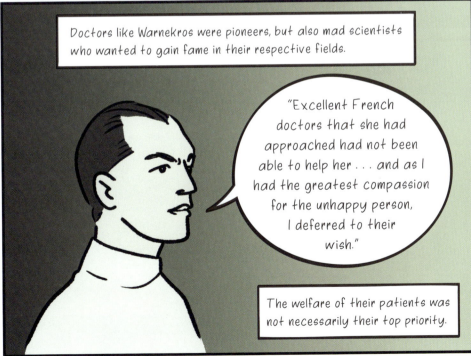

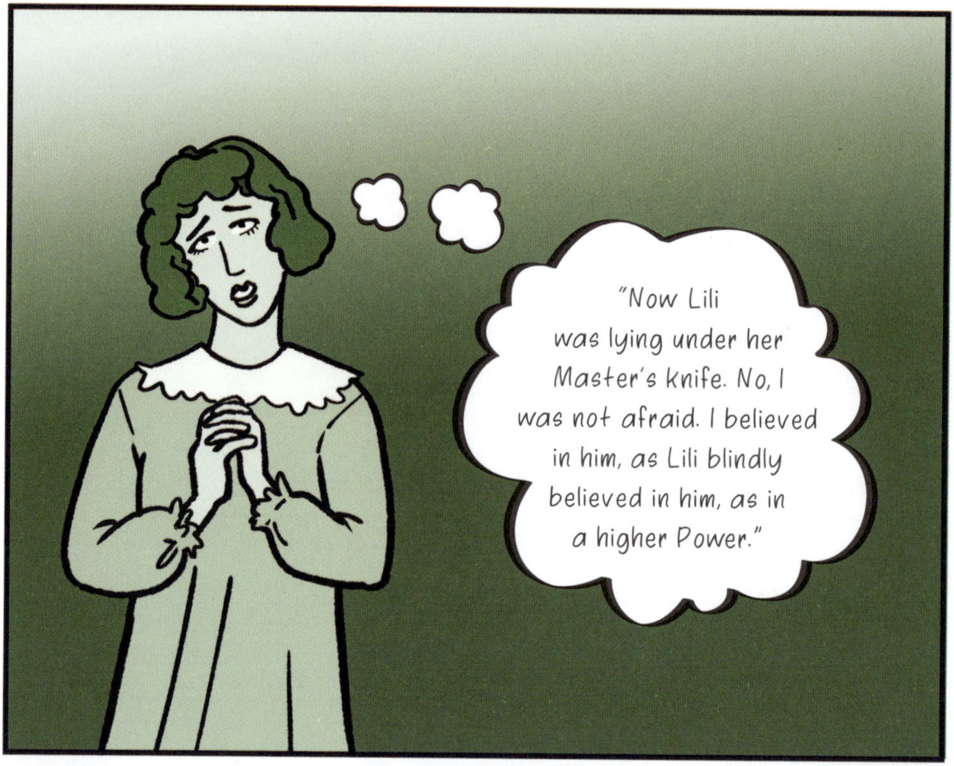
"Now Lili was lying under her Master's knife. No, I was not afraid. I believed in him, as Lili blindly believed in him, as in a higher Power."

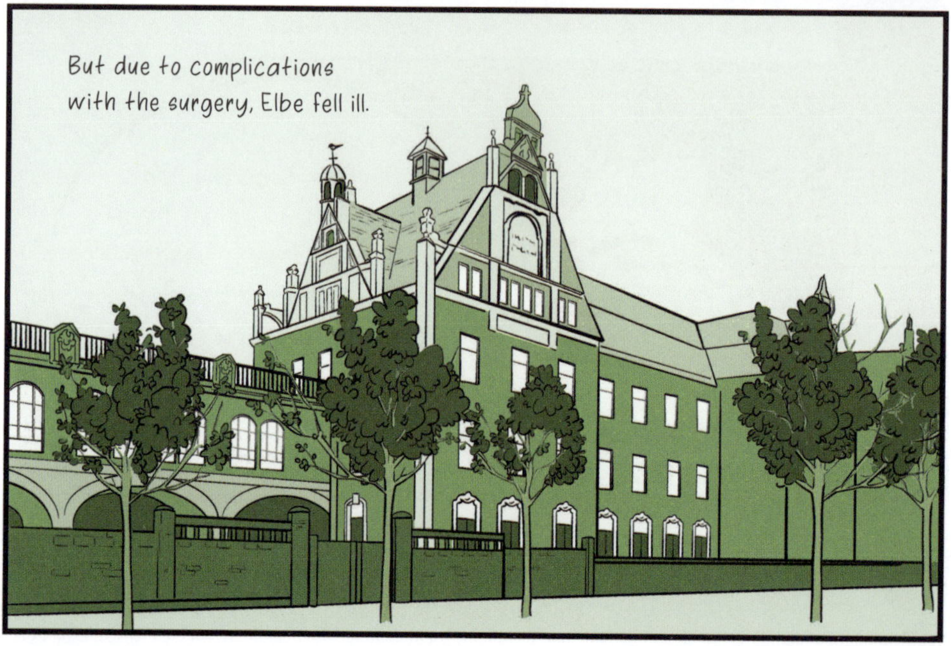
But due to complications with the surgery, Elbe fell ill.

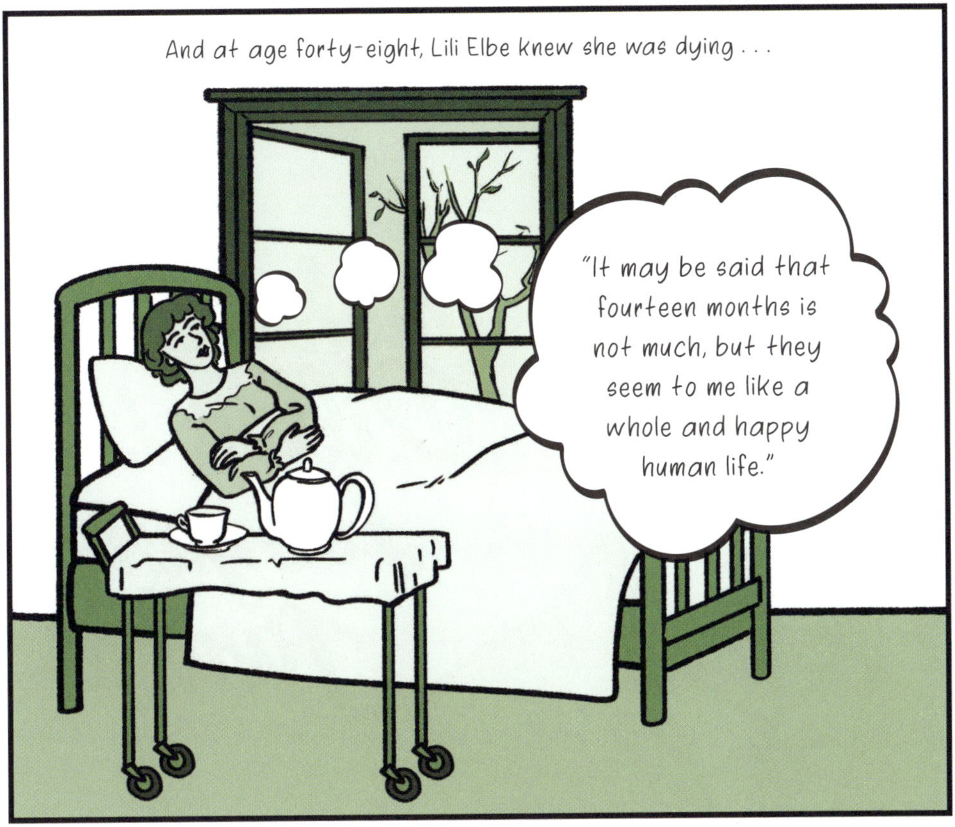
And at age forty-eight, Lili Elbe knew she was dying . . .
"It may be said that fourteen months is not much, but they seem to me like a whole and happy human life."

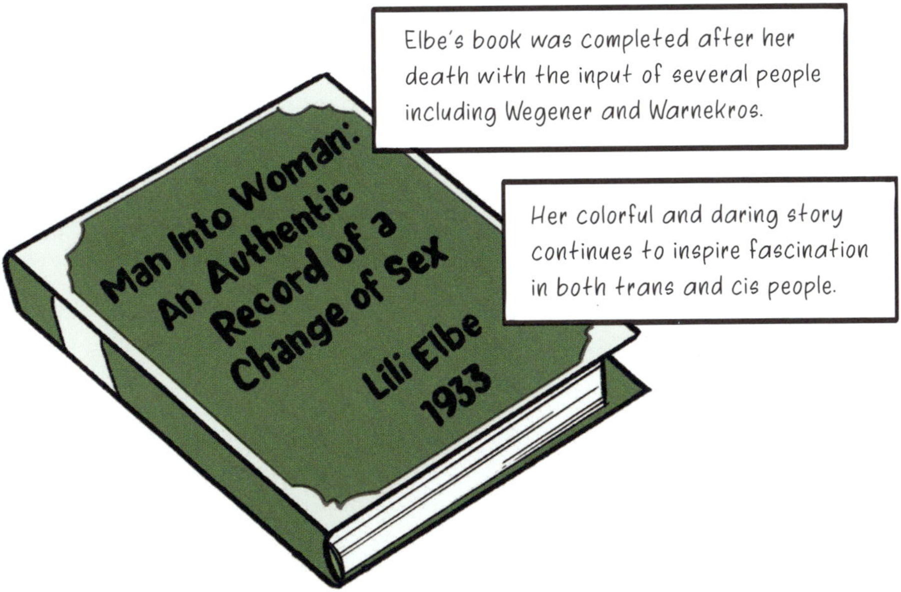
Elbe's book was completed after her death with the input of several people including Wegener and Warnekros.
Man Into Woman: An Authentic Record of a Change of Sex
Lili Elbe
1933
Her colorful and daring story continues to inspire fascination in both trans and cis people.

Throughout most of the twentieth century, trans-affirming medical care remained almost nonexistent.

Even so, sometimes people found a way to access the newly developing medical technologies.

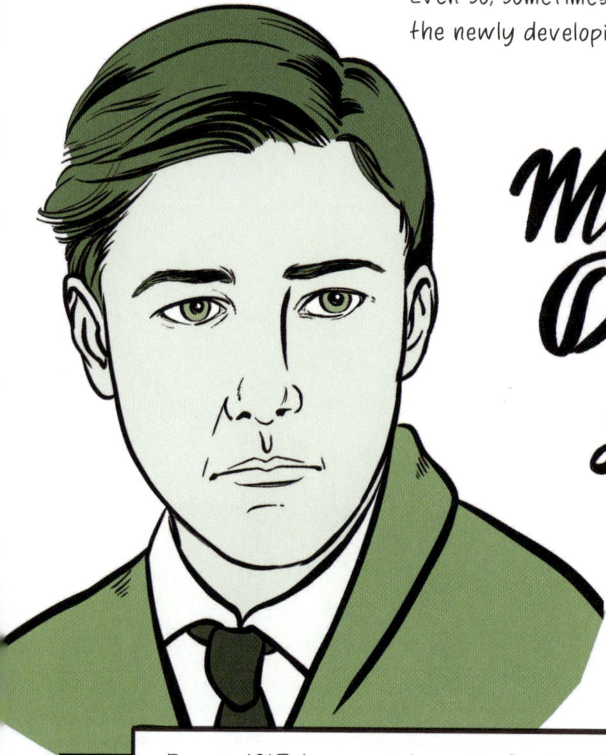

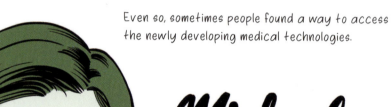

Michael Dillon / Lobzang Jivaka

Based on a photo courtesy of Liz Hodgkinson's private collection

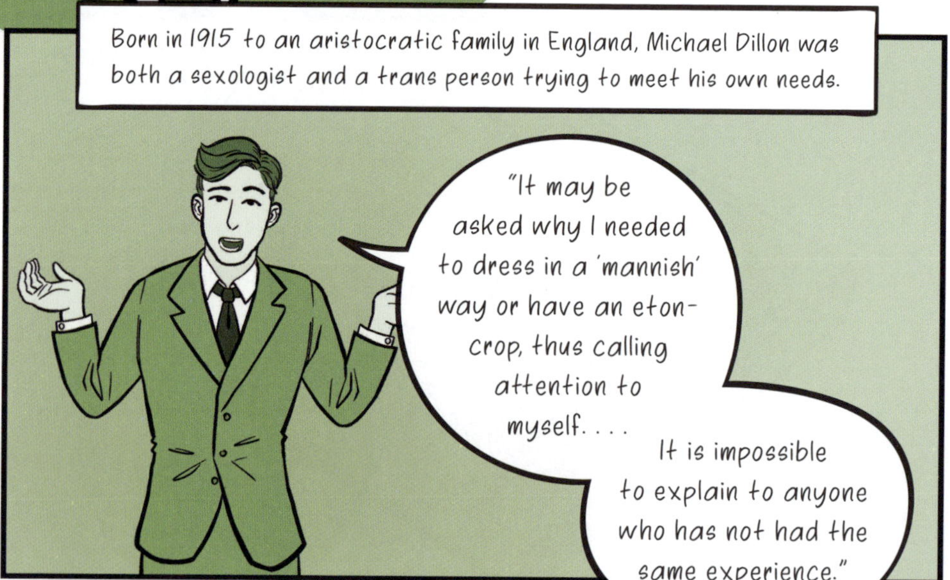

Born in 1915 to an aristocratic family in England, Michael Dillon was both a sexologist and a trans person trying to meet his own needs.
"It may be asked why I needed to dress in a 'mannish' way or have an eton-crop, thus calling attention to myself. . . .
It is impossible to explain to anyone who has not had the same experience."

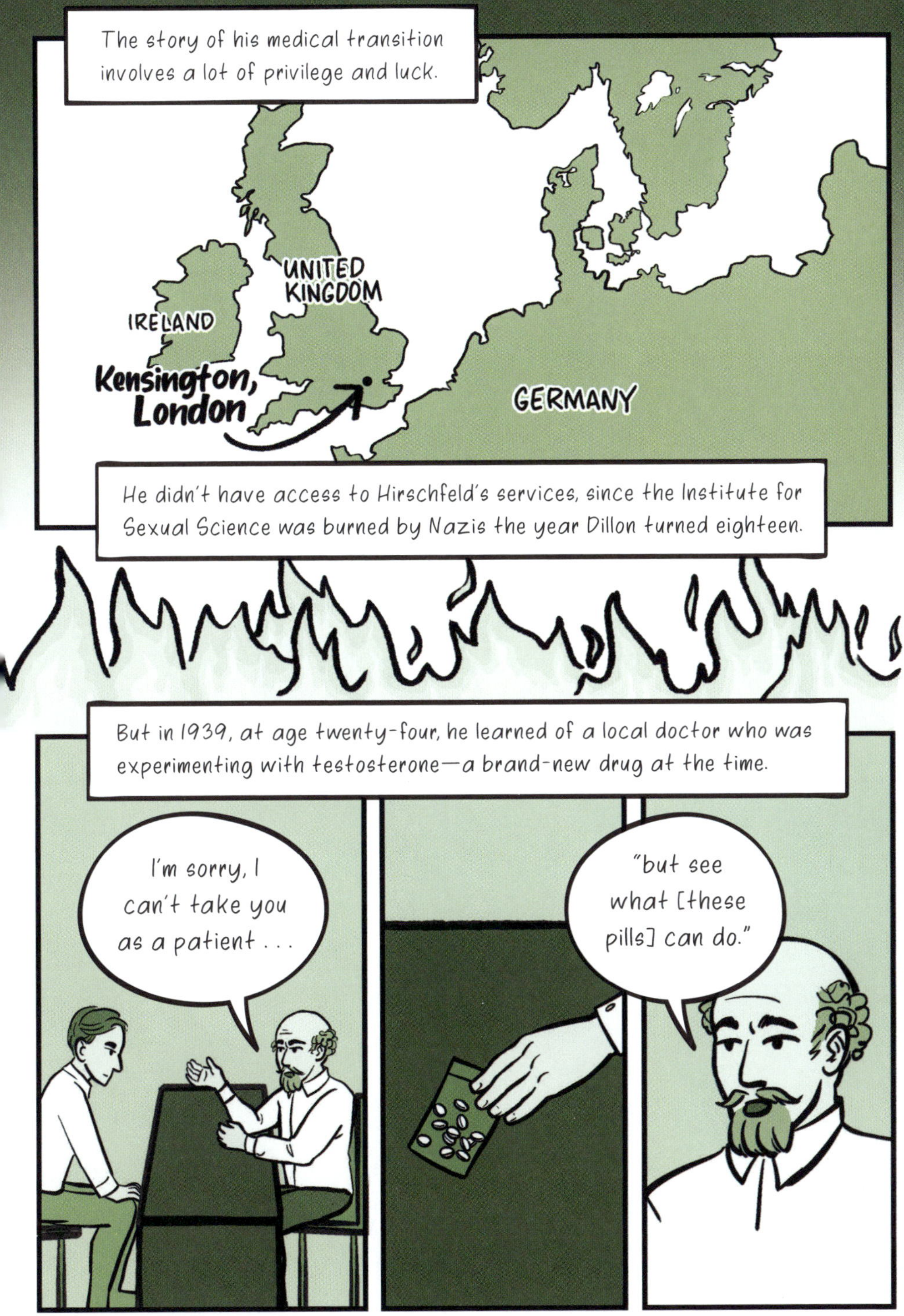
The story of his medical transition involves a lot of privilege and luck.
UNITED KINGDOM
IRELAND
Kensington, London
GERMANY
He didn't have access to Hirschfeld's services, since the Institute for Sexual Science was burned by Nazis the year Dillon turned eighteen.
But in 1939, at age twenty-four, he learned of a local doctor who was experimenting with testosterone—a brand-new drug at the time.
I'm sorry, I can't take you as a patient . . .
"but see what [these pills] can do."

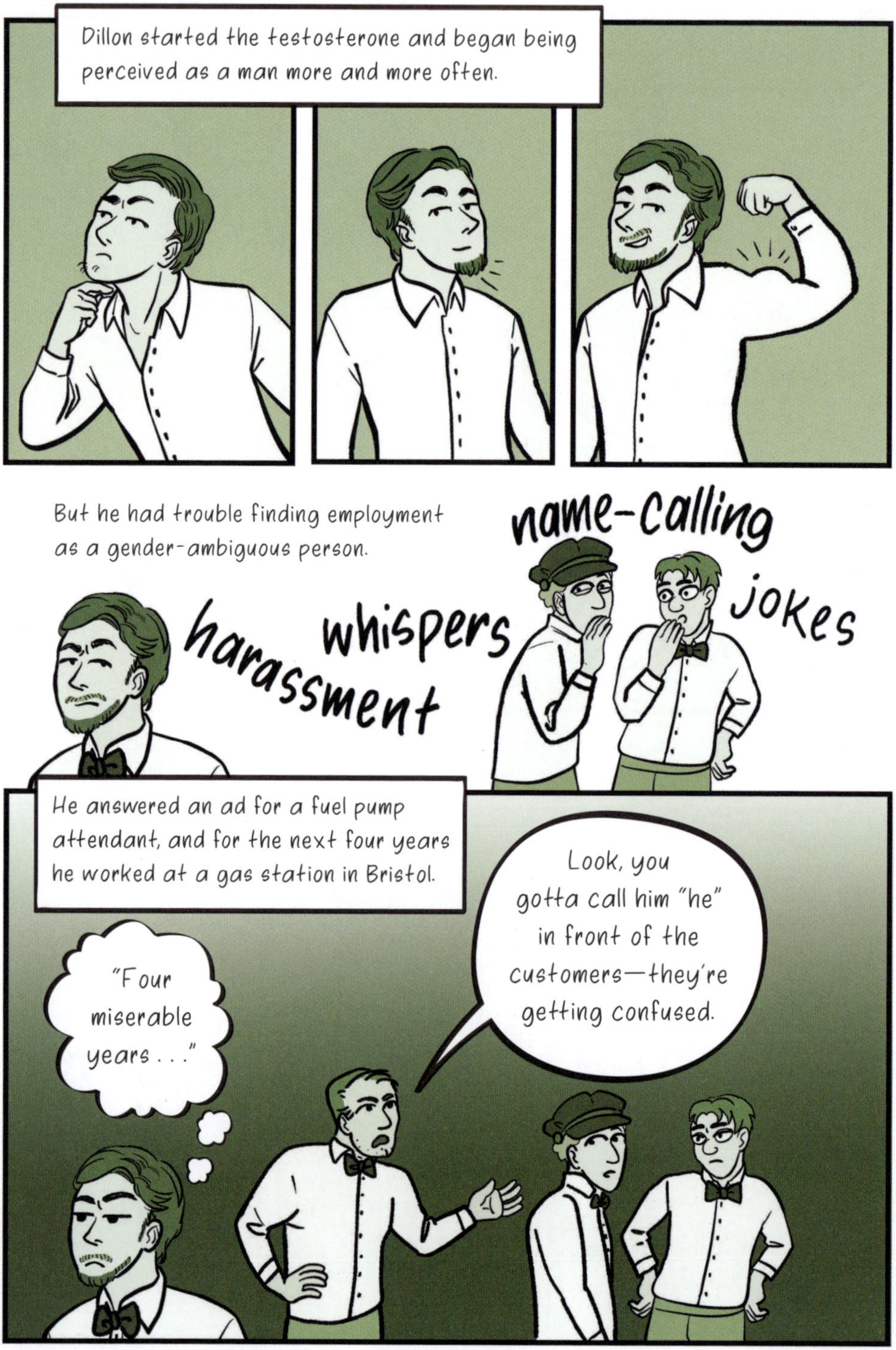
Dillon started the testosterone and began being perceived as a man more and more often.
But he had trouble finding employment as a gender-ambiguous person.
name-calling
jokes
whispers
harassment
He answered an ad for a fuel pump attendant, and for the next four years he worked at a gas station in Bristol.
"Four miserable years . . ."
Look, you gotta call him "he" in front of the customers—they're getting confused.

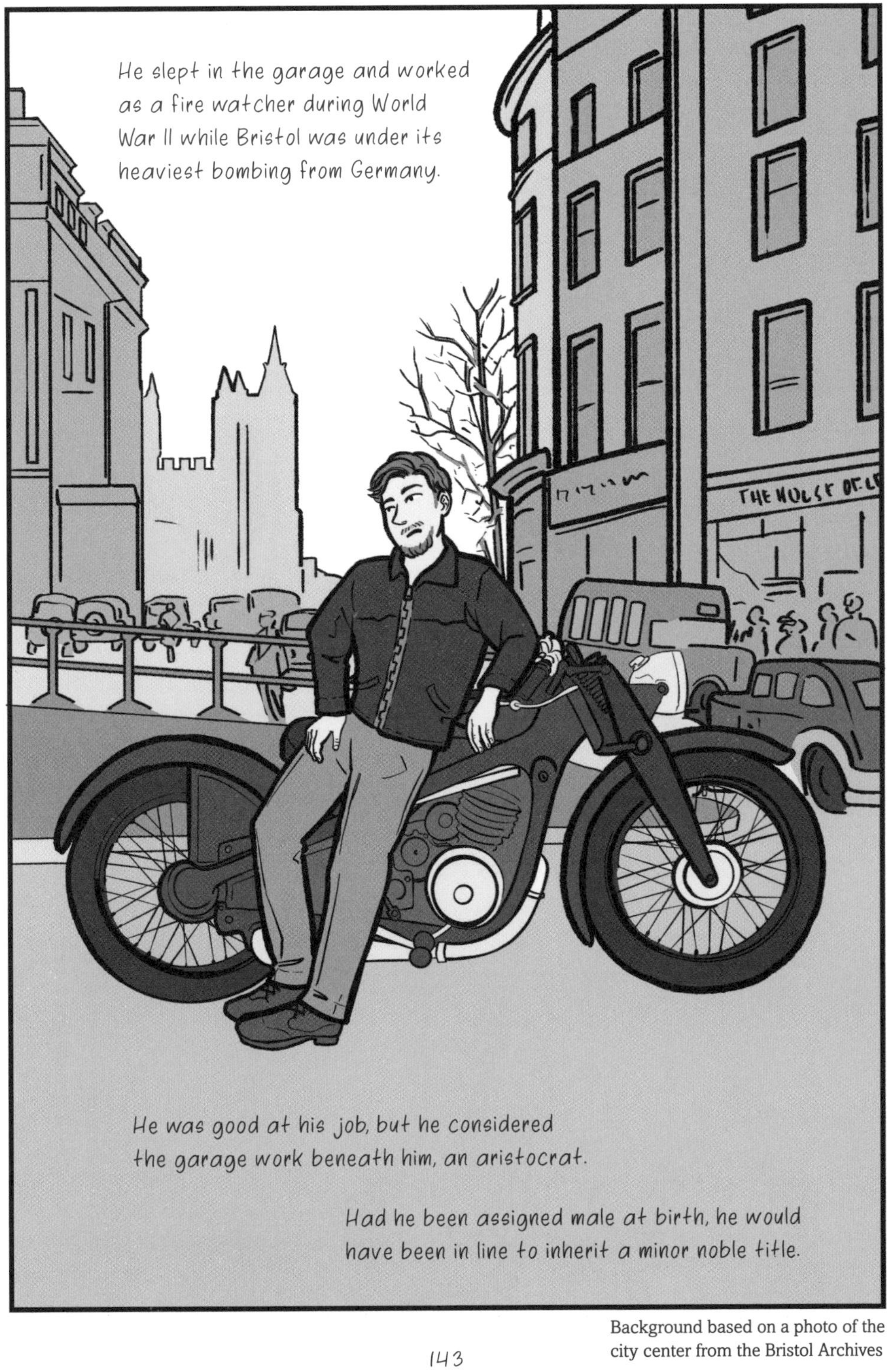
He slept in the garage and worked as a fire watcher during World War II while Bristol was under its heaviest bombing from Germany.
He was good at his job, but he considered the garage work beneath him, an aristocrat.
Had he been assigned male at birth, he would have been in line to inherit a minor noble title.

Background based on a photo of the city center from the Bristol Archives

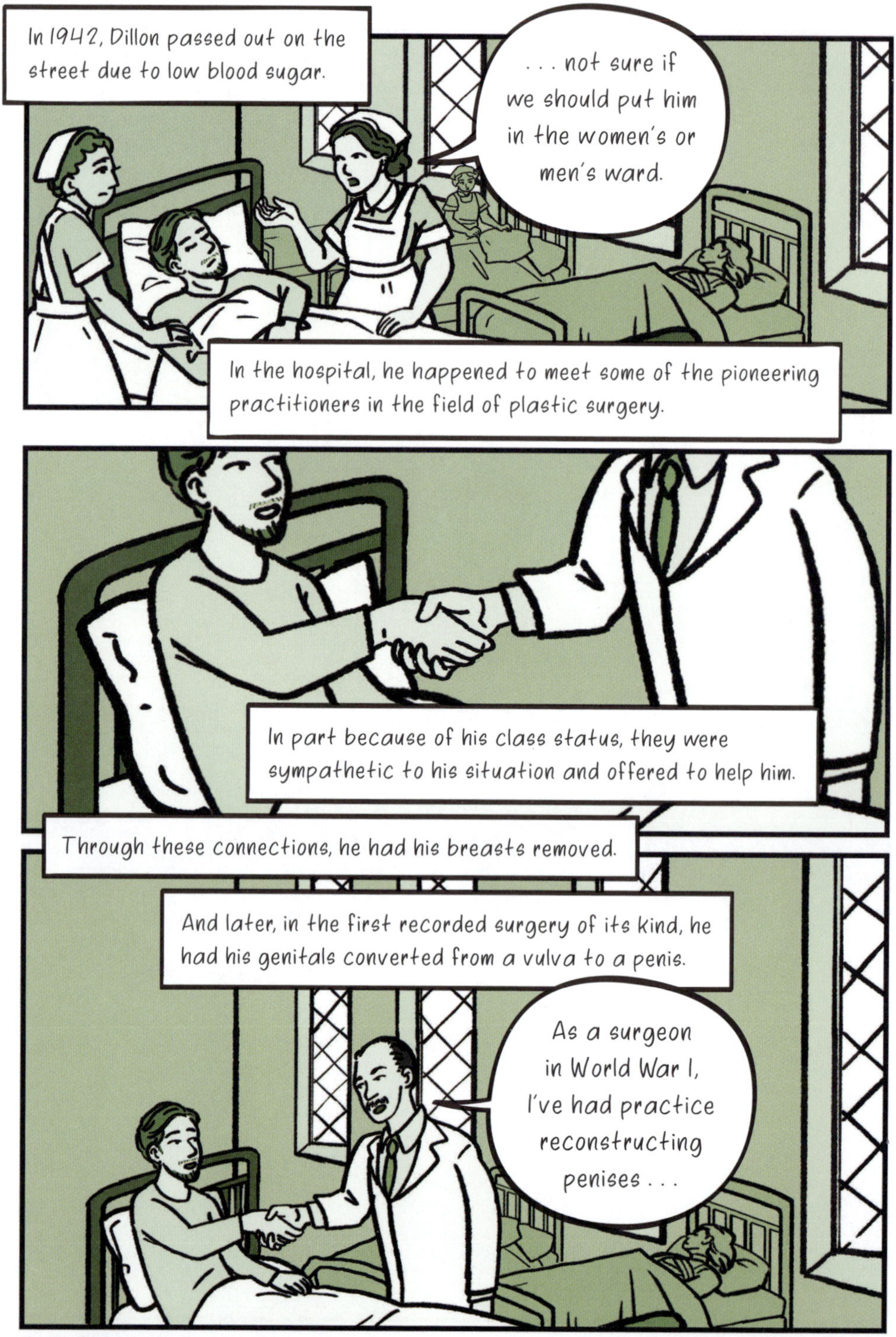
In 1942, Dillon passed out on the street due to low blood sugar.
. . . not sure if we should put him in the women's or men's ward.
In the hospital, he happened to meet some of the pioneering practitioners in the field of plastic surgery.
In part because of his class status, they were sympathetic to his situation and offered to help him.
Through these connections, he had his breasts removed.
And later, in the first recorded surgery of its kind, he had his genitals converted from a vulva to a penis.
As a surgeon in World War I, I've had practice reconstructing penises . . .
Harold Gillies, father of modern plastic surgery

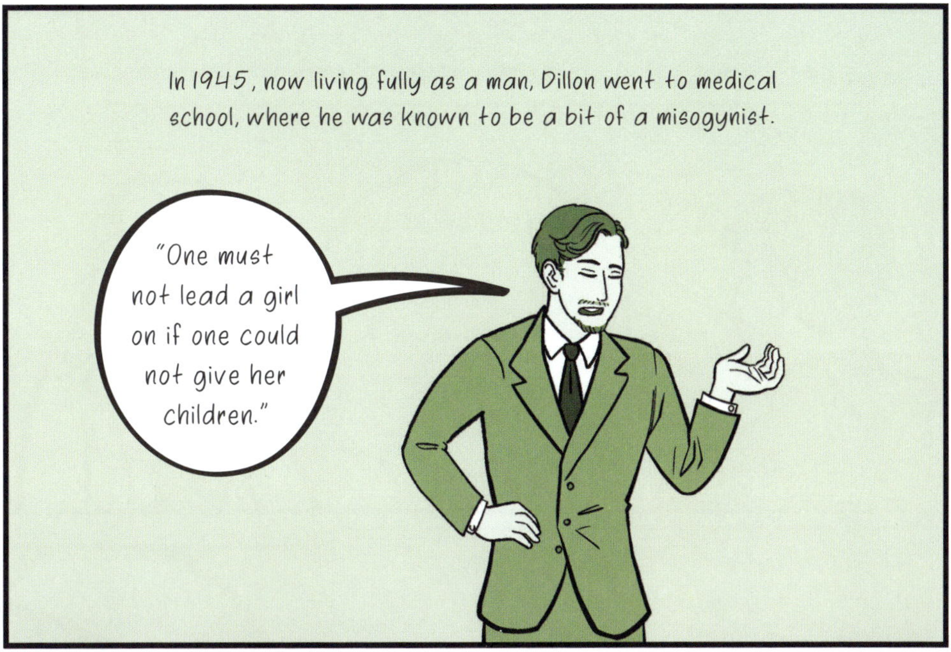
In 1945, now living fully as a man, Dillon went to medical school, where he was known to be a bit of a misogynist.
"One must not lead a girl on if one could not give her children."

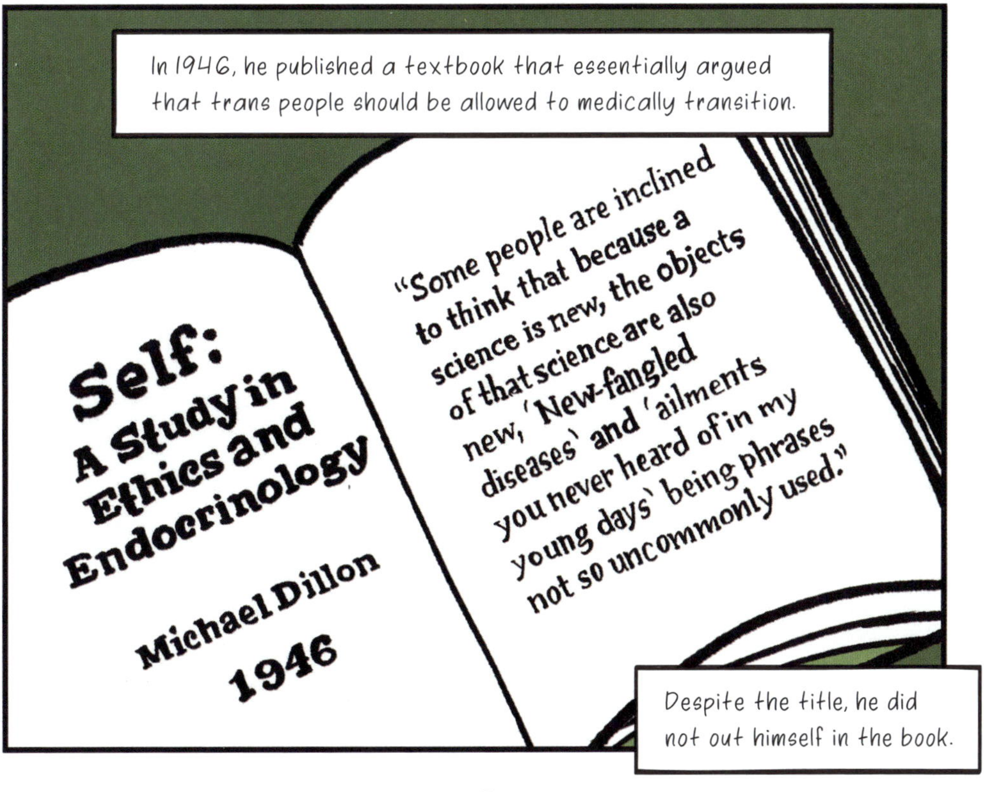
In 1946, he published a textbook that essentially argued that trans people should be allowed to medically transition.
Self: A Study in Ethics and Endocrinology
Michael Dillon
1946
"Some people are inclined to think that because a science is new, the objects of that science are also new, 'New-fangled diseases' and 'ailments you never heard of in my young days' being phrases not so uncommonly used."
Despite the title, he did not out himself in the book.

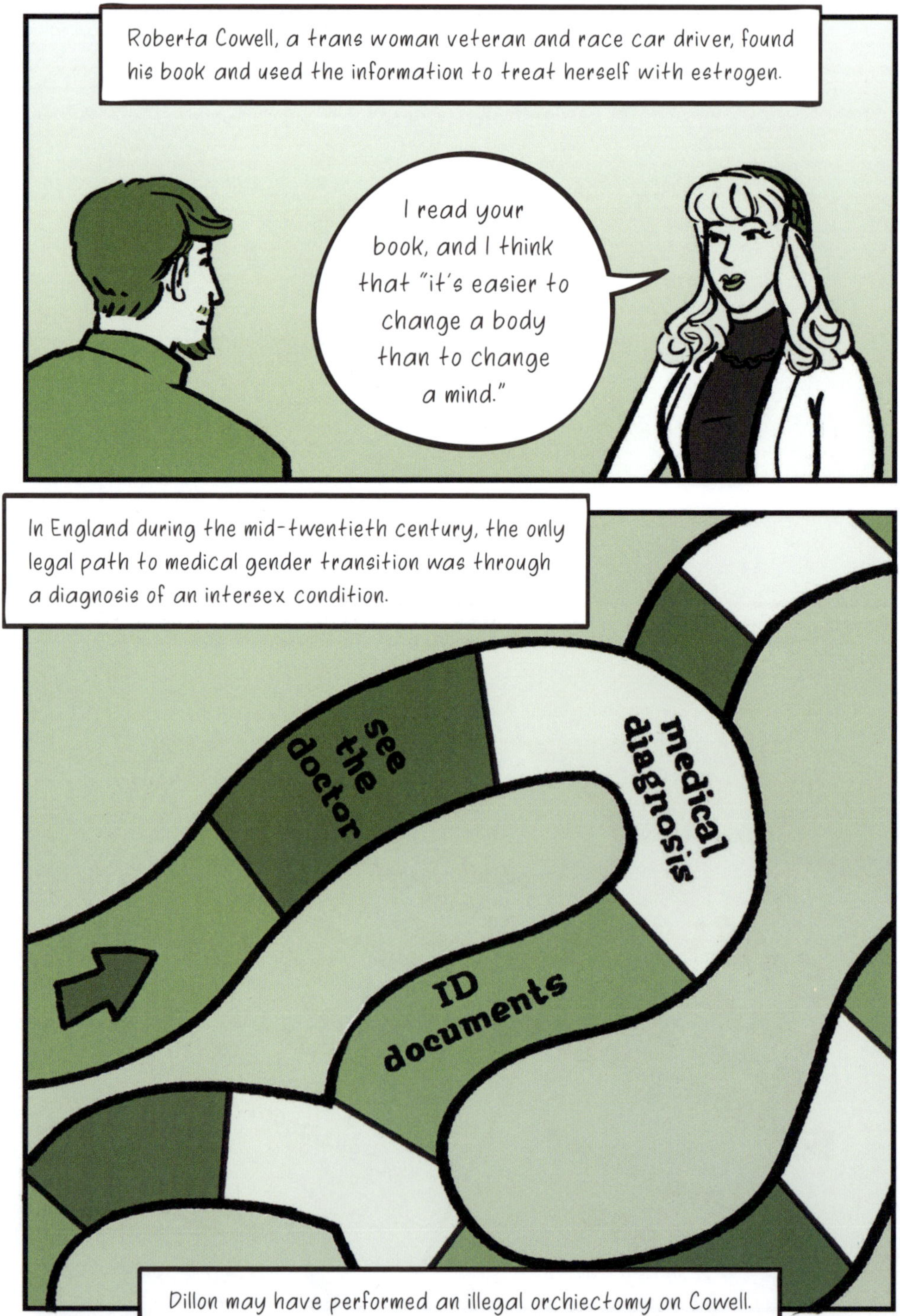
Roberta Cowell, a trans woman veteran and race car driver, found his book and used the information to treat herself with estrogen.
I read your book, and I think that "it's easier to change a body than to change a mind."
In England during the mid-twentieth century, the only legal path to medical gender transition was through a diagnosis of an intersex condition.
see the doctor
medical diagnosis
ID documents
Dillon may have performed an illegal orchiectomy on Cowell.

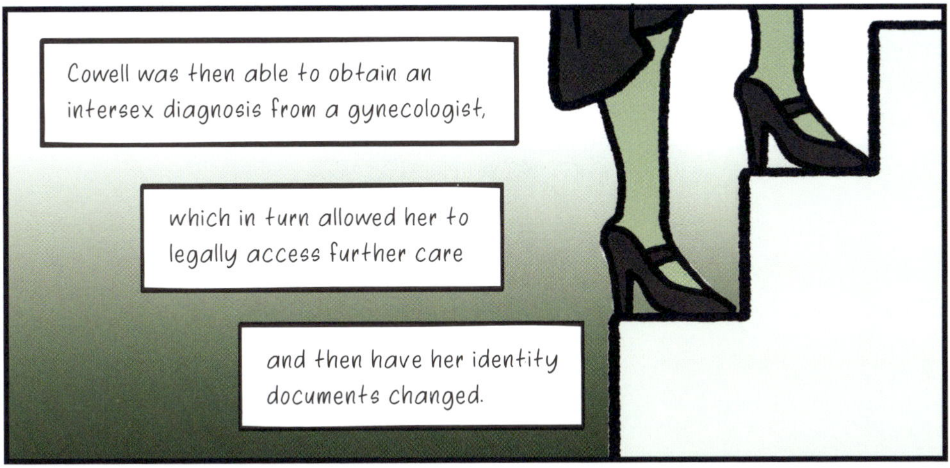
Cowell was then able to obtain an intersex diagnosis from a gynecologist,
which in turn allowed her to legally access further care
and then have her identity documents changed.

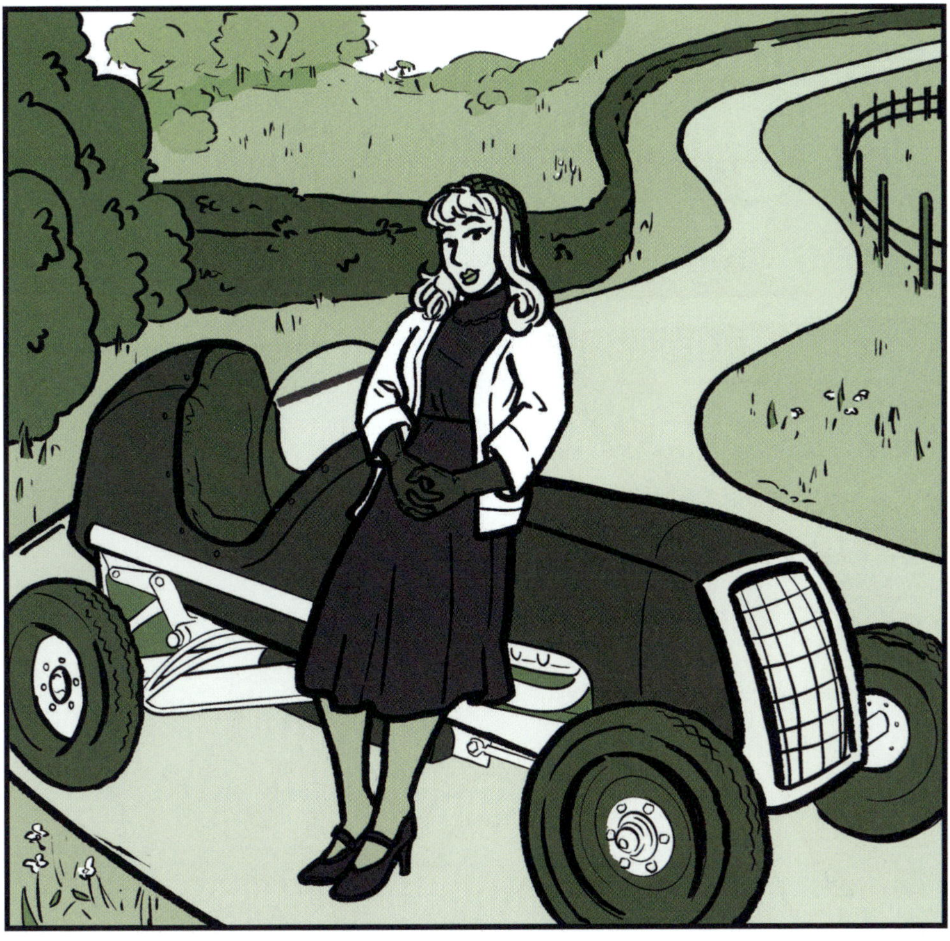

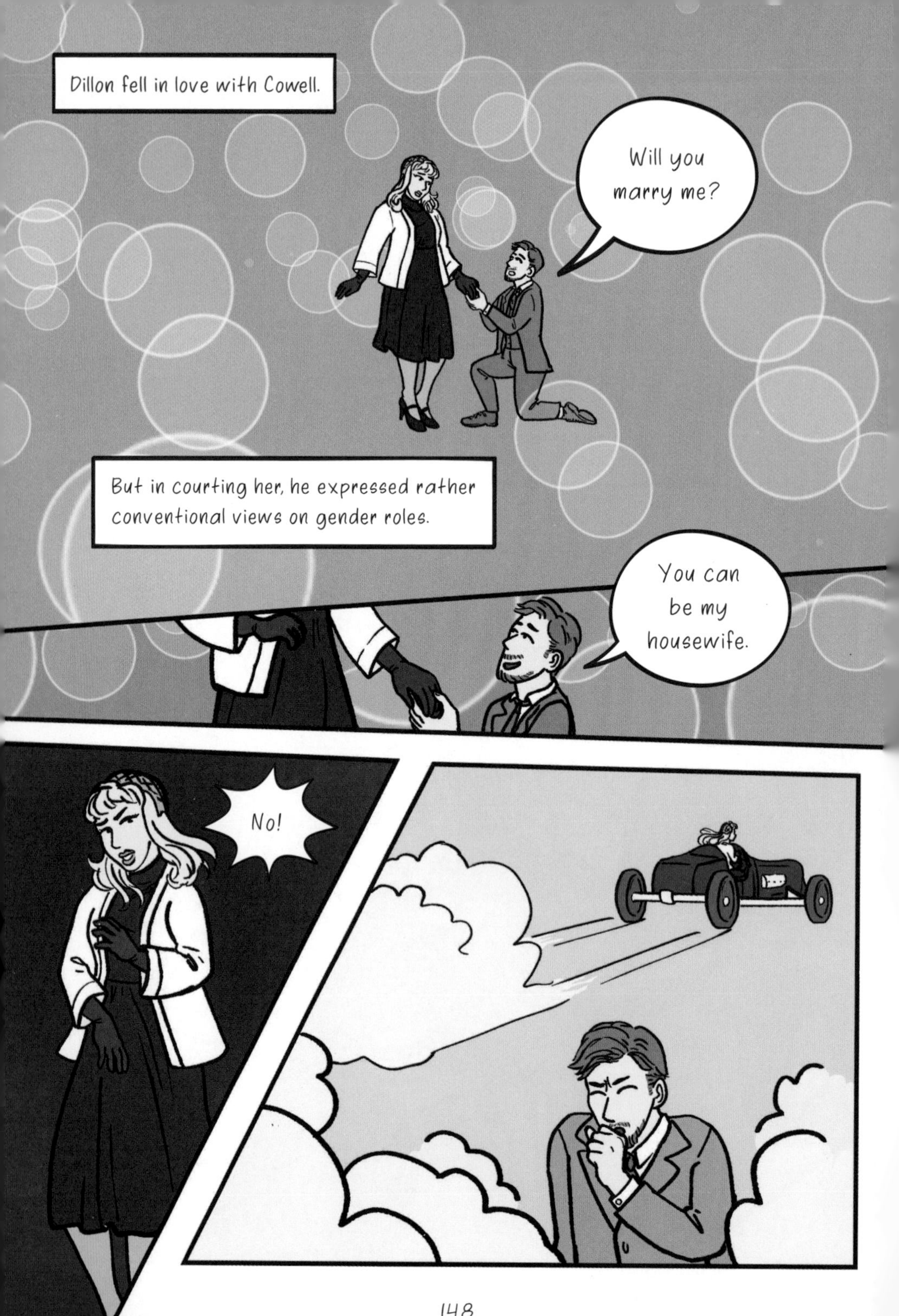
Dillon fell in love with Cowell.
Will you marry me?
But in courting her, he expressed rather conventional views on gender roles.
You can be my housewife.
No!

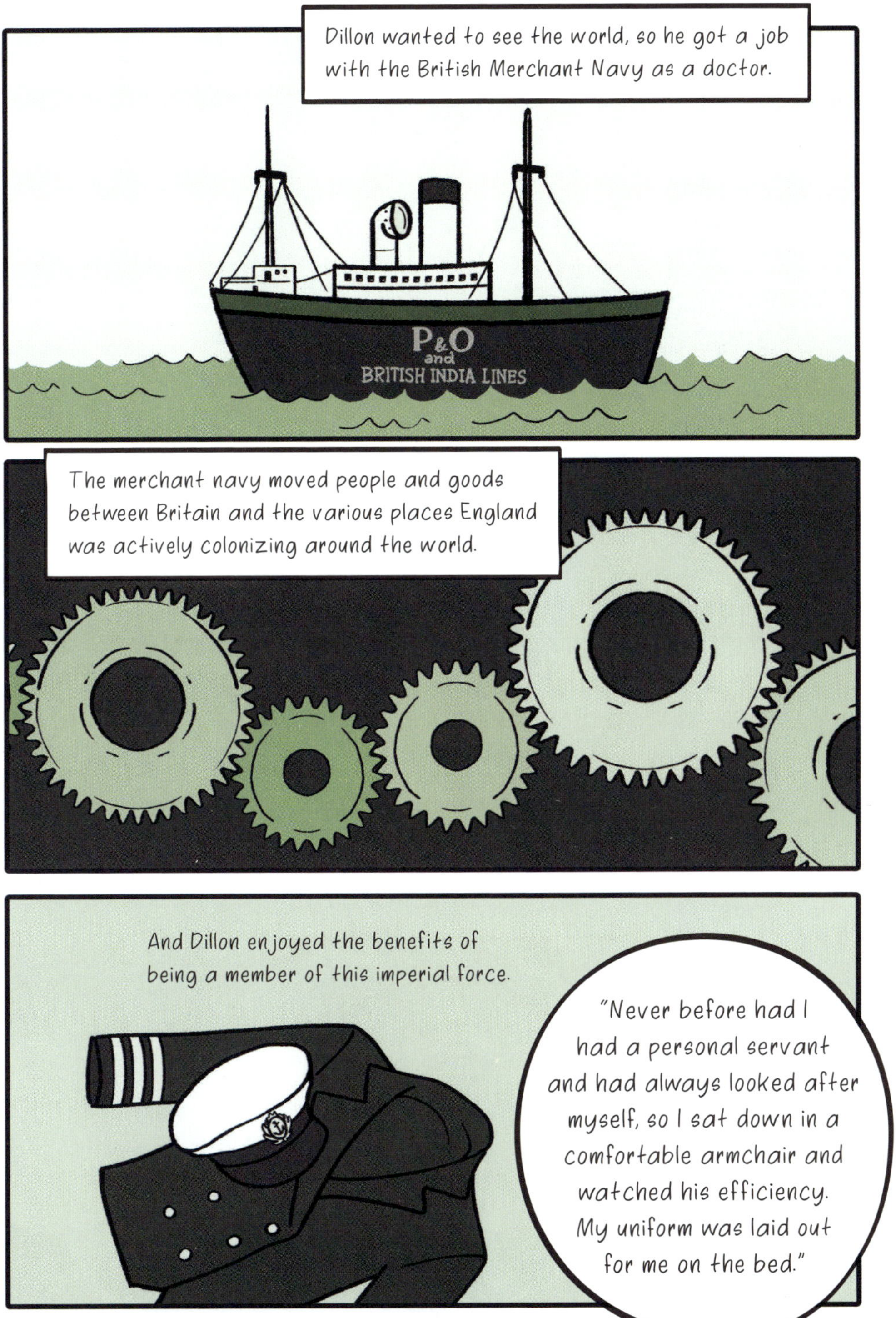
Dillon wanted to see the world, so he got a job with the British Merchant Navy as a doctor.
P&O and BRITISH INDIA LINES
The merchant navy moved people and goods between Britain and the various places England was actively colonizing around the world.
And Dillon enjoyed the benefits of being a member of this imperial force.
"Never before had I had a personal servant and had always looked after myself, so I sat down in a comfortable armchair and watched his efficiency. My uniform was laid out for me on the bed."

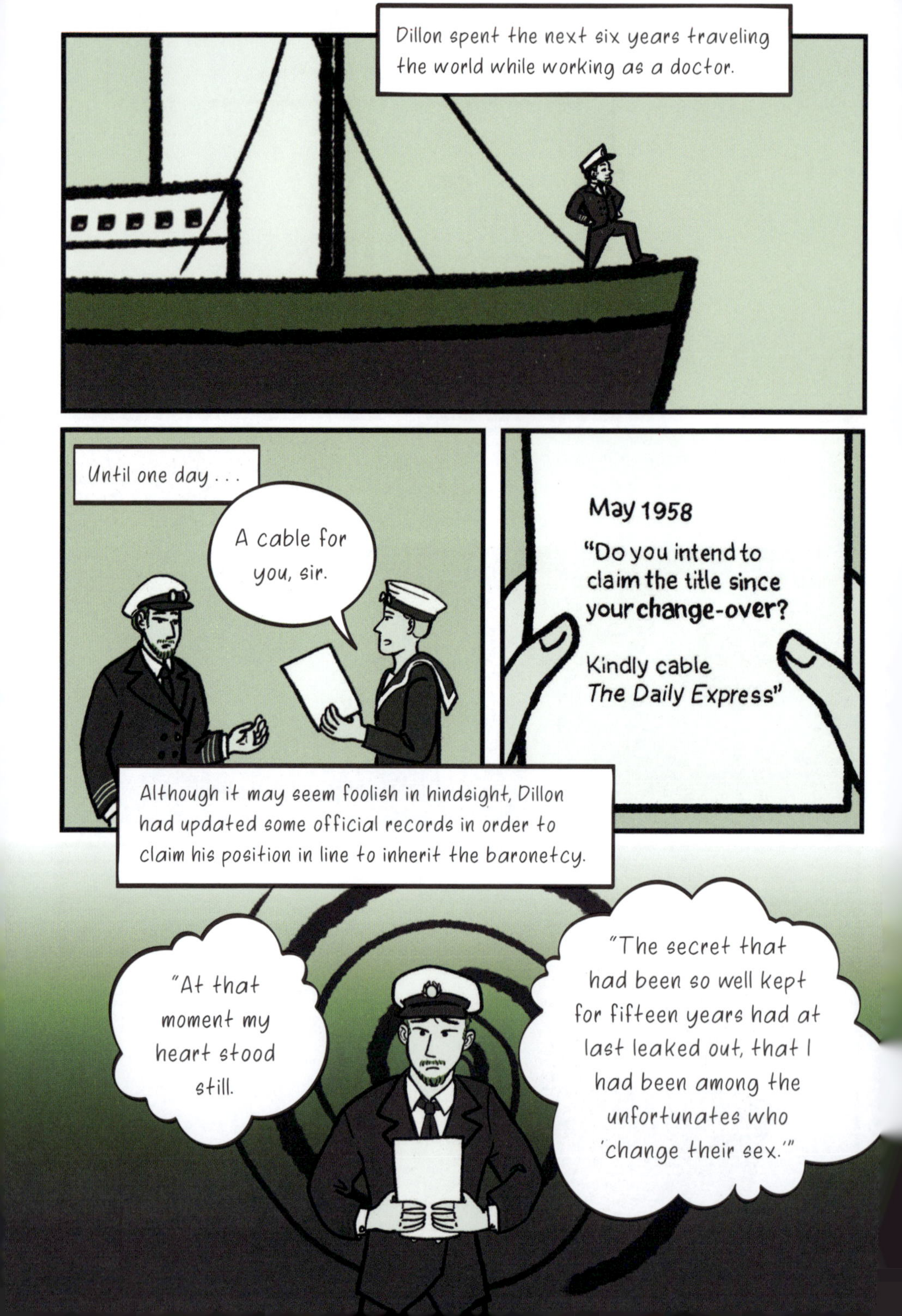
Dillon spent the next six years traveling the world while working as a doctor.
Until one day . . .
A cable for you, sir.
May 1958
"Do you intend to claim the title since your change-over?
Kindly cable *The Daily Express*"
Although it may seem foolish in hindsight, Dillon had updated some official records in order to claim his position in line to inherit the baronetcy.
"At that moment my heart stood still.
"The secret that had been so well kept for fifteen years had at last leaked out, that I had been among the unfortunates who 'change their sex.'"

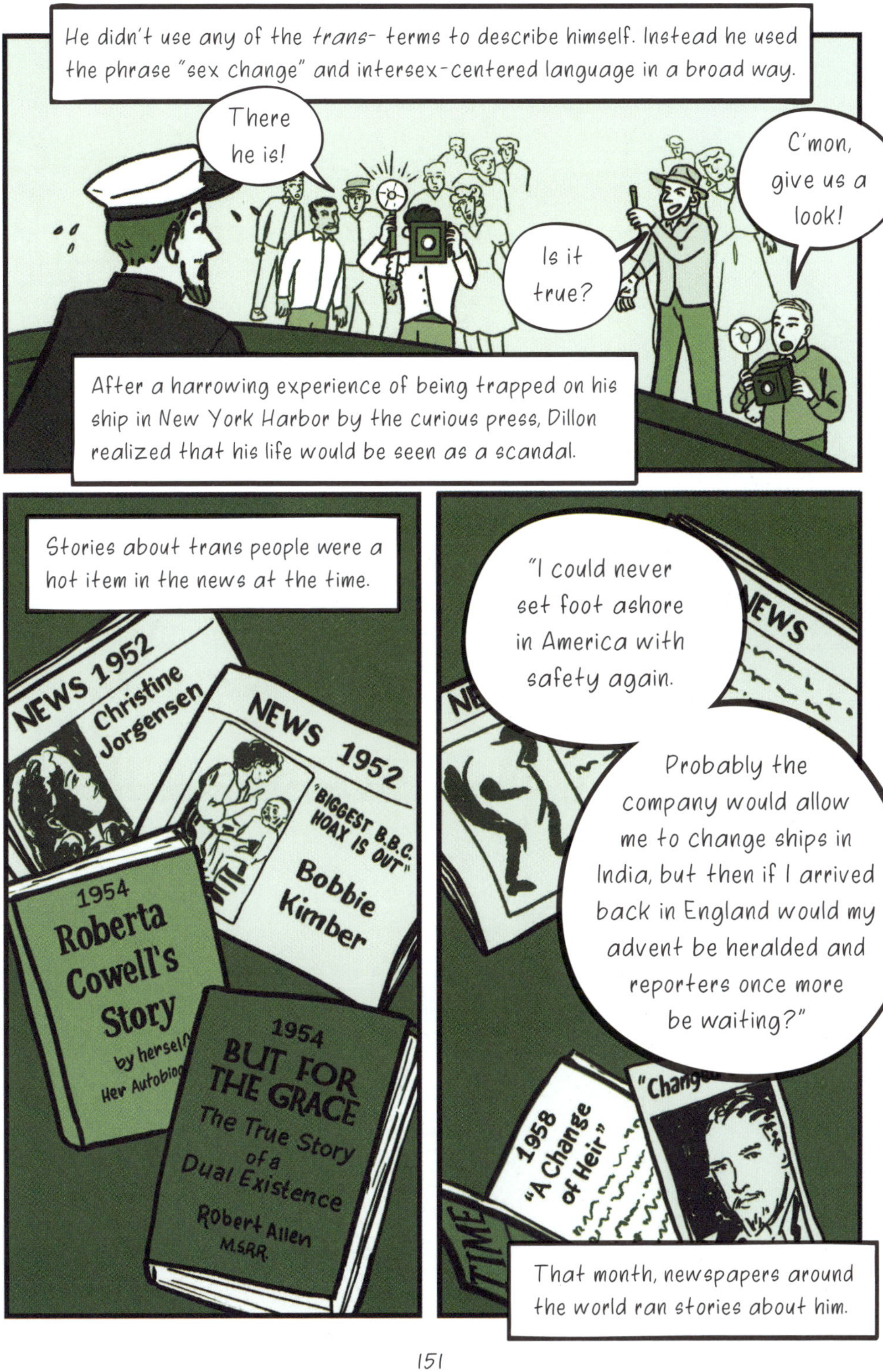
He didn't use any of the *trans-* terms to describe himself. Instead he used the phrase "sex change" and intersex-centered language in a broad way.
There he is!
Is it true?
C'mon, give us a look!
After a harrowing experience of being trapped on his ship in New York Harbor by the curious press, Dillon realized that his life would be seen as a scandal.
Stories about trans people were a hot item in the news at the time.
NEWS 1952 Christine Jorgensen
NEWS 1952 "BIGGEST B.B.C. HOAX IS OUT" Bobbie Kimber
1954 Roberta Cowell's Story by herself Her Autobio
1954 BUT FOR THE GRACE The True Story of a Dual Existence Robert Allen M.S.R.R.
"I could never set foot ashore in America with safety again.
Probably the company would allow me to change ships in India, but then if I arrived back in England would my advent be heralded and reporters once more be waiting?"
NEWS
1958 "A Change of Heir"
TIME
That month, newspapers around the world ran stories about him.

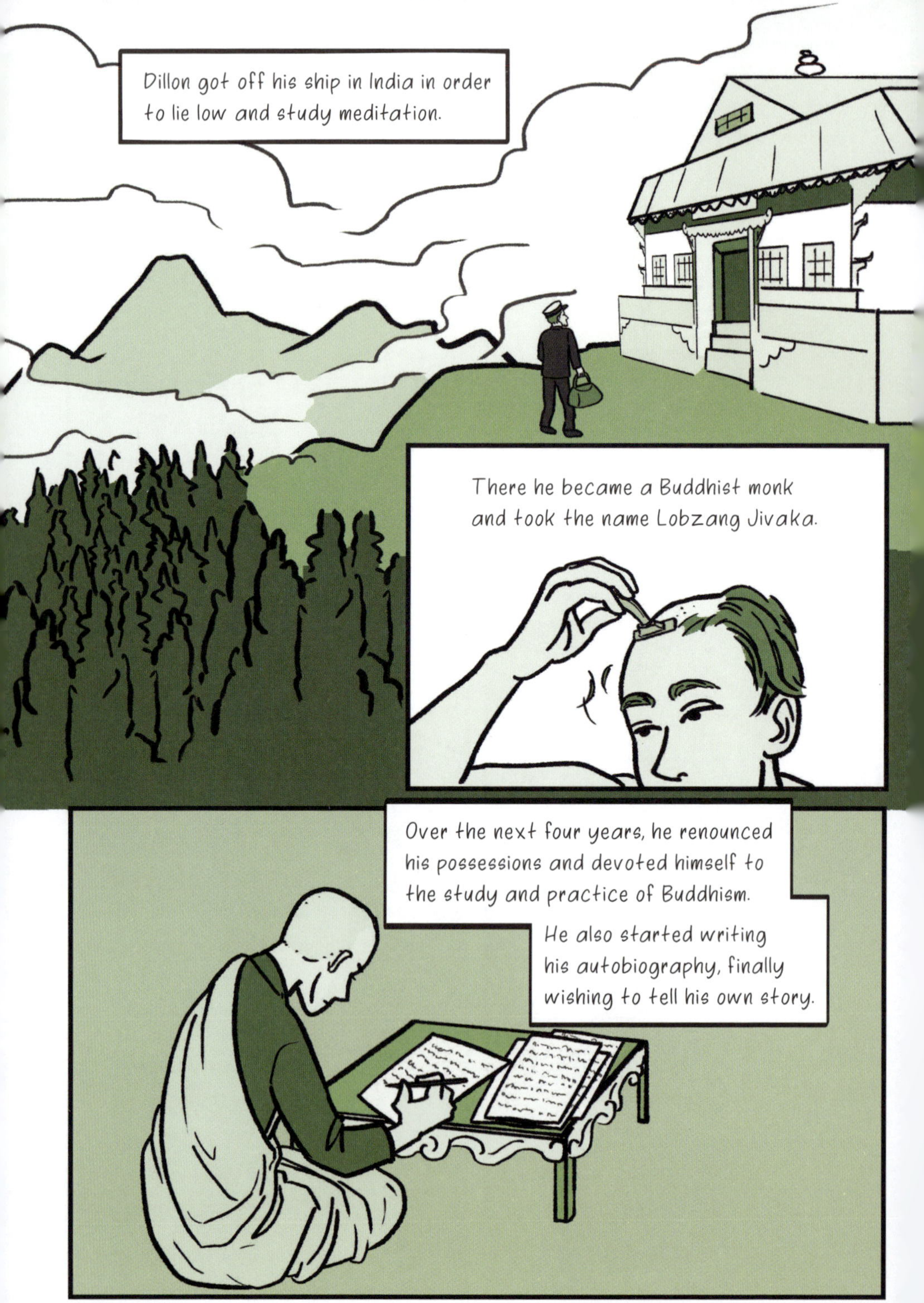

Dillon got off his ship in India in order to lie low and study meditation.
There he became a Buddhist monk and took the name Lobzang Jivaka.
Over the next four years, he renounced his possessions and devoted himself to the study and practice of Buddhism.
He also started writing his autobiography, finally wishing to tell his own story.

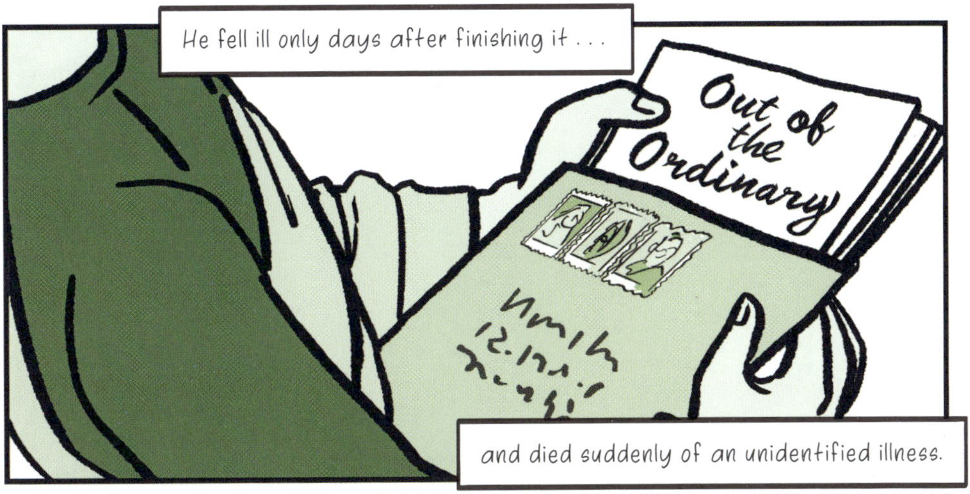
He fell ill only days after finishing it . . .
Out of the Ordinary
and died suddenly of an unidentified illness.

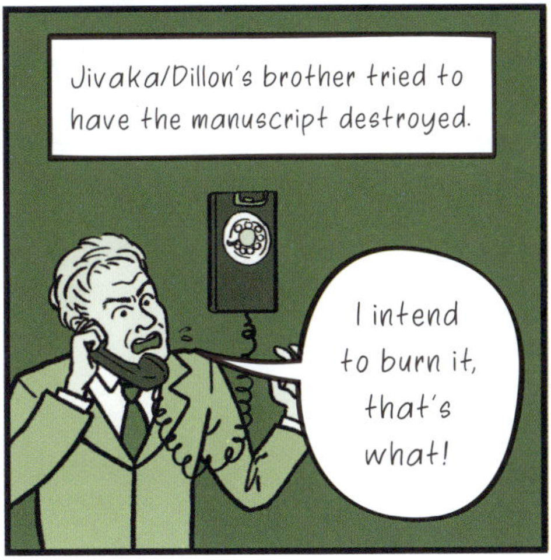
Jivaka/Dillon's brother tried to have the manuscript destroyed.
I intend to burn it, that's what!

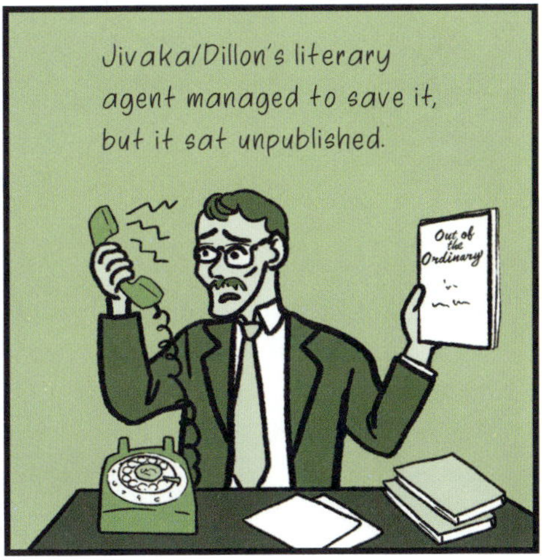
Jivaka/Dillon's literary agent managed to save it, but it sat unpublished.
Out of the Ordinary

It was eventually published in 2017, fifty-five years later.

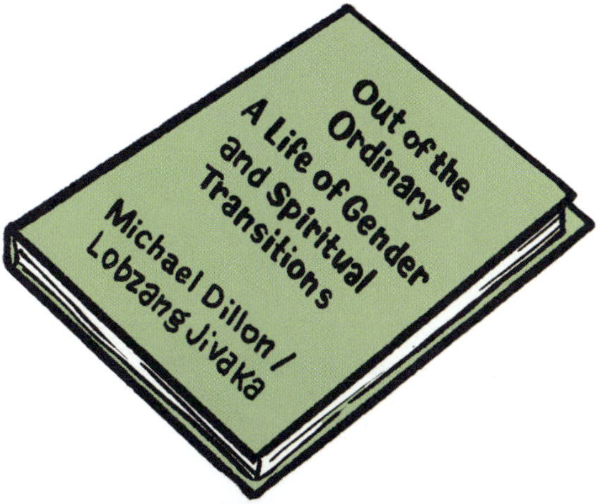
Out of the Ordinary
A Life of Gender and Spiritual Transitions
Michael Dillon / Lobzang Jivaka

How does sexology's history affect current understandings of what it means to be trans?

Does sexology's history help explain why it's often assumed that all trans people want to medically transition?

How might these understandings be benefiting and/or failing us today?

How did sexologists work with and/or push back against their own culture's norms about sex, gender, and sexuality?

How has sexology been used both as a tool of oppression and a means of self-actualization for trans people?

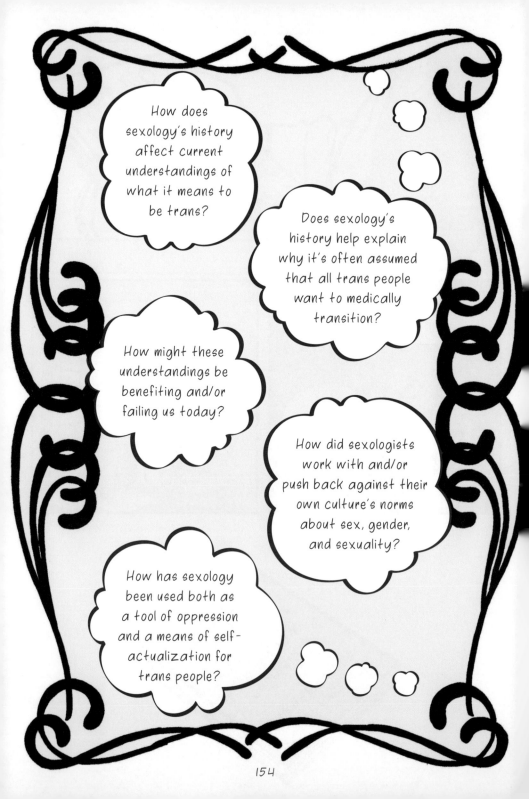

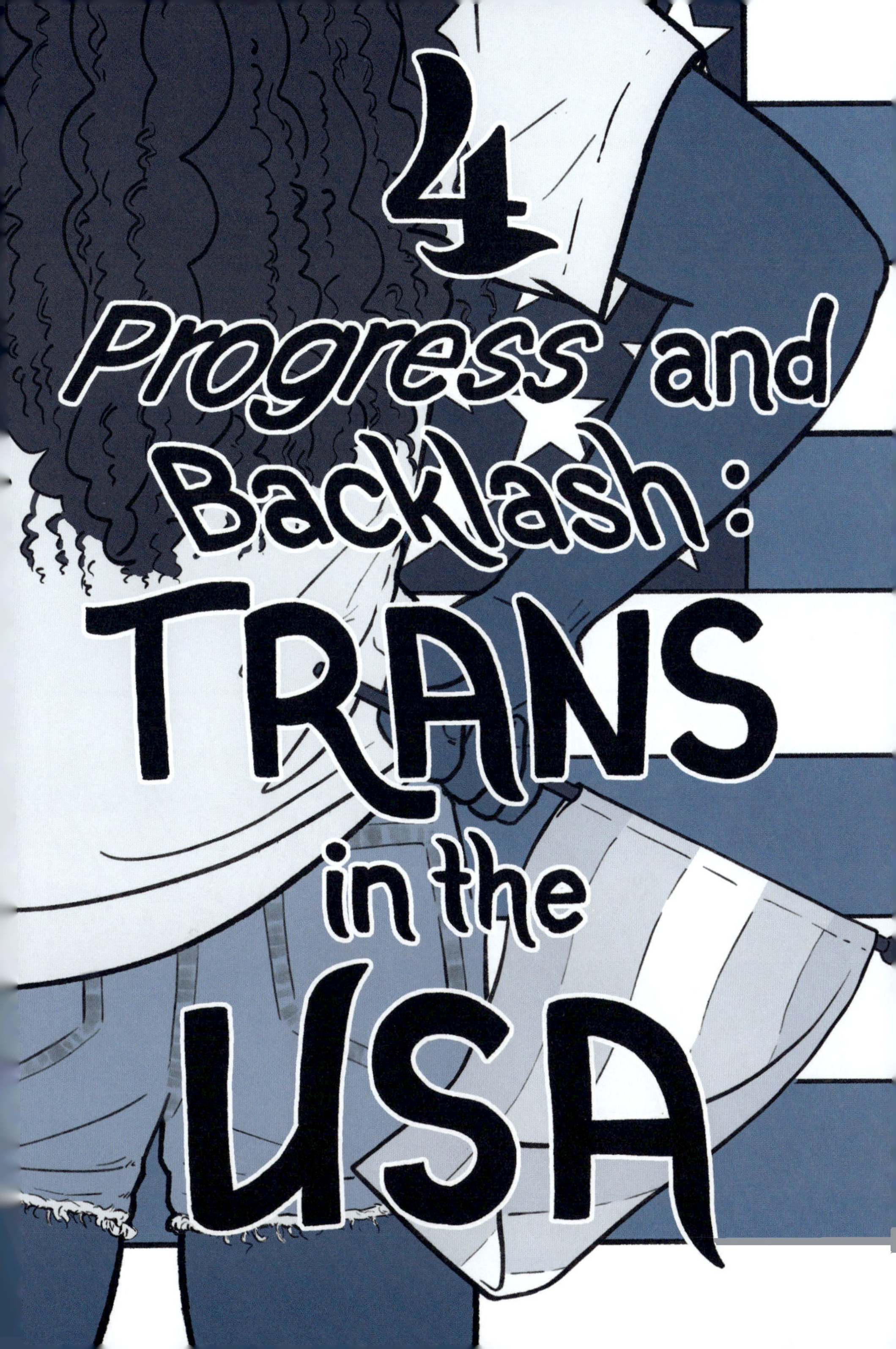
4
Progress and Backlash:
TRANS
in the
USA

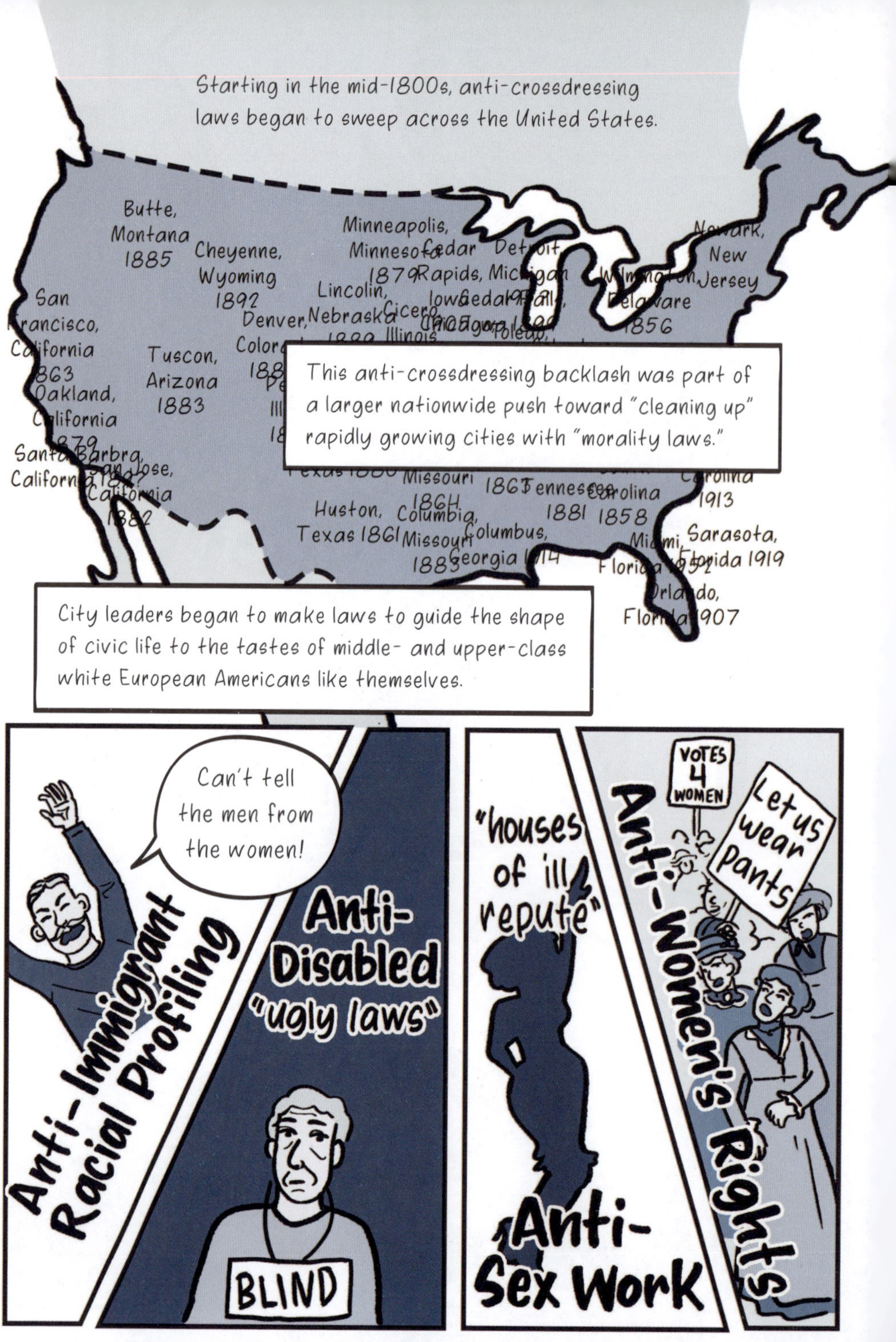

Starting in the mid-1800s, anti-crossdressing laws began to sweep across the United States.
Butte, Montana 1885
Cheyenne, Wyoming 1892
San Francisco, California 1863
Oakland, California 1879
Tuscon, Arizona 1883
Minneapolis, Minnesota 1879
Lincoln, Nebraska
Newark, New Jersey
Delaware 1856
Huston, Texas 1861
Columbia, Missouri 1883
Tennessee 1881
Carolina 1858
Sarasota, Florida 1919
Orlando, Florida 1907
This anti-crossdressing backlash was part of a larger nationwide push toward "cleaning up" rapidly growing cities with "morality laws."
City leaders began to make laws to guide the shape of civic life to the tastes of middle- and upper-class white European Americans like themselves.
Can't tell the men from the women!
Anti-Immigrant Racial Profiling
Anti-Disabled "ugly laws"
BLIND
"houses of ill repute"
Anti-Sex Work
VOTES 4 WOMEN
Let us wear pants
Anti-Women's Rights

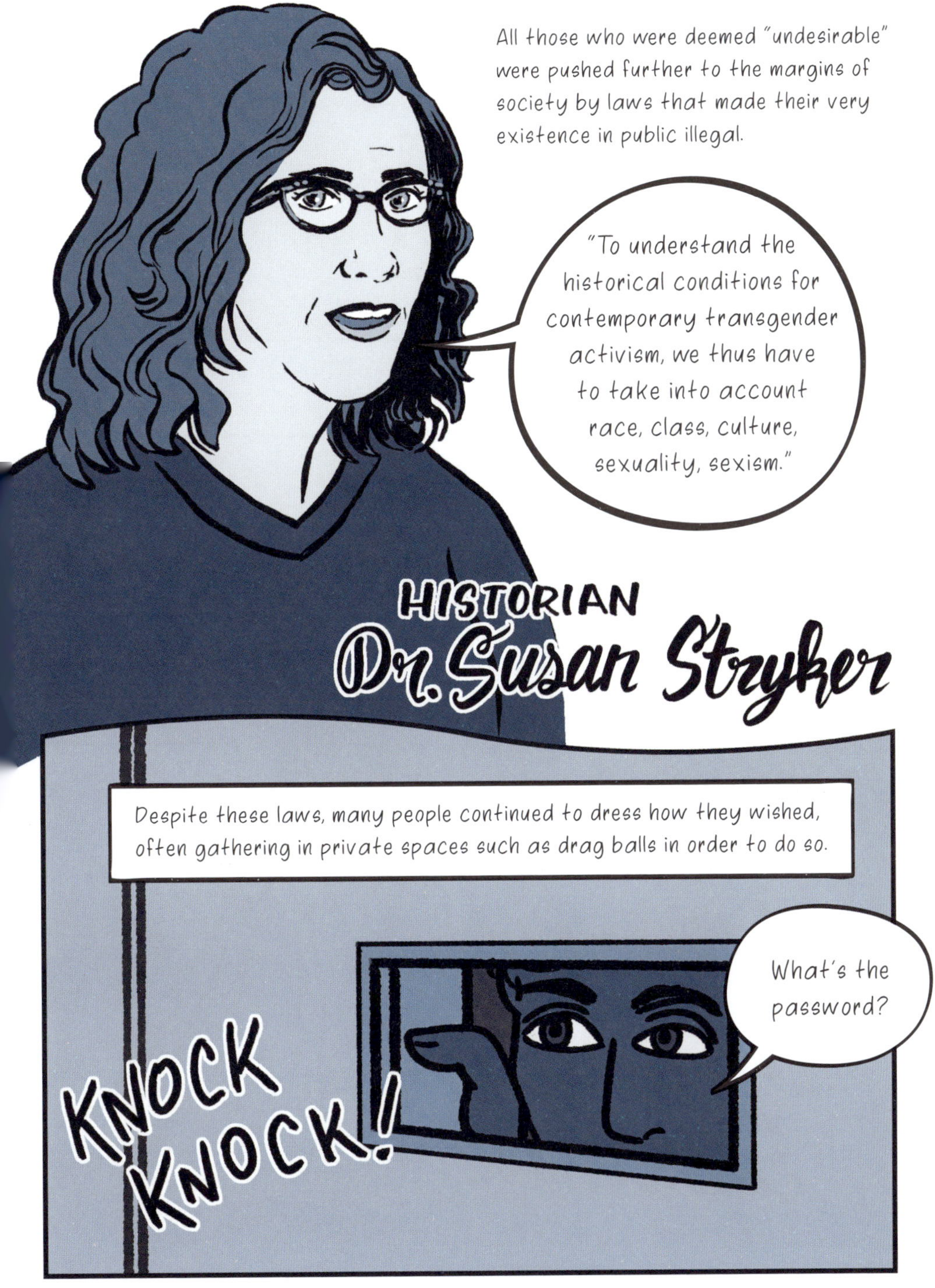
All those who were deemed "undesirable" were pushed further to the margins of society by laws that made their very existence in public illegal.
"To understand the historical conditions for contemporary transgender activism, we thus have to take into account race, class, culture, sexuality, sexism."
HISTORIAN
Dr. Susan Stryker
Despite these laws, many people continued to dress how they wished, often gathering in private spaces such as drag balls in order to do so.
KNOCK KNOCK!
What's the password?

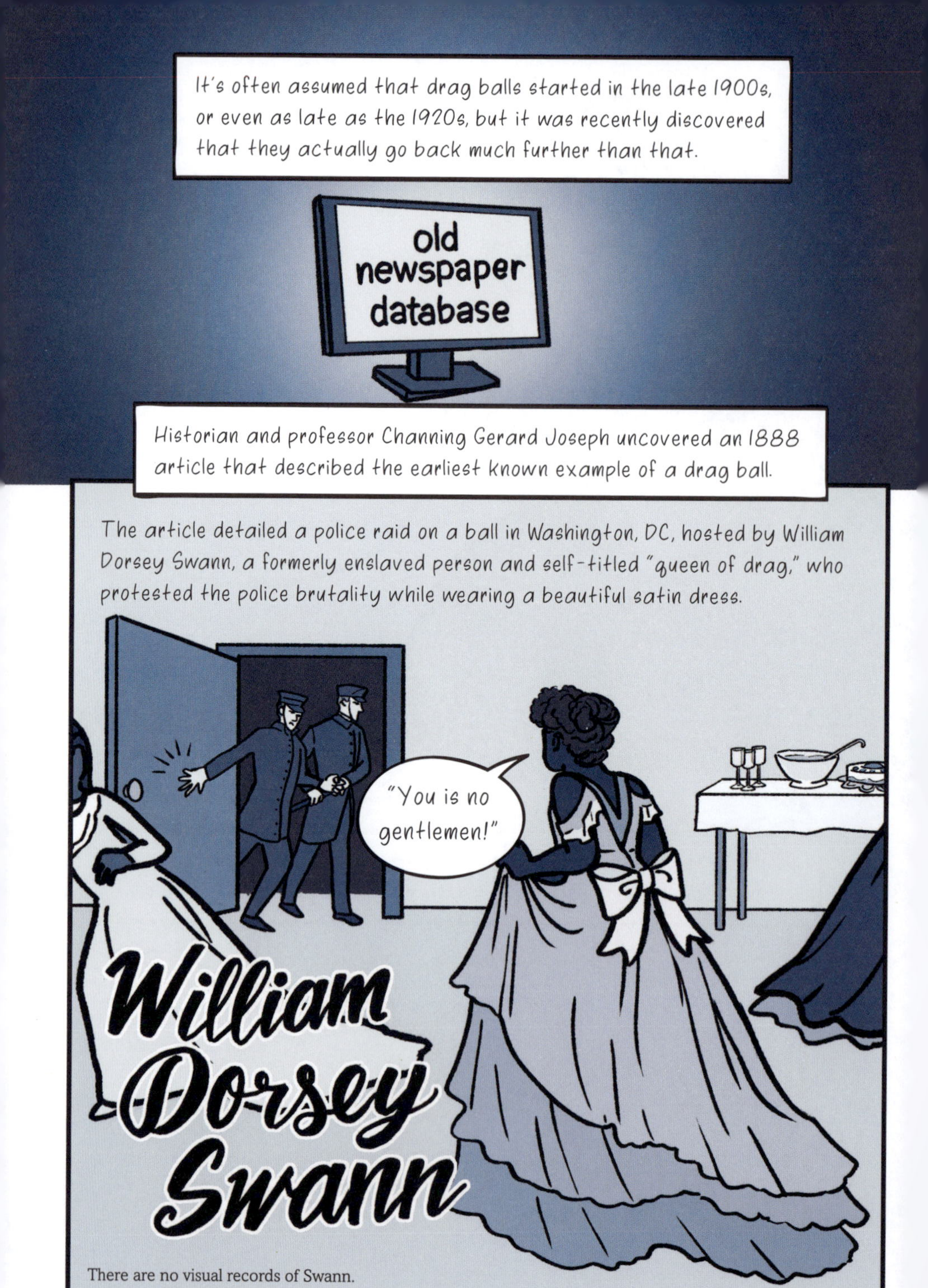
It's often assumed that drag balls started in the late 1900s, or even as late as the 1920s, but it was recently discovered that they actually go back much further than that.
old newspaper database
Historian and professor Channing Gerard Joseph uncovered an 1888 article that described the earliest known example of a drag ball.
The article detailed a police raid on a ball in Washington, DC, hosted by William Dorsey Swann, a formerly enslaved person and self-titled "queen of drag," who protested the police brutality while wearing a beautiful satin dress.
"You is no gentlemen!"
William Dorsey Swann
There are no visual records of Swann.

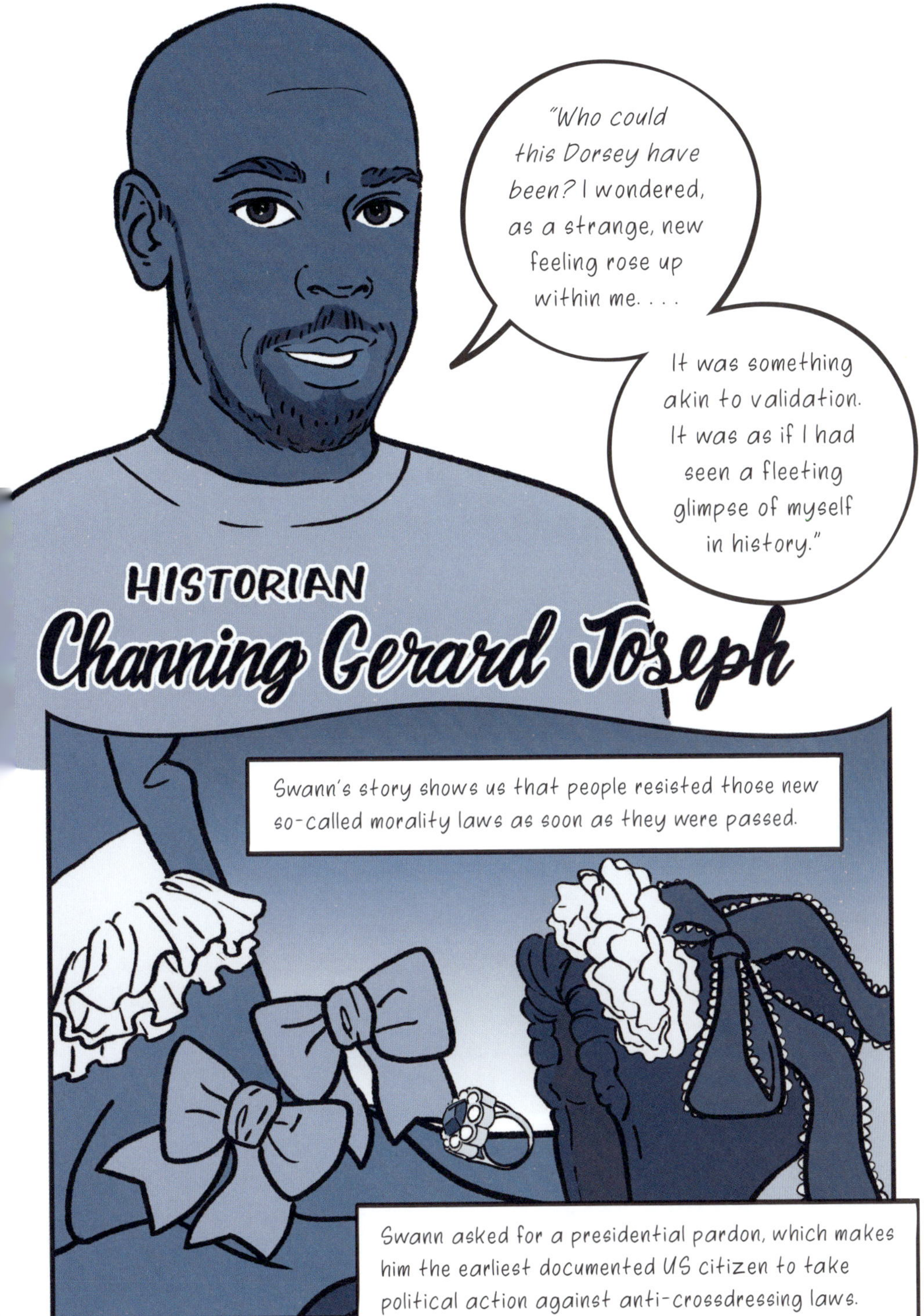
"Who could this Dorsey have been? I wondered, as a strange, new feeling rose up within me. . . .
It was something akin to validation. It was as if I had seen a fleeting glimpse of myself in history."
HISTORIAN
Channing Gerard Joseph
Swann's story shows us that people resisted those new so-called morality laws as soon as they were passed.
Swann asked for a presidential pardon, which makes him the earliest documented US citizen to take political action against anti-crossdressing laws.

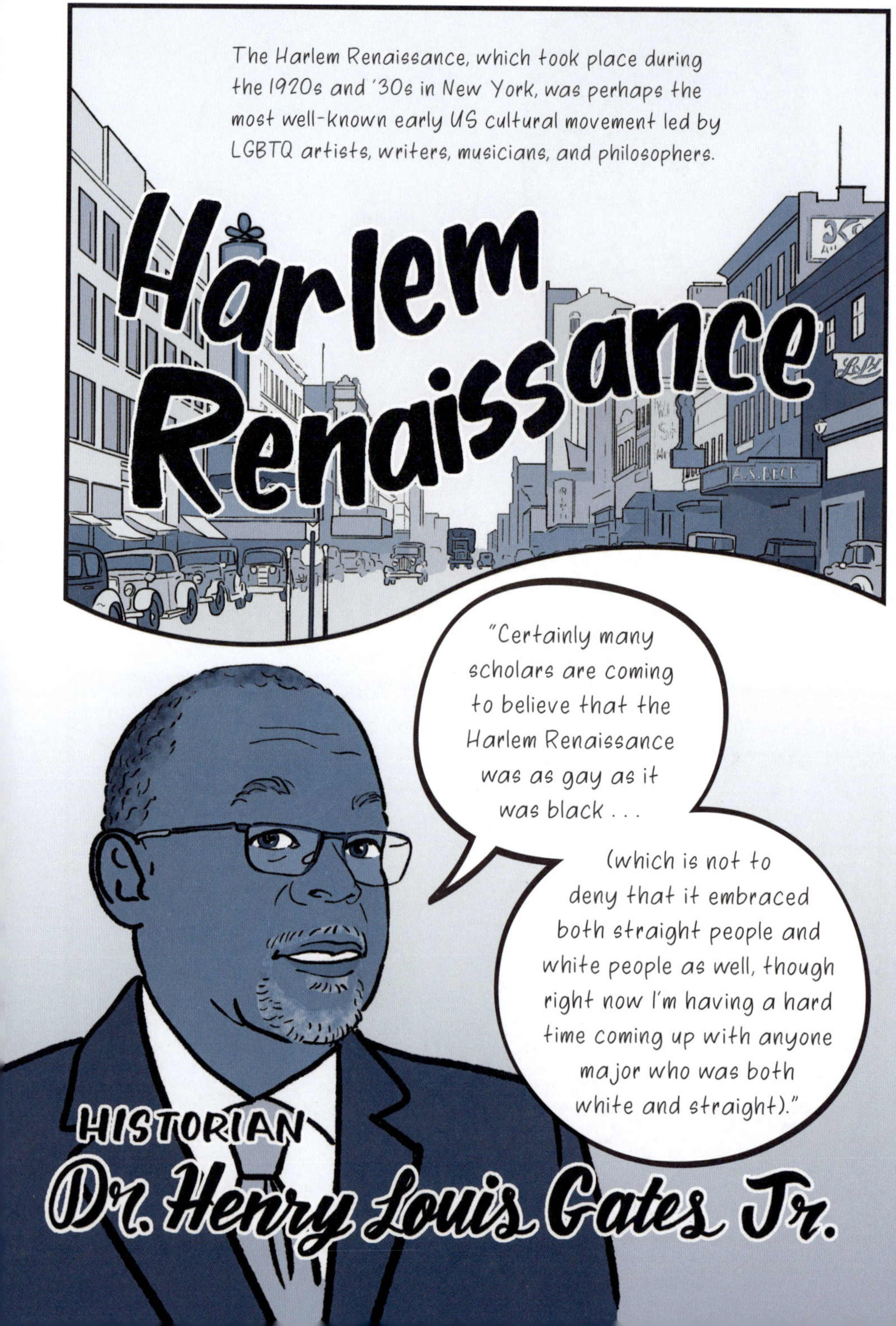

The Harlem Renaissance, which took place during the 1920s and '30s in New York, was perhaps the most well-known early US cultural movement led by LGBTQ artists, writers, musicians, and philosophers.
Harlem Renaissance
A.S. BECK
"Certainly many scholars are coming to believe that the Harlem Renaissance was as gay as it was black . . .
(which is not to deny that it embraced both straight people and white people as well, though right now I'm having a hard time coming up with anyone major who was both white and straight)."
HISTORIAN
Dr. Henry Louis Gates Jr.

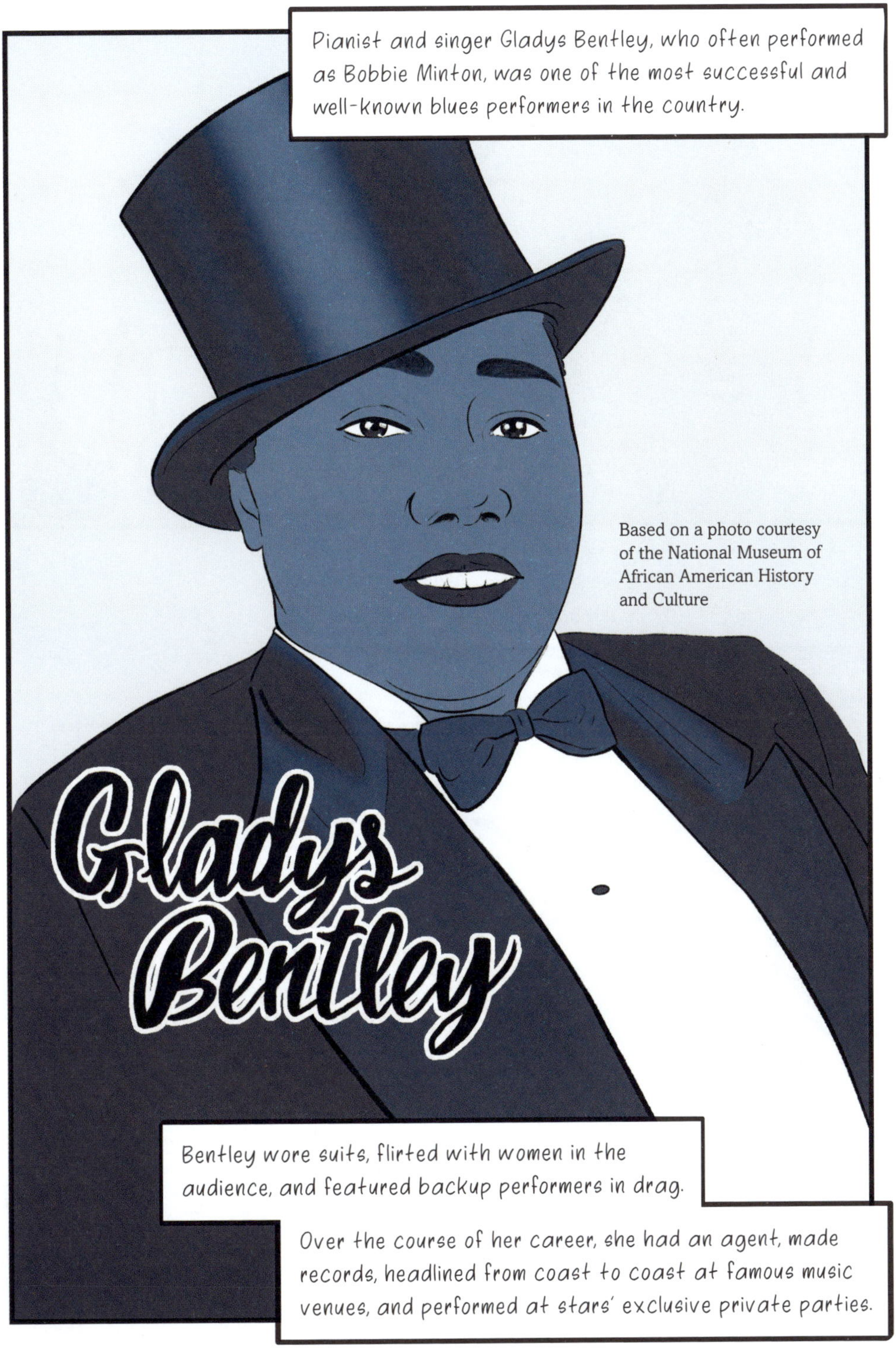
Pianist and singer Gladys Bentley, who often performed as Bobbie Minton, was one of the most successful and well-known blues performers in the country.
Based on a photo courtesy of the National Museum of African American History and Culture
Gladys Bentley
Bentley wore suits, flirted with women in the audience, and featured backup performers in drag.
Over the course of her career, she had an agent, made records, headlined from coast to coast at famous music venues, and performed at stars' exclusive private parties.

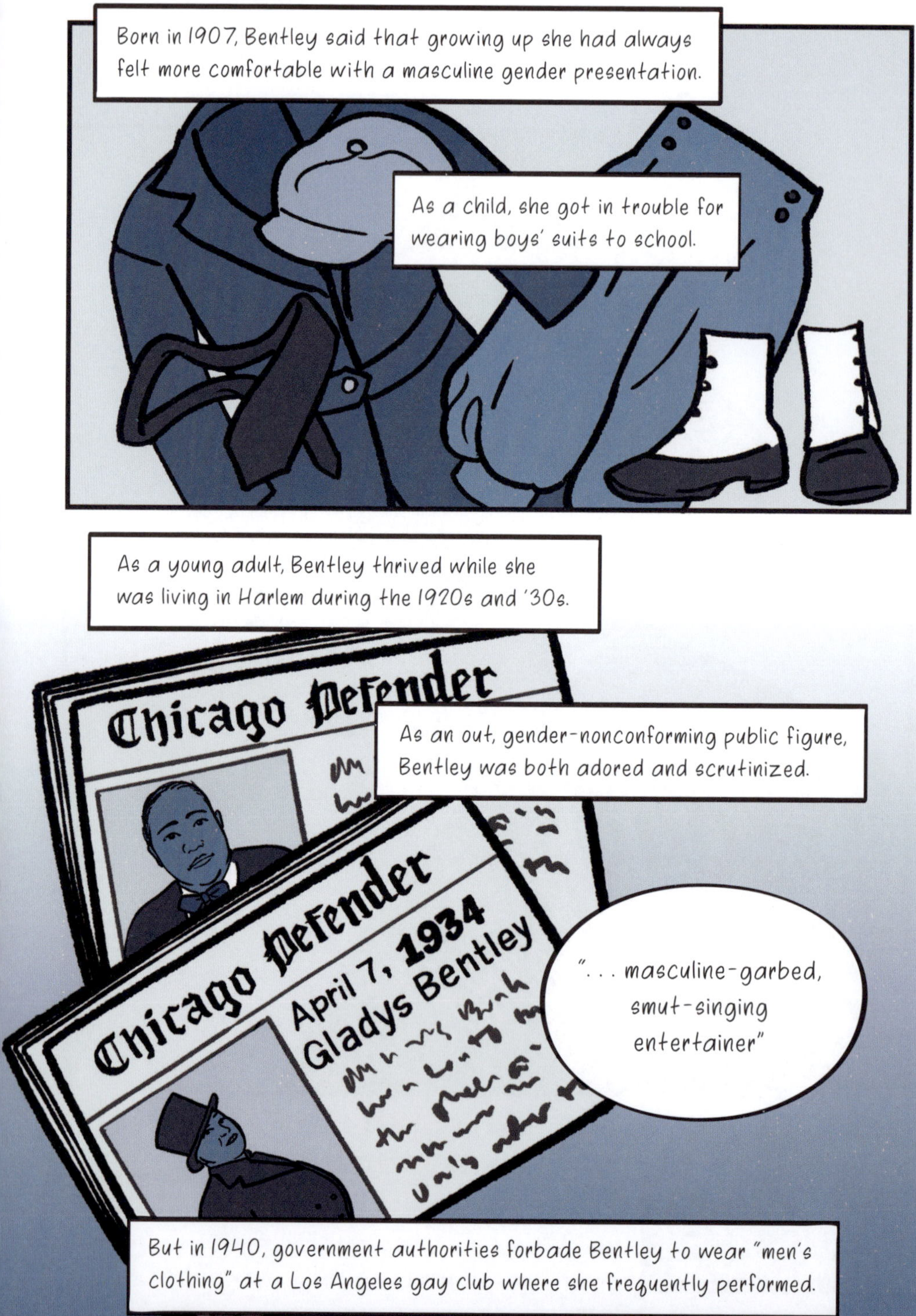
Born in 1907, Bentley said that growing up she had always felt more comfortable with a masculine gender presentation.
As a child, she got in trouble for wearing boys' suits to school.
As a young adult, Bentley thrived while she was living in Harlem during the 1920s and '30s.
Chicago Defender
As an out, gender-nonconforming public figure, Bentley was both adored and scrutinized.
Chicago Defender
April 7, 1934
Gladys Bentley
". . . masculine-garbed, smut-singing entertainer"
But in 1940, government authorities forbade Bentley to wear "men's clothing" at a Los Angeles gay club where she frequently performed.

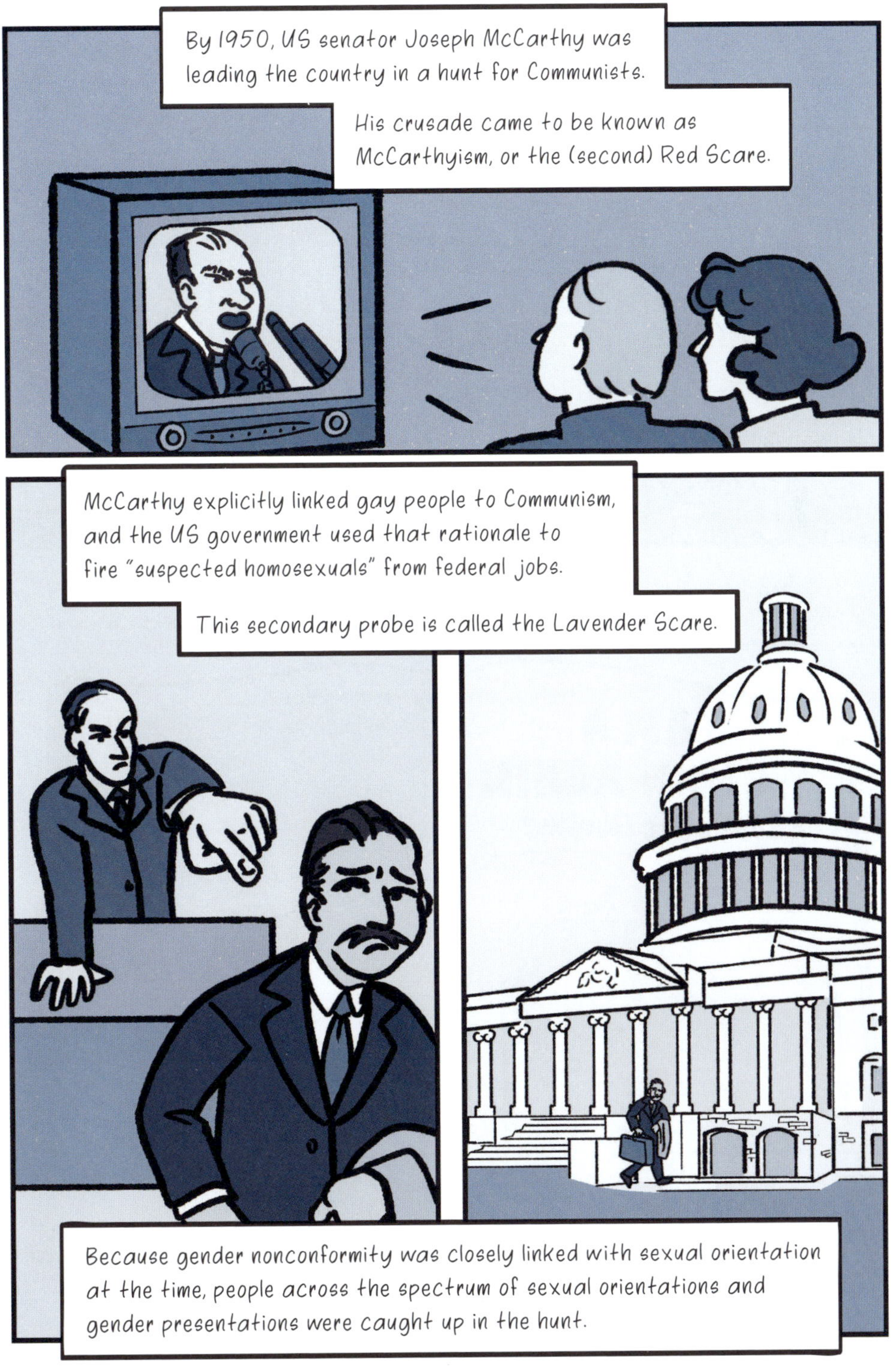
By 1950, US senator Joseph McCarthy was leading the country in a hunt for Communists.
His crusade came to be known as McCarthyism, or the (second) Red Scare.
McCarthy explicitly linked gay people to Communism, and the US government used that rationale to fire "suspected homosexuals" from federal jobs.
This secondary probe is called the Lavender Scare.
Because gender nonconformity was closely linked with sexual orientation at the time, people across the spectrum of sexual orientations and gender presentations were caught up in the hunt.

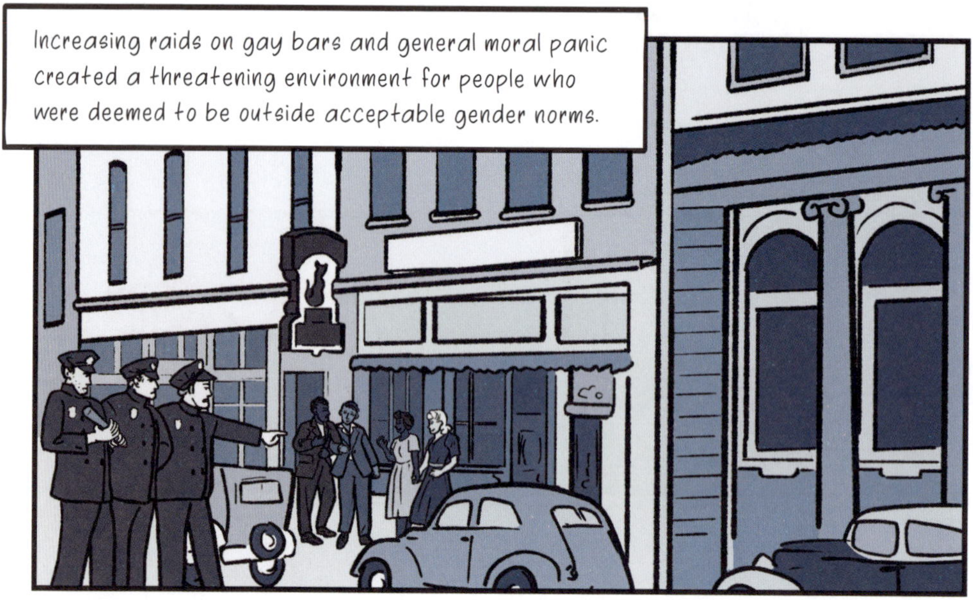
Increasing raids on gay bars and general moral panic created a threatening environment for people who were deemed to be outside acceptable gender norms.

In 1952, Bentley wrote an article titled "I Am a Woman Again," in which she said she'd been cured of her lesbian gender-bending lifestyle by taking "female hormones."

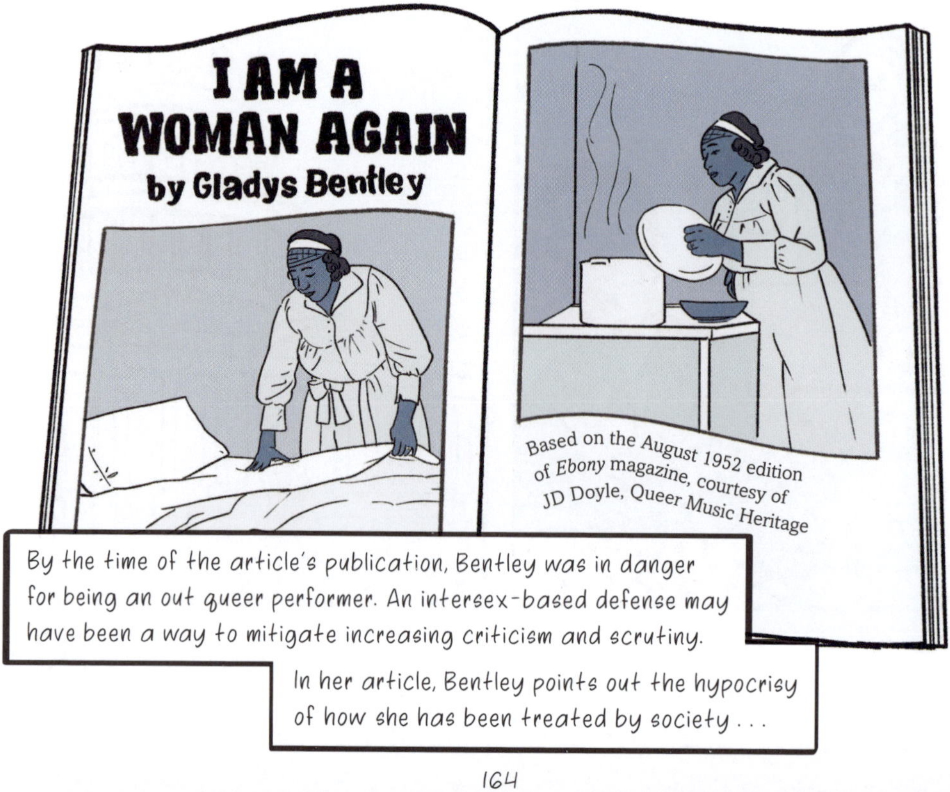
I AM A WOMAN AGAIN
by Gladys Bentley
Based on the August 1952 edition of *Ebony* magazine, courtesy of JD Doyle, Queer Music Heritage
By the time of the article's publication, Bentley was in danger for being an out queer performer. An intersex-based defense may have been a way to mitigate increasing criticism and scrutiny.
In her article, Bentley points out the hypocrisy of how she has been treated by society . . .

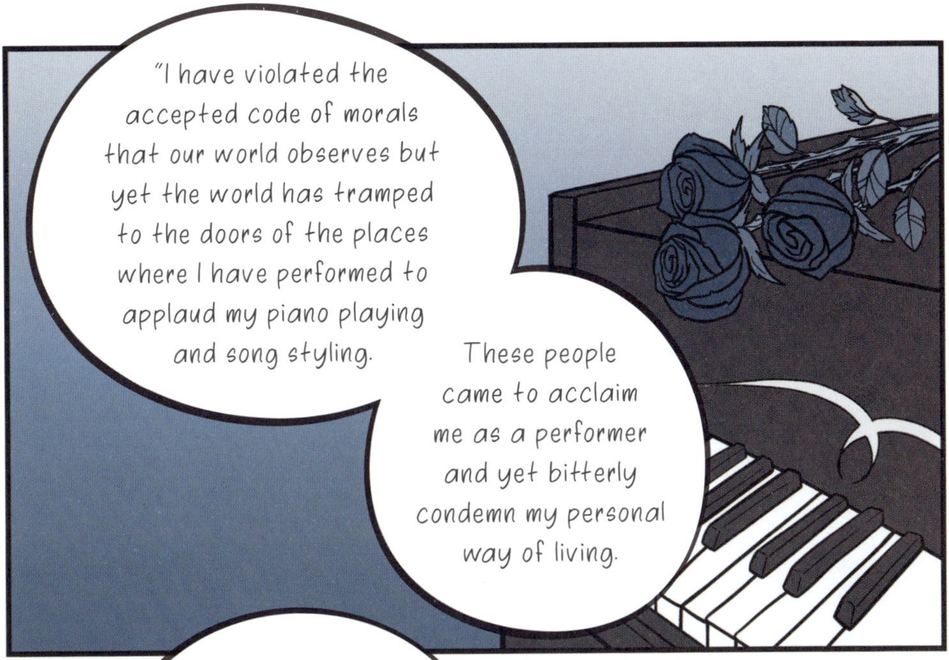
"I have violated the accepted code of morals that our world observes but yet the world has tramped to the doors of the places where I have performed to applaud my piano playing and song styling.
These people came to acclaim me as a performer and yet bitterly condemn my personal way of living.

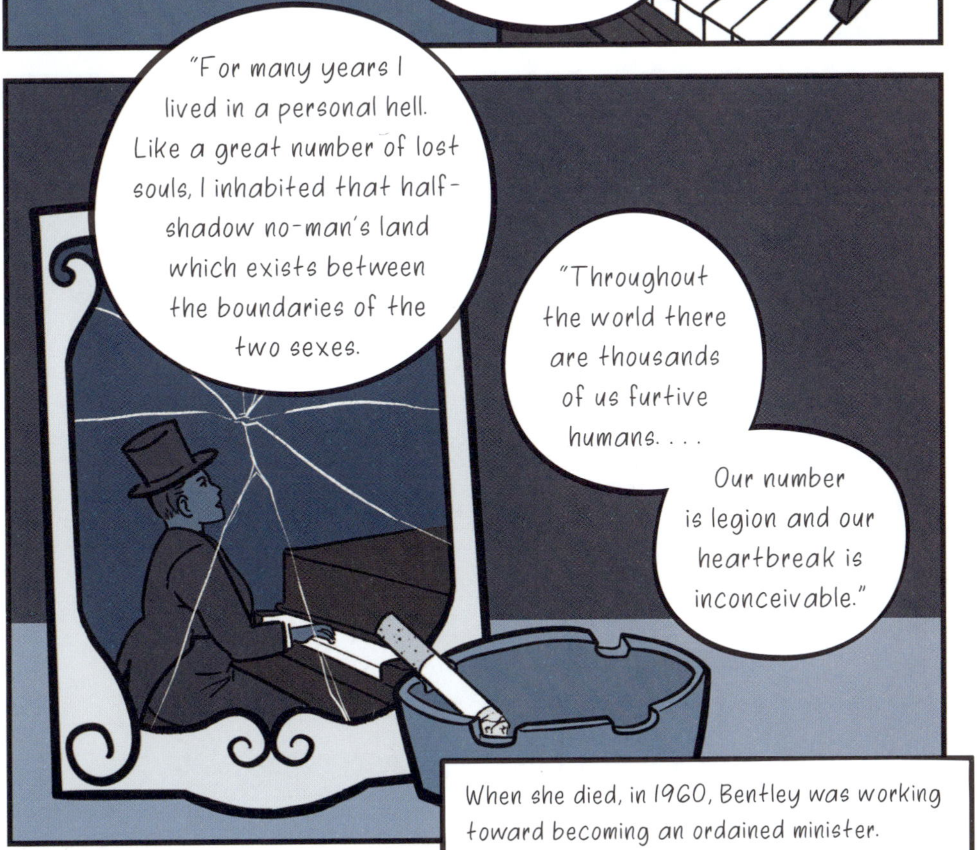
"For many years I lived in a personal hell. Like a great number of lost souls, I inhabited that half-shadow no-man's land which exists between the boundaries of the two sexes.
"Throughout the world there are thousands of us furtive humans. . . .
Our number is legion and our heartbreak is inconceivable."
When she died, in 1960, Bentley was working toward becoming an ordained minister.

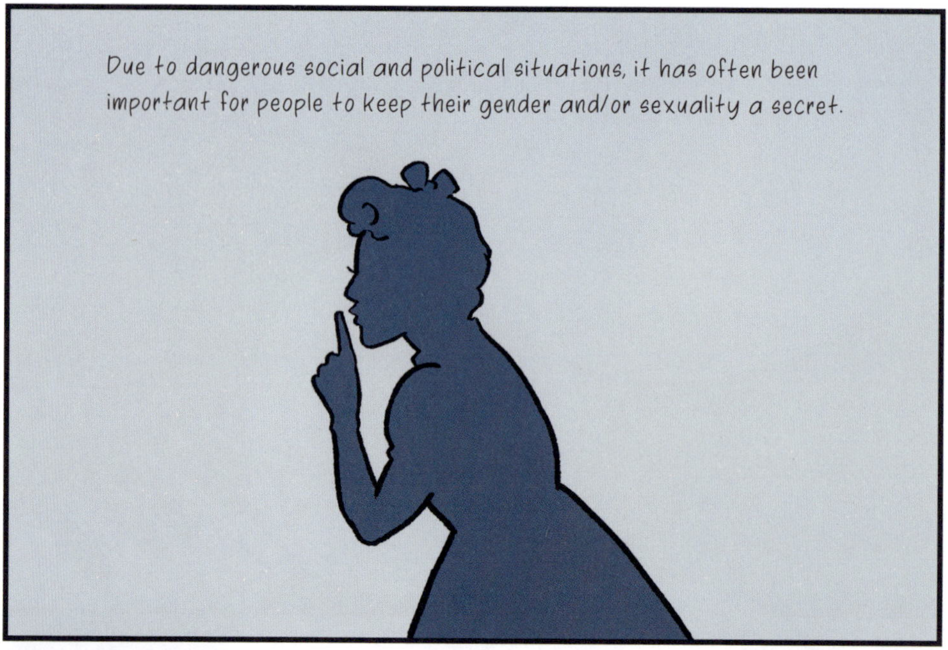
Due to dangerous social and political situations, it has often been important for people to keep their gender and/or sexuality a secret.

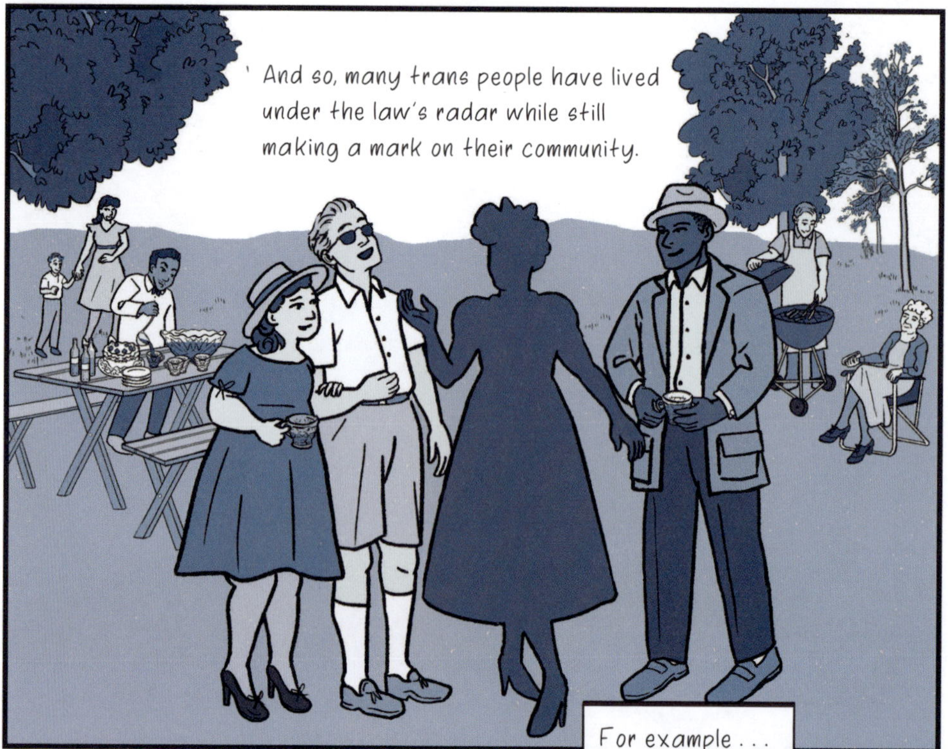
And so, many trans people have lived under the law's radar while still making a mark on their community.
For example . . .

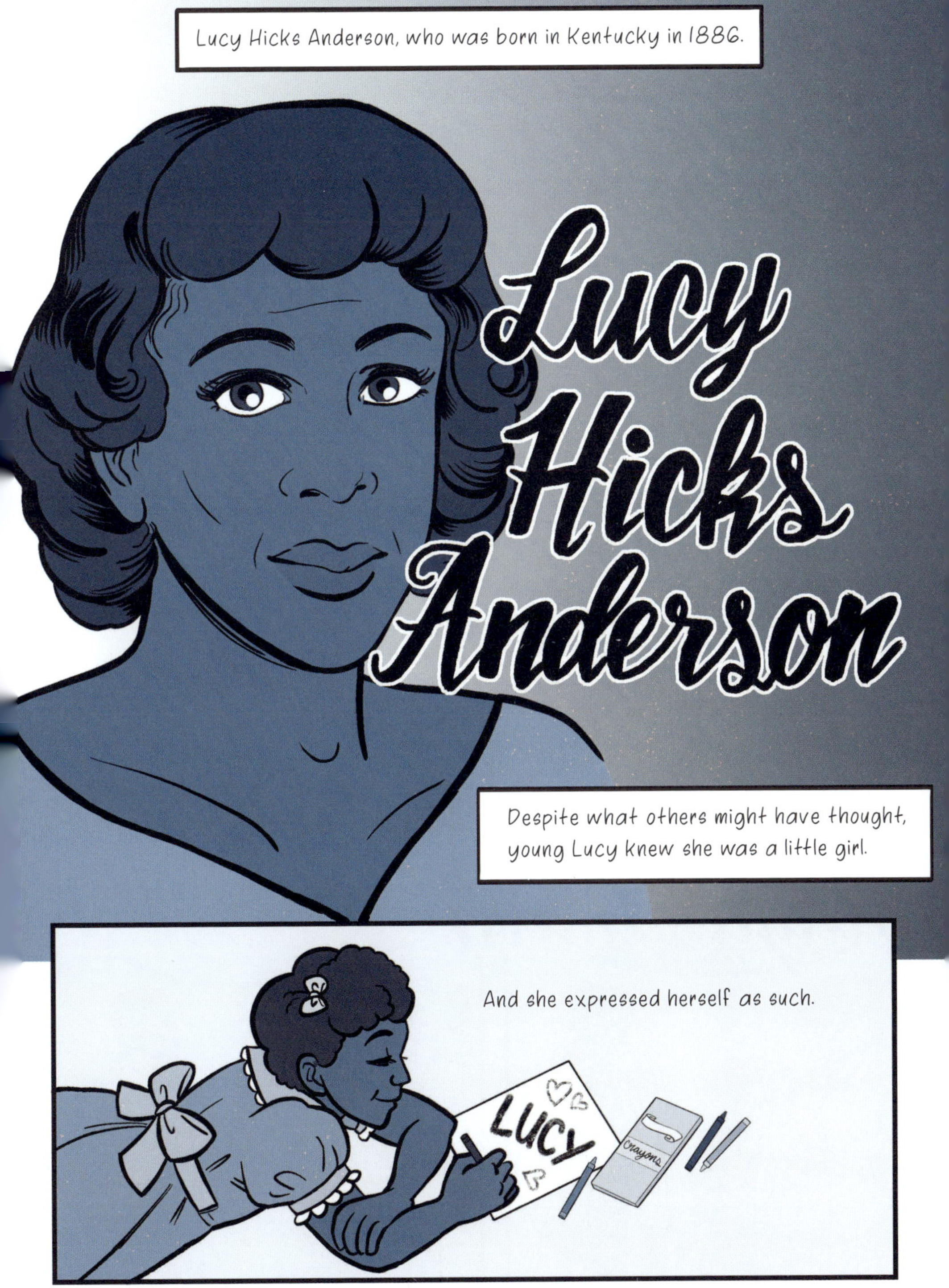
Lucy Hicks Anderson, who was born in Kentucky in 1886.
Lucy Hicks Anderson
Despite what others might have thought, young Lucy knew she was a little girl.
And she expressed herself as such.
LUCY
Crayons

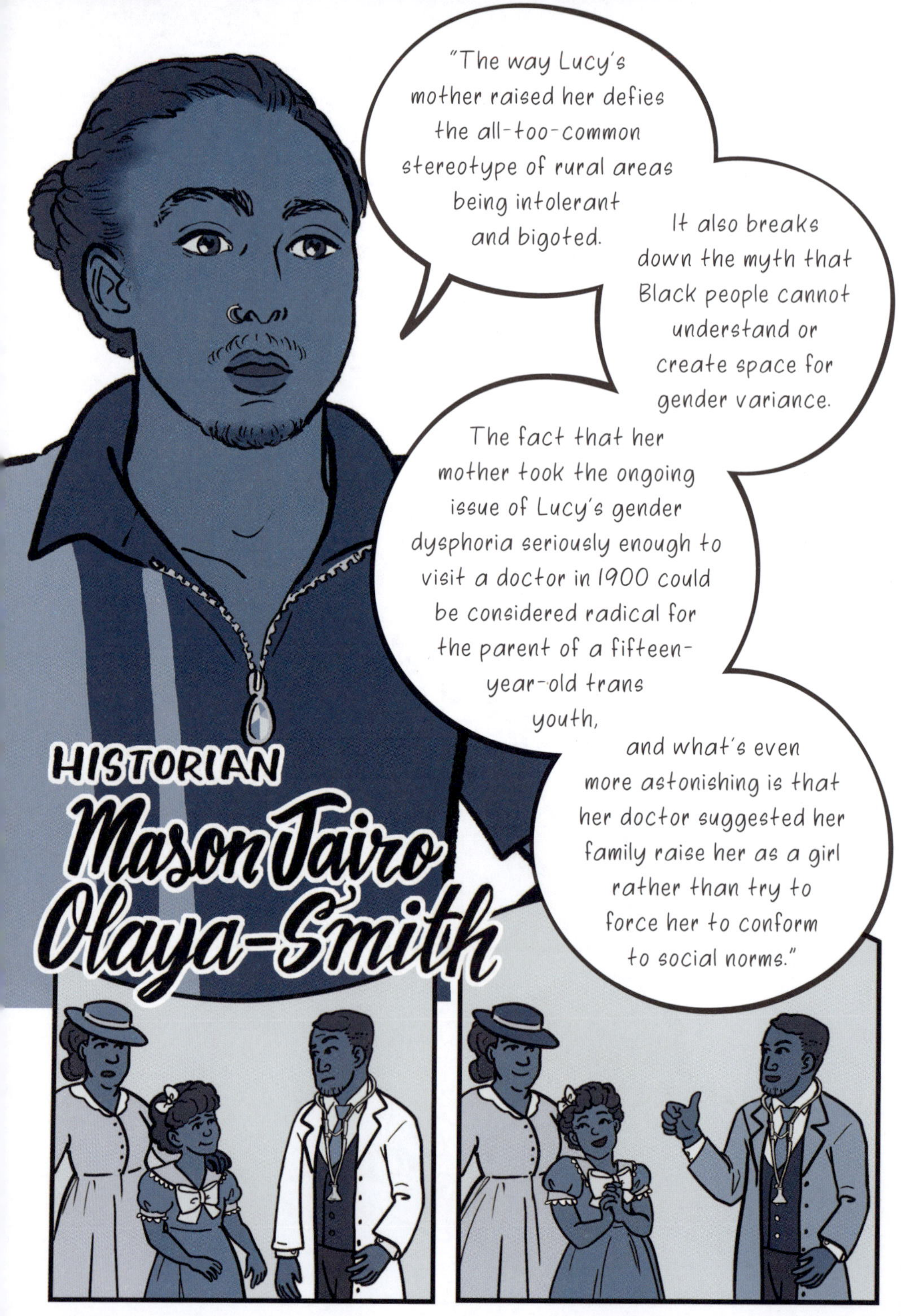
"The way Lucy's mother raised her defies the all-too-common stereotype of rural areas being intolerant and bigoted.
It also breaks down the myth that Black people cannot understand or create space for gender variance.
The fact that her mother took the ongoing issue of Lucy's gender dysphoria seriously enough to visit a doctor in 1900 could be considered radical for the parent of a fifteen-year-old trans youth,
and what's even more astonishing is that her doctor suggested her family raise her as a girl rather than try to force her to conform to social norms."
HISTORIAN
Mason Jairo Olaya-Smith

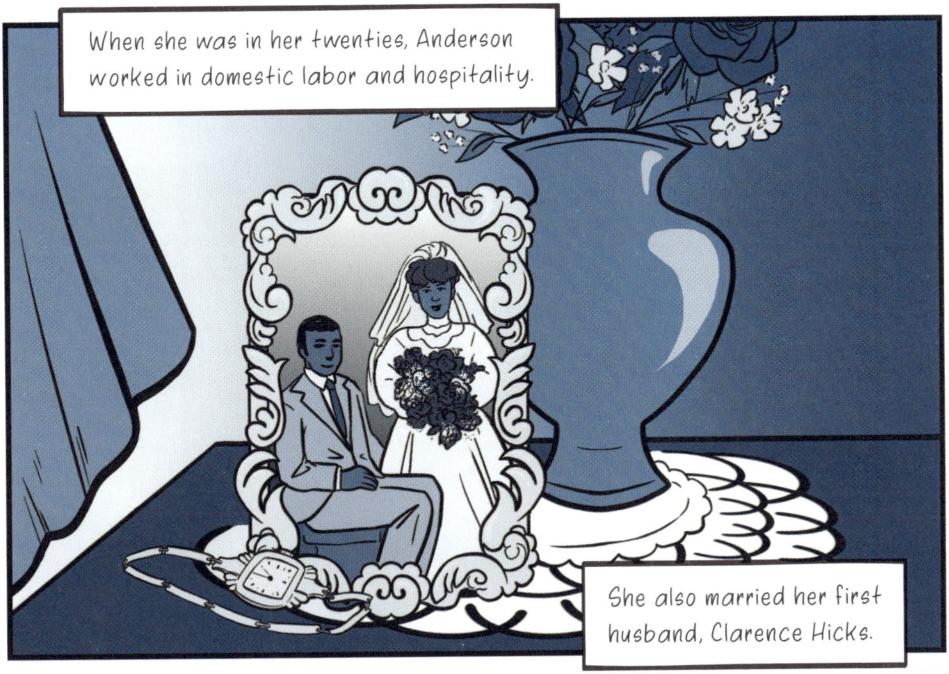
When she was in her twenties, Anderson worked in domestic labor and hospitality.
She also married her first husband, Clarence Hicks.

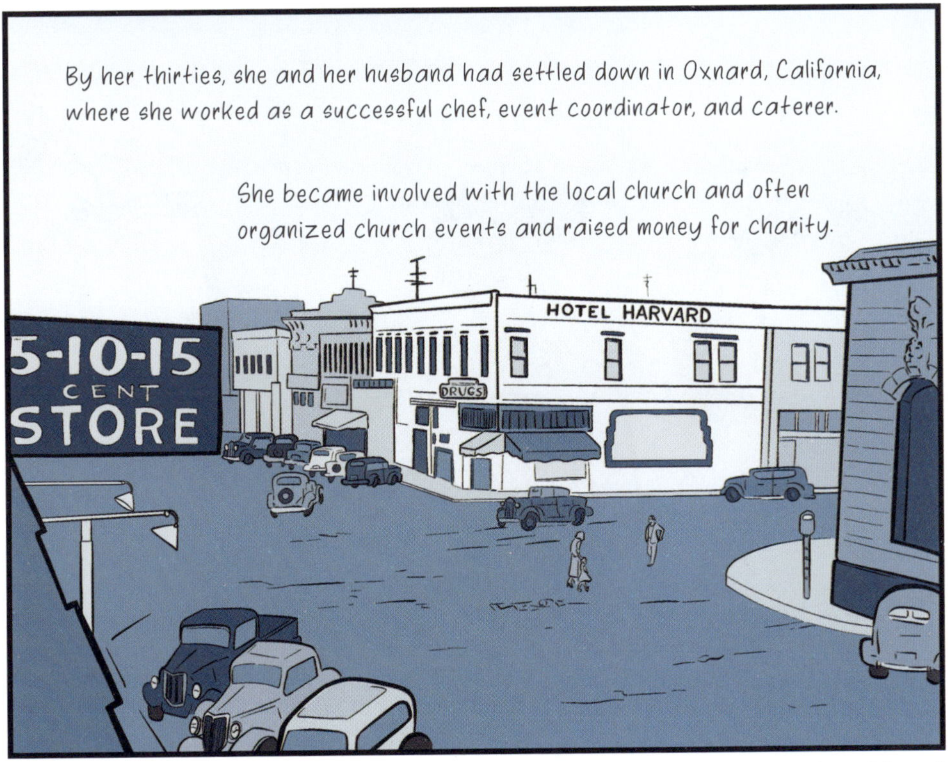
By her thirties, she and her husband had settled down in Oxnard, California, where she worked as a successful chef, event coordinator, and caterer.
She became involved with the local church and often organized church events and raised money for charity.
5-10-15 CENT STORE
HOTEL HARVARD
DRUGS

Based on a 1939 photo of Oxnard from the Oxnard Public Library

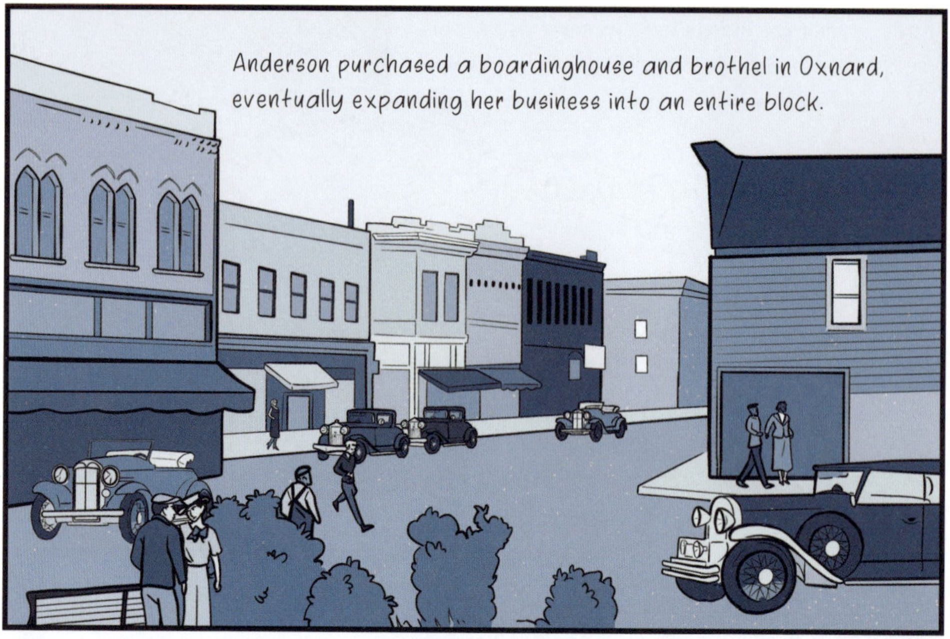
Anderson purchased a boardinghouse and brothel in Oxnard, eventually expanding her business into an entire block.

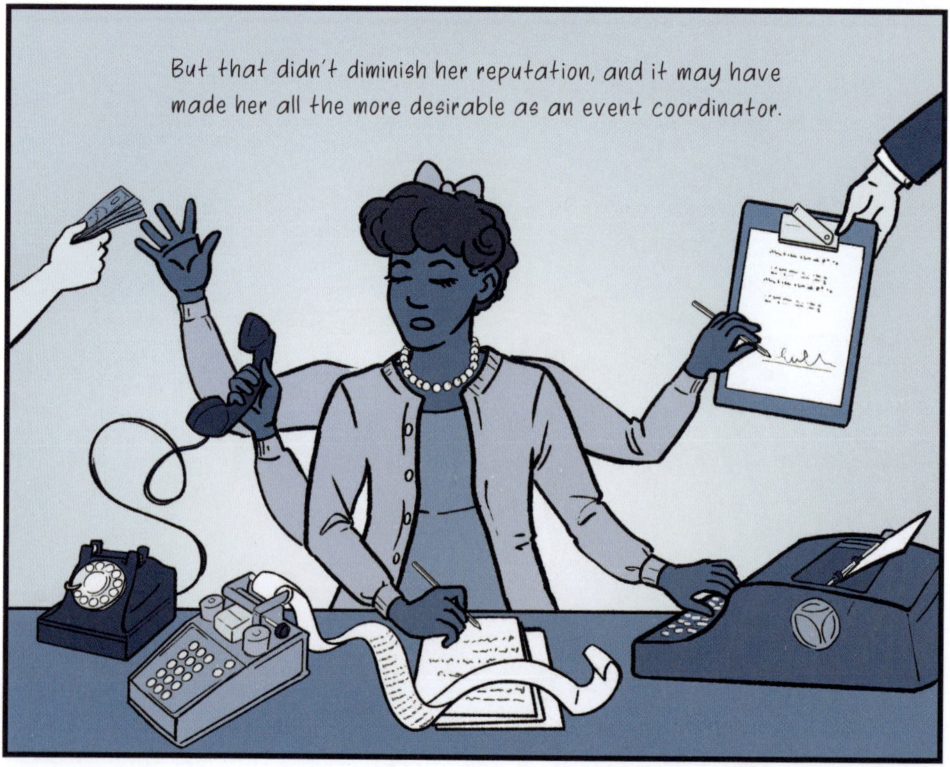
But that didn't diminish her reputation, and it may have made her all the more desirable as an event coordinator.

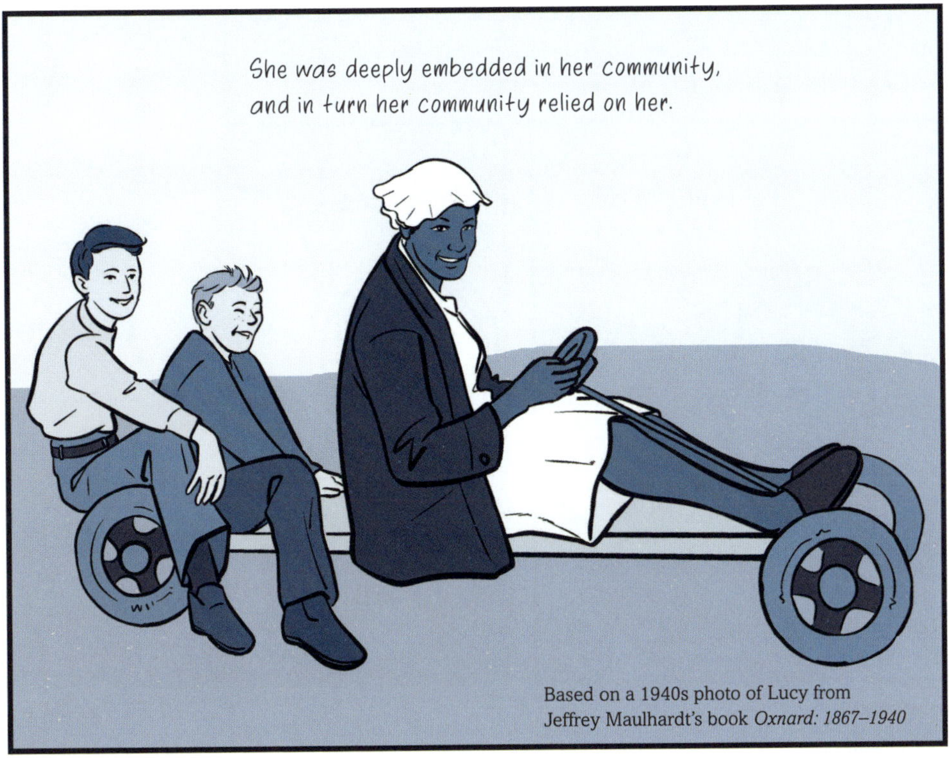
She was deeply embedded in her community,
and in turn her community relied on her.
Based on a 1940s photo of Lucy from
Jeffrey Maulhardt's book *Oxnard: 1867–1940*

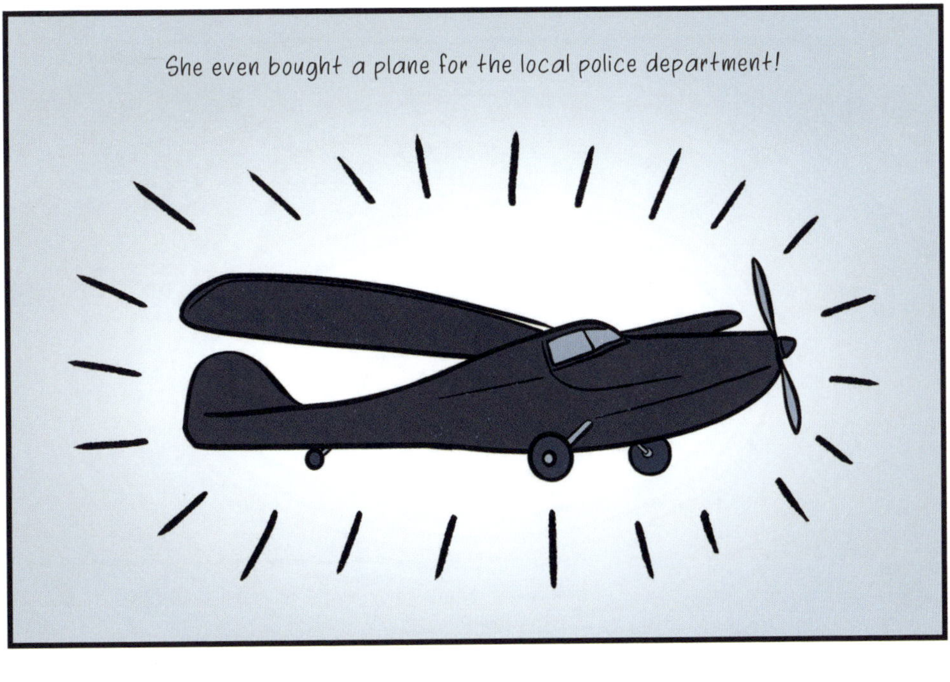
She even bought a plane for the local police department!

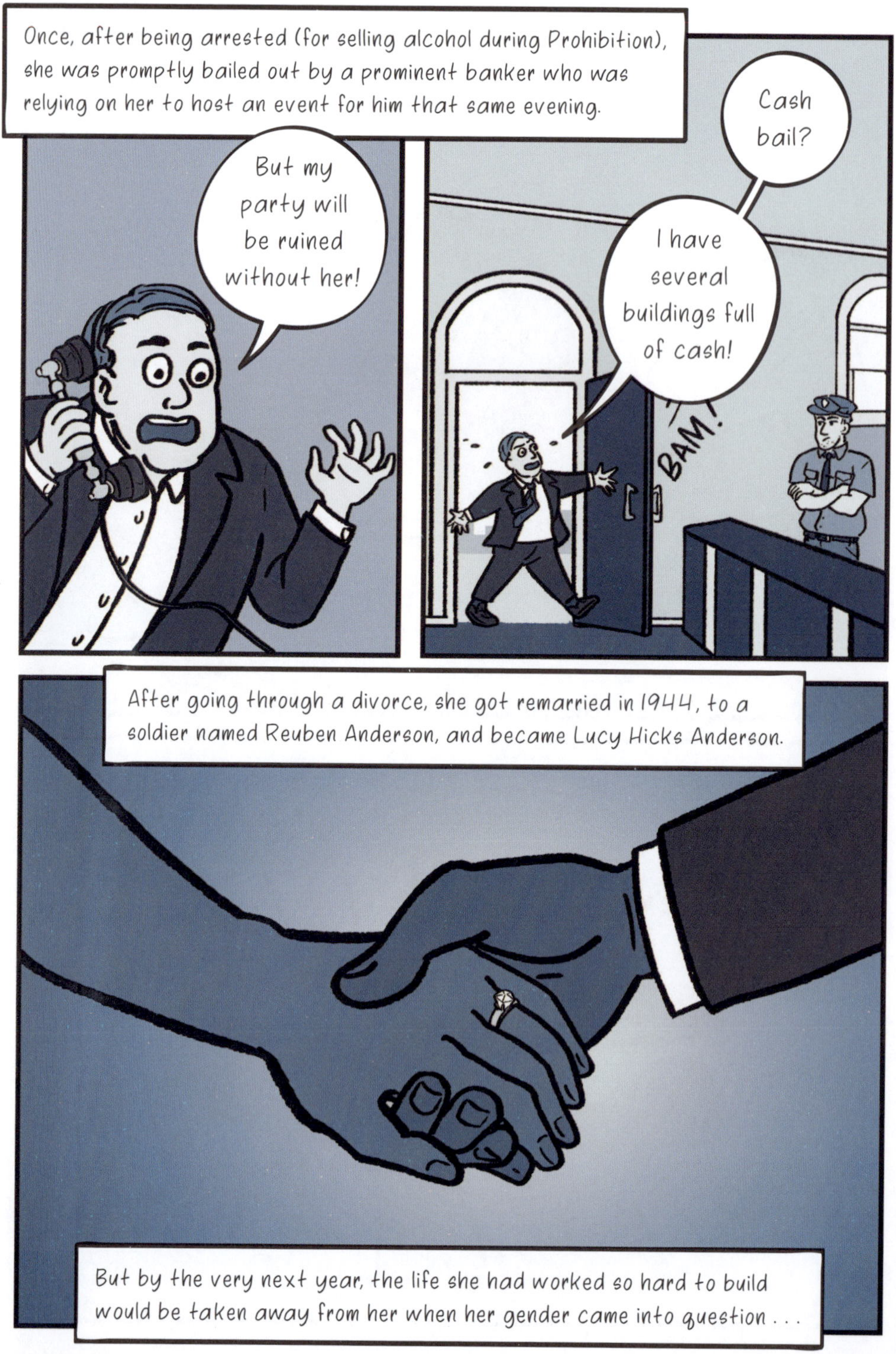
Once, after being arrested (for selling alcohol during Prohibition), she was promptly bailed out by a prominent banker who was relying on her to host an event for him that same evening.
But my party will be ruined without her!
I have several buildings full of cash!
Cash bail?
BAM!
After going through a divorce, she got remarried in 1944, to a soldier named Reuben Anderson, and became Lucy Hicks Anderson.
But by the very next year, the life she had worked so hard to build would be taken away from her when her gender came into question . . .

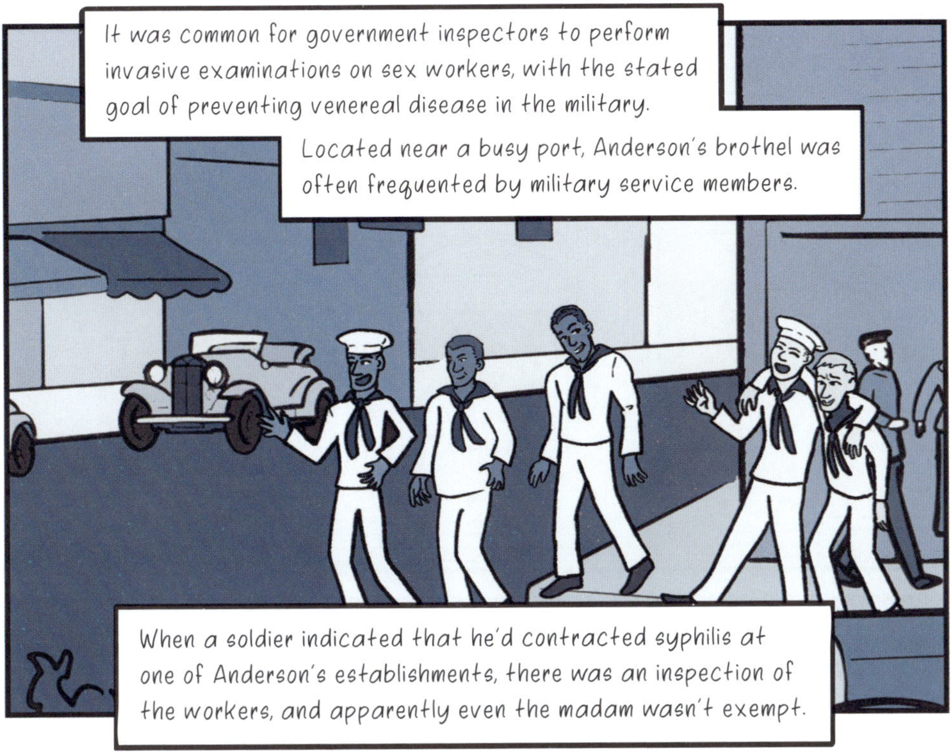
It was common for government inspectors to perform invasive examinations on sex workers, with the stated goal of preventing venereal disease in the military.
Located near a busy port, Anderson's brothel was often frequented by military service members.
When a soldier indicated that he'd contracted syphilis at one of Anderson's establishments, there was an inspection of the workers, and apparently even the madam wasn't exempt.

Upon inspecting her, the doctor decided she was a man, and said so publicly.

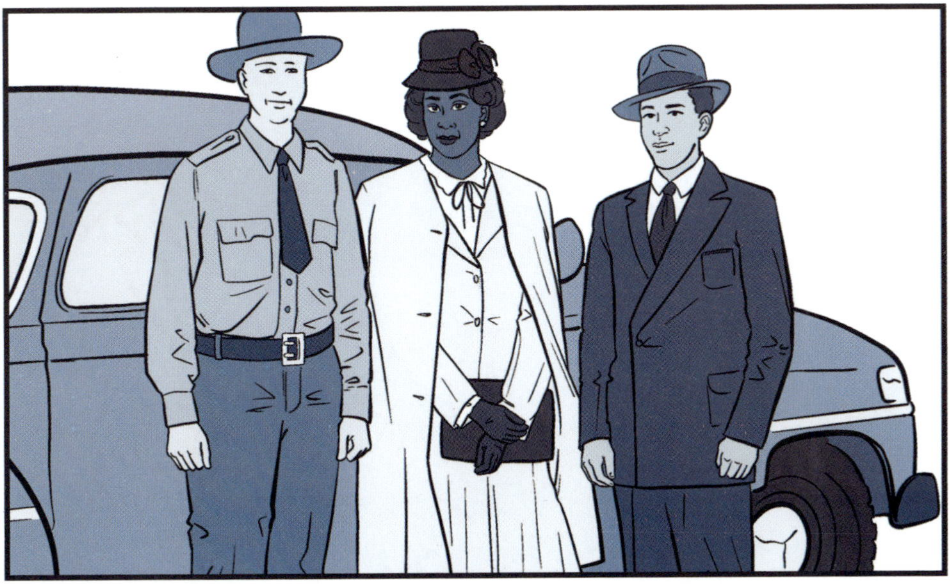

Based on a photo of Lucy, courtesy of the Museum of Ventura County

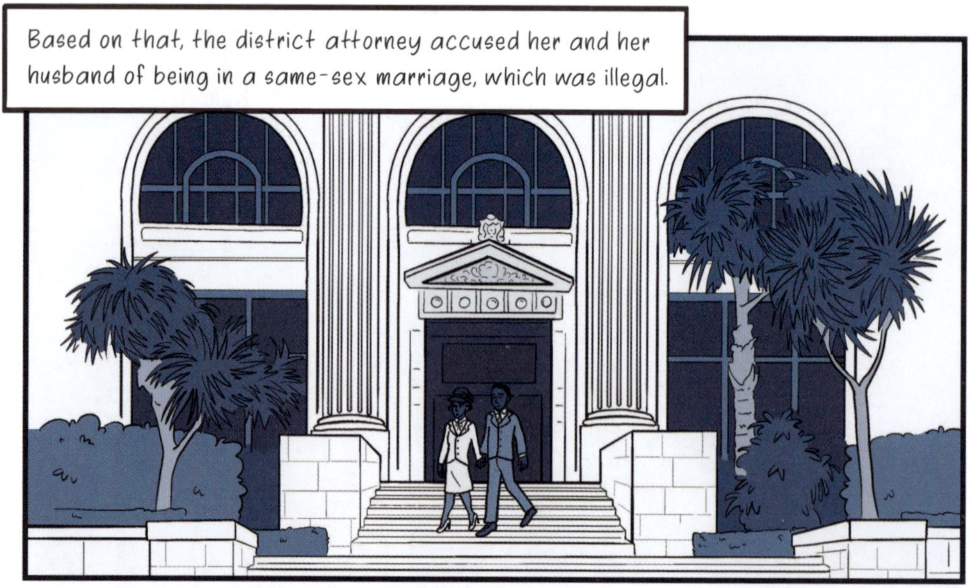
Based on that, the district attorney accused her and her husband of being in a same-sex marriage, which was illegal.

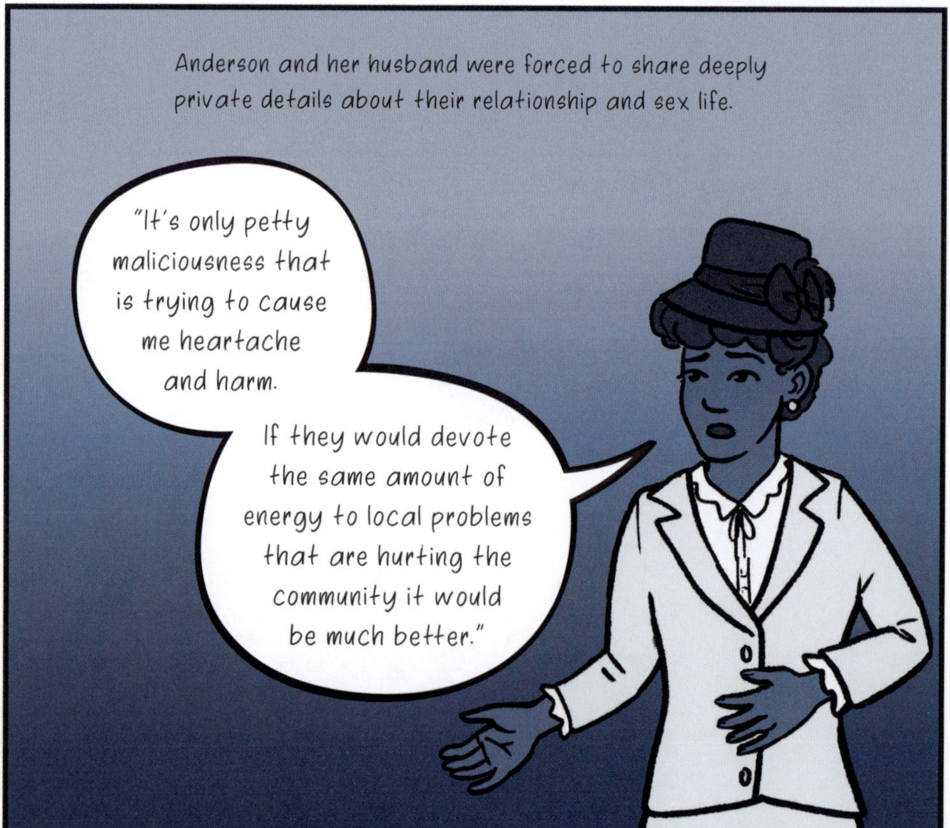
Anderson and her husband were forced to share deeply private details about their relationship and sex life.
"It's only petty maliciousness that is trying to cause me heartache and harm.
If they would devote the same amount of energy to local problems that are hurting the community it would be much better."

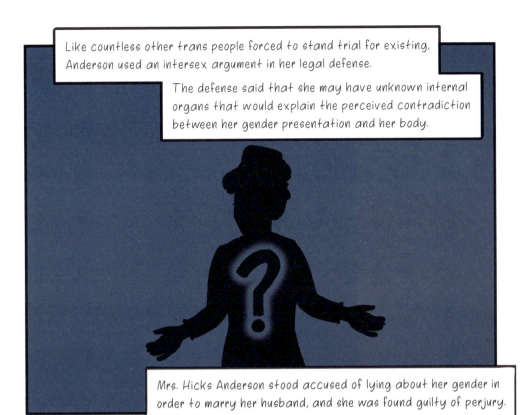

Like countless other trans people forced to stand trial for existing, Anderson used an intersex argument in her legal defense.

The defense said that she may have unknown internal organs that would explain the perceived contradiction between her gender presentation and her body.

Mrs. Hicks Anderson stood accused of lying about her gender in order to marry her husband, and she was found guilty of perjury.

Once the federal government got wind of her trial, she was put on trial yet again. This time she was accused of fraud and draft dodging. If found guilty, any money she had received as a benefit for being the wife of a GI would have to be returned.

Perhaps this could be pointed to as the first example of a US federal court case in defense of gay marriage, although that certainly wasn't how Anderson saw it.

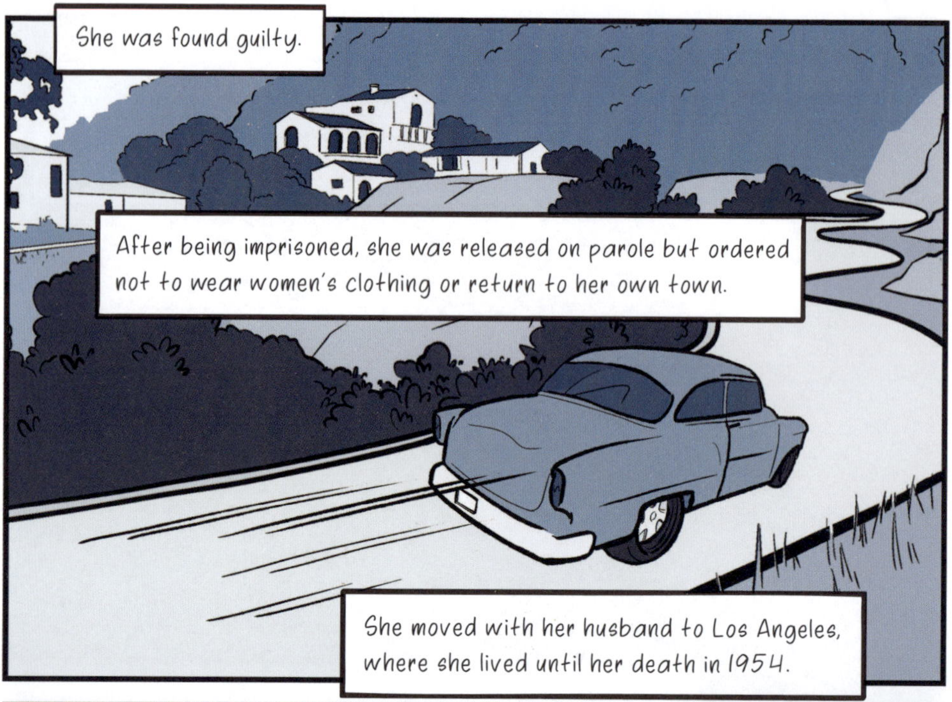
She was found guilty.
After being imprisoned, she was released on parole but ordered not to wear women's clothing or return to her own town.
She moved with her husband to Los Angeles, where she lived until her death in 1954.

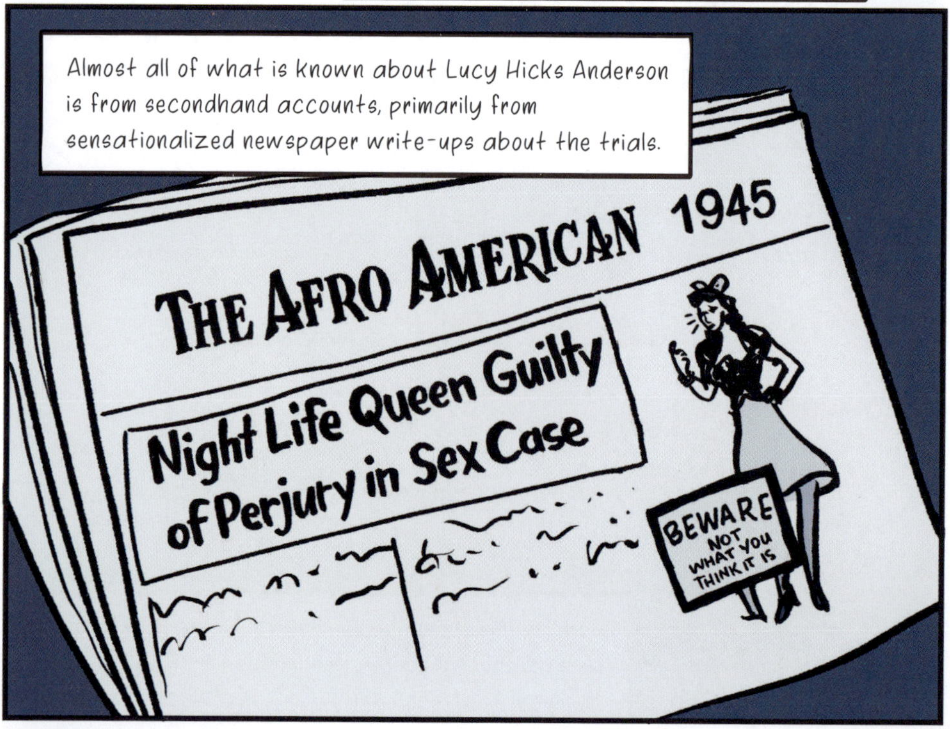
Almost all of what is known about Lucy Hicks Anderson is from secondhand accounts, primarily from sensationalized newspaper write-ups about the trials.
THE AFRO AMERICAN 1945
Night Life Queen Guilty of Perjury in Sex Case
BEWARE NOT WHAT YOU THINK IT IS

A headline and cartoon from shortly after Anderson's trial

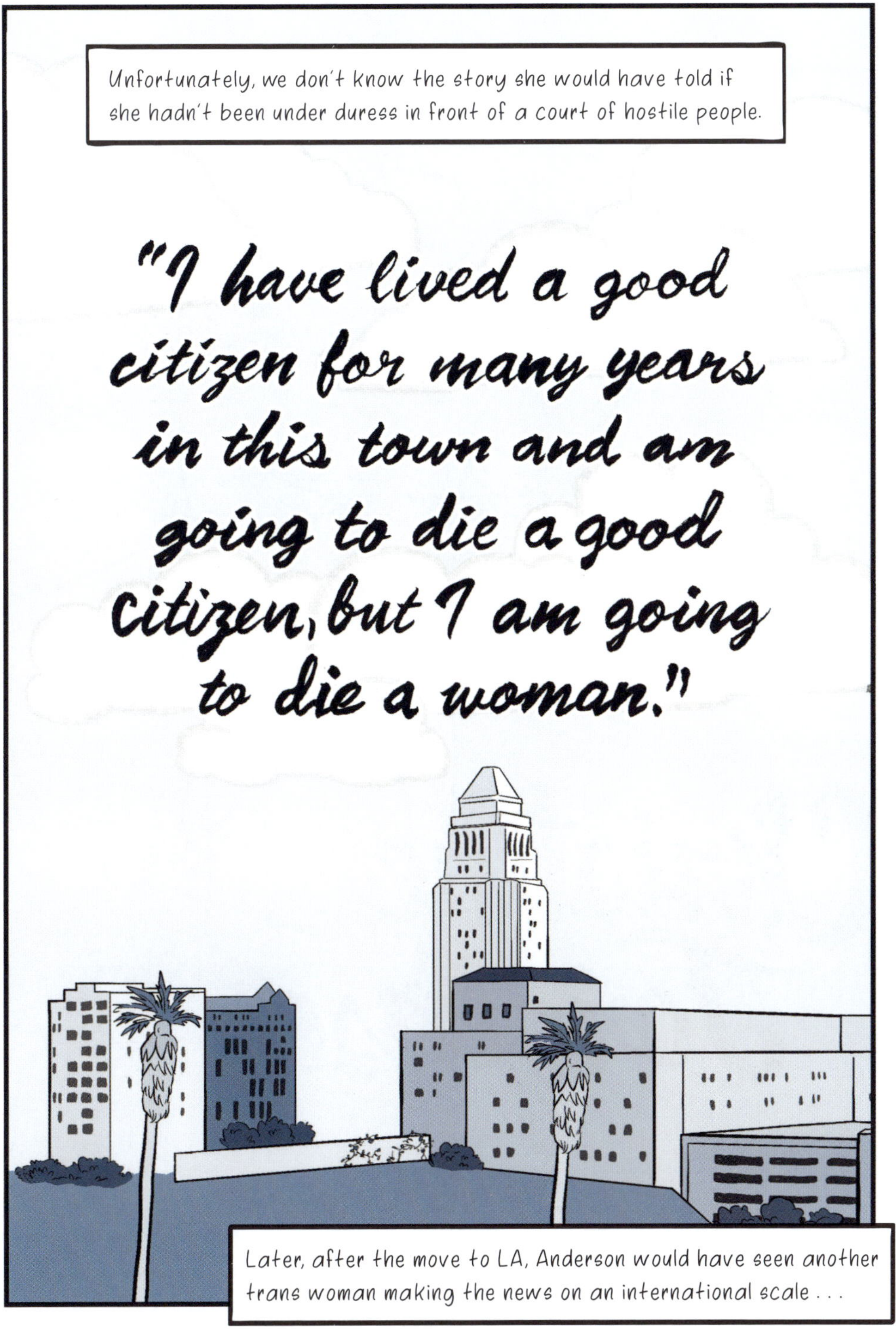
Unfortunately, we don't know the story she would have told if she hadn't been under duress in front of a court of hostile people.
"I have lived a good citizen for many years in this town and am going to die a good citizen, but I am going to die a woman."
Later, after the move to LA, Anderson would have seen another trans woman making the news on an international scale . . .

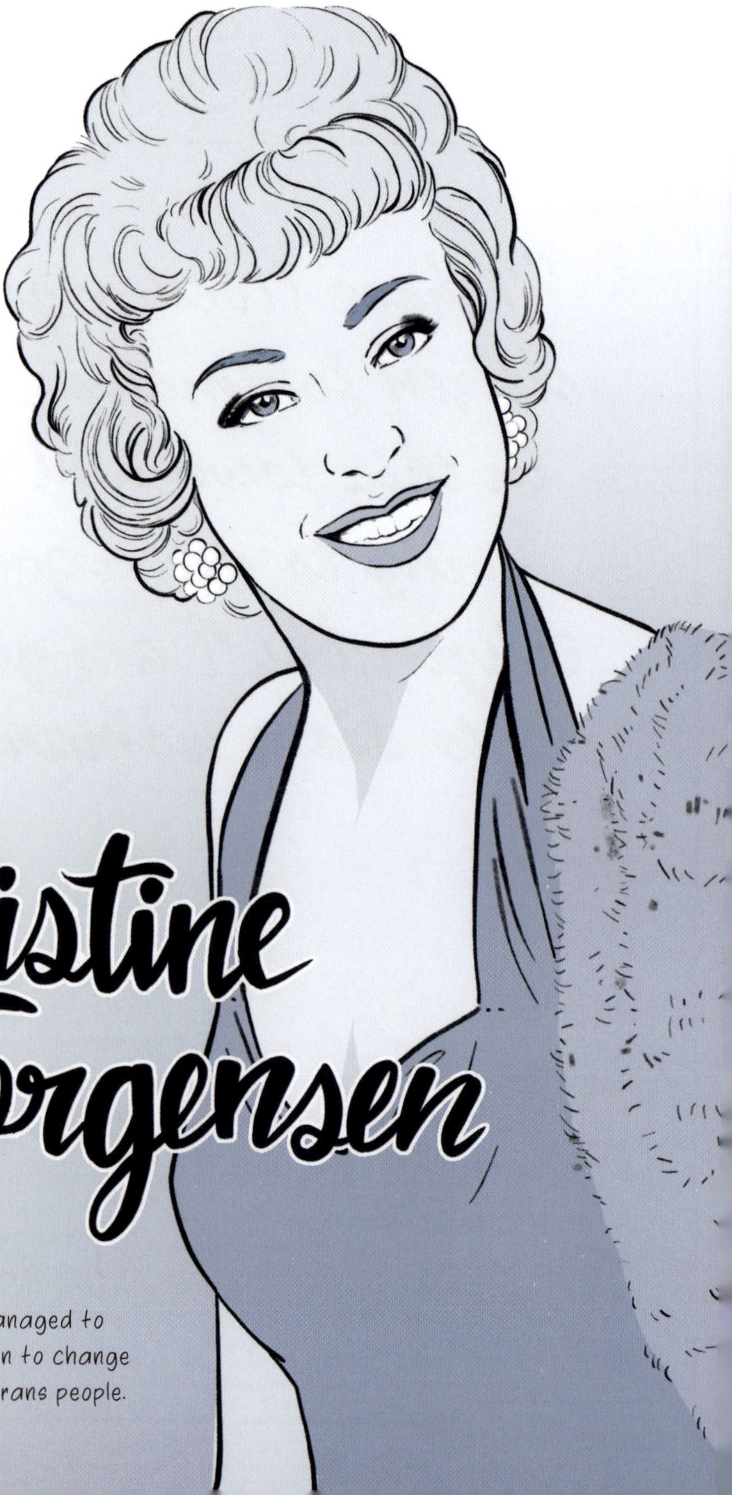

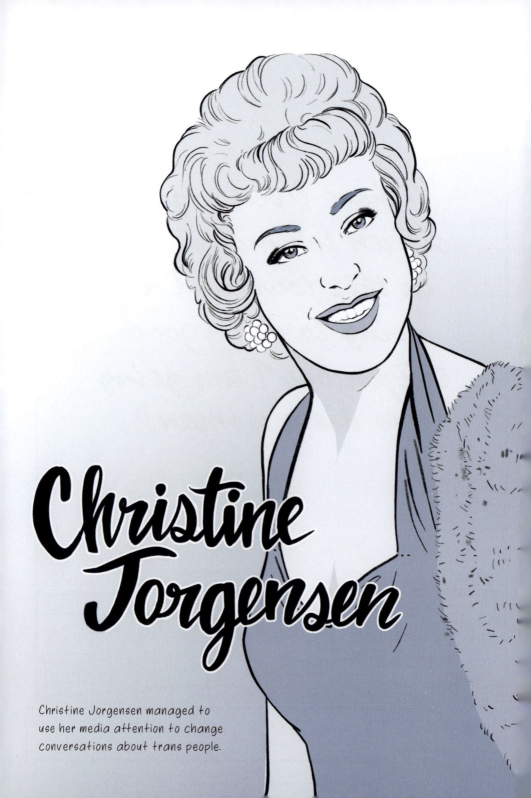

Christine Jorgensen

Christine Jorgensen managed to use her media attention to change conversations about trans people.

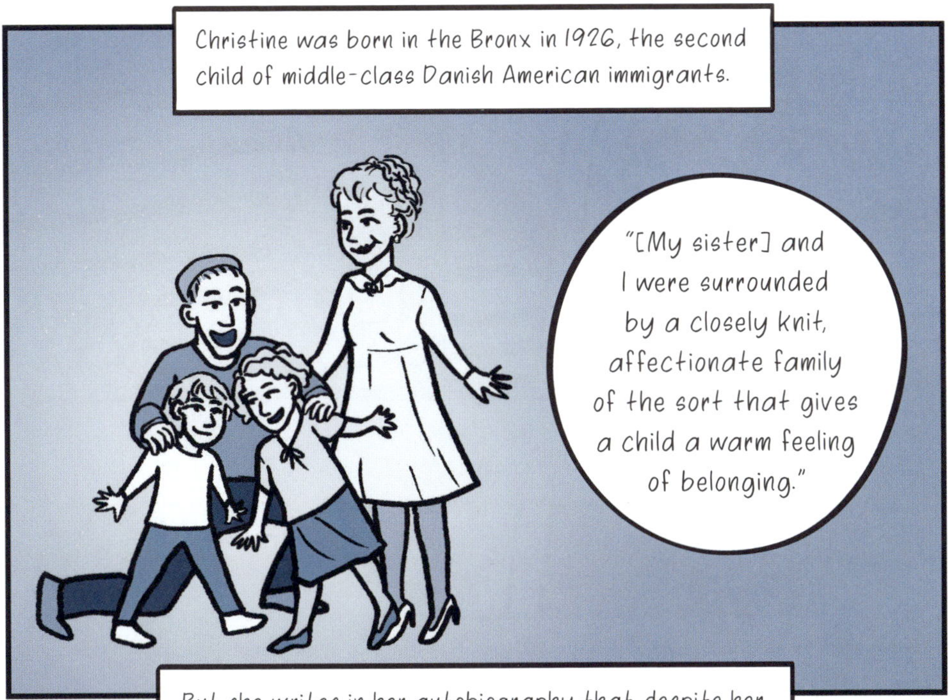
Christine was born in the Bronx in 1926, the second child of middle-class Danish American immigrants.
"[My sister] and I were surrounded by a closely knit, affectionate family of the sort that gives a child a warm feeling of belonging."

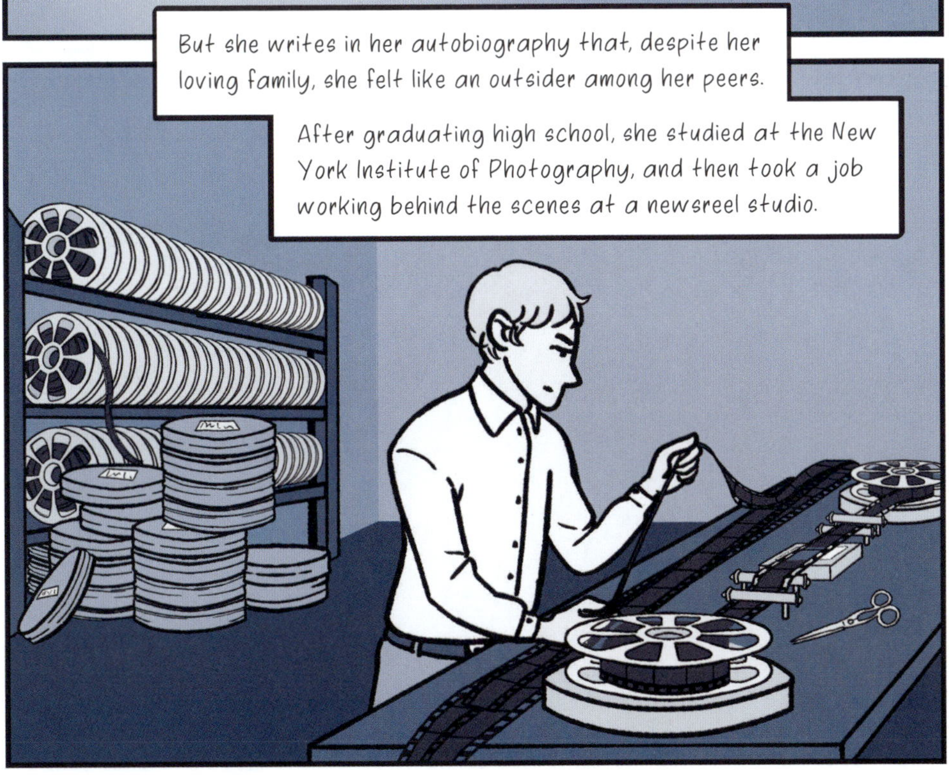
But she writes in her autobiography that, despite her loving family, she felt like an outsider among her peers.
After graduating high school, she studied at the New York Institute of Photography, and then took a job working behind the scenes at a newsreel studio.

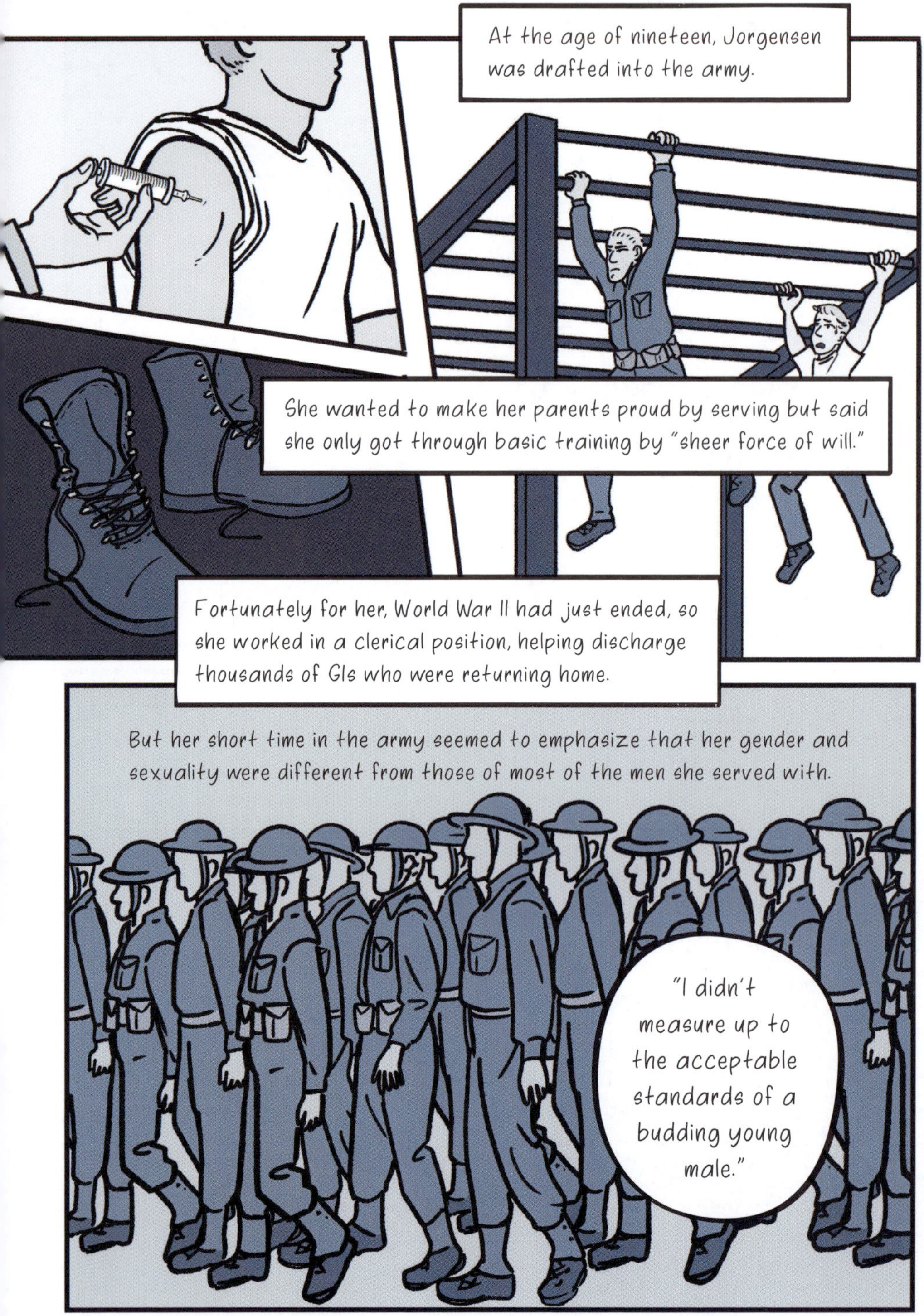
At the age of nineteen, Jorgensen was drafted into the army.
She wanted to make her parents proud by serving but said she only got through basic training by "sheer force of will."
Fortunately for her, World War II had just ended, so she worked in a clerical position, helping discharge thousands of GIs who were returning home.
But her short time in the army seemed to emphasize that her gender and sexuality were different from those of most of the men she served with.
"I didn't measure up to the acceptable standards of a budding young male."

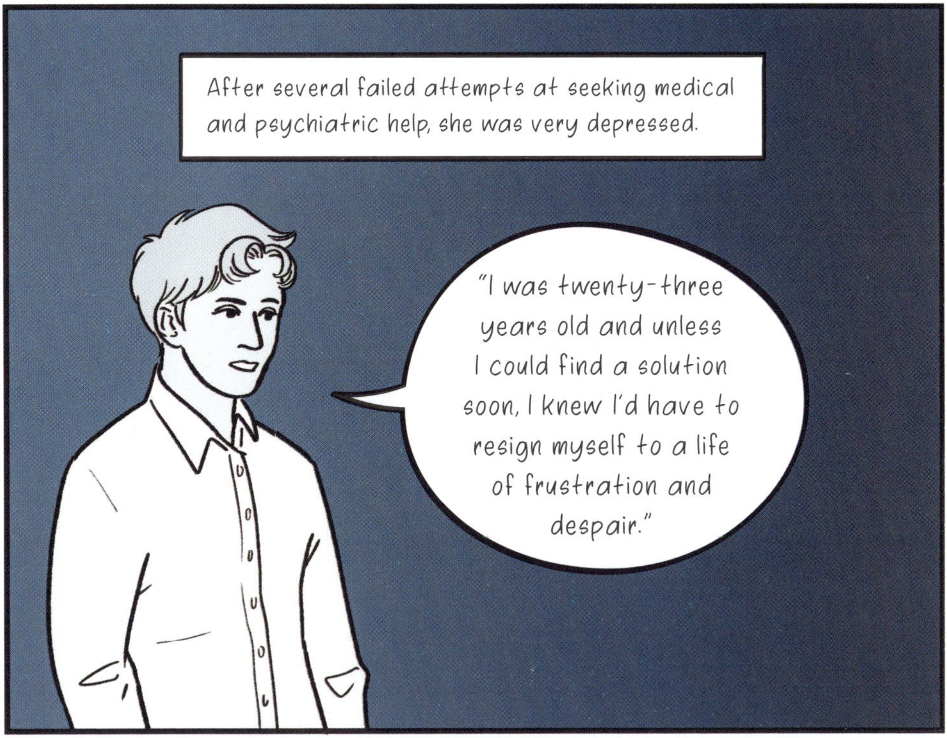
After several failed attempts at seeking medical and psychiatric help, she was very depressed.
"I was twenty-three years old and unless I could find a solution soon, I knew I'd have to resign myself to a life of frustration and despair."

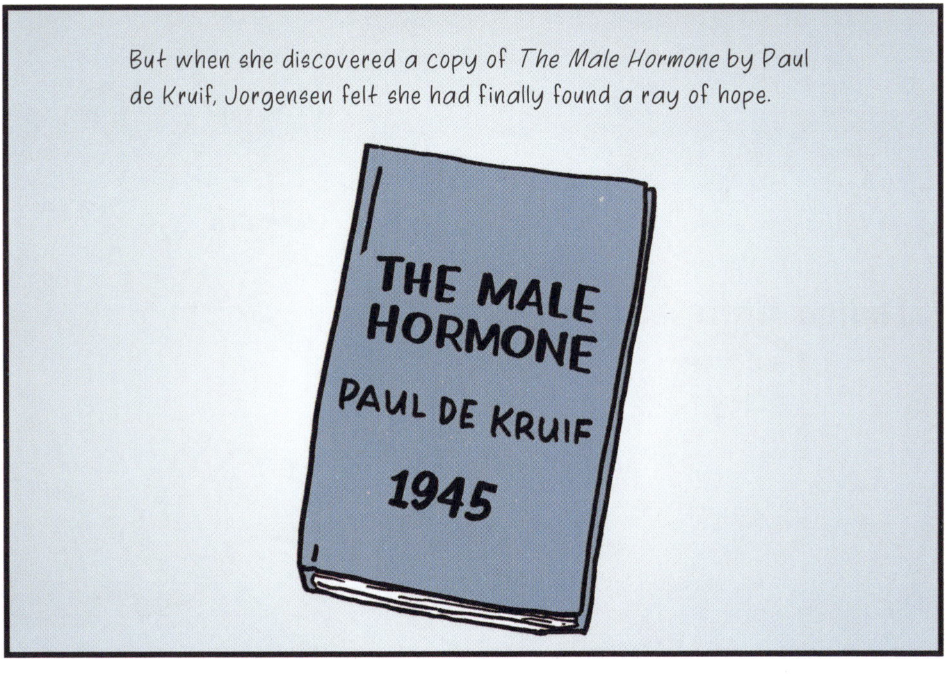
But when she discovered a copy of *The Male Hormone* by Paul de Kruif, Jorgensen felt she had finally found a ray of hope.
THE MALE HORMONE
PAUL DE KRUIF
1945

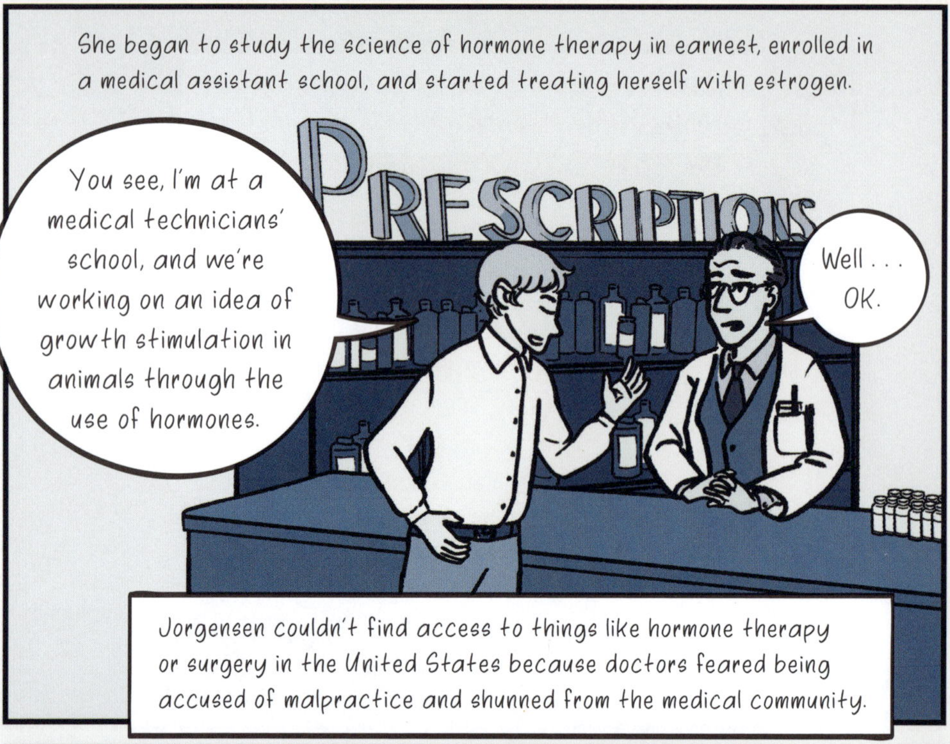
She began to study the science of hormone therapy in earnest, enrolled in a medical assistant school, and started treating herself with estrogen.
PRESCRIPTIONS
You see, I'm at a medical technicians' school, and we're working on an idea of growth stimulation in animals through the use of hormones.
Well . . . OK.
Jorgensen couldn't find access to things like hormone therapy or surgery in the United States because doctors feared being accused of malpractice and shunned from the medical community.

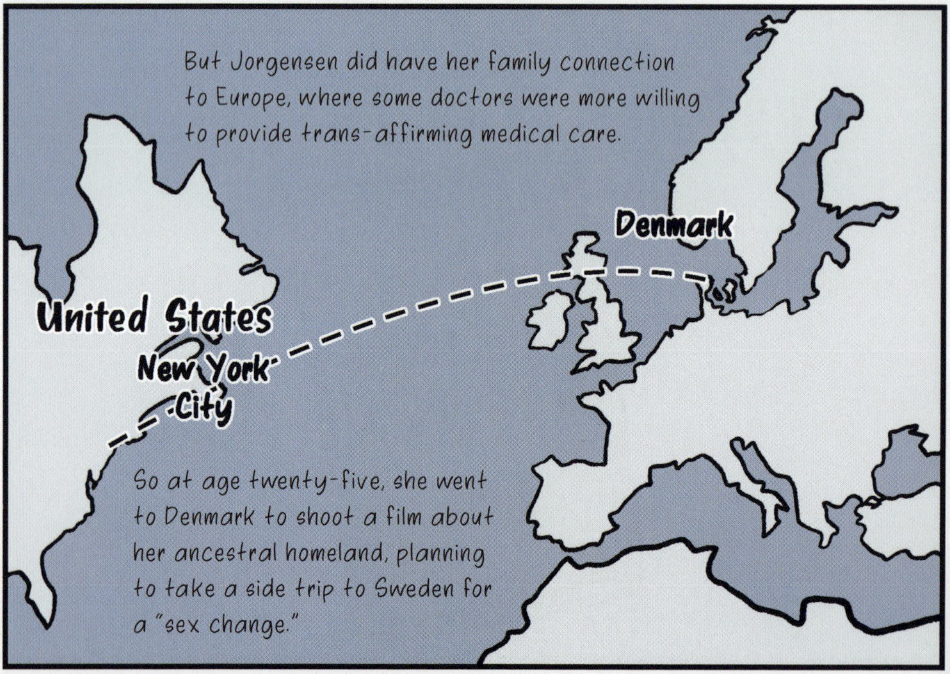
But Jorgensen did have her family connection to Europe, where some doctors were more willing to provide trans-affirming medical care.
Denmark
United States
New York City
So at age twenty-five, she went to Denmark to shoot a film about her ancestral homeland, planning to take a side trip to Sweden for a "sex change."

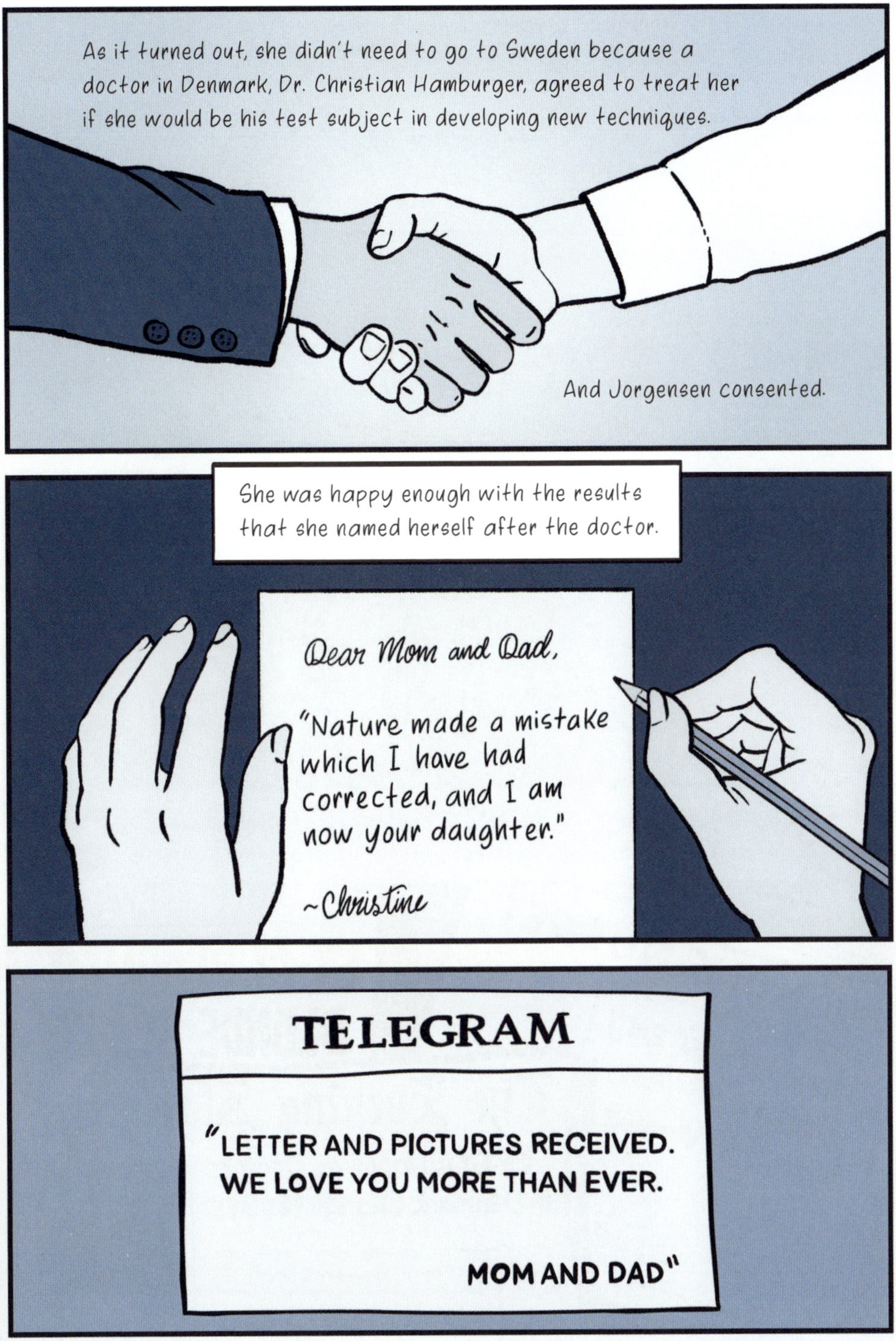
As it turned out, she didn't need to go to Sweden because a doctor in Denmark, Dr. Christian Hamburger, agreed to treat her if she would be his test subject in developing new techniques.
And Jorgensen consented.
She was happy enough with the results that she named herself after the doctor.
Dear Mom and Dad,
"Nature made a mistake which I have had corrected, and I am now your daughter."
~Christine
TELEGRAM
"LETTER AND PICTURES RECEIVED.
WE LOVE YOU MORE THAN EVER.
MOM AND DAD"

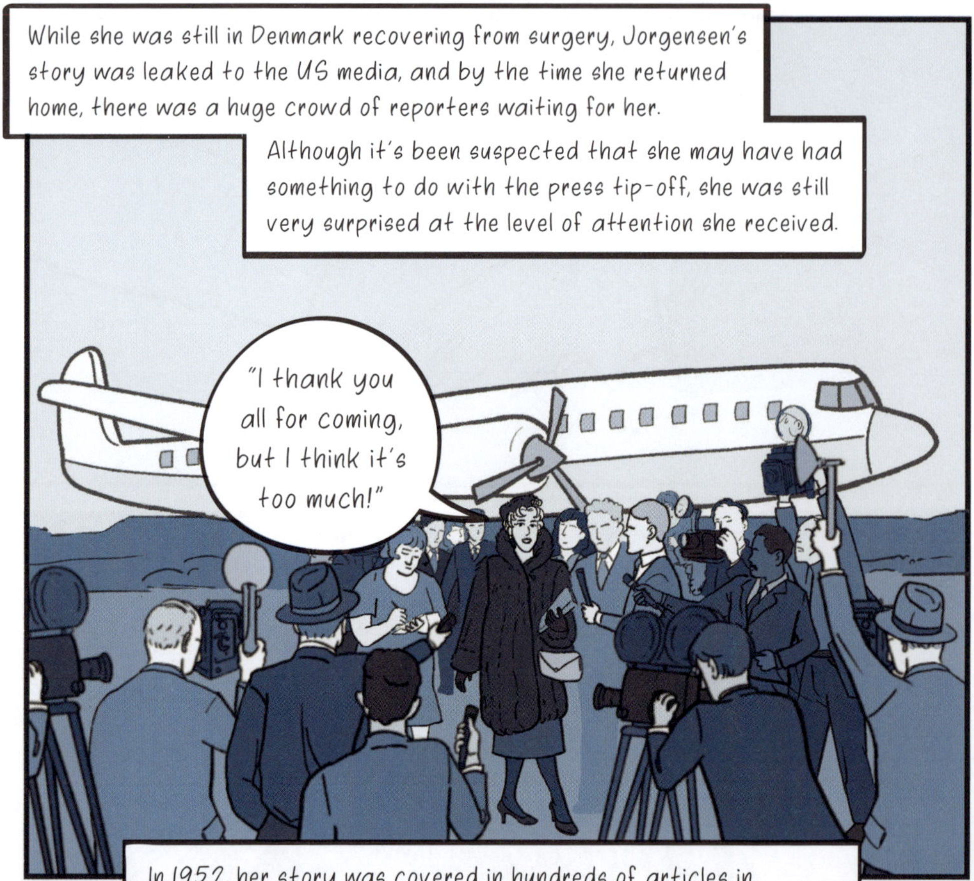
While she was still in Denmark recovering from surgery, Jorgensen's story was leaked to the US media, and by the time she returned home, there was a huge crowd of reporters waiting for her.
Although it's been suspected that she may have had something to do with the press tip-off, she was still very surprised at the level of attention she received.
"I thank you all for coming, but I think it's too much!"
In 1952, her story was covered in hundreds of articles in newspapers and magazines both stateside and internationally.

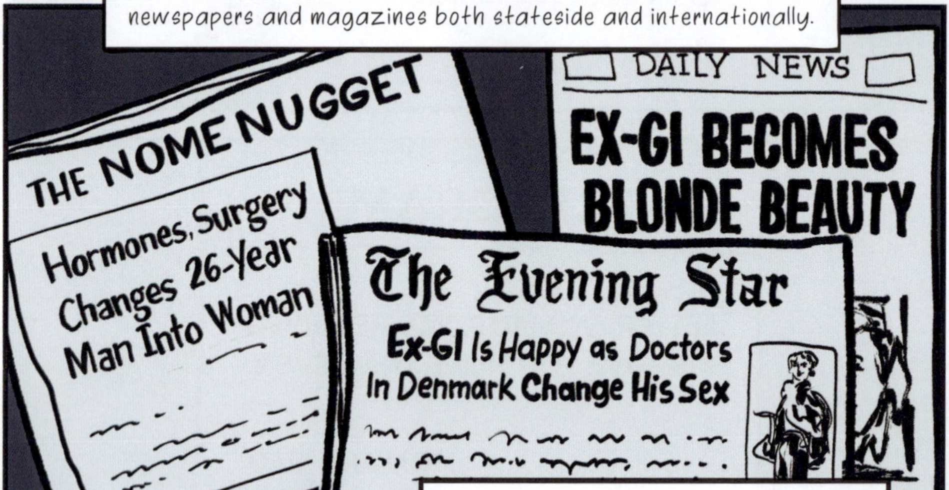
THE NOME NUGGET
Hormones, Surgery Changes 26-Year Man Into Woman
DAILY NEWS
EX-GI BECOMES BLONDE BEAUTY
The Evening Star
Ex-GI Is Happy as Doctors In Denmark Change His Sex
But she stayed cool under the pressure.

Headlines from 1952

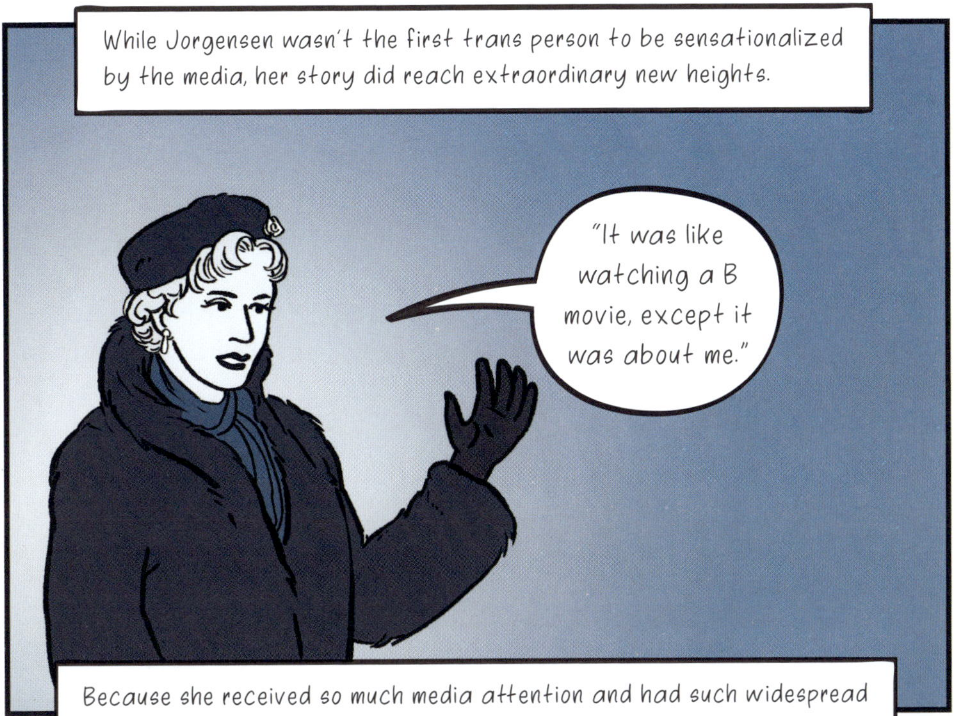
While Jorgensen wasn't the first trans person to be sensationalized by the media, her story did reach extraordinary new heights.
"It was like watching a B movie, except it was about me."

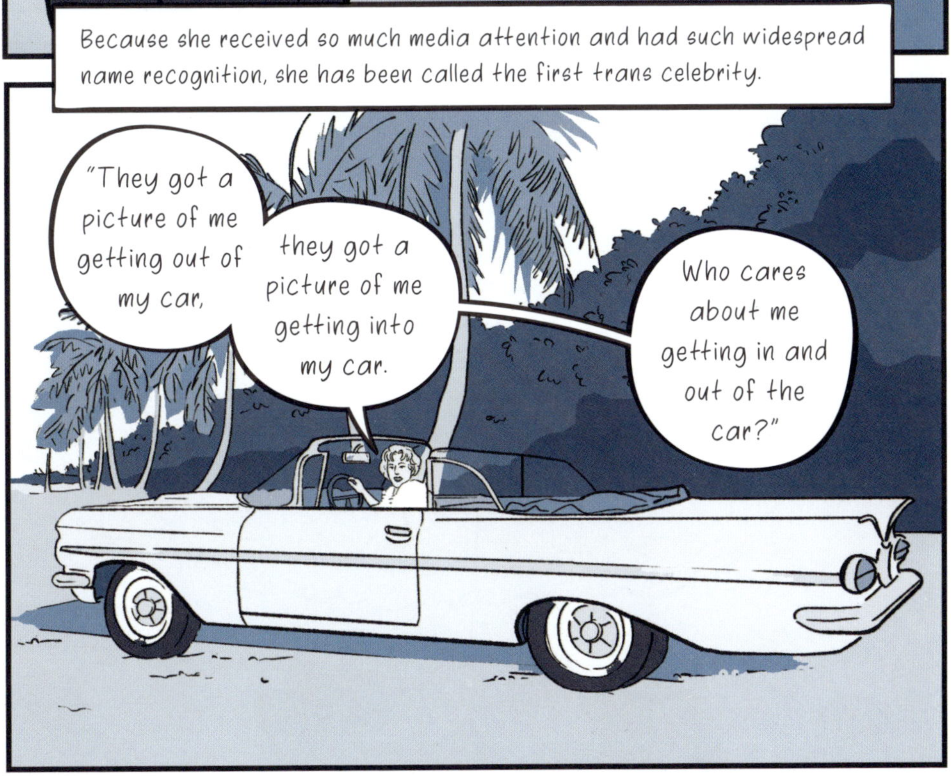
Because she received so much media attention and had such widespread name recognition, she has been called the first trans celebrity.
"They got a picture of me getting out of my car,
they got a picture of me getting into my car.
Who cares about me getting in and out of the car?"

Based on a 1960 photo, courtesy of Transas City and the Digital Transgender Archive

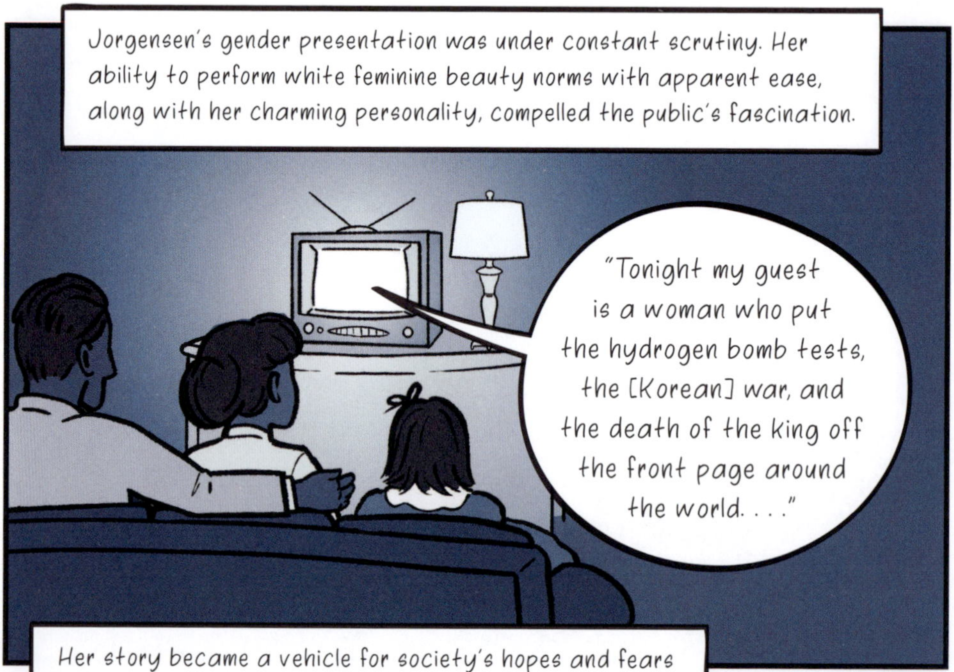
Jorgensen's gender presentation was under constant scrutiny. Her ability to perform white feminine beauty norms with apparent ease, along with her charming personality, compelled the public's fascination.
"Tonight my guest is a woman who put the hydrogen bomb tests, the [Korean] war, and the death of the king off the front page around the world. . . ."

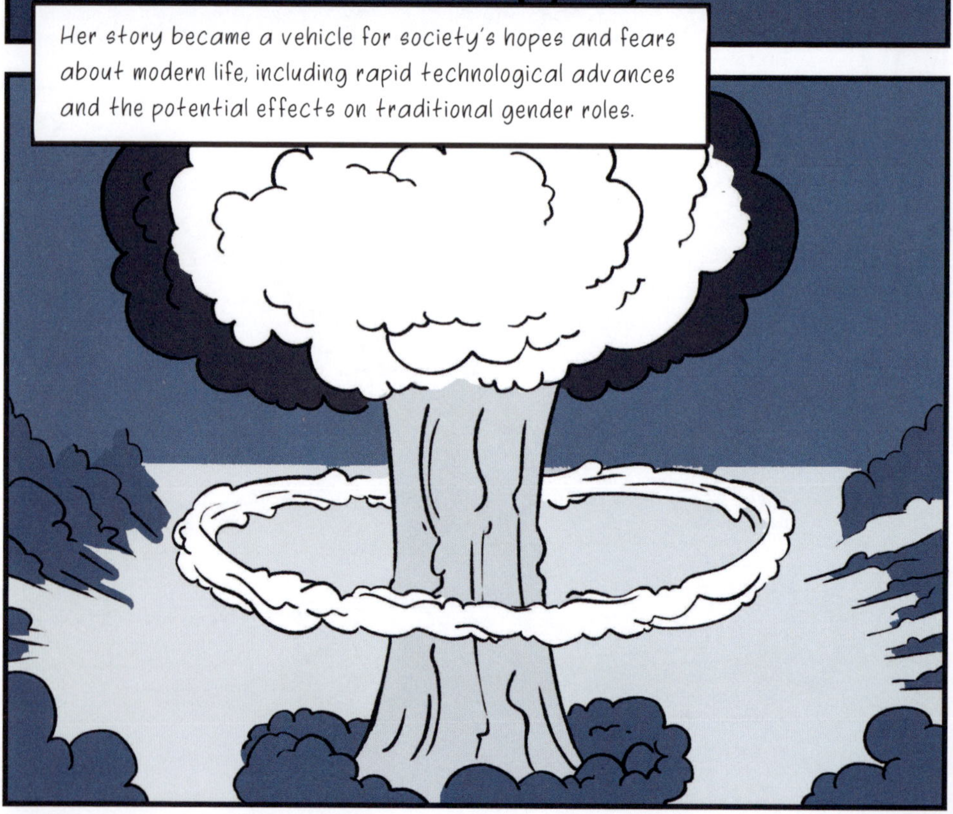
Her story became a vehicle for society's hopes and fears about modern life, including rapid technological advances and the potential effects on traditional gender roles.

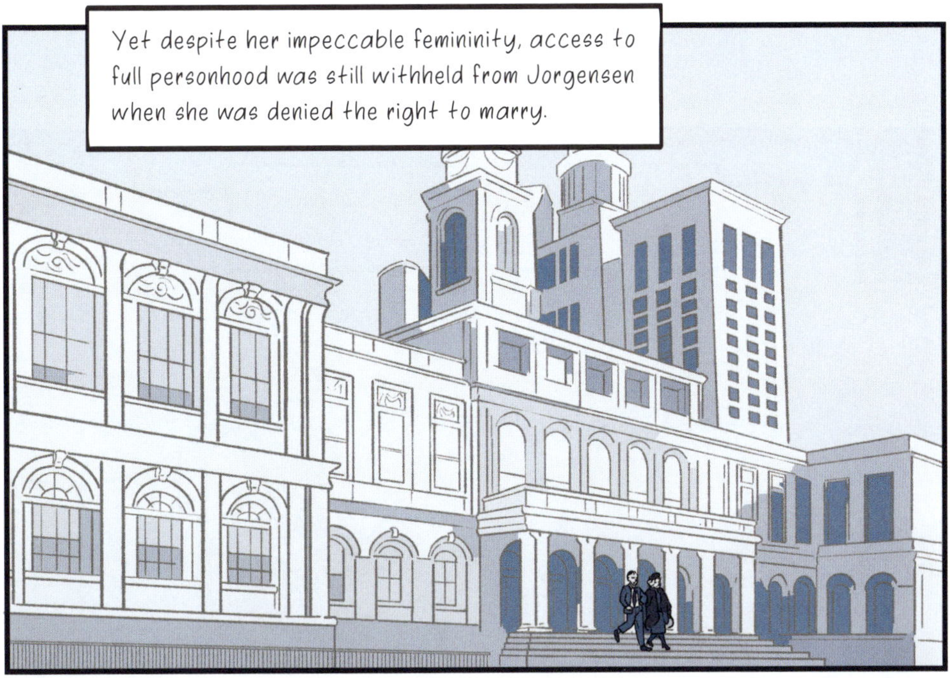
Yet despite her impeccable femininity, access to full personhood was still withheld from Jorgensen when she was denied the right to marry.

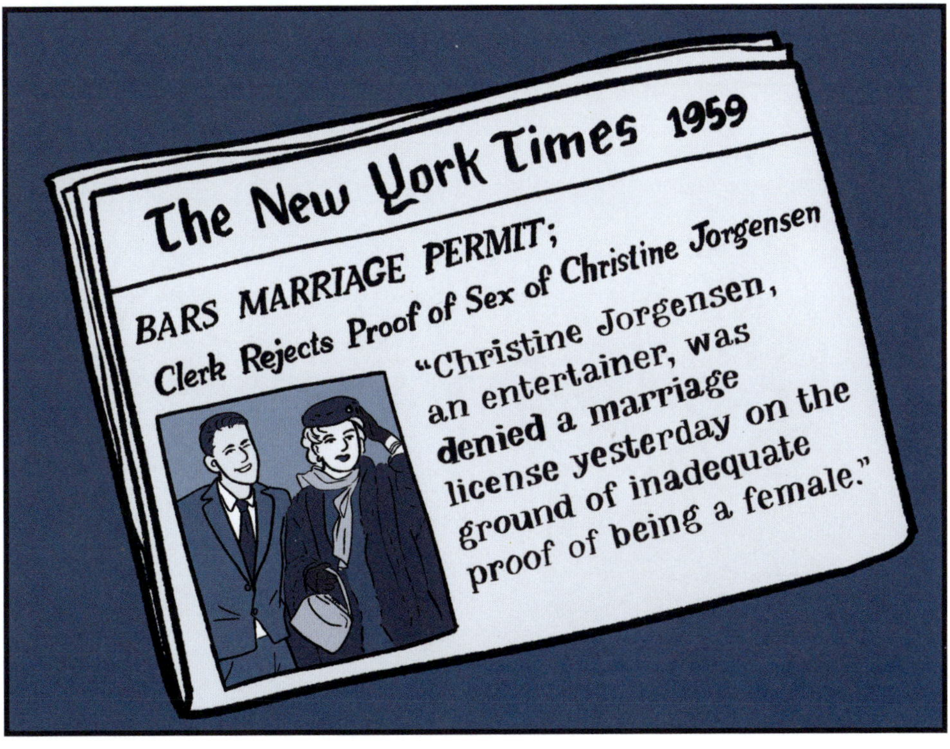
The New York Times 1959
BARS MARRIAGE PERMIT;
Clerk Rejects Proof of Sex of Christine Jorgensen
"Christine Jorgensen, an entertainer, was denied a marriage license yesterday on the ground of inadequate proof of being a female."

Jorgensen endured jokes, harassment, and many hateful lies.

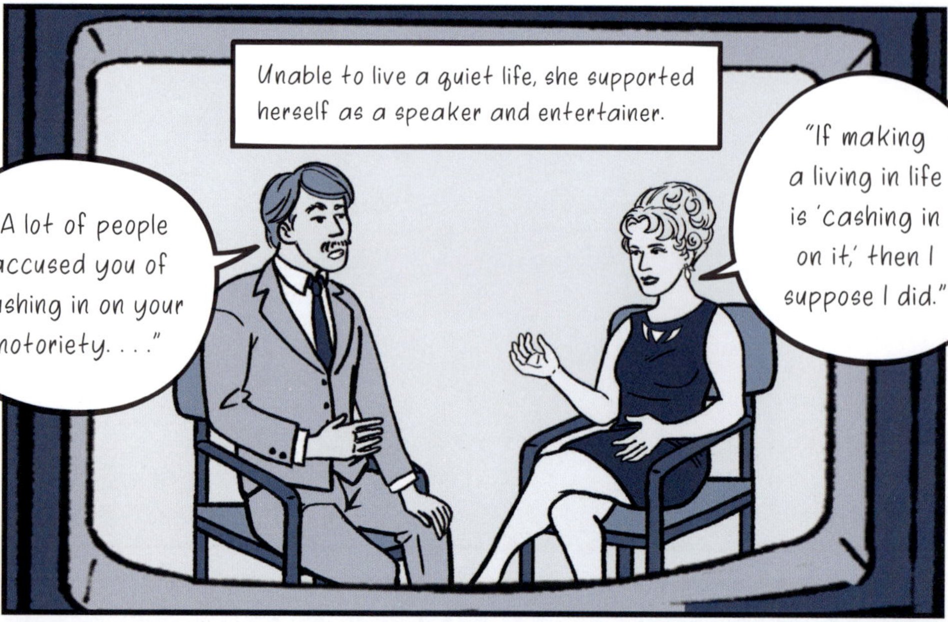
Unable to live a quiet life, she supported herself as a speaker and entertainer.
"A lot of people accused you of cashing in on your notoriety. . . ."
"If making a living in life is 'cashing in on it,' then I suppose I did."

BBC interview, 1970

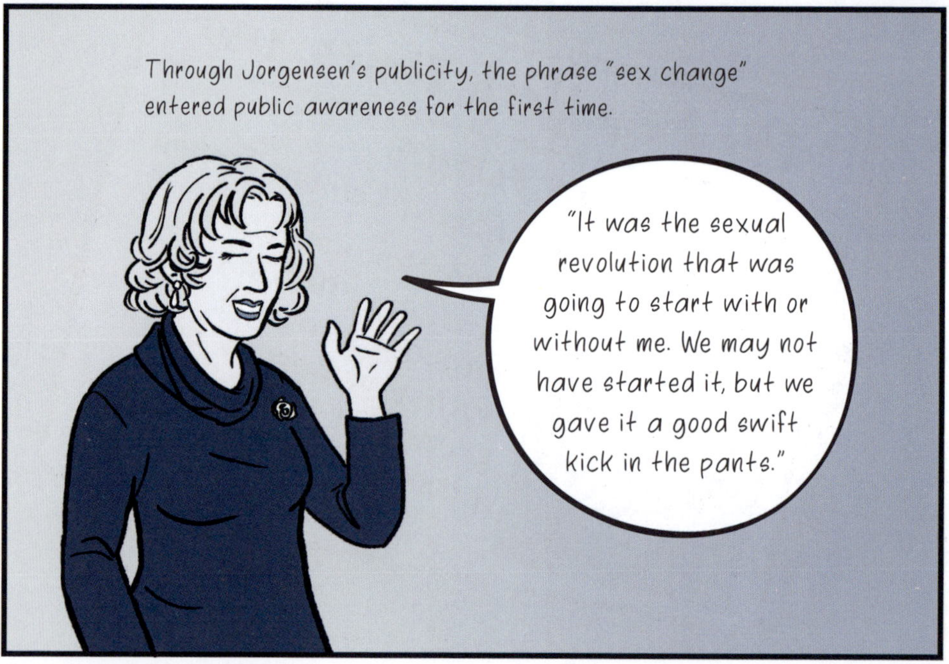
Through Jorgensen's publicity, the phrase "sex change" entered public awareness for the first time.
"It was the sexual revolution that was going to start with or without me. We may not have started it, but we gave it a good swift kick in the pants."

Los Angeles Times interview, 1988

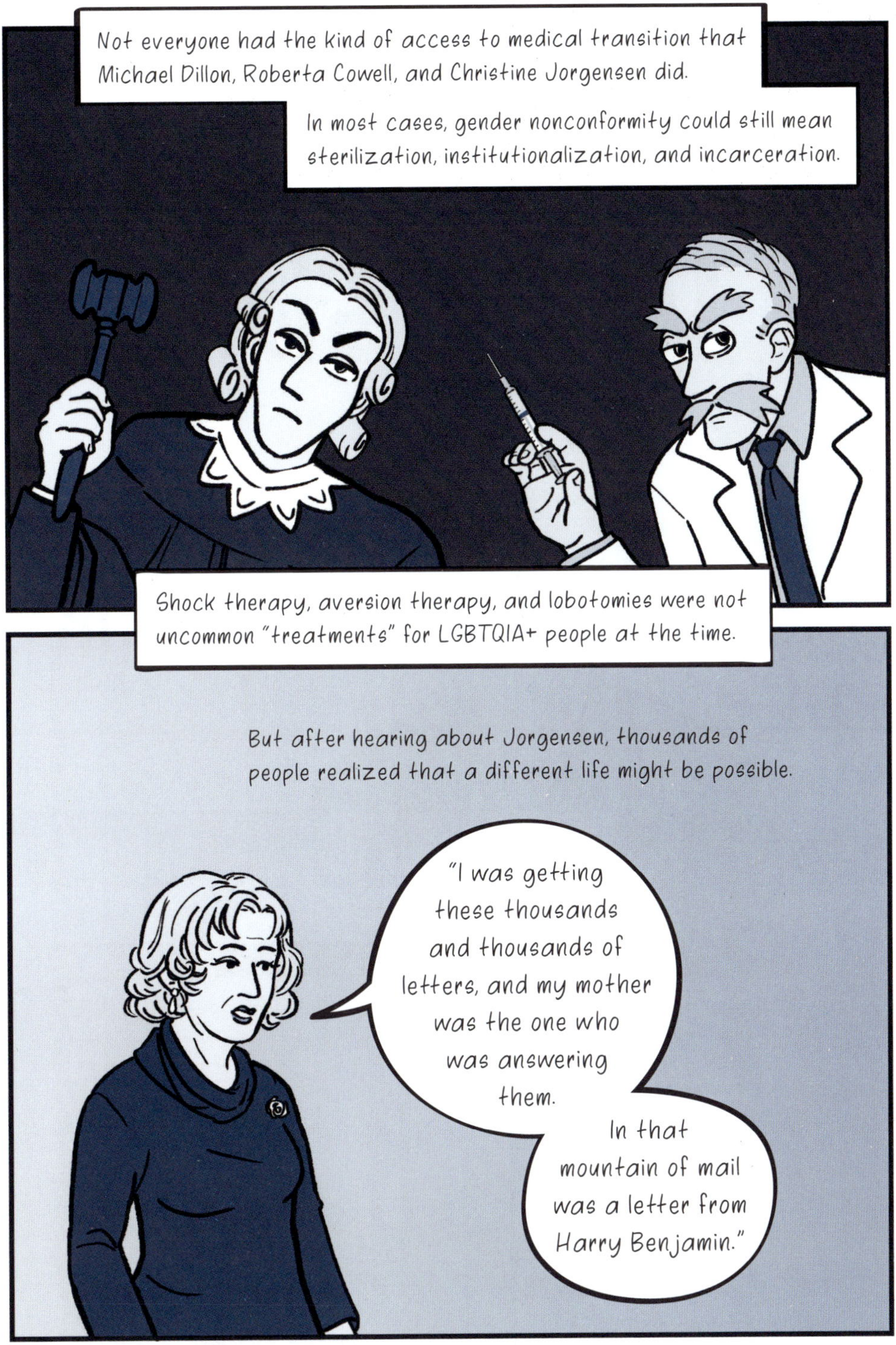
Not everyone had the kind of access to medical transition that Michael Dillon, Roberta Cowell, and Christine Jorgensen did.
In most cases, gender nonconformity could still mean sterilization, institutionalization, and incarceration.
Shock therapy, aversion therapy, and lobotomies were not uncommon "treatments" for LGBTQIA+ people at the time.
But after hearing about Jorgensen, thousands of people realized that a different life might be possible.
"I was getting these thousands and thousands of letters, and my mother was the one who was answering them.
In that mountain of mail was a letter from Harry Benjamin."

Trans-Affirming (-ish) Medical Care in the United States

Harry Benjamin, a younger colleague of Magnus Hirschfeld, took trans medical care in the United States to a new level.

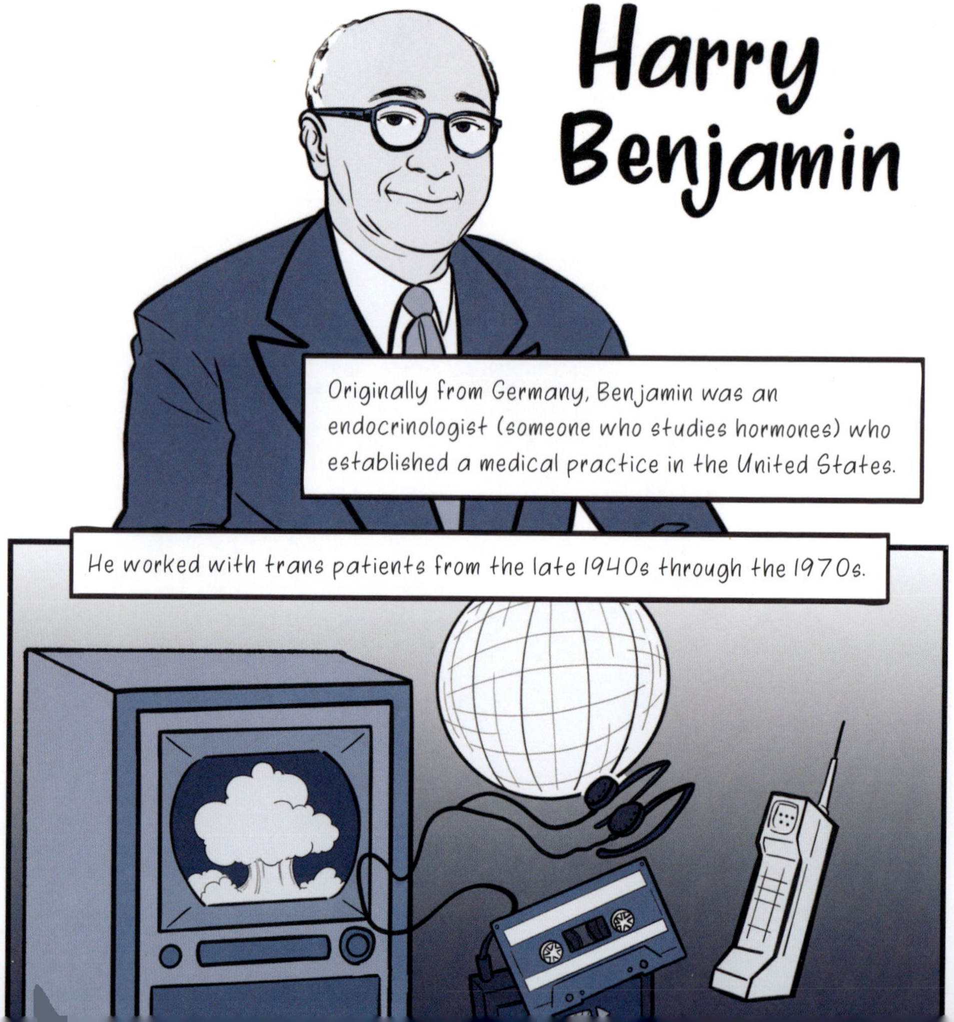
Harry Benjamin
Originally from Germany, Benjamin was an endocrinologist (someone who studies hormones) who established a medical practice in the United States.
He worked with trans patients from the late 1940s through the 1970s.

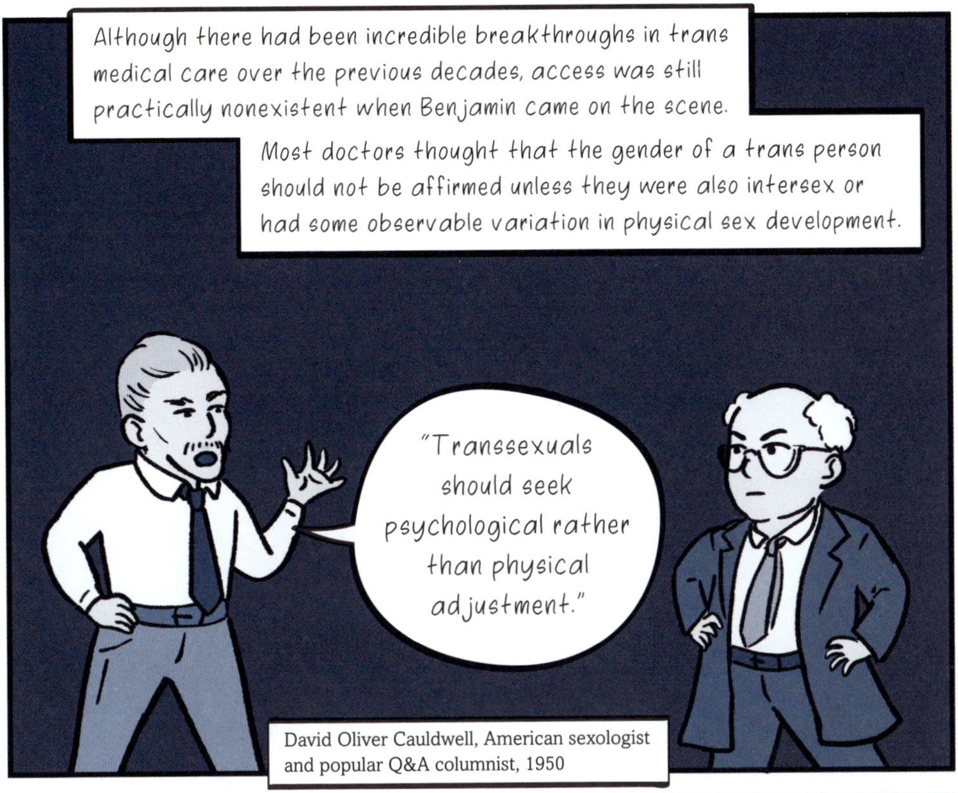
Although there had been incredible breakthroughs in trans medical care over the previous decades, access was still practically nonexistent when Benjamin came on the scene.
Most doctors thought that the gender of a trans person should not be affirmed unless they were also intersex or had some observable variation in physical sex development.
"Transsexuals should seek psychological rather than physical adjustment."
David Oliver Cauldwell, American sexologist and popular Q&A columnist, 1950

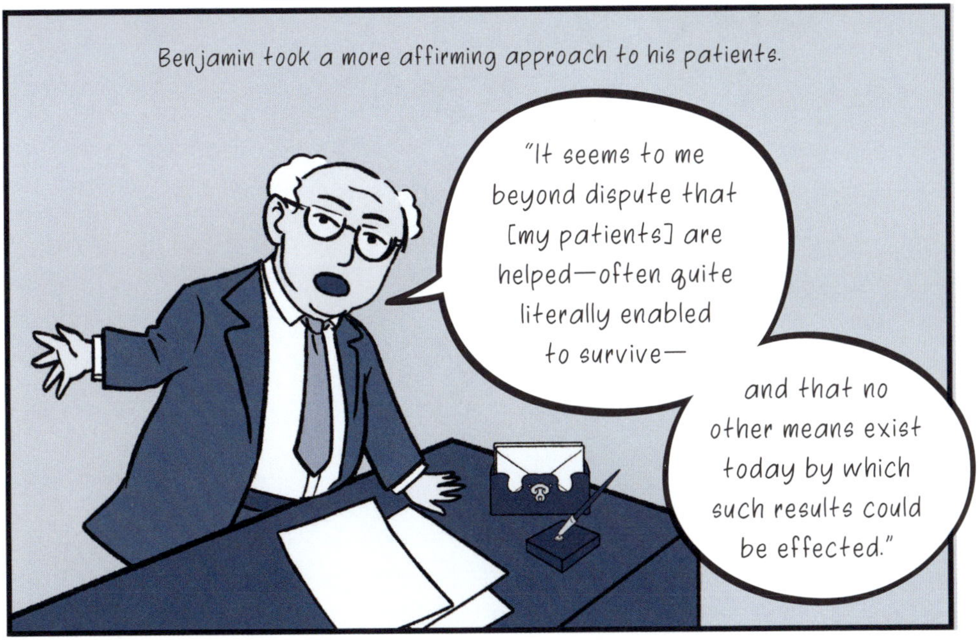
Benjamin took a more affirming approach to his patients.
"It seems to me beyond dispute that [my patients] are helped—often quite literally enabled to survive—
and that no other means exist today by which such results could be effected."

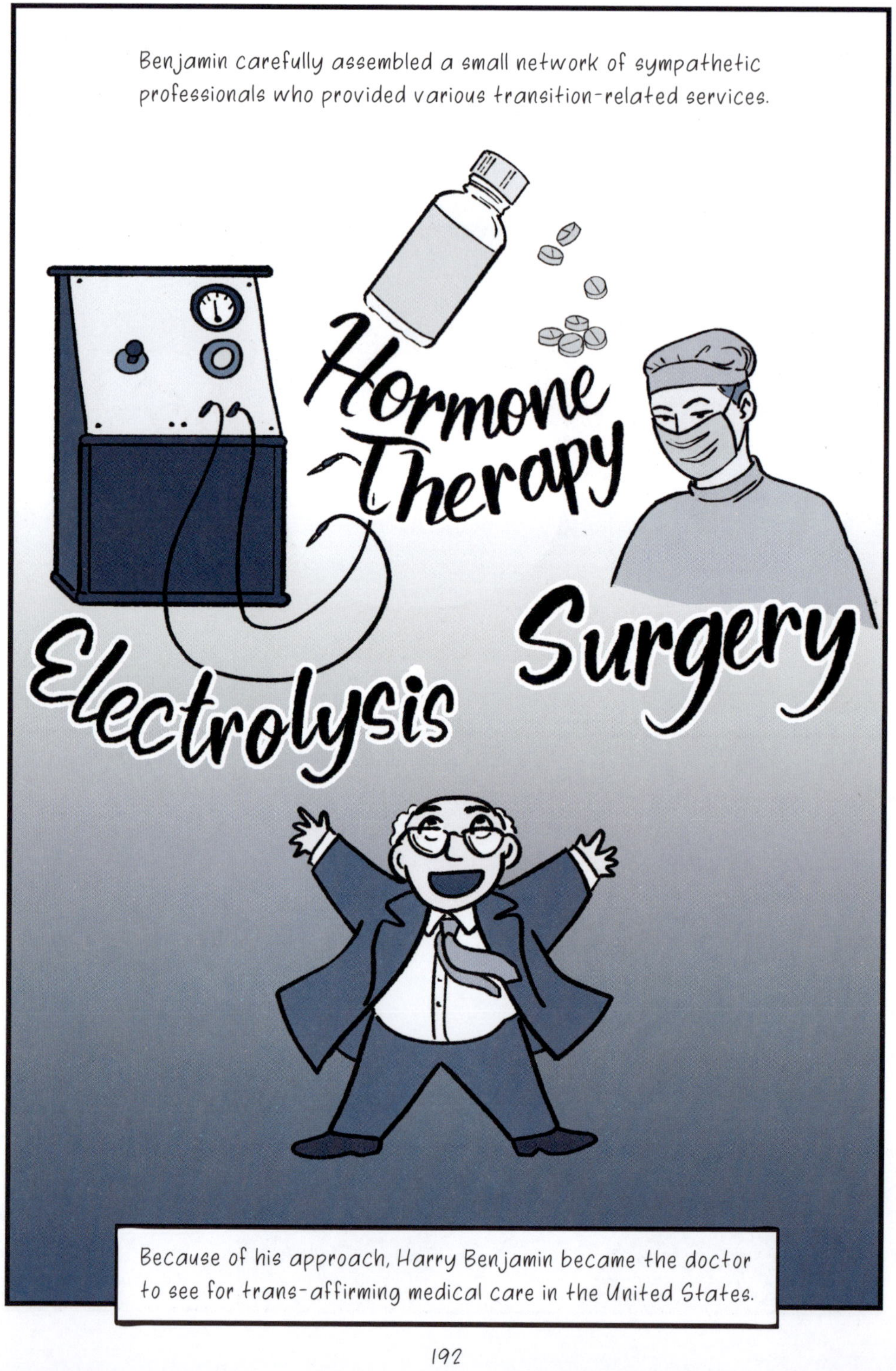
Benjamin carefully assembled a small network of sympathetic professionals who provided various transition-related services.
Hormone Therapy
Electrolysis
Surgery
Because of his approach, Harry Benjamin became the doctor to see for trans-affirming medical care in the United States.

He was also known for his kind manner toward patients.

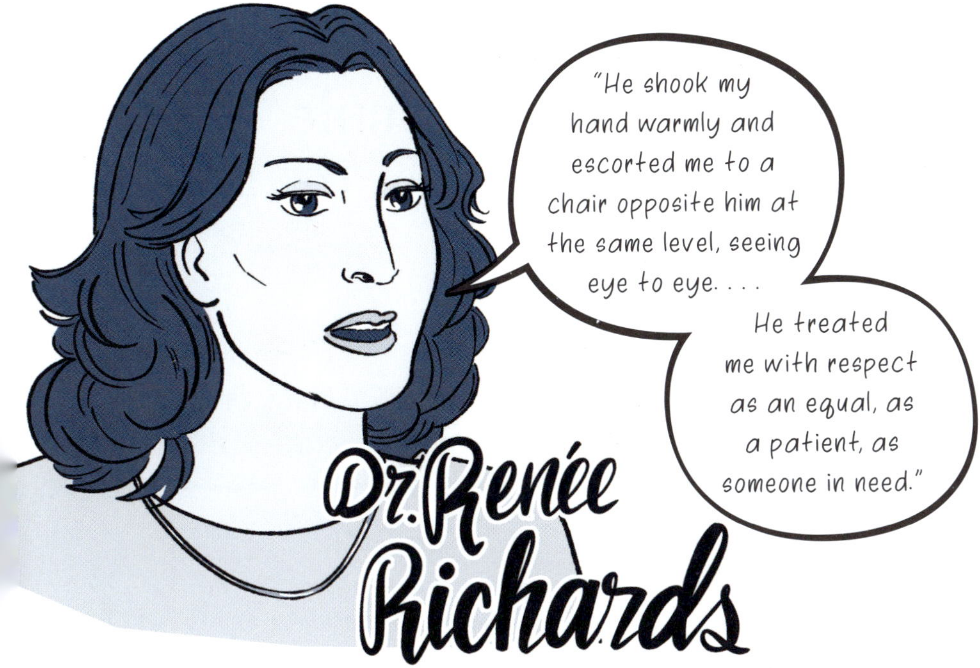
"He shook my hand warmly and escorted me to a chair opposite him at the same level, seeing eye to eye. . . .
He treated me with respect as an equal, as a patient, as someone in need."
Dr. Renée Richards

Ophthalmologist, tennis player, and former patient speaking at Harry Benjamin's funeral in 1987

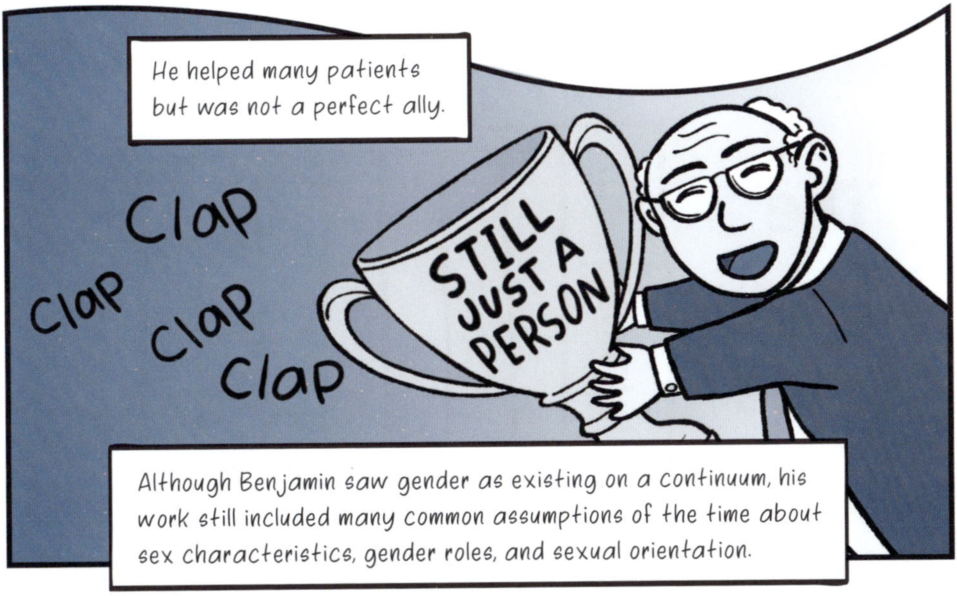
He helped many patients but was not a perfect ally.
Clap
Clap
Clap
Clap
STILL JUST A PERSON
Although Benjamin saw gender as existing on a continuum, his work still included many common assumptions of the time about sex characteristics, gender roles, and sexual orientation.

Benjamin created a now obsolete diagnostic scale that would become the basis on which future trans medical care in the United States would be built.

"The Benjamin Sex Orientation Scale" (SOS)

"TYPE I: Transvestite Pseudo

TYPE II: Transvestite Fetishistic

TYPE III: Transvestite True

TYPE IV: Transsexual Non-Surgical

TYPE V: True Transsexual Moderate Intensity

TYPE VI: True Transsexual High Intensity"

Benjamin's scale considered transness to essentially be an extreme version of gayness. At the low end of the scale were gay cis men who occasionally crossdressed, and at the high end were straight trans women who wanted surgery.

Benjamin had been influenced by the work of a contemporary, the American sexologist Alfred Kinsey, who introduced the idea that many people are somewhere in between "exclusively heterosexual" and "exclusively homosexual."

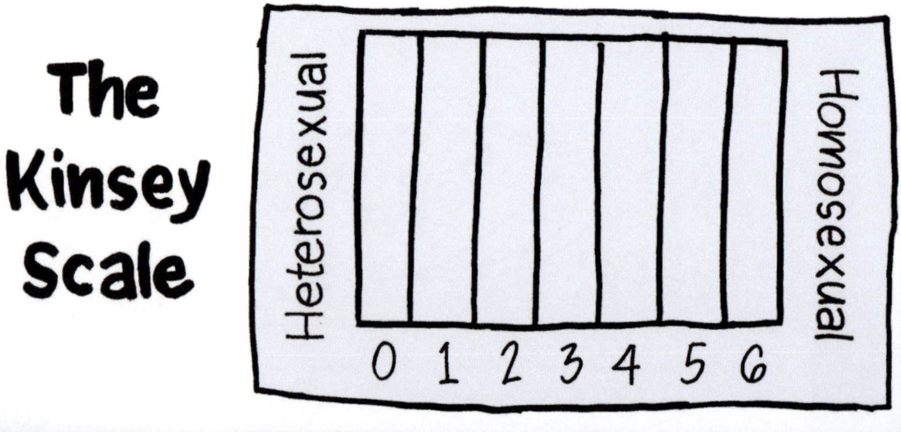
The Kinsey Scale
Heterosexual
Homosexual
0 1 2 3 4 5 6

These scales were often applied to create a hierarchy based on the assumption that straight and cis-appearing people should be the outcome of any trans-affirming medical intervention.

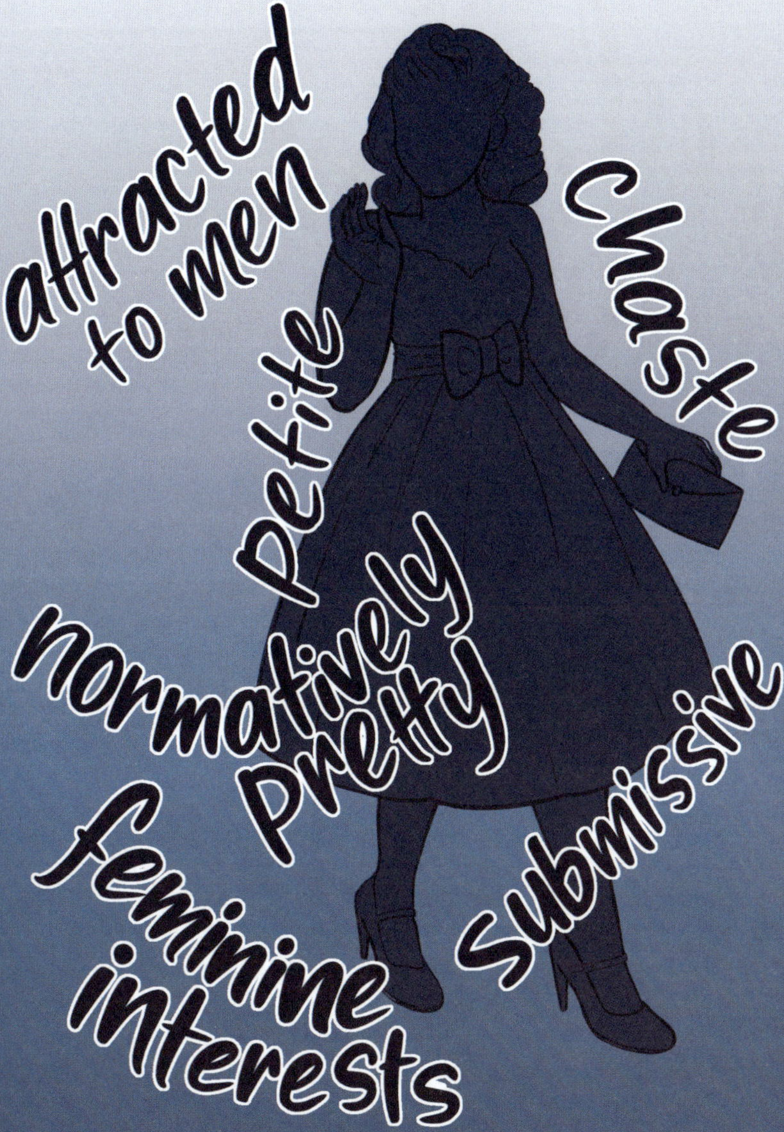
attracted to men
chaste
petite
normatively pretty
submissive
feminine interests

Therefore, medical access was prioritized based on whoever was judged most likely to align with cis-heterosexual stereotypes after transition.

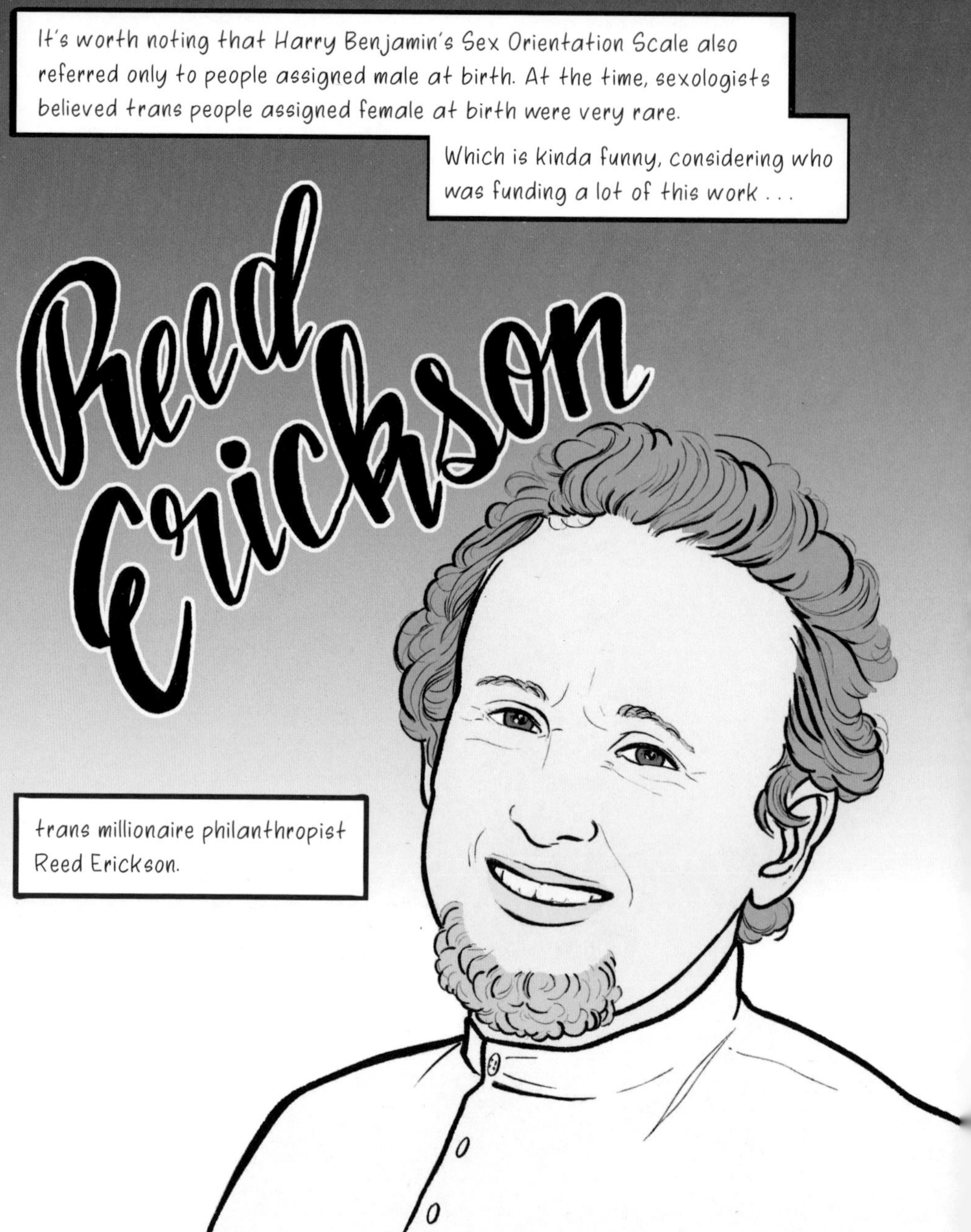
It's worth noting that Harry Benjamin's Sex Orientation Scale also referred only to people assigned male at birth. At the time, sexologists believed trans people assigned female at birth were very rare.
Which is kinda funny, considering who was funding a lot of this work . . .
Reed Erickson
trans millionaire philanthropist Reed Erickson.

Based on a photo courtesy of the Transgender Archives at the University of Victoria Libraries

In 1917, Reed Erickson was born to a well-off family in Texas.

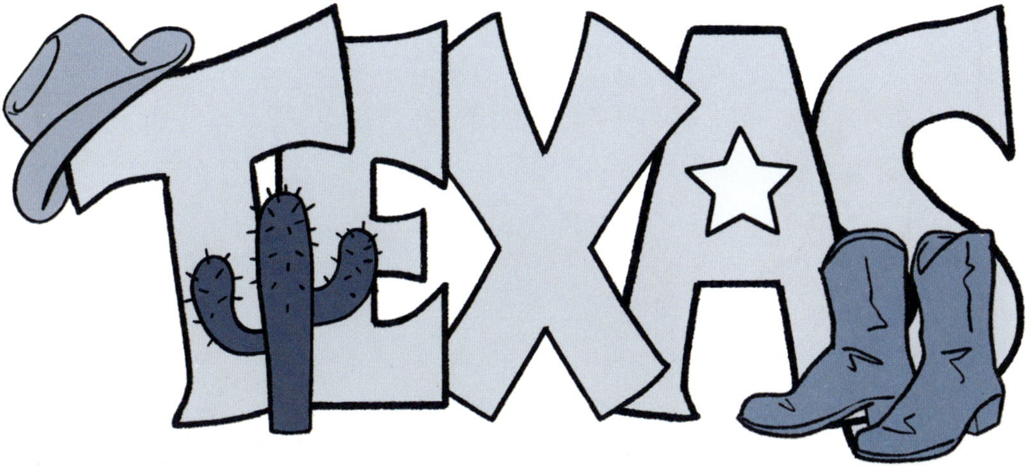
TEXAS

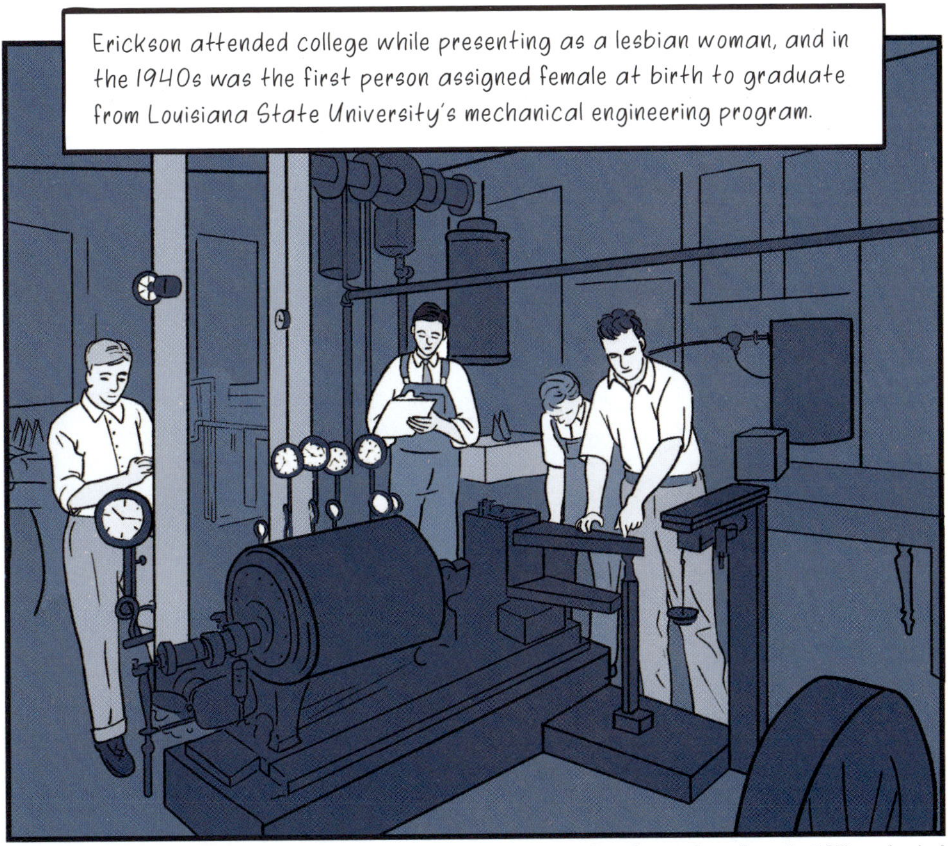
Erickson attended college while presenting as a lesbian woman, and in the 1940s was the first person assigned female at birth to graduate from Louisiana State University's mechanical engineering program.

Based on a photo from the LSU mechanical engineering program, taken sometime between 1886 and 1926

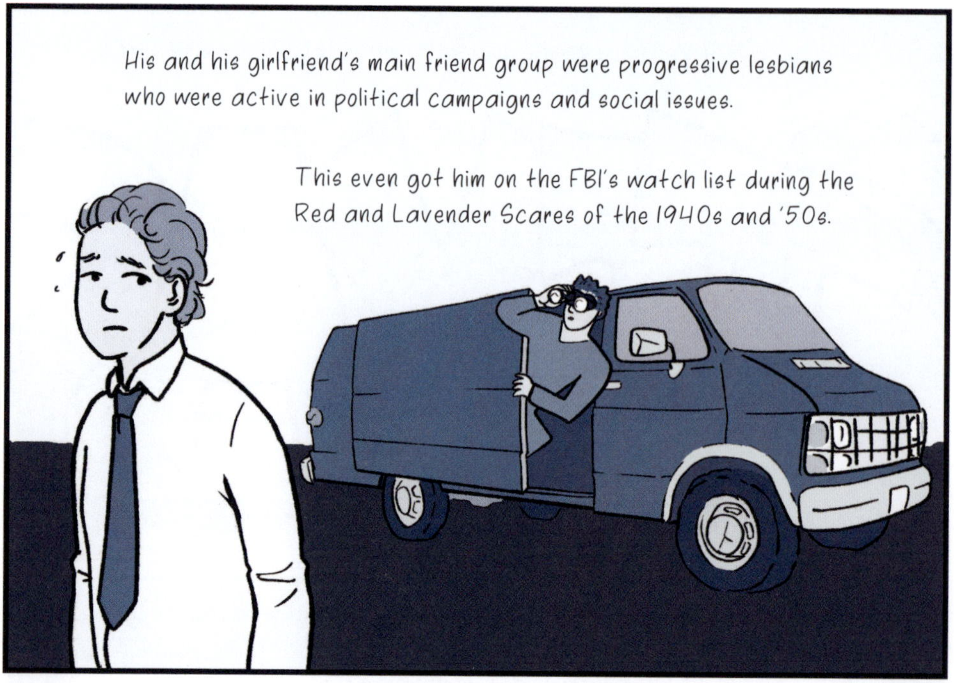
His and his girlfriend's main friend group were progressive lesbians who were active in political campaigns and social issues.
This even got him on the FBI's watch list during the Red and Lavender Scares of the 1940s and '50s.

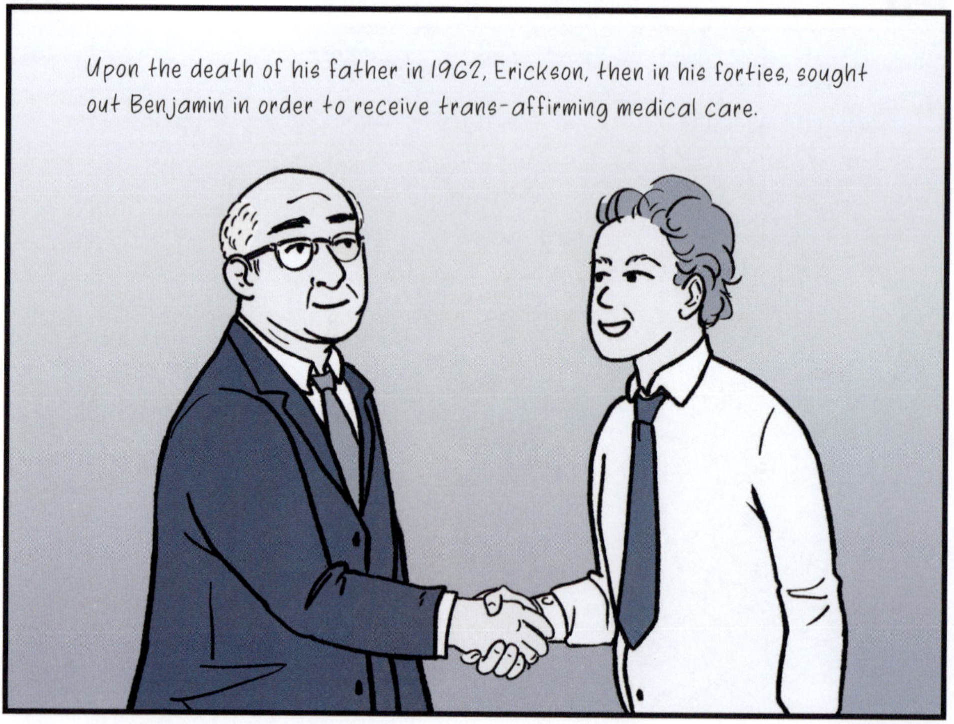
Upon the death of his father in 1962, Erickson, then in his forties, sought out Benjamin in order to receive trans-affirming medical care.

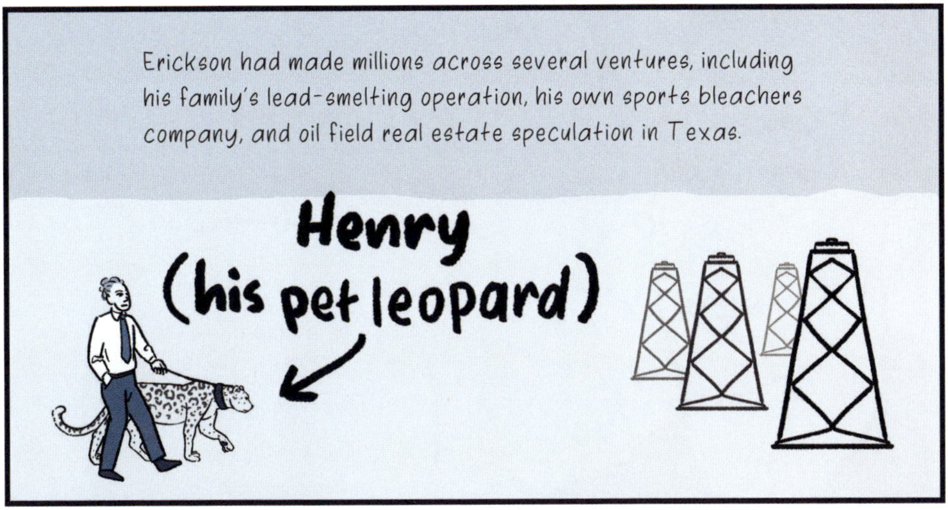
Erickson had made millions across several ventures, including his family's lead-smelting operation, his own sports bleachers company, and oil field real estate speculation in Texas.
Henry (his pet leopard)

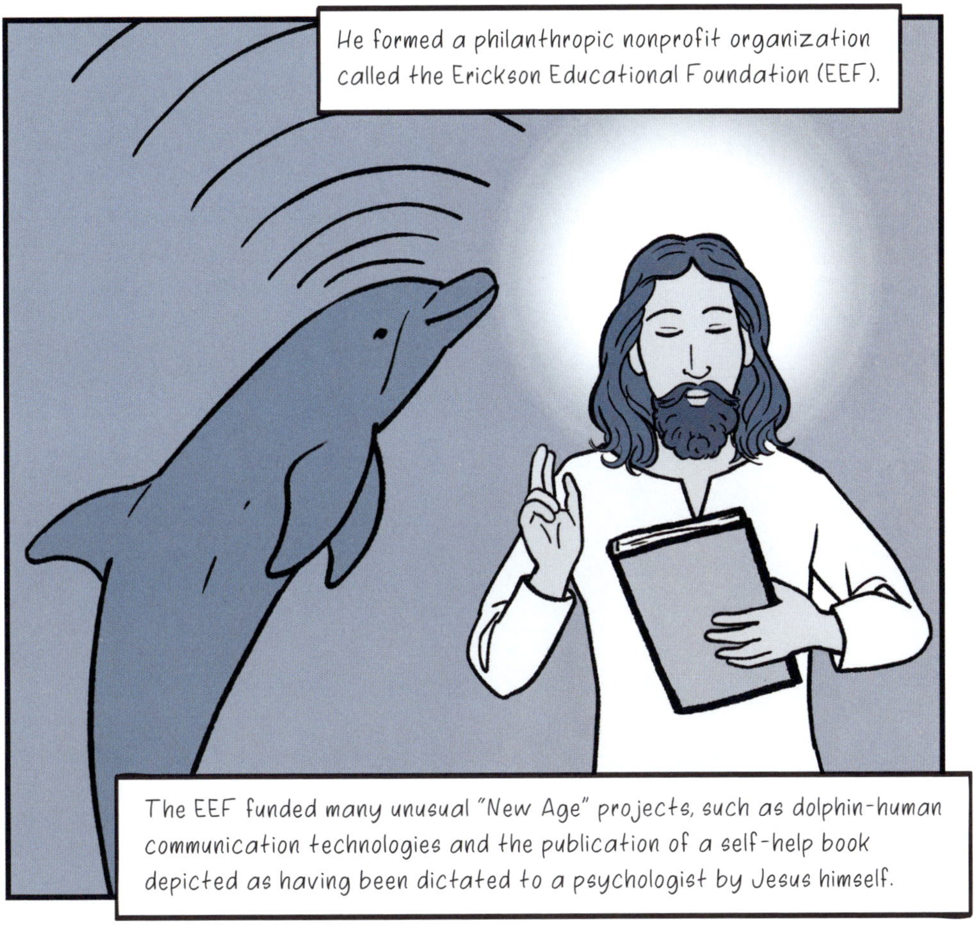
He formed a philanthropic nonprofit organization called the Erickson Educational Foundation (EEF).
The EEF funded many unusual "New Age" projects, such as dolphin-human communication technologies and the publication of a self-help book depicted as having been dictated to a psychologist by Jesus himself.

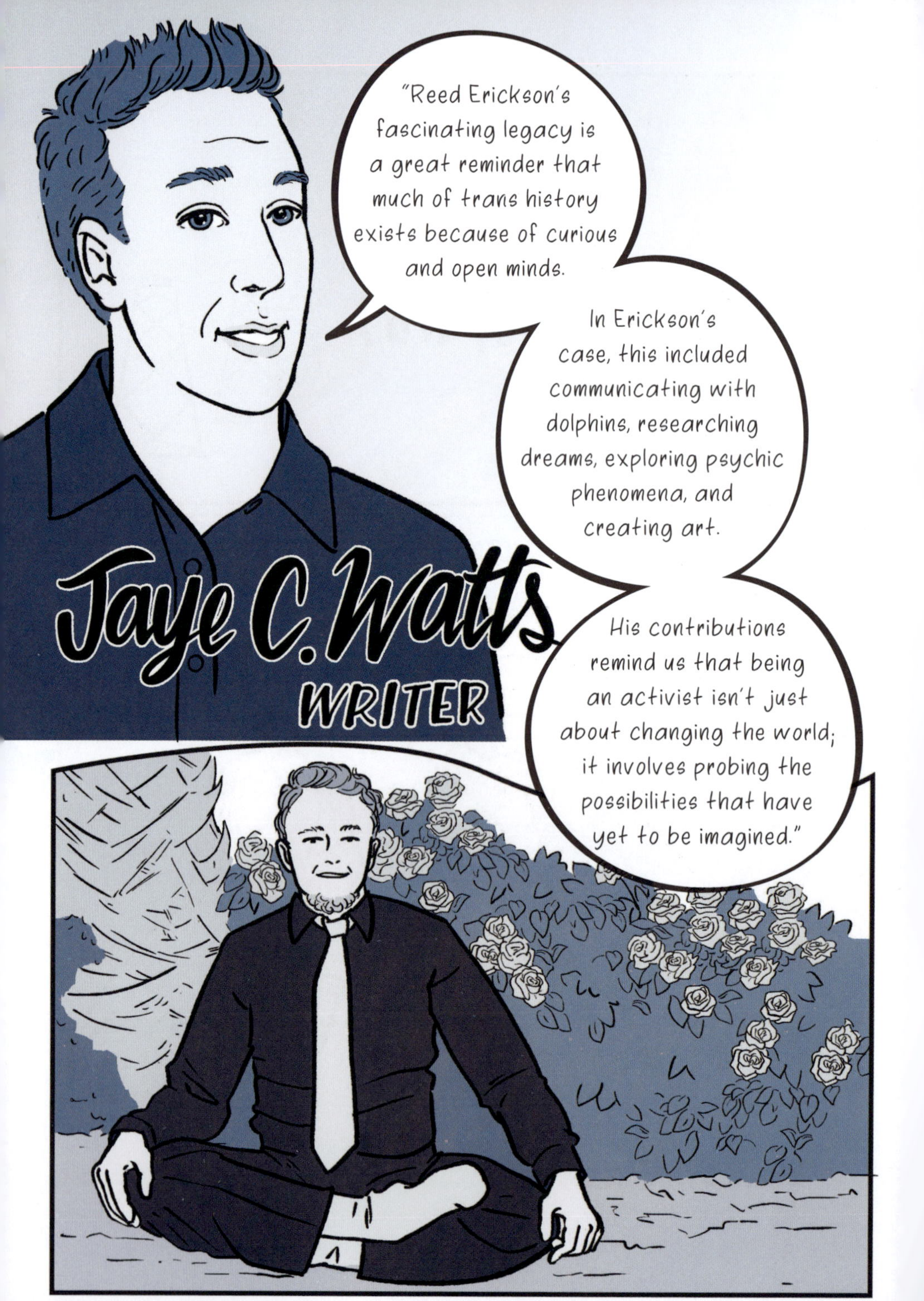
"Reed Erickson's fascinating legacy is a great reminder that much of trans history exists because of curious and open minds.
In Erickson's case, this included communicating with dolphins, researching dreams, exploring psychic phenomena, and creating art.
His contributions remind us that being an activist isn't just about changing the world; it involves probing the possibilities that have yet to be imagined."
Jaye C. Watts
WRITER

Based on a photo of Erickson, courtesy of the Transgender Archives at the University of Victoria Libraries

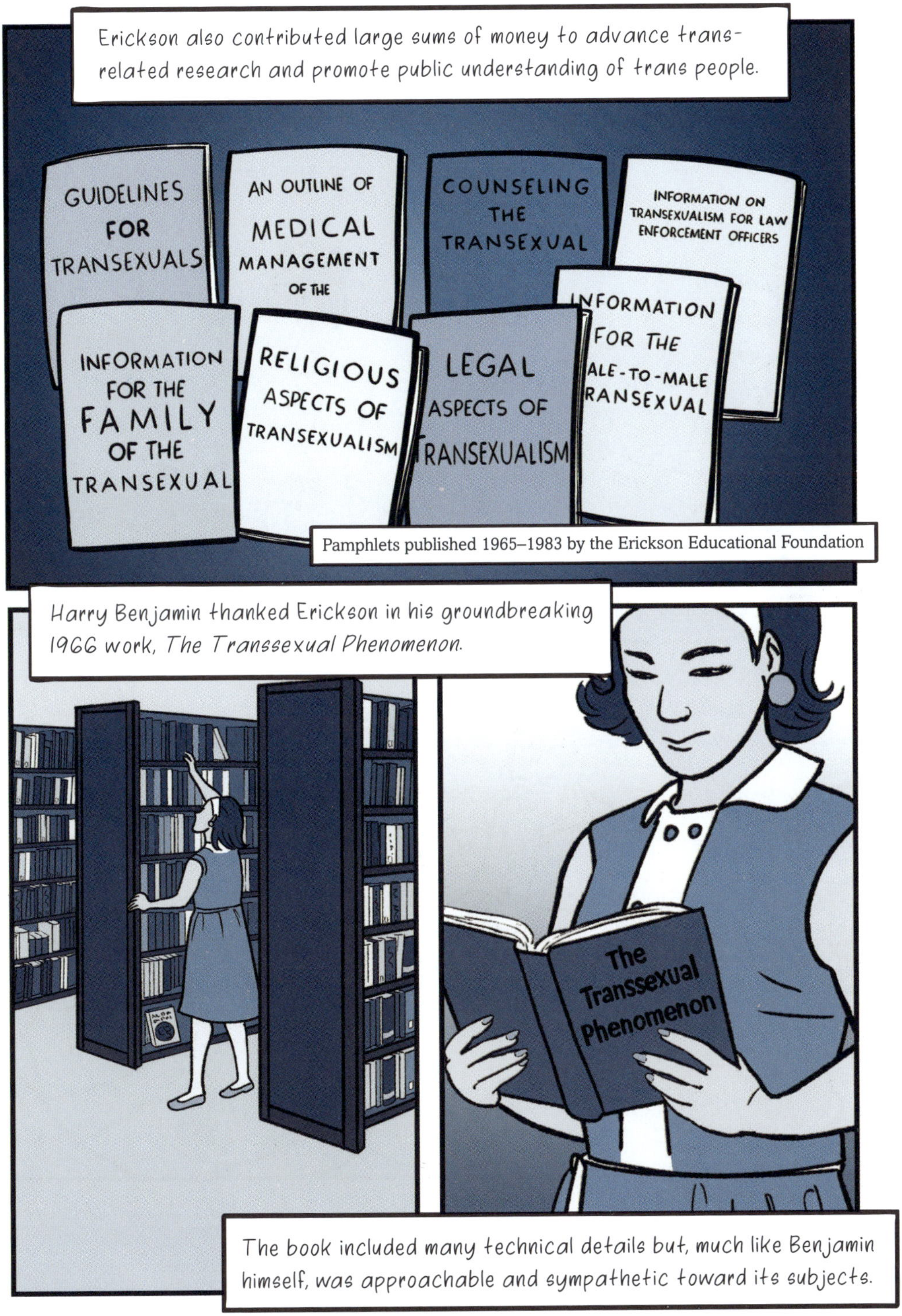
Erickson also contributed large sums of money to advance trans-related research and promote public understanding of trans people.
GUIDELINES FOR TRANSEXUALS
AN OUTLINE OF MEDICAL MANAGEMENT OF THE
COUNSELING THE TRANSEXUAL
INFORMATION ON TRANSEXUALISM FOR LAW ENFORCEMENT OFFICERS
INFORMATION FOR THE FAMILY OF THE TRANSEXUAL
RELIGIOUS ASPECTS OF TRANSEXUALISM
LEGAL ASPECTS OF TRANSEXUALISM
NFORMATION FOR THE ALE-TO-MALE RANSEXUAL
Pamphlets published 1965–1983 by the Erickson Educational Foundation
Harry Benjamin thanked Erickson in his groundbreaking 1966 work, *The Transsexual Phenomenon*.
The Transsexual Phenomenon
The book included many technical details but, much like Benjamin himself, was approachable and sympathetic toward its subjects.

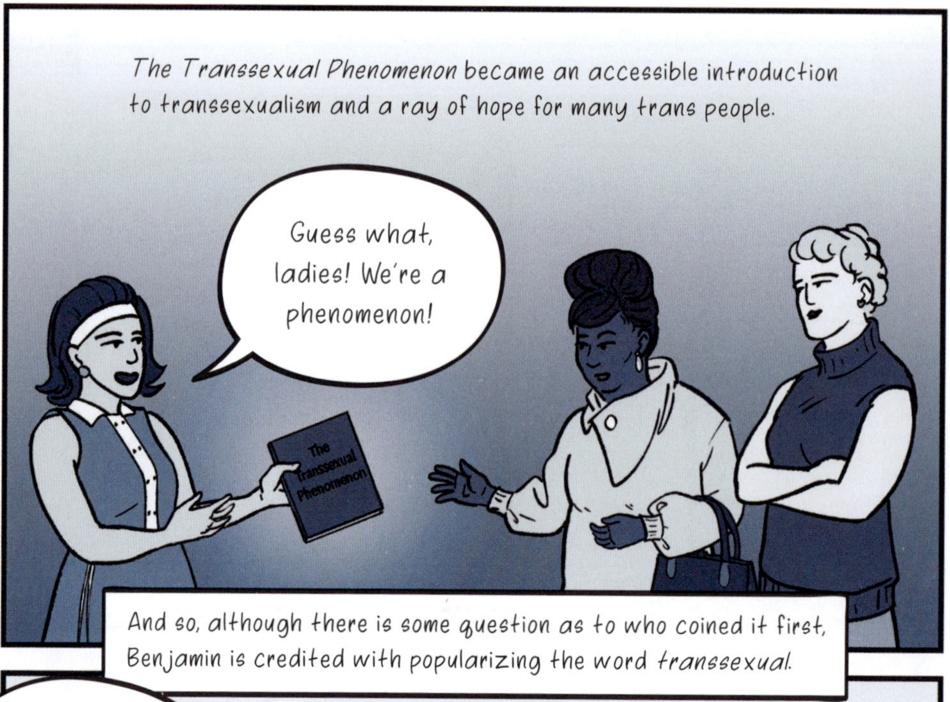
The Transsexual Phenomenon became an accessible introduction to transsexualism and a ray of hope for many trans people.
Guess what, ladies! We're a phenomenon!
The Transsexual Phenomenon
And so, although there is some question as to who coined it first, Benjamin is credited with popularizing the word *transsexual*.

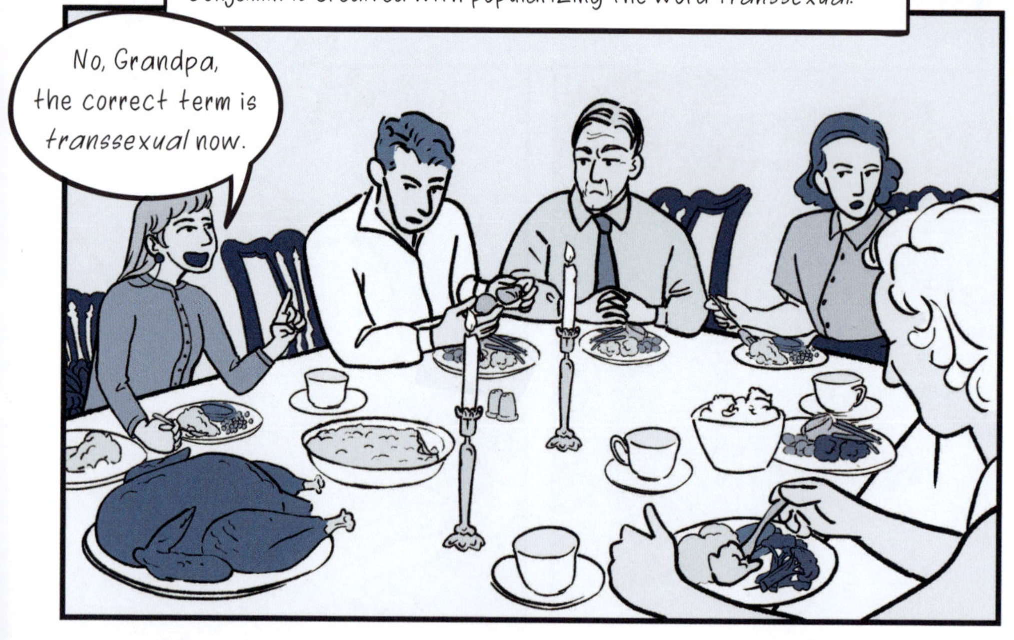
No, Grandpa, the correct term is *transsexual* now.

Benjamin would also later say that his degree of professional success "probably [wouldn't] have happened" without Christine Jorgensen.

Erickson provided financial backing for Johns Hopkins University, which formed the first gender identity clinic in 1965.

Many other similar clinics would open across the United States and beyond over the next few decades.

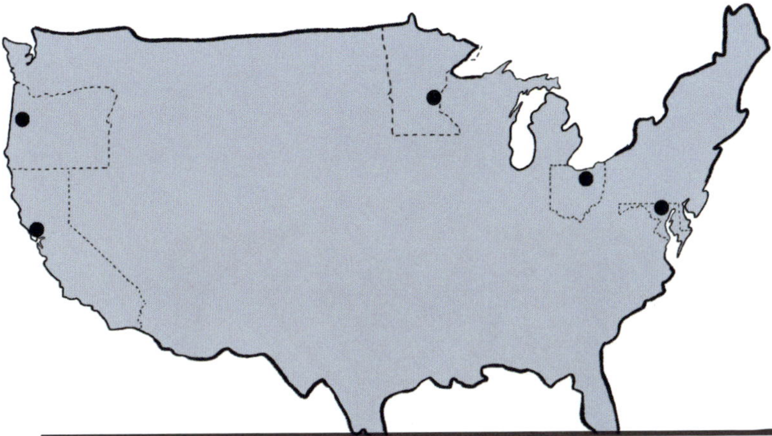

Also with Erickson's backing, the International Symposium on Gender Identity, the first conference of its kind, began in 1969.

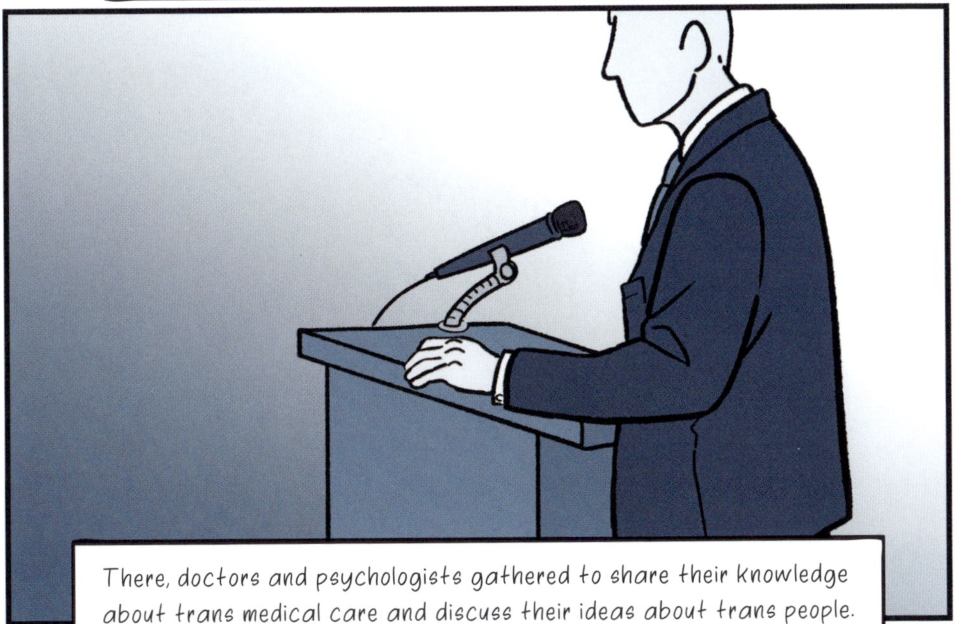

There, doctors and psychologists gathered to share their knowledge about trans medical care and discuss their ideas about trans people.

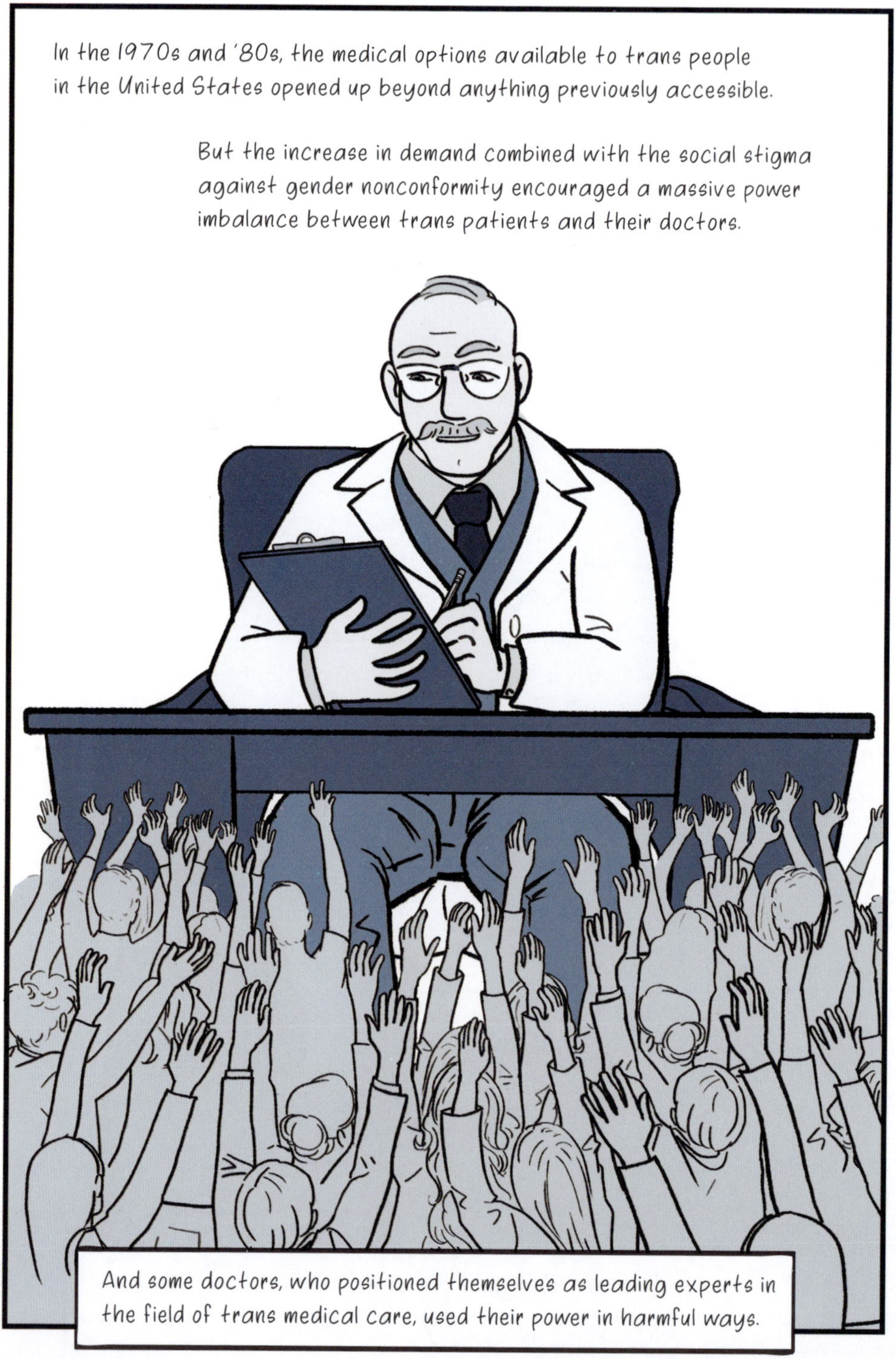
In the 1970s and '80s, the medical options available to trans people in the United States opened up beyond anything previously accessible.
But the increase in demand combined with the social stigma against gender nonconformity encouraged a massive power imbalance between trans patients and their doctors.
And some doctors, who positioned themselves as leading experts in the field of trans medical care, used their power in harmful ways.

Dr. John Money, founder of the 1965 Johns Hopkins Gender Identity Clinic, based his theories on his work with intersex children.

Money popularized many terms still used today, such as:

Gender Identity

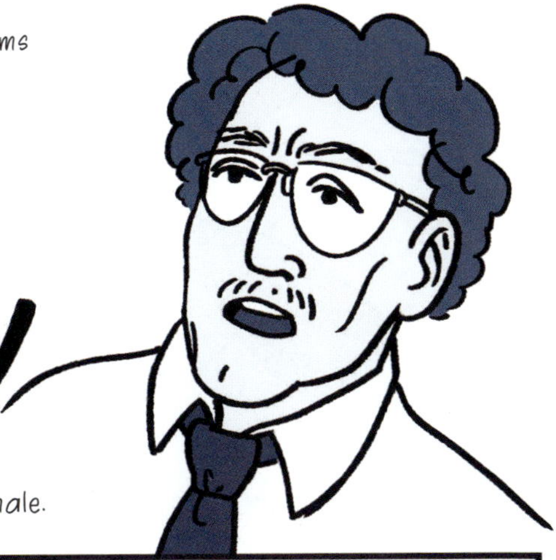

He used it to refer to an internal experience of oneself as male or female.

Feminists had previously introduced the concept of gender being influenced by social forces:

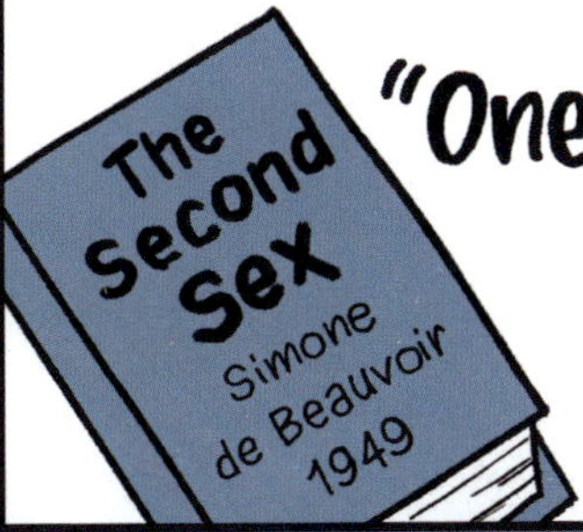
The Second Sex
Simone de Beauvoir
1949

"One is not born, but rather becomes, woman."

But Money's now-debunked theory posited that a child's gender identity could be actively manipulated until a "gender identity gate" closed.

A theory that he tested nonconsensually on his patients.

He was later described by two patients as forcing sexually abusive "treatment" on them as young children.

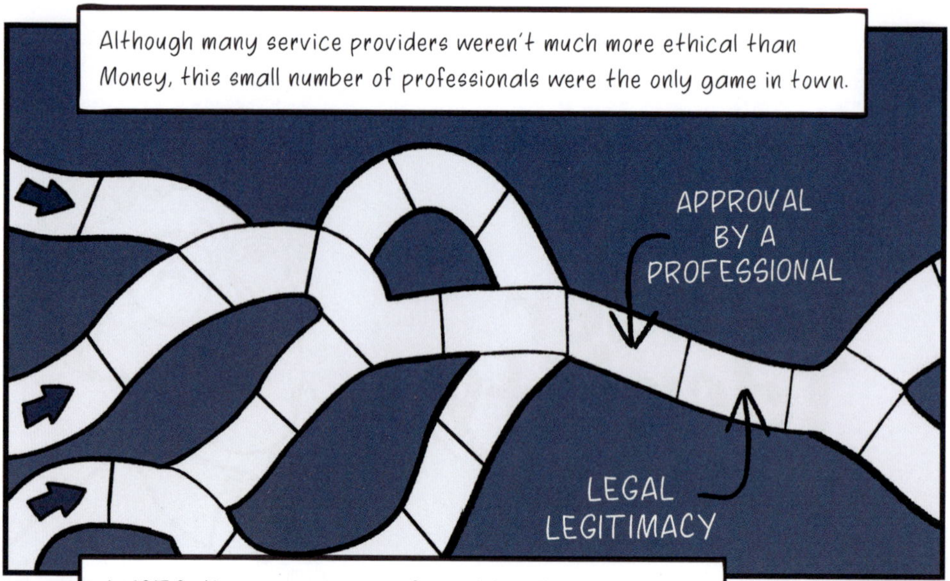
Although many service providers weren't much more ethical than Money, this small number of professionals were the only game in town.
APPROVAL BY A PROFESSIONAL
LEGAL LEGITIMACY

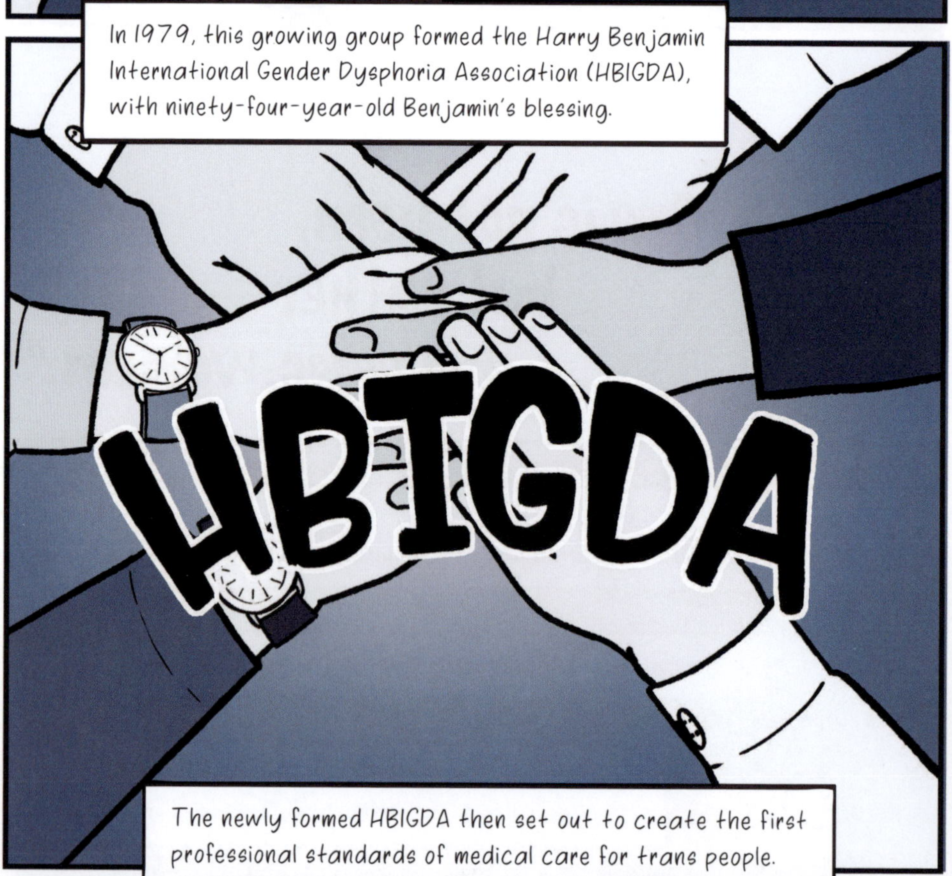
In 1979, this growing group formed the Harry Benjamin International Gender Dysphoria Association (HBIGDA), with ninety-four-year-old Benjamin's blessing.
HBIGDA
The newly formed HBIGDA then set out to create the first professional standards of medical care for trans people.

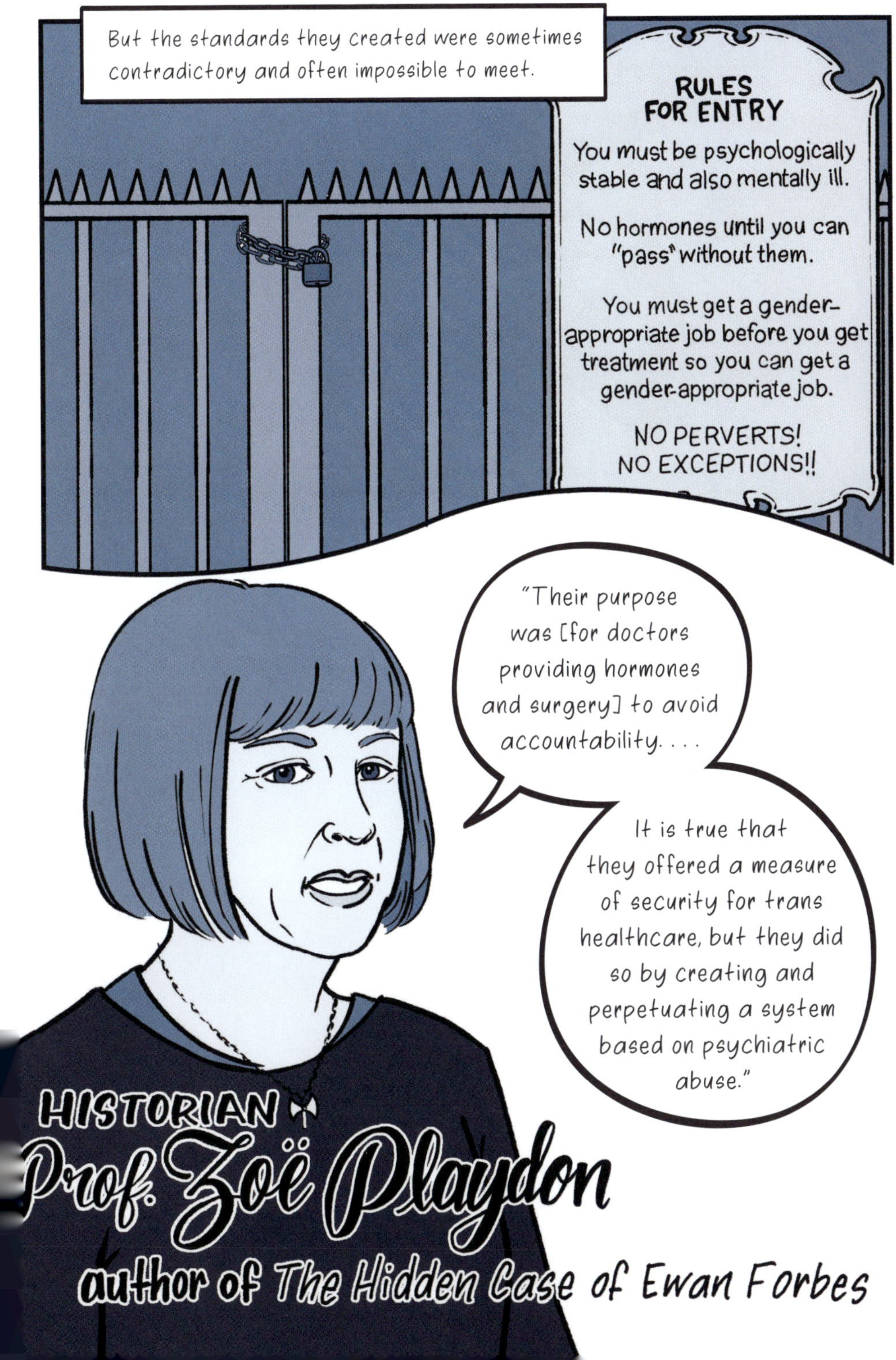

But the standards they created were sometimes contradictory and often impossible to meet.
RULES FOR ENTRY
You must be psychologically stable and also mentally ill.
No hormones until you can "pass" without them.
You must get a gender-appropriate job before you get treatment so you can get a gender-appropriate job.
NO PERVERTS! NO EXCEPTIONS!!
"Their purpose was [for doctors providing hormones and surgery] to avoid accountability. . . .
It is true that they offered a measure of security for trans healthcare, but they did so by creating and perpetuating a system based on psychiatric abuse."
HISTORIAN
Prof. Zoë Playdon
author of The Hidden Case of Ewan Forbes

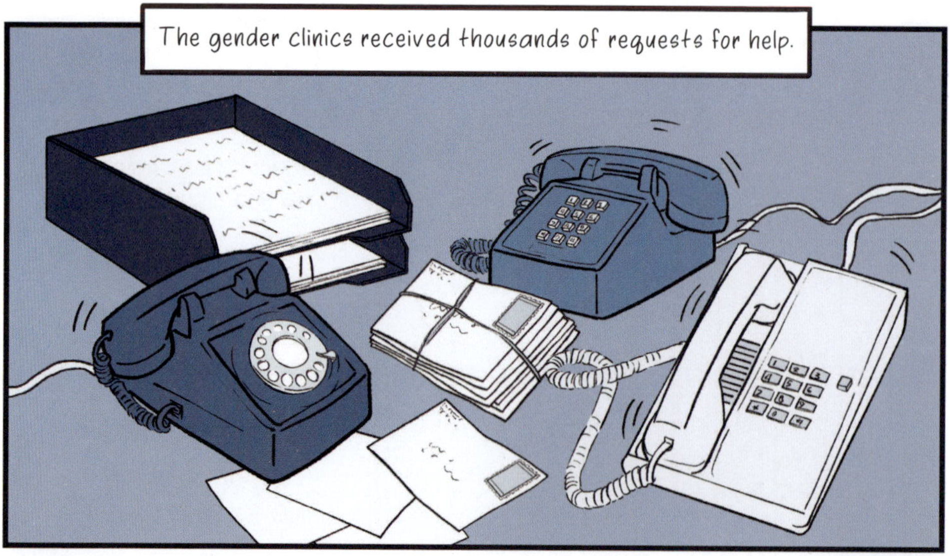
The gender clinics received thousands of requests for help.

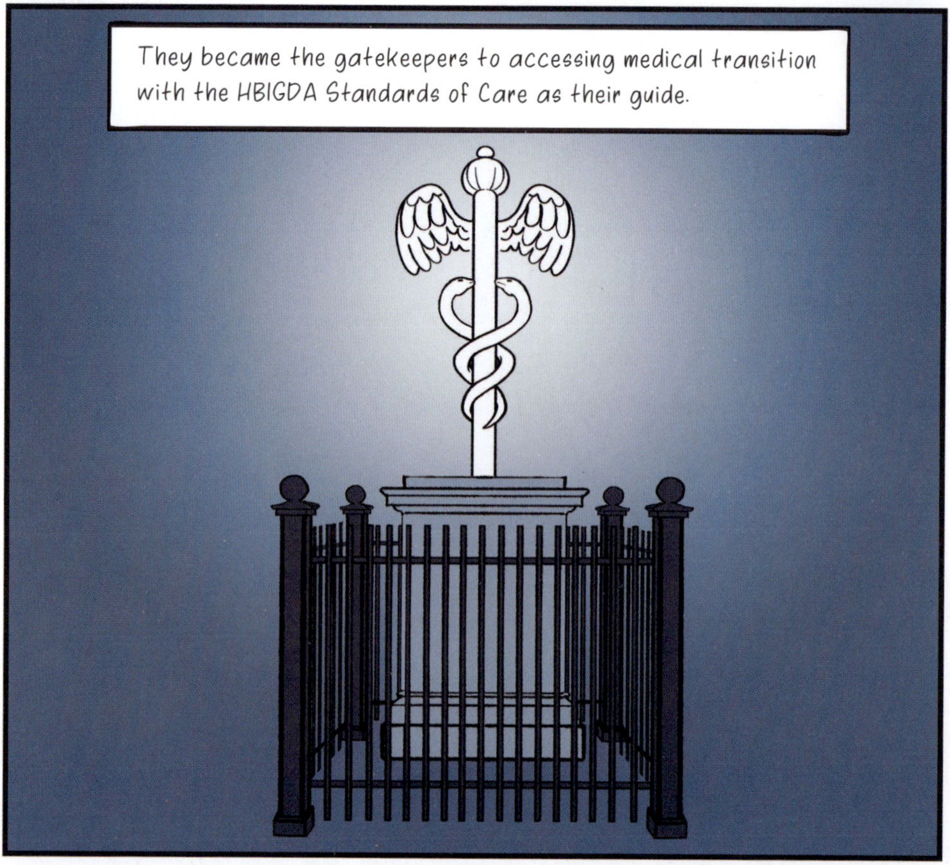
They became the gatekeepers to accessing medical transition with the HBIGDA Standards of Care as their guide.

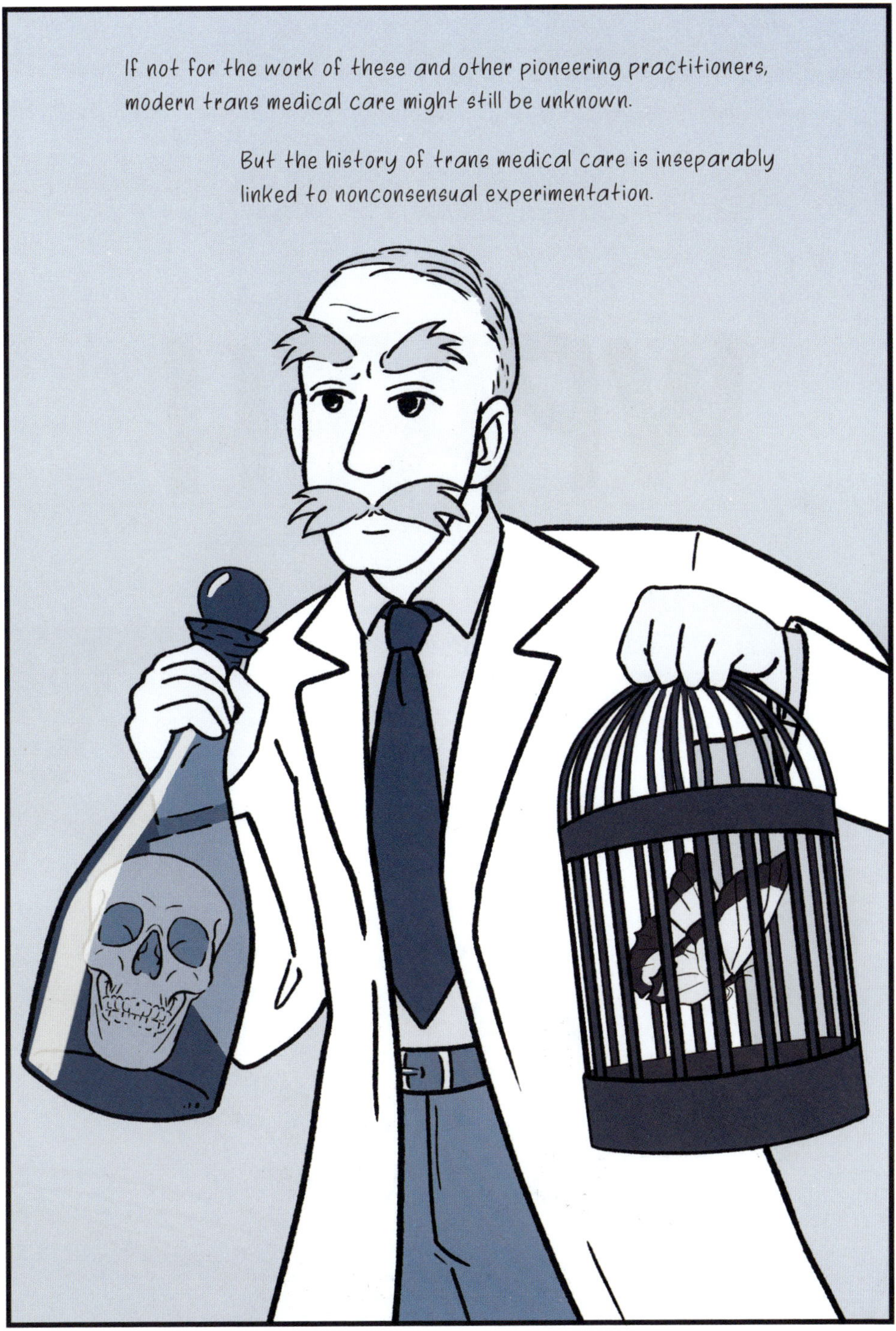
If not for the work of these and other pioneering practitioners, modern trans medical care might still be unknown.
But the history of trans medical care is inseparably linked to nonconsensual experimentation.

The original HBIGDA standards have been revised multiple times, but they formed the basis for the guidelines that are still used today.

In 2007, the Harry Benjamin International Gender Dysphoria Association changed its name to the World Professional Association for Transgender Health (WPATH).

WPATH

WPATH proposed the diagnosis of gender dysphoria for the fifth edition of the *Diagnostic and Statistical Manual of Mental Disorders* (DSM).

DSM 5th Edition 2013

Gender Dysphoria:

"A. A marked incongruence between one's experienced/expressed gender and assigned gender...

B. The condition is associated with clinically significant distress..."

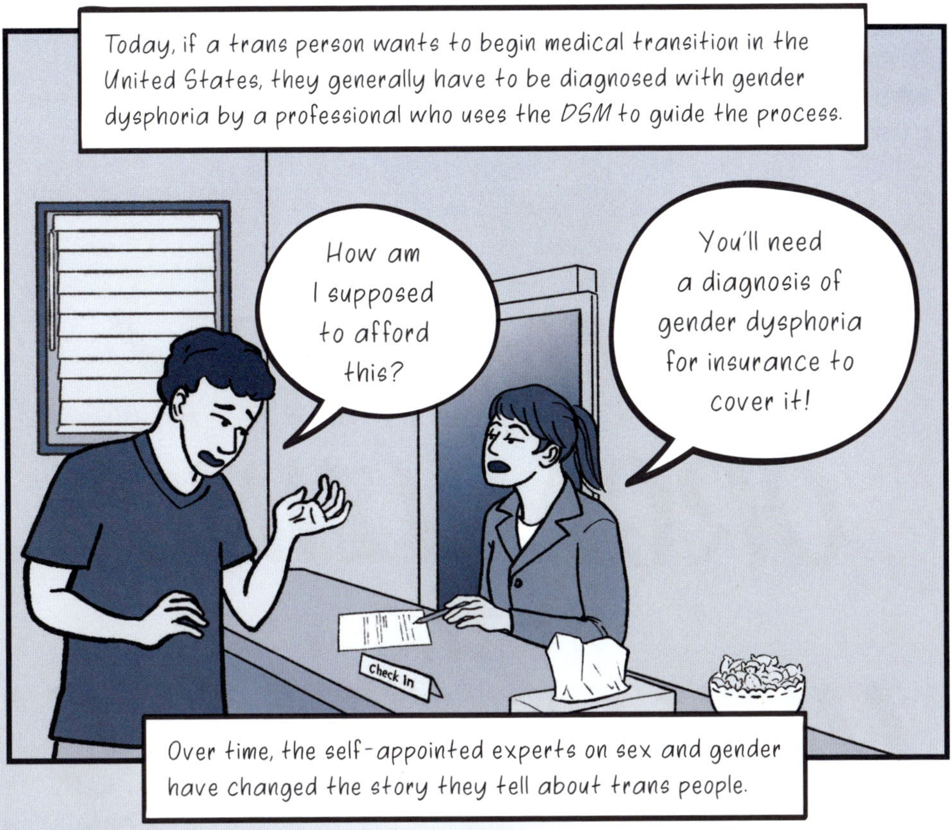
Today, if a trans person wants to begin medical transition in the United States, they generally have to be diagnosed with gender dysphoria by a professional who uses the *DSM* to guide the process.
How am I supposed to afford this?
You'll need a diagnosis of gender dysphoria for insurance to cover it!
Check In
Over time, the self-appointed experts on sex and gender have changed the story they tell about trans people.

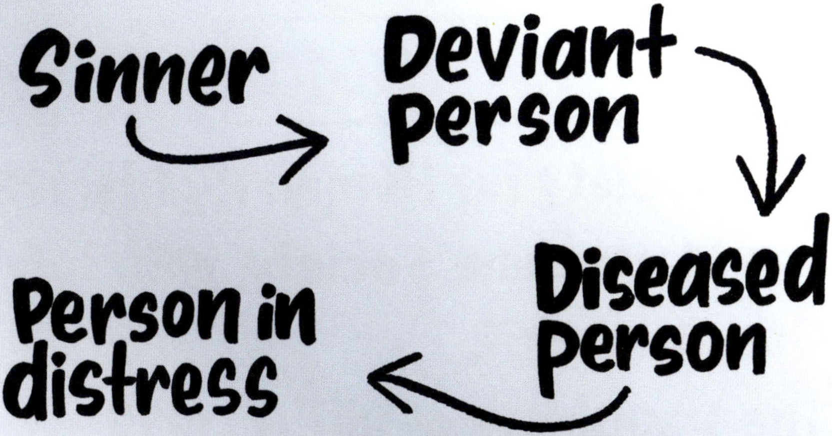
Sinner
Deviant person
Diseased person
Person in distress

But the old viewpoints haven't gone away, and they continue shaping a world that's still hostile to the idea of affirming trans people's existence.

Medical transition continued (and continues) to be important to many trans people, and because of the gender clinics, more people were "changing sex" than ever before.

But even for those who didn't want or couldn't access medical transition, a life-changing awareness was building.

COMMUNITY ORGANIZING in the UNITED STATES

At the beginning of the 1960s, there were already several gay and lesbian groups in the United States:

The Society for Human Rights, 1924
The Mattachine Society, 1950
One, Inc., 1952
The Daughters of Bilitis, 1955
The Janus Society, 1962

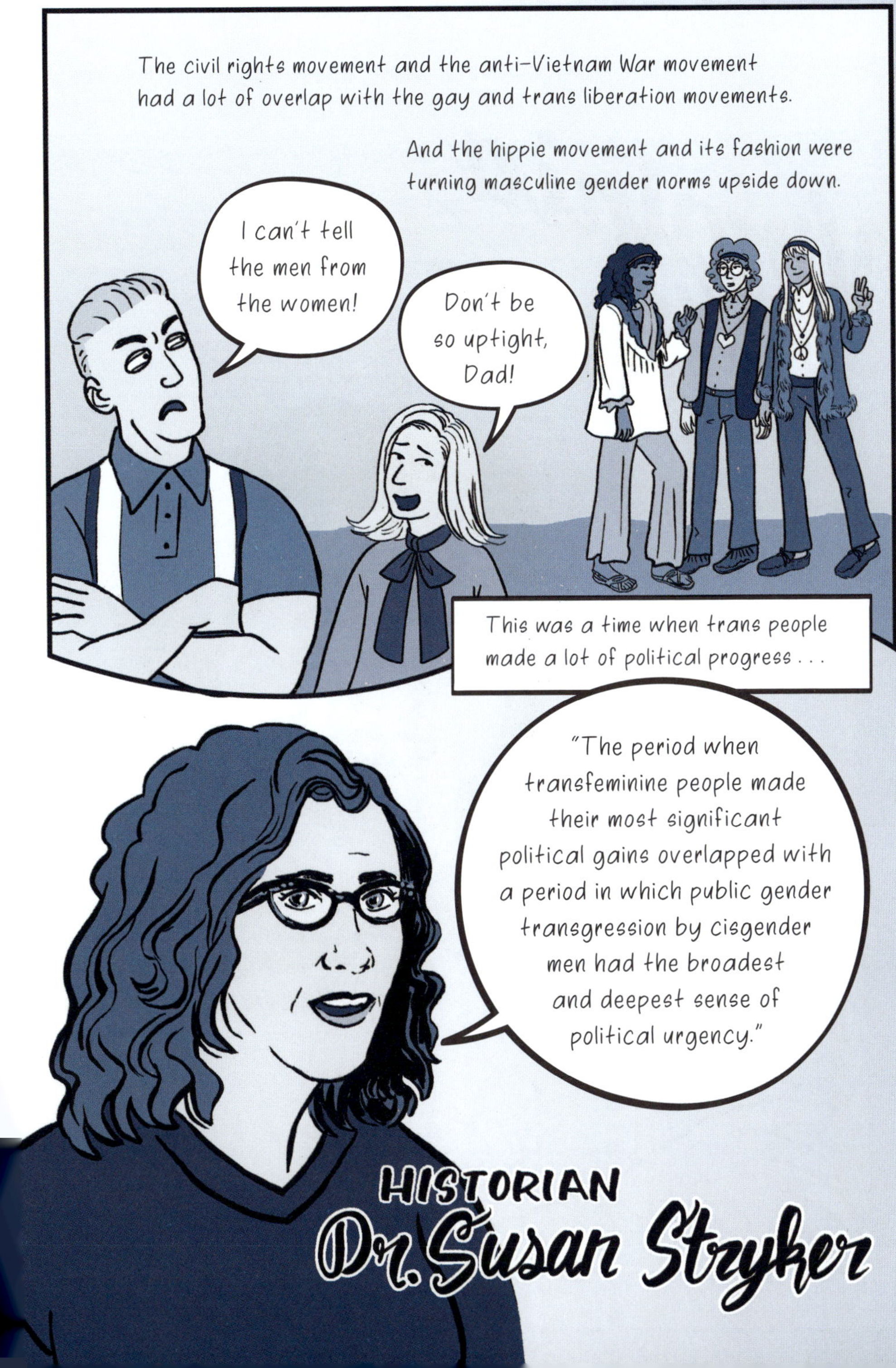

The civil rights movement and the anti-Vietnam War movement had a lot of overlap with the gay and trans liberation movements.
And the hippie movement and its fashion were turning masculine gender norms upside down.
I can't tell the men from the women!
Don't be so uptight, Dad!
This was a time when trans people made a lot of political progress . . .
"The period when transfeminine people made their most significant political gains overlapped with a period in which public gender transgression by cisgender men had the broadest and deepest sense of political urgency."
HISTORIAN
Dr. Susan Stryker

However, the first well-documented group to form specifically around gender expression actually excluded most forms of trans experience.

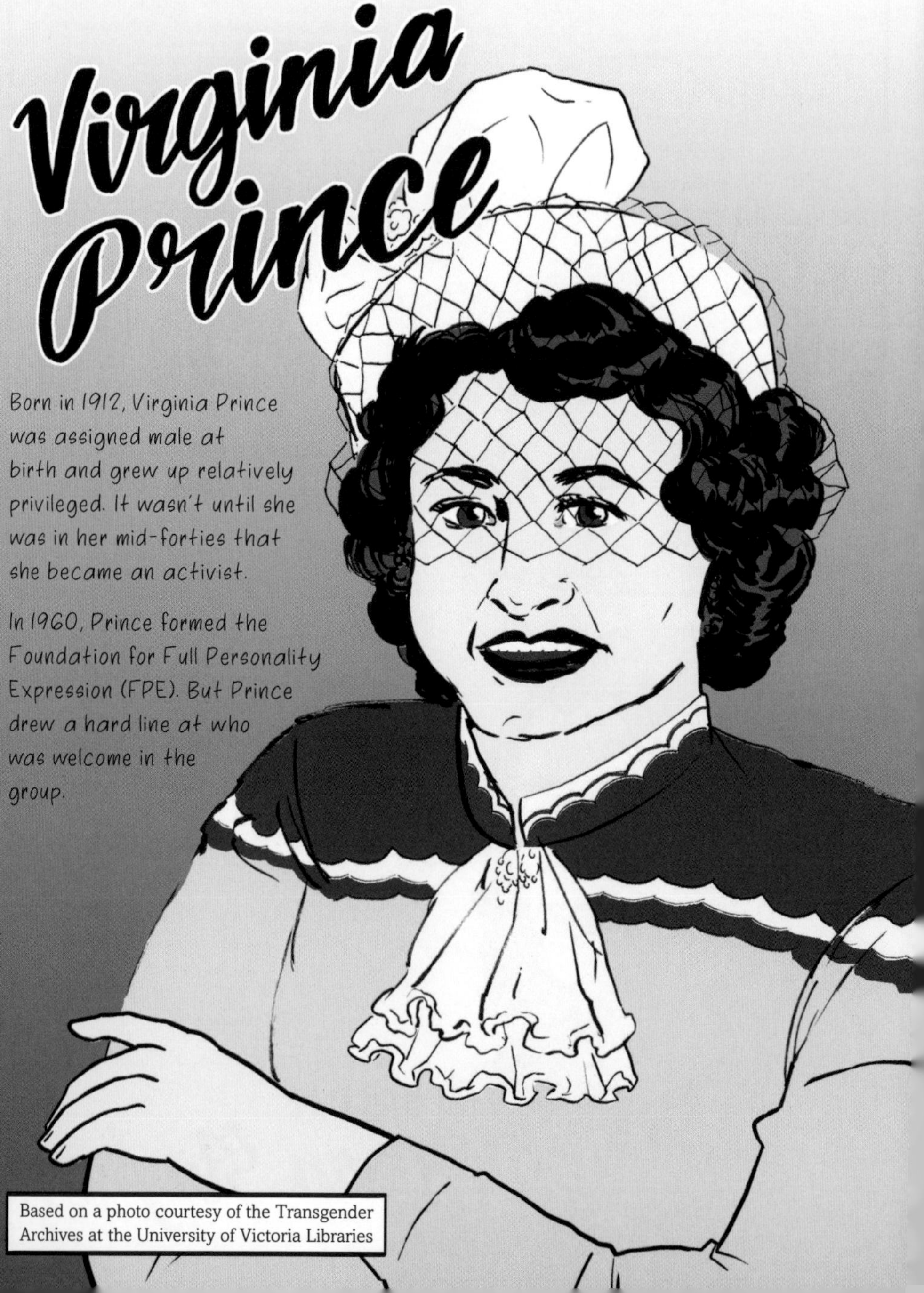
Virginia Prince
Born in 1912, Virginia Prince was assigned male at birth and grew up relatively privileged. It wasn't until she was in her mid-forties that she became an activist.
In 1960, Prince formed the Foundation for Full Personality Expression (FPE). But Prince drew a hard line at who was welcome in the group.

Based on a photo courtesy of the Transgender Archives at the University of Victoria Libraries

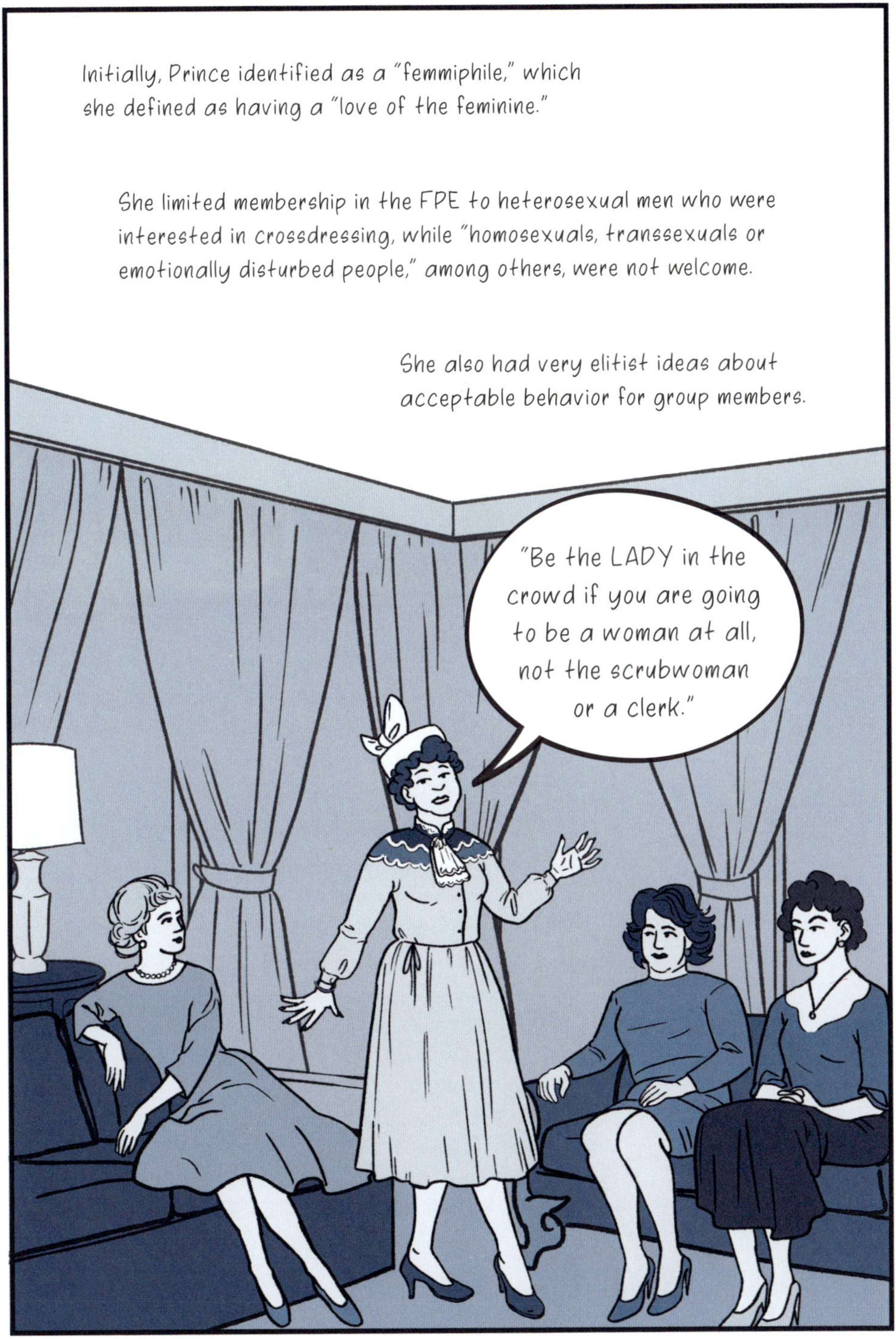
Initially, Prince identified as a "femmiphile," which she defined as having a "love of the feminine."
She limited membership in the FPE to heterosexual men who were interested in crossdressing, while "homosexuals, transsexuals or emotionally disturbed people," among others, were not welcome.
She also had very elitist ideas about acceptable behavior for group members.
"Be the LADY in the crowd if you are going to be a woman at all, not the scrubwoman or a clerk."

Prince is also well-known for publishing *Transvestia*, a community magazine "dedicated to the needs of those heterosexual persons who have become aware of their 'other side' and seek to express it."

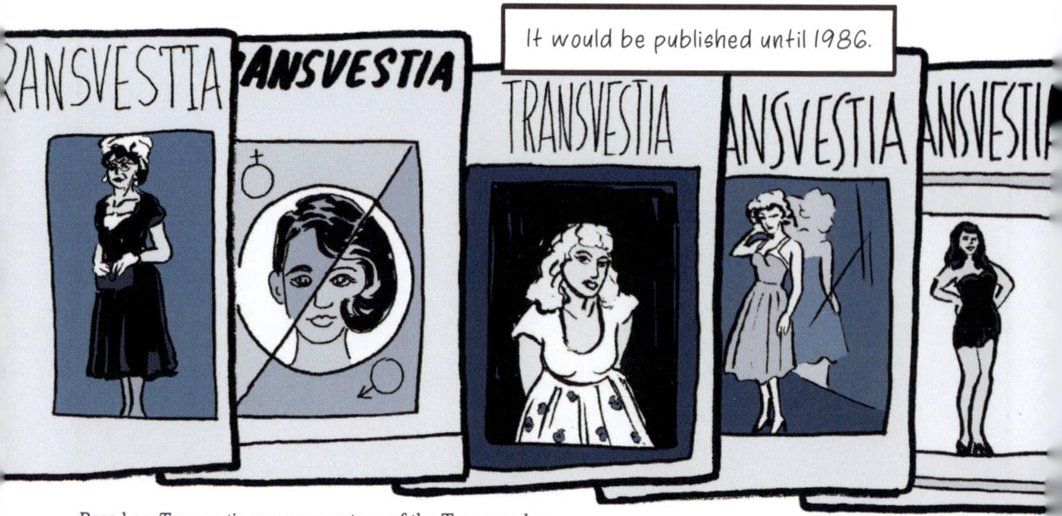
It would be published until 1986.
TRANSVESTIA

Based on *Transvestia* covers, courtesy of the Transgender Archives at the University of Victoria Libraries

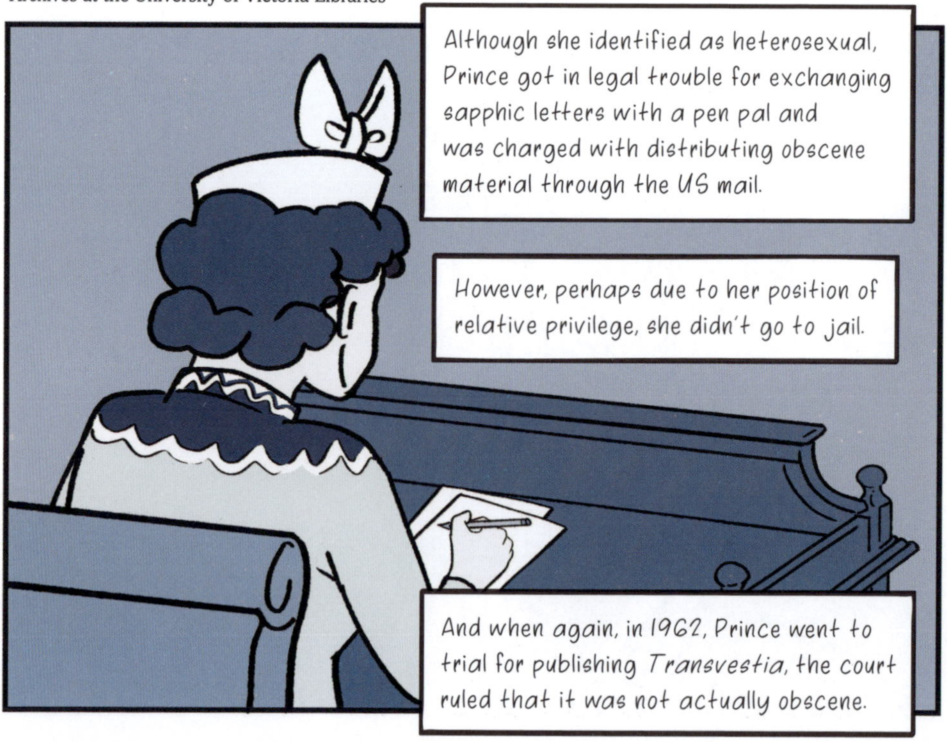
Although she identified as heterosexual, Prince got in legal trouble for exchanging sapphic letters with a pen pal and was charged with distributing obscene material through the US mail.
However, perhaps due to her position of relative privilege, she didn't go to jail.
And when again, in 1962, Prince went to trial for publishing *Transvestia*, the court ruled that it was not actually obscene.

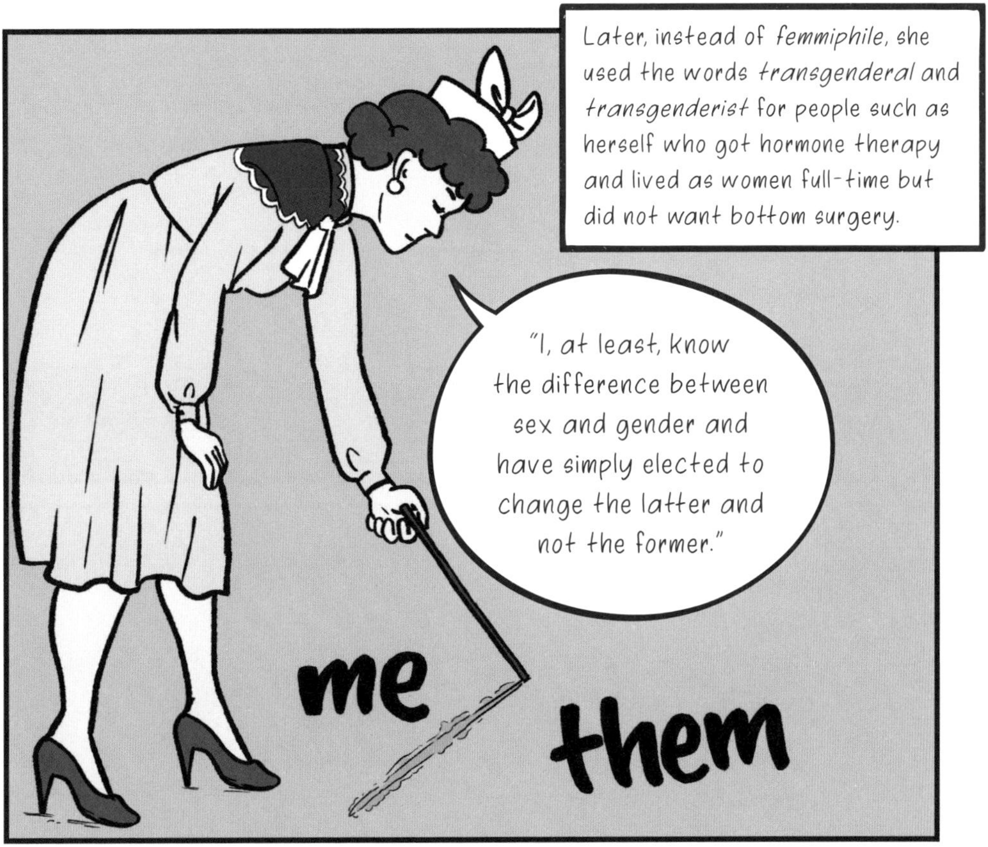
Later, instead of *femmiphile*, she used the words *transgenderal* and *transgenderist* for people such as herself who got hormone therapy and lived as women full-time but did not want bottom surgery.
"I, at least, know the difference between sex and gender and have simply elected to change the latter and not the former."
me
them

Because of this, she claimed to have coined the word *transgender*.

But there had been several previously proposed combinations of *trans* and *gender* with varying meanings, so it's difficult to pinpoint one exact origin of the word.

TRANS___

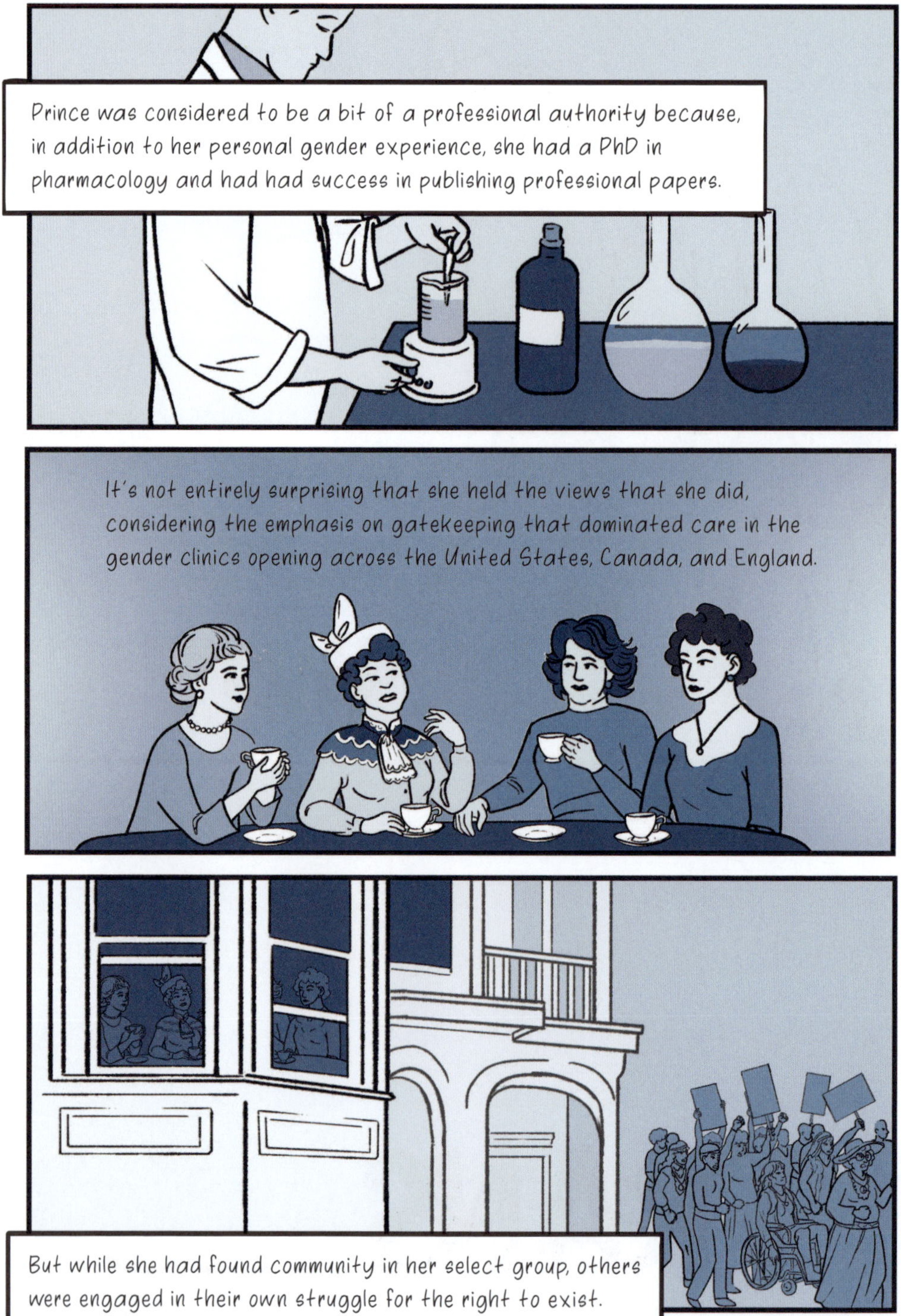
Prince was considered to be a bit of a professional authority because, in addition to her personal gender experience, she had a PhD in pharmacology and had had success in publishing professional papers.
It's not entirely surprising that she held the views that she did, considering the emphasis on gatekeeping that dominated care in the gender clinics opening across the United States, Canada, and England.
But while she had found community in her select group, others were engaged in their own struggle for the right to exist.

During the 1960s, there were many instances of disenfranchised trans people coming together to resist discrimination and harassment.

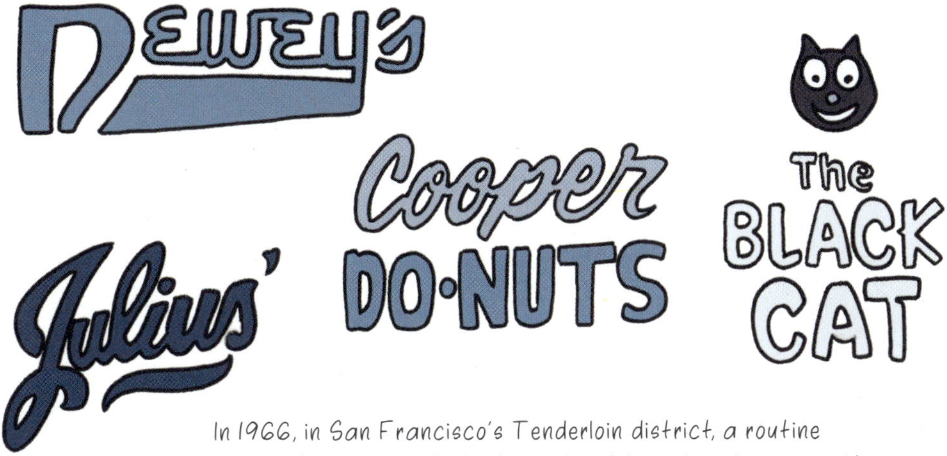
Dewey's
Cooper
DO-NUTS
The
BLACK
CAT
Julius'

In 1966, in San Francisco's Tenderloin district, a routine abuse of power erupted into a street brawl—police against trans people, street kids, gay sex workers, and others.

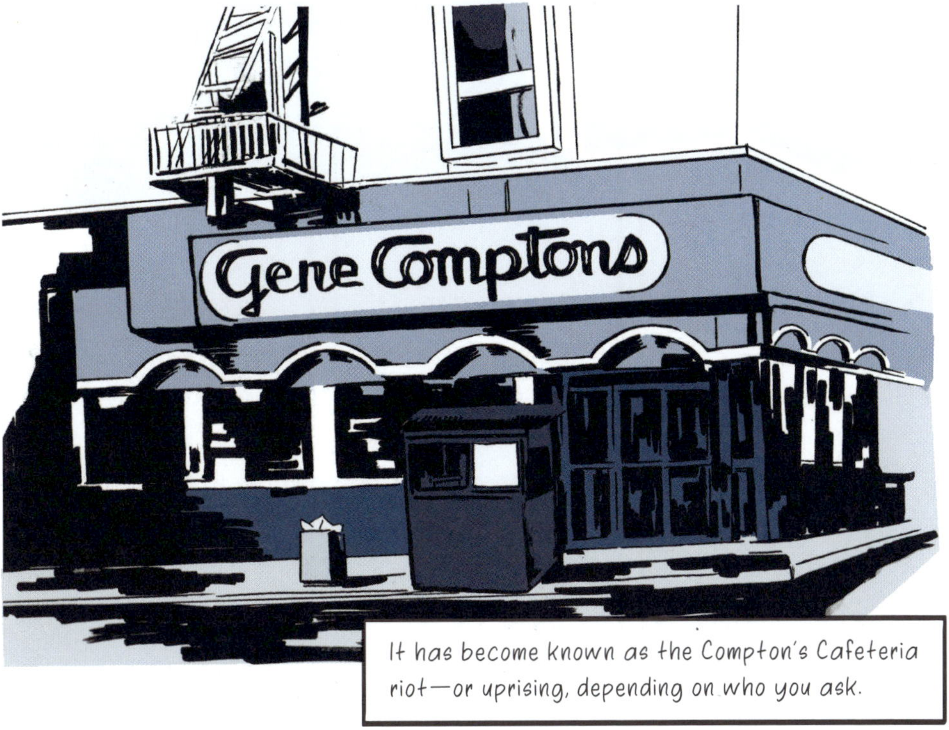
Gene Comptons
It has become known as the Compton's Cafeteria riot—or uprising, depending on who you ask.

Based on footage from the documentary *Screaming Queens*, courtesy of Susan Stryker

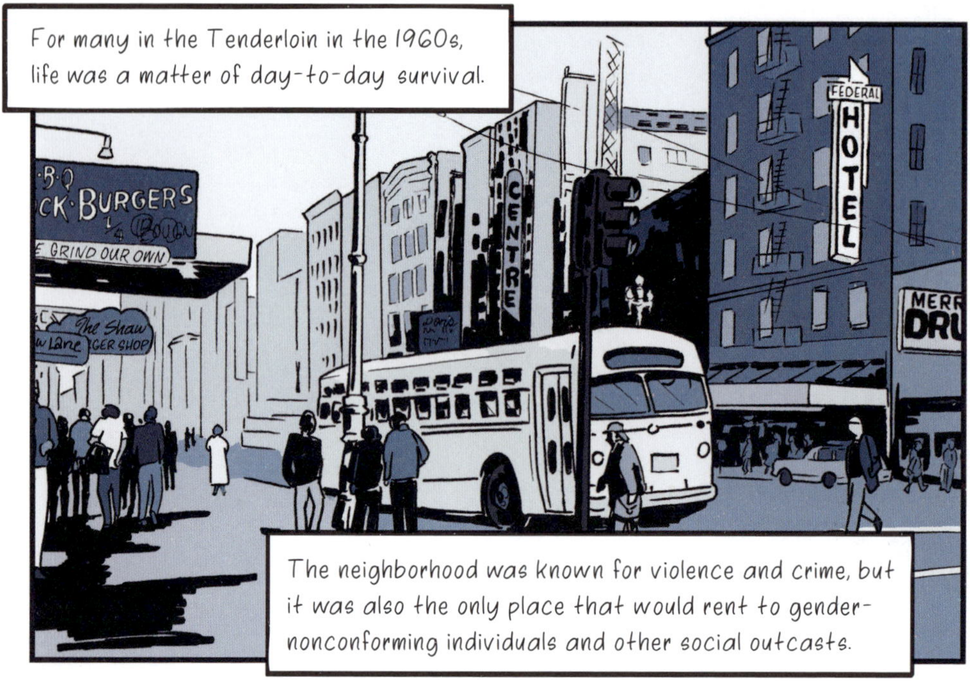

For many in the Tenderloin in the 1960s, life was a matter of day-to-day survival.
CK·BURGERS
E GRIND OUR OWN
The Shaw
GER SHOP
FEDERAL
HOTEL
CENTRE
MERR
DRU
The neighborhood was known for violence and crime, but it was also the only place that would rent to gender-nonconforming individuals and other social outcasts.

Based on a 1964 photo, courtesy of OpenSFHistory

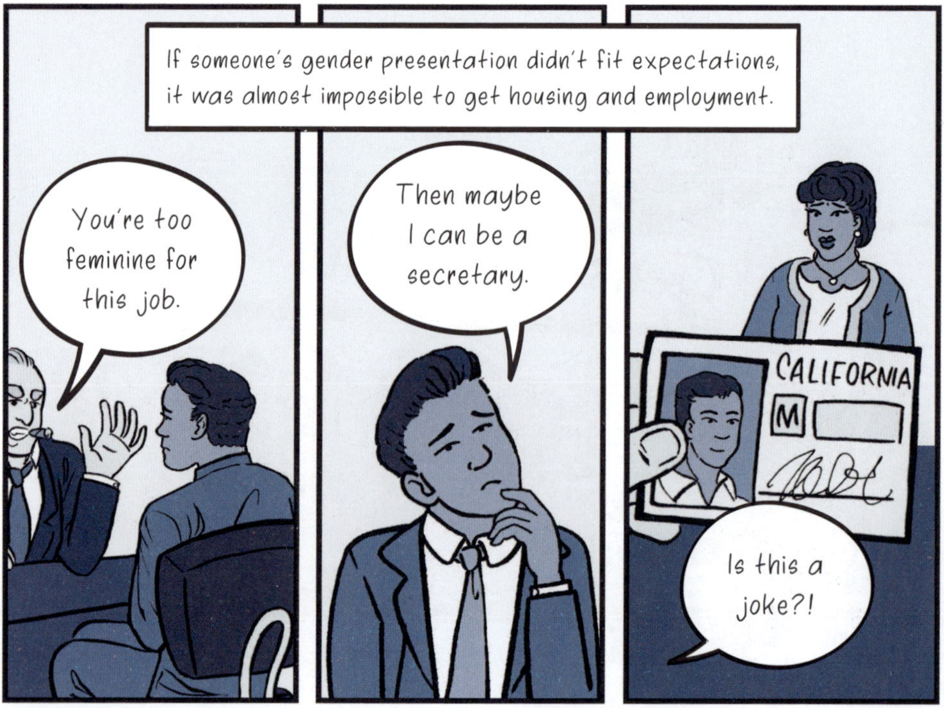

If someone's gender presentation didn't fit expectations, it was almost impossible to get housing and employment.
You're too feminine for this job.
Then maybe I can be a secretary.
CALIFORNIA
M
Is this a joke?!

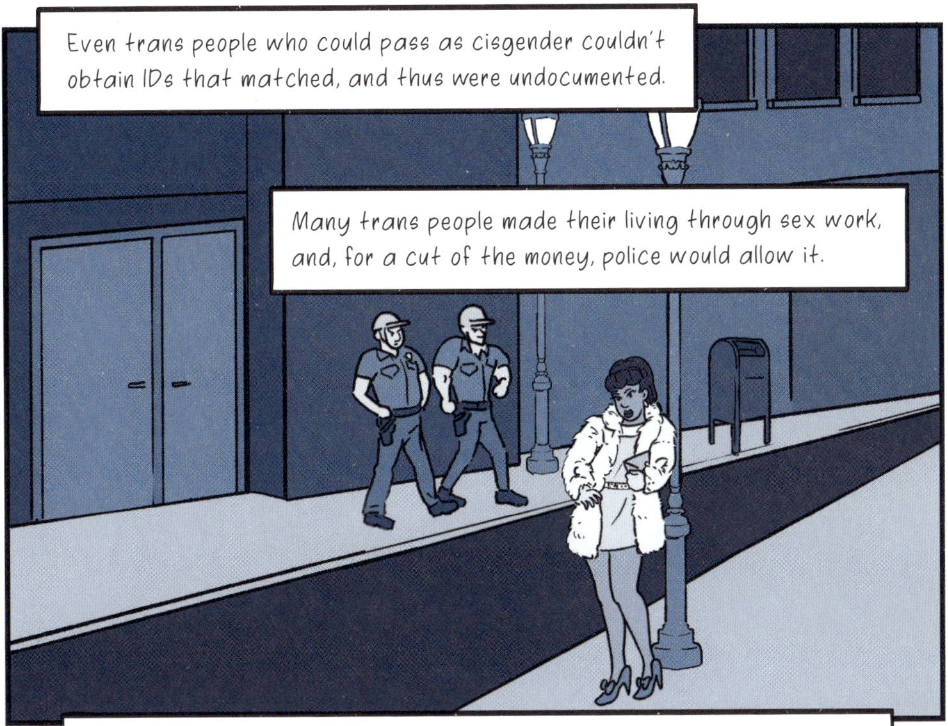
Even trans people who could pass as cisgender couldn't obtain IDs that matched, and thus were undocumented.
Many trans people made their living through sex work, and, for a cut of the money, police would allow it.

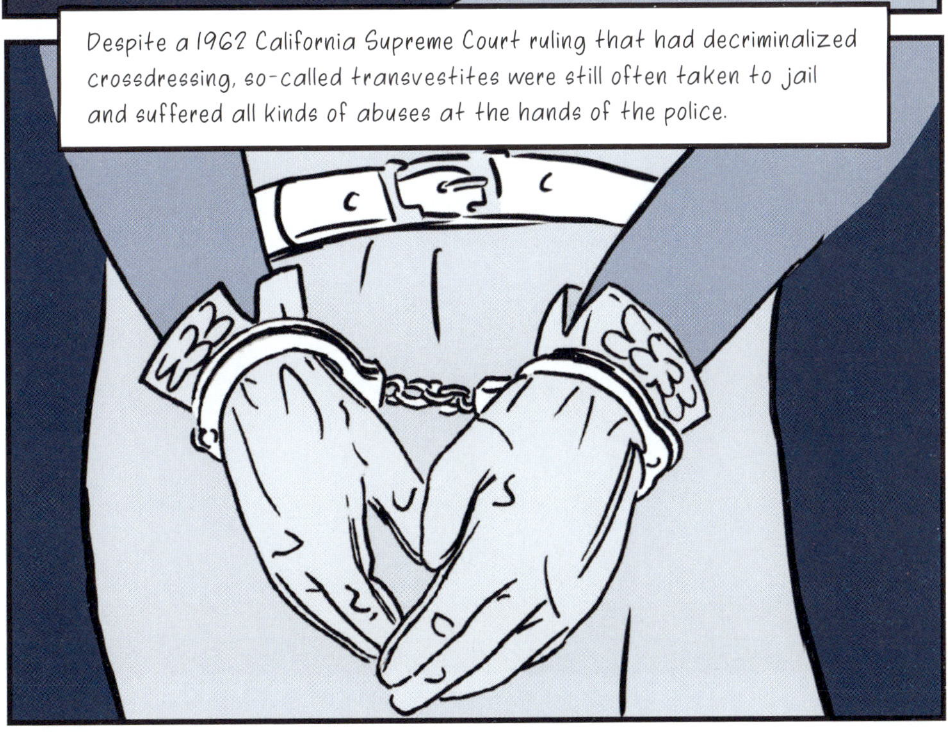
Despite a 1962 California Supreme Court ruling that had decriminalized crossdressing, so-called transvestites were still often taken to jail and suffered all kinds of abuses at the hands of the police.

But there were some places that trans people would claim space...

Open twenty-four hours, Compton's was clean and brightly lit, with a long menu of cheap food.

All kinds of people gathered there.

A local group of street kids would frequently hang out and talk politics but not spend much money.

When management blacklisted them, they organized a picket line to protest unfair treatment.

This political action helped set the stage for the Compton's uprising.

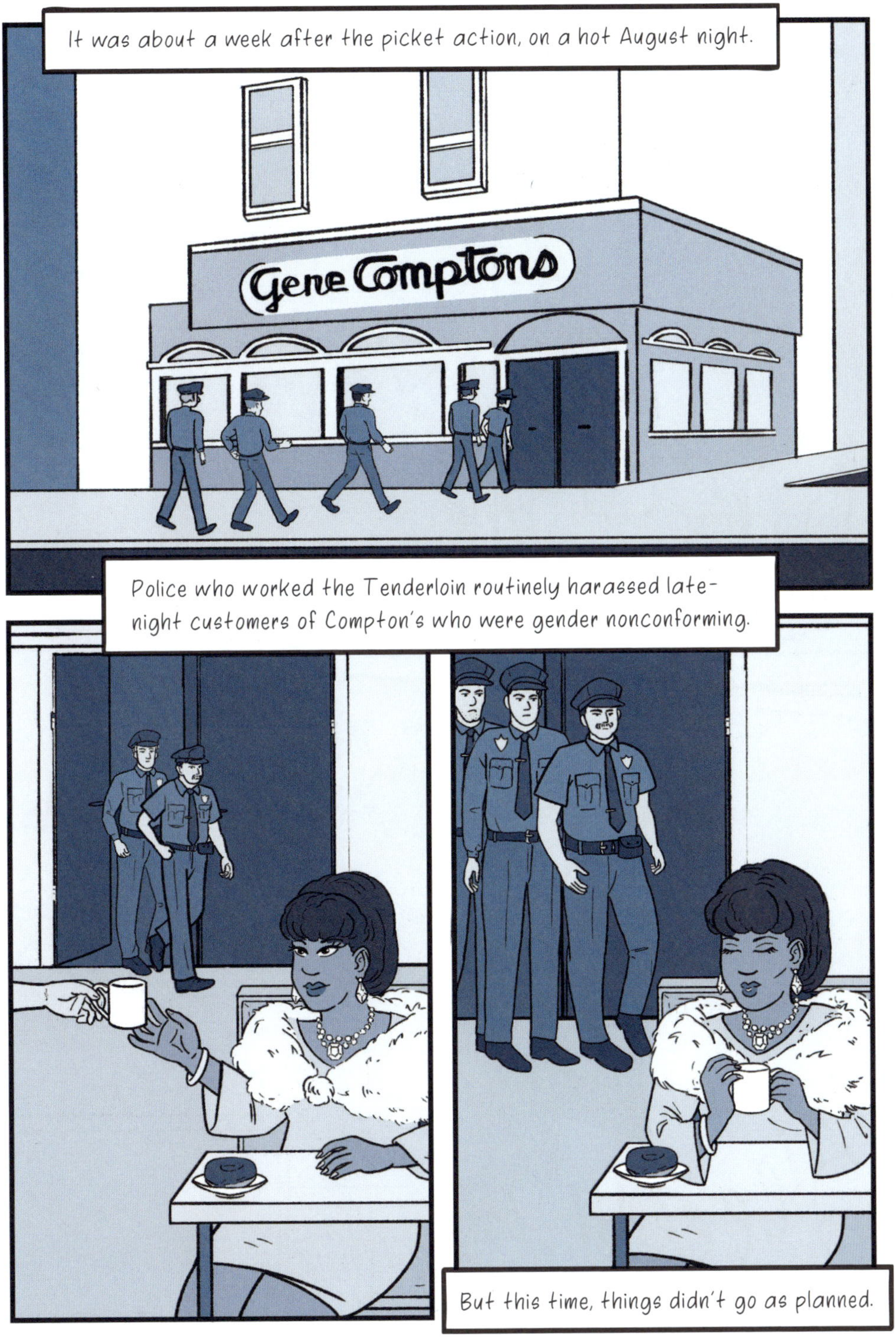
It was about a week after the picket action, on a hot August night.
Gene Comptons
Police who worked the Tenderloin routinely harassed late-night customers of Compton's who were gender nonconforming.
But this time, things didn't go as planned.

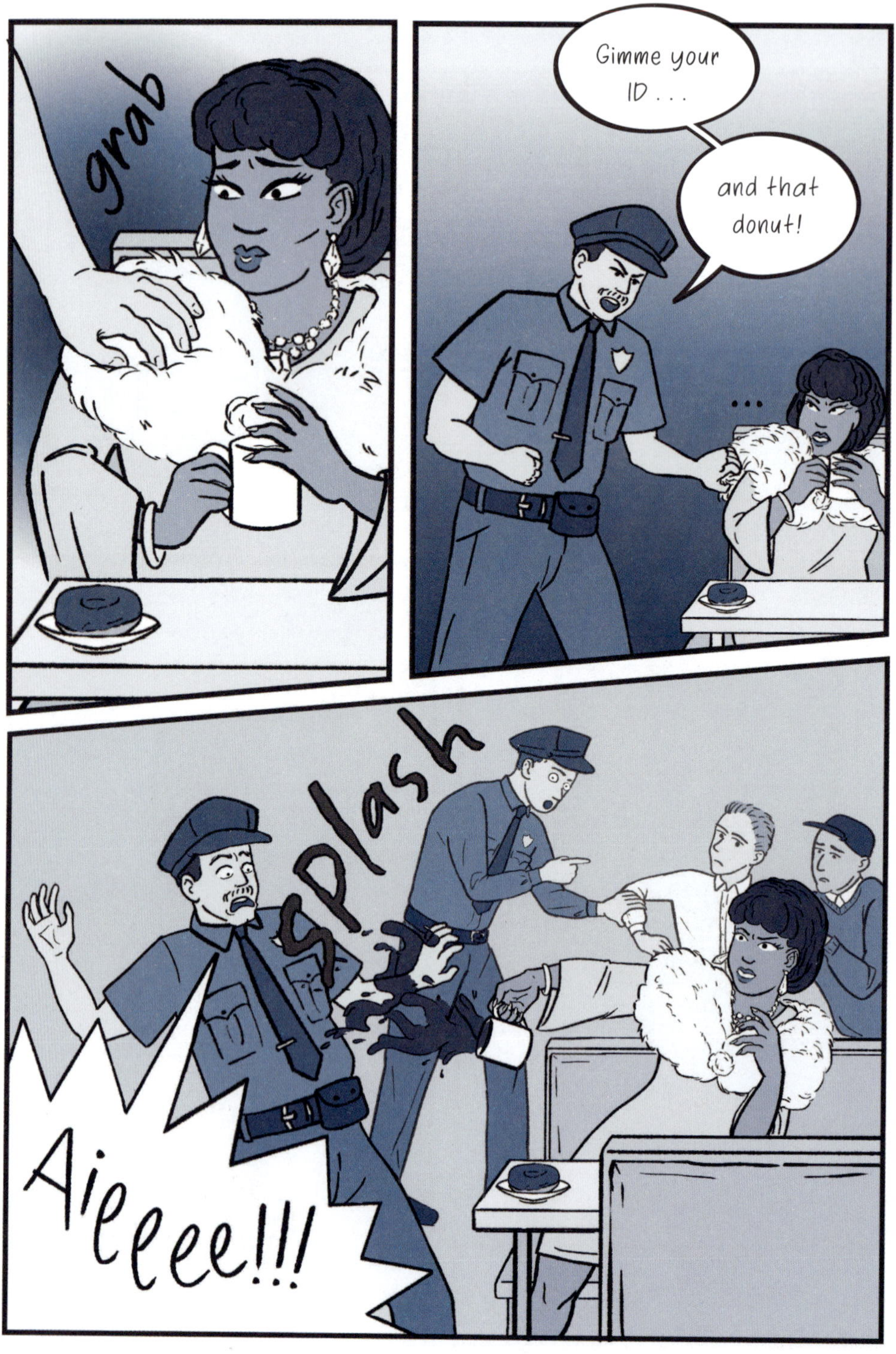
grab
Gimme your ID . . .
and that donut!
...
Splash
Aieeee!!!

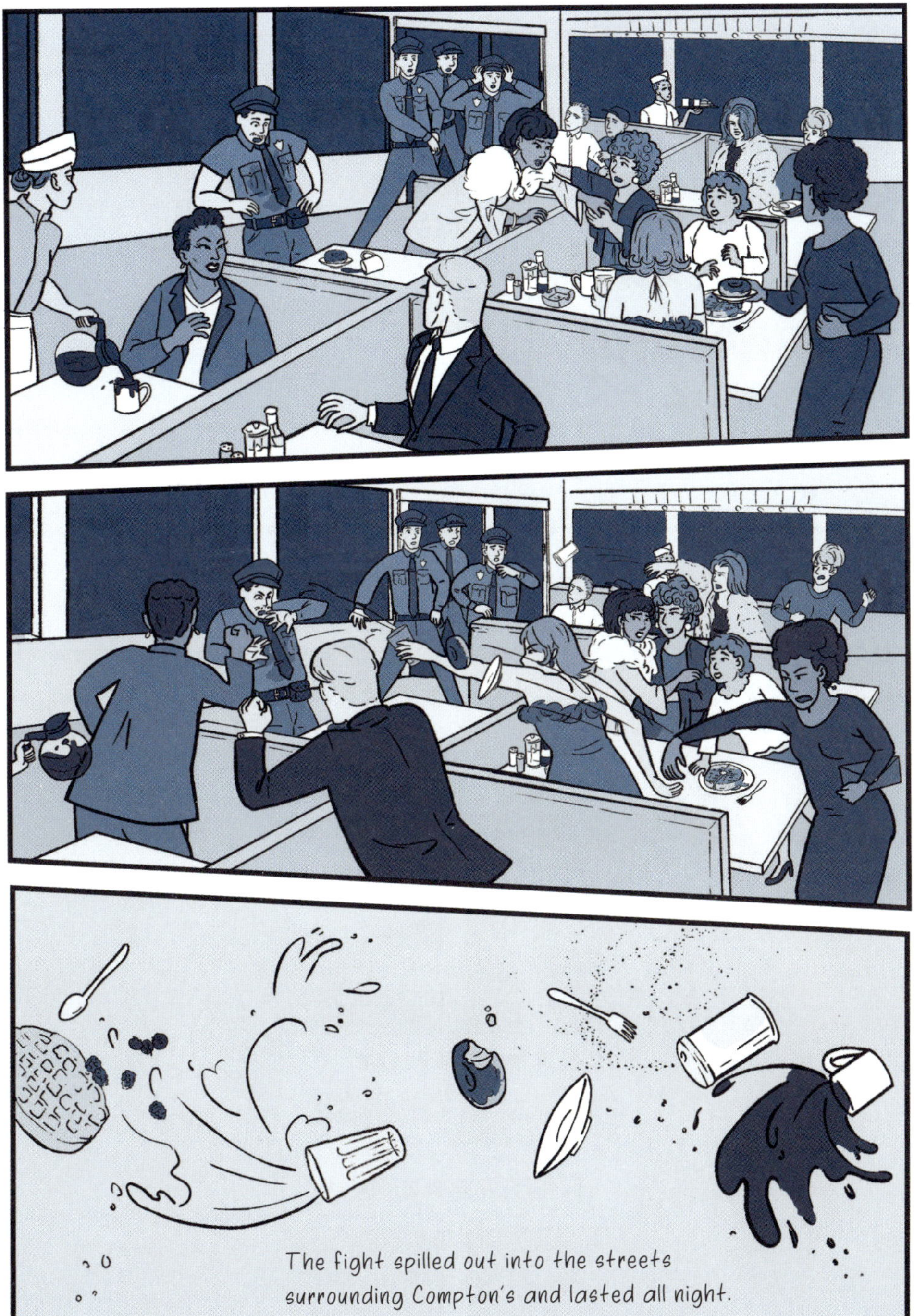
The fight spilled out into the streets surrounding Compton's and lasted all night.

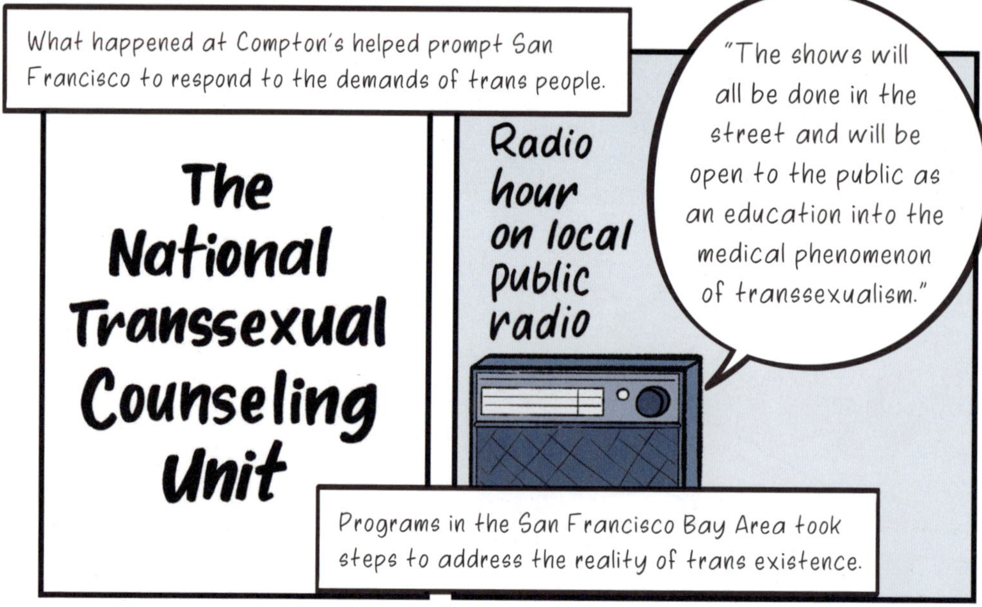
What happened at Compton's helped prompt San Francisco to respond to the demands of trans people.
The National Transsexual Counseling Unit
Radio hour on local public radio
"The shows will all be done in the street and will be open to the public as an education into the medical phenomenon of transsexualism."
Programs in the San Francisco Bay Area took steps to address the reality of trans existence.

Similar to Berlin's "transvestite passes" of three decades prior, the city of San Francisco began issuing special IDs to trans people to help them get housing and employment, open bank accounts, and avoid police harassment.

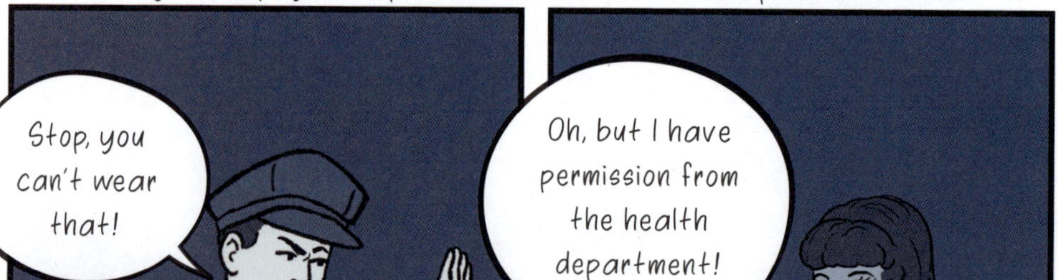
Stop, you can't wear that!
Oh, but I have permission from the health department!
THIS IS TO CERTIFY THAT
______________ IS UNDER TREATMENT AT THE CENTER FOR SPECIAL PROBLEMS FOR TRANSSEXUALISM
S.F. DEPT. OF PUBLIC HEALTH

Based on a real "transvestite pass" as seen in the documentary *Screaming Queens*

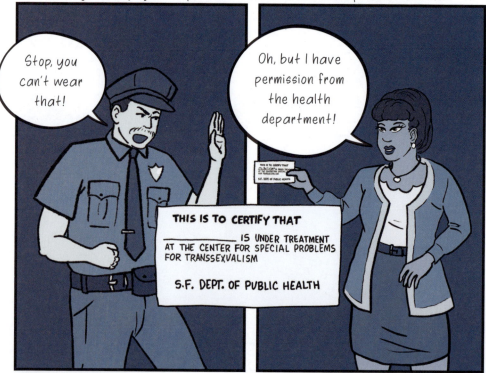

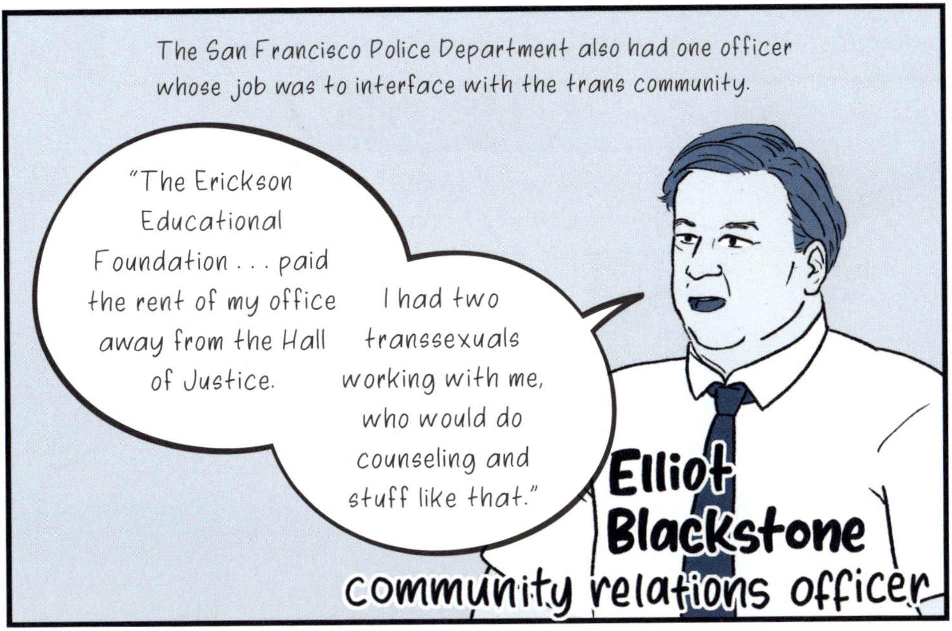
The San Francisco Police Department also had one officer whose job was to interface with the trans community.
"The Erickson Educational Foundation . . . paid the rent of my office away from the Hall of Justice.
I had two transsexuals working with me, who would do counseling and stuff like that."
Elliot Blackstone
community relations officer

These services were made possible in large part due to Harry Benjamin having a part-time trans medical practice in San Francisco and to Reed Erickson's financial involvement in everything from medical care to city initiatives.

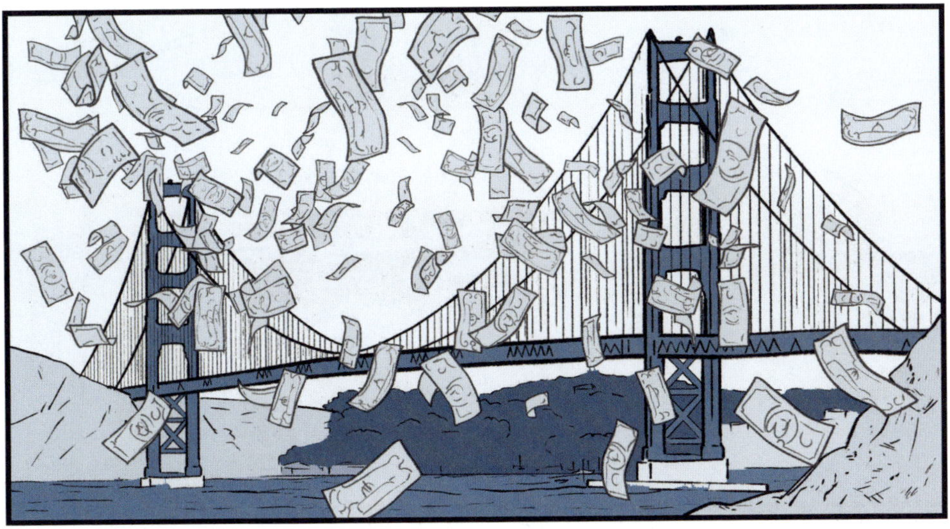

Meanwhile, on the East Coast, things were also changing . . .

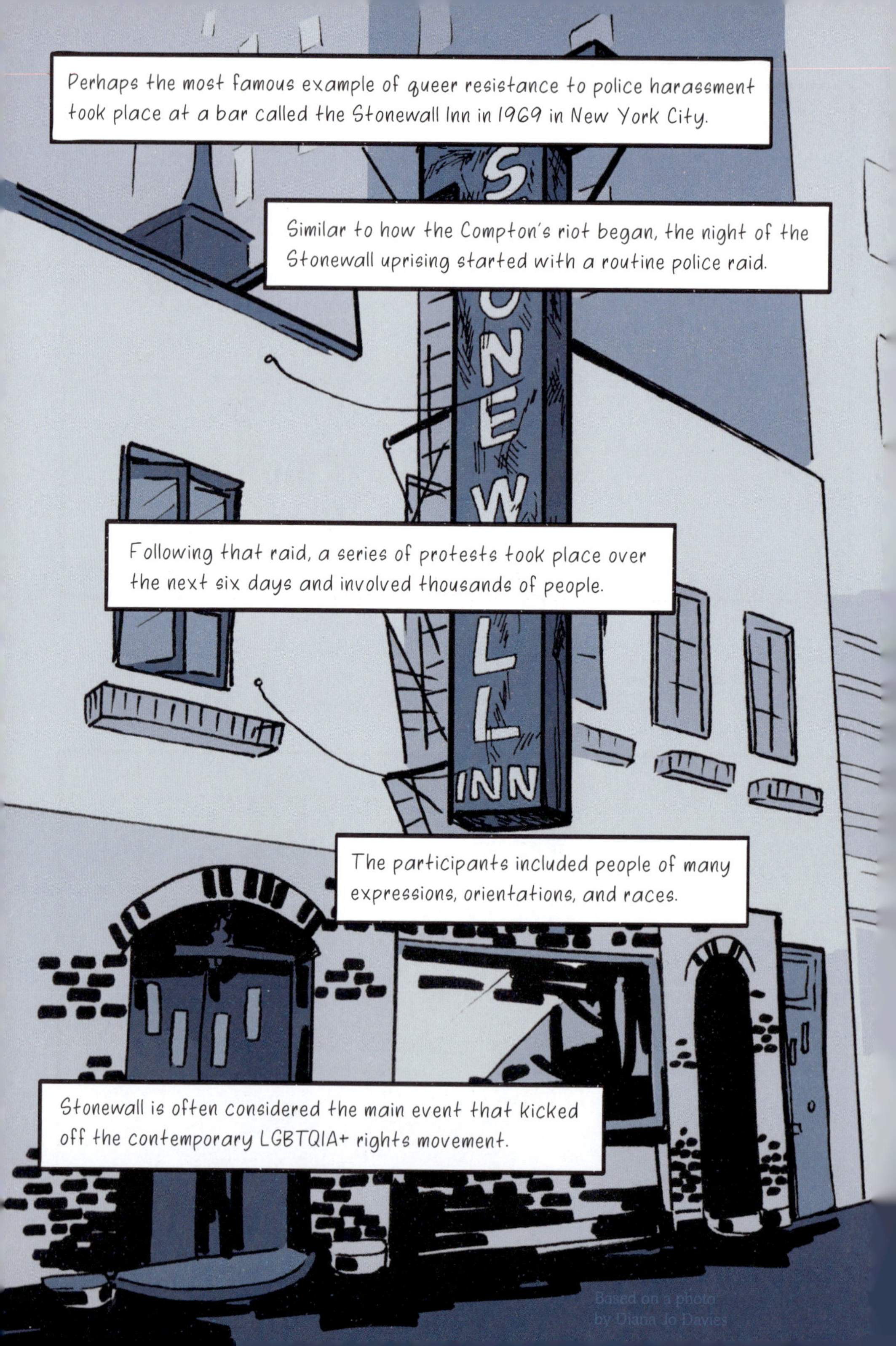
Perhaps the most famous example of queer resistance to police harassment took place at a bar called the Stonewall Inn in 1969 in New York City.
Similar to how the Compton's riot began, the night of the Stonewall uprising started with a routine police raid.
Following that raid, a series of protests took place over the next six days and involved thousands of people.
The participants included people of many expressions, orientations, and races.
Stonewall is often considered the main event that kicked off the contemporary LGBTQIA+ rights movement.
Based on a photo by Diana Jo Davies

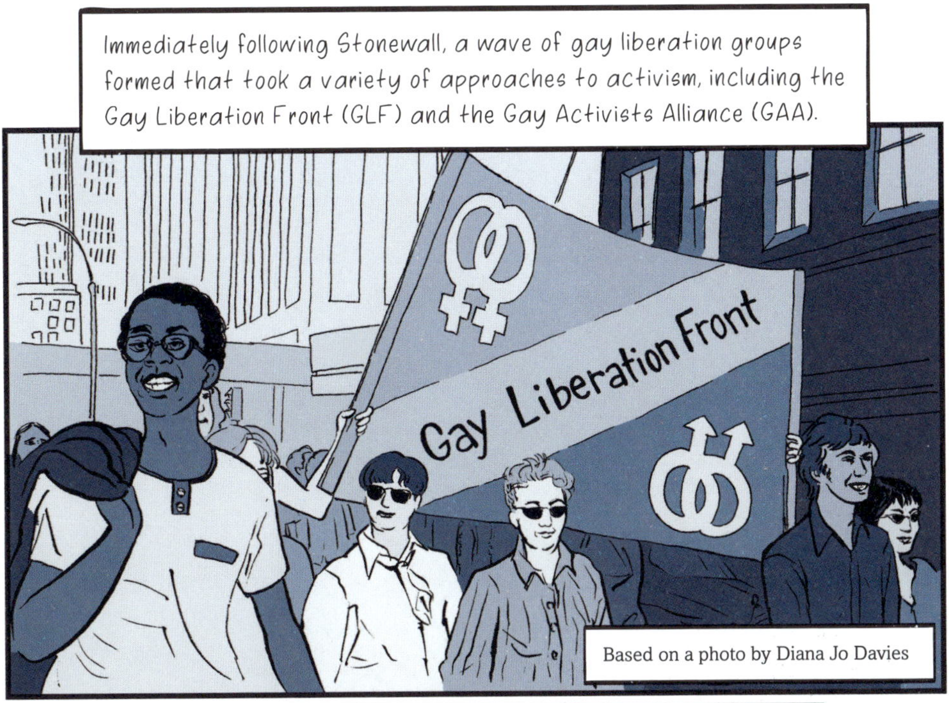
Immediately following Stonewall, a wave of gay liberation groups formed that took a variety of approaches to activism, including the Gay Liberation Front (GLF) and the Gay Activists Alliance (GAA).
Gay Liberation Front
Based on a photo by Diana Jo Davies

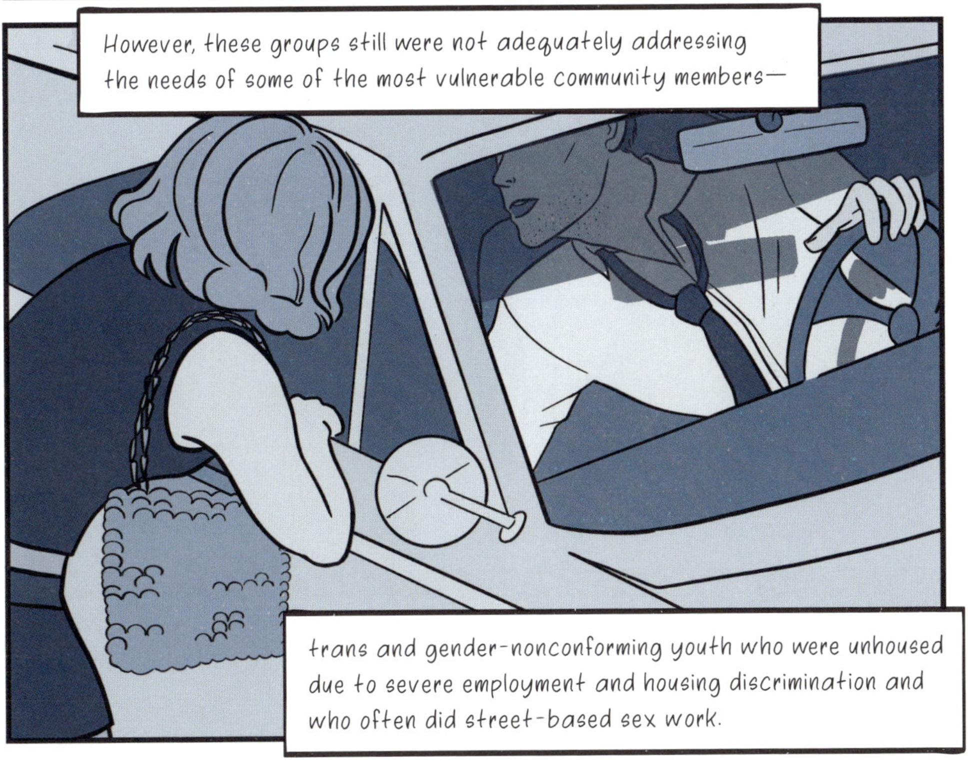
However, these groups still were not adequately addressing the needs of some of the most vulnerable community members—
trans and gender-nonconforming youth who were unhoused due to severe employment and housing discrimination and who often did street-based sex work.

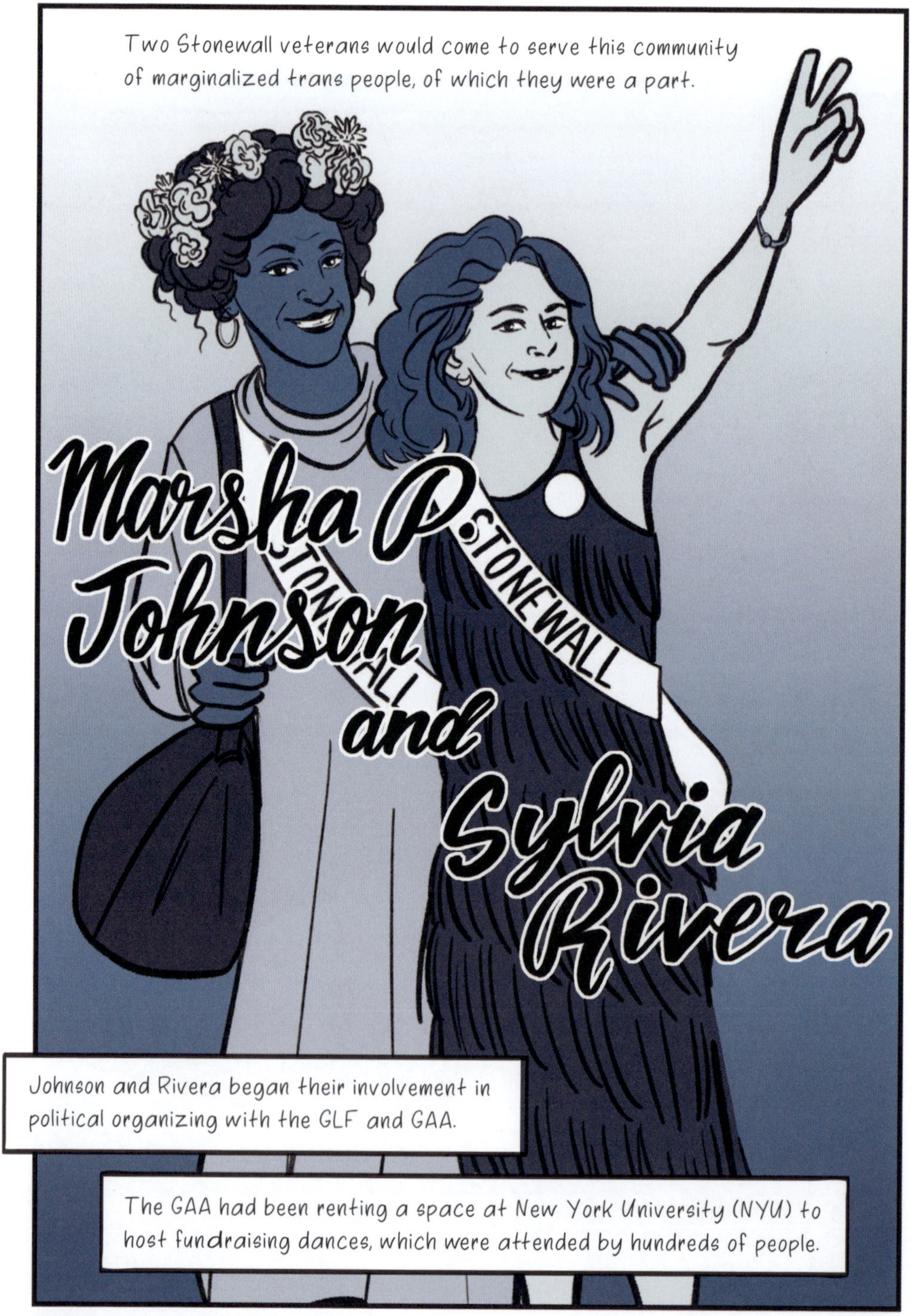
Two Stonewall veterans would come to serve this community of marginalized trans people, of which they were a part.
Marsha P. Johnson and Sylvia Rivera
STONEWALL
STONEWALL
Johnson and Rivera began their involvement in political organizing with the GLF and GAA.
The GAA had been renting a space at New York University (NYU) to host fundraising dances, which were attended by hundreds of people.

Based on a ca. 1990 photo by Rudy Grillo, courtesy of the Lesbian, Gay, Bisexual & Transgender Community Center

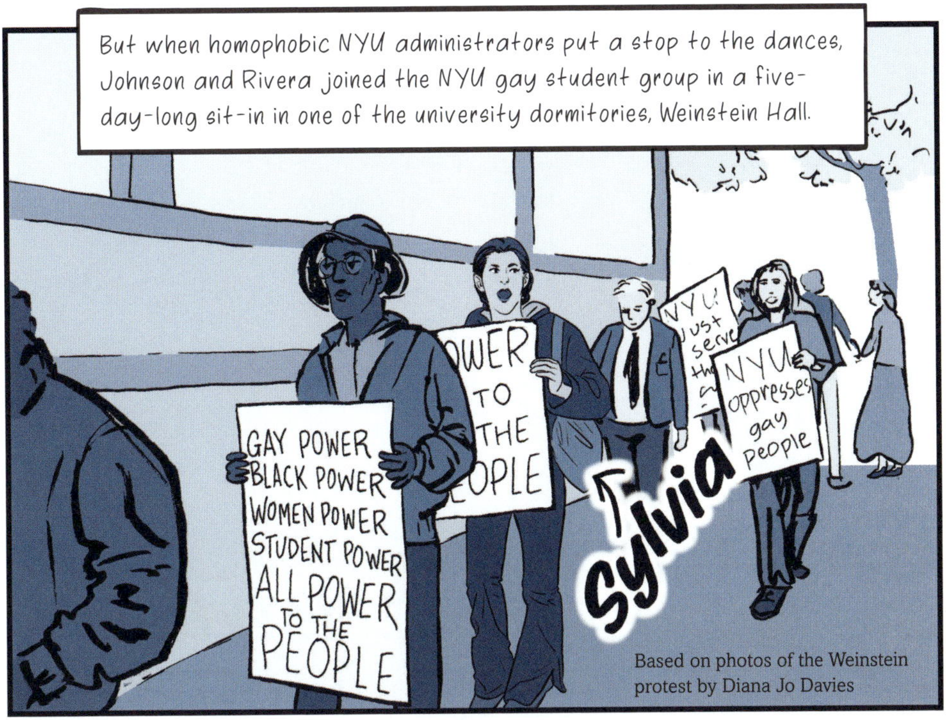
But when homophobic NYU administrators put a stop to the dances, Johnson and Rivera joined the NYU gay student group in a five-day-long sit-in in one of the university dormitories, Weinstein Hall.
GAY POWER BLACK POWER WOMEN POWER STUDENT POWER ALL POWER TO THE PEOPLE
OWER TO THE EOPLE
NYU! Just serve
NYU oppresses gay people
Sylvia
Based on photos of the Weinstein protest by Diana Jo Davies

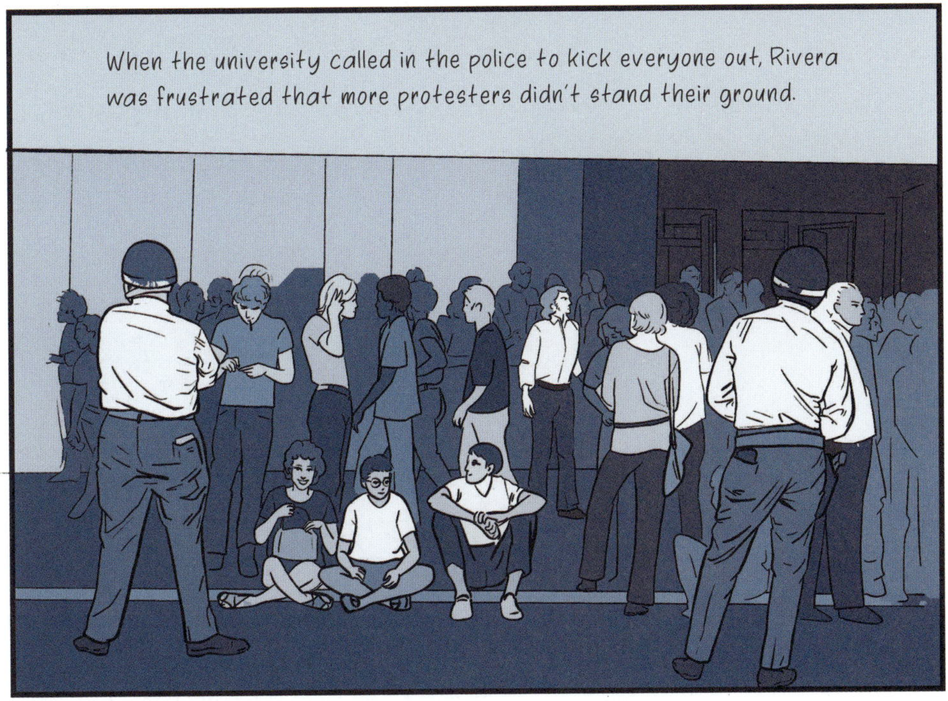
When the university called in the police to kick everyone out, Rivera was frustrated that more protesters didn't stand their ground.

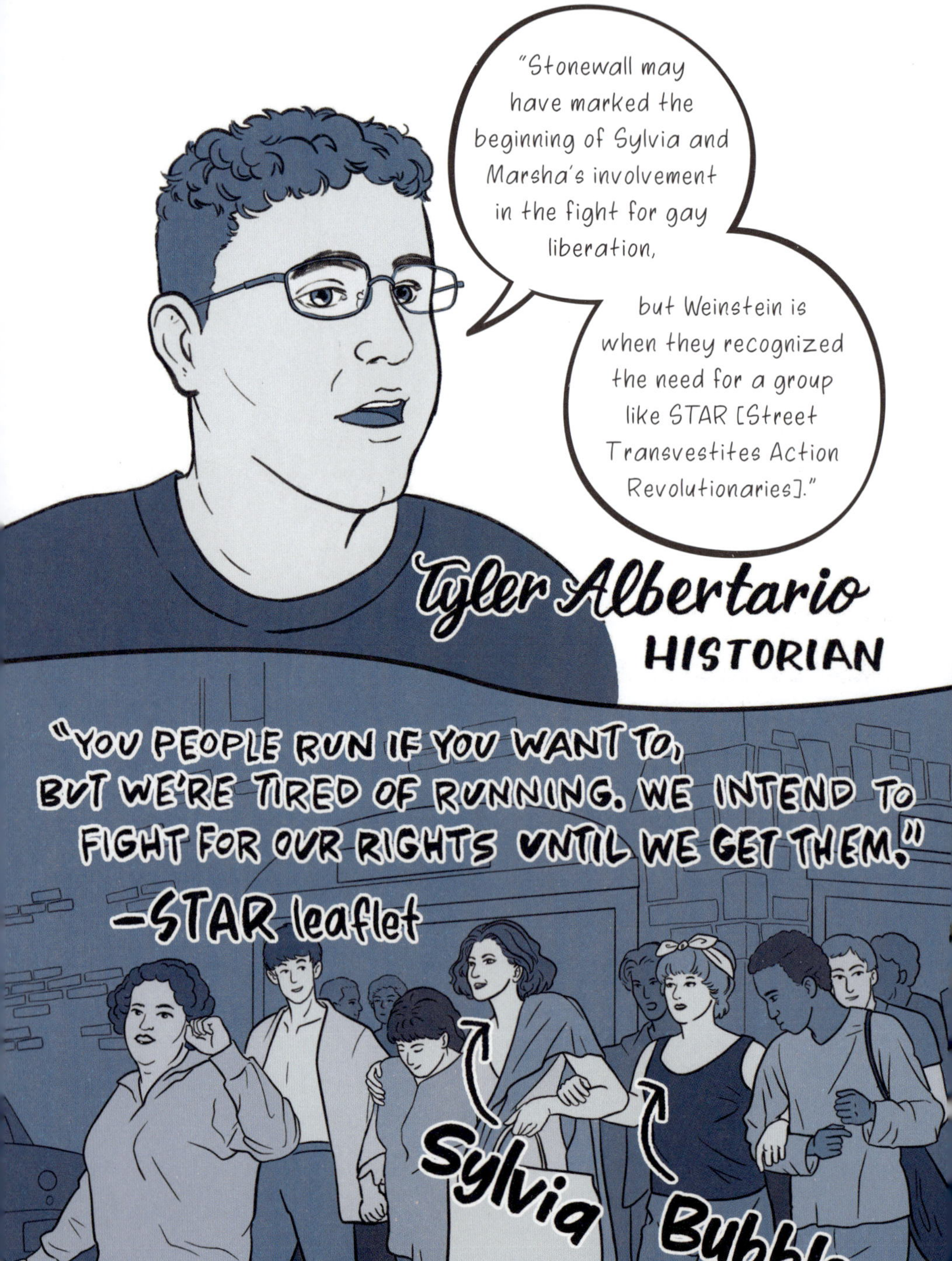
"Stonewall may have marked the beginning of Sylvia and Marsha's involvement in the fight for gay liberation,
but Weinstein is when they recognized the need for a group like STAR [Street Transvestites Action Revolutionaries]."
Tyler Albertario
HISTORIAN
"YOU PEOPLE RUN IF YOU WANT TO, BUT WE'RE TIRED OF RUNNING. WE INTEND TO FIGHT FOR OUR RIGHTS UNTIL WE GET THEM."
-STAR leaflet
Sylvia
Bubbles

From a photo of the Weinstein protest by Diana Jo Davies

Bubbles Rose Lee was another founding member of STAR.

Johnson and Rivera both did sex work to support themselves and provide for others in need.

They founded STAR House, which provided food and shelter to poor trans youth and other gender-marginalized people.

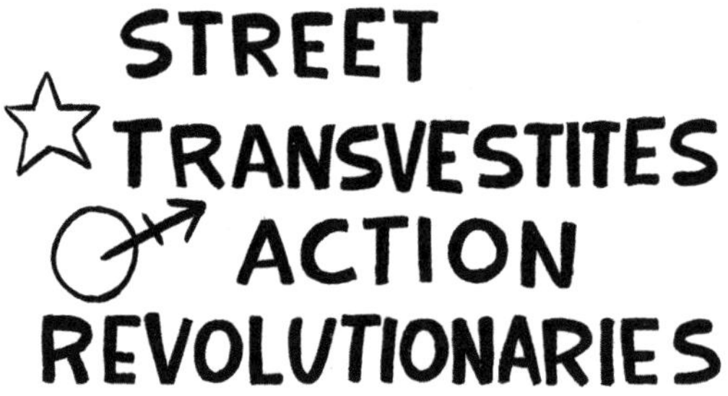
STREET
TRANSVESTITES
ACTION
REVOLUTIONARIES

Based on a banner made by STAR

STAR explained who they were:

"The oppression against transvestites of either sex arises from sexist values and this oppression is manifested by heterosexuals and homosexuals of both sexes in [the] form of exploitation, ridicule, harassment, beatings, rapes, murders.

Because of this oppression the majority of transvestites are forced into the streets we have framed a strong alliance with our gay sisters and brothers of the street. Who we are a part of and represent we are; a part of the revolutionaries armies fighting against the system."

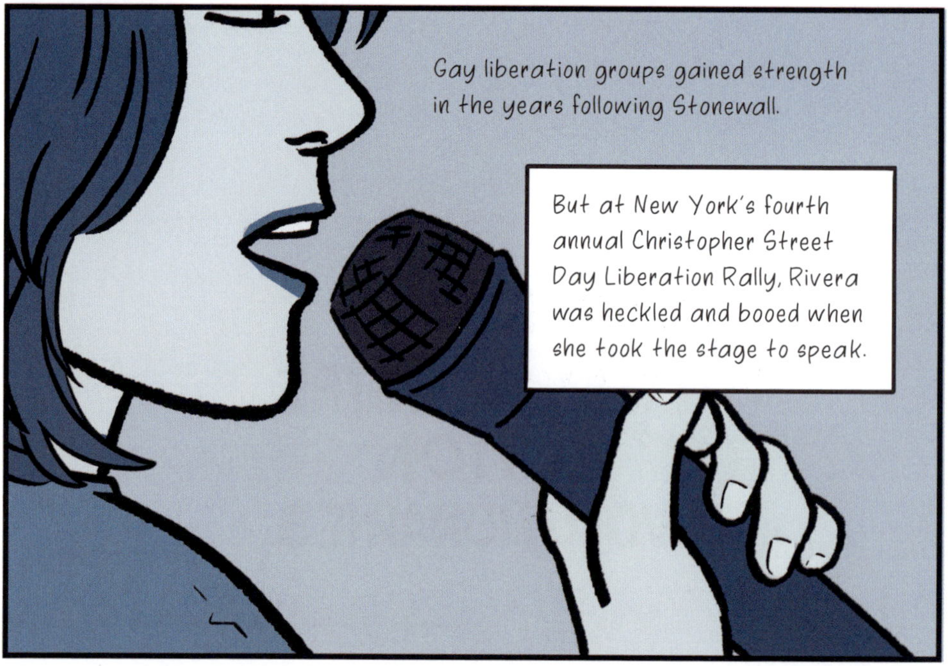
Gay liberation groups gained strength in the years following Stonewall.
But at New York's fourth annual Christopher Street Day Liberation Rally, Rivera was heckled and booed when she took the stage to speak.

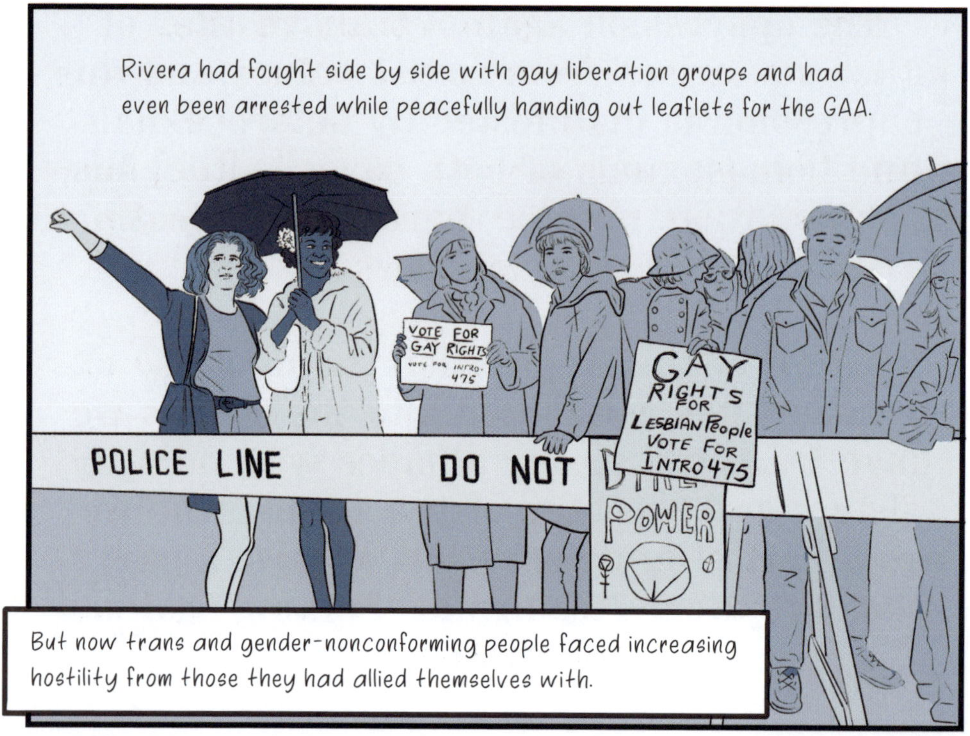
Rivera had fought side by side with gay liberation groups and had even been arrested while peacefully handing out leaflets for the GAA.
VOTE FOR GAY RIGHTS
VOTE FOR INTRO-475
GAY RIGHTS FOR LESBIAN People VOTE FOR INTRO 475
POLICE LINE DO NOT
POWER
But now trans and gender-nonconforming people faced increasing hostility from those they had allied themselves with.

Based on a ca. 1973 photo by Diana Jo Davies

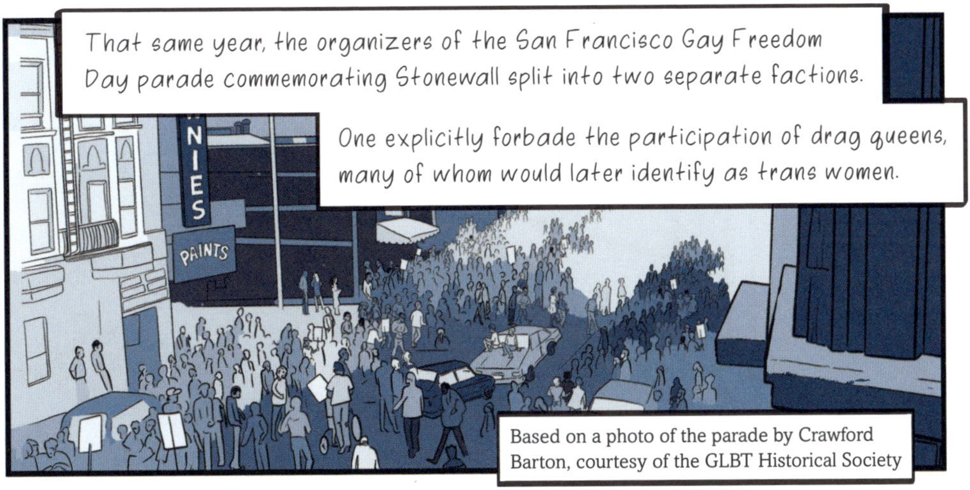
That same year, the organizers of the San Francisco Gay Freedom Day parade commemorating Stonewall split into two separate factions.
One explicitly forbade the participation of drag queens, many of whom would later identify as trans women.
NIES
PAINTS
Based on a photo of the parade by Crawford Barton, courtesy of the GLBT Historical Society

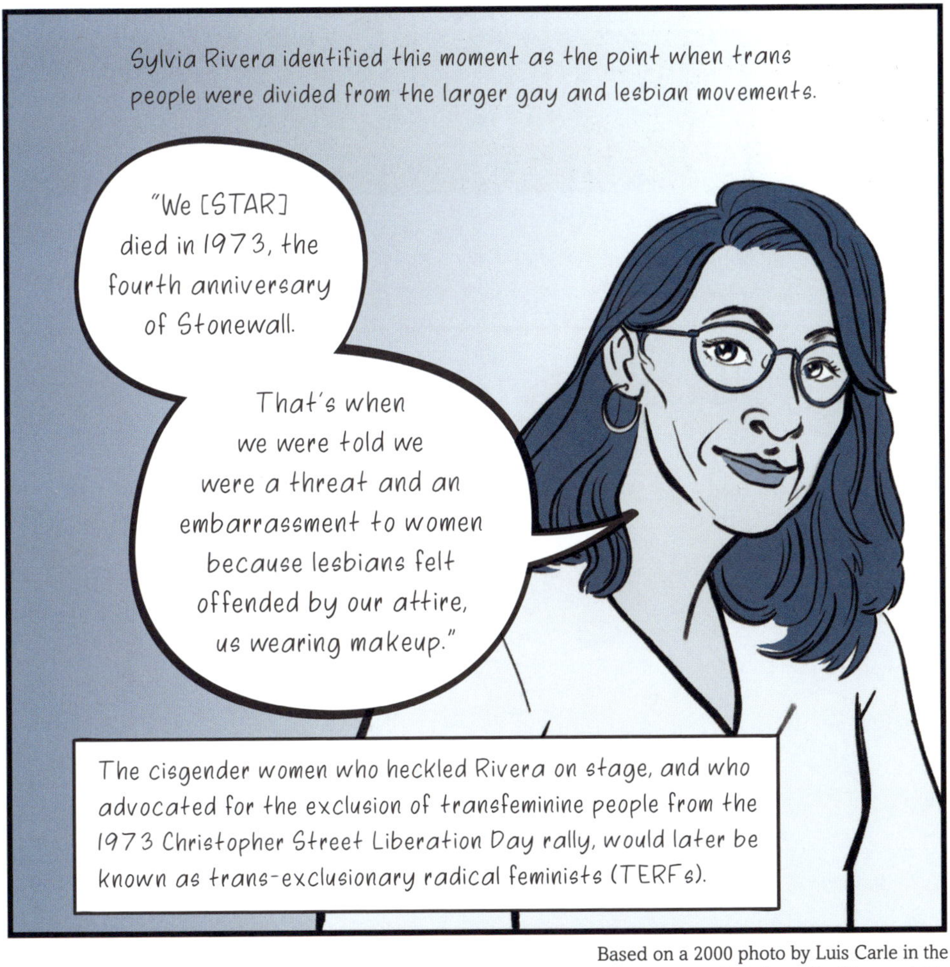
Sylvia Rivera identified this moment as the point when trans people were divided from the larger gay and lesbian movements.
"We [STAR] died in 1973, the fourth anniversary of Stonewall.
That's when we were told we were a threat and an embarrassment to women because lesbians felt offended by our attire, us wearing makeup."
The cisgender women who heckled Rivera on stage, and who advocated for the exclusion of transfeminine people from the 1973 Christopher Street Liberation Day rally, would later be known as trans-exclusionary radical feminists (TERFs).
Based on a 2000 photo by Luis Carle in the National Portrait Gallery, Washington, DC

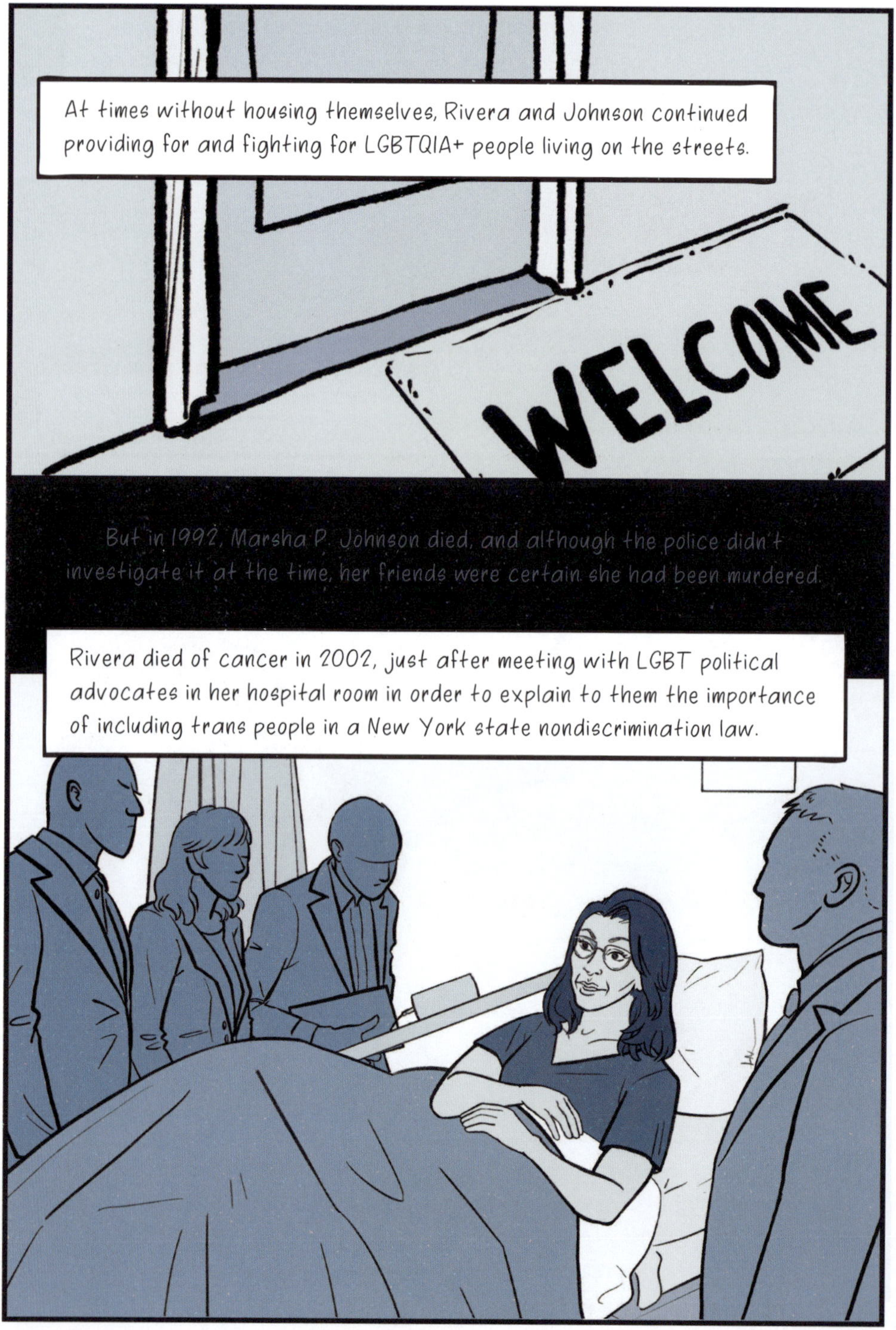
At times without housing themselves, Rivera and Johnson continued providing for and fighting for LGBTQIA+ people living on the streets.
WELCOME
But in 1992, Marsha P. Johnson died, and although the police didn't investigate it at the time, her friends were certain she had been murdered.
Rivera died of cancer in 2002, just after meeting with LGBT political advocates in her hospital room in order to explain to them the importance of including trans people in a New York state nondiscrimination law.

Based on a ca. 1970 photo by Diana Jo Davies

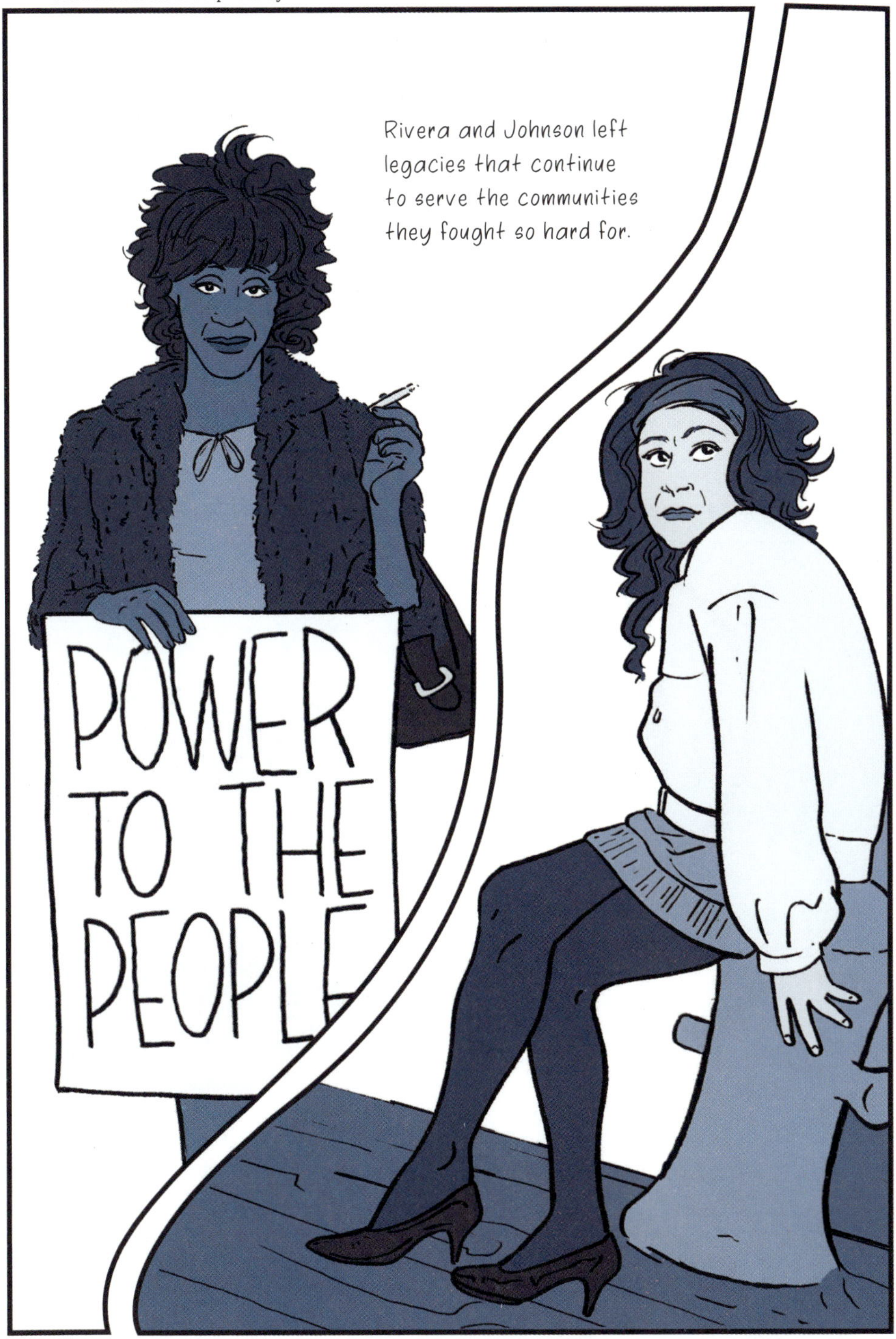

Rivera and Johnson left legacies that continue to serve the communities they fought so hard for.
POWER TO THE PEOPLE

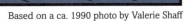

Based on a ca. 1990 photo by Valerie Shaff

BUILDING MOMENTUM

The commercial success of gender-bending imagery throughout the 1970s and '80s may seem to indicate acceptance...

but there was a larger shift happening in the United States toward narrowing gender roles and restricting gender expression.

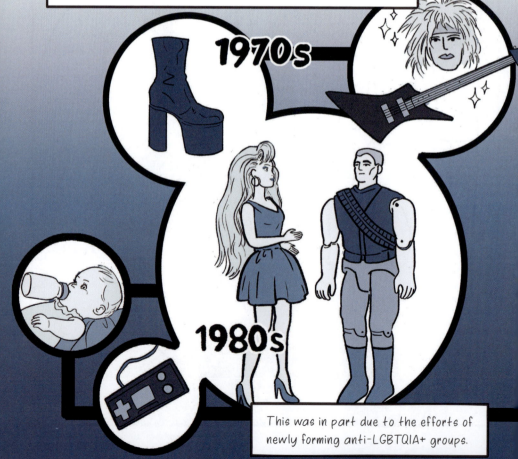

1970s

1980s

This was in part due to the efforts of newly forming anti-LGBTQIA+ groups.

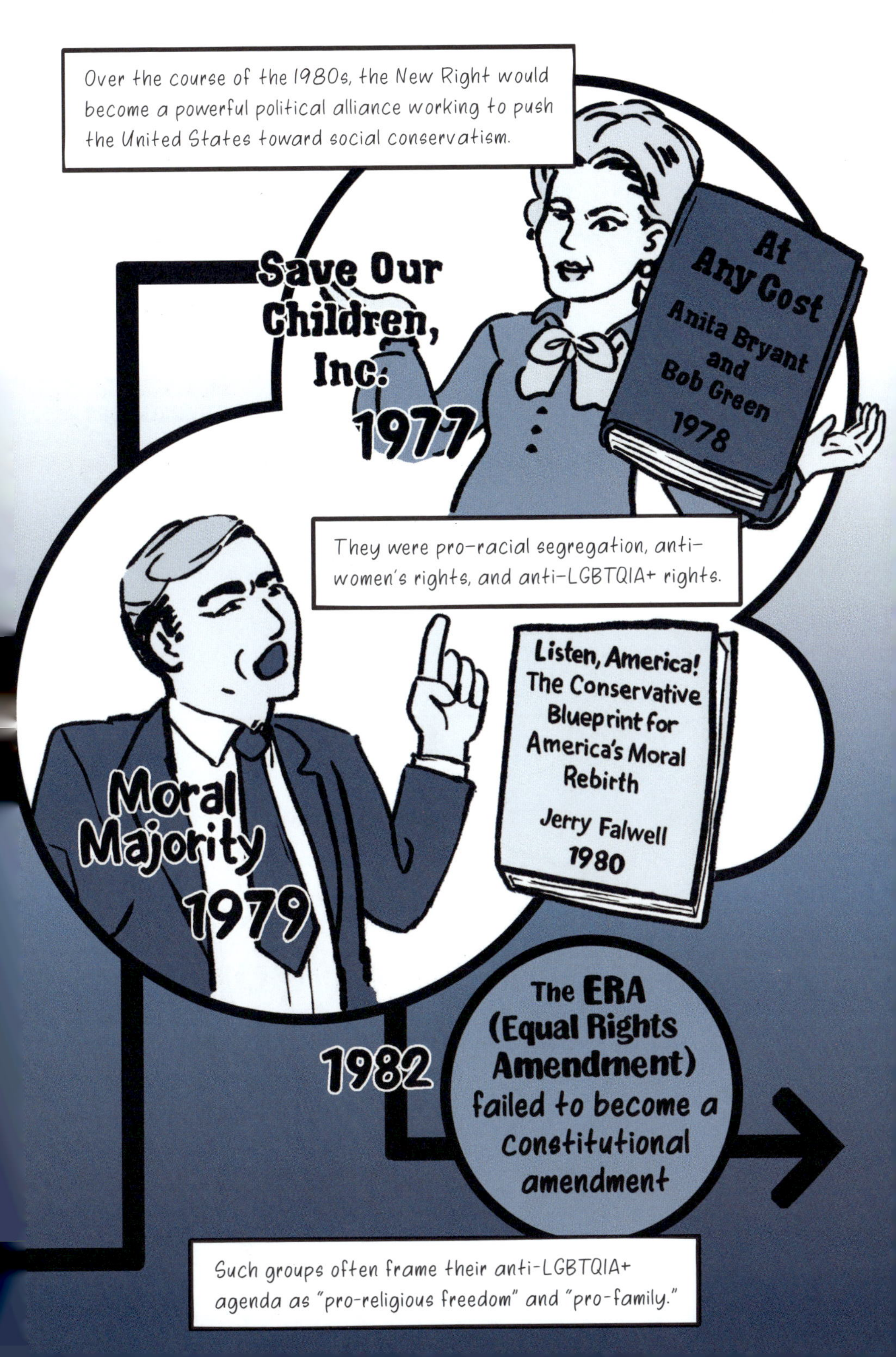

Over the course of the 1980s, the New Right would become a powerful political alliance working to push the United States toward social conservatism.
Save Our Children, Inc. 1977
At Any Cost
Anita Bryant and Bob Green
1978
They were pro-racial segregation, anti-women's rights, and anti-LGBTQIA+ rights.
Moral Majority 1979
Listen, America! The Conservative Blueprint for America's Moral Rebirth
Jerry Falwell
1980
1982
The ERA (Equal Rights Amendment) failed to become a constitutional amendment
Such groups often frame their anti-LGBTQIA+ agenda as "pro-religious freedom" and "pro-family."

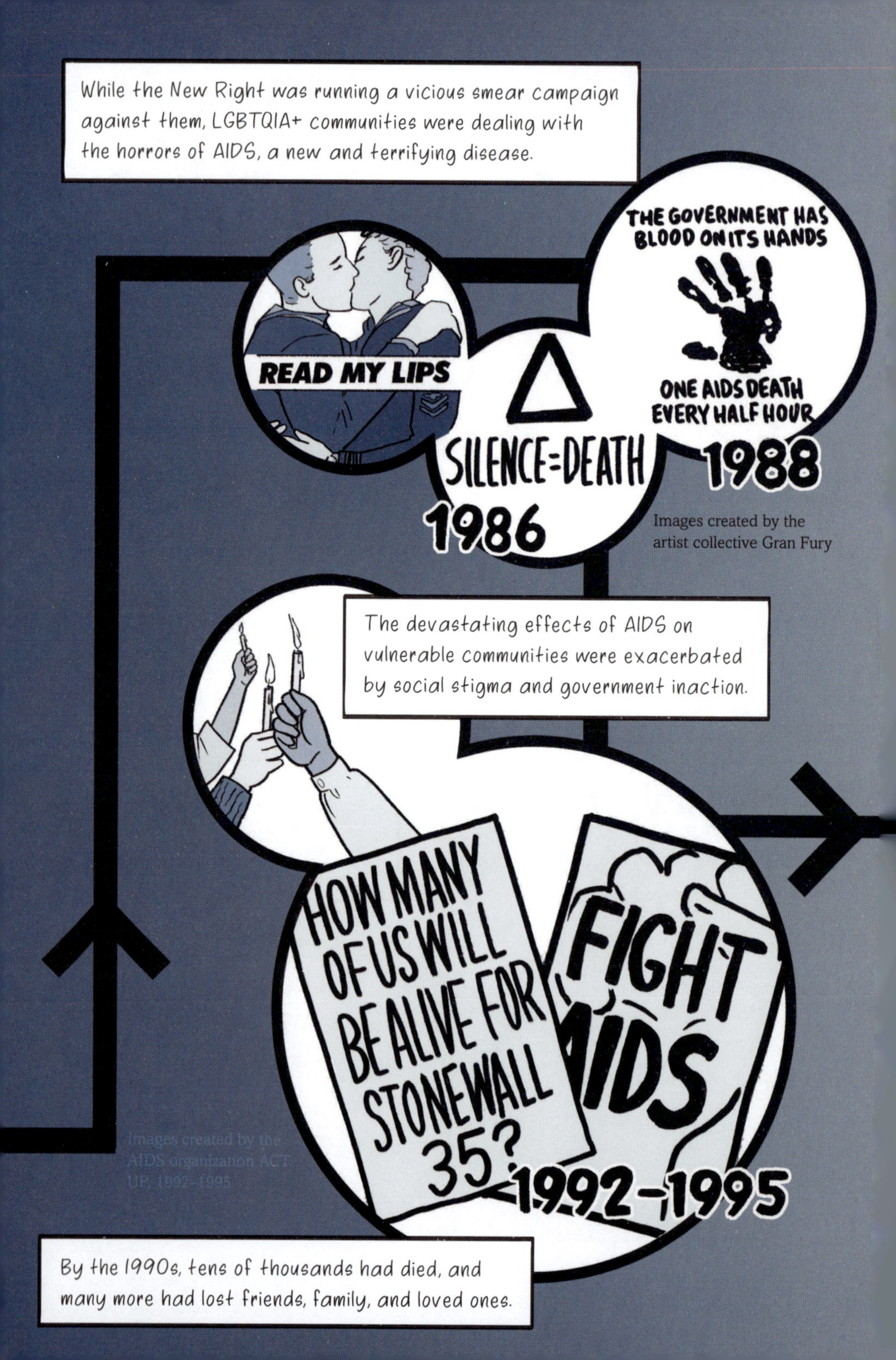
While the New Right was running a vicious smear campaign against them, LGBTQIA+ communities were dealing with the horrors of AIDS, a new and terrifying disease.
READ MY LIPS
SILENCE=DEATH
1986
THE GOVERNMENT HAS BLOOD ON ITS HANDS
ONE AIDS DEATH EVERY HALF HOUR
1988
Images created by the artist collective Gran Fury
The devastating effects of AIDS on vulnerable communities were exacerbated by social stigma and government inaction.
HOW MANY OF US WILL BE ALIVE FOR STONEWALL 35?
FIGHT AIDS
1992–1995
Images created by the AIDS organization ACT UP, 1992–1995
By the 1990s, tens of thousands had died, and many more had lost friends, family, and loved ones.

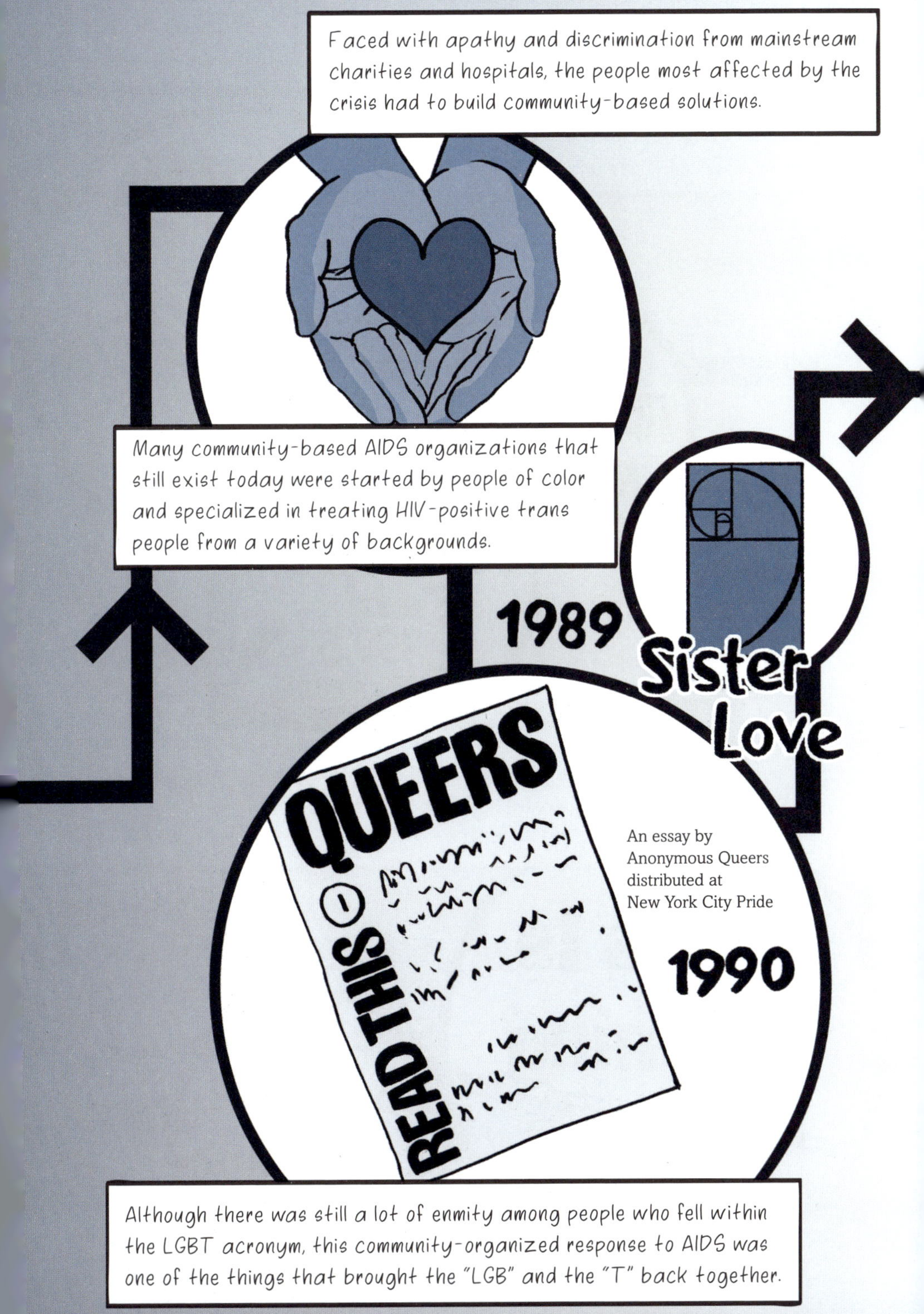
Faced with apathy and discrimination from mainstream charities and hospitals, the people most affected by the crisis had to build community-based solutions.
Many community-based AIDS organizations that still exist today were started by people of color and specialized in treating HIV-positive trans people from a variety of backgrounds.
1989
Sister Love
QUEERS READ THIS
An essay by Anonymous Queers distributed at New York City Pride
1990
Although there was still a lot of enmity among people who fell within the LGBT acronym, this community-organized response to AIDS was one of the things that brought the "LGB" and the "T" back together.

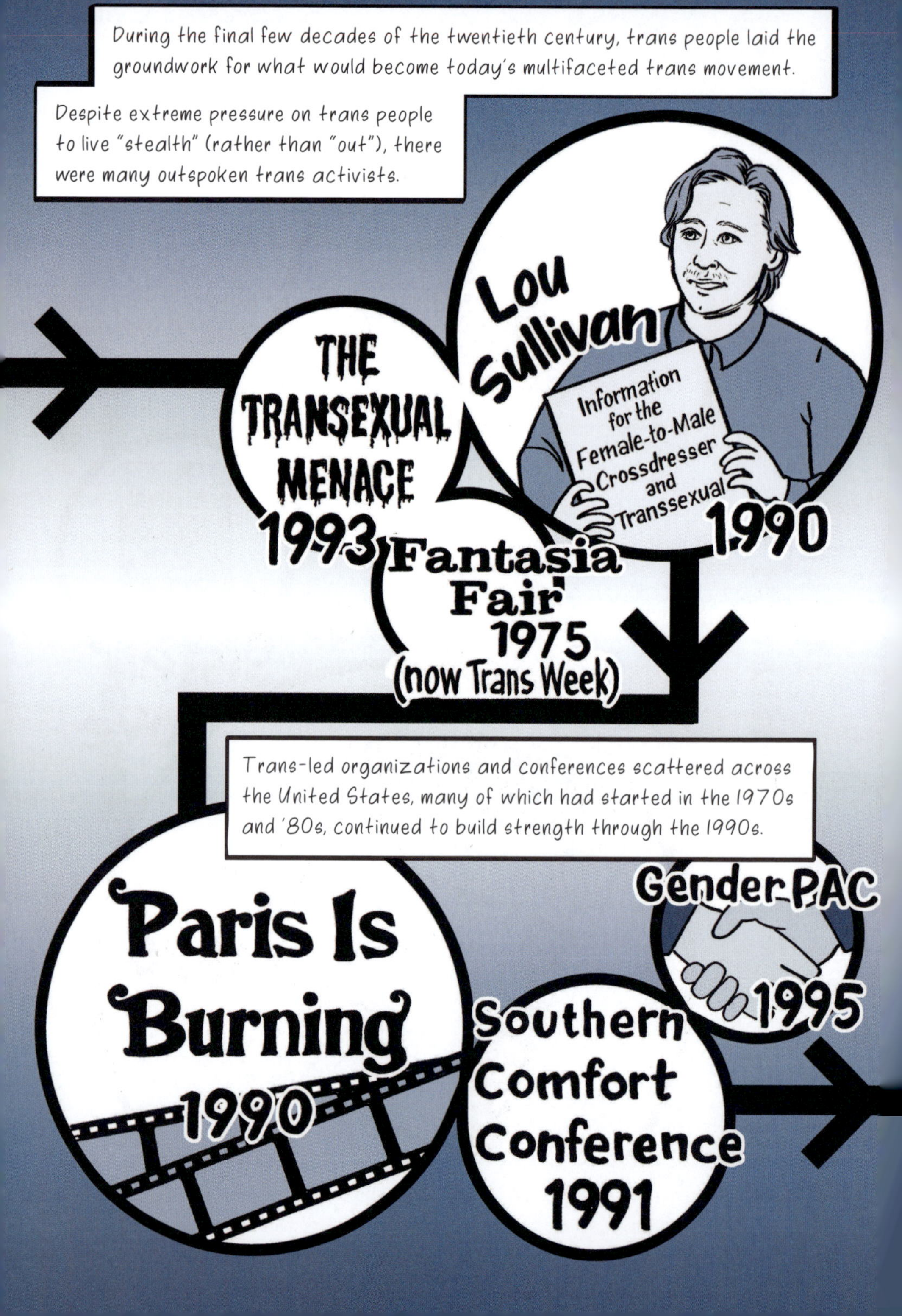
During the final few decades of the twentieth century, trans people laid the groundwork for what would become today's multifaceted trans movement.
Despite extreme pressure on trans people to live "stealth" (rather than "out"), there were many outspoken trans activists.
Lou Sullivan
Information for the Female-to-Male Crossdresser and Transsexual
1990
THE TRANSEXUAL MENACE
1993
Fantasia Fair
1975
(now Trans Week)
Trans-led organizations and conferences scattered across the United States, many of which had started in the 1970s and '80s, continued to build strength through the 1990s.
Paris Is Burning
1990
Gender PAC
1995
Southern Comfort Conference
1991

From making art to advancing state law to publishing books about trans history, politics, and theory, trans people were breaking down barriers and building coalitions.

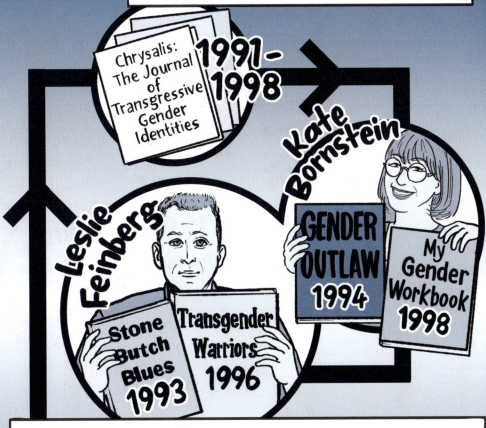

Chrysalis: The Journal of Transgressive Gender Identities 1991–1998

Leslie Feinberg — *Stone Butch Blues* 1993, *Transgender Warriors* 1996

Kate Bornstein — *Gender Outlaw* 1994, *My Gender Workbook* 1998

And with a new tool—the Internet—trans people were connecting with one another and had the power to tell their stories in a way that had previously been impossible.

AOL chat room The Gazebo 1994

Transgender Tapestry 1970s–2000s 1999

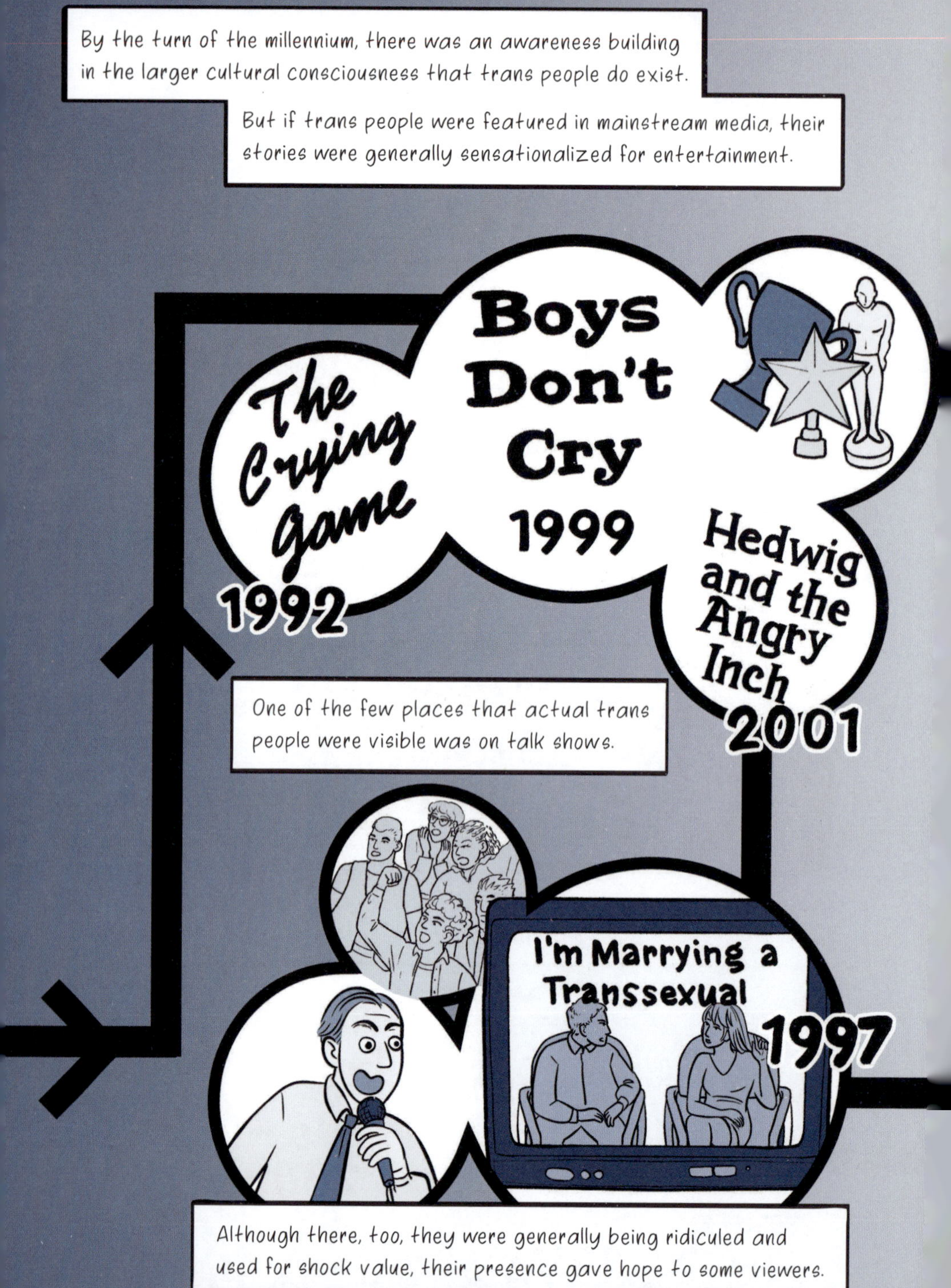
By the turn of the millennium, there was an awareness building in the larger cultural consciousness that trans people do exist.
But if trans people were featured in mainstream media, their stories were generally sensationalized for entertainment.
The Crying Game
1992
Boys Don't Cry
1999
Hedwig and the Angry Inch
2001
One of the few places that actual trans people were visible was on talk shows.
I'm Marrying a Transsexual
1997
Although there, too, they were generally being ridiculed and used for shock value, their presence gave hope to some viewers.

One of many *Jerry Springer* episodes featuring a trans person

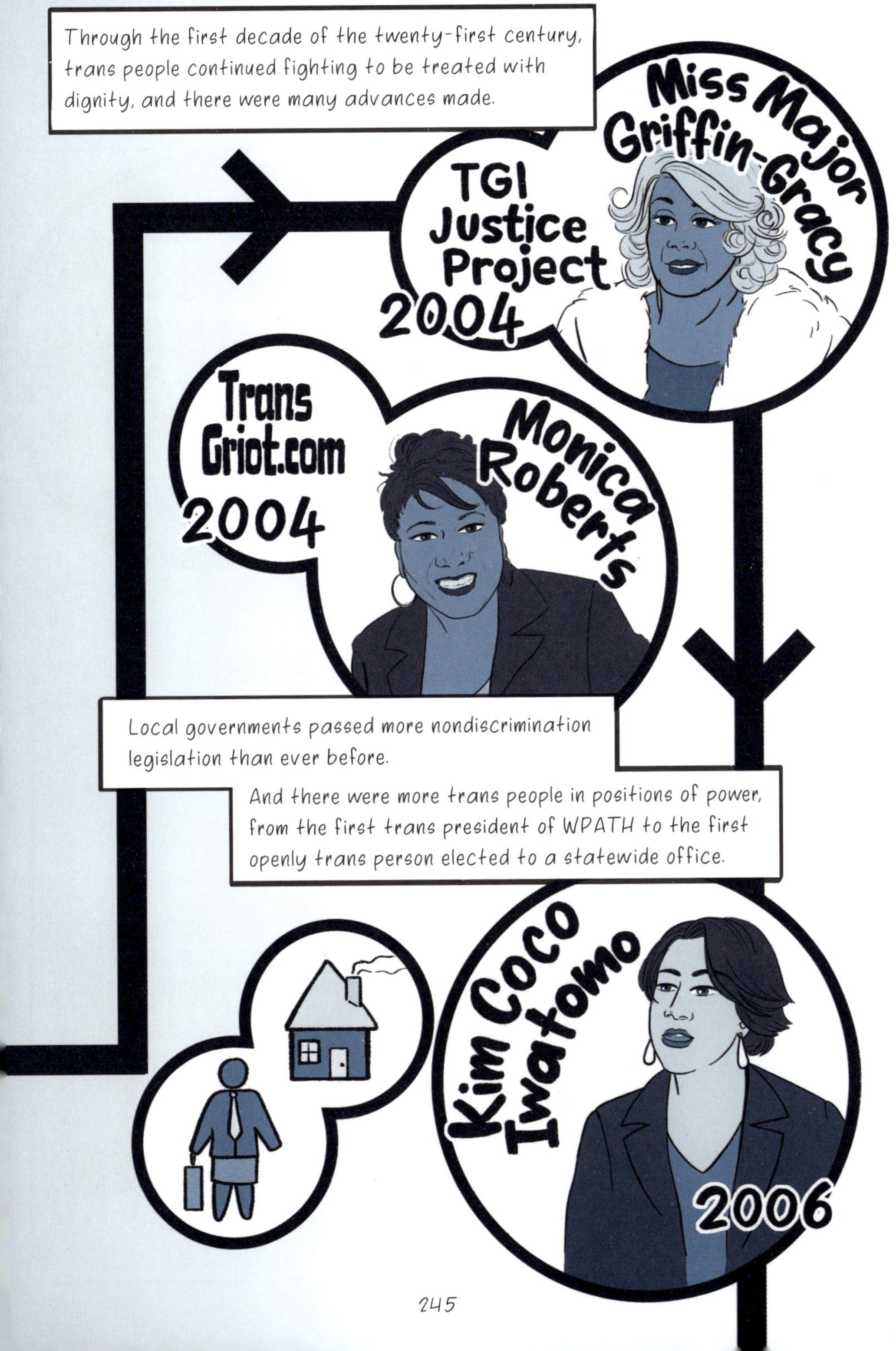

Through the first decade of the twenty-first century, trans people continued fighting to be treated with dignity, and there were many advances made.
Miss Major Griffin-Gracy
TGI Justice Project 2004
TransGriot.com 2004
Monica Roberts
Local governments passed more nondiscrimination legislation than ever before.
And there were more trans people in positions of power, from the first trans president of WPATH to the first openly trans person elected to a statewide office.
Kim Coco Iwatomo
2006

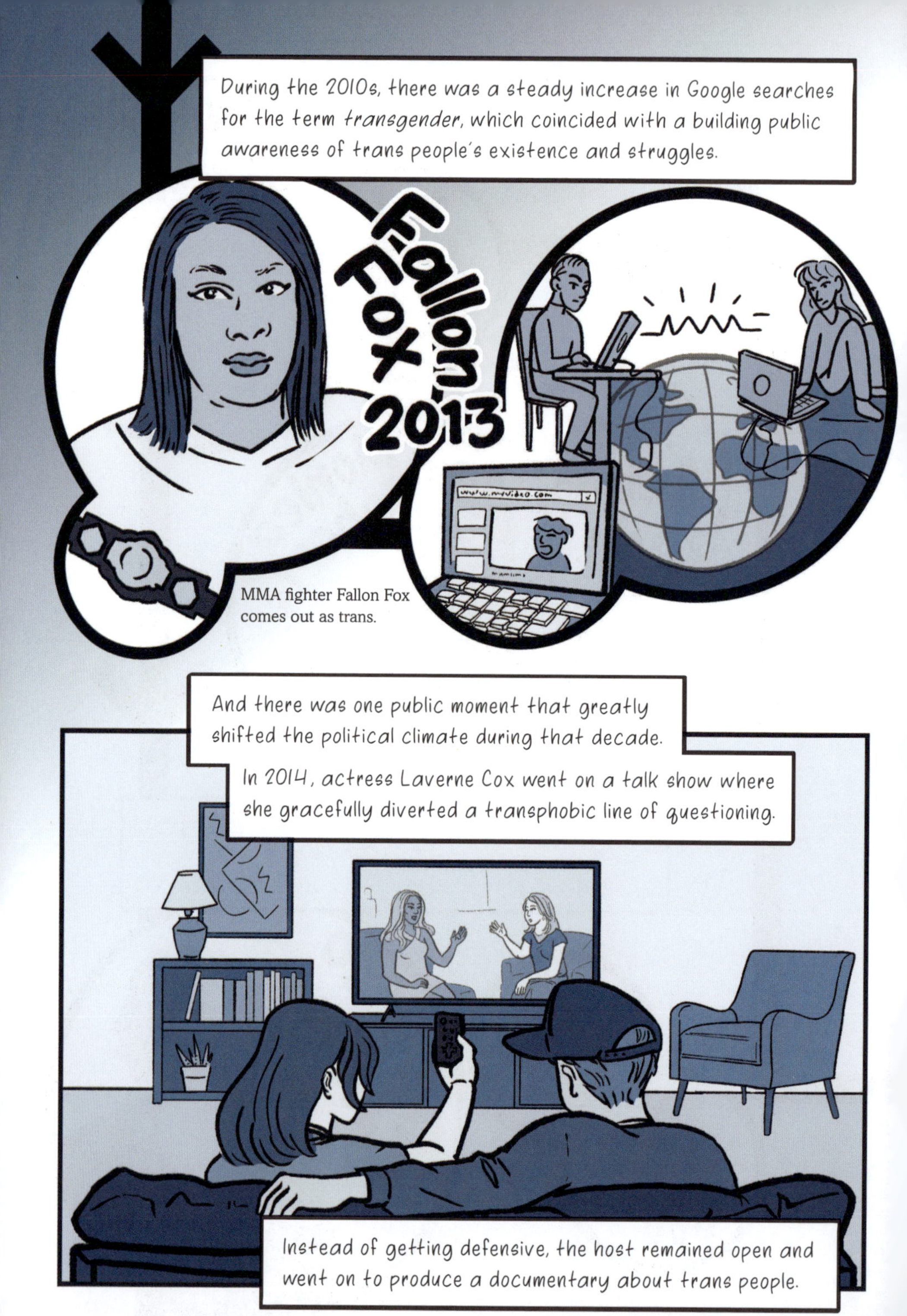
During the 2010s, there was a steady increase in Google searches for the term *transgender*, which coincided with a building public awareness of trans people's existence and struggles.
Fallon Fox, 2013
www.myvideo.com
And there was one public moment that greatly shifted the political climate during that decade.
In 2014, actress Laverne Cox went on a talk show where she gracefully diverted a transphobic line of questioning.
Instead of getting defensive, the host remained open and went on to produce a documentary about trans people.
MMA fighter Fallon Fox comes out as trans.

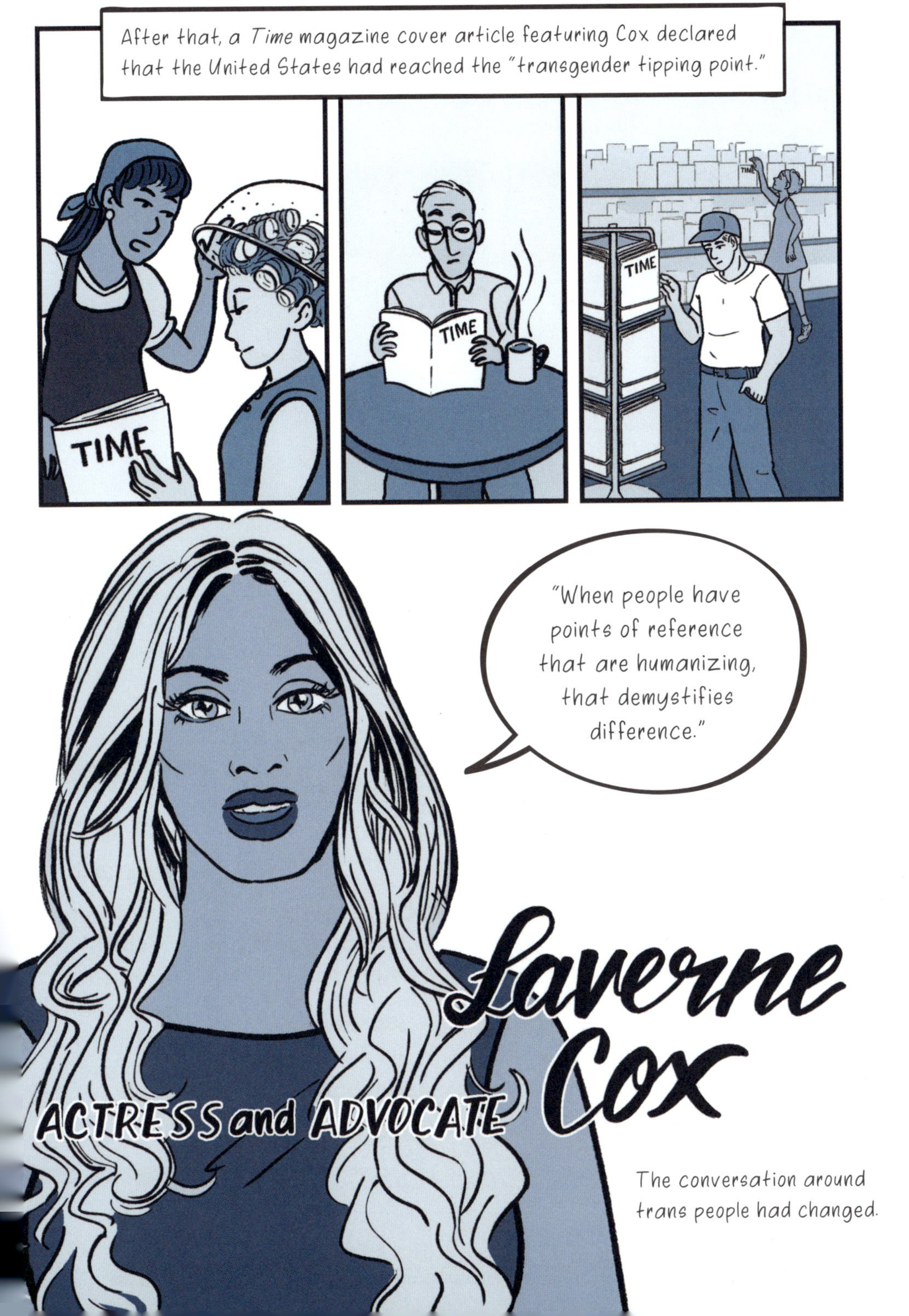
After that, a *Time* magazine cover article featuring Cox declared that the United States had reached the "transgender tipping point."
TIME
TIME
TIME
"When people have points of reference that are humanizing, that demystifies difference."
Laverne Cox
ACTRESS and ADVOCATE
The conversation around trans people had changed.

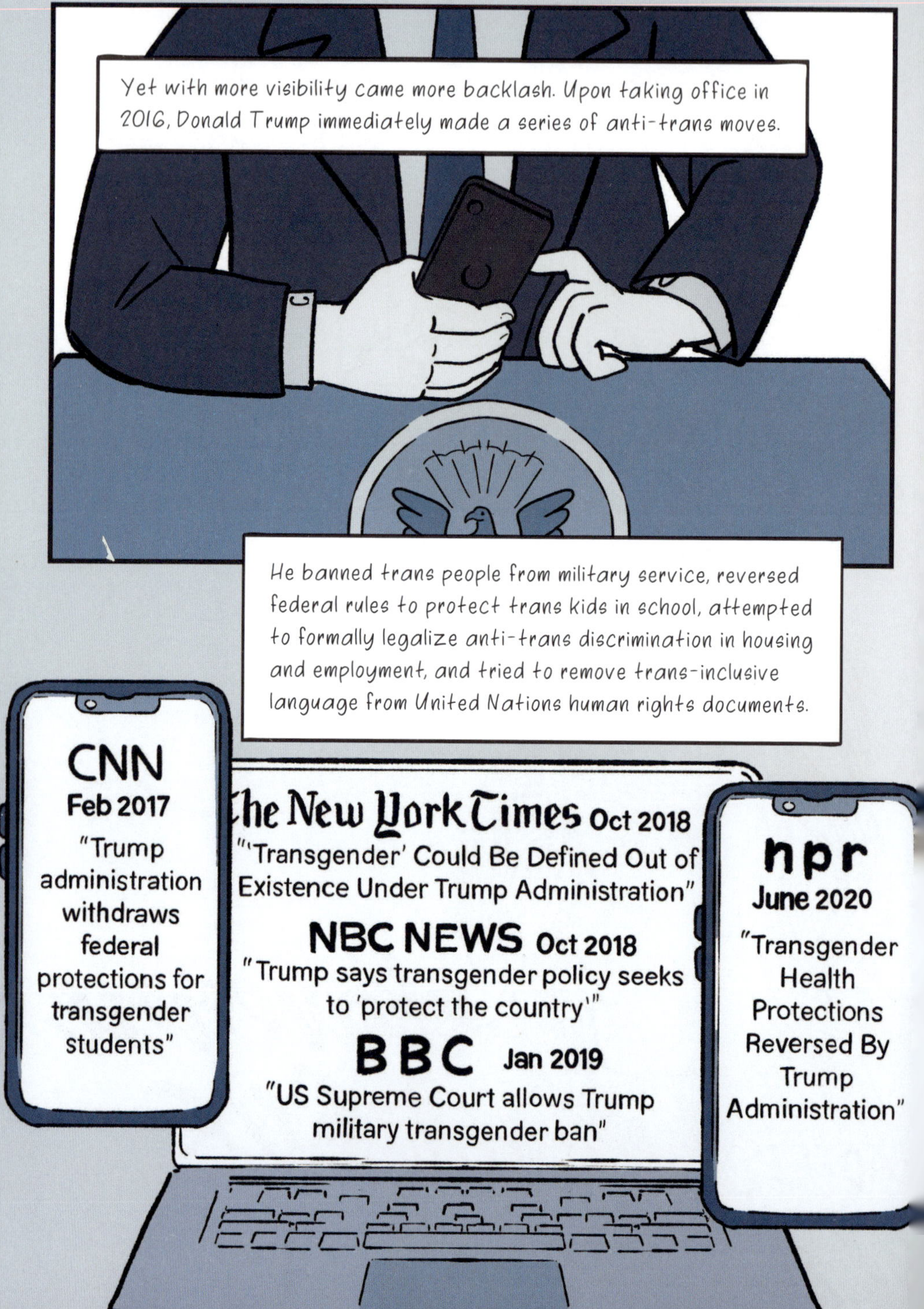
Yet with more visibility came more backlash. Upon taking office in 2016, Donald Trump immediately made a series of anti-trans moves.
He banned trans people from military service, reversed federal rules to protect trans kids in school, attempted to formally legalize anti-trans discrimination in housing and employment, and tried to remove trans-inclusive language from United Nations human rights documents.
CNN
Feb 2017
"Trump administration withdraws federal protections for transgender students"
The New York Times Oct 2018
"'Transgender' Could Be Defined Out of Existence Under Trump Administration"
NBC NEWS Oct 2018
"Trump says transgender policy seeks to 'protect the country'"
BBC Jan 2019
"US Supreme Court allows Trump military transgender ban"
npr
June 2020
"Transgender Health Protections Reversed By Trump Administration"

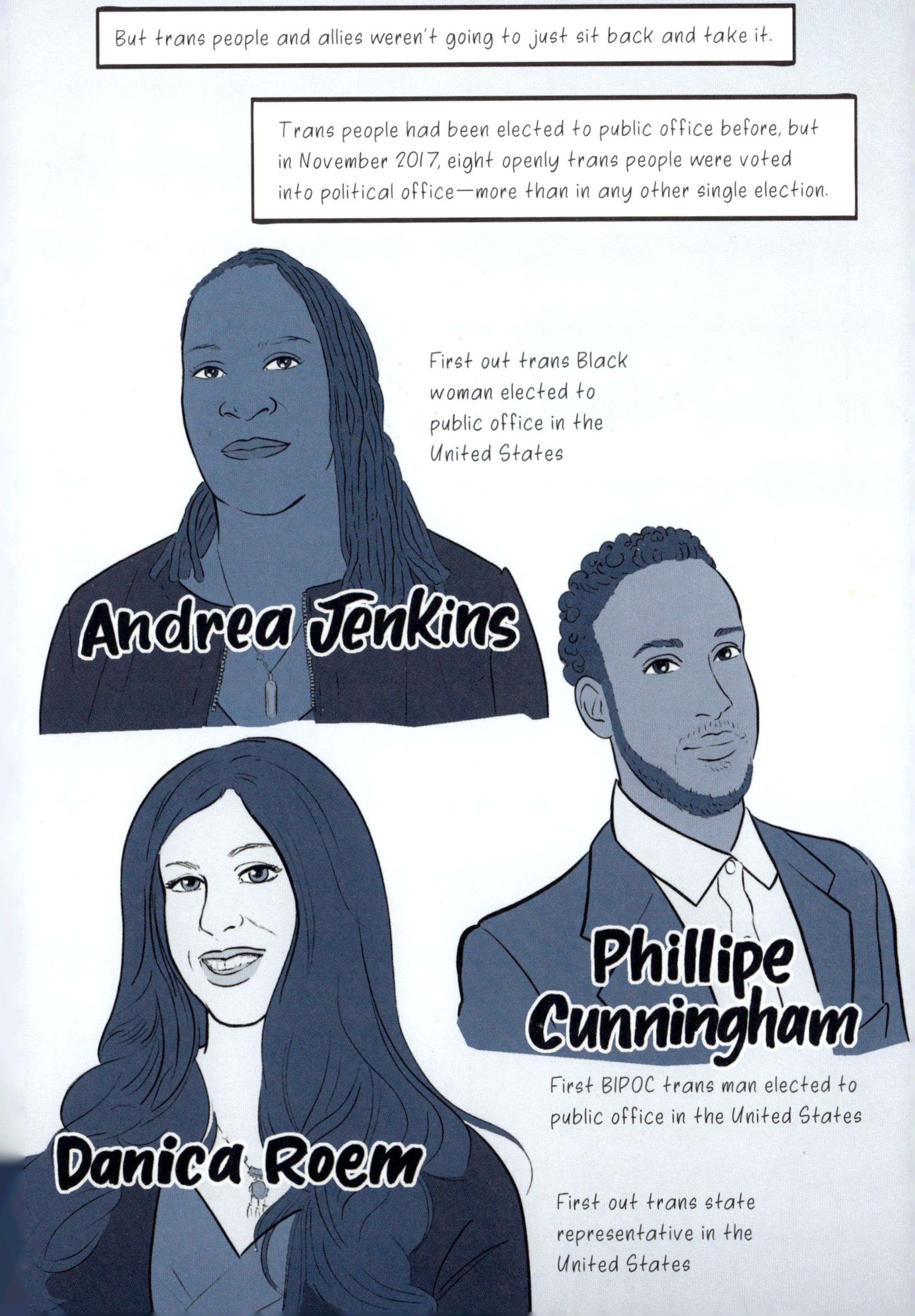
But trans people and allies weren't going to just sit back and take it.
Trans people had been elected to public office before, but in November 2017, eight openly trans people were voted into political office—more than in any other single election.
Andrea Jenkins
First out trans Black woman elected to public office in the United States
Phillipe Cunningham
First BIPOC trans man elected to public office in the United States
Danica Roem
First out trans state representative in the United States

But as exciting as it is to finally have trans people in positions of political power, there are influential and well-funded opponents to trans rights.

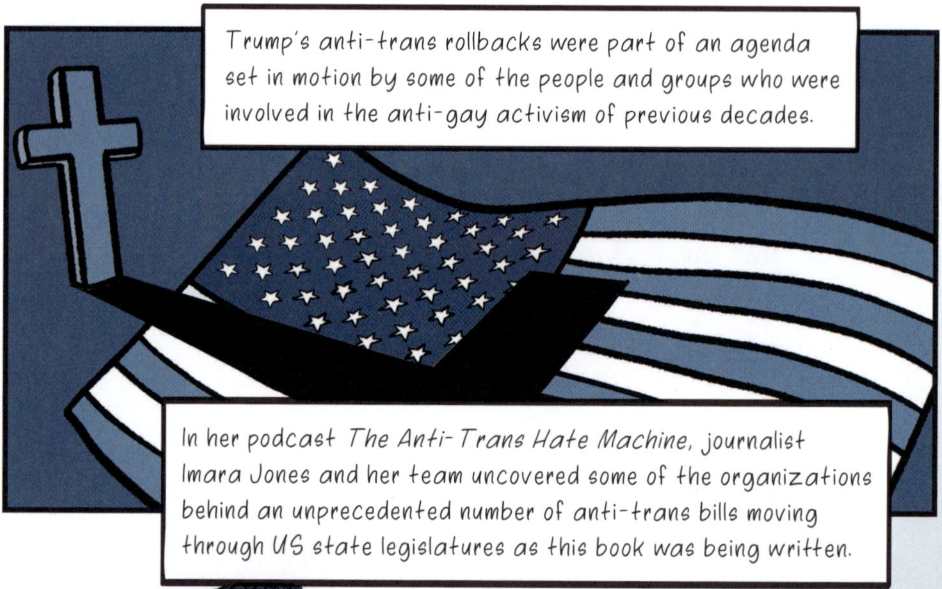
Trump's anti-trans rollbacks were part of an agenda set in motion by some of the people and groups who were involved in the anti-gay activism of previous decades.
In her podcast *The Anti-Trans Hate Machine*, journalist Imara Jones and her team uncovered some of the organizations behind an unprecedented number of anti-trans bills moving through US state legislatures as this book was being written.

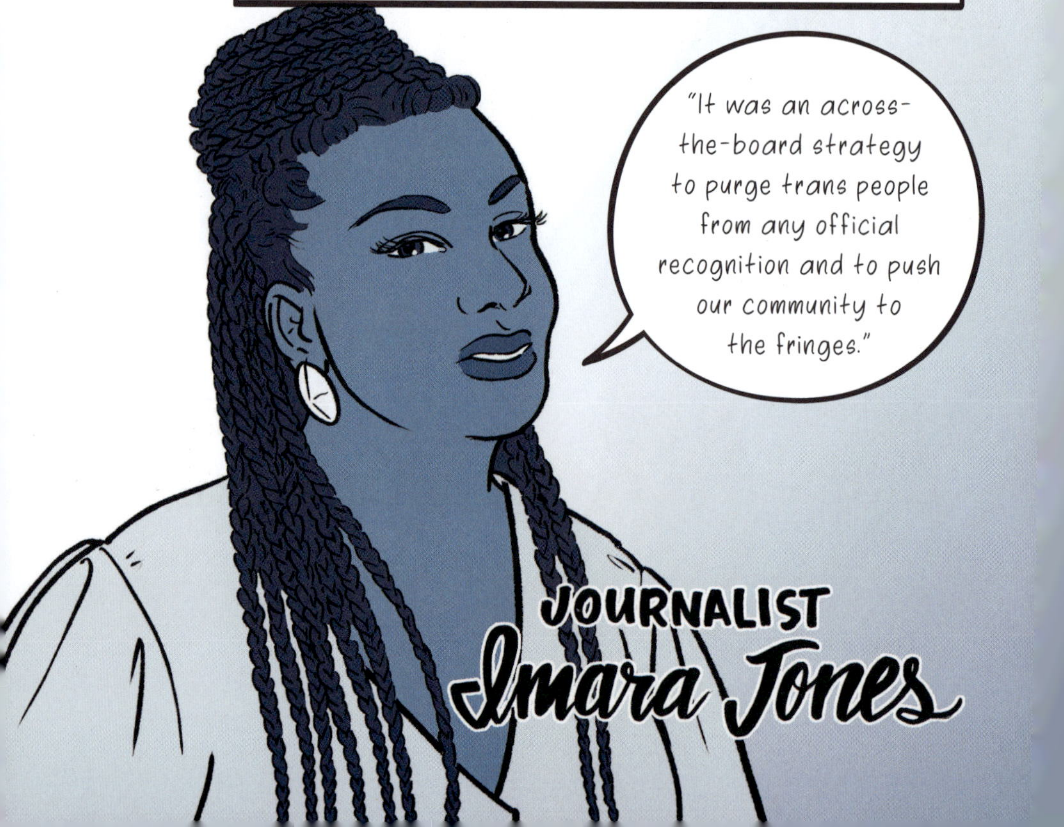
"It was an across-the-board strategy to purge trans people from any official recognition and to push our community to the fringes."
JOURNALIST
Imara Jones

These groups have been involved in designing numerous bills and providing money and lawyers to help pass them:

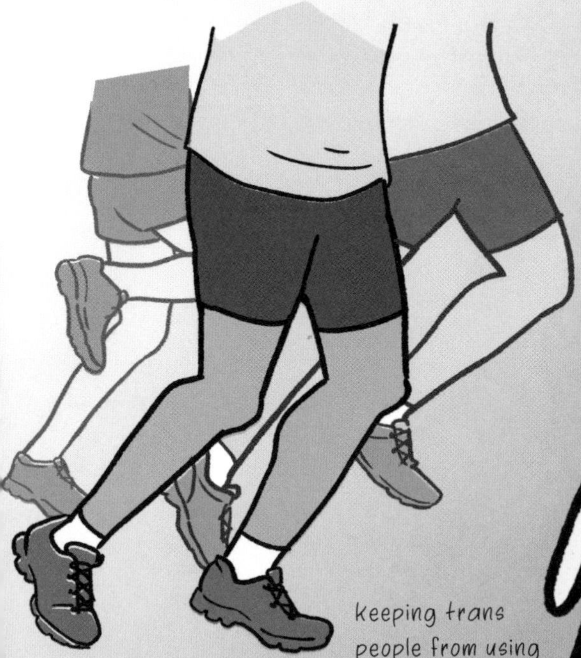

stopping trans athletes from playing on school sports teams

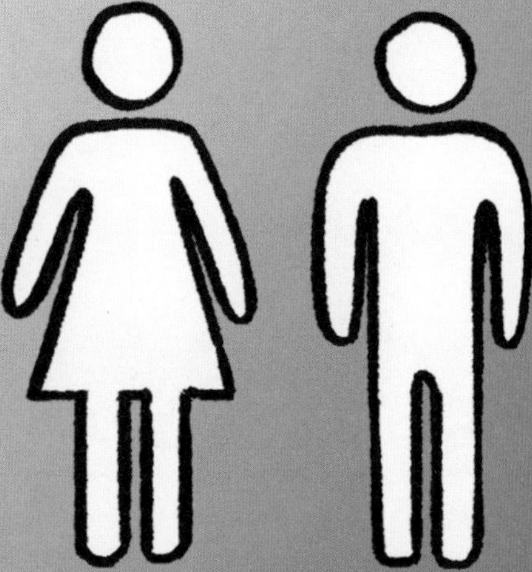

keeping trans people from using public bathrooms

making it a crime to give trans children puberty blockers and/or hormone therapy

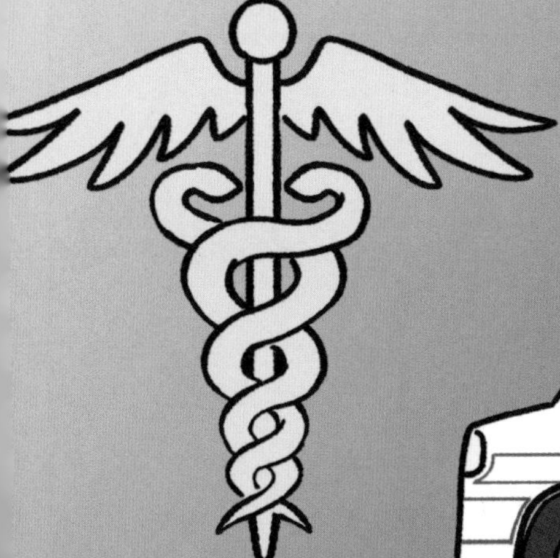

legalizing discrimination by transphobic service providers, including any kind of medical care

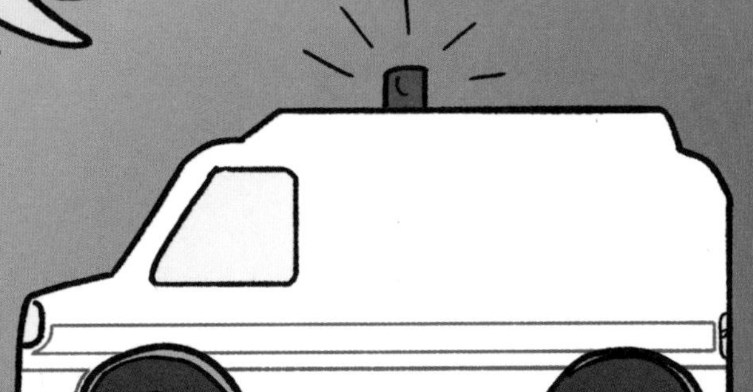

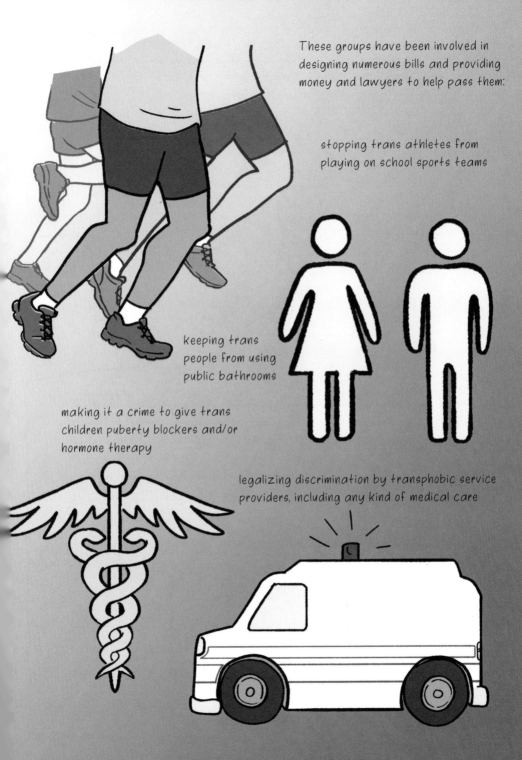

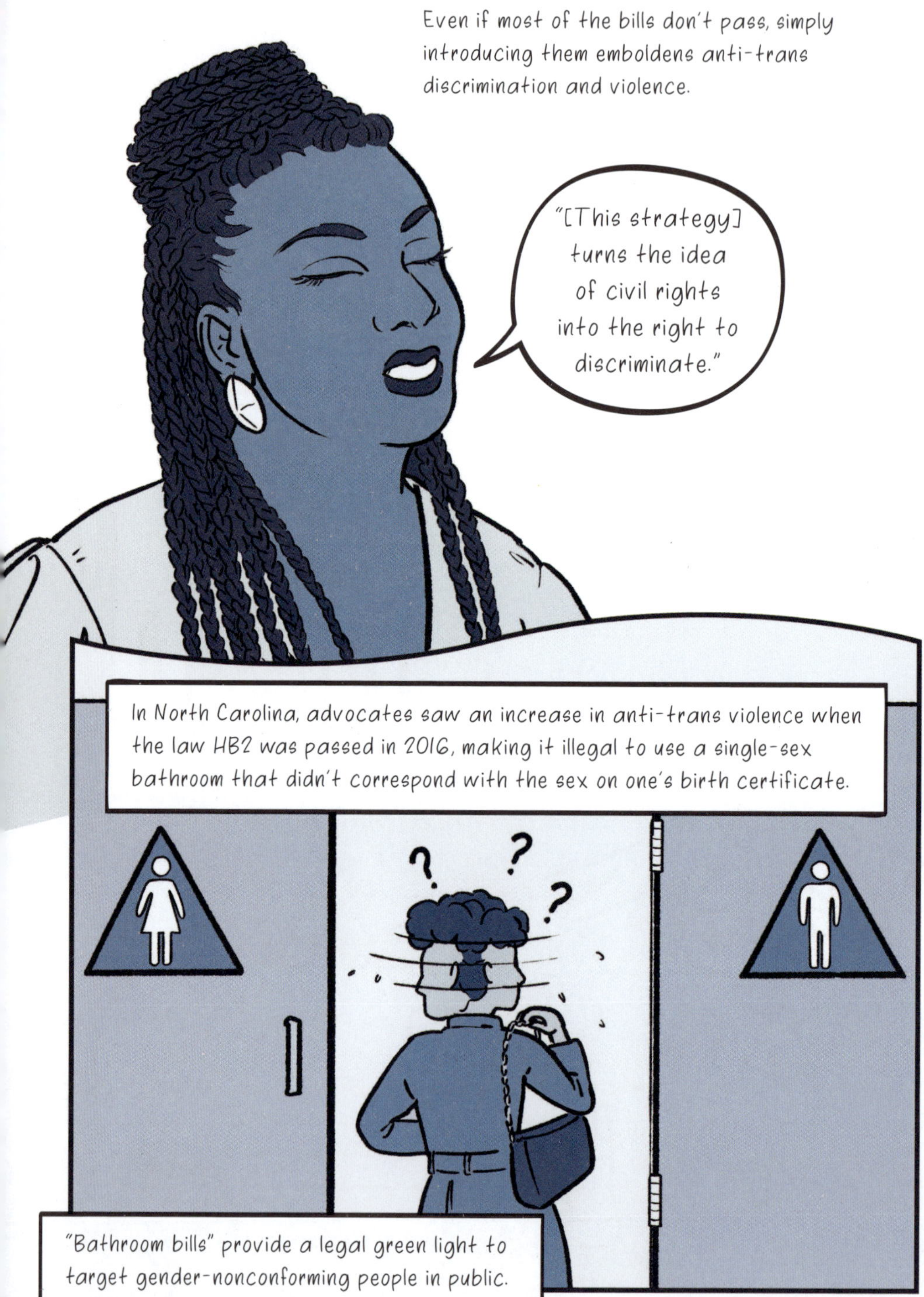
Even if most of the bills don't pass, simply introducing them emboldens anti-trans discrimination and violence.
"[This strategy] turns the idea of civil rights into the right to discriminate."
In North Carolina, advocates saw an increase in anti-trans violence when the law HB2 was passed in 2016, making it illegal to use a single-sex bathroom that didn't correspond with the sex on one's birth certificate.
? ? ?
"Bathroom bills" provide a legal green light to target gender-nonconforming people in public.

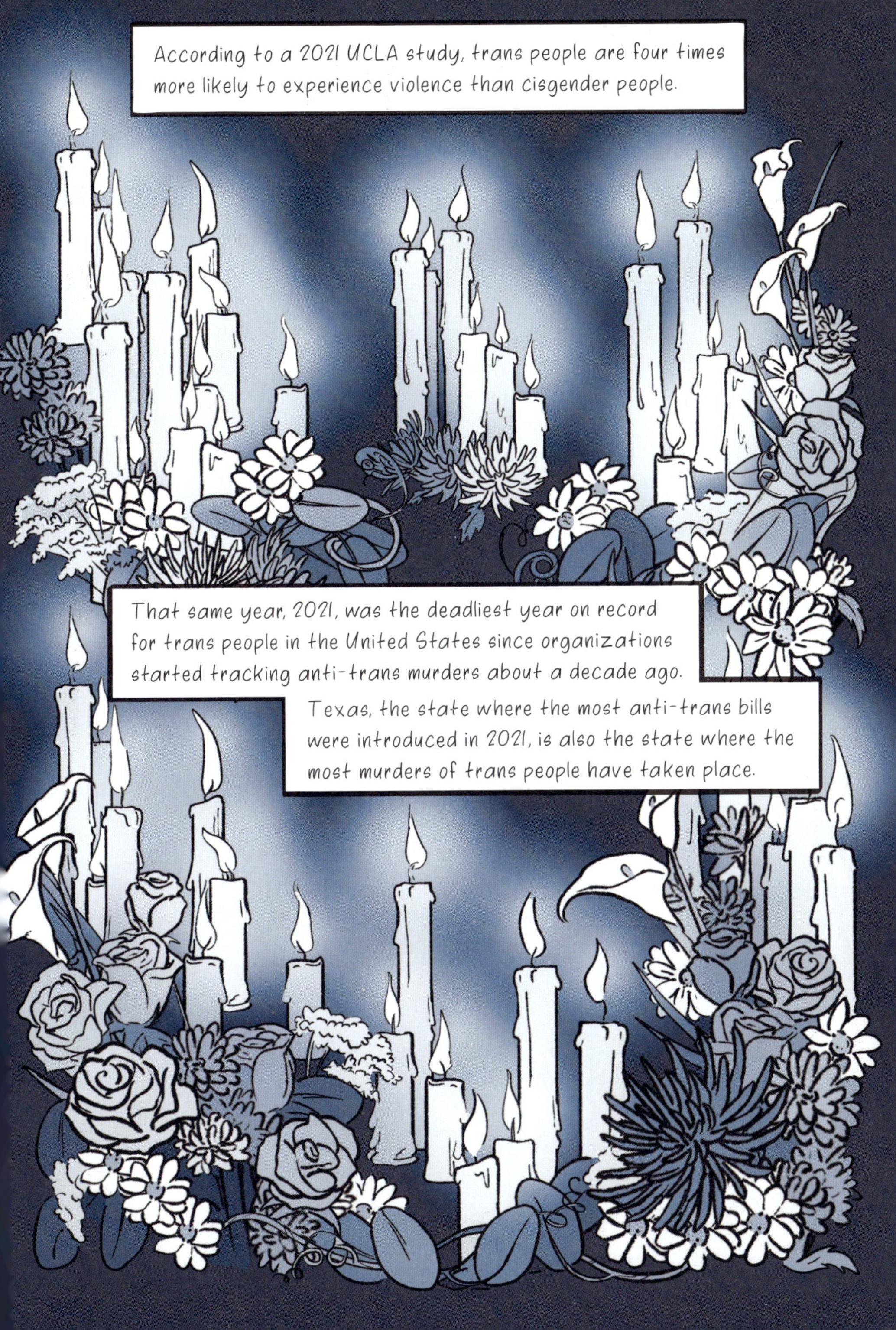
According to a 2021 UCLA study, trans people are four times more likely to experience violence than cisgender people.
That same year, 2021, was the deadliest year on record for trans people in the United States since organizations started tracking anti-trans murders about a decade ago.
Texas, the state where the most anti-trans bills were introduced in 2021, is also the state where the most murders of trans people have taken place.

Is there really such a thing as a "trans community"?

What does learning about trans history reveal about modern views on gender?

If there is, what are some of the values that hold it together?

How do racism, classism, sexism, ableism, and other forms of oppression keep trans people divided?

Who benefits when trans history is shared?

Who benefits when it's repressed?

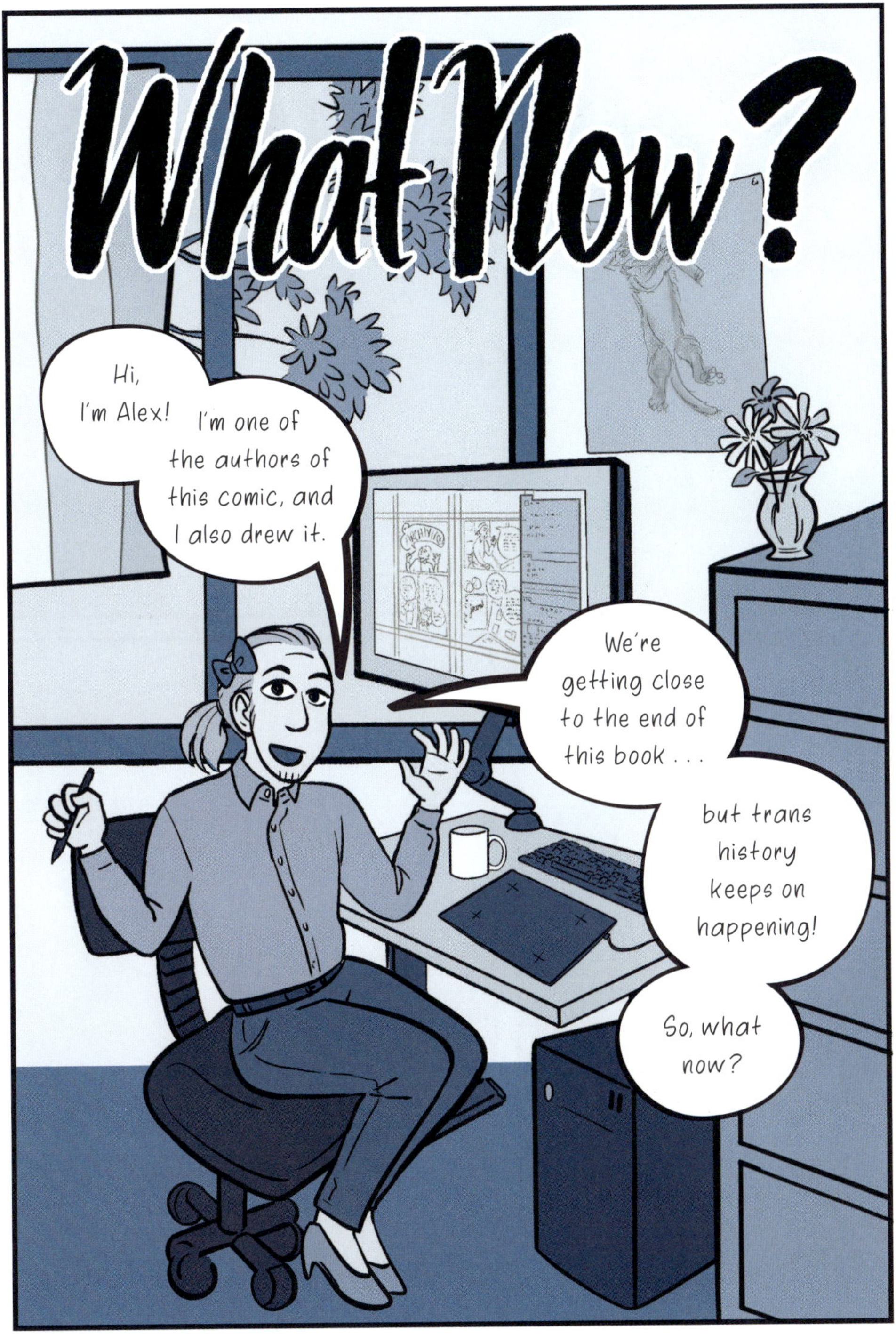
What Now?
Hi, I'm Alex!
I'm one of the authors of this comic, and I also drew it.
We're getting close to the end of this book . . .
but trans history keeps on happening!
So, what now?

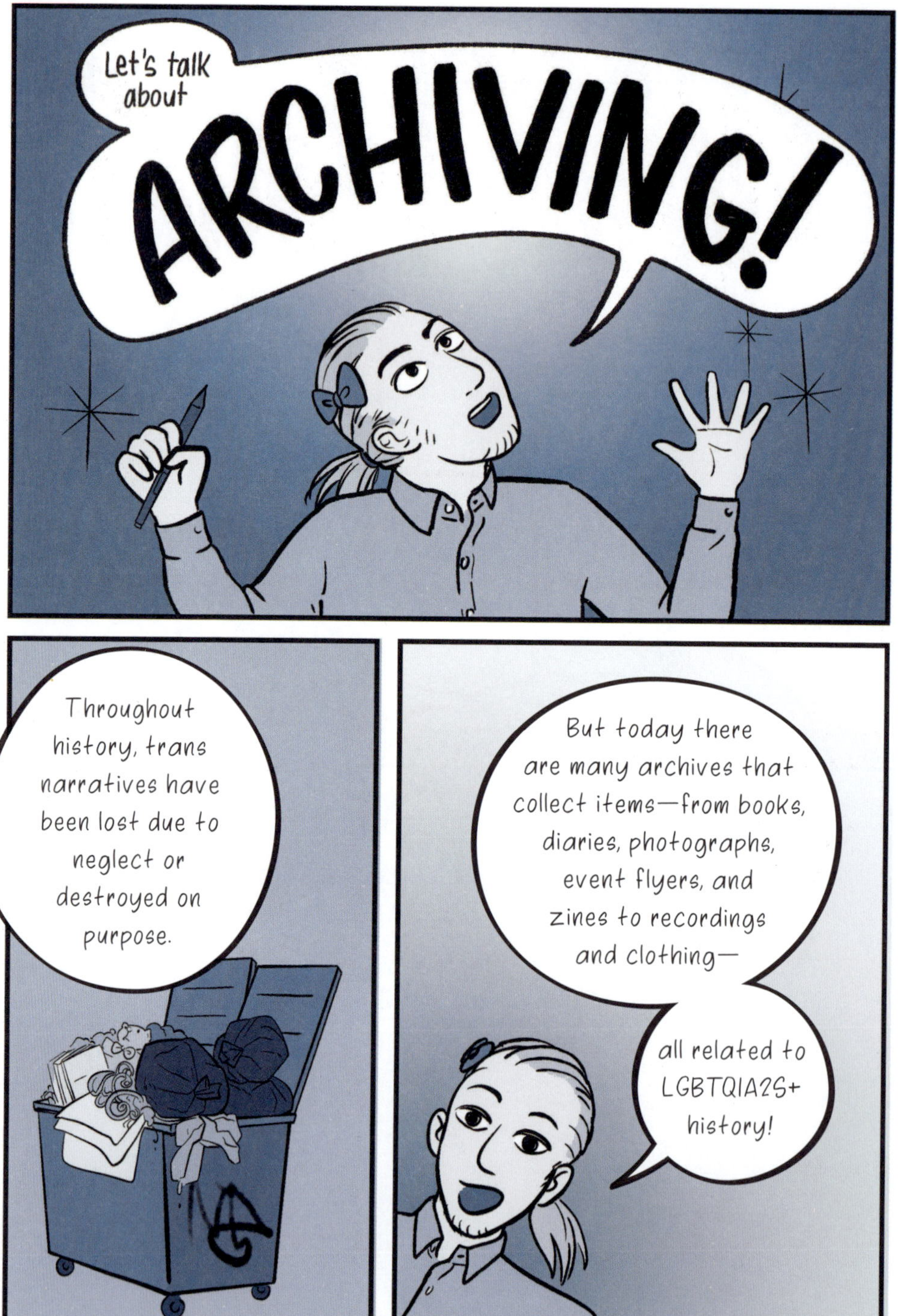
Let's talk about ARCHIVING!
Throughout history, trans narratives have been lost due to neglect or destroyed on purpose.
But today there are many archives that collect items—from books, diaries, photographs, event flyers, and zines to recordings and clothing—
all related to LGBTQIA2S+ history!

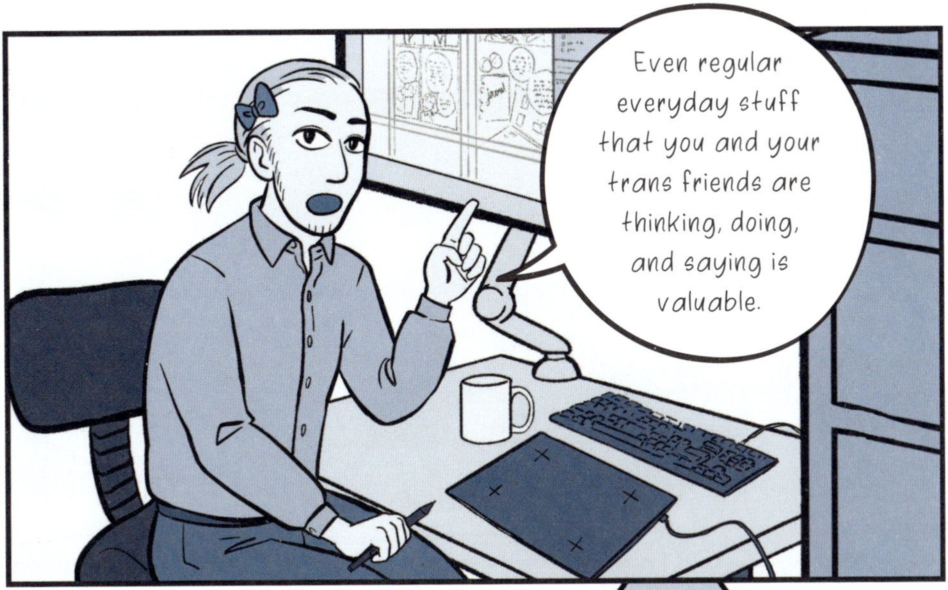
Even regular everyday stuff that you and your trans friends are thinking, doing, and saying is valuable.

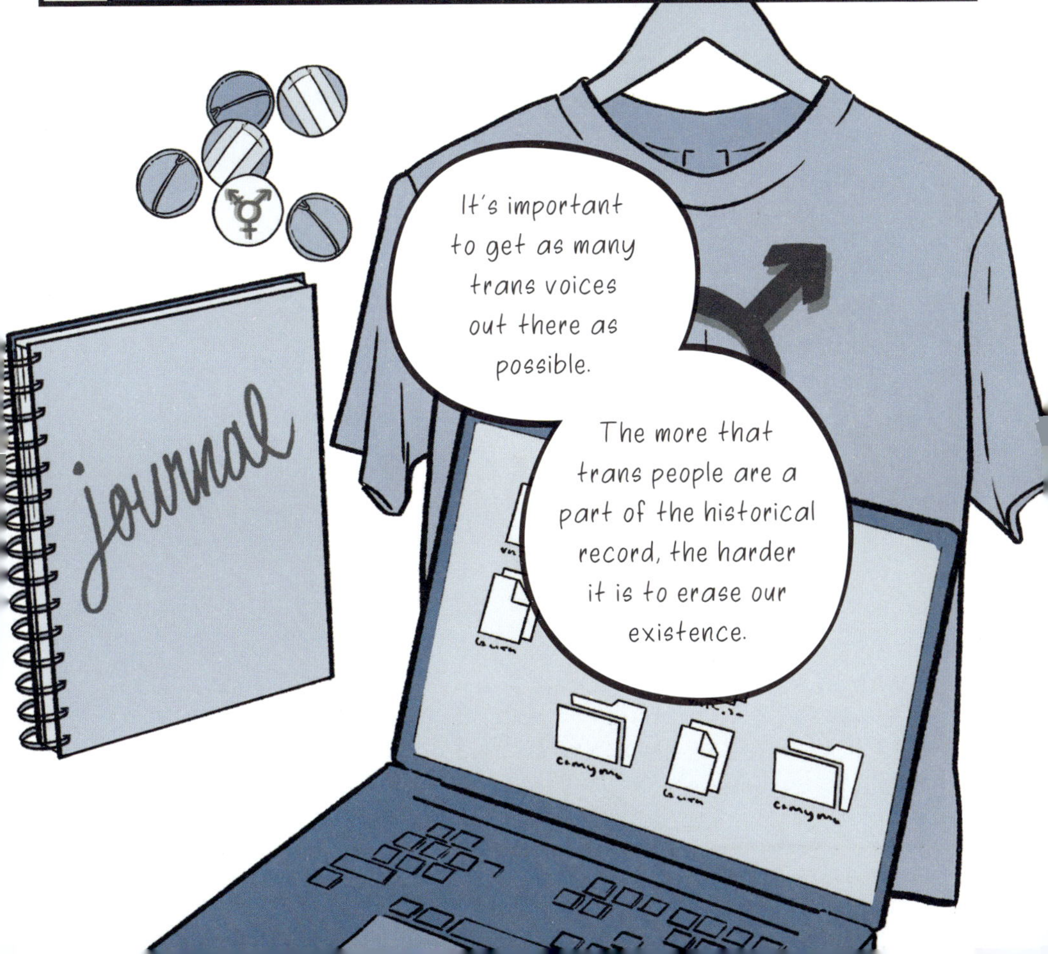
journal
It's important to get as many trans voices out there as possible.
The more that trans people are a part of the historical record, the harder it is to erase our existence.

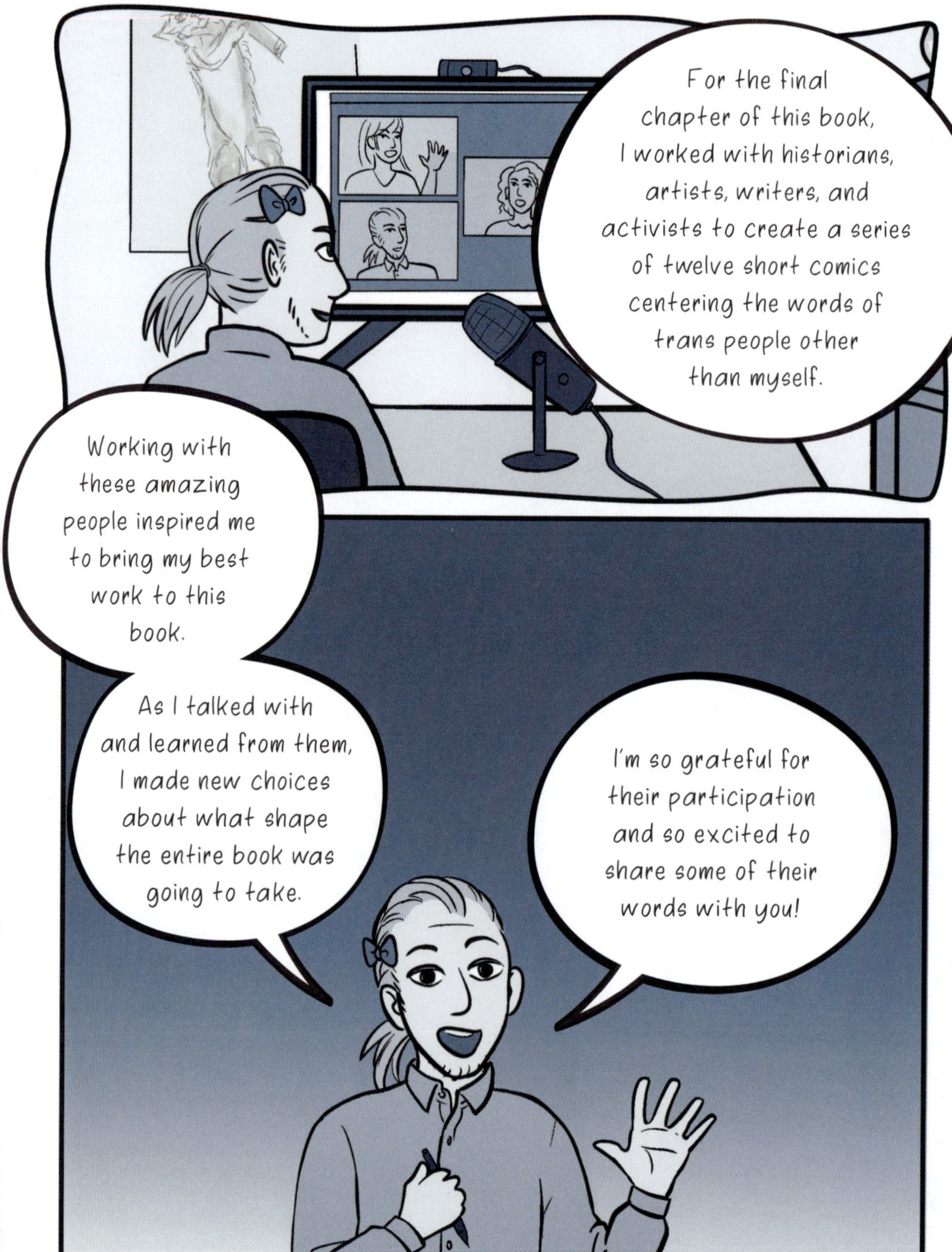
For the final chapter of this book, I worked with historians, artists, writers, and activists to create a series of twelve short comics centering the words of trans people other than myself.
Working with these amazing people inspired me to bring my best work to this book.
As I talked with and learned from them, I made new choices about what shape the entire book was going to take.
I'm so grateful for their participation and so excited to share some of their words with you!

5

The Present Moment: Community Voices

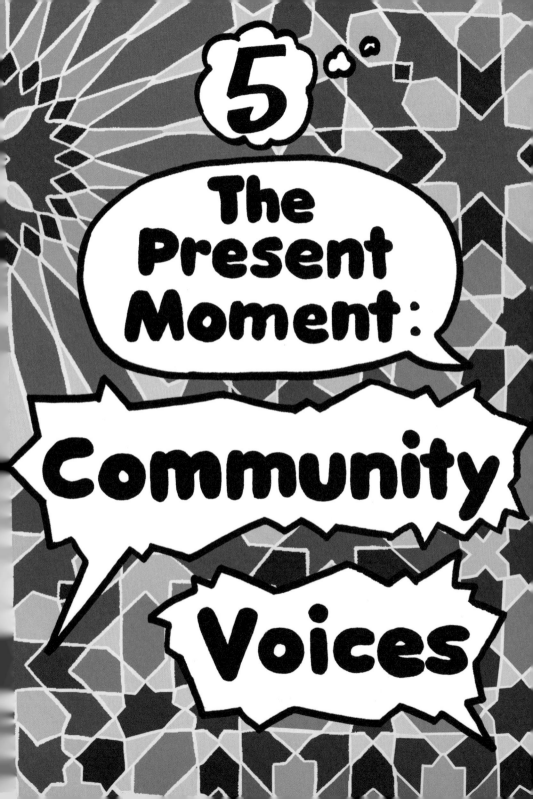

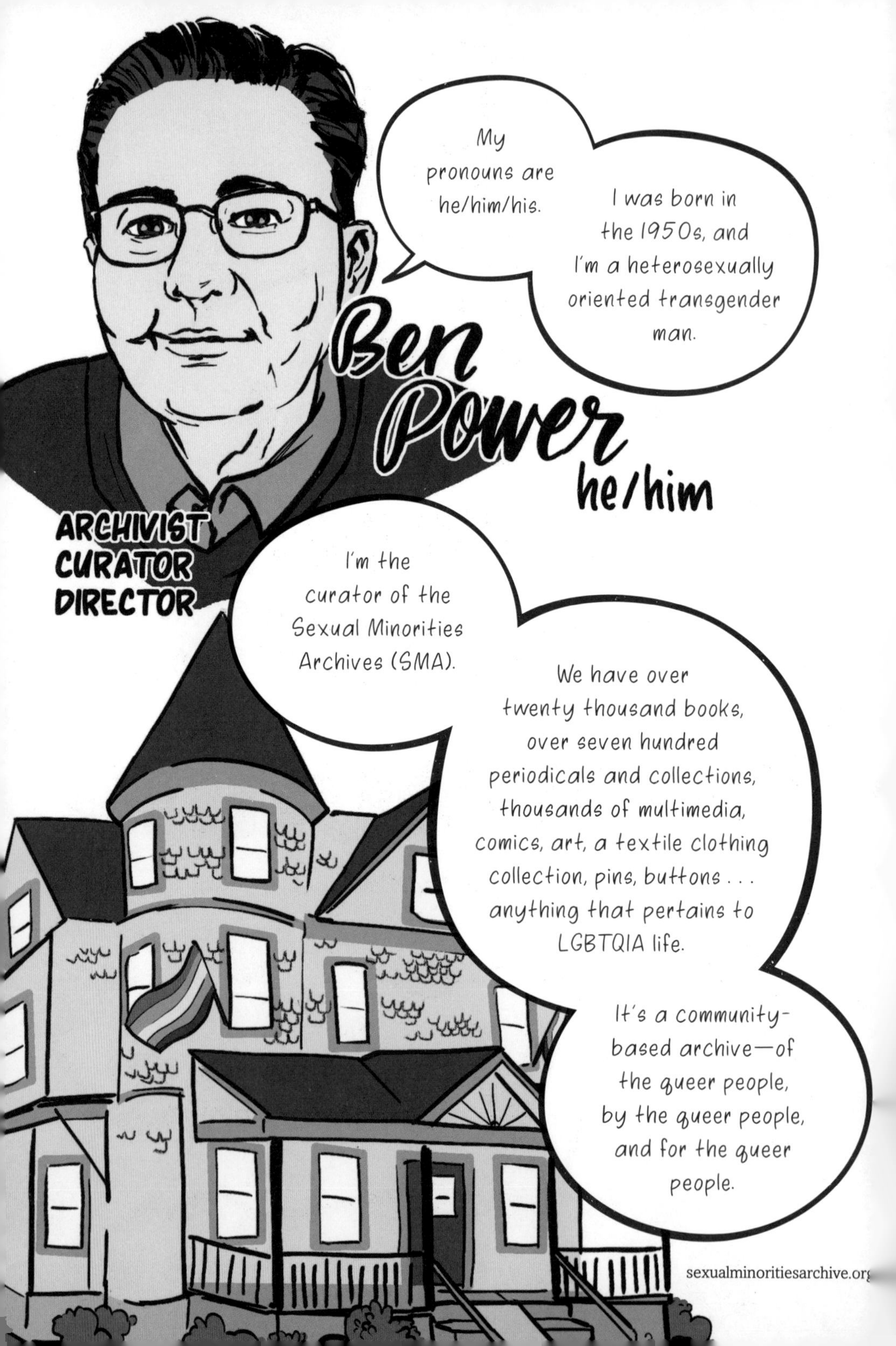
My pronouns are he/him/his.
I was born in the 1950s, and I'm a heterosexually oriented transgender man.
Ben Power
he/him
ARCHIVIST
CURATOR
DIRECTOR
I'm the curator of the Sexual Minorities Archives (SMA).
We have over twenty thousand books, over seven hundred periodicals and collections, thousands of multimedia, comics, art, a textile clothing collection, pins, buttons . . . anything that pertains to LGBTQIA life.
It's a community-based archive—of the queer people, by the queer people, and for the queer people.
sexualminoritiesarchive.org

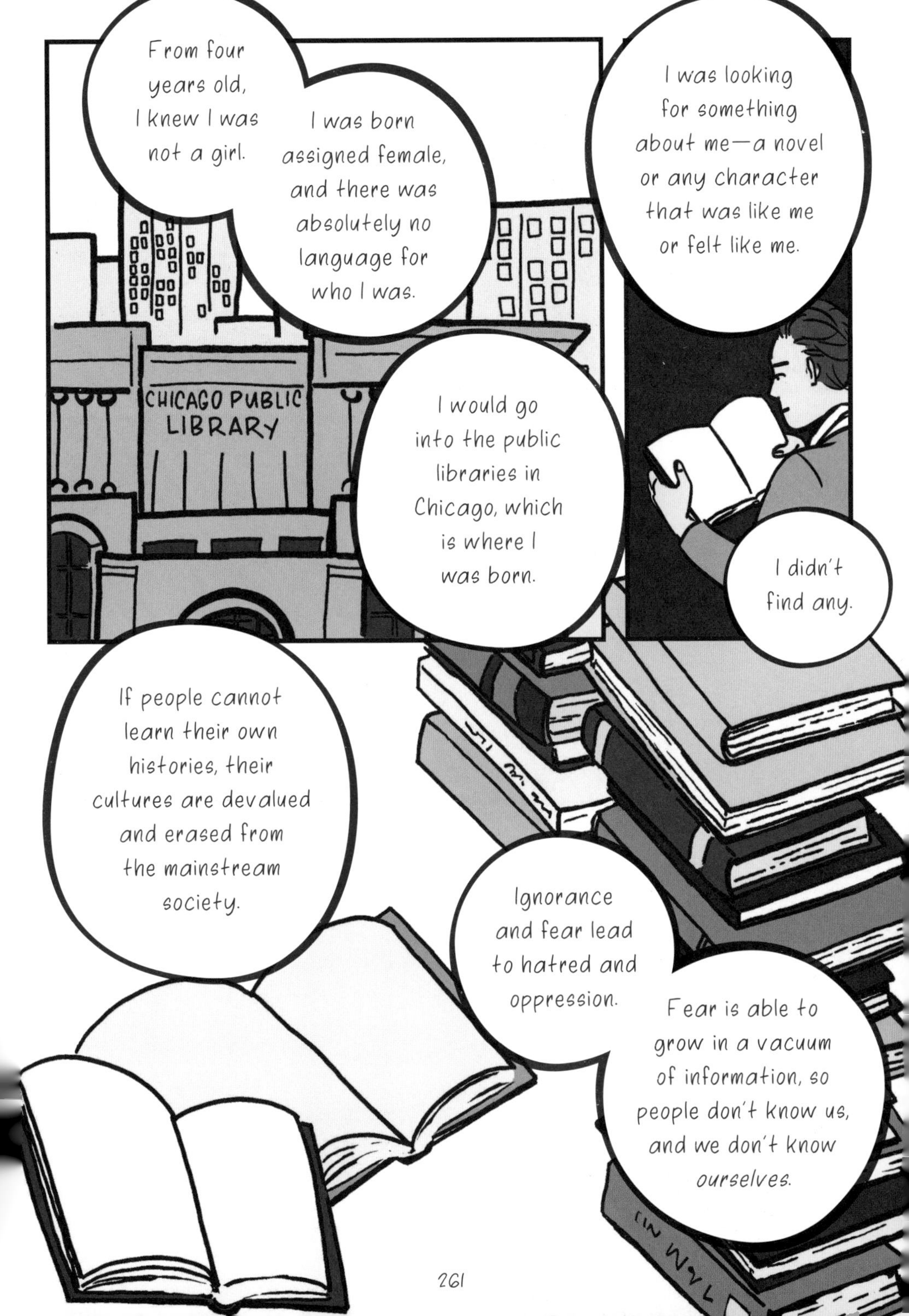
From four years old, I knew I was not a girl.
I was born assigned female, and there was absolutely no language for who I was.
CHICAGO PUBLIC LIBRARY
I would go into the public libraries in Chicago, which is where I was born.
I was looking for something about me—a novel or any character that was like me or felt like me.
I didn't find any.
If people cannot learn their own histories, their cultures are devalued and erased from the mainstream society.
Ignorance and fear lead to hatred and oppression.
Fear is able to grow in a vacuum of information, so people don't know us, and we don't know ourselves.

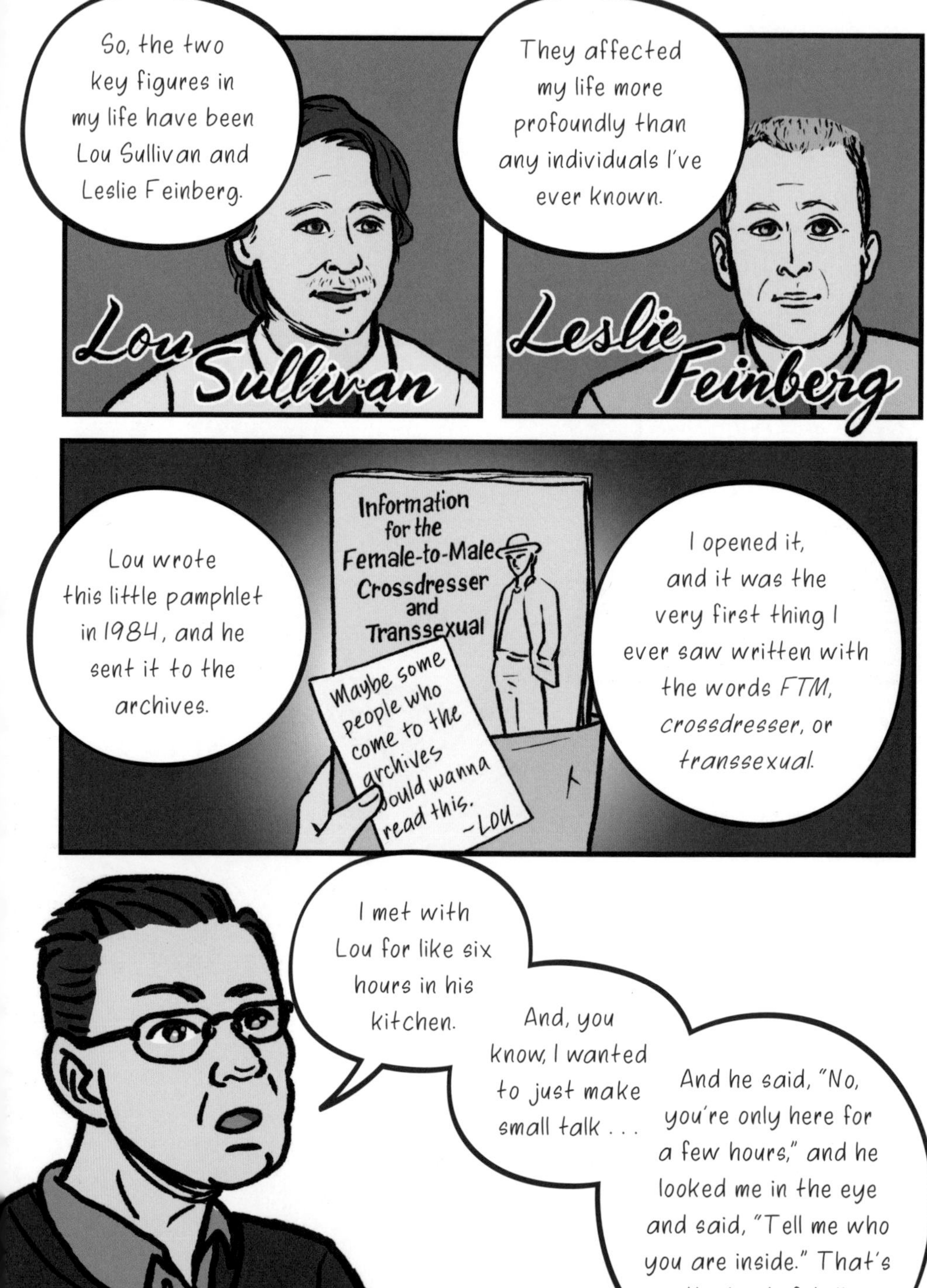
So, the two key figures in my life have been Lou Sullivan and Leslie Feinberg.
They affected my life more profoundly than any individuals I've ever known.
Lou Sullivan
Leslie Feinberg
Lou wrote this little pamphlet in 1984, and he sent it to the archives.
Information for the Female-to-Male Crossdresser and Transsexual
Maybe some people who come to the archives ould wanna read this. –LOU
I opened it, and it was the very first thing I ever saw written with the words *FTM*, *crossdresser*, or *transsexual*.
I met with Lou for like six hours in his kitchen.
And, you know, I wanted to just make small talk . . .
And he said, "No, you're only here for a few hours," and he looked me in the eye and said, "Tell me who you are inside." That's the kind of talk we had.

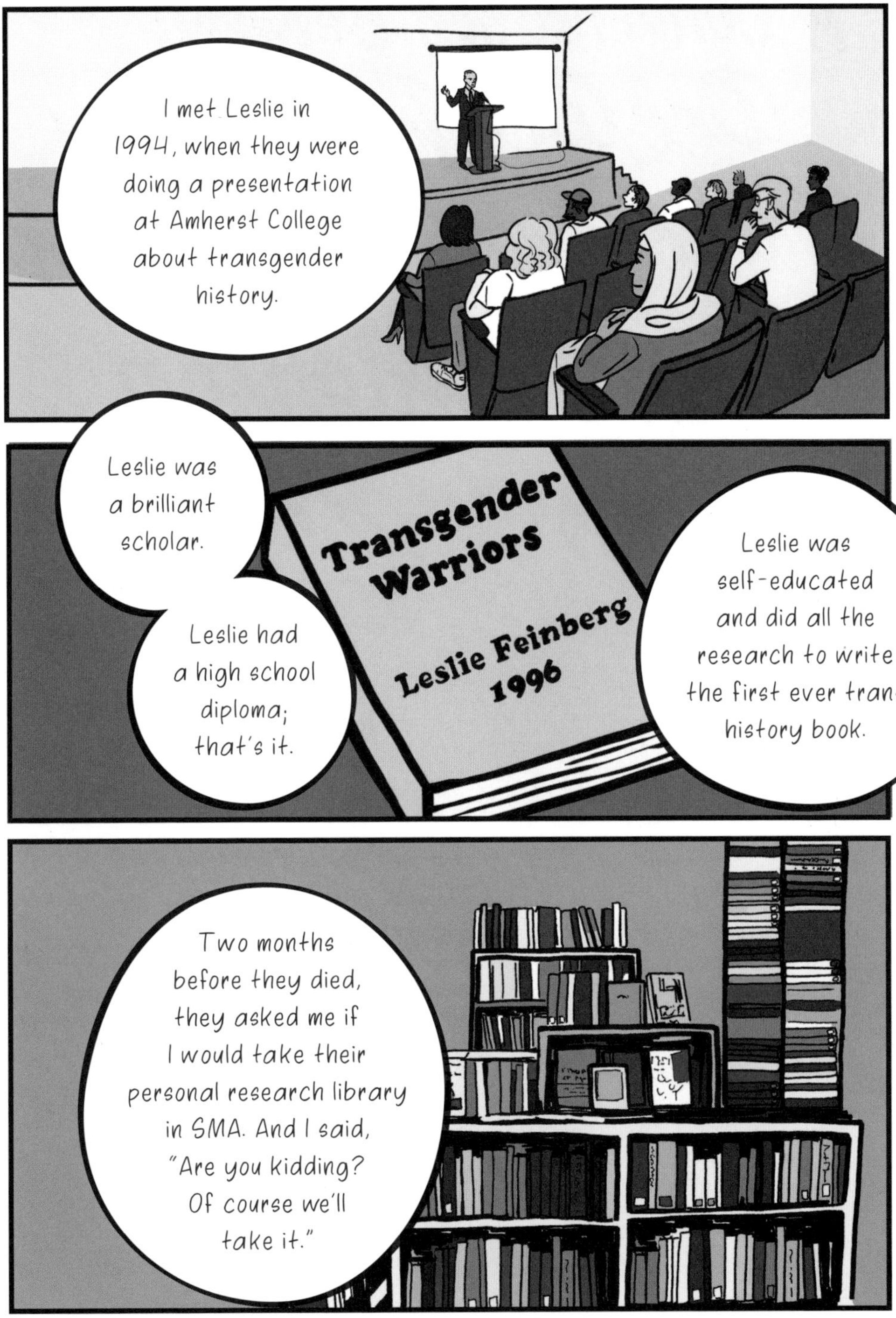
I met Leslie in 1994, when they were doing a presentation at Amherst College about transgender history.
Leslie was a brilliant scholar.
Leslie had a high school diploma; that's it.
Transgender Warriors
Leslie Feinberg 1996
Leslie was self-educated and did all the research to write the first ever trans history book.
Two months before they died, they asked me if I would take their personal research library in SMA. And I said, "Are you kidding? Of course we'll take it."

A Conversation Between Dee Dee Watters and Marie Angel Venarsian about Monica Roberts

1962–2020
she/her

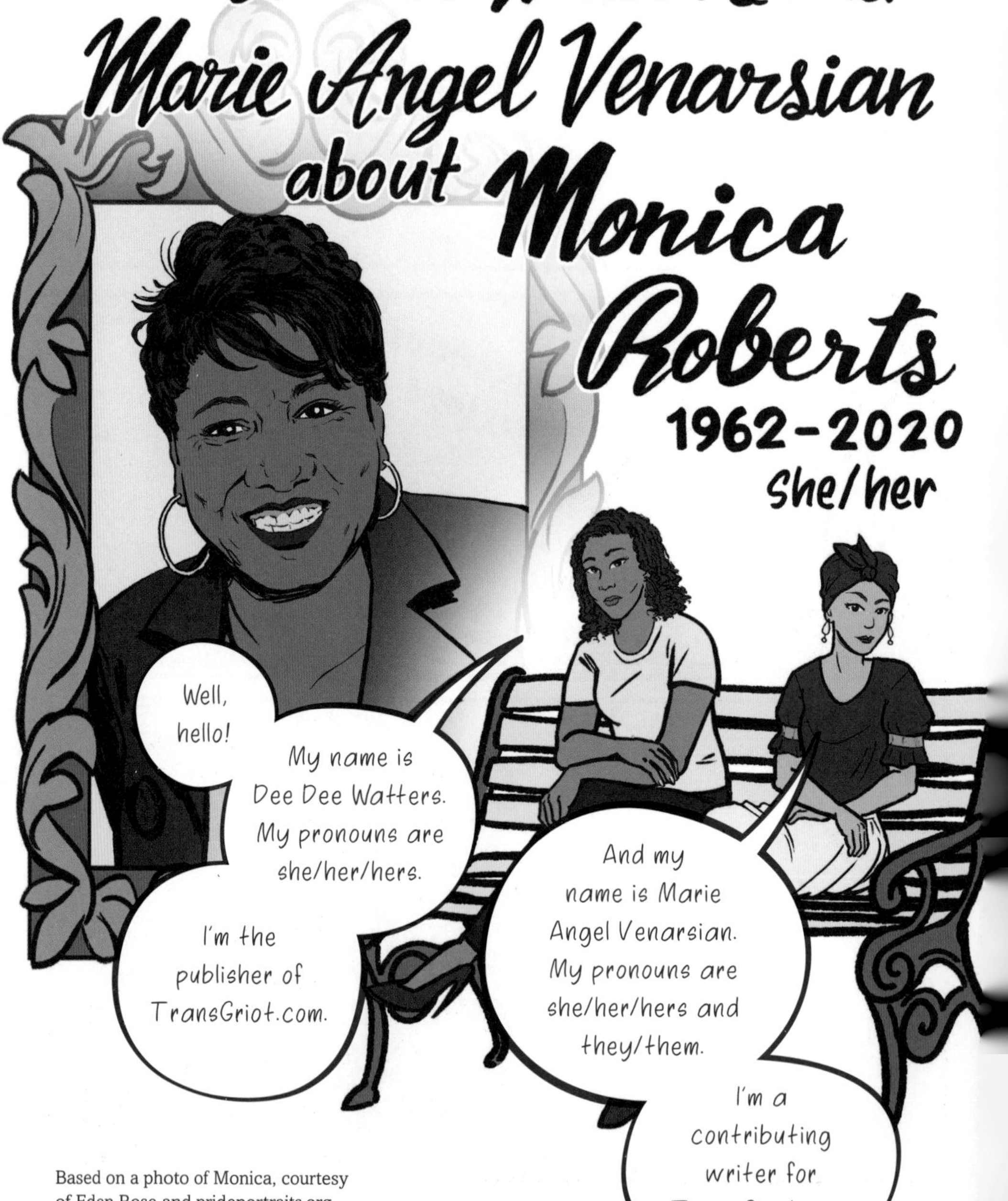
Well, hello!
My name is Dee Dee Watters. My pronouns are she/her/hers.
I'm the publisher of TransGriot.com.
And my name is Marie Angel Venarsian. My pronouns are she/her/hers and they/them.
I'm a contributing writer for TransGriot.com.

Based on a photo of Monica, courtesy of Eden Rose and prideportraits.org

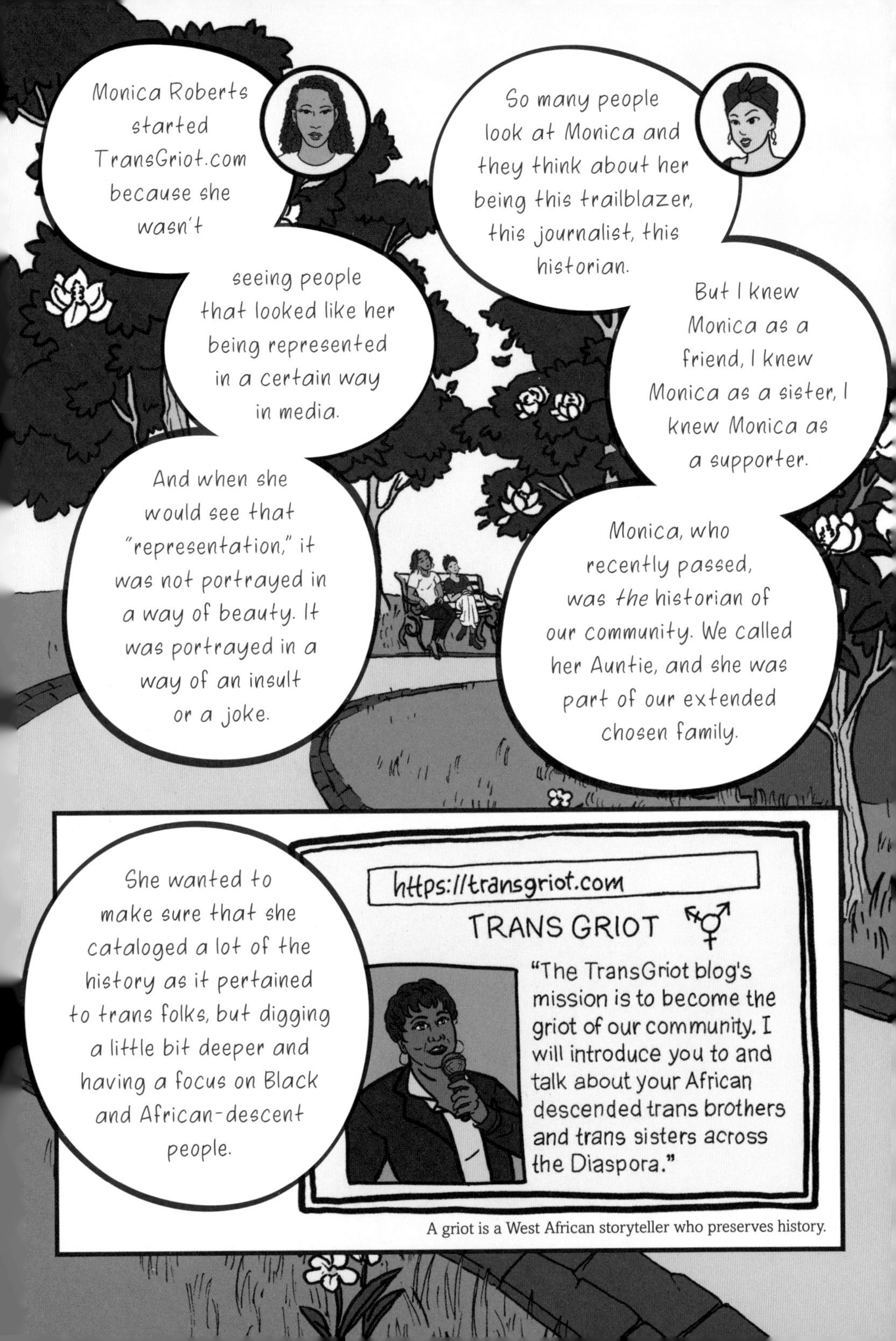
Monica Roberts started TransGriot.com because she wasn't
seeing people that looked like her being represented in a certain way in media.
And when she would see that "representation," it was not portrayed in a way of beauty. It was portrayed in a way of an insult or a joke.
So many people look at Monica and they think about her being this trailblazer, this journalist, this historian.
But I knew Monica as a friend, I knew Monica as a sister, I knew Monica as a supporter.
Monica, who recently passed, was *the* historian of our community. We called her Auntie, and she was part of our extended chosen family.
She wanted to make sure that she cataloged a lot of the history as it pertained to trans folks, but digging a little bit deeper and having a focus on Black and African-descent people.
https://transgriot.com
TRANS GRIOT
"The TransGriot blog's mission is to become the griot of our community. I will introduce you to and talk about your African descended trans brothers and trans sisters across the Diaspora."
A griot is a West African storyteller who preserves history.

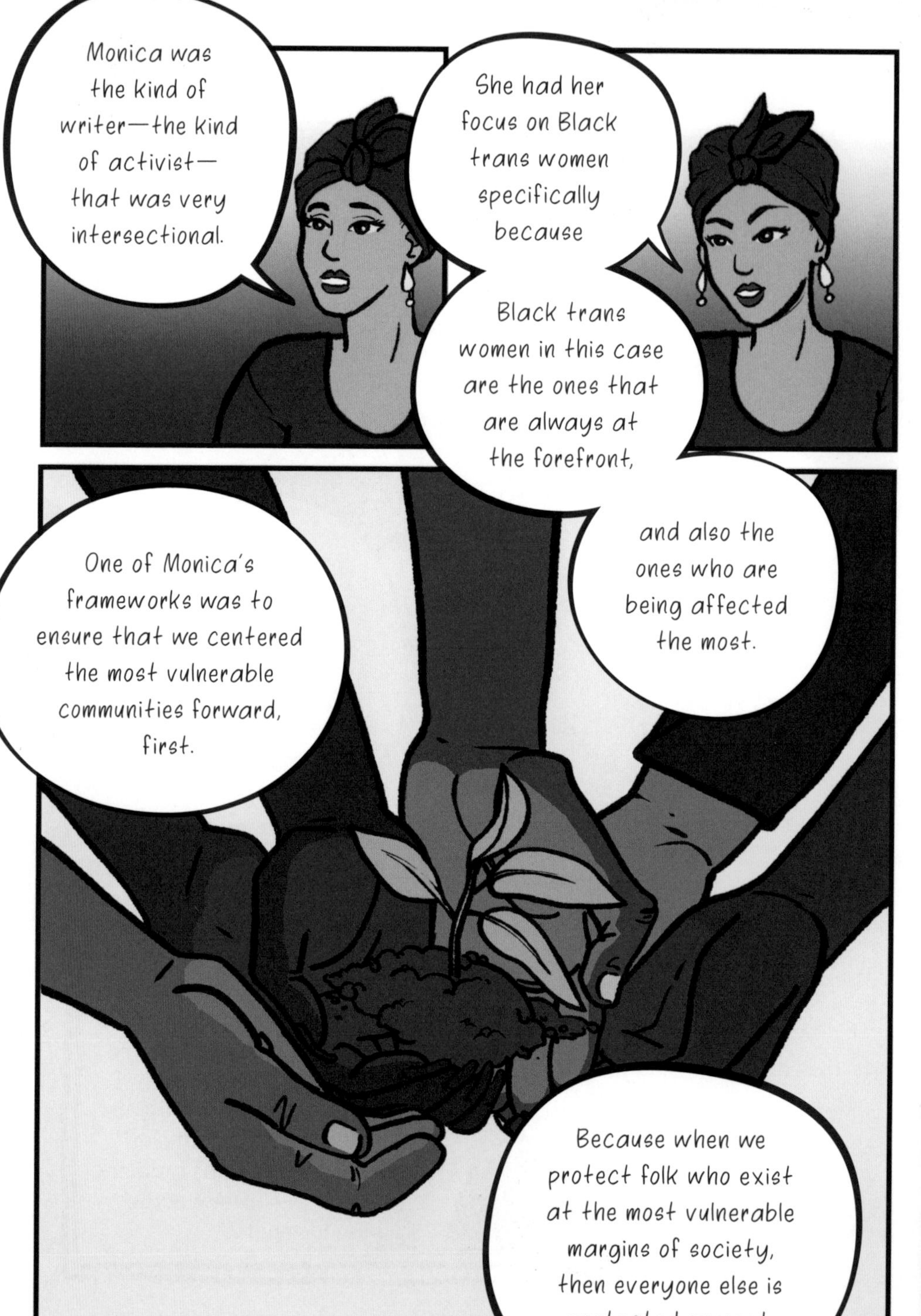
Monica was the kind of writer—the kind of activist—that was very intersectional.
She had her focus on Black trans women specifically because
Black trans women in this case are the ones that are always at the forefront,
and also the ones who are being affected the most.
One of Monica's frameworks was to ensure that we centered the most vulnerable communities forward, first.
Because when we protect folk who exist at the most vulnerable margins of society, then everyone else is protected onward.

"Witnessing Dee Dee Watters's work throughout my life has been also a learning process for me."

"She's been able to carry through a very important aspect of trans advocacy, which is honoring and documenting trans murders beyond the usual gnarly lens of media."

"A lot of times I have identified bodies in the morgue; I have been the first point of contact to family members and let them know that their children have been murdered."

"And so when those things would come about, it was even more complicated to have to deal with the media outlets that were misgendering these individuals."

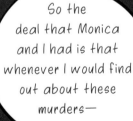

"So the deal that Monica and I had is that whenever I would find out about these murders—"

CLICK

"if it was anything, bad articles, that kind of stuff, she'd get right on it and she would address it."

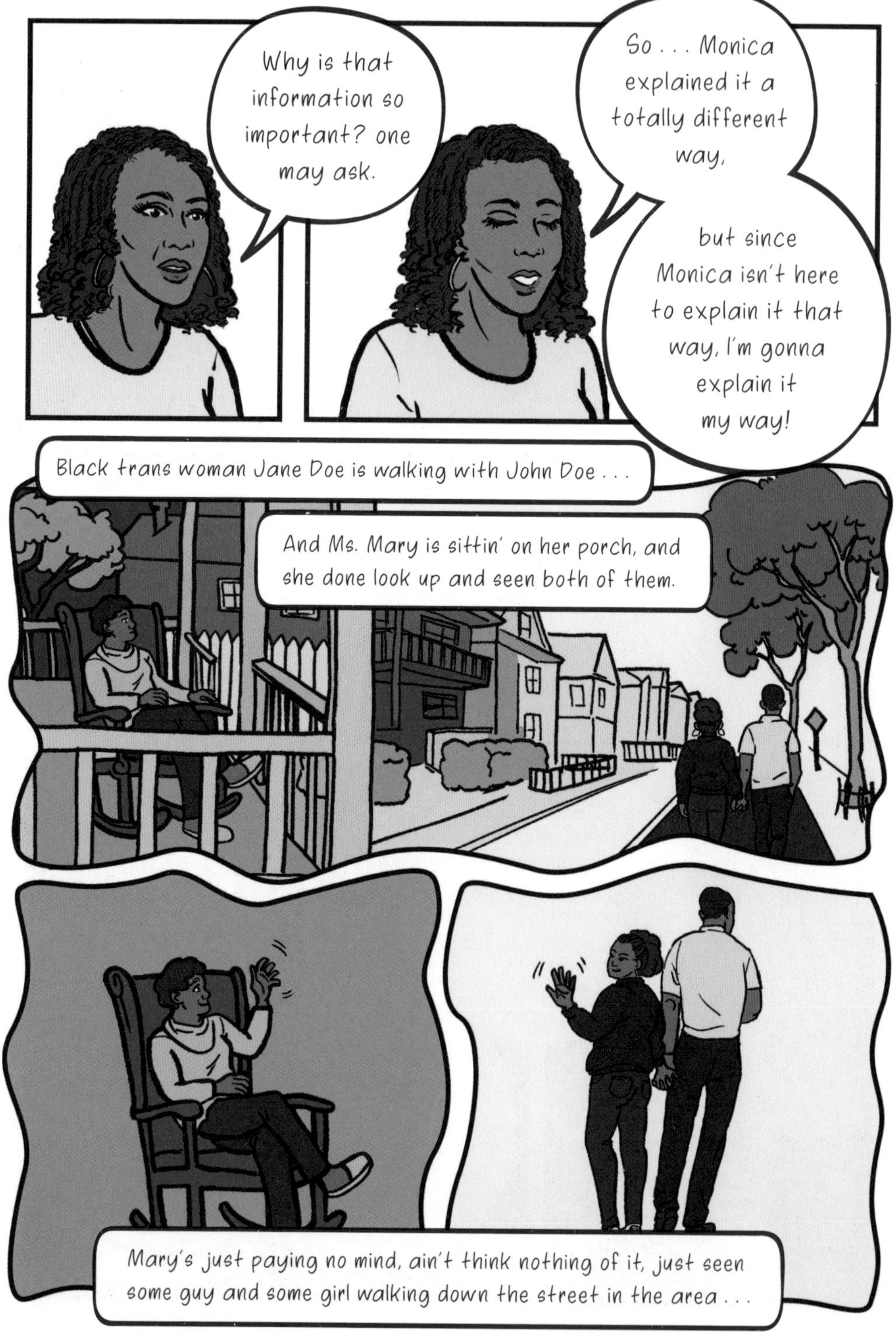
Why is that information so important? one may ask.
So . . . Monica explained it a totally different way,
but since Monica isn't here to explain it that way, I'm gonna explain it my way!
Black trans woman Jane Doe is walking with John Doe . . .
And Ms. Mary is sittin' on her porch, and she done look up and seen both of them.
Mary's just paying no mind, ain't think nothing of it, just seen some guy and some girl walking down the street in the area . . .

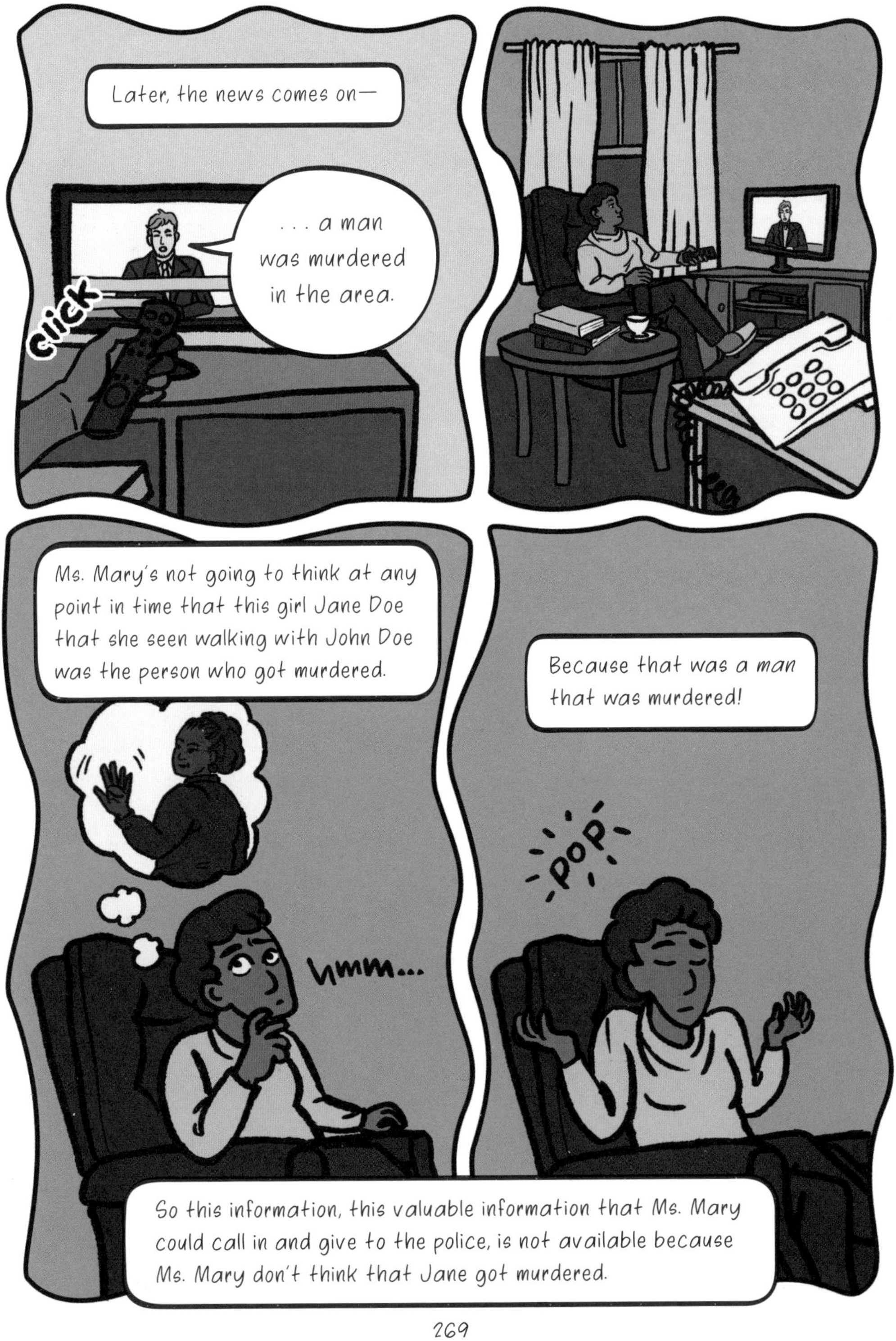

Later, the news comes on—
CLICK
. . . a man was murdered in the area.
Ms. Mary's not going to think at any point in time that this girl Jane Doe that she seen walking with John Doe was the person who got murdered.
hmm...
Because that was a man that was murdered!
POP
So this information, this valuable information that Ms. Mary could call in and give to the police, is not available because Ms. Mary don't think that Jane got murdered.

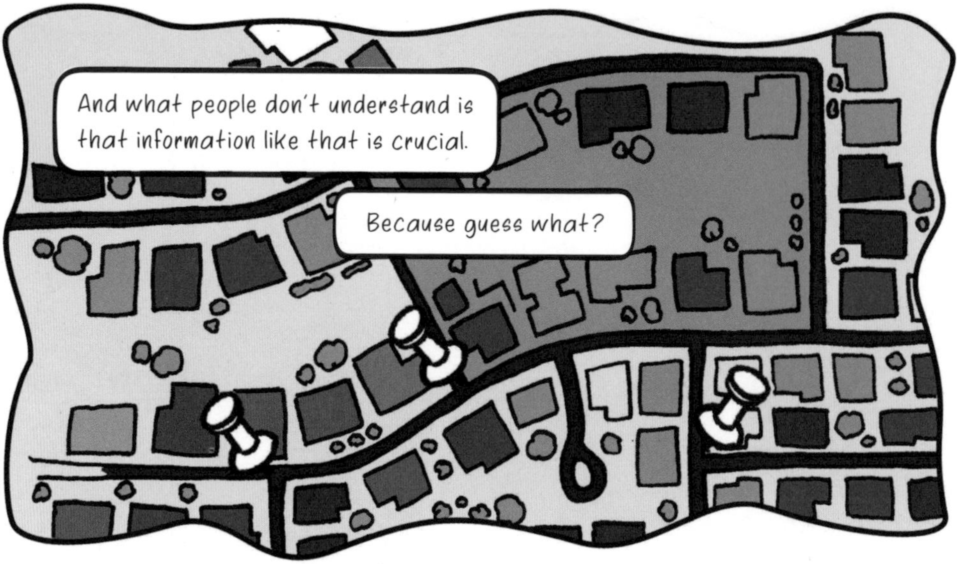
And what people don't understand is that information like that is crucial.
Because guess what?

John Doe could have been at the corner right up the street from that location, but nobody put John and Jane together.

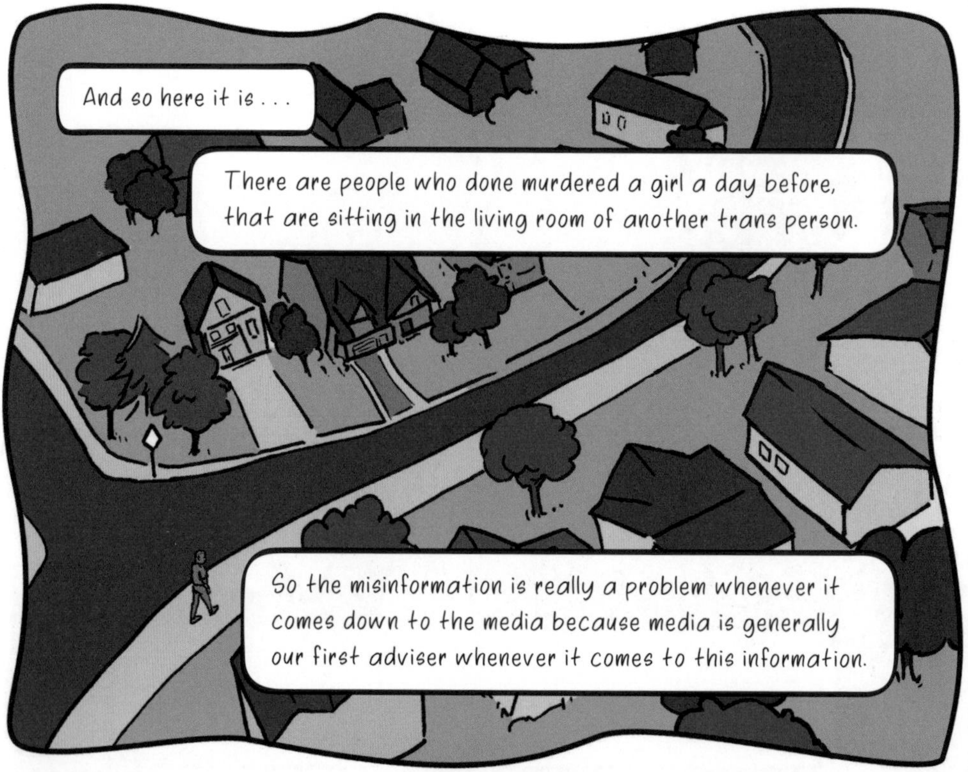
And so here it is . . .
There are people who done murdered a girl a day before, that are sitting in the living room of another trans person.
So the misinformation is really a problem whenever it comes down to the media because media is generally our first adviser whenever it comes to this information.

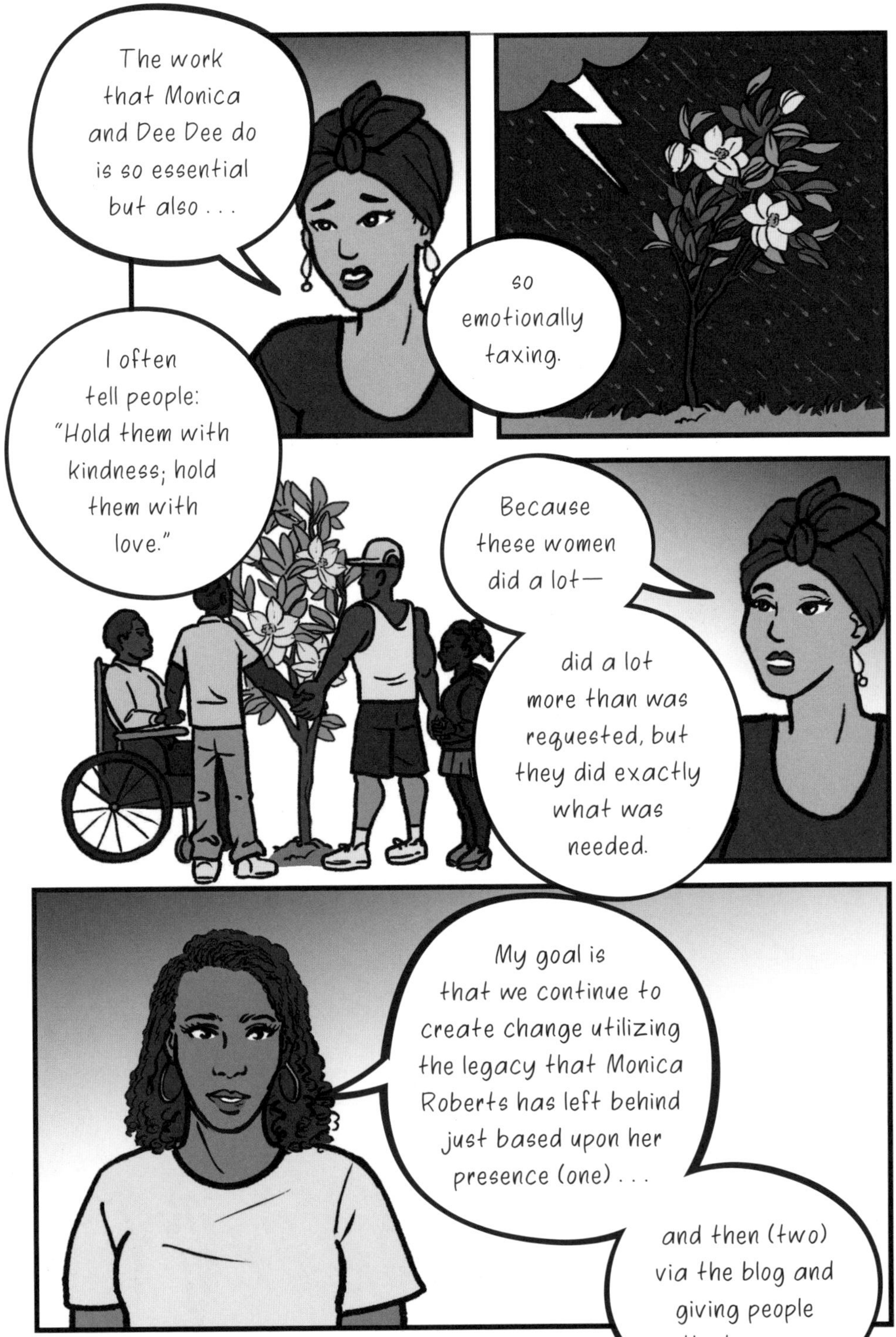
The work that Monica and Dee Dee do is so essential but also . . .
so emotionally taxing.
I often tell people: "Hold them with kindness; hold them with love."
Because these women did a lot—
did a lot more than was requested, but they did exactly what was needed.
My goal is that we continue to create change utilizing the legacy that Monica Roberts has left behind just based upon her presence (one) . . .
and then (two) via the blog and giving people that space.

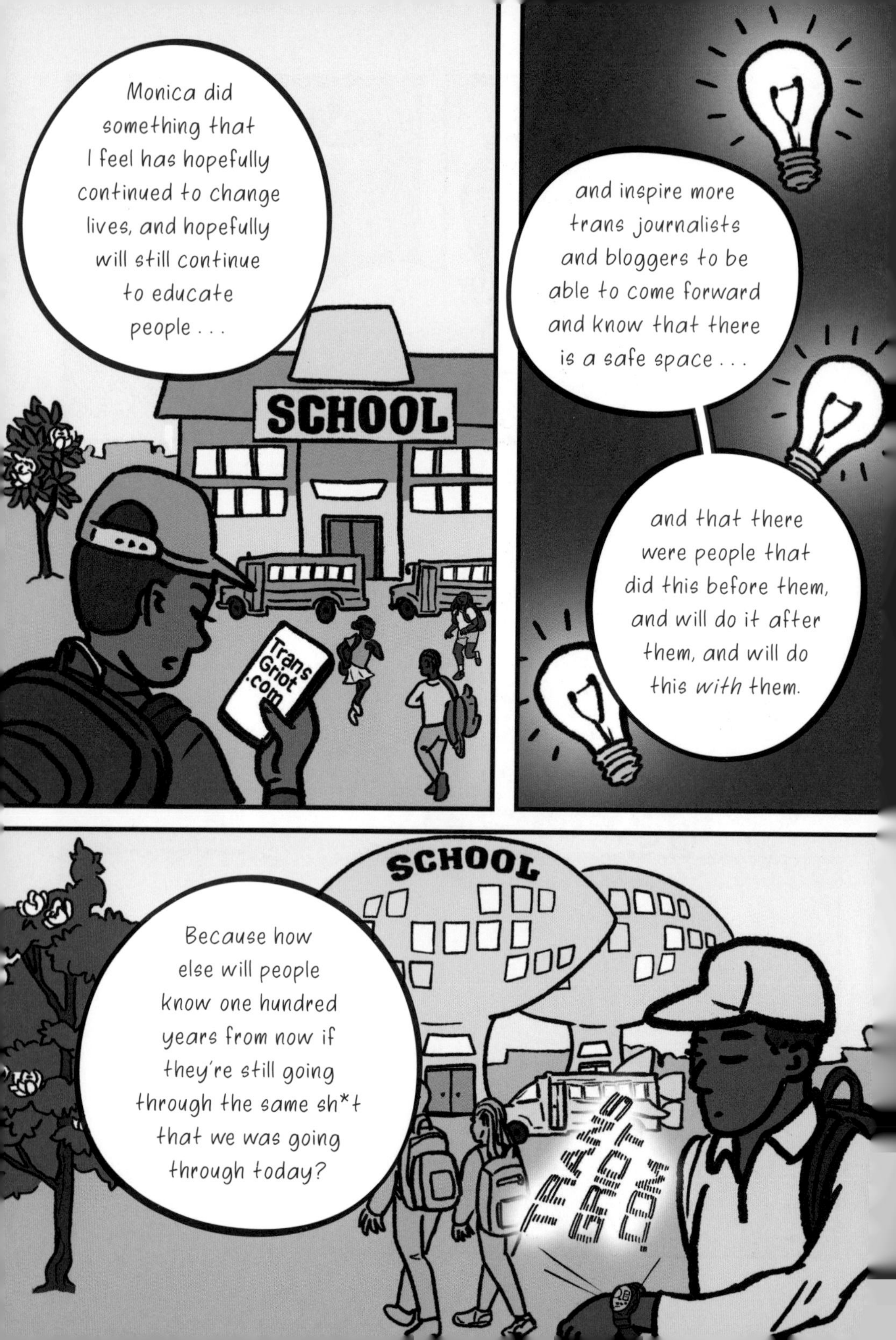
Monica did something that I feel has hopefully continued to change lives, and hopefully will still continue to educate people . . .
SCHOOL
TransGriot.com
and inspire more trans journalists and bloggers to be able to come forward and know that there is a safe space . . .
and that there were people that did this before them, and will do it after them, and will do this *with* them.
SCHOOL
Because how else will people know one hundred years from now if they're still going through the same sh*t that we was going through today?
TRANSGRIOT.COM

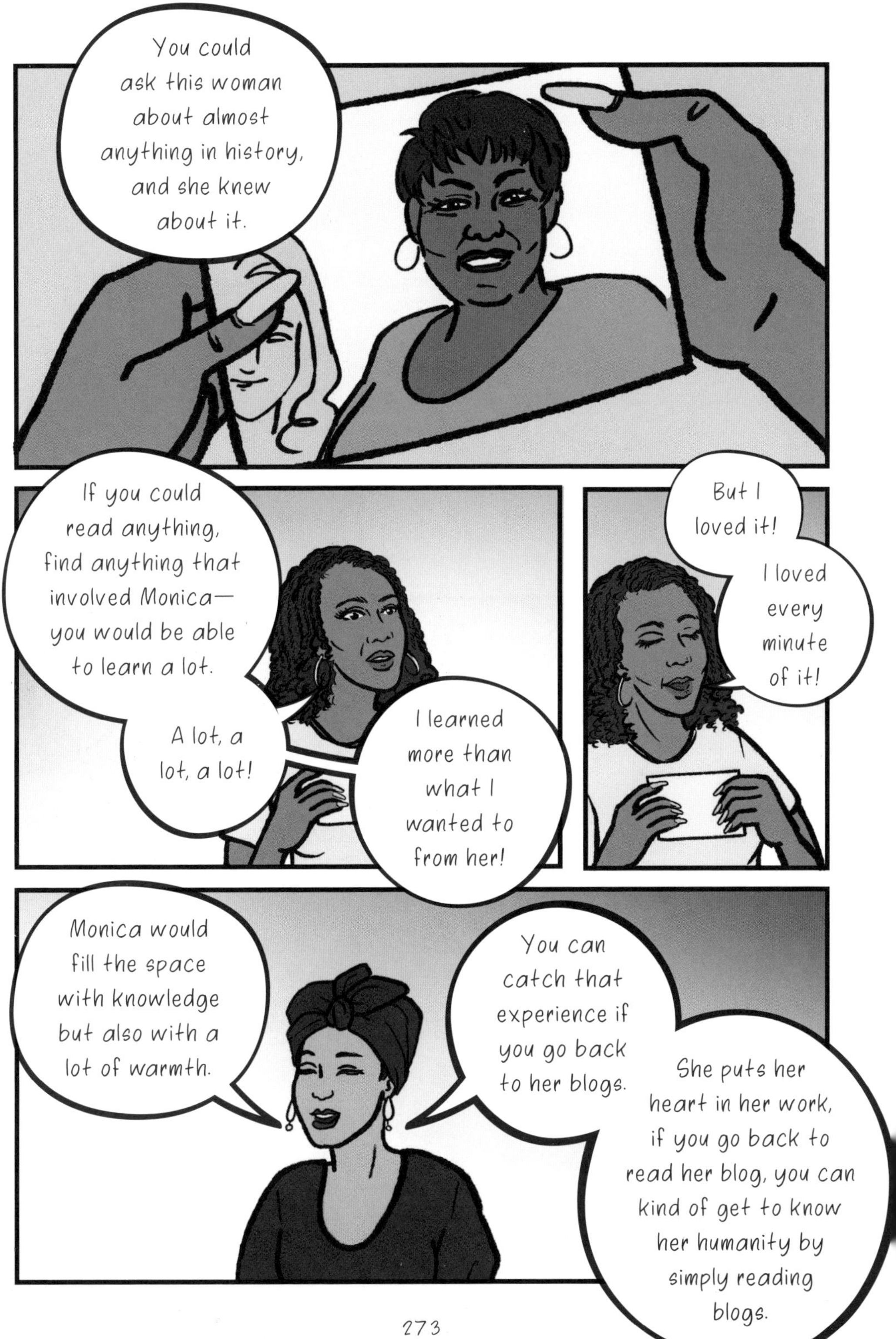
You could ask this woman about almost anything in history, and she knew about it.
If you could read anything, find anything that involved Monica— you would be able to learn a lot.
A lot, a lot, a lot!
I learned more than what I wanted to from her!
But I loved it!
I loved every minute of it!
Monica would fill the space with knowledge but also with a lot of warmth.
You can catch that experience if you go back to her blogs.
She puts her heart in her work, if you go back to read her blog, you can kind of get to know her humanity by simply reading blogs.

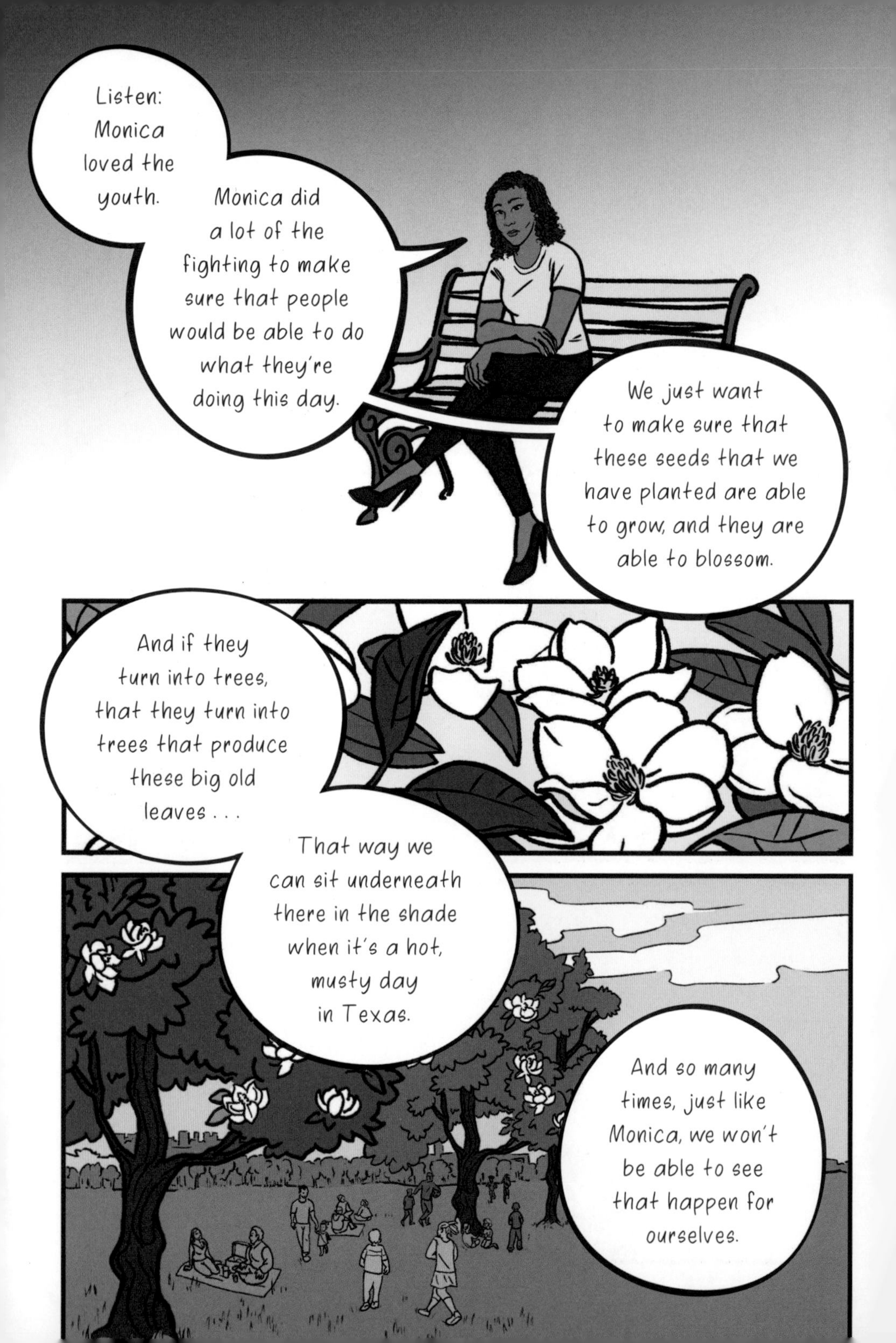
Listen: Monica loved the youth.
Monica did a lot of the fighting to make sure that people would be able to do what they're doing this day.
We just want to make sure that these seeds that we have planted are able to grow, and they are able to blossom.
And if they turn into trees, that they turn into trees that produce these big old leaves . . .
That way we can sit underneath there in the shade when it's a hot, musty day in Texas.
And so many times, just like Monica, we won't be able to see that happen for ourselves.

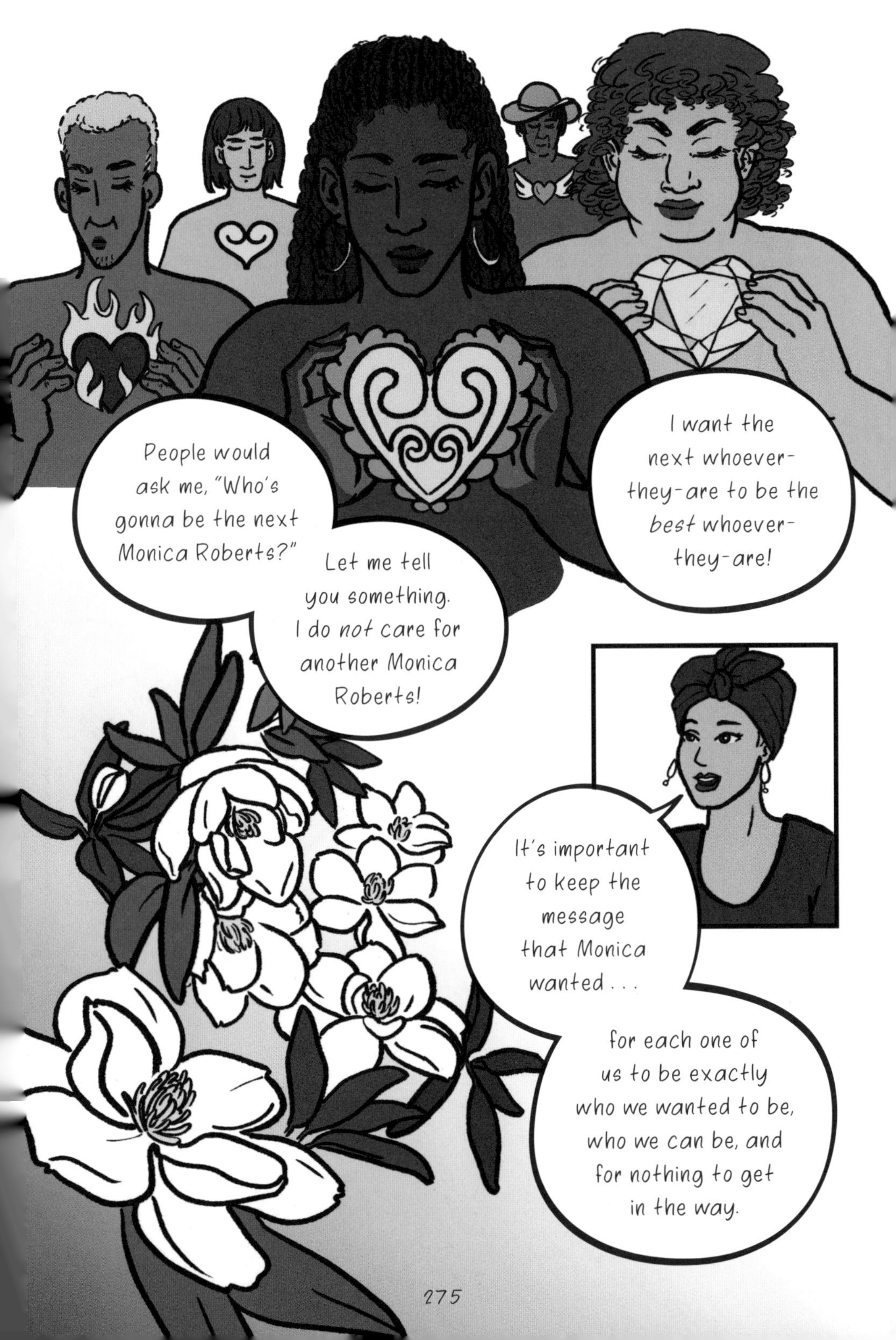
People would ask me, "Who's gonna be the next Monica Roberts?"
Let me tell you something. I do *not* care for another Monica Roberts!
I want the next whoever-they-are to be the *best* whoever-they-are!
It's important to keep the message that Monica wanted . . .
for each one of us to be exactly who we wanted to be, who we can be, and for nothing to get in the way.

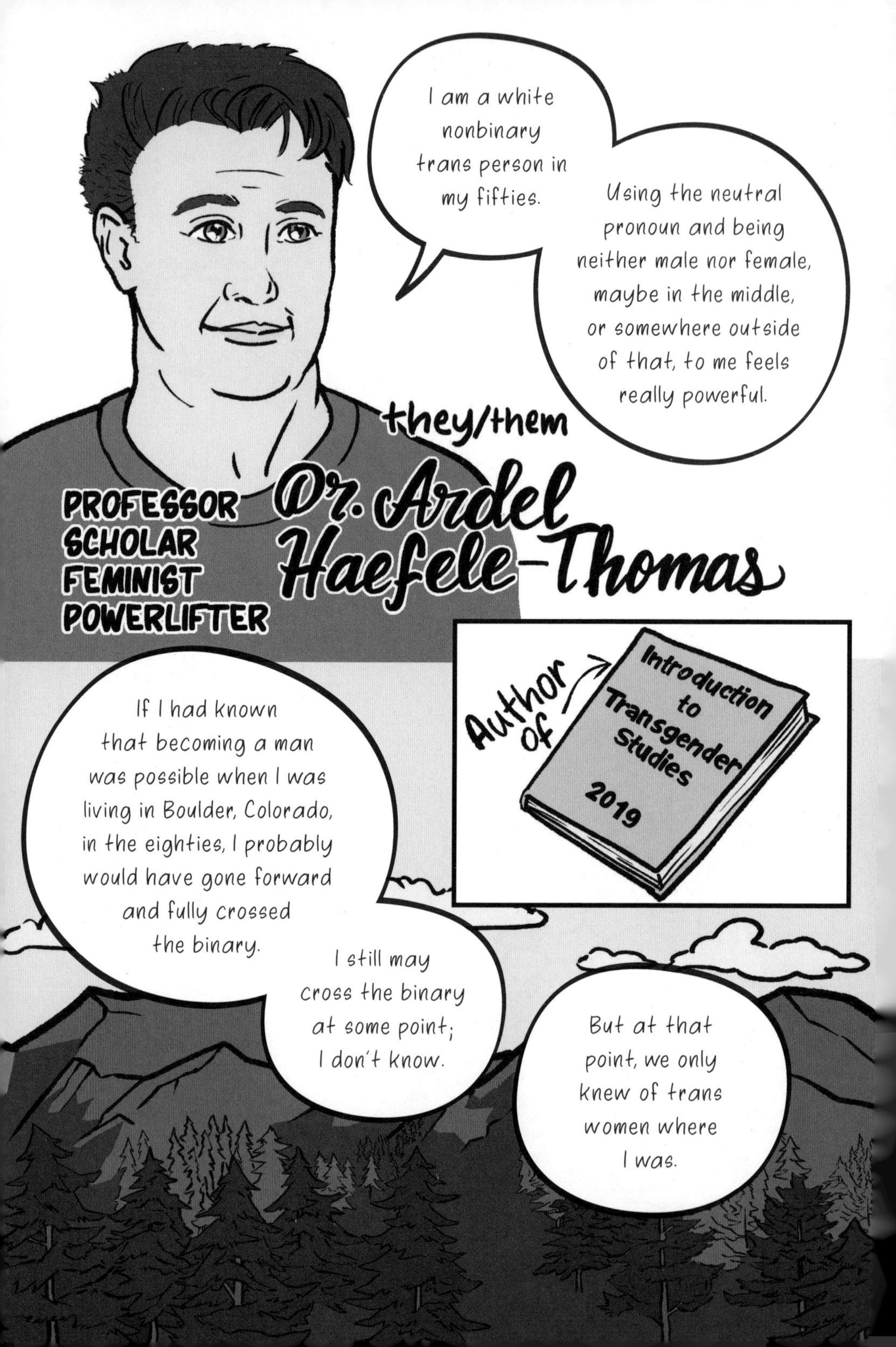
I am a white nonbinary trans person in my fifties.
Using the neutral pronoun and being neither male nor female, maybe in the middle, or somewhere outside of that, to me feels really powerful.
they/them
PROFESSOR
SCHOLAR
FEMINIST
POWERLIFTER
Dr. Ardel Haefele-Thomas
Author of
Introduction to Transgender Studies
2019
If I had known that becoming a man was possible when I was living in Boulder, Colorado, in the eighties, I probably would have gone forward and fully crossed the binary.
I still may cross the binary at some point; I don't know.
But at that point, we only knew of trans women where I was.

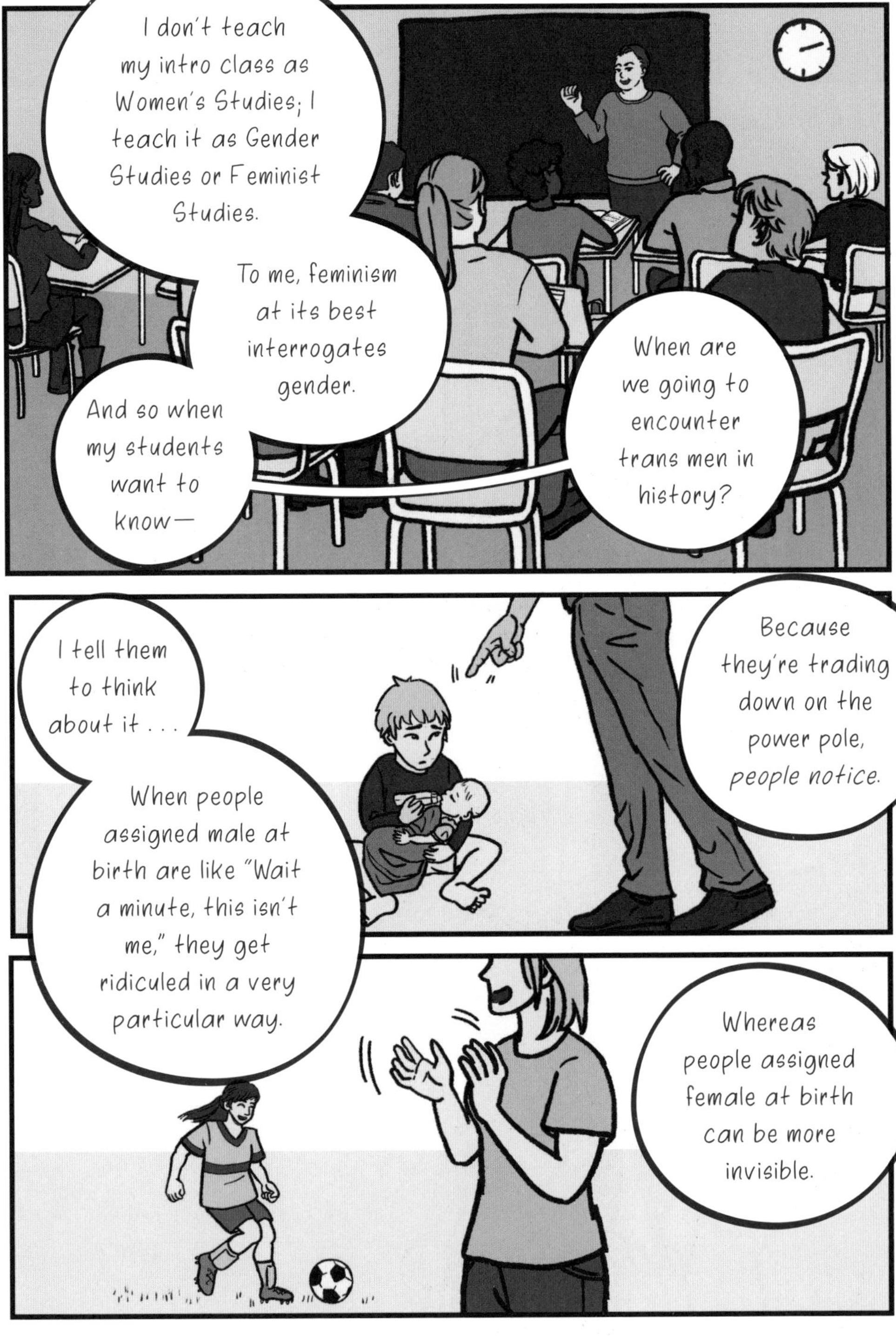

I don't teach my intro class as Women's Studies; I teach it as Gender Studies or Feminist Studies.
To me, feminism at its best interrogates gender.
And so when my students want to know—
When are we going to encounter trans men in history?
I tell them to think about it . . .
When people assigned male at birth are like "Wait a minute, this isn't me," they get ridiculed in a very particular way.
Because they're trading down on the power pole, *people notice.*
Whereas people assigned female at birth can be more invisible.

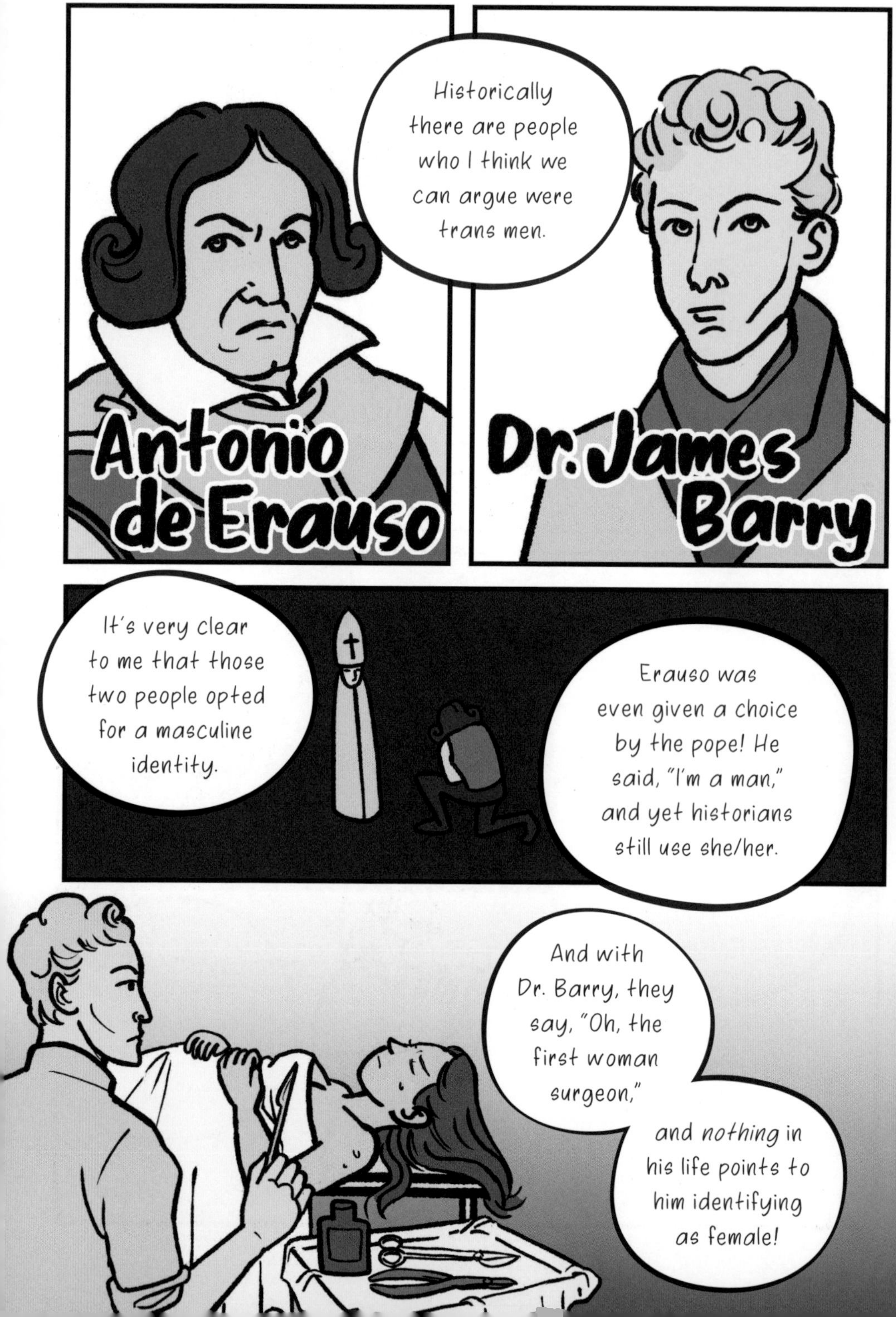
Historically there are people who I think we can argue were trans men.
Antonio de Erauso
Dr. James Barry
It's very clear to me that those two people opted for a masculine identity.
Erauso was even given a choice by the pope! He said, "I'm a man," and yet historians still use she/her.
And with Dr. Barry, they say, "Oh, the first woman surgeon,"
and *nothing* in his life points to him identifying as female!

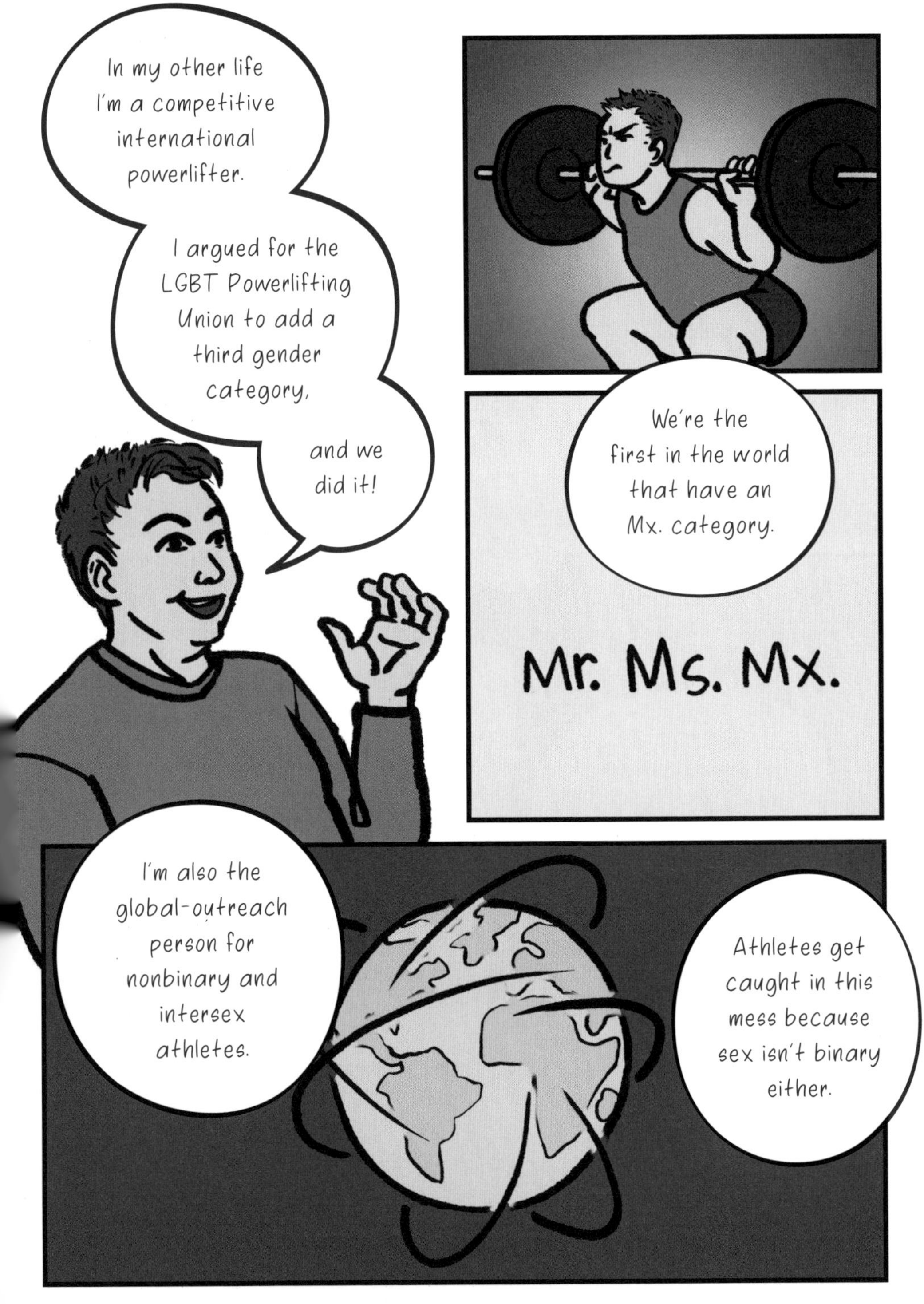
In my other life I'm a competitive international powerlifter.
I argued for the LGBT Powerlifting Union to add a third gender category,
and we did it!
We're the first in the world that have an Mx. category.
Mr. Ms. Mx.
I'm also the global-outreach person for nonbinary and intersex athletes.
Athletes get caught in this mess because sex isn't binary either.

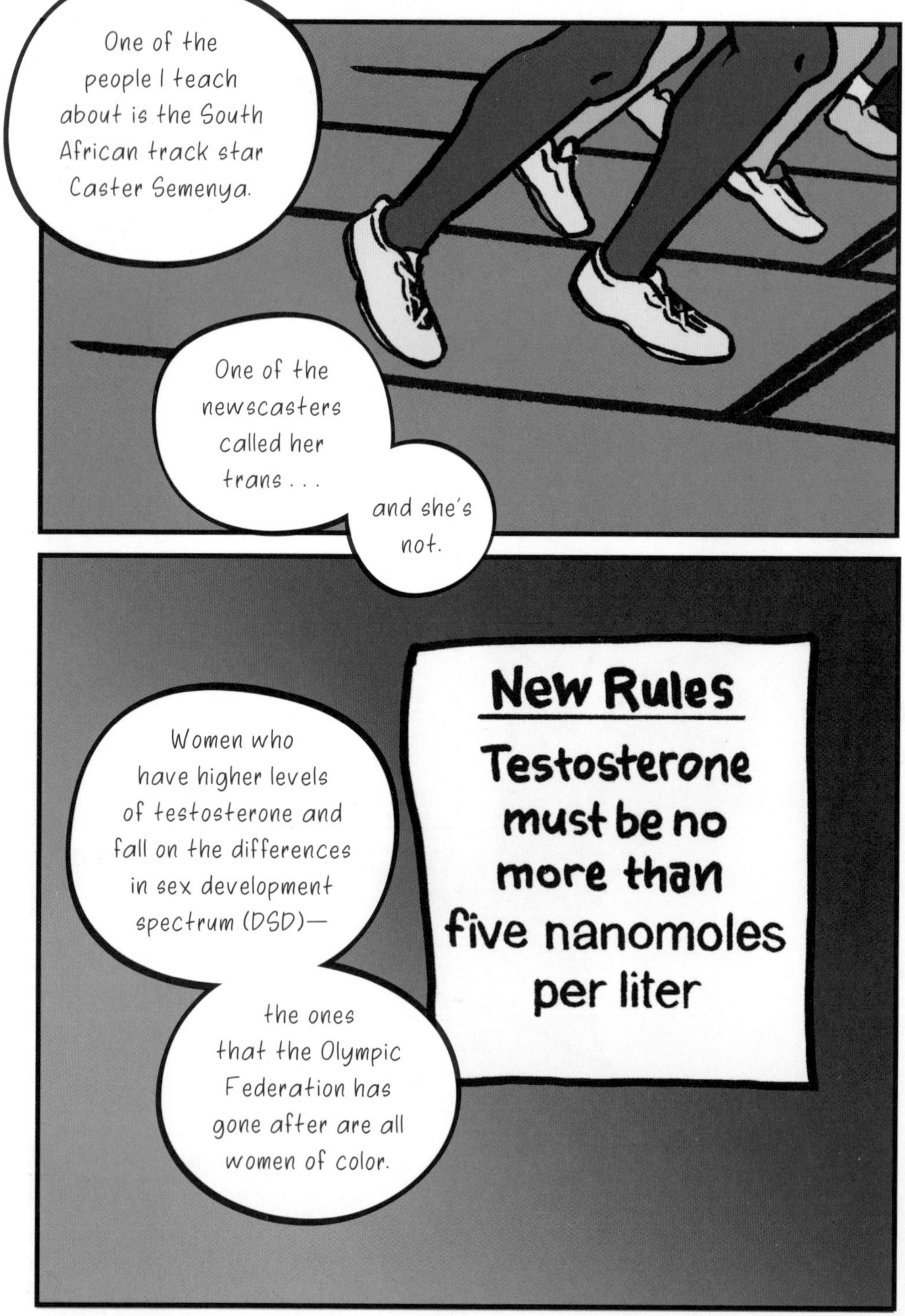
One of the people I teach about is the South African track star Caster Semenya.
One of the newscasters called her trans . . .
and she's not.
Women who have higher levels of testosterone and fall on the differences in sex development spectrum (DSD)—
New Rules
Testosterone must be no more than five nanomoles per liter
the ones that the Olympic Federation has gone after are all women of color.

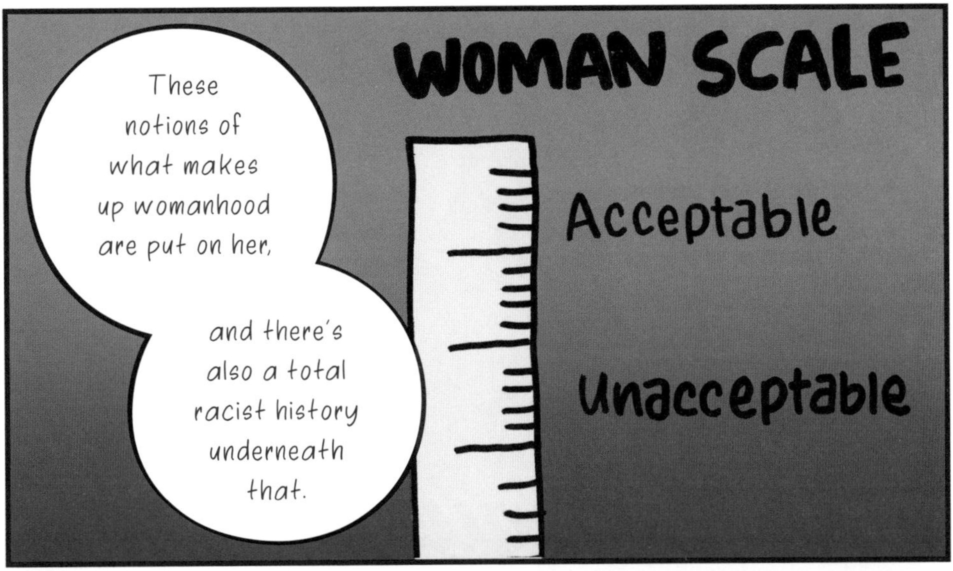
These notions of what makes up womanhood are put on her,
WOMAN SCALE
Acceptable
Unacceptable
and there's also a total racist history underneath that.

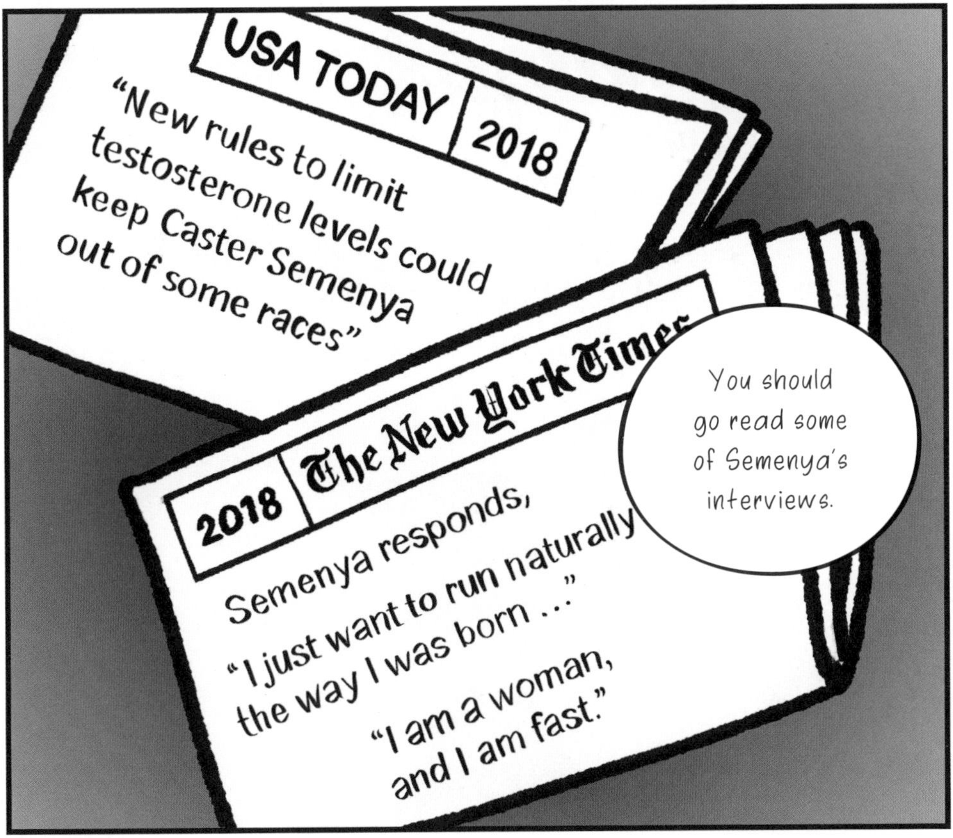
USA TODAY
2018
"New rules to limit testosterone levels could keep Caster Semenya out of some races"
2018
The New York Times
Semenya responds,
"I just want to run naturally the way I was born ..."
"I am a woman, and I am fast."
You should go read some of Semenya's interviews.

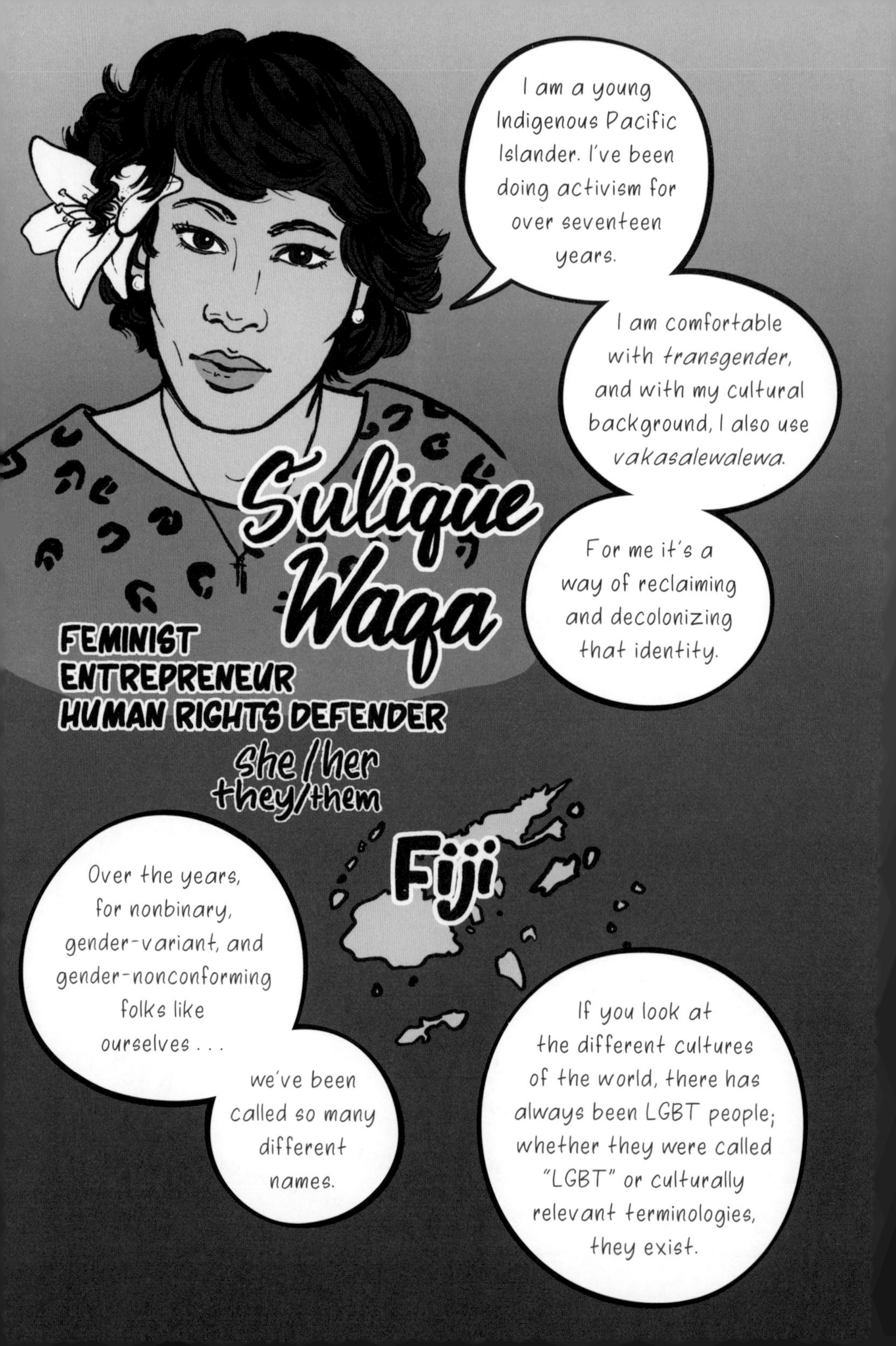

I am a young Indigenous Pacific Islander. I've been doing activism for over seventeen years.
I am comfortable with *transgender*, and with my cultural background, I also use *vakasalewalewa*.
For me it's a way of reclaiming and decolonizing that identity.
Sulique Waqa
FEMINIST
ENTREPRENEUR
HUMAN RIGHTS DEFENDER
she/her
they/them
Fiji
Over the years, for nonbinary, gender-variant, and gender-nonconforming folks like ourselves . . .
we've been called so many different names.
If you look at the different cultures of the world, there has always been LGBT people; whether they were called "LGBT" or culturally relevant terminologies, they exist.

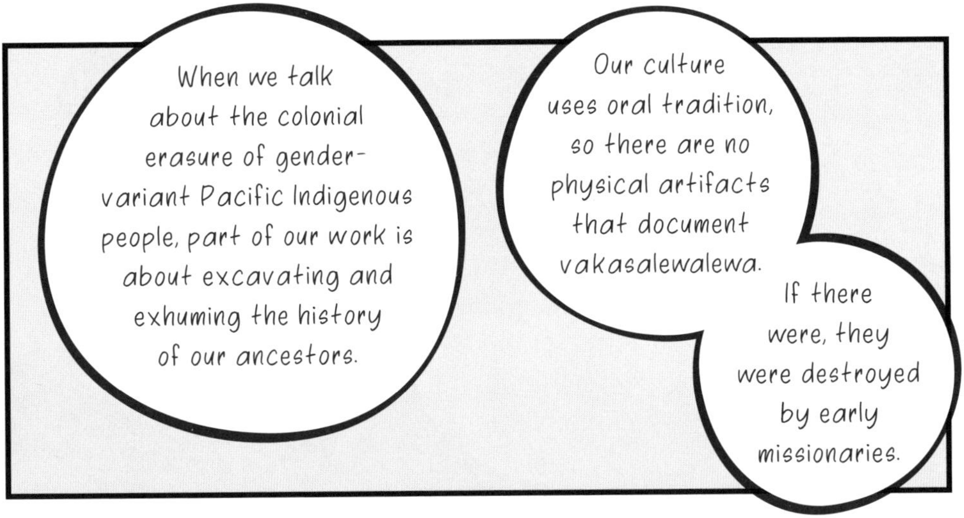
When we talk about the colonial erasure of gender-variant Pacific Indigenous people, part of our work is about excavating and exhuming the history of our ancestors.
Our culture uses oral tradition, so there are no physical artifacts that document vakasalewalewa.
If there were, they were destroyed by early missionaries.

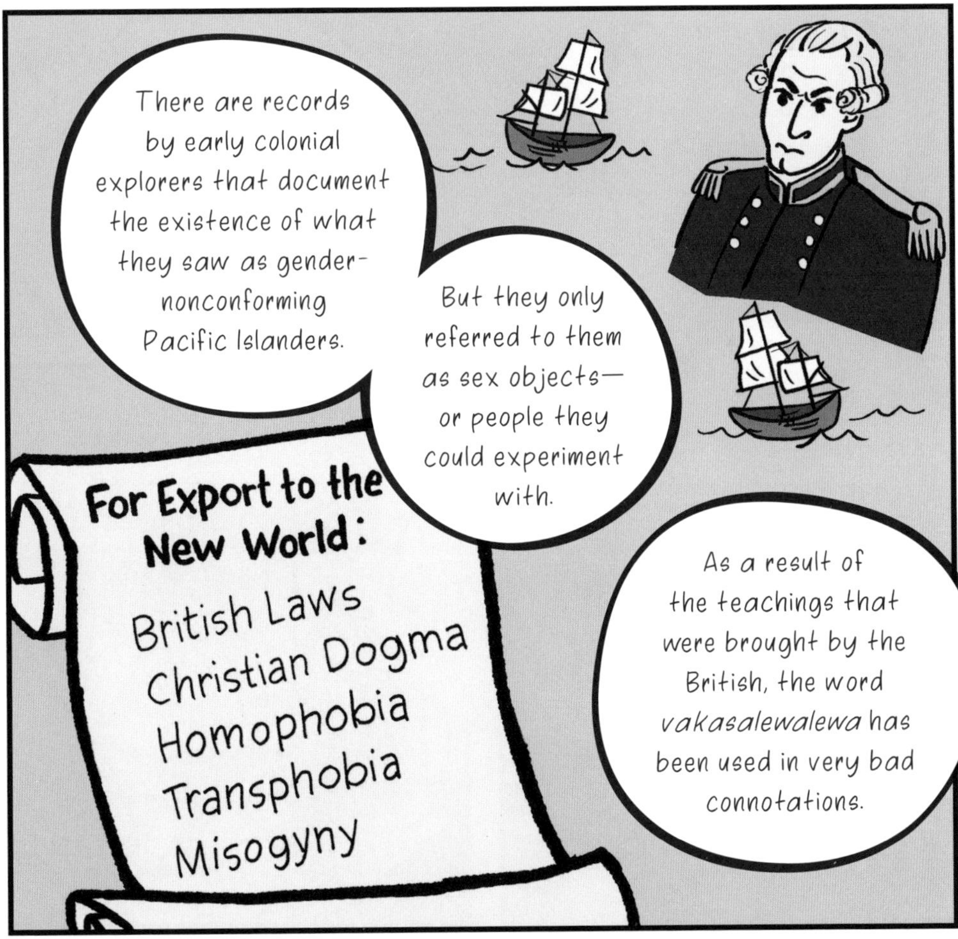
There are records by early colonial explorers that document the existence of what they saw as gender-nonconforming Pacific Islanders.
But they only referred to them as sex objects— or people they could experiment with.
For Export to the New World:
British Laws
Christian Dogma
Homophobia
Transphobia
Misogyny
As a result of the teachings that were brought by the British, the word *vakasalewalewa* has been used in very bad connotations.

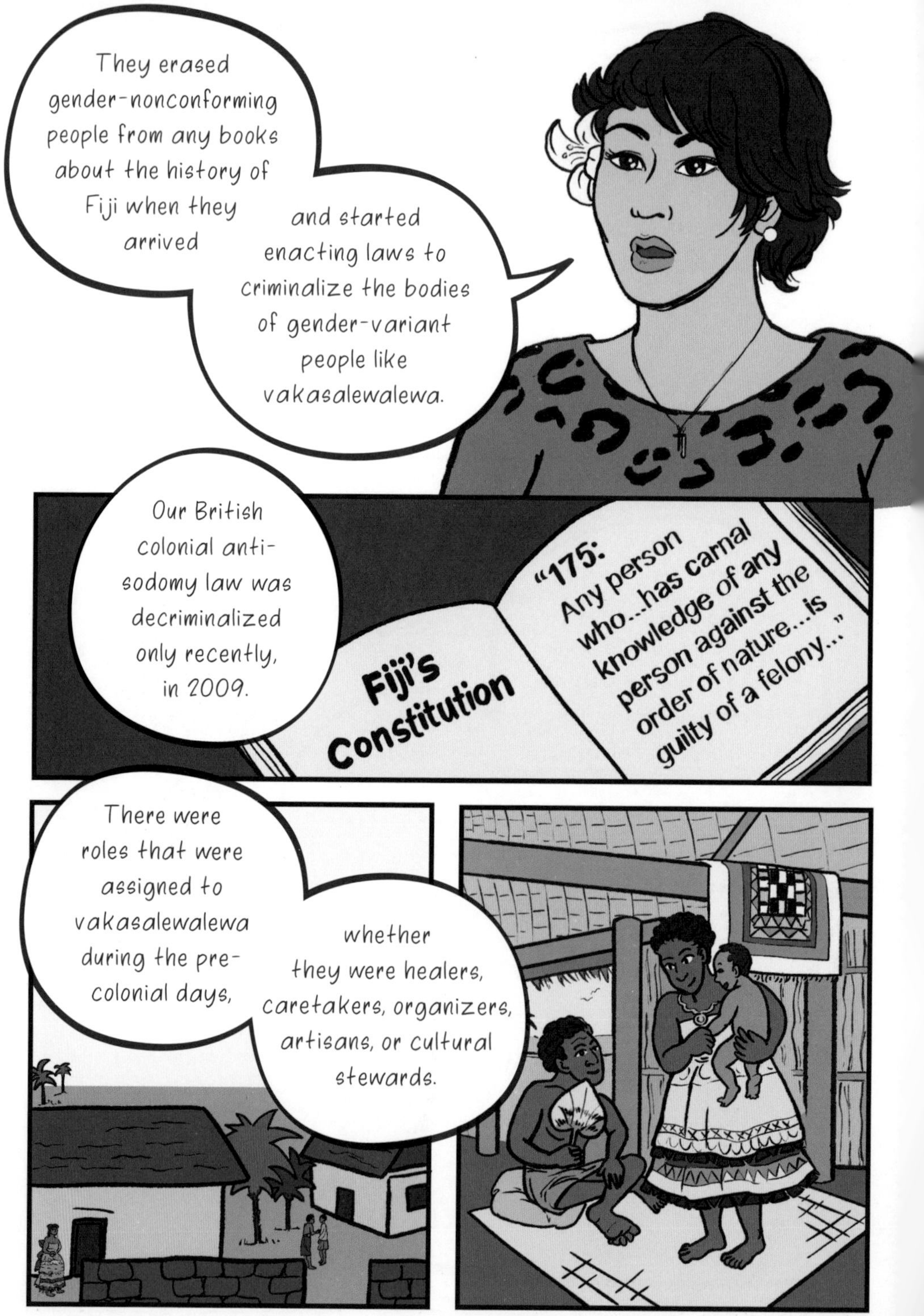
They erased gender-nonconforming people from any books about the history of Fiji when they arrived
and started enacting laws to criminalize the bodies of gender-variant people like vakasalewalewa.
Our British colonial anti-sodomy law was decriminalized only recently, in 2009.
Fiji's Constitution
"175: Any person who...has carnal knowledge of any person against the order of nature...is guilty of a felony..."
There were roles that were assigned to vakasalewalewa during the pre-colonial days,
whether they were healers, caretakers, organizers, artisans, or cultural stewards.

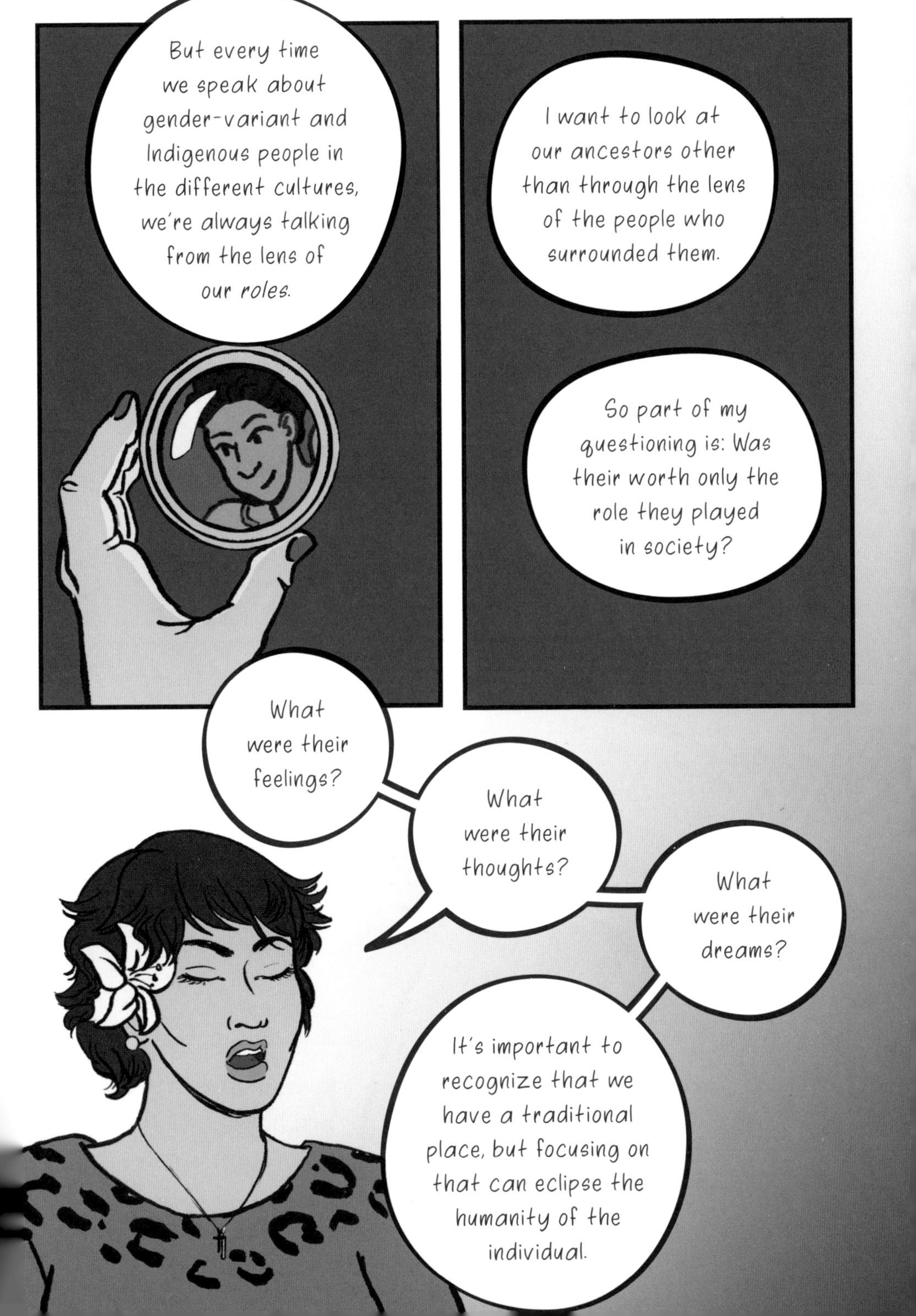
But every time we speak about gender-variant and Indigenous people in the different cultures, we're always talking from the lens of our *roles*.
I want to look at our ancestors other than through the lens of the people who surrounded them.
So part of my questioning is: Was their worth only the role they played in society?
What were their feelings?
What were their thoughts?
What were their dreams?
It's important to recognize that we have a traditional place, but focusing on that can eclipse the humanity of the individual.

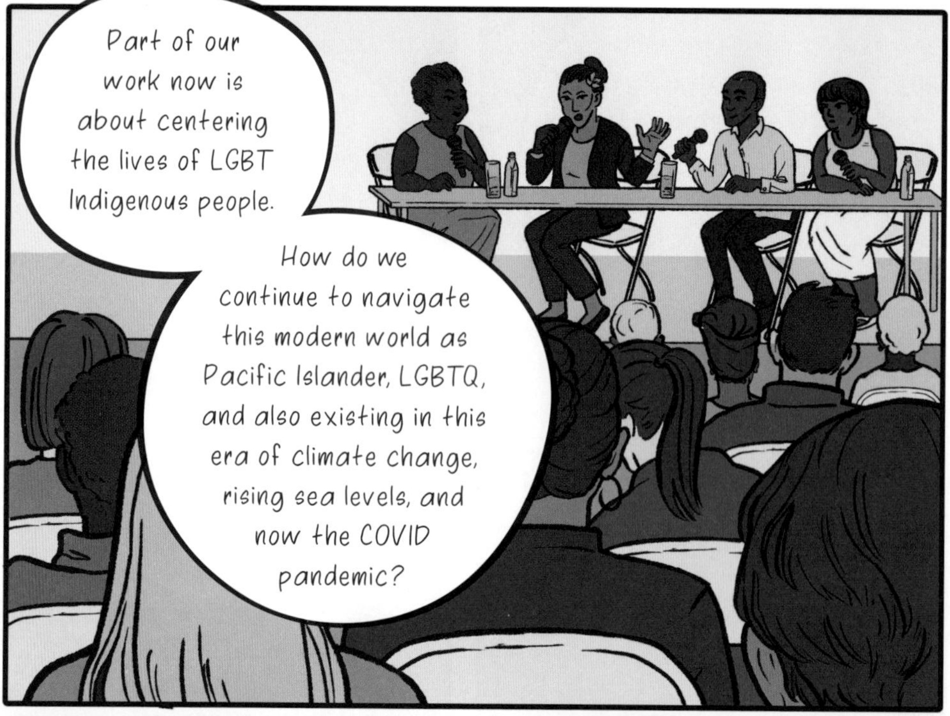
Part of our work now is about centering the lives of LGBT Indigenous people.
How do we continue to navigate this modern world as Pacific Islander, LGBTQ, and also existing in this era of climate change, rising sea levels, and now the COVID pandemic?

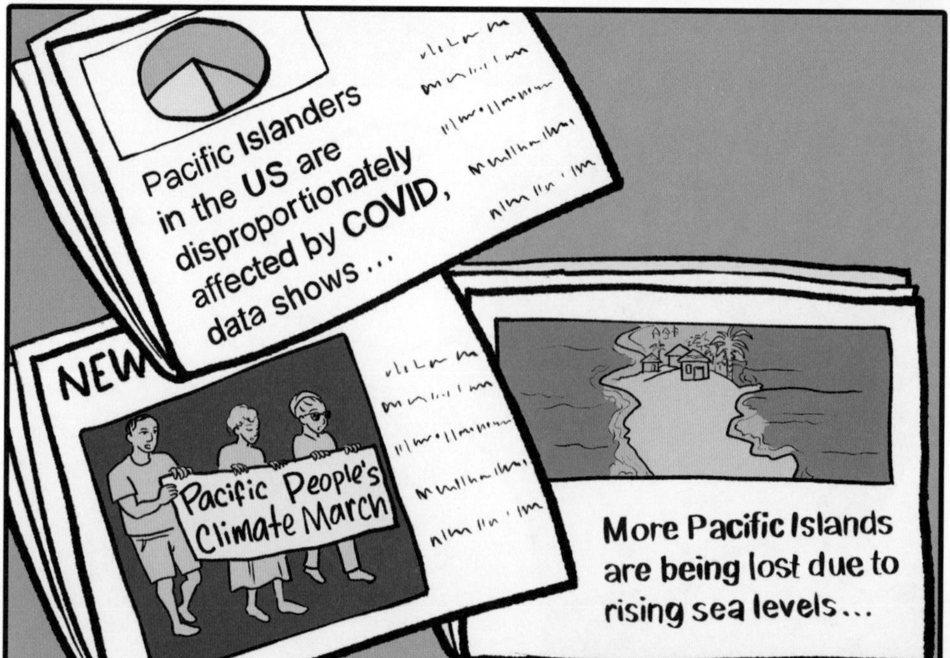
Pacific Islanders in the US are disproportionately affected by COVID, data shows ...
NEW
Pacific People's Climate March
More Pacific Islands are being lost due to rising sea levels...

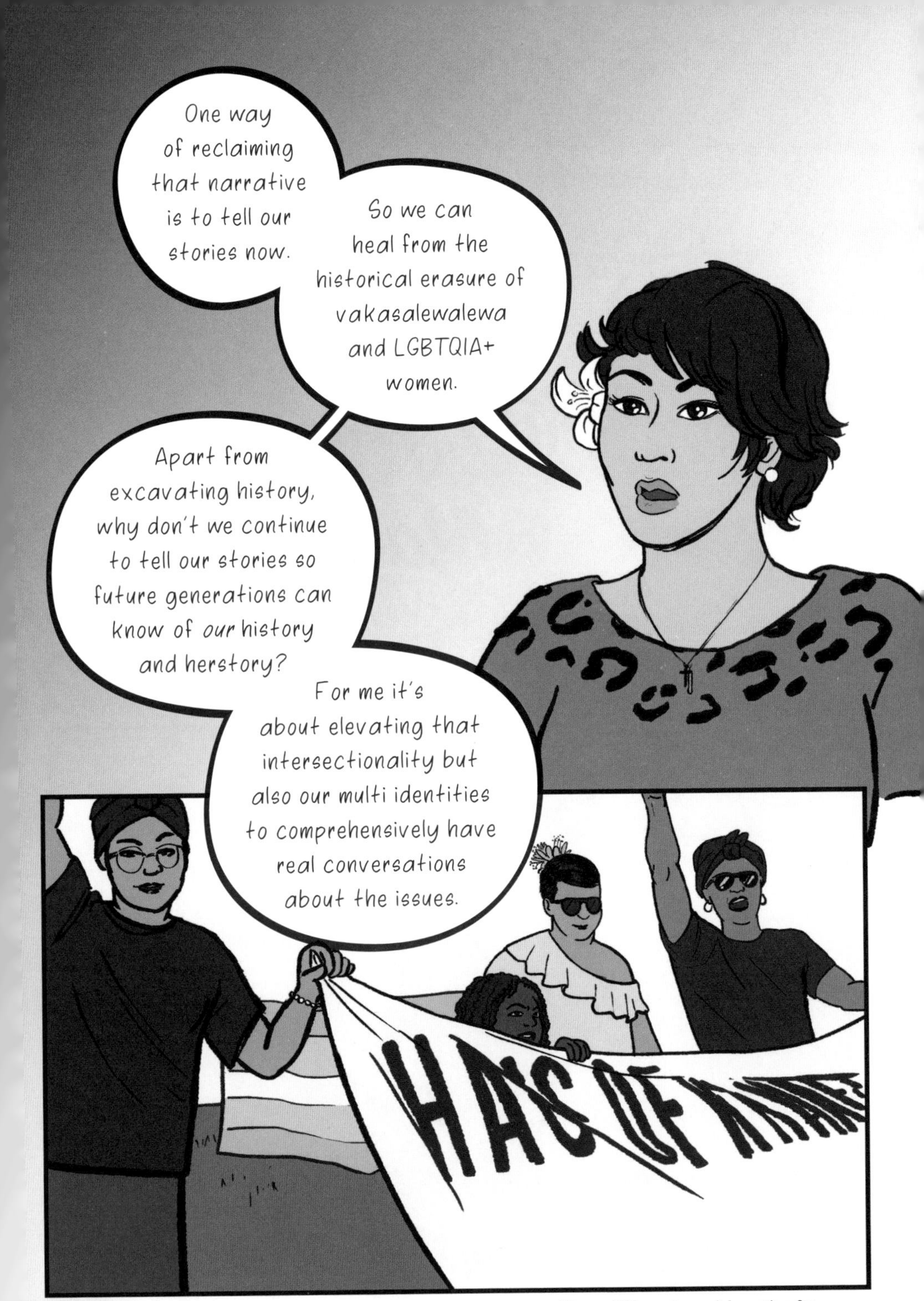
One way of reclaiming that narrative is to tell our stories now.
So we can heal from the historical erasure of vakasalewalewa and LGBTQIA+ women.
Apart from excavating history, why don't we continue to tell our stories so future generations can know of *our* history and herstory?
For me it's about elevating that intersectionality but also our multi identities to comprehensively have real conversations about the issues.

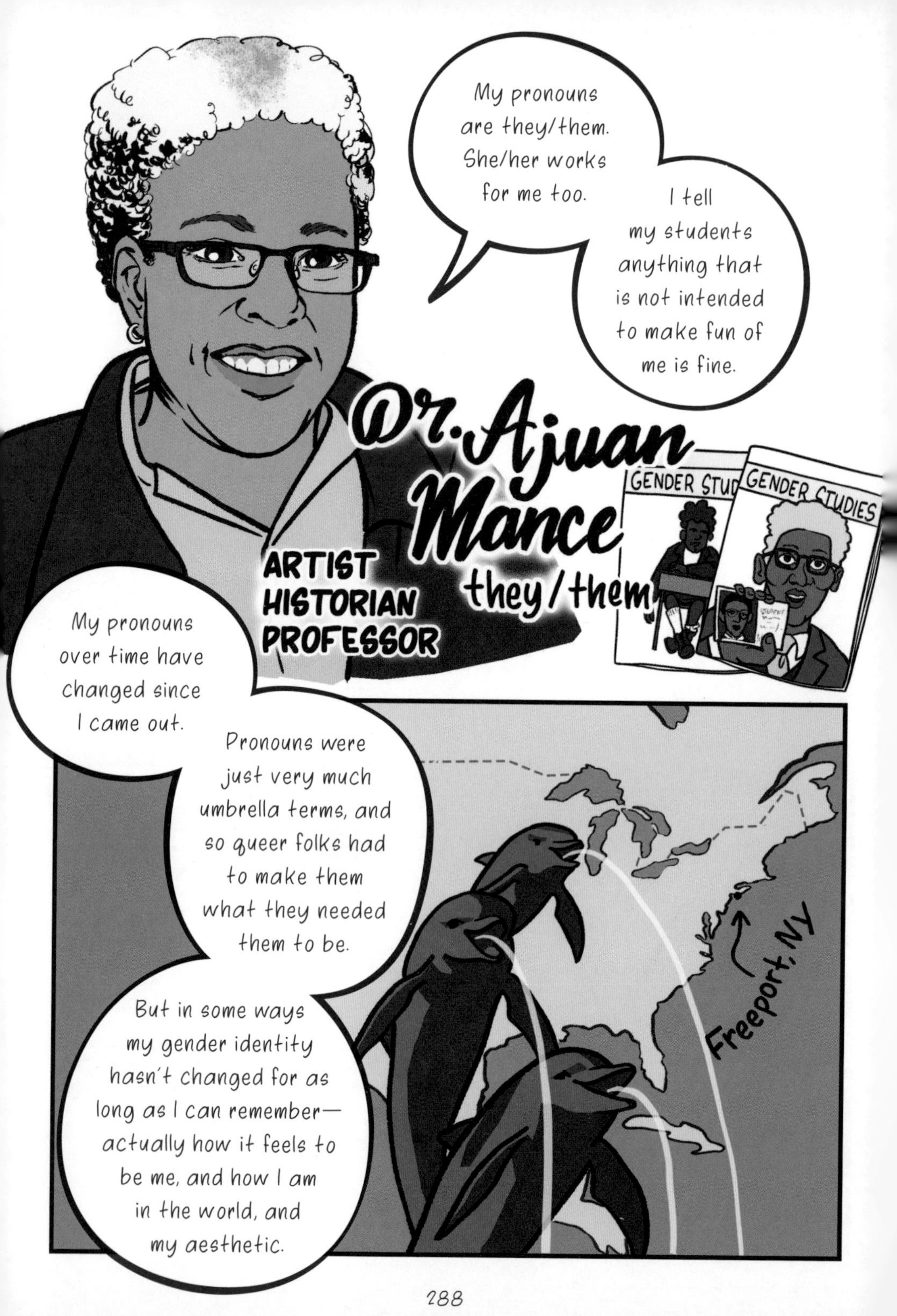
My pronouns are they/them. She/her works for me too.
I tell my students anything that is not intended to make fun of me is fine.
Dr. Ajuan Mance
they/them
ARTIST
HISTORIAN
PROFESSOR
GENDER STUD
GENDER STUDIES
My pronouns over time have changed since I came out.
Pronouns were just very much umbrella terms, and so queer folks had to make them what they needed them to be.
But in some ways my gender identity hasn't changed for as long as I can remember—actually how it feels to be me, and how I am in the world, and my aesthetic.
Freeport, NY

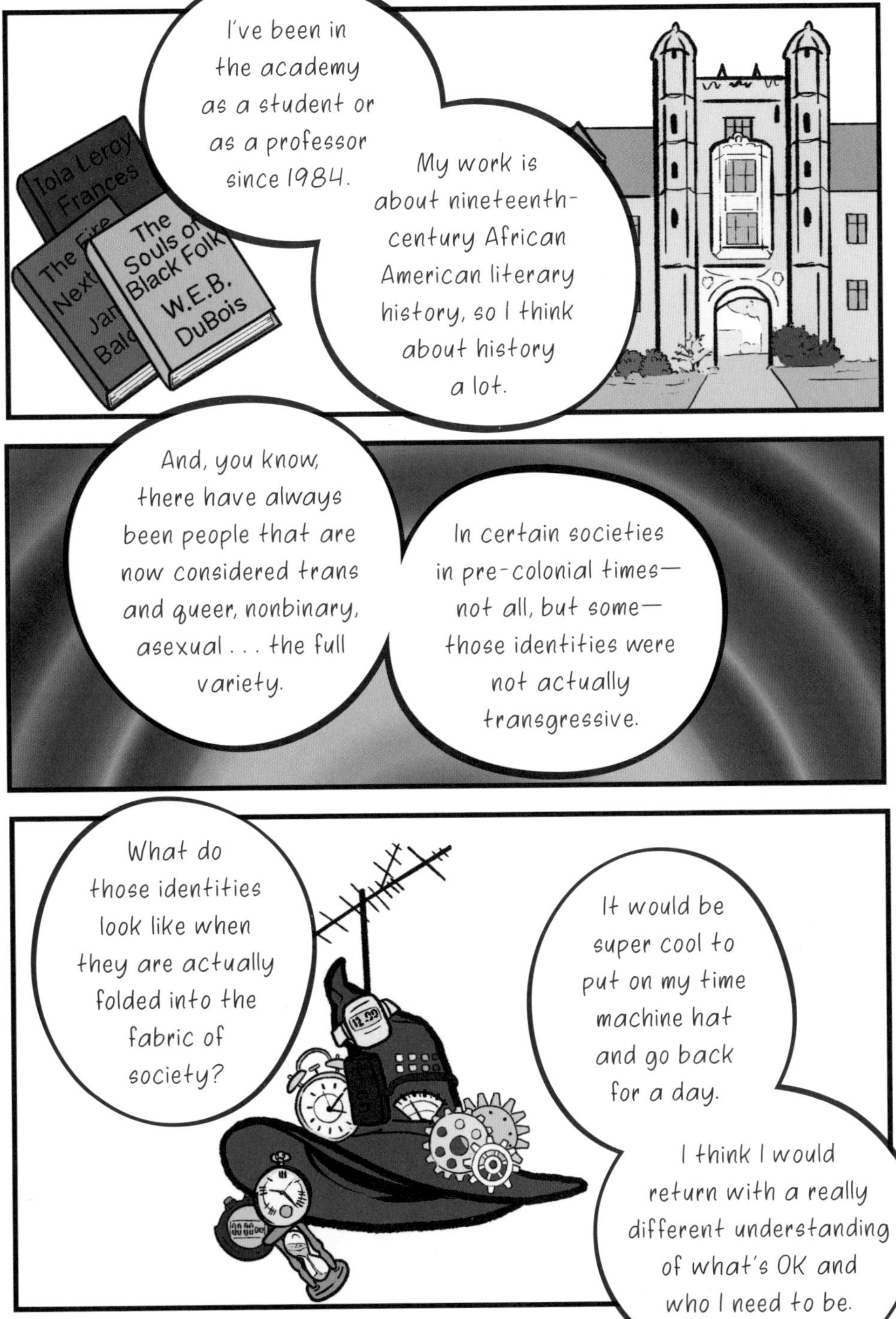
I've been in the academy as a student or as a professor since 1984.
My work is about nineteenth-century African American literary history, so I think about history a lot.
Iola Leroy
Frances
The Souls of Black Folk
W.E.B. DuBois
And, you know, there have always been people that are now considered trans and queer, nonbinary, asexual . . . the full variety.
In certain societies in pre-colonial times—not all, but some—those identities were not actually transgressive.
What do those identities look like when they are actually folded into the fabric of society?
It would be super cool to put on my time machine hat and go back for a day.
I think I would return with a really different understanding of what's OK and who I need to be.

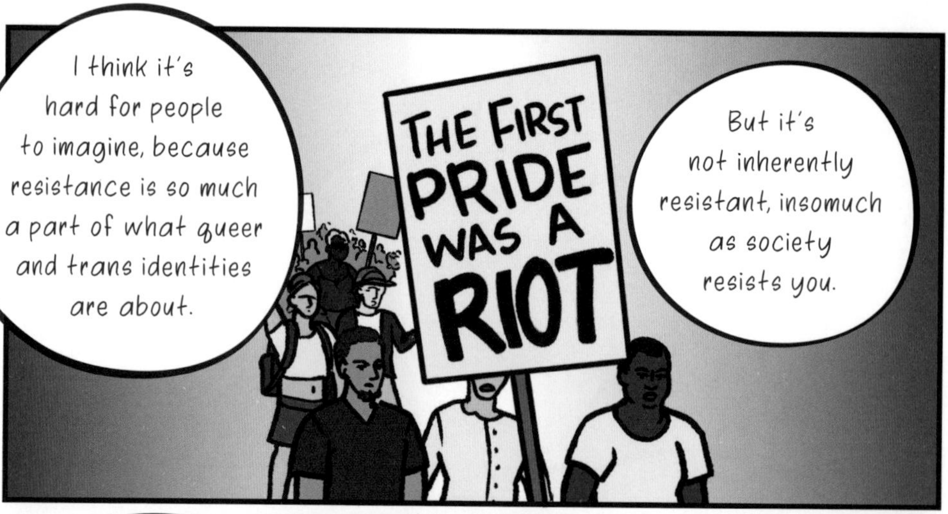
I think it's hard for people to imagine, because resistance is so much a part of what queer and trans identities are about.
THE FIRST PRIDE WAS A RIOT
But it's not inherently resistant, insomuch as society resists you.

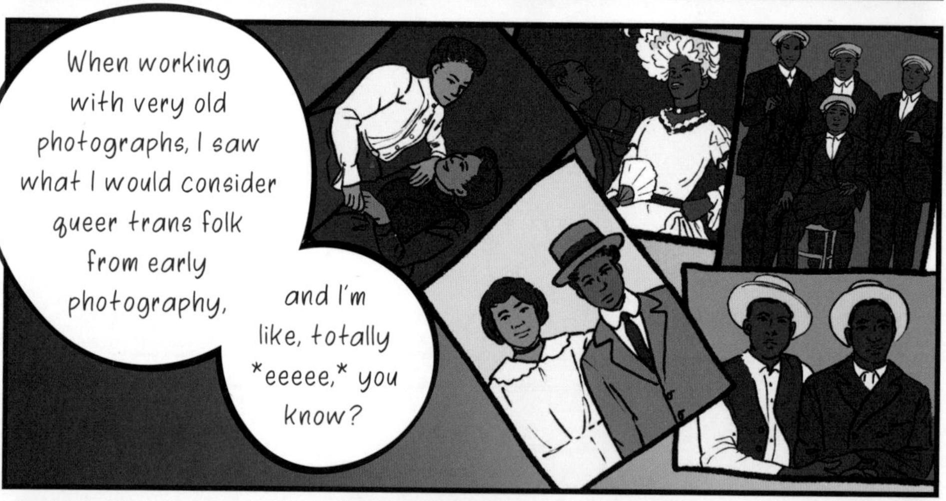
When working with very old photographs, I saw what I would consider queer trans folk from early photography,
and I'm like, totally *eeeee,* you know?

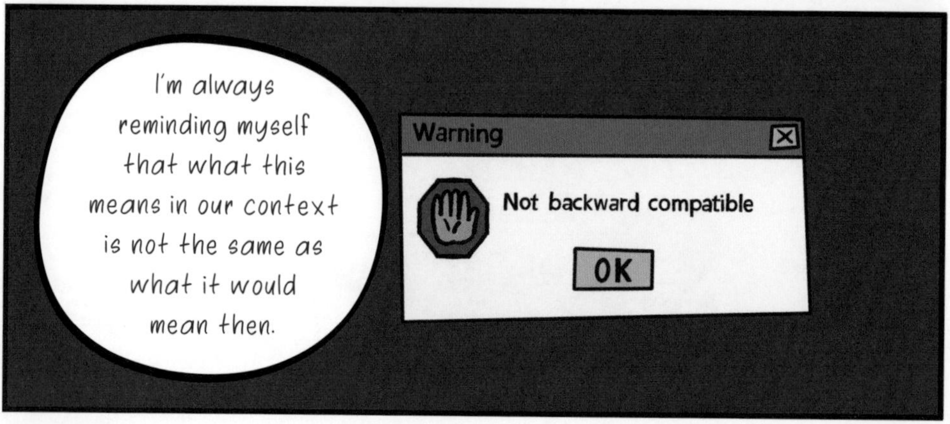
I'm always reminding myself that what this means in our context is not the same as what it would mean then.
Warning
Not backward compatible
OK

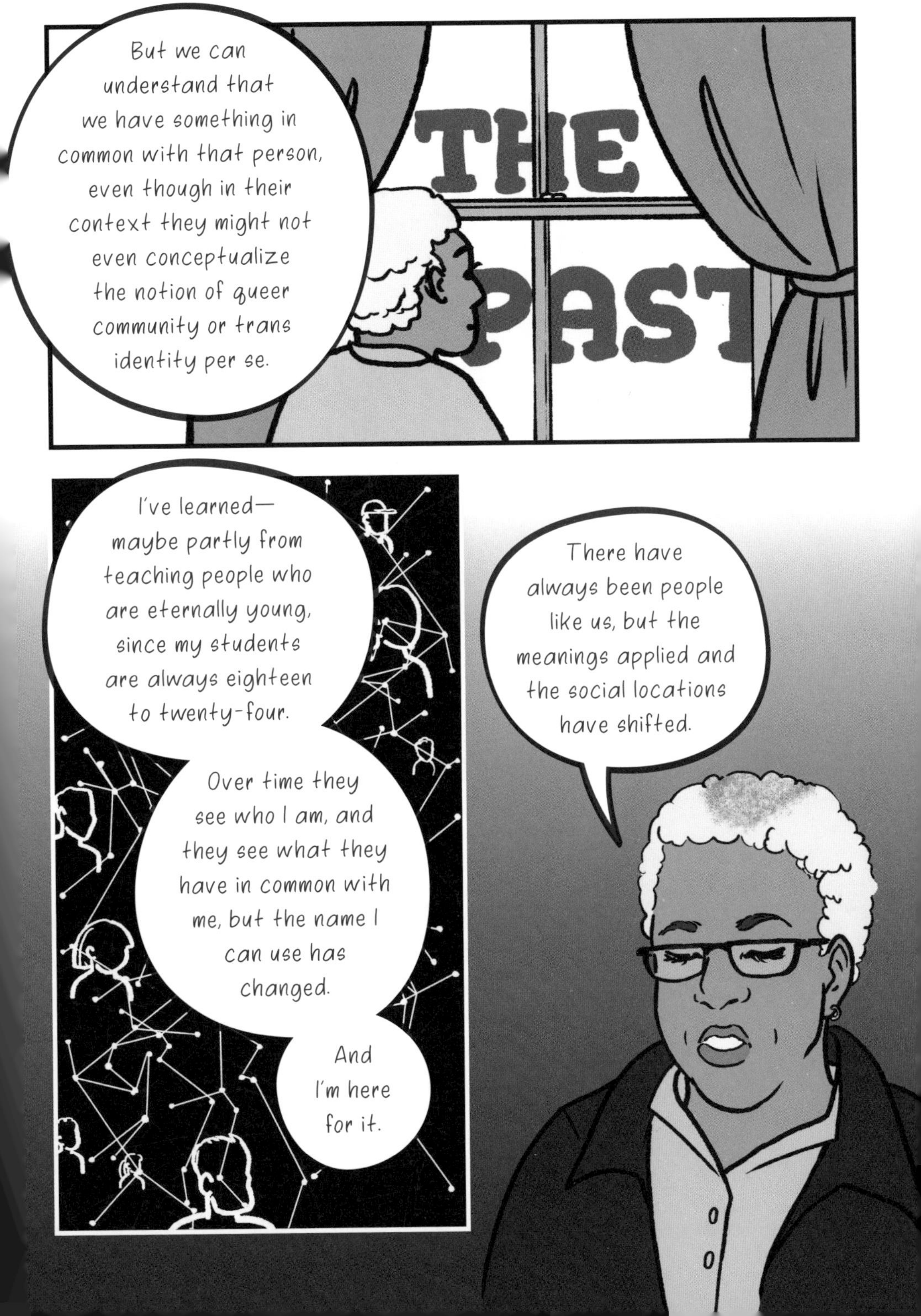

But we can understand that we have something in common with that person, even though in their context they might not even conceptualize the notion of queer community or trans identity per se.
THE PAST
I've learned— maybe partly from teaching people who are eternally young, since my students are always eighteen to twenty-four.
Over time they see who I am, and they see what they have in common with me, but the name I can use has changed.
And I'm here for it.
There have always been people like us, but the meanings applied and the social locations have shifted.

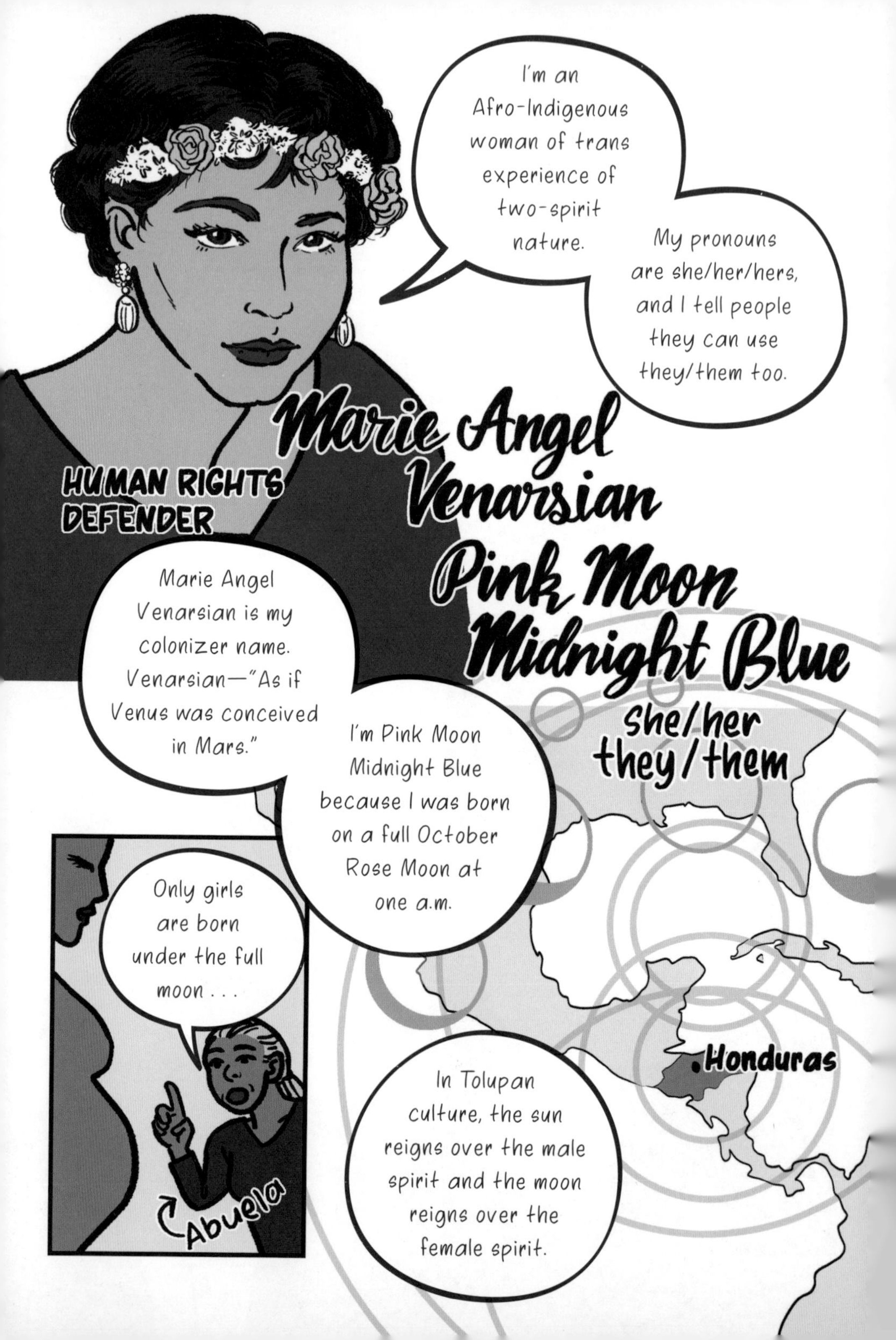
I'm an Afro-Indigenous woman of trans experience of two-spirit nature.
My pronouns are she/her/hers, and I tell people they can use they/them too.
Marie Angel Venarsian
Pink Moon Midnight Blue
HUMAN RIGHTS DEFENDER
she/her they/them
Marie Angel Venarsian is my colonizer name. Venarsian—"As if Venus was conceived in Mars."
I'm Pink Moon Midnight Blue because I was born on a full October Rose Moon at one a.m.
Only girls are born under the full moon . . .
Abuela
Honduras
In Tolupan culture, the sun reigns over the male spirit and the moon reigns over the female spirit.

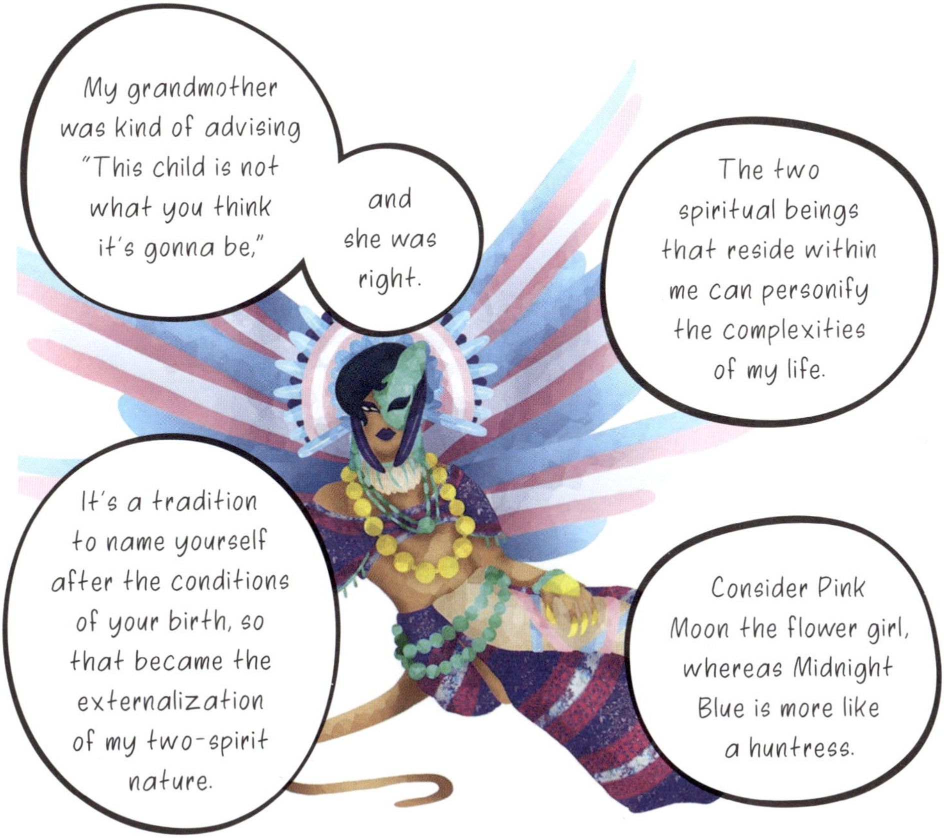
My grandmother was kind of advising "This child is not what you think it's gonna be,"
and she was right.
The two spiritual beings that reside within me can personify the complexities of my life.
It's a tradition to name yourself after the conditions of your birth, so that became the externalization of my two-spirit nature.
Consider Pink Moon the flower girl, whereas Midnight Blue is more like a huntress.

Illustration by Julie and MAV

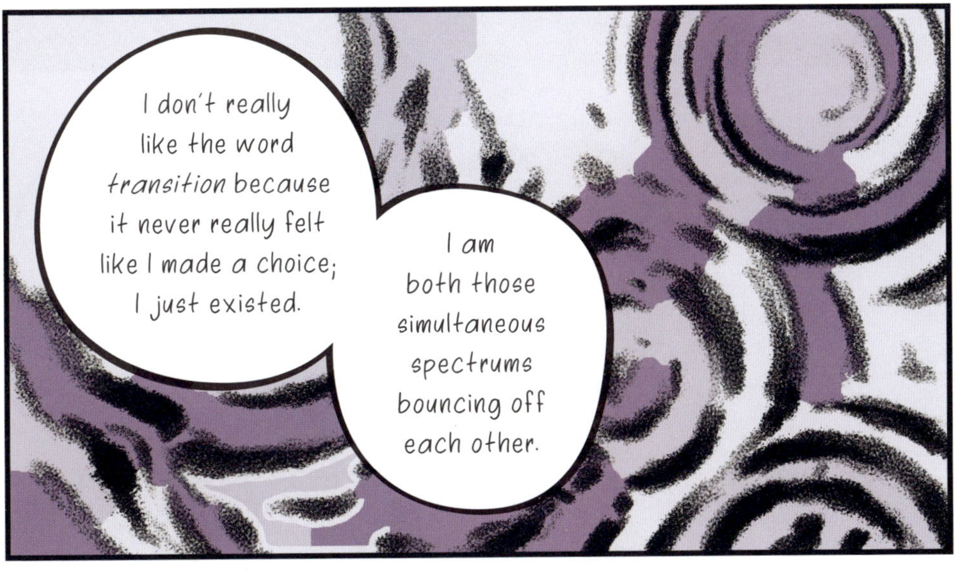
I don't really like the word *transition* because it never really felt like I made a choice; I just existed.
I am both those simultaneous spectrums bouncing off each other.

Rosalila Mayan Temple, Copán Ruinas, Honduras

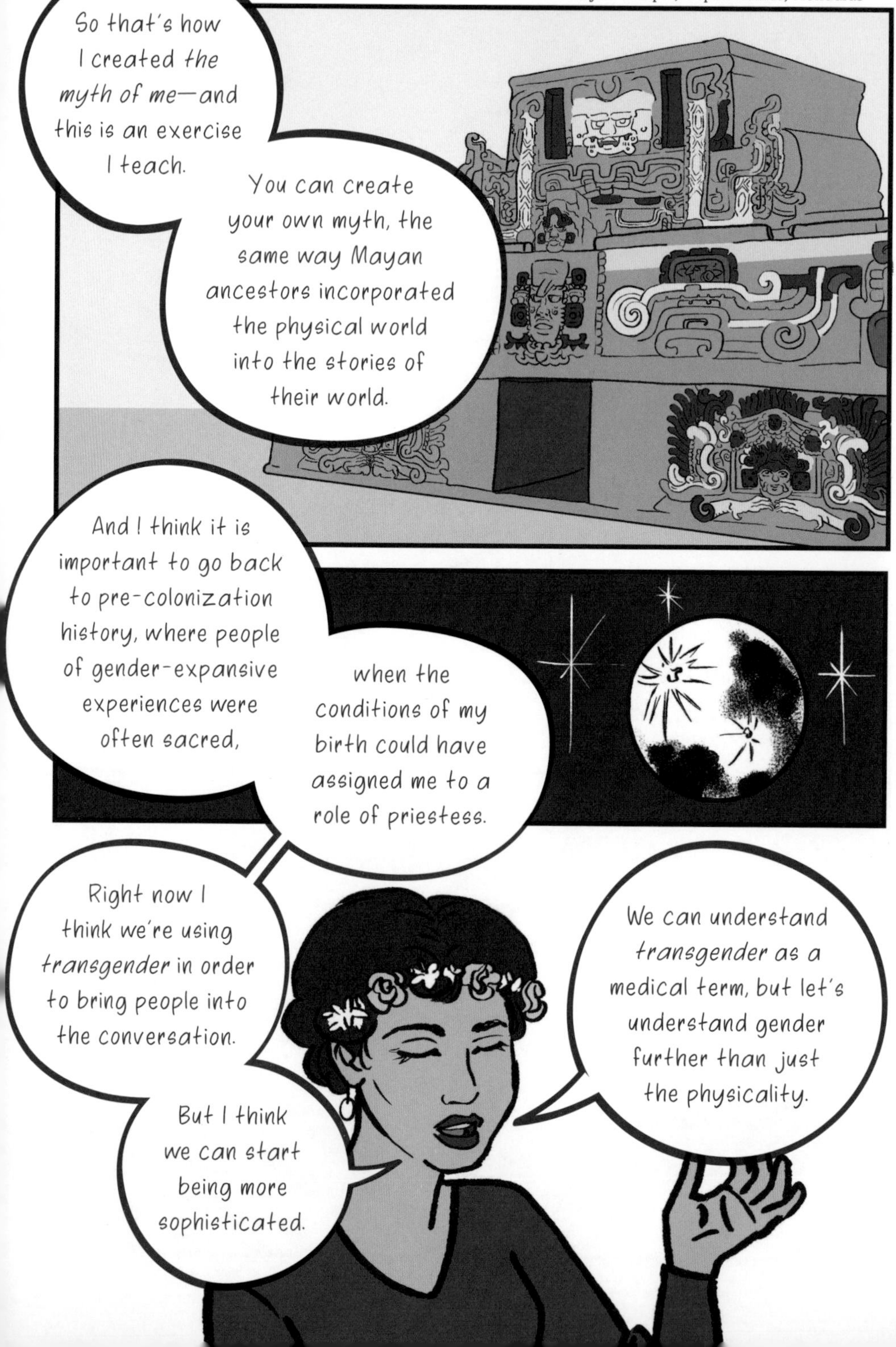
So that's how I created *the myth of me*—and this is an exercise I teach.
You can create your own myth, the same way Mayan ancestors incorporated the physical world into the stories of their world.
And I think it is important to go back to pre-colonization history, where people of gender-expansive experiences were often sacred,
when the conditions of my birth could have assigned me to a role of priestess.
Right now I think we're using *transgender* in order to bring people into the conversation.
But I think we can start being more sophisticated.
We can understand *transgender* as a medical term, but let's understand gender further than just the physicality.

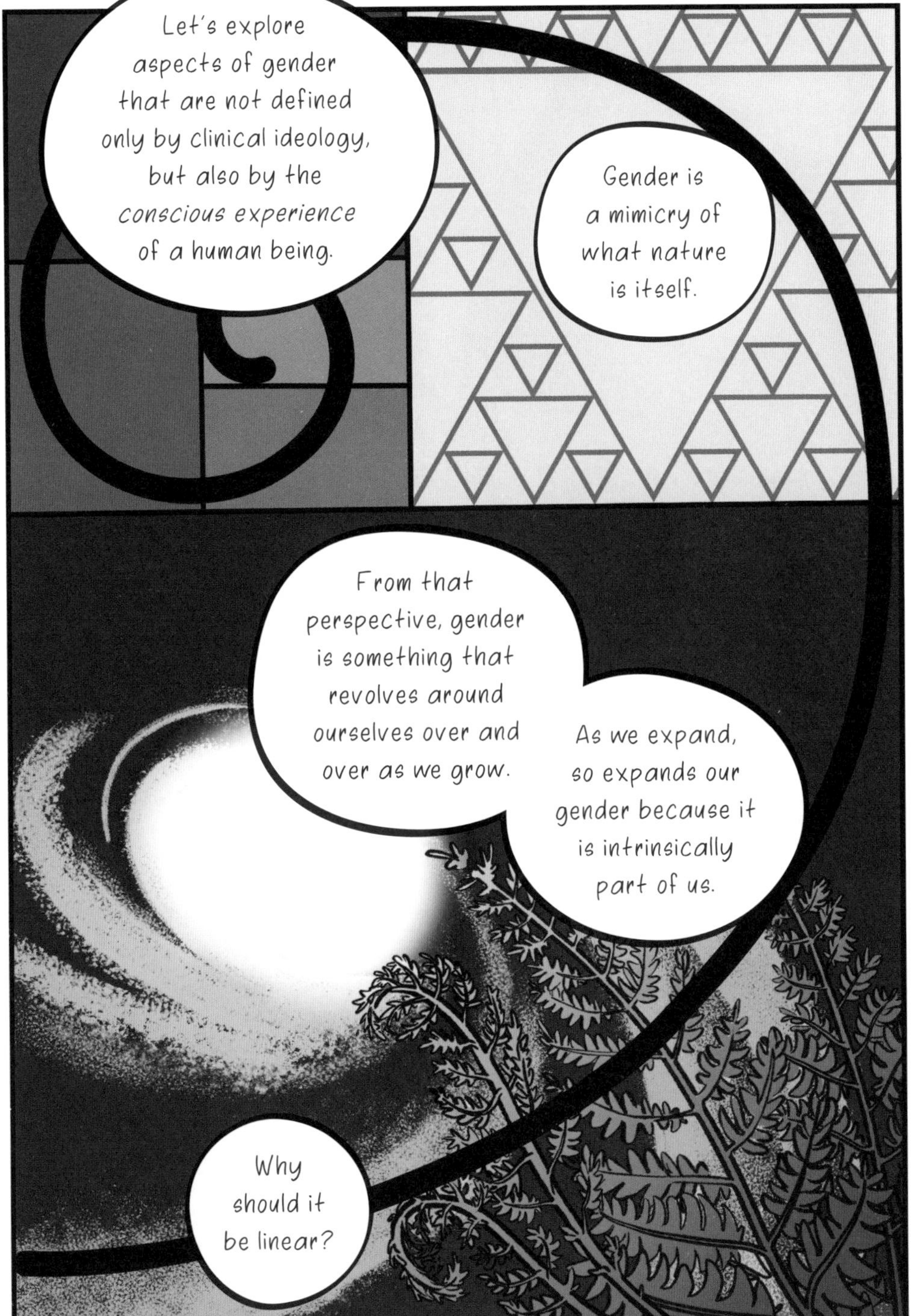
Let's explore aspects of gender that are not defined only by clinical ideology, but also by the *conscious experience* of a human being.
Gender is a mimicry of what nature is itself.
From that perspective, gender is something that revolves around ourselves over and over as we grow.
As we expand, so expands our gender because it is intrinsically part of us.
Why should it be linear?

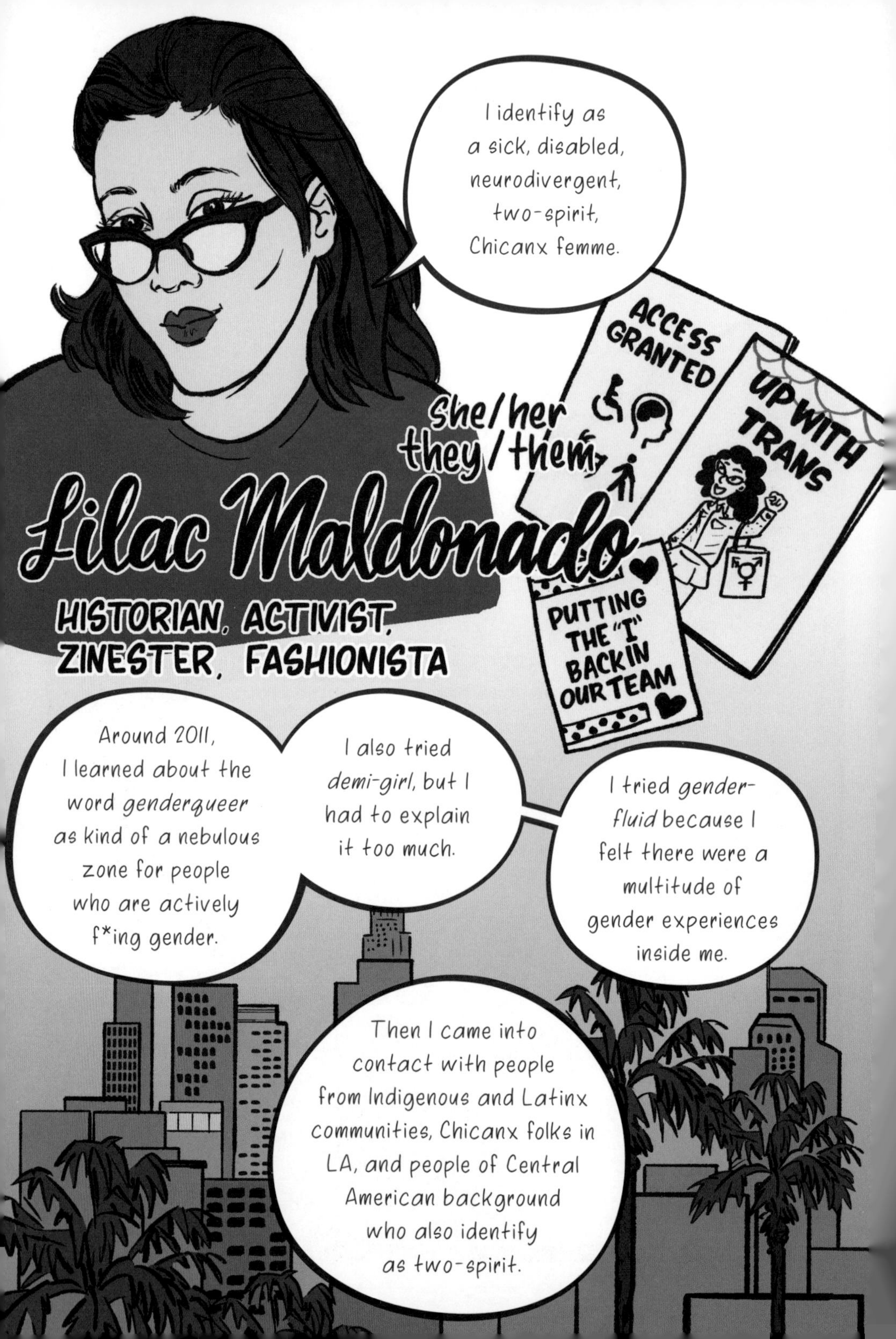
I identify as a sick, disabled, neurodivergent, two-spirit, Chicanx femme.
ACCESS GRANTED
UP WITH TRANS
she/her they/them
Lilac Maldonado
HISTORIAN, ACTIVIST, ZINESTER, FASHIONISTA
PUTTING THE "I" BACK IN OUR TEAM
Around 2011, I learned about the word *genderqueer* as kind of a nebulous zone for people who are actively f*ing gender.
I also tried *demi-girl*, but I had to explain it too much.
I tried *gender-fluid* because I felt there were a multitude of gender experiences inside me.
Then I came into contact with people from Indigenous and Latinx communities, Chicanx folks in LA, and people of Central American background who also identify as two-spirit.

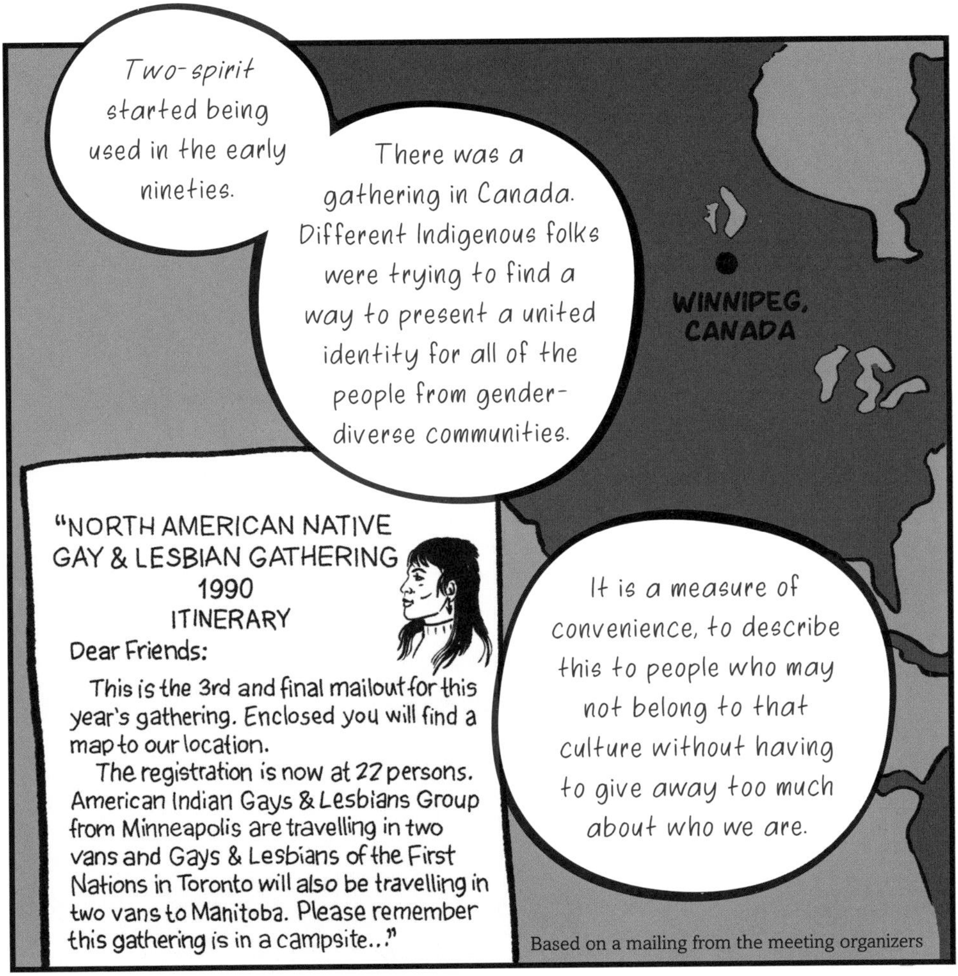
Two-spirit started being used in the early nineties.
There was a gathering in Canada. Different Indigenous folks were trying to find a way to present a united identity for all of the people from gender-diverse communities.
WINNIPEG, CANADA
"NORTH AMERICAN NATIVE GAY & LESBIAN GATHERING 1990 ITINERARY
Dear Friends:
This is the 3rd and final mailout for this year's gathering. Enclosed you will find a map to our location.
The registration is now at 22 persons. American Indian Gays & Lesbians Group from Minneapolis are travelling in two vans and Gays & Lesbians of the First Nations in Toronto will also be travelling in two vans to Manitoba. Please remember this gathering is in a campsite..."
It is a measure of convenience, to describe this to people who may not belong to that culture without having to give away too much about who we are.
Based on a mailing from the meeting organizers

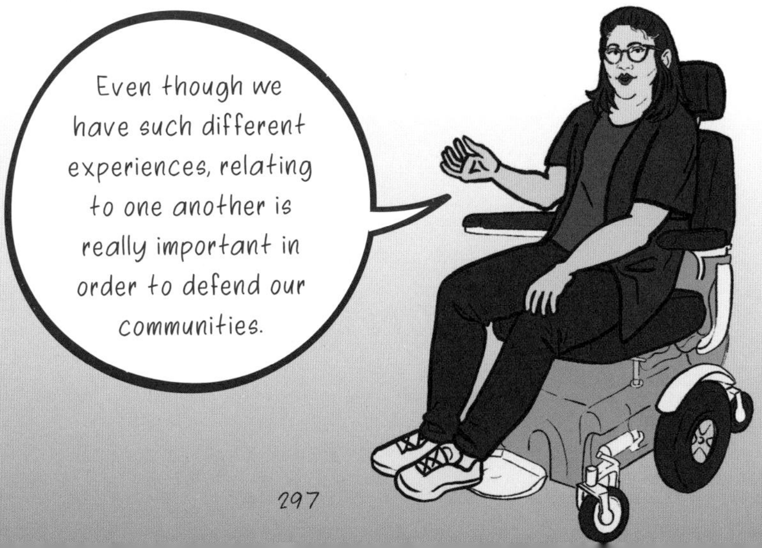
Even though we have such different experiences, relating to one another is really important in order to defend our communities.

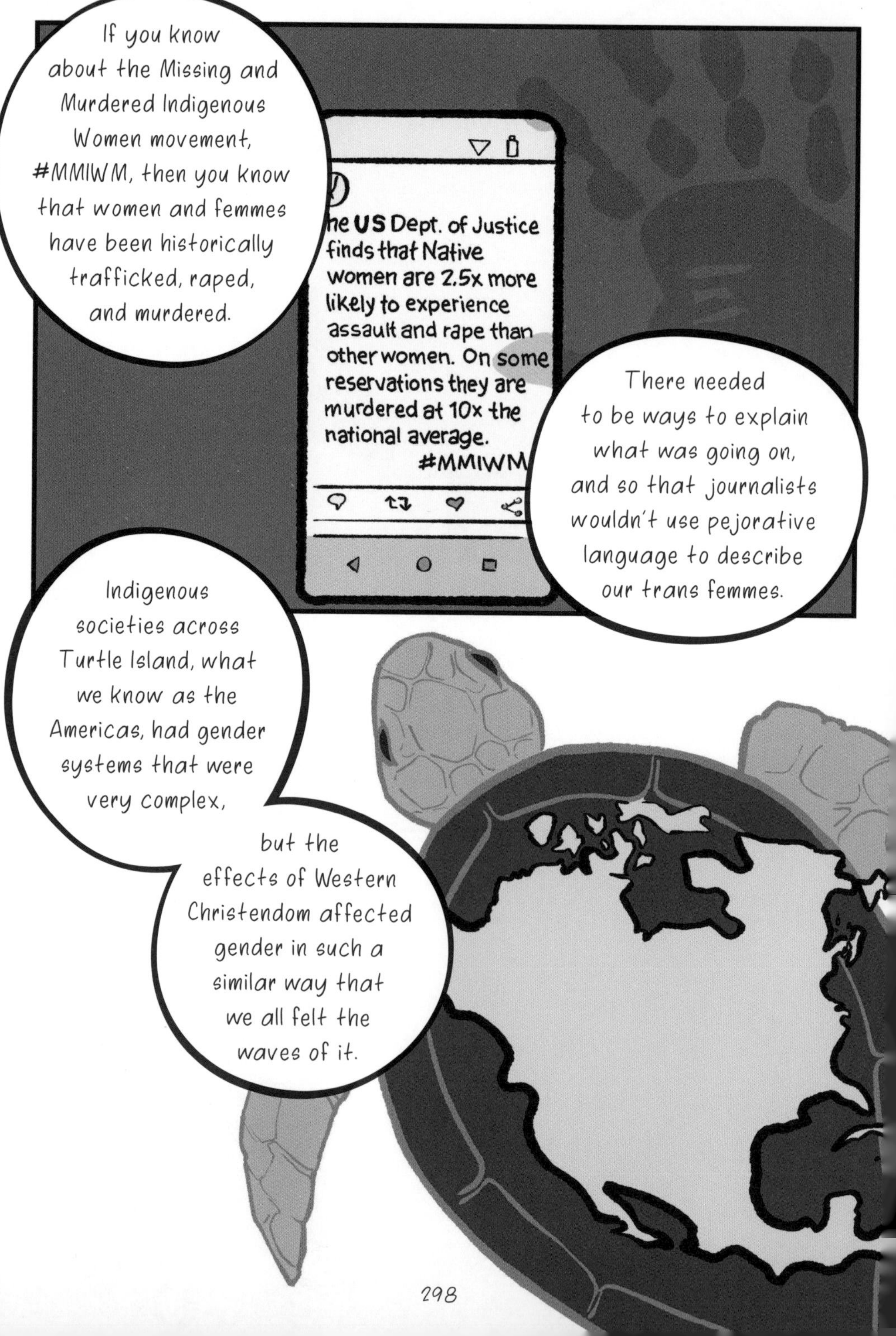
If you know about the Missing and Murdered Indigenous Women movement, #MMIWM, then you know that women and femmes have been historically trafficked, raped, and murdered.
he US Dept. of Justice finds that Native women are 2.5x more likely to experience assault and rape than other women. On some reservations they are murdered at 10x the national average. #MMIWM
There needed to be ways to explain what was going on, and so that journalists wouldn't use pejorative language to describe our trans femmes.
Indigenous societies across Turtle Island, what we know as the Americas, had gender systems that were very complex,
but the effects of Western Christendom affected gender in such a similar way that we all felt the waves of it.

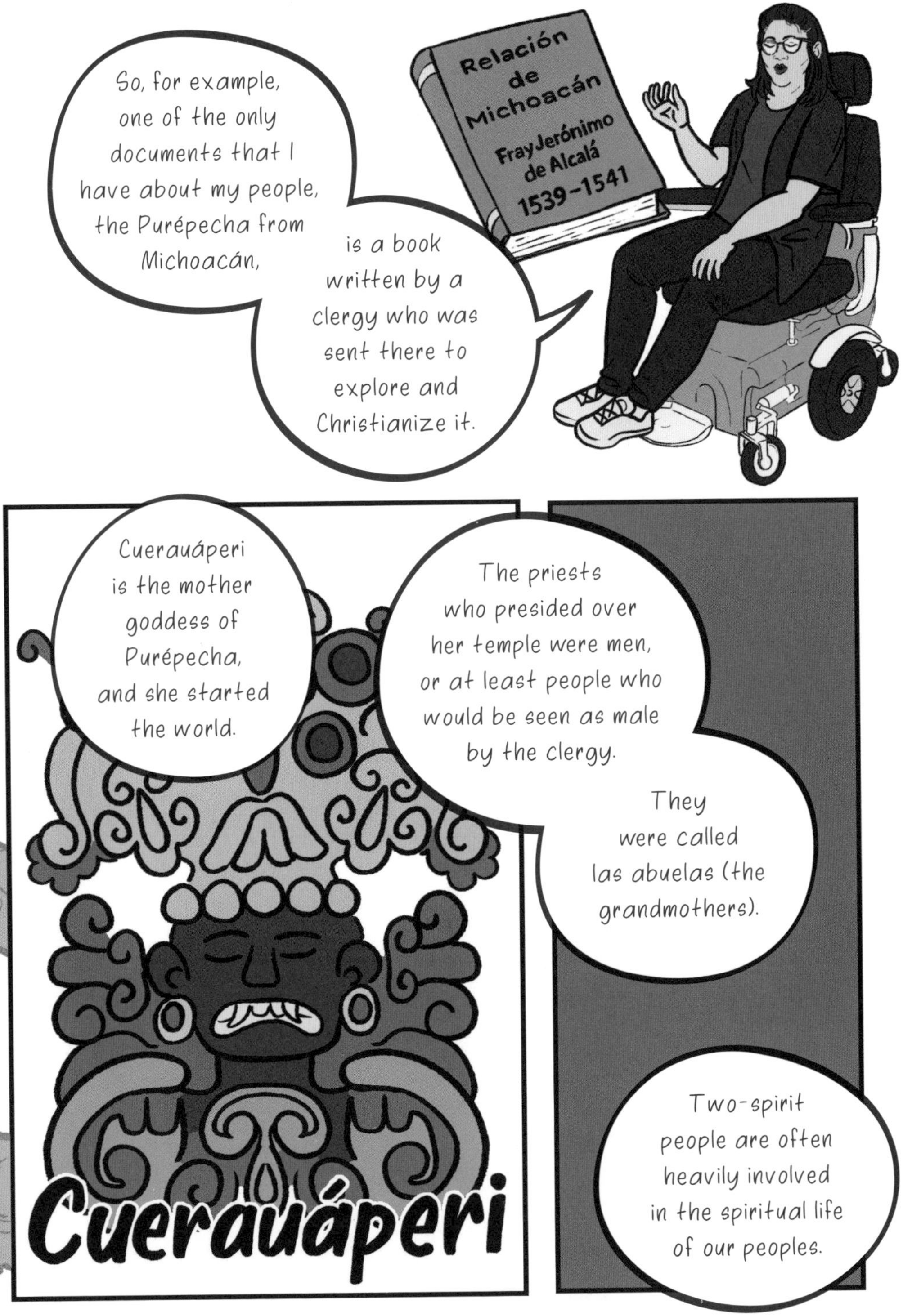
So, for example, one of the only documents that I have about my people, the Purépecha from Michoacán,
is a book written by a clergy who was sent there to explore and Christianize it.
Relación de Michoacán Fray Jerónimo de Alcalá 1539–1541
Cuerauáperi is the mother goddess of Purépecha, and she started the world.
Cuerauáperi
The priests who presided over her temple were men, or at least people who would be seen as male by the clergy.
They were called las abuelas (the grandmothers).
Two-spirit people are often heavily involved in the spiritual life of our peoples.

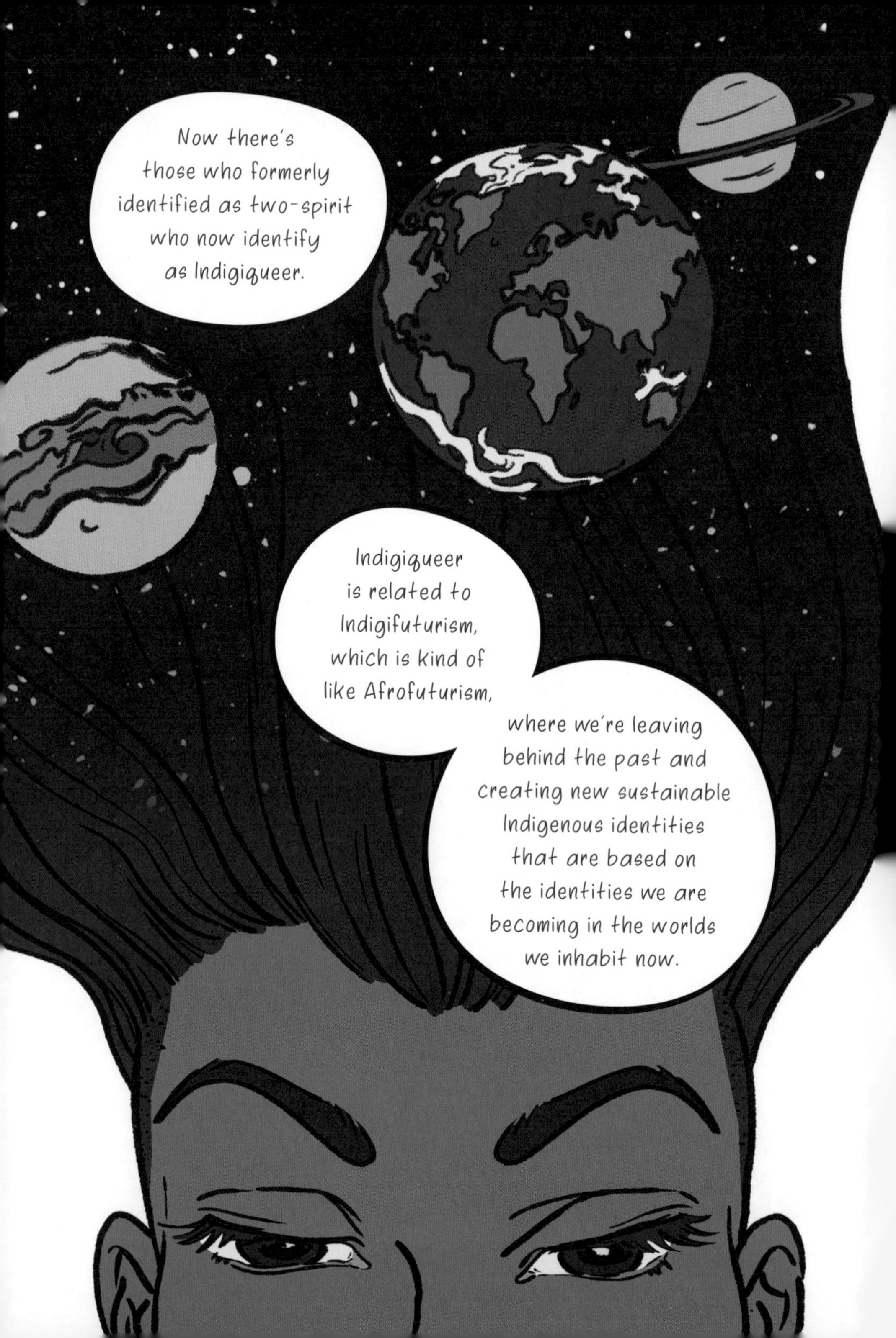
Now there's those who formerly identified as two-spirit who now identify as Indigiqueer.
Indigiqueer is related to Indigifuturism, which is kind of like Afrofuturism,
where we're leaving behind the past and creating new sustainable Indigenous identities that are based on the identities we are becoming in the worlds we inhabit now.

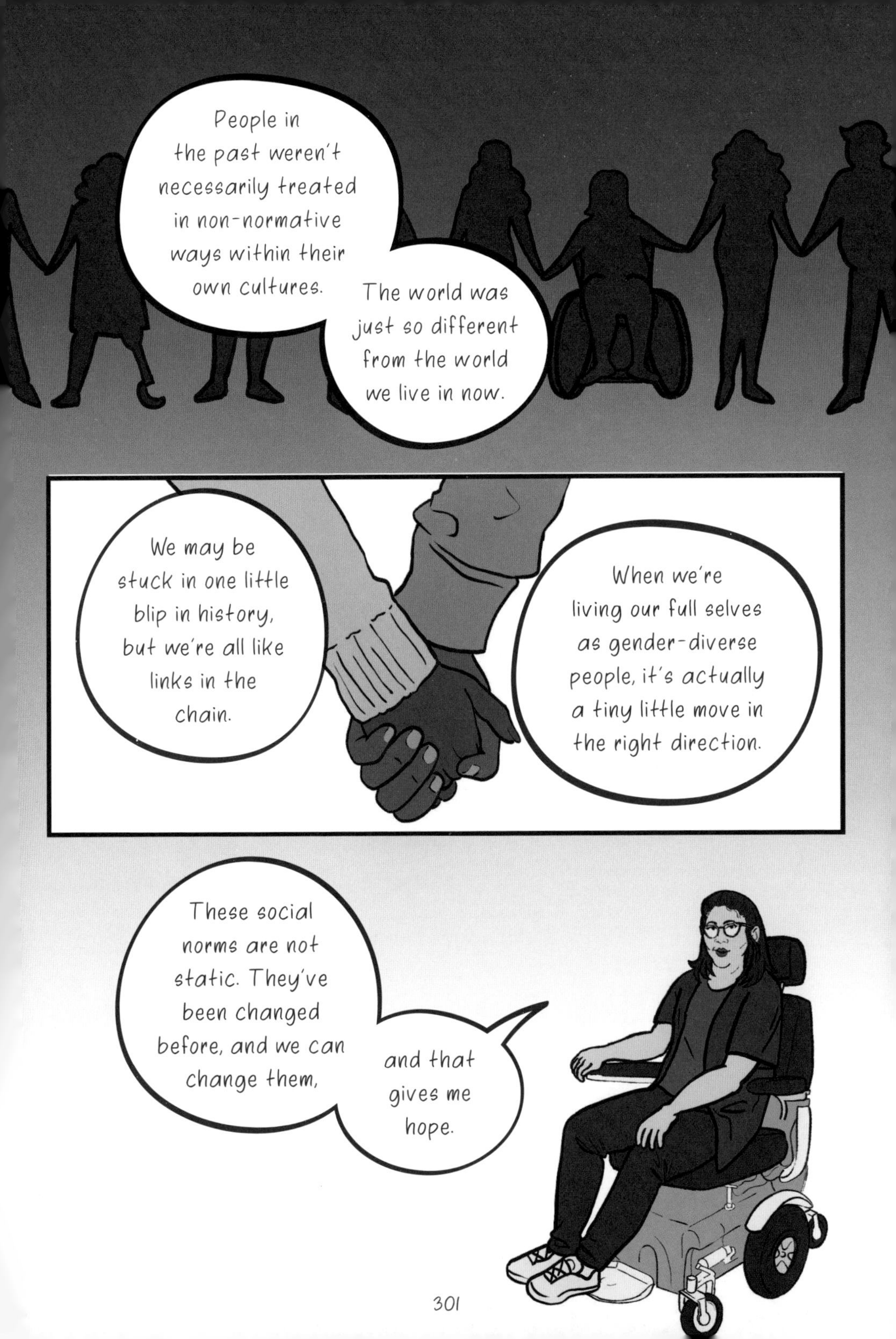
People in the past weren't necessarily treated in non-normative ways within their own cultures.
The world was just so different from the world we live in now.
We may be stuck in one little blip in history, but we're all like links in the chain.
When we're living our full selves as gender-diverse people, it's actually a tiny little move in the right direction.
These social norms are not static. They've been changed before, and we can change them,
and that gives me hope.

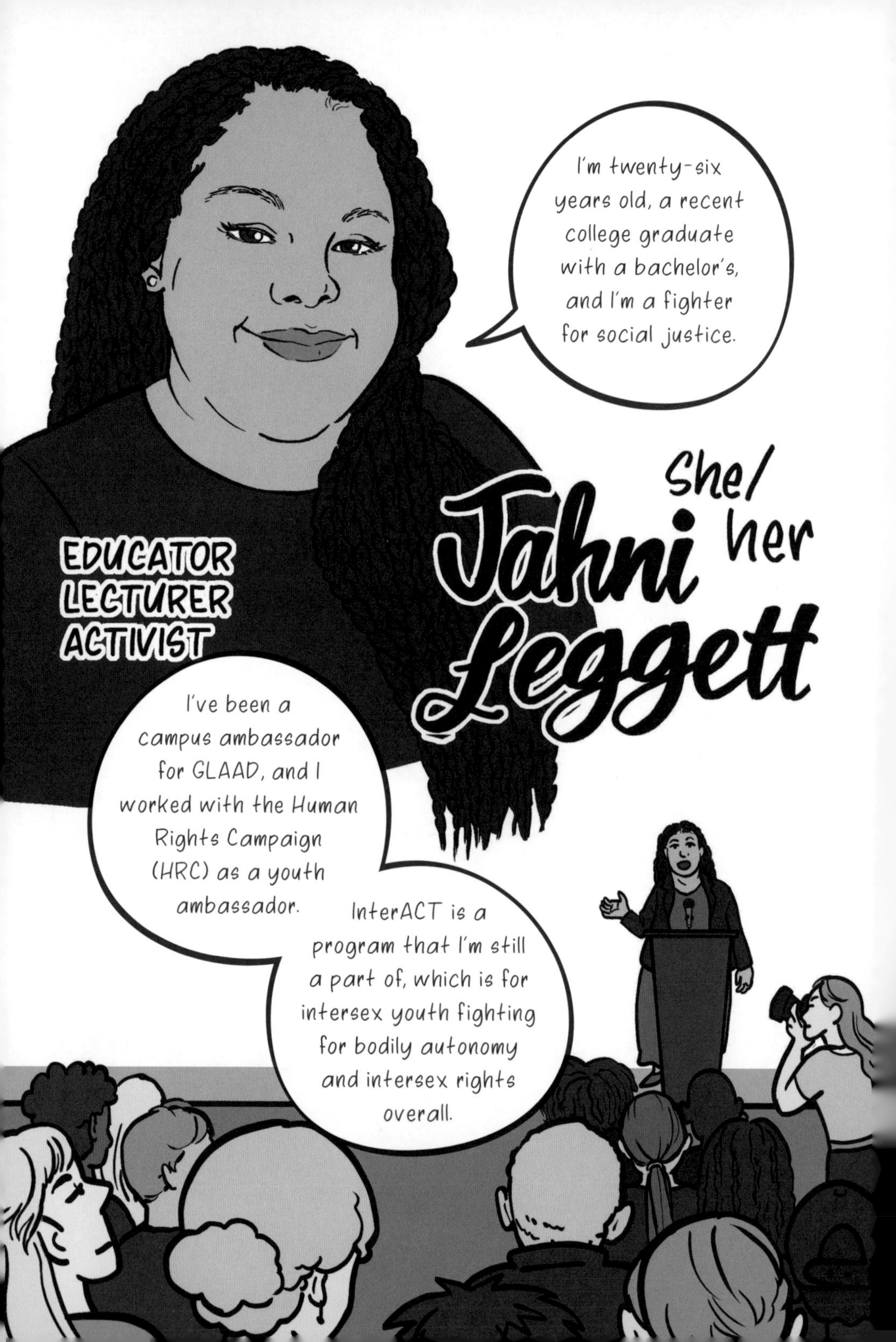

I'm twenty-six years old, a recent college graduate with a bachelor's, and I'm a fighter for social justice.
EDUCATOR
LECTURER
ACTIVIST
Jahni Leggett
She/her
I've been a campus ambassador for GLAAD, and I worked with the Human Rights Campaign (HRC) as a youth ambassador.
InterACT is a program that I'm still a part of, which is for intersex youth fighting for bodily autonomy and intersex rights overall.

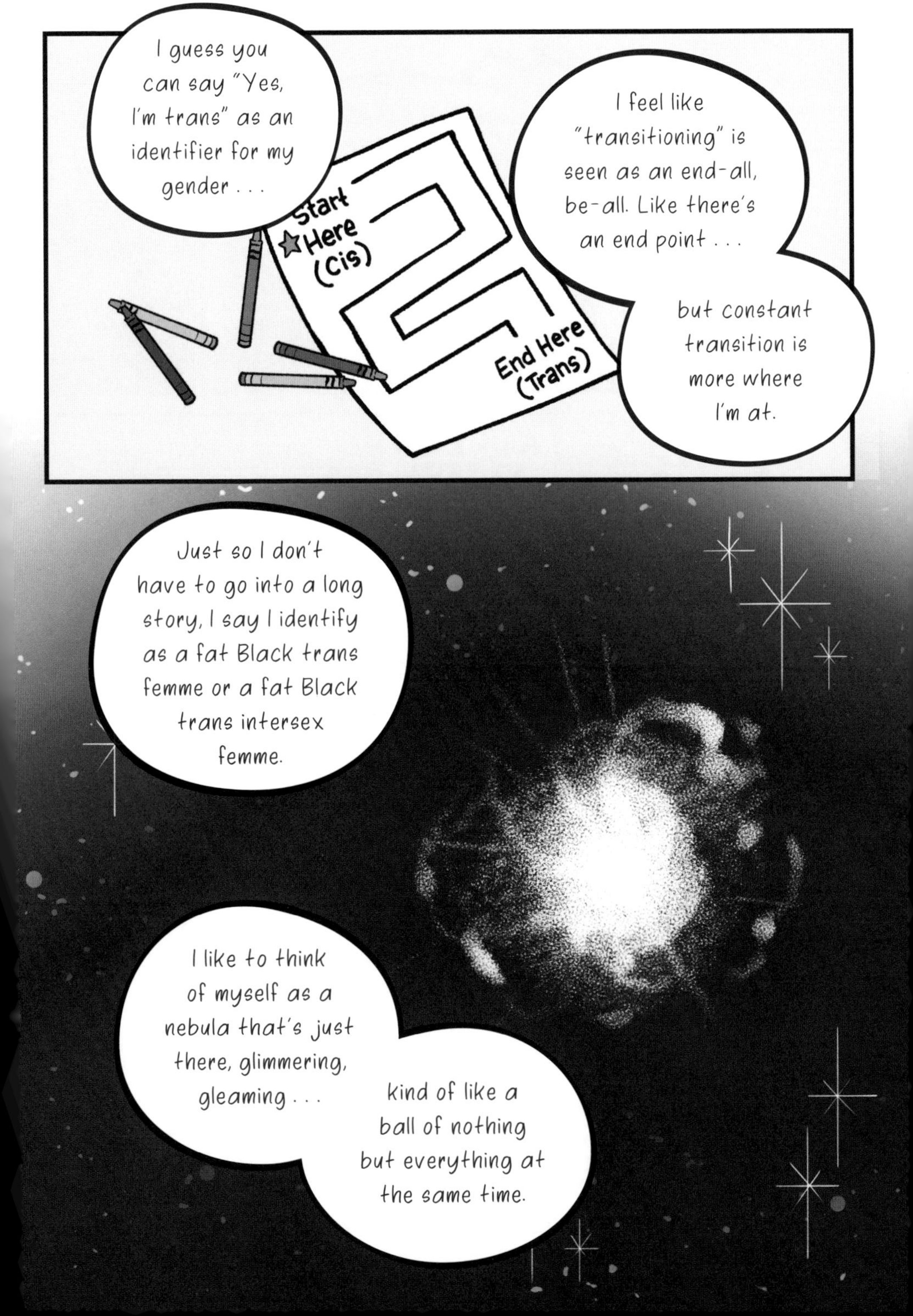
I guess you can say "Yes, I'm trans" as an identifier for my gender . . .
Start Here (Cis)
End Here (Trans)
I feel like "transitioning" is seen as an end-all, be-all. Like there's an end point . . .
but constant transition is more where I'm at.
Just so I don't have to go into a long story, I say I identify as a fat Black trans femme or a fat Black trans intersex femme.
I like to think of myself as a nebula that's just there, glimmering, gleaming . . .
kind of like a ball of nothing but everything at the same time.

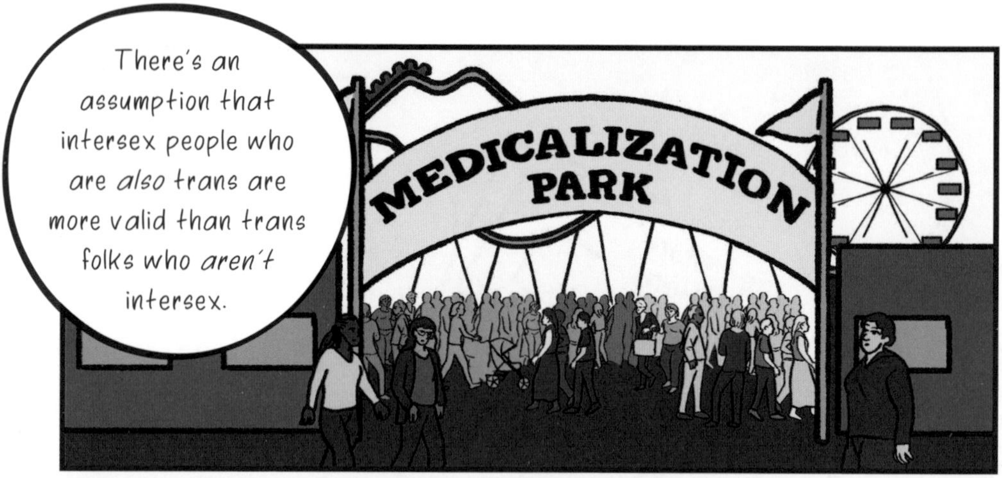
There's an assumption that intersex people who are *also* trans are more valid than trans folks who *aren't* intersex.
MEDICALIZATION PARK

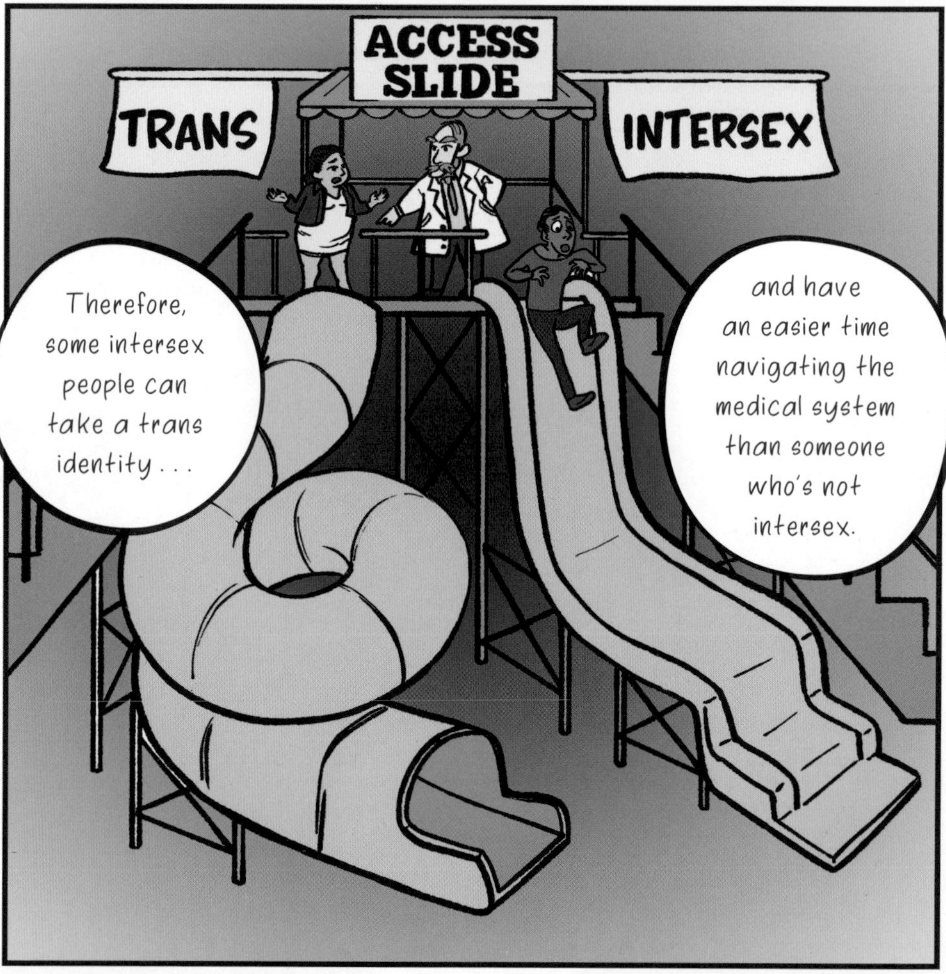
ACCESS SLIDE
TRANS
INTERSEX
Therefore, some intersex people can take a trans identity . . .
and have an easier time navigating the medical system than someone who's not intersex.

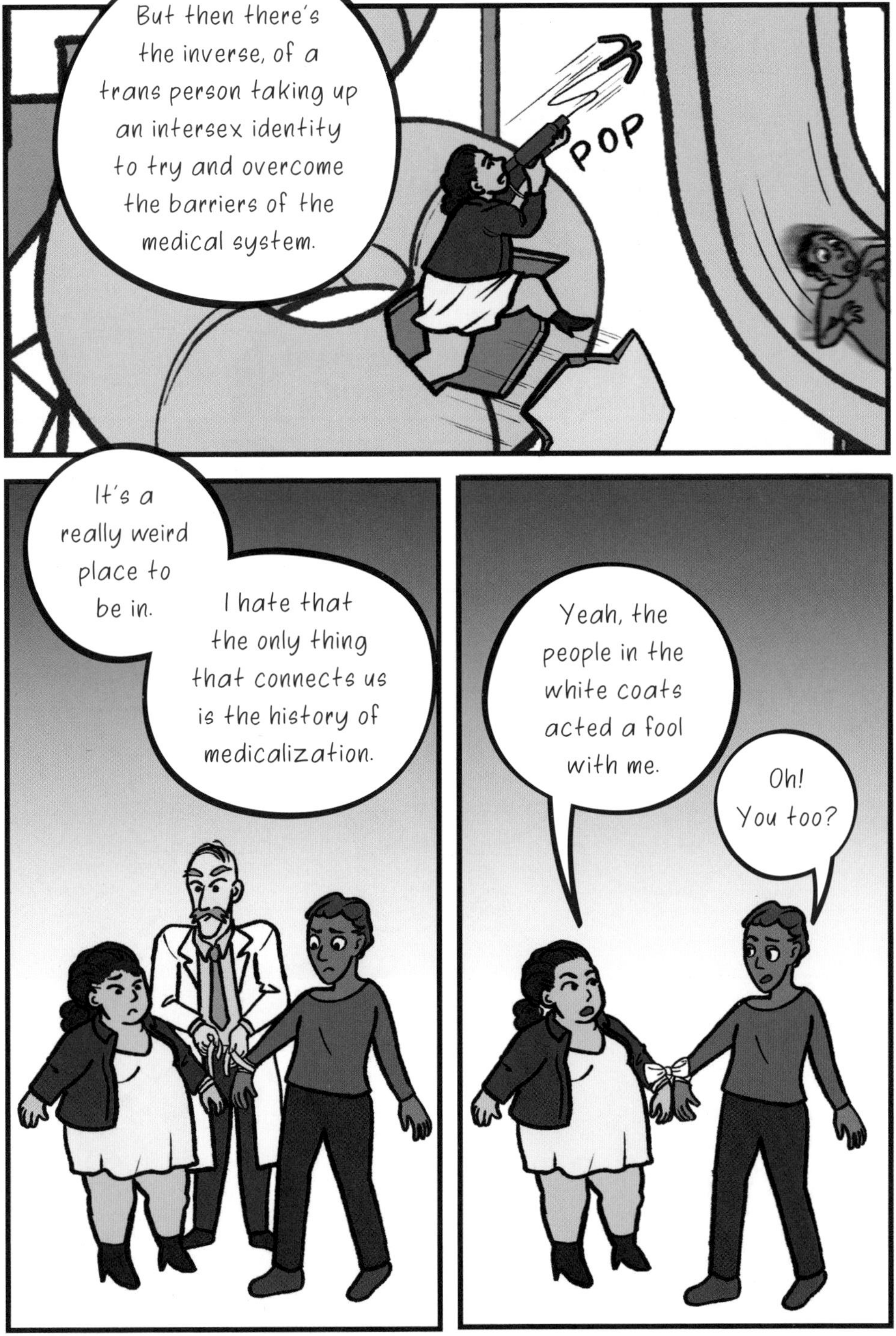
But then there's the inverse, of a trans person taking up an intersex identity to try and overcome the barriers of the medical system.
POP
It's a really weird place to be in.
I hate that the only thing that connects us is the history of medicalization.
Yeah, the people in the white coats acted a fool with me.
Oh! You too?

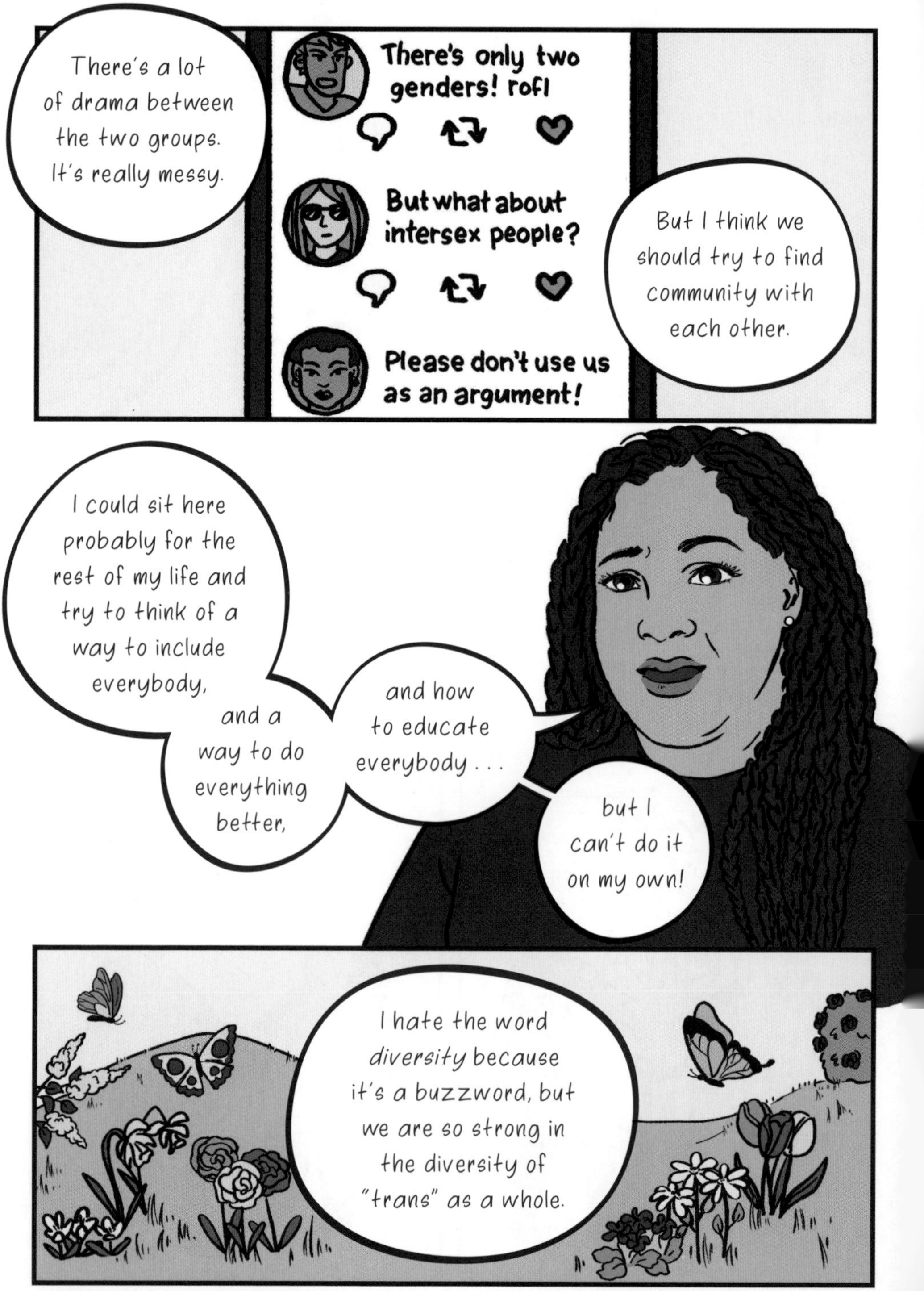
There's a lot of drama between the two groups. It's really messy.
There's only two genders! rofl
But what about intersex people?
Please don't use us as an argument!
But I think we should try to find community with each other.
I could sit here probably for the rest of my life and try to think of a way to include everybody,
and a way to do everything better,
and how to educate everybody . . .
but I can't do it on my own!
I hate the word *diversity* because it's a buzzword, but we are so strong in the diversity of "trans" as a whole.

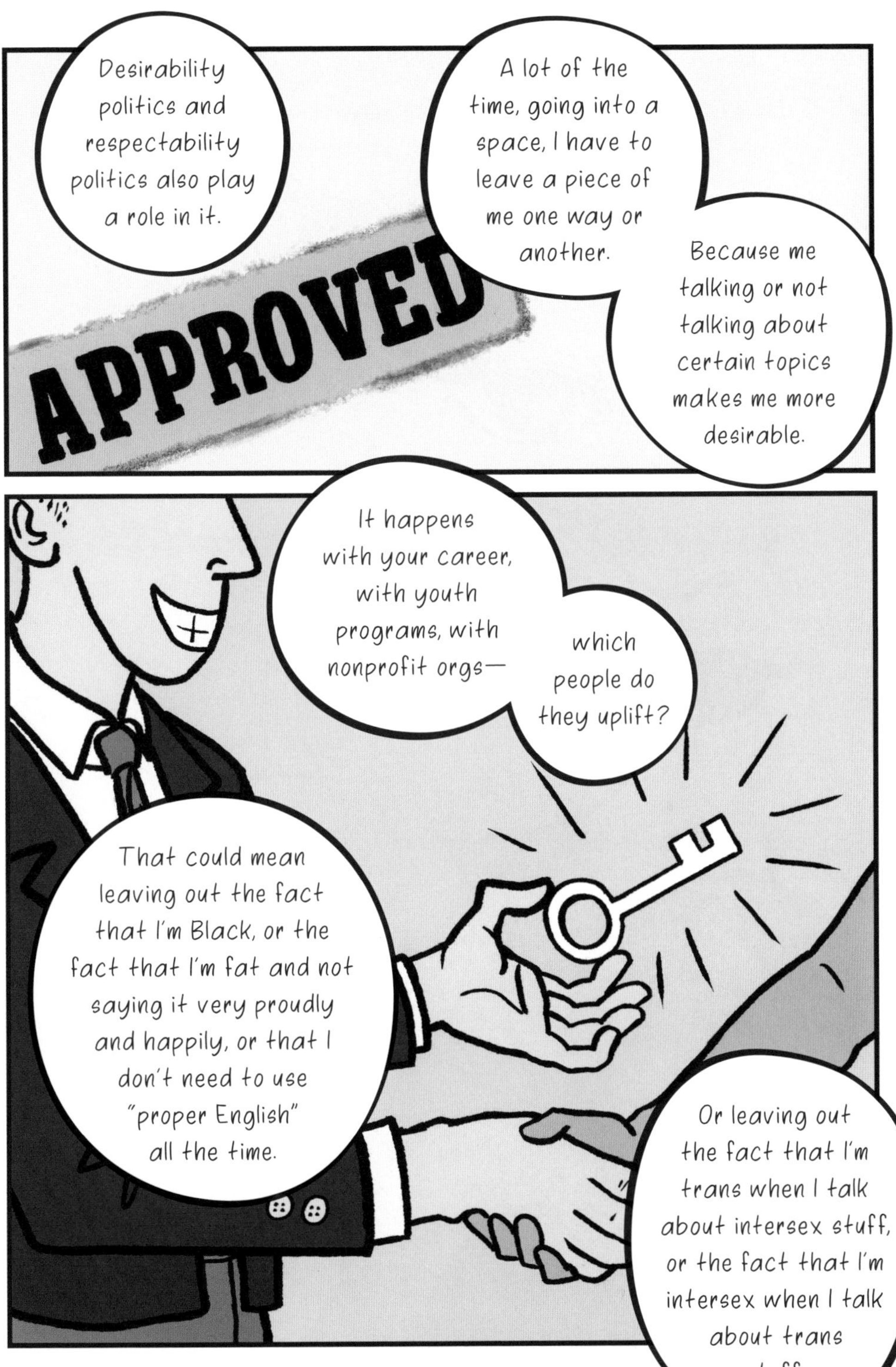
Desirability politics and respectability politics also play a role in it.
APPROVED
A lot of the time, going into a space, I have to leave a piece of me one way or another.
Because me talking or not talking about certain topics makes me more desirable.
It happens with your career, with youth programs, with nonprofit orgs—
which people do they uplift?
That could mean leaving out the fact that I'm Black, or the fact that I'm fat and not saying it very proudly and happily, or that I don't need to use "proper English" all the time.
Or leaving out the fact that I'm trans when I talk about intersex stuff, or the fact that I'm intersex when I talk about trans stuff.

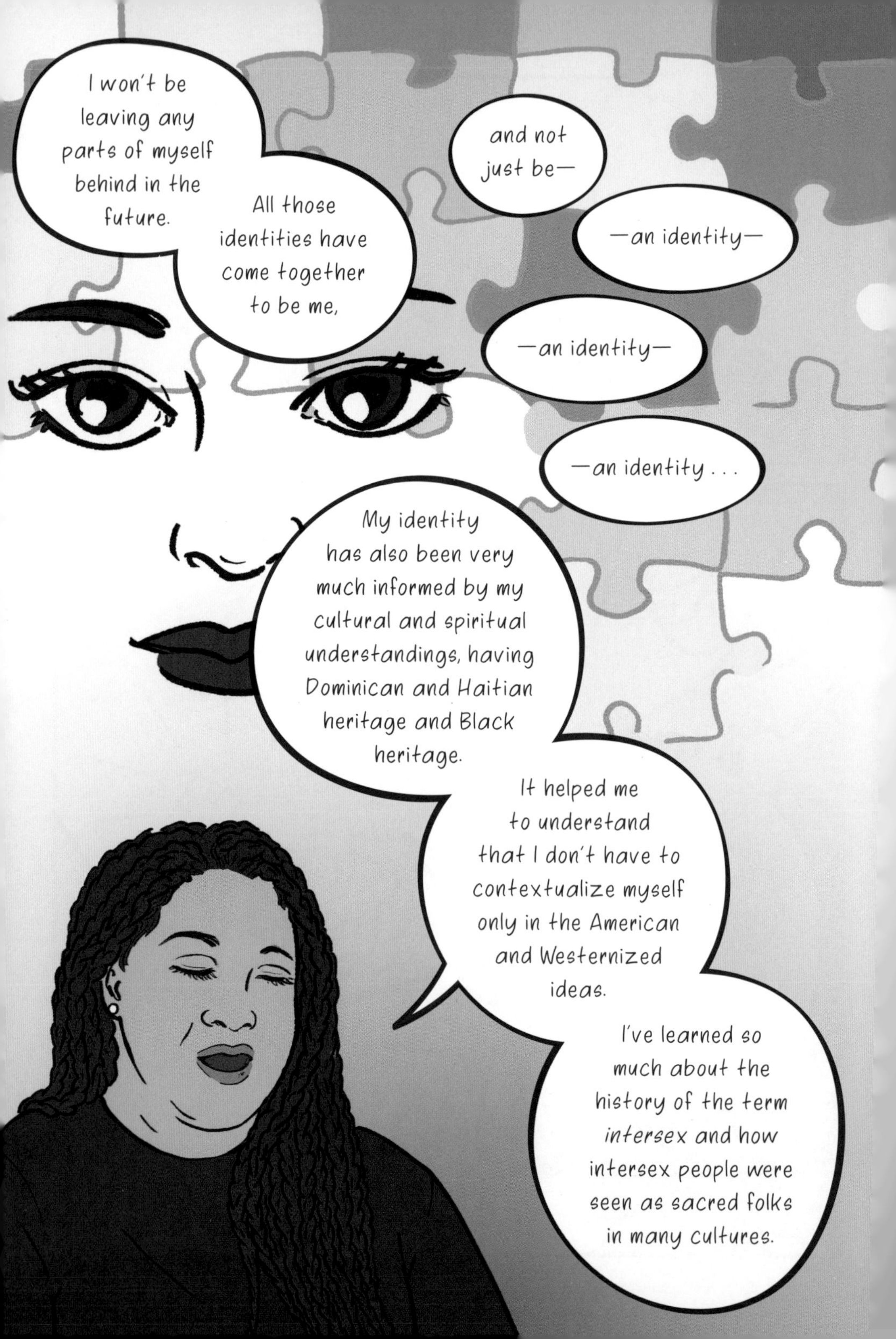
I won't be leaving any parts of myself behind in the future.
All those identities have come together to be me,
and not just be—
—an identity—
—an identity—
—an identity . . .
My identity has also been very much informed by my cultural and spiritual understandings, having Dominican and Haitian heritage and Black heritage.
It helped me to understand that I don't have to contextualize myself only in the American and Westernized ideas.
I've learned so much about the history of the term *intersex* and how intersex people were seen as sacred folks in many cultures.

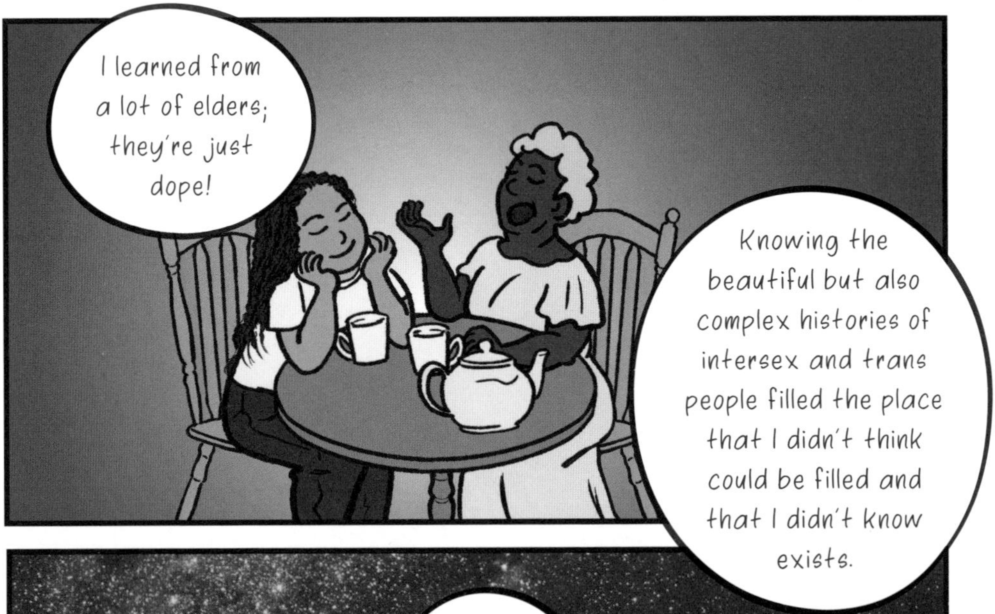
I learned from a lot of elders; they're just dope!
Knowing the beautiful but also complex histories of intersex and trans people filled the place that I didn't think could be filled and that I didn't know exists.

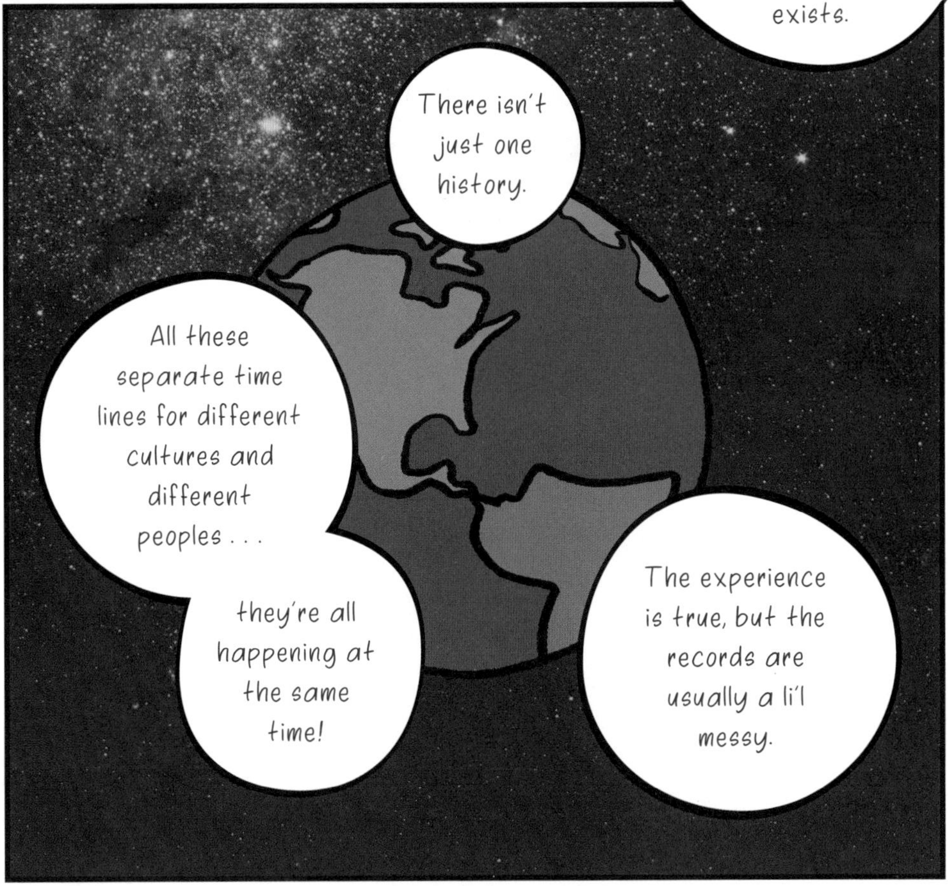
There isn't just one history.
All these separate time lines for different cultures and different peoples . . .
they're all happening at the same time!
The experience is true, but the records are usually a li'l messy.

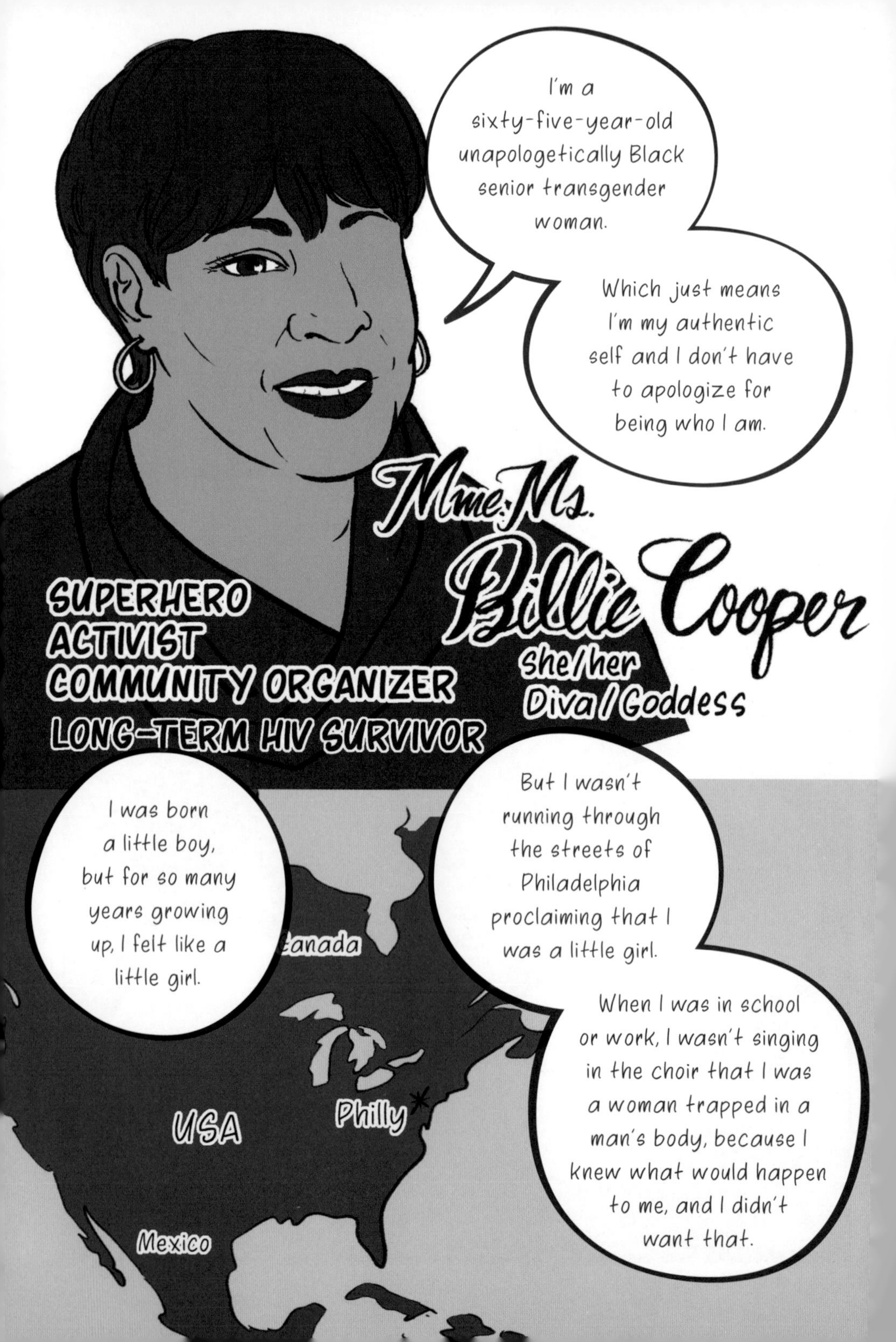
I'm a sixty-five-year-old unapologetically Black senior transgender woman.
Which just means I'm my authentic self and I don't have to apologize for being who I am.
Mme. Ms. Billie Cooper
SUPERHERO
ACTIVIST
COMMUNITY ORGANIZER
LONG-TERM HIV SURVIVOR
She/her
Diva/Goddess
I was born a little boy, but for so many years growing up, I felt like a little girl.
But I wasn't running through the streets of Philadelphia proclaiming that I was a little girl.
When I was in school or work, I wasn't singing in the choir that I was a woman trapped in a man's body, because I knew what would happen to me, and I didn't want that.
Canada
USA
Philly
Mexico

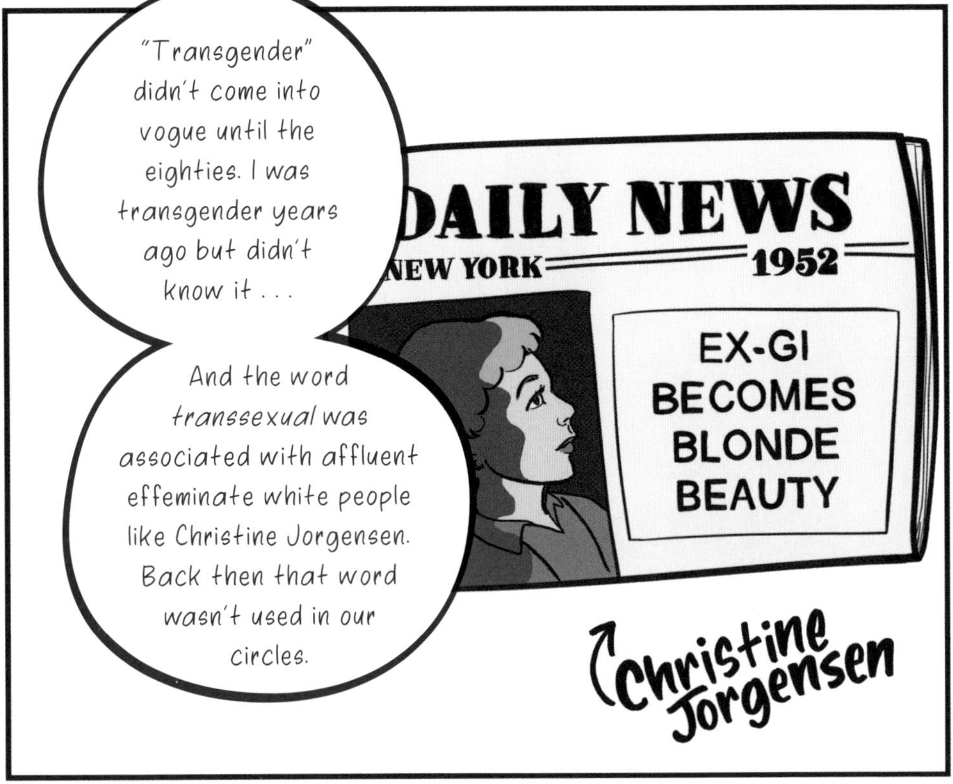
"Transgender" didn't come into vogue until the eighties. I was transgender years ago but didn't know it . . .
And the word *transsexual* was associated with affluent effeminate white people like Christine Jorgensen. Back then that word wasn't used in our circles.
DAILY NEWS
NEW YORK
1952
EX-GI BECOMES BLONDE BEAUTY
Christine Jorgensen

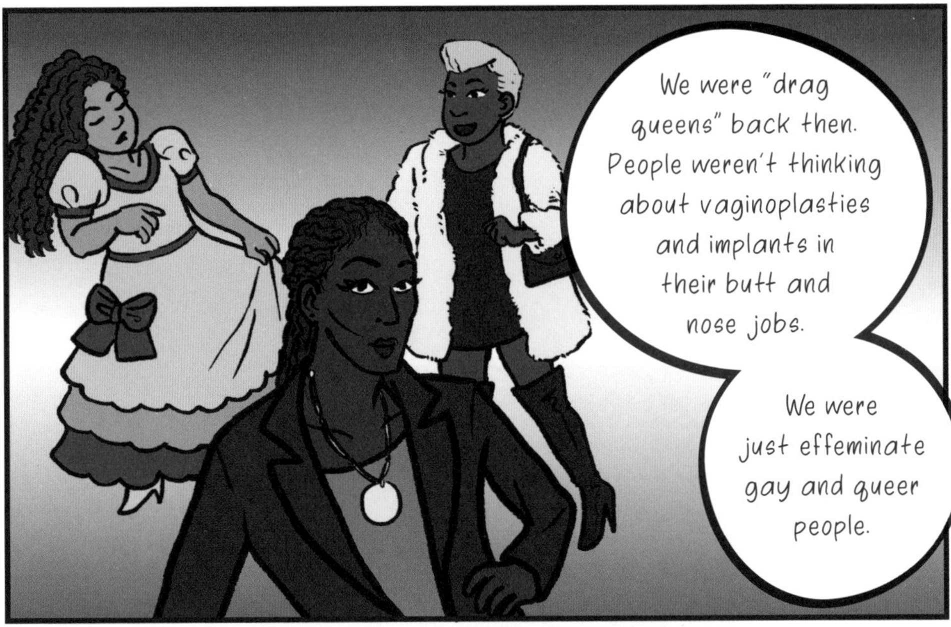
We were "drag queens" back then. People weren't thinking about vaginoplasties and implants in their butt and nose jobs.
We were just effeminate gay and queer people.

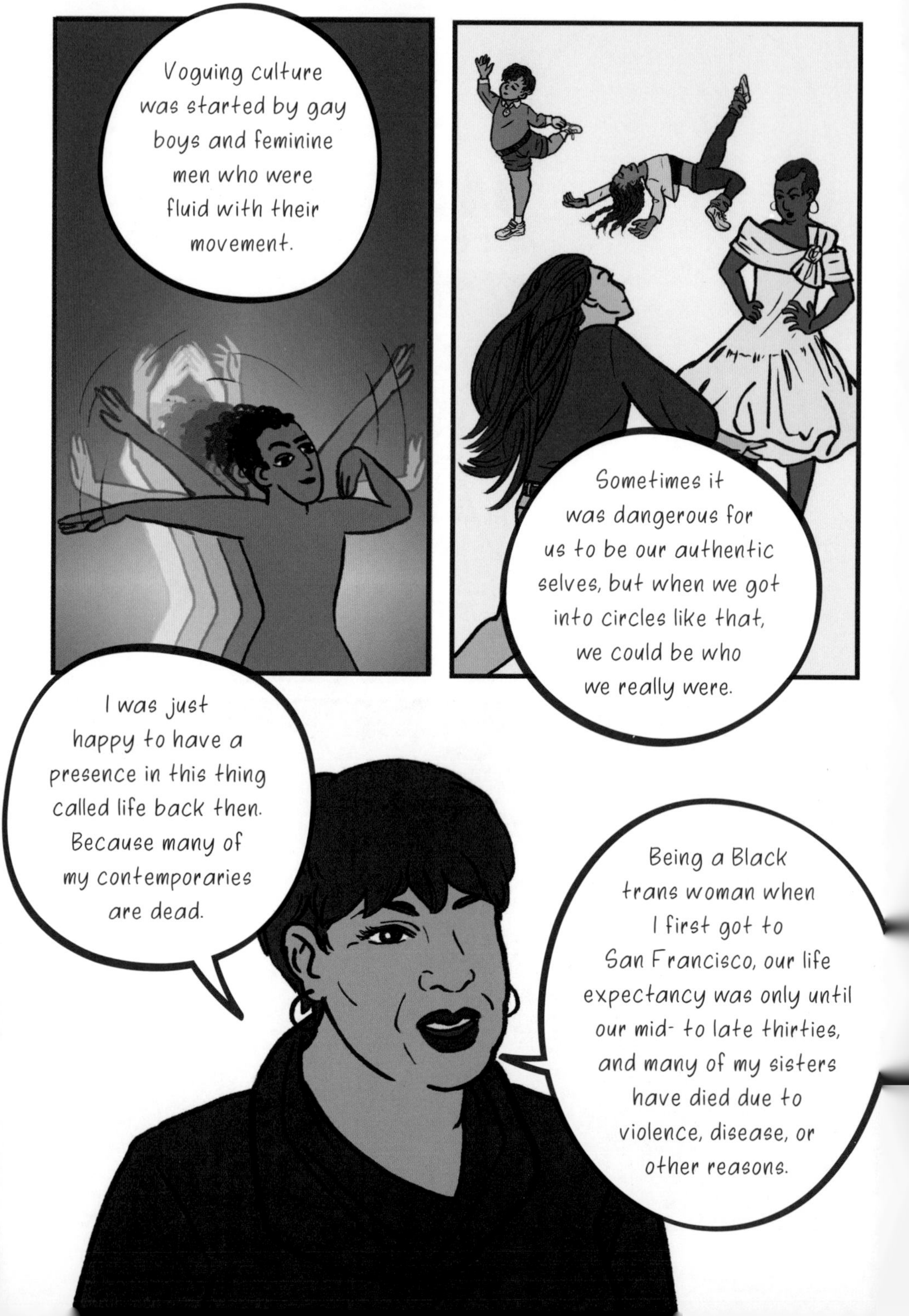
Voguing culture was started by gay boys and feminine men who were fluid with their movement.
Sometimes it was dangerous for us to be our authentic selves, but when we got into circles like that, we could be who we really were.
I was just happy to have a presence in this thing called life back then. Because many of my contemporaries are dead.
Being a Black trans woman when I first got to San Francisco, our life expectancy was only until our mid- to late thirties, and many of my sisters have died due to violence, disease, or other reasons.

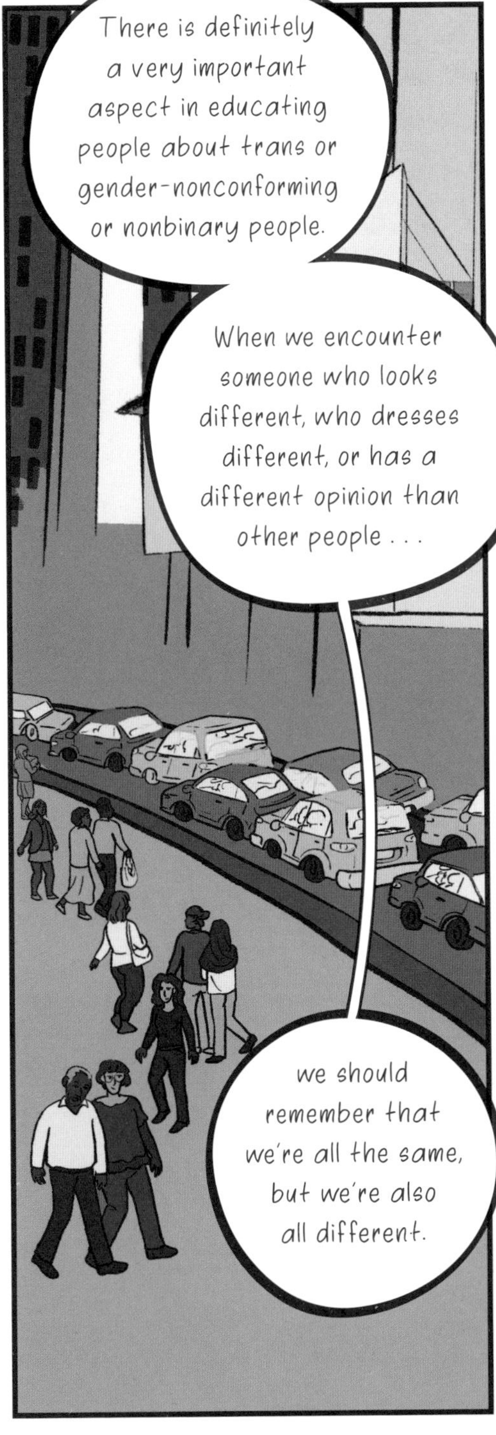
There is definitely a very important aspect in educating people about trans or gender-nonconforming or nonbinary people.
When we encounter someone who looks different, who dresses different, or has a different opinion than other people . . .
we should remember that we're all the same, but we're also all different.

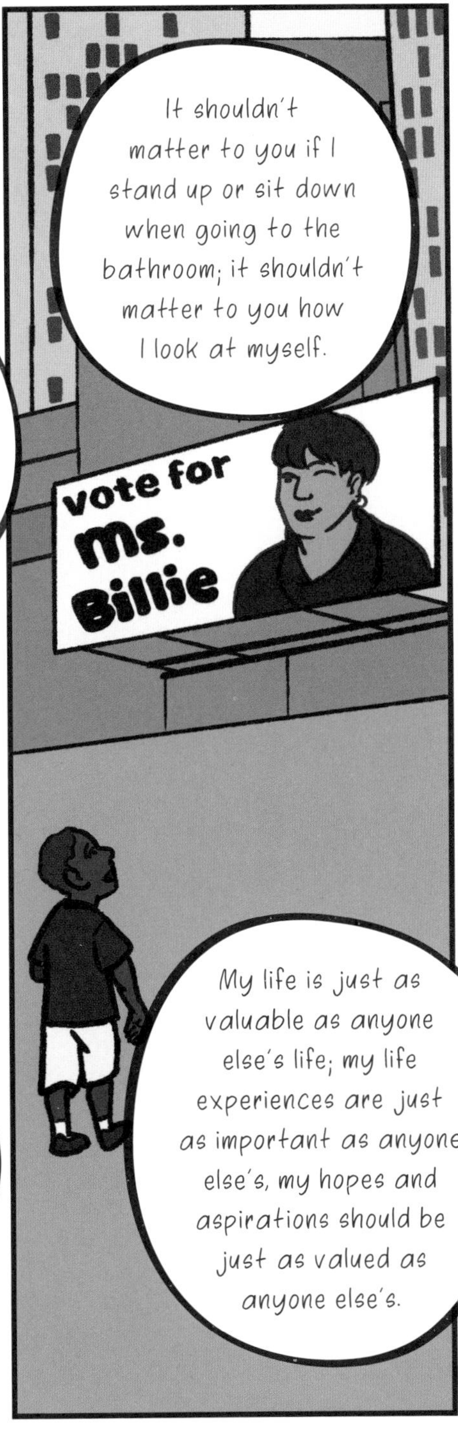
It shouldn't matter to you if I stand up or sit down when going to the bathroom; it shouldn't matter to you how I look at myself.
vote for Ms. Billie
My life is just as valuable as anyone else's life; my life experiences are just as important as anyone else's, my hopes and aspirations should be just as valued as anyone else's.

THE GENESIS OF SUPER COOPER

BY MS. BILLIE COOPER

ILLUSTRATED BY ALEX L. COMBS

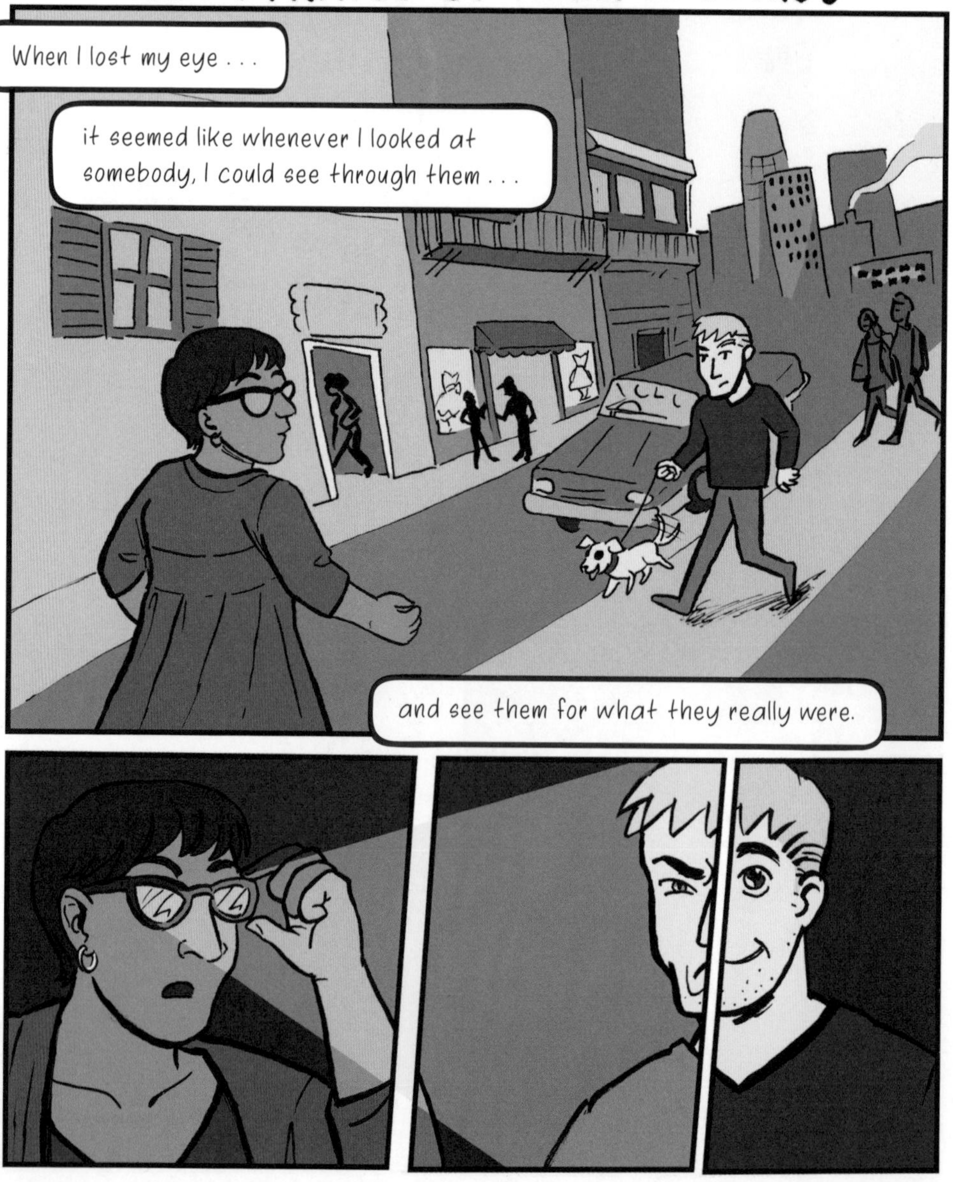
When I lost my eye . . .
it seemed like whenever I looked at somebody, I could see through them . . .
and see them for what they really were.

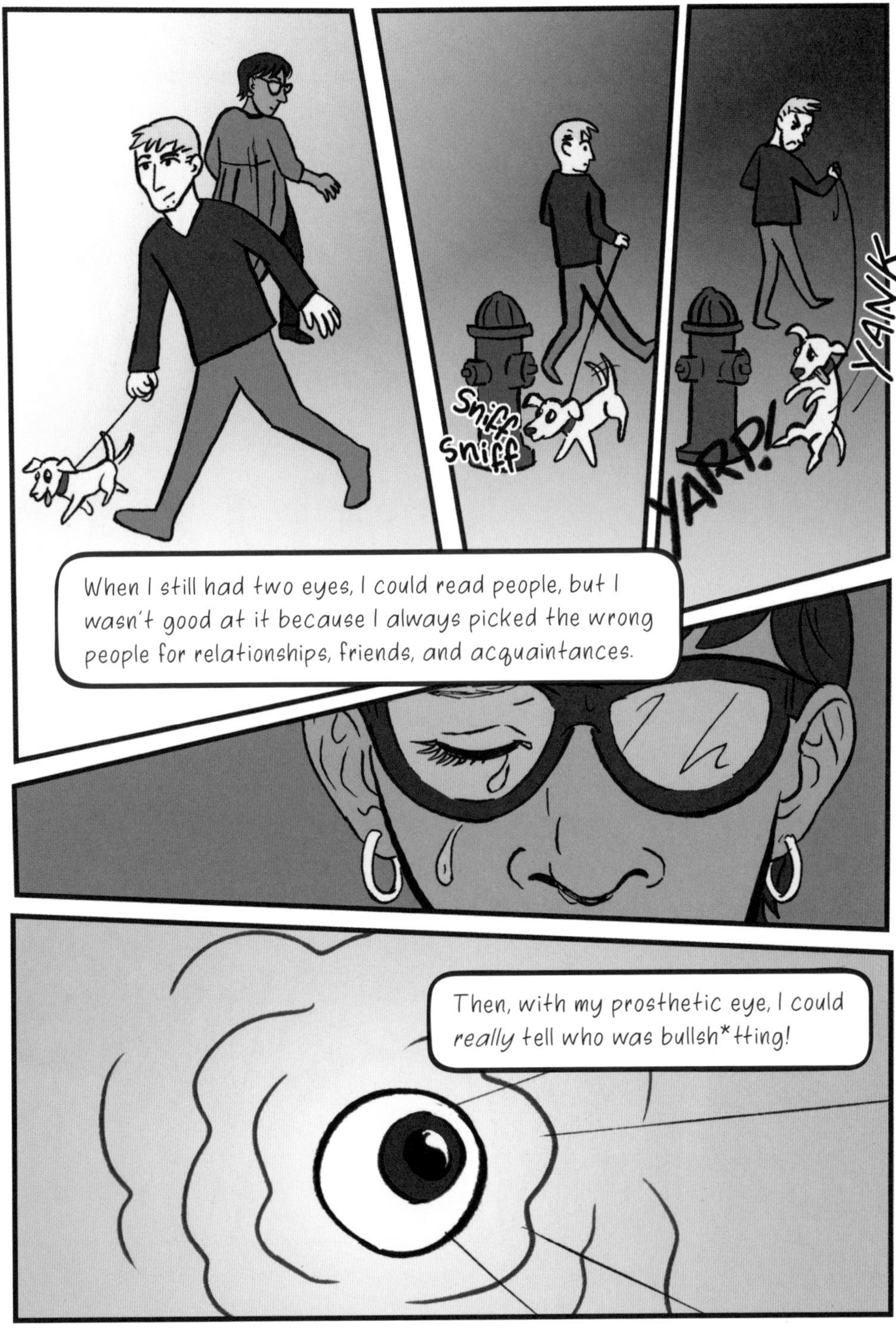
Sniff sniff
HARP!
YANK
When I still had two eyes, I could read people, but I wasn't good at it because I always picked the wrong people for relationships, friends, and acquaintances.
Then, with my prosthetic eye, I could *really* tell who was bullsh*tting!

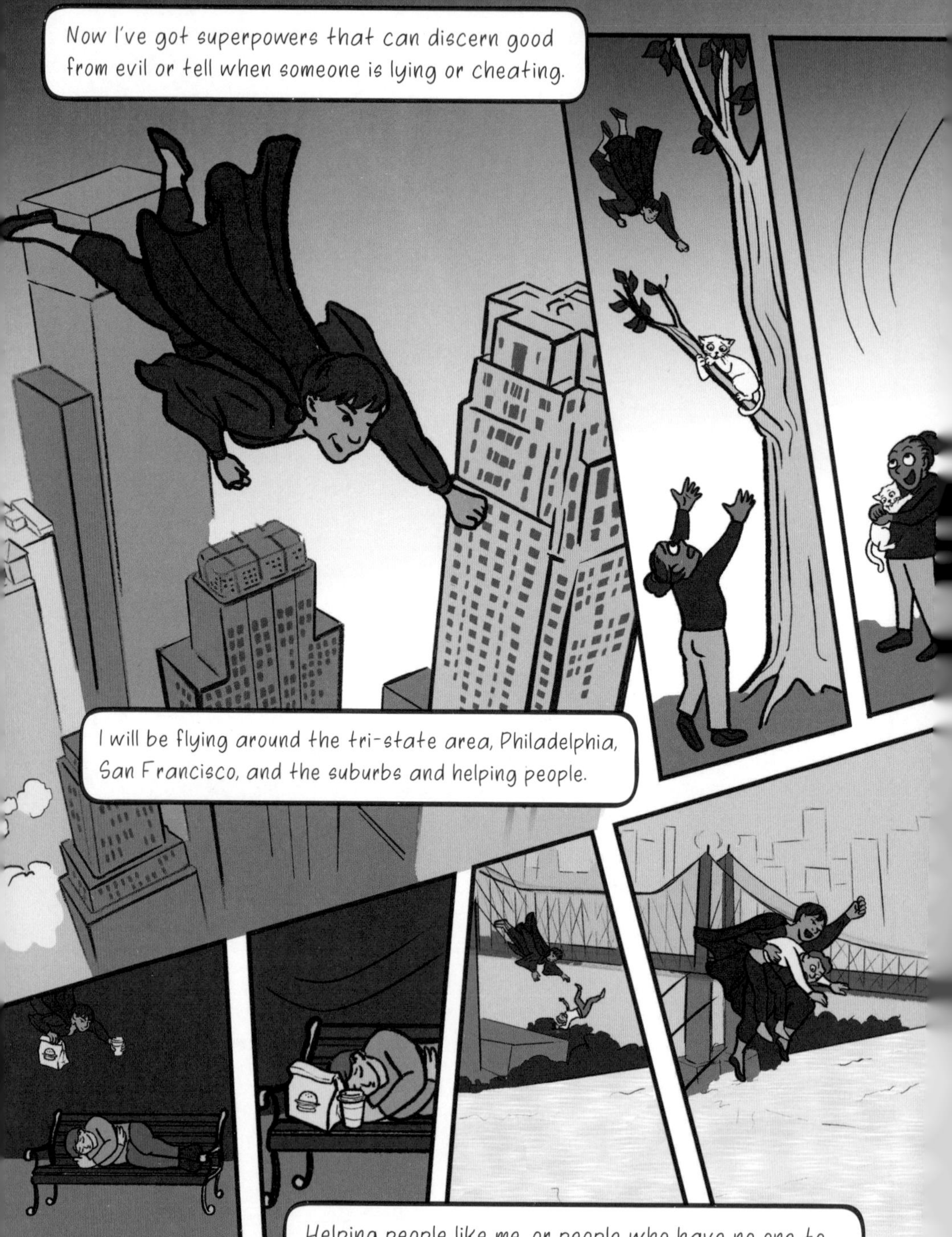
Now I've got superpowers that can discern good from evil or tell when someone is lying or cheating.
I will be flying around the tri-state area, Philadelphia, San Francisco, and the suburbs and helping people.
Helping people like me, or people who have no one to confide in, and helping people to believe in themselves.

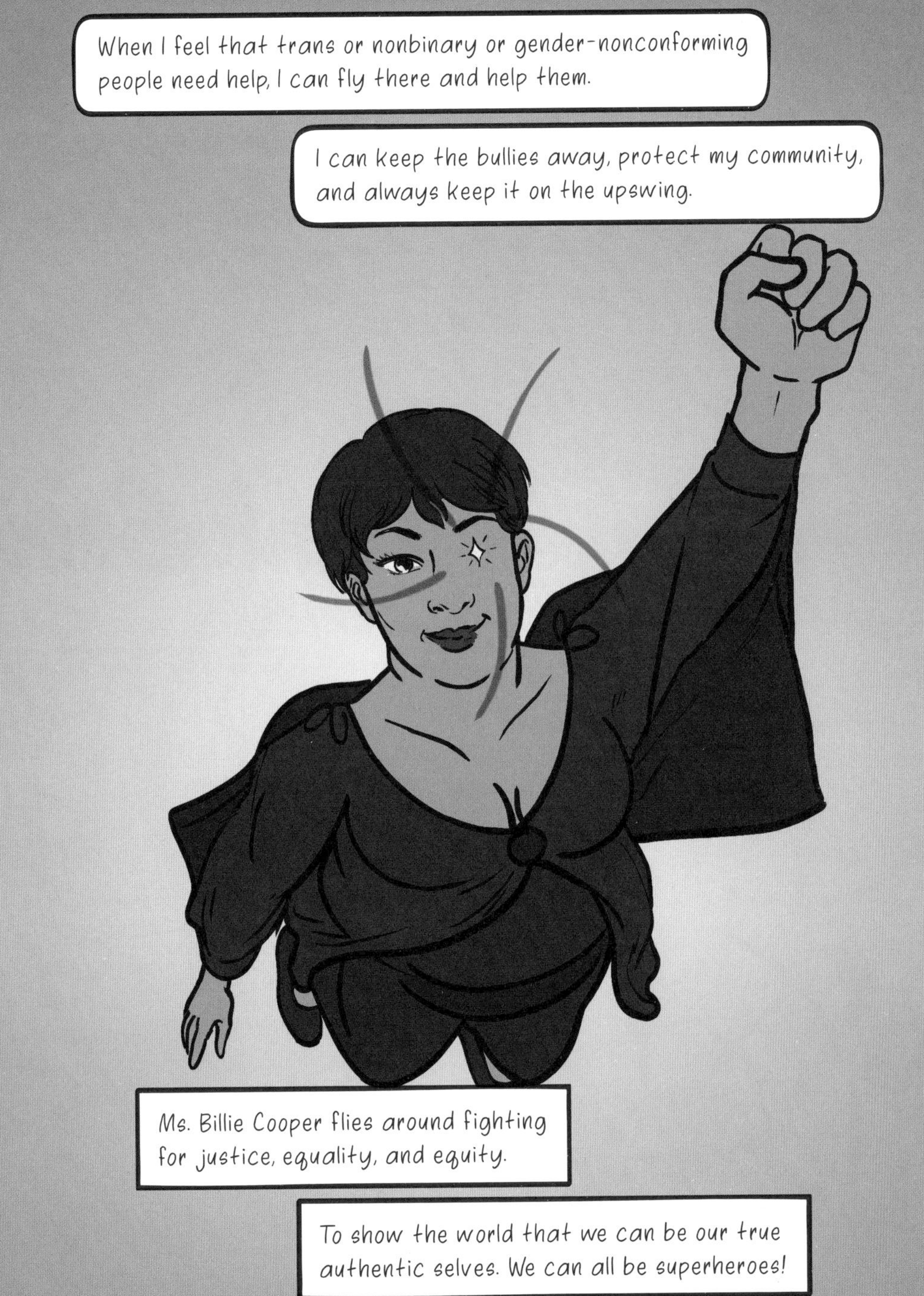
When I feel that trans or nonbinary or gender-nonconforming people need help, I can fly there and help them.
I can keep the bullies away, protect my community, and always keep it on the upswing.
Ms. Billie Cooper flies around fighting for justice, equality, and equity.
To show the world that we can be our true authentic selves. We can all be superheroes!
If you see her fly by . . . just wave!

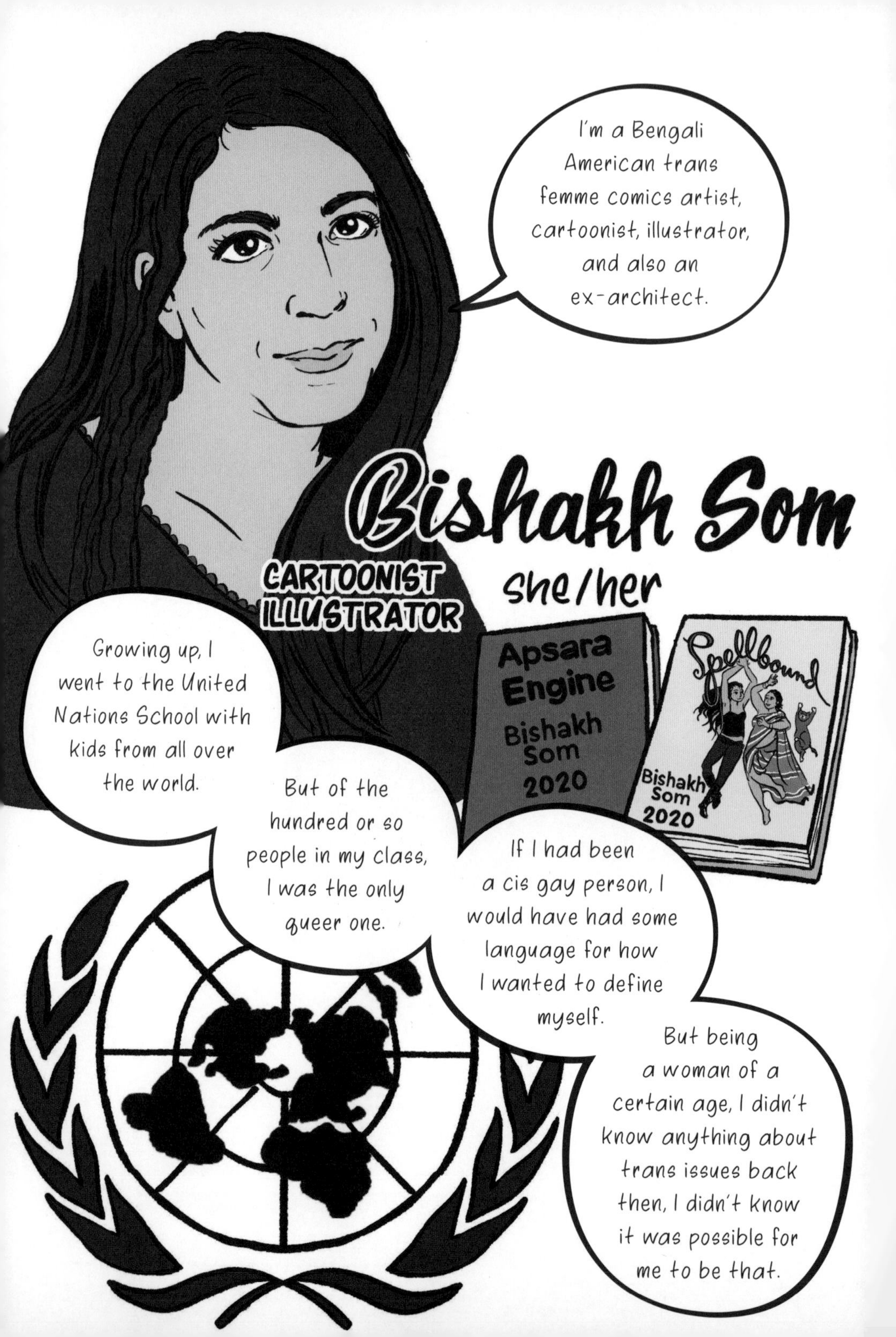
I'm a Bengali American trans femme comics artist, cartoonist, illustrator, and also an ex-architect.
Bishakh Som
CARTOONIST ILLUSTRATOR
she/her
Apsara Engine Bishakh Som 2020
Spellbound Bishakh Som 2020
Growing up, I went to the United Nations School with kids from all over the world.
But of the hundred or so people in my class, I was the only queer one.
If I had been a cis gay person, I would have had some language for how I wanted to define myself.
But being a woman of a certain age, I didn't know anything about trans issues back then, I didn't know it was possible for me to be that.

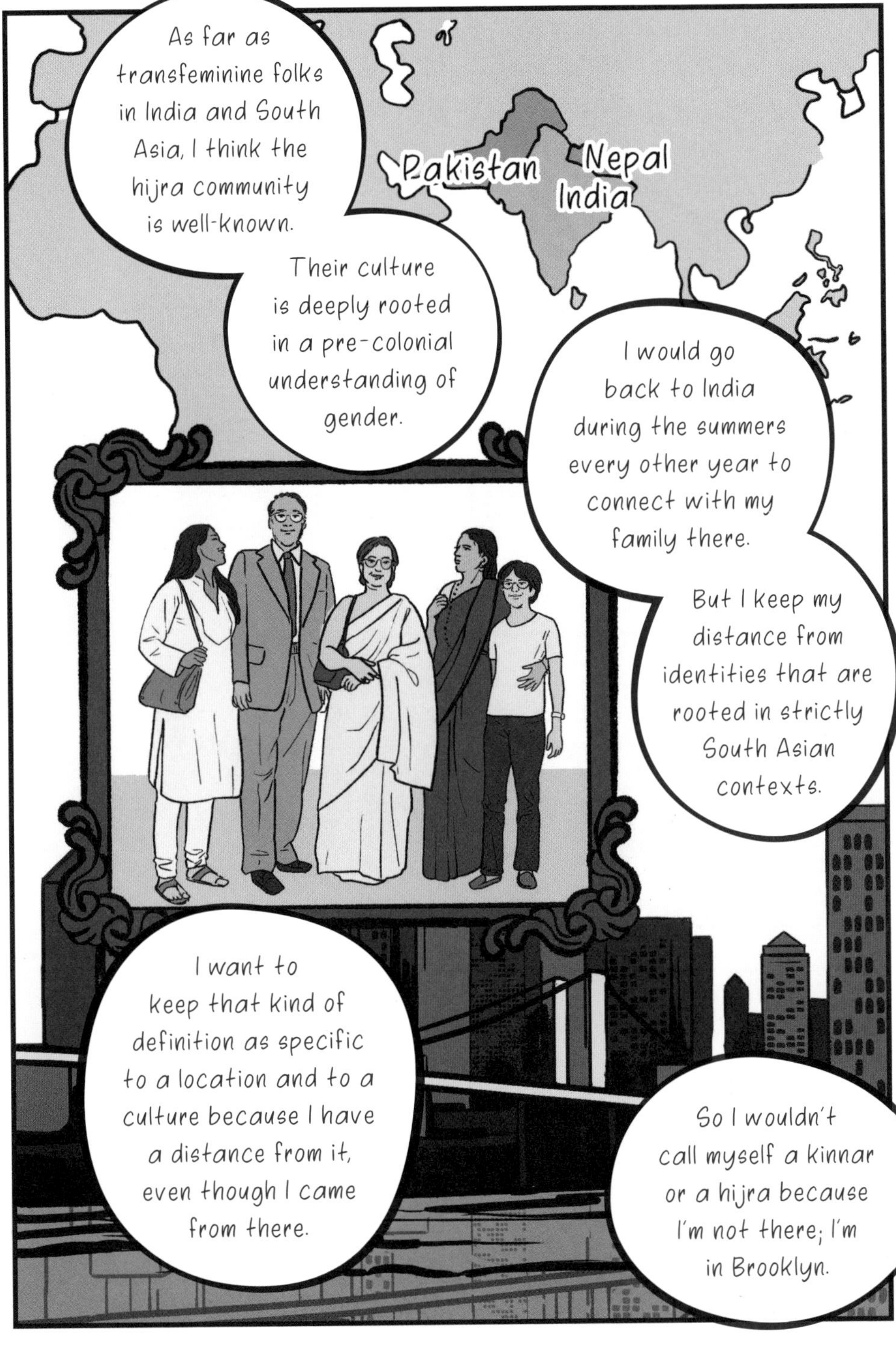
As far as transfeminine folks in India and South Asia, I think the hijra community is well-known.
Pakistan
Nepal
India
Their culture is deeply rooted in a pre-colonial understanding of gender.
I would go back to India during the summers every other year to connect with my family there.
But I keep my distance from identities that are rooted in strictly South Asian contexts.
I want to keep that kind of definition as specific to a location and to a culture because I have a distance from it, even though I came from there.
So I wouldn't call myself a kinnar or a hijra because I'm not there; I'm in Brooklyn.

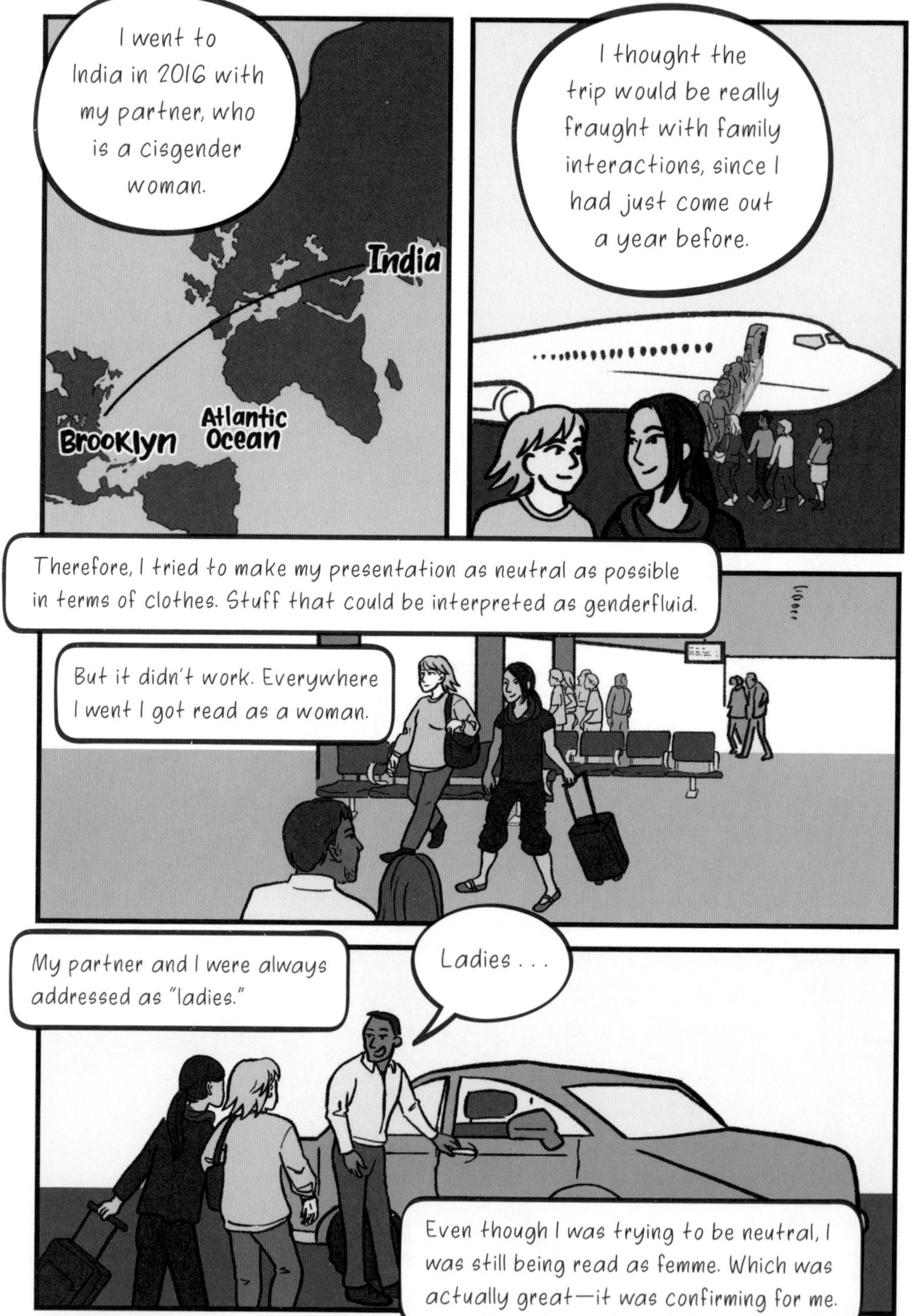
I went to India in 2016 with my partner, who is a cisgender woman.
India
Brooklyn
Atlantic Ocean
I thought the trip would be really fraught with family interactions, since I had just come out a year before.
Therefore, I tried to make my presentation as neutral as possible in terms of clothes. Stuff that could be interpreted as genderfluid.
But it didn't work. Everywhere I went I got read as a woman.
My partner and I were always addressed as "ladies."
Ladies . . .
Even though I was trying to be neutral, I was still being read as femme. Which was actually great—it was confirming for me.

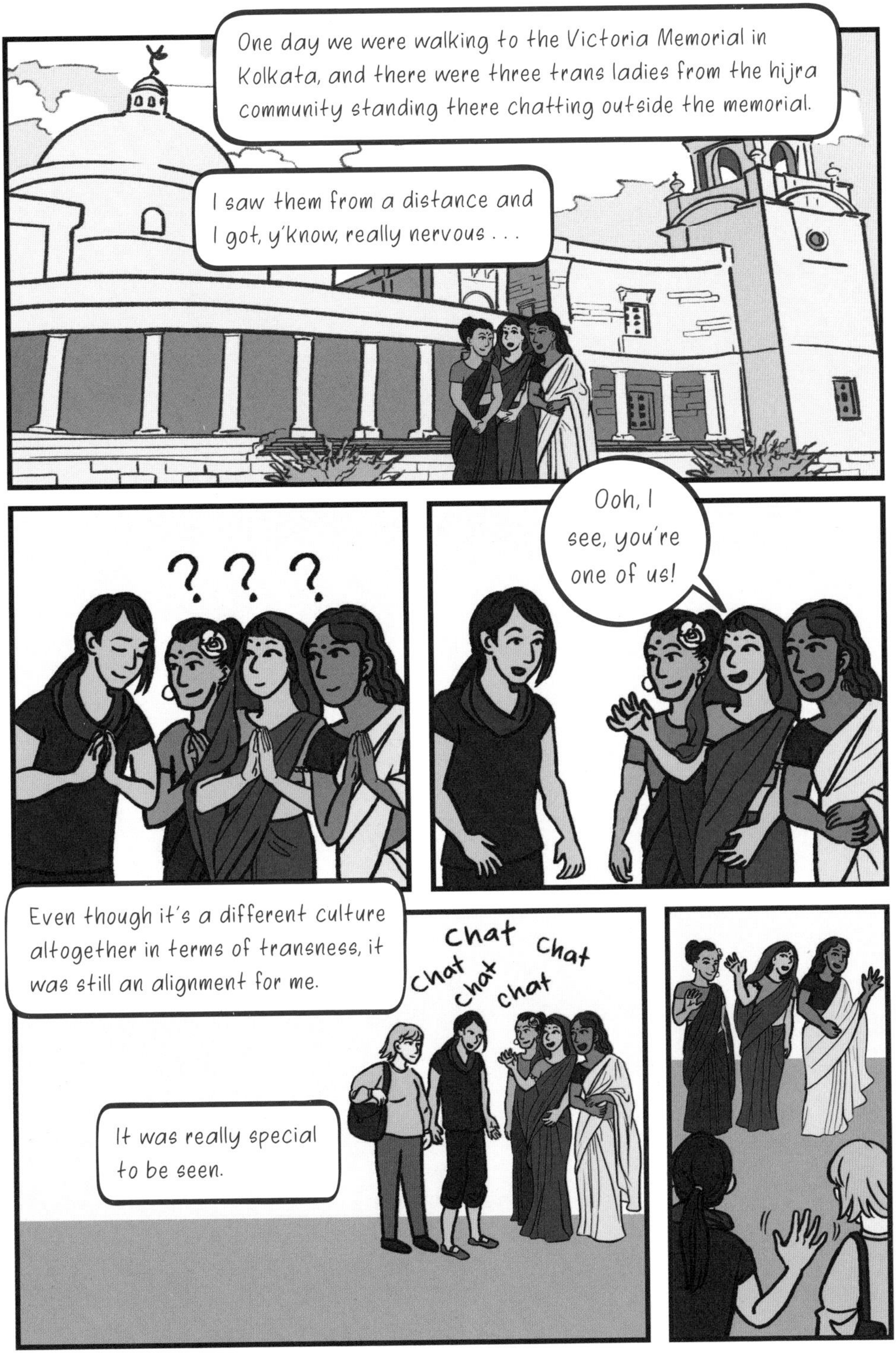
One day we were walking to the Victoria Memorial in Kolkata, and there were three trans ladies from the hijra community standing there chatting outside the memorial.
I saw them from a distance and I got, y'know, really nervous . . .
? ? ?
Ooh, I see, you're one of us!
Even though it's a different culture altogether in terms of transness, it was still an alignment for me.
Chat
Chat
Chat
Chat
Chat
It was really special to be seen.

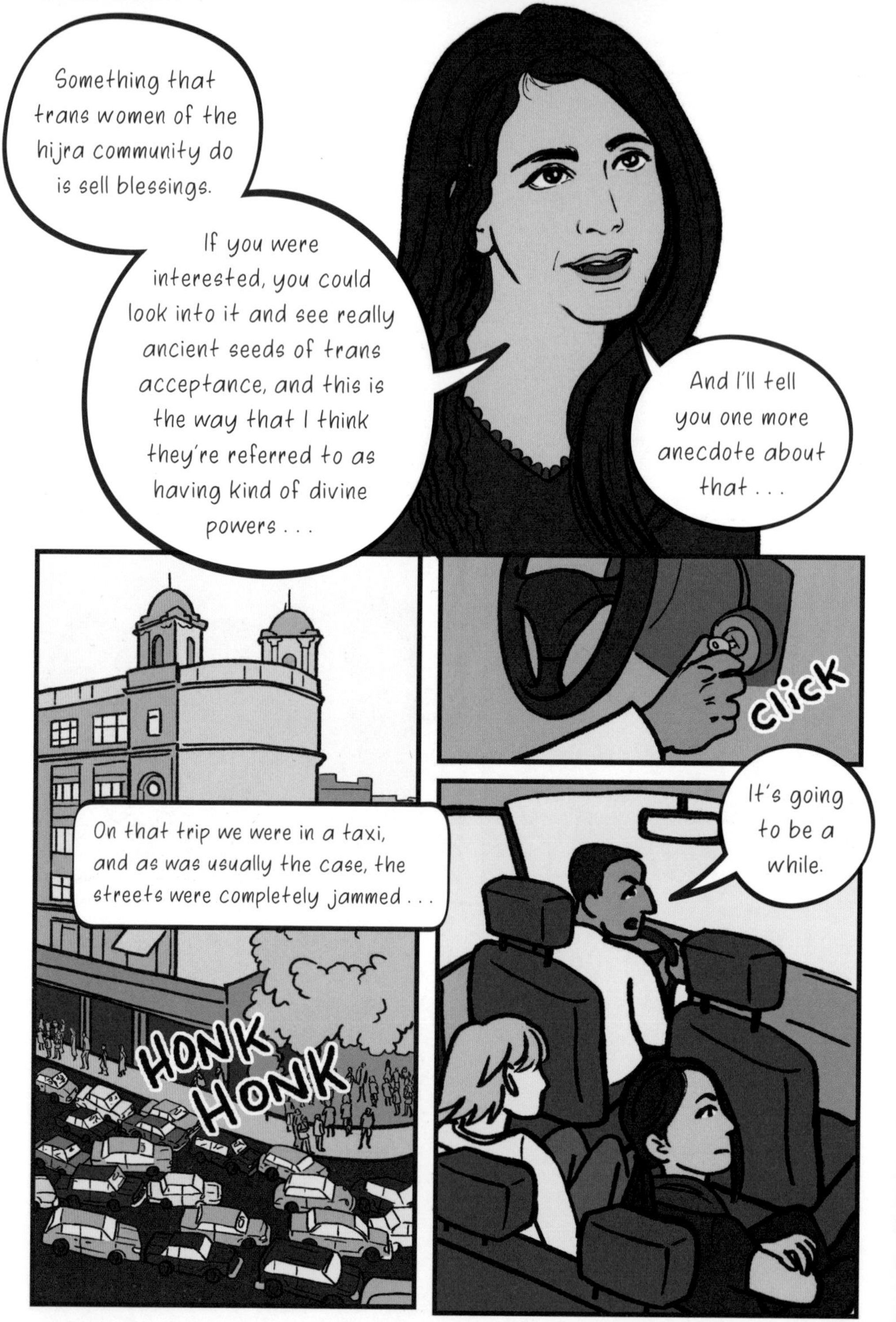
Something that trans women of the hijra community do is sell blessings.
If you were interested, you could look into it and see really ancient seeds of trans acceptance, and this is the way that I think they're referred to as having kind of divine powers . . .
And I'll tell you one more anecdote about that . . .
On that trip we were in a taxi, and as was usually the case, the streets were completely jammed . . .
HONK HONK
CLICK
It's going to be a while.

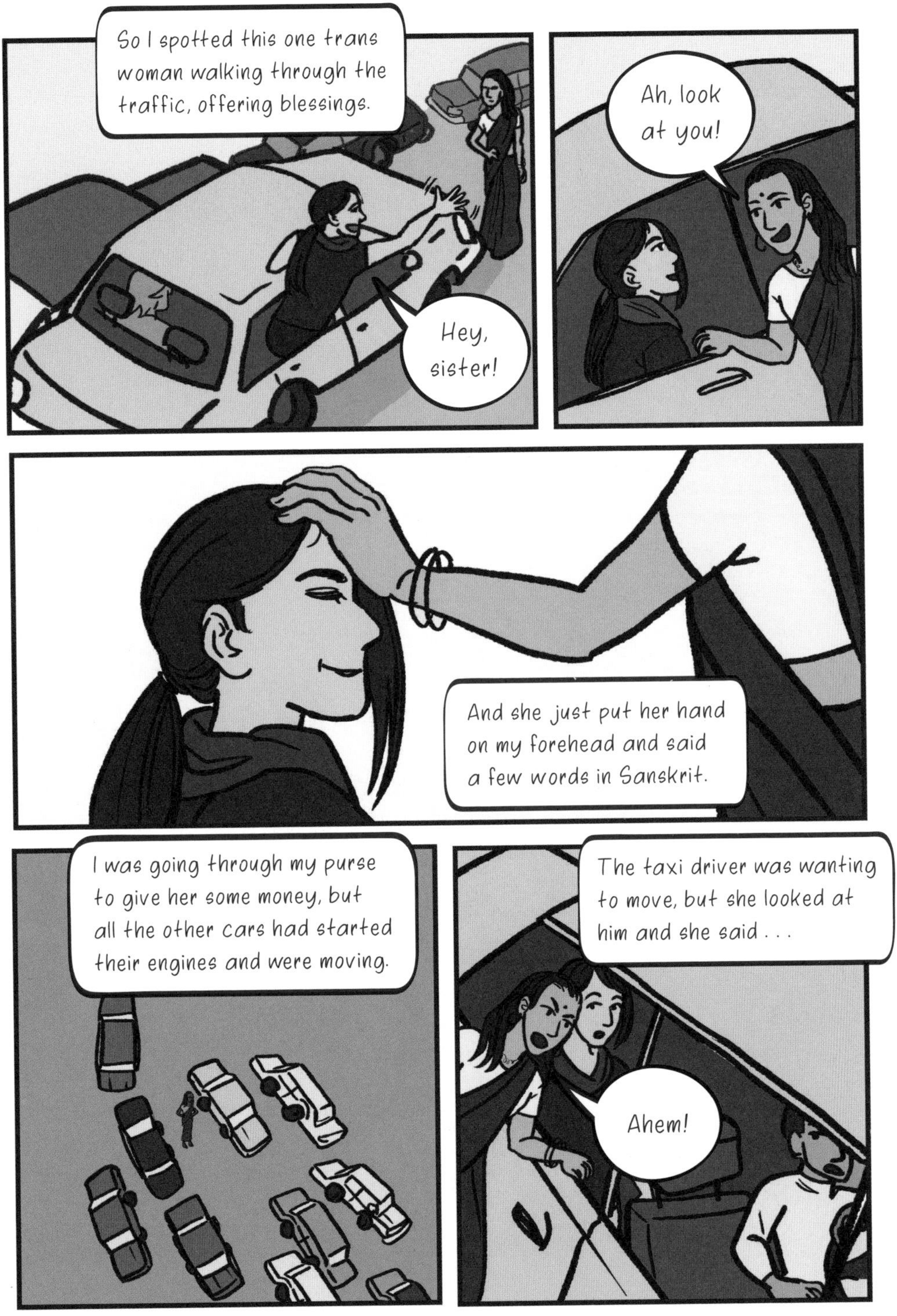
So I spotted this one trans woman walking through the traffic, offering blessings.
Hey, sister!
Ah, look at you!
And she just put her hand on my forehead and said a few words in Sanskrit.
I was going through my purse to give her some money, but all the other cars had started their engines and were moving.
The taxi driver was wanting to move, but she looked at him and she said . . .
Ahem!

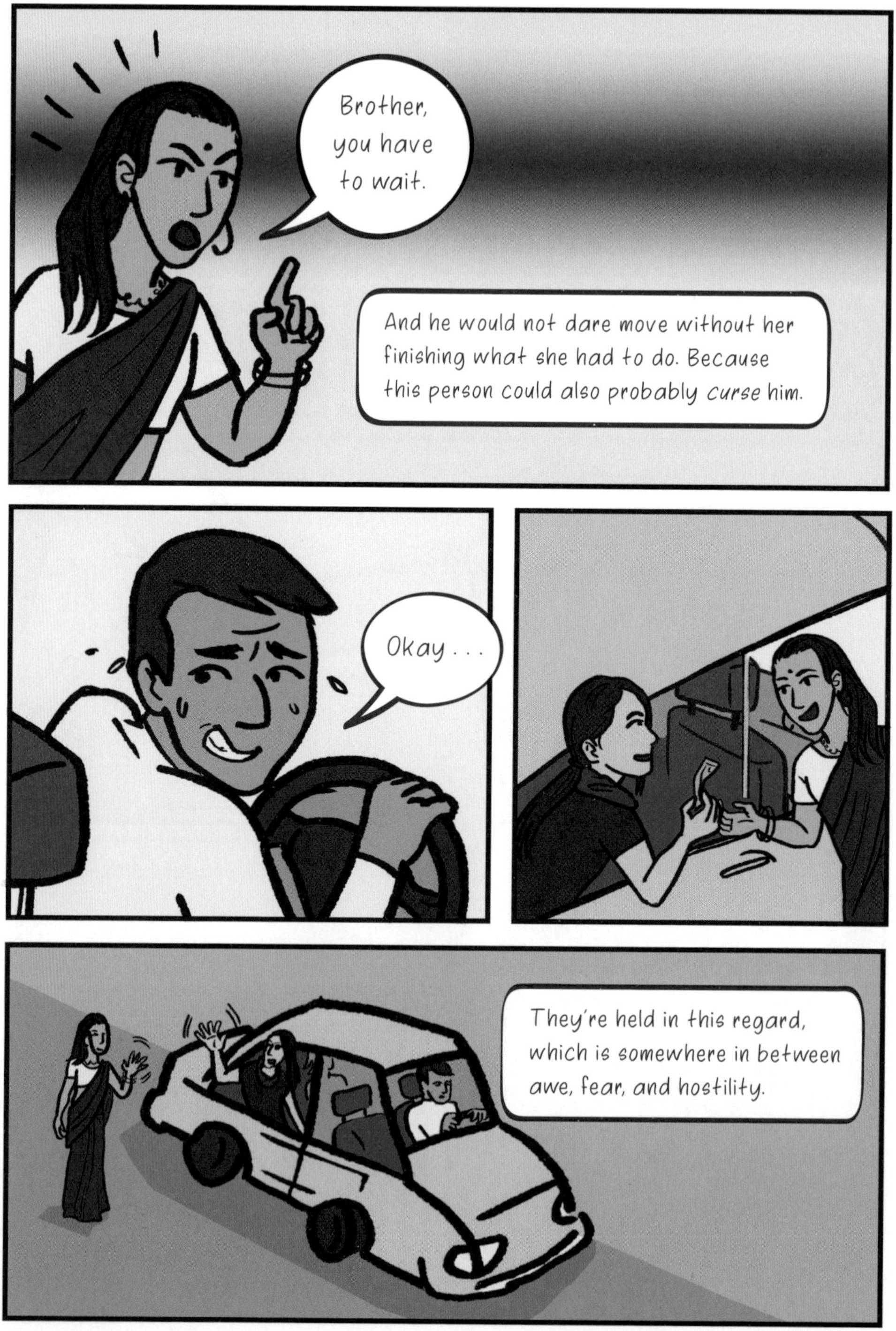
Brother, you have to wait.
And he would not dare move without her finishing what she had to do. Because this person could also probably *curse* him.
Okay . . .
They're held in this regard, which is somewhere in between awe, fear, and hostility.

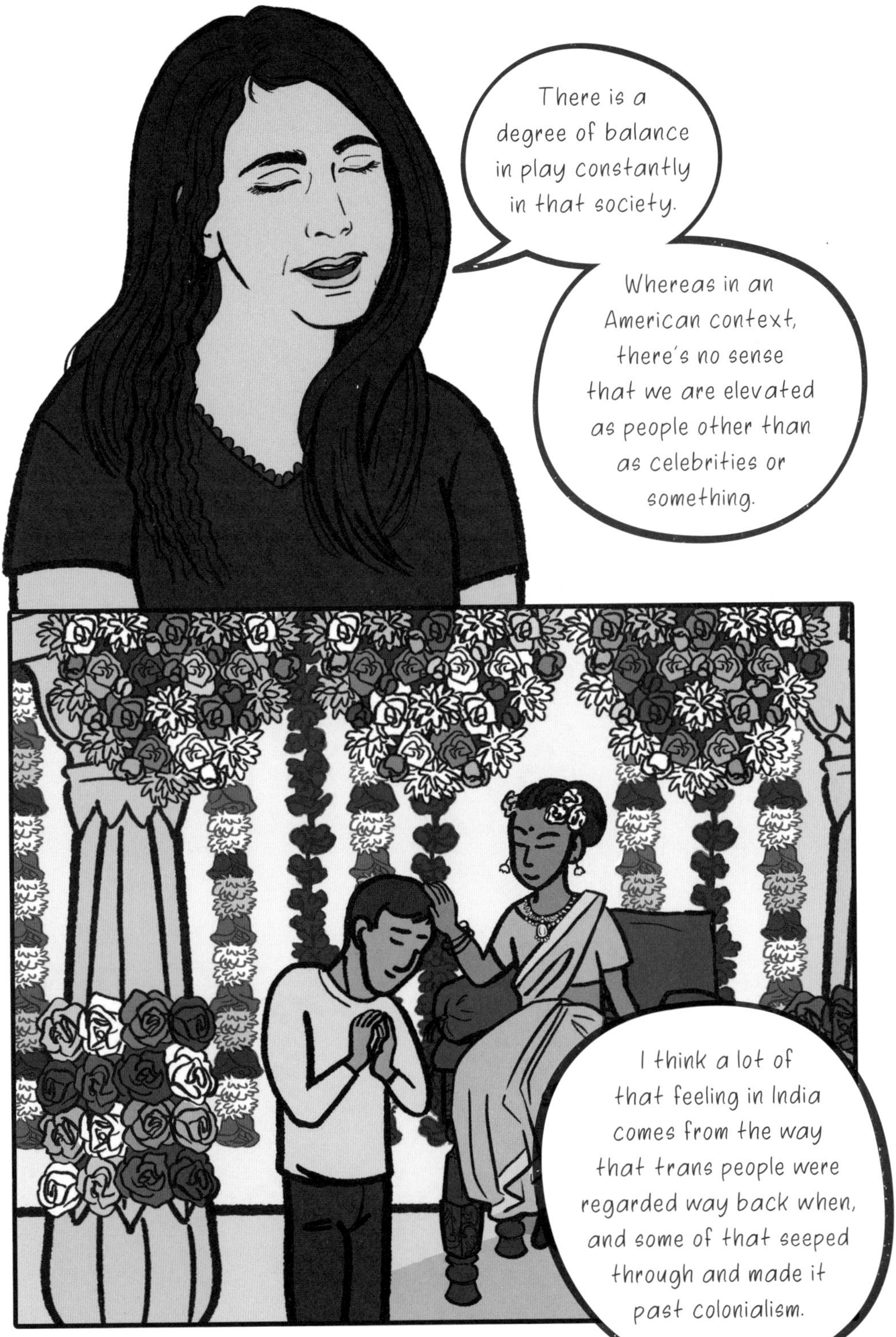
There is a degree of balance in play constantly in that society.
Whereas in an American context, there's no sense that we are elevated as people other than as celebrities or something.
I think a lot of that feeling in India comes from the way that trans people were regarded way back when, and some of that seeped through and made it past colonialism.

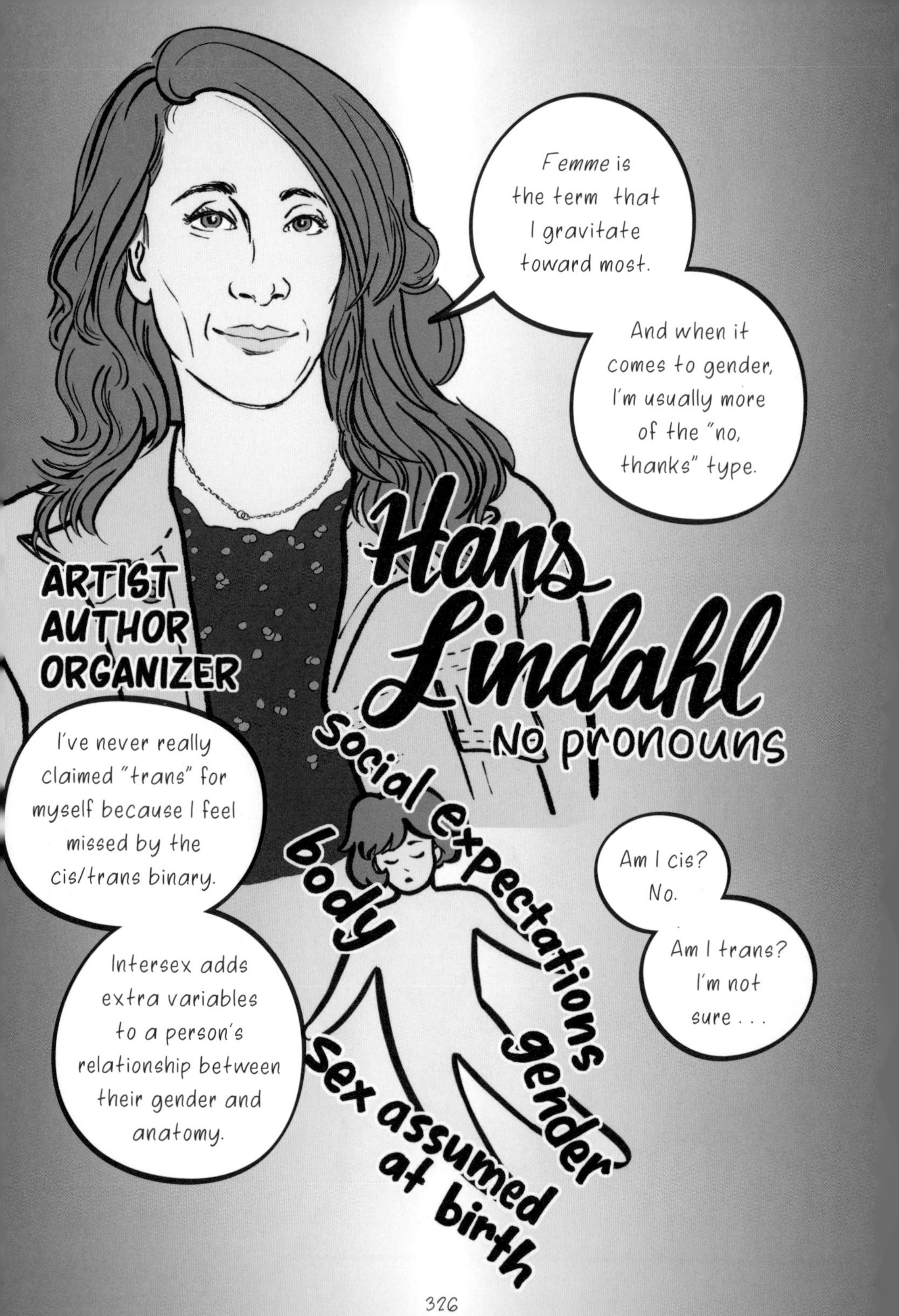

Femme is the term that I gravitate toward most.
And when it comes to gender, I'm usually more of the "no, thanks" type.
Hans Lindahl
No pronouns
ARTIST
AUTHOR
ORGANIZER
I've never really claimed "trans" for myself because I feel missed by the cis/trans binary.
Intersex adds extra variables to a person's relationship between their gender and anatomy.
social expectations
body
gender
sex assumed at birth
Am I cis? No.
Am I trans? I'm not sure . . .

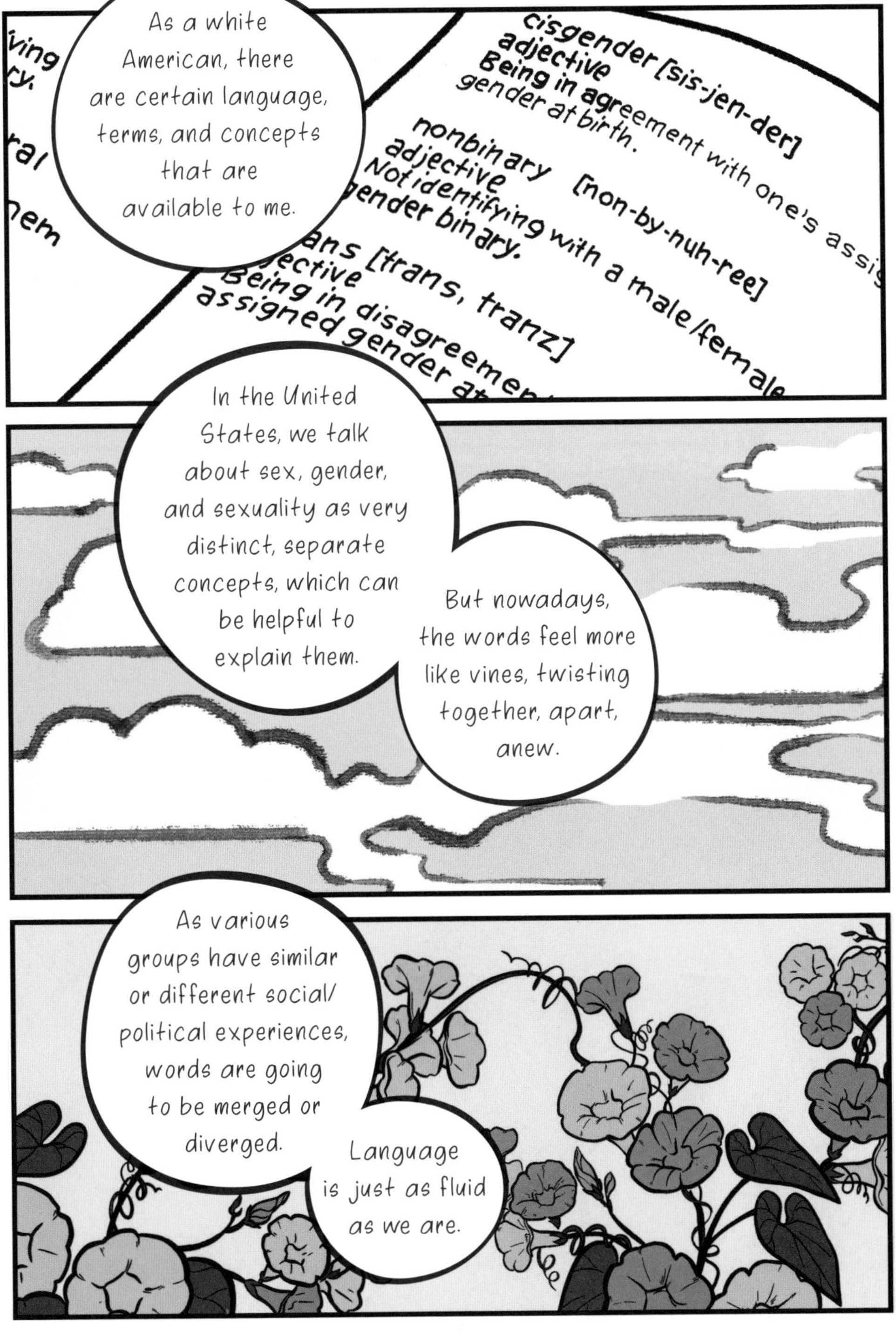
As a white American, there are certain language, terms, and concepts that are available to me.
cisgender [sis-jen-der]
adjective
Being in agreement with one's assi
gender at birth.
nonbinary [non-by-nuh-ree]
adjective
Not identifying with a male/female
gender binary.
ans [trans, tranz]
jective
Being in disagreemen
assigned gender at
In the United States, we talk about sex, gender, and sexuality as very distinct, separate concepts, which can be helpful to explain them.
But nowadays, the words feel more like vines, twisting together, apart, anew.
As various groups have similar or different social/political experiences, words are going to be merged or diverged.
Language is just as fluid as we are.

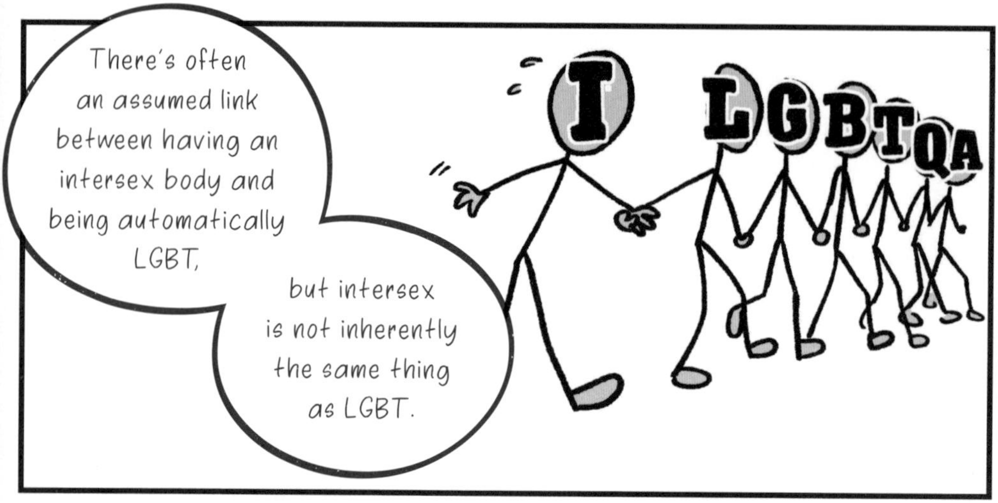
There's often an assumed link between having an intersex body and being automatically LGBT,
but intersex is not inherently the same thing as LGBT.
I
LGBTQA

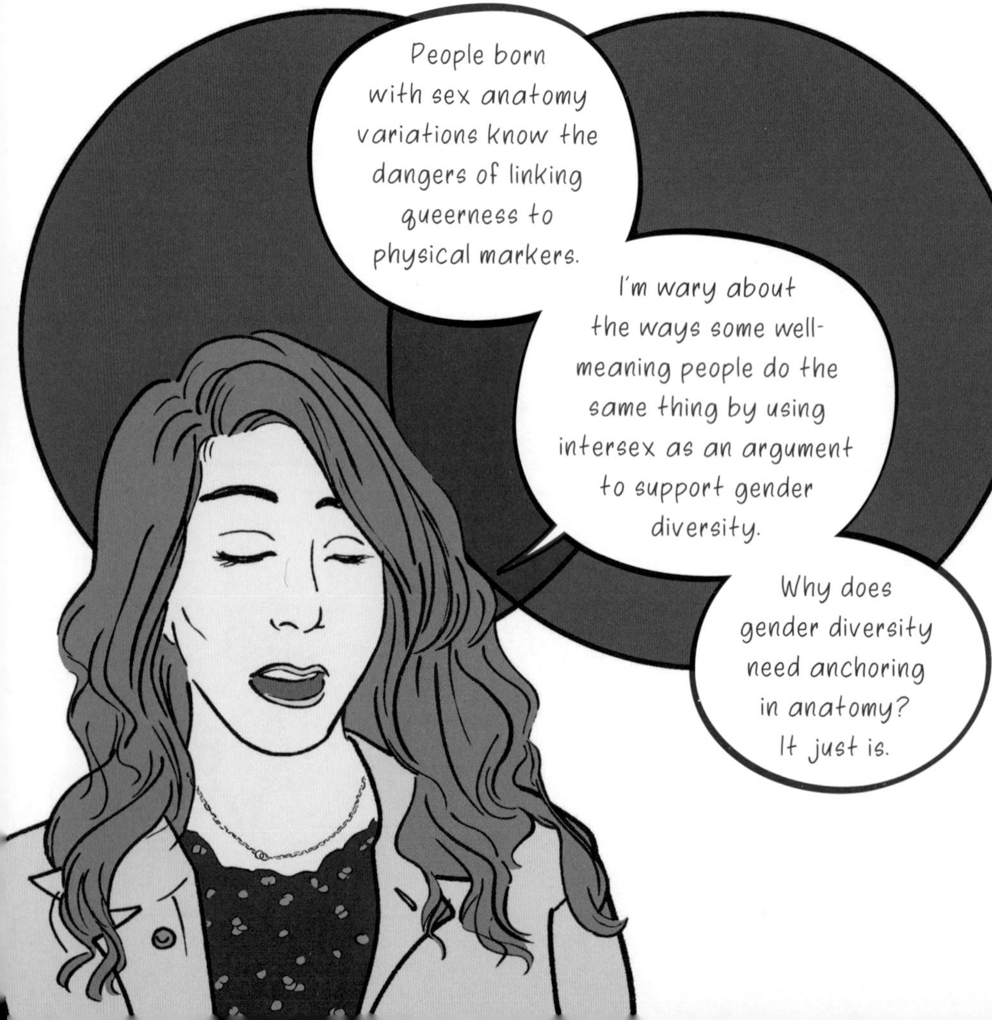
People born with sex anatomy variations know the dangers of linking queerness to physical markers.
I'm wary about the ways some well-meaning people do the same thing by using intersex as an argument to support gender diversity.
Why does gender diversity need anchoring in anatomy? It just is.

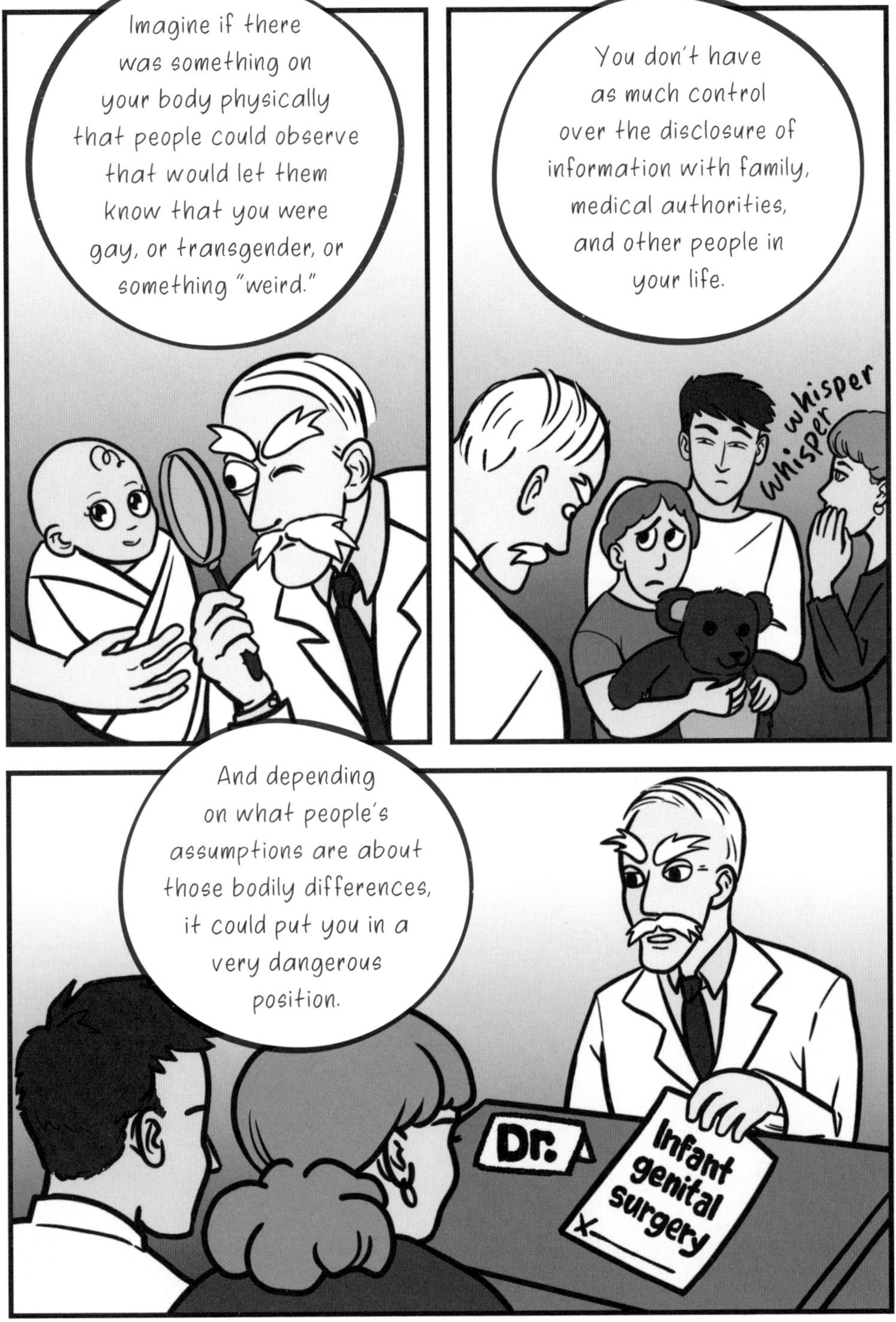
Imagine if there was something on your body physically that people could observe that would let them know that you were gay, or transgender, or something "weird."
You don't have as much control over the disclosure of information with family, medical authorities, and other people in your life.
whisper whisper
And depending on what people's assumptions are about those bodily differences, it could put you in a very dangerous position.
Dr.
Infant genital surgery
X

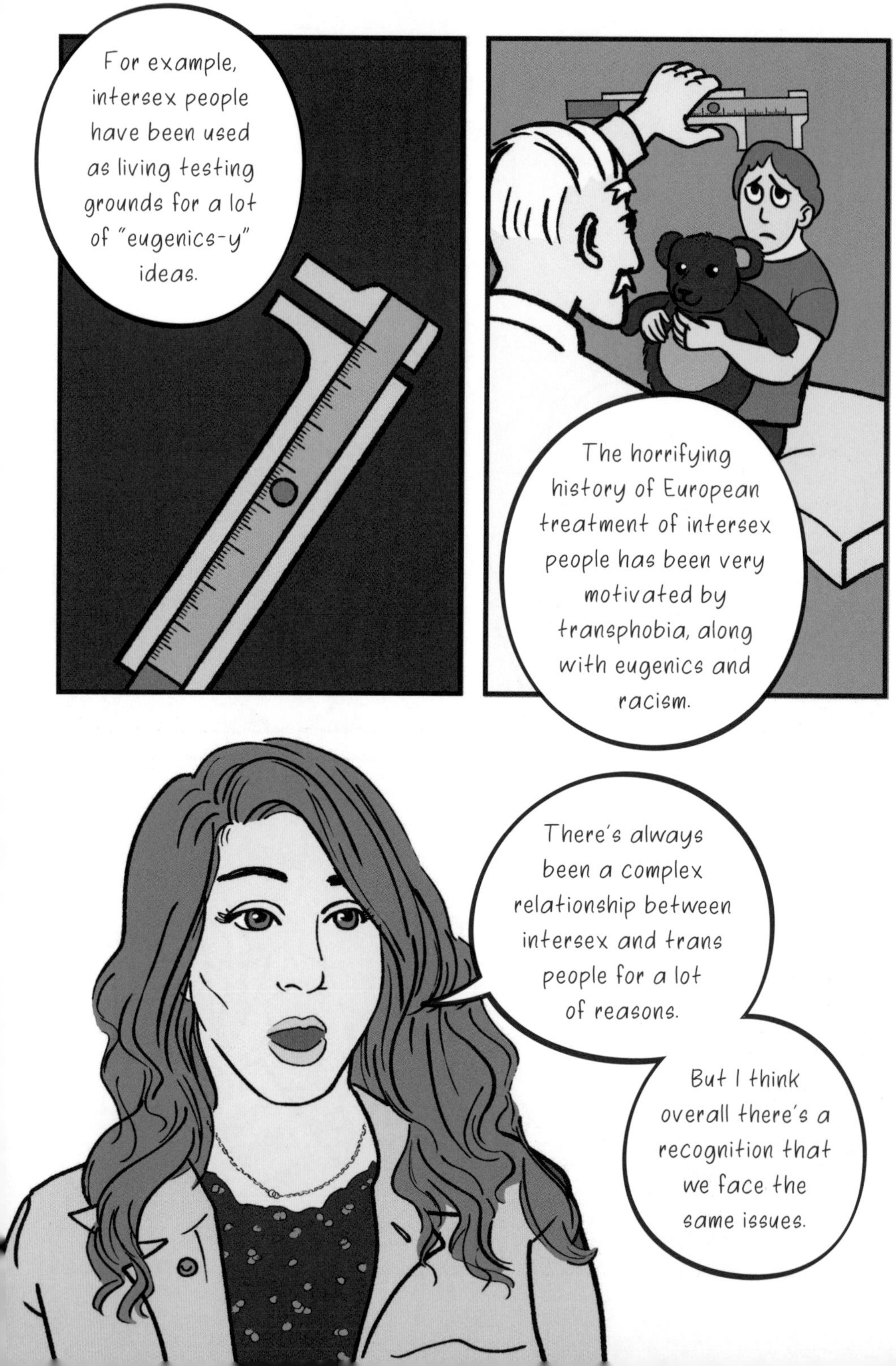
For example, intersex people have been used as living testing grounds for a lot of "eugenics-y" ideas.
The horrifying history of European treatment of intersex people has been very motivated by transphobia, along with eugenics and racism.
There's always been a complex relationship between intersex and trans people for a lot of reasons.
But I think overall there's a recognition that we face the same issues.

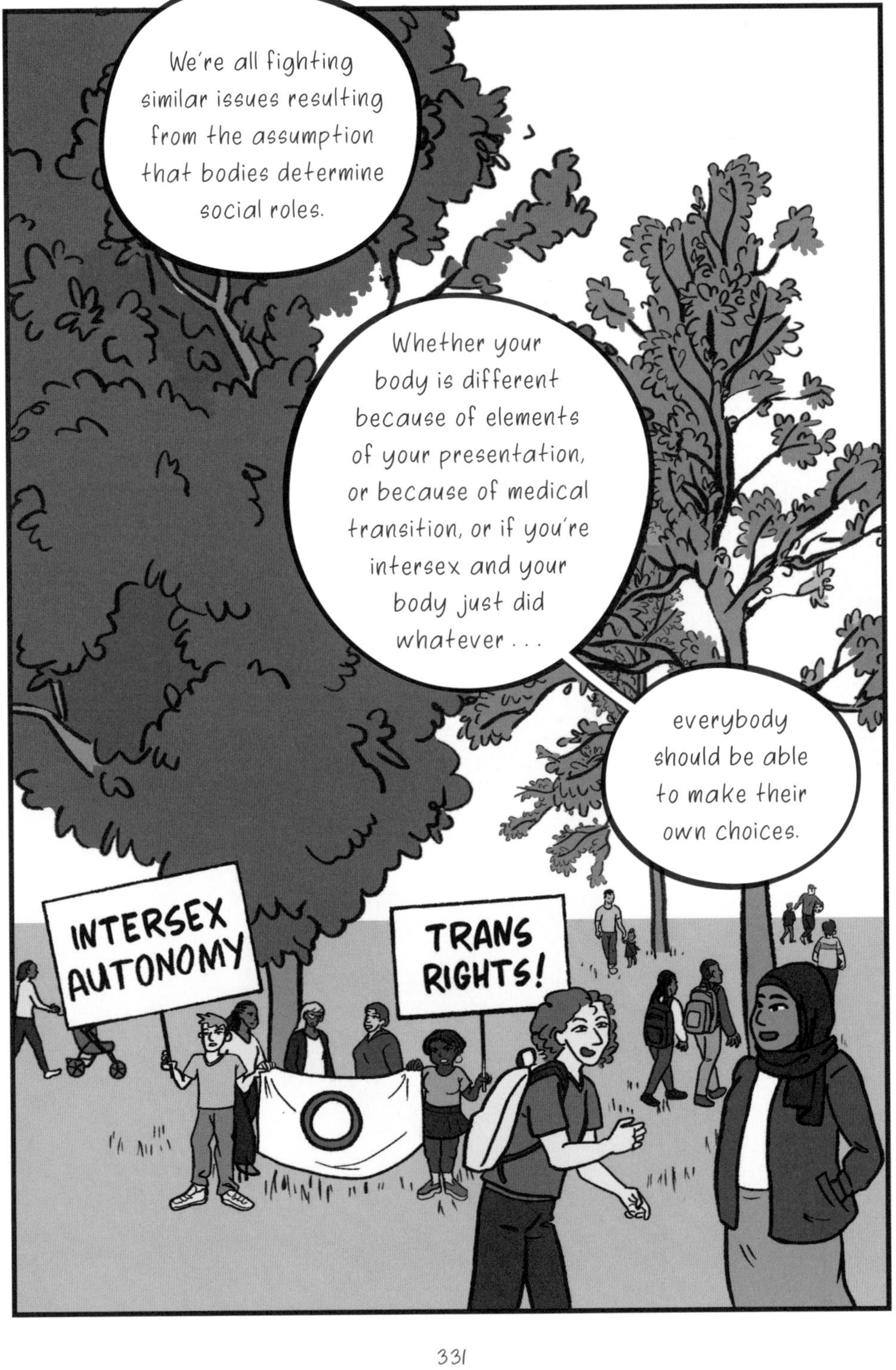
We're all fighting similar issues resulting from the assumption that bodies determine social roles.
Whether your body is different because of elements of your presentation, or because of medical transition, or if you're intersex and your body just did whatever . . .
everybody should be able to make their own choices.
INTERSEX AUTONOMY
TRANS RIGHTS!

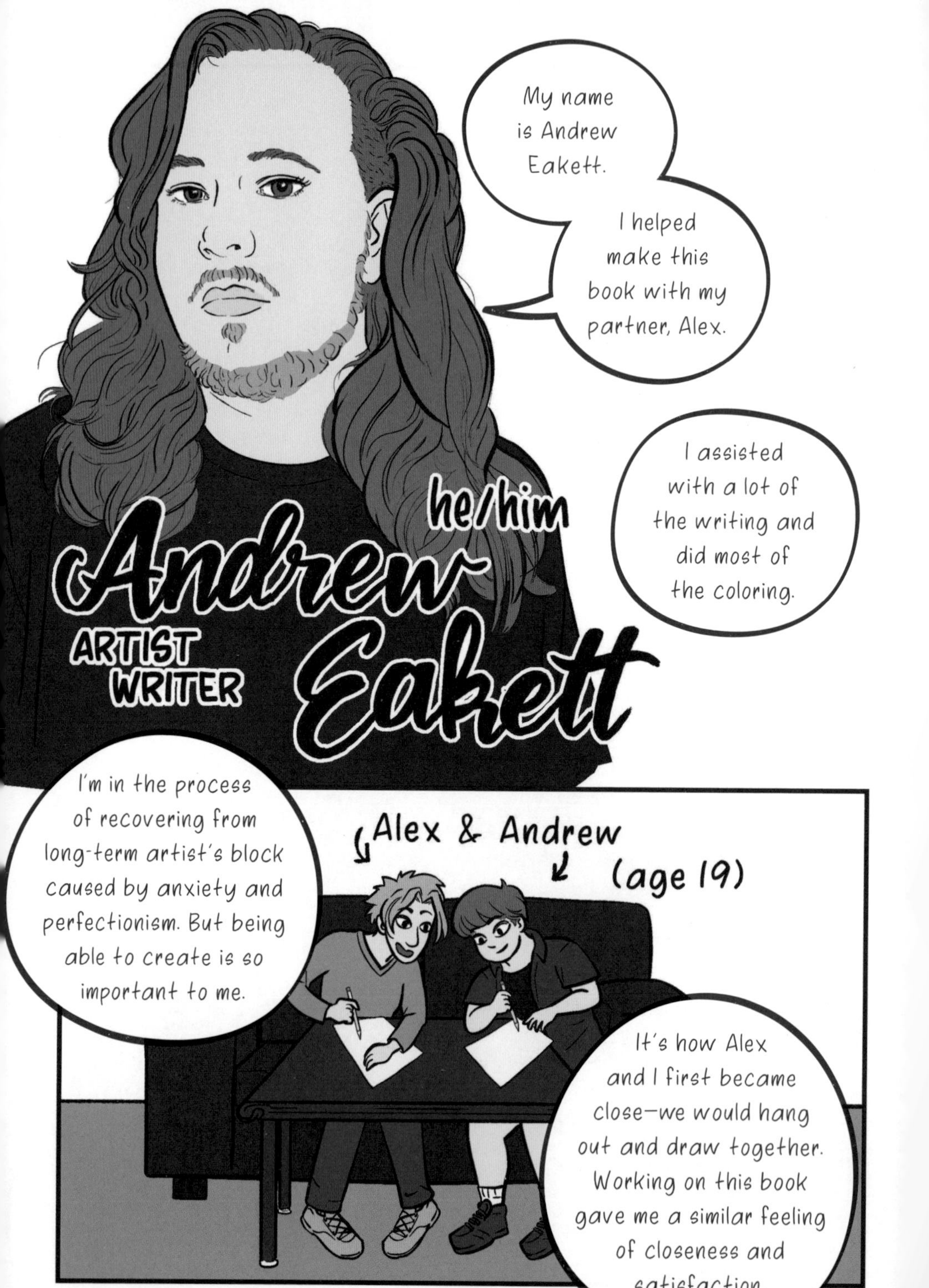
My name is Andrew Eakett.
I helped make this book with my partner, Alex.
he/him
Andrew Eakett
ARTIST
WRITER
I assisted with a lot of the writing and did most of the coloring.
I'm in the process of recovering from long-term artist's block caused by anxiety and perfectionism. But being able to create is so important to me.
Alex & Andrew
(age 19)
It's how Alex and I first became close—we would hang out and draw together. Working on this book gave me a similar feeling of closeness and satisfaction.

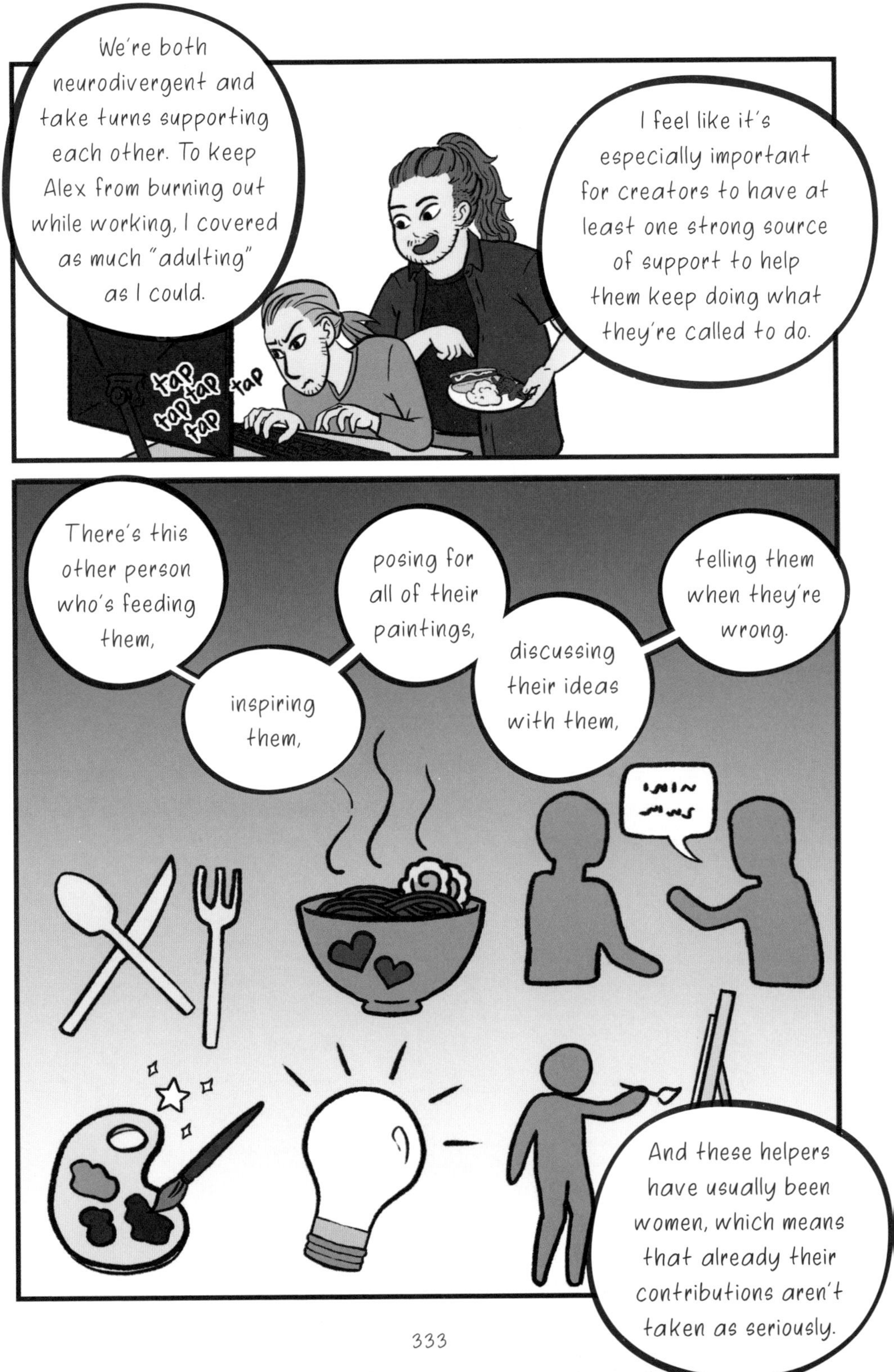
We're both neurodivergent and take turns supporting each other. To keep Alex from burning out while working, I covered as much "adulting" as I could.
I feel like it's especially important for creators to have at least one strong source of support to help them keep doing what they're called to do.
tap tap tap tap tap
There's this other person who's feeding them,
inspiring them,
posing for all of their paintings,
discussing their ideas with them,
telling them when they're wrong.
And these helpers have usually been women, which means that already their contributions aren't taken as seriously.

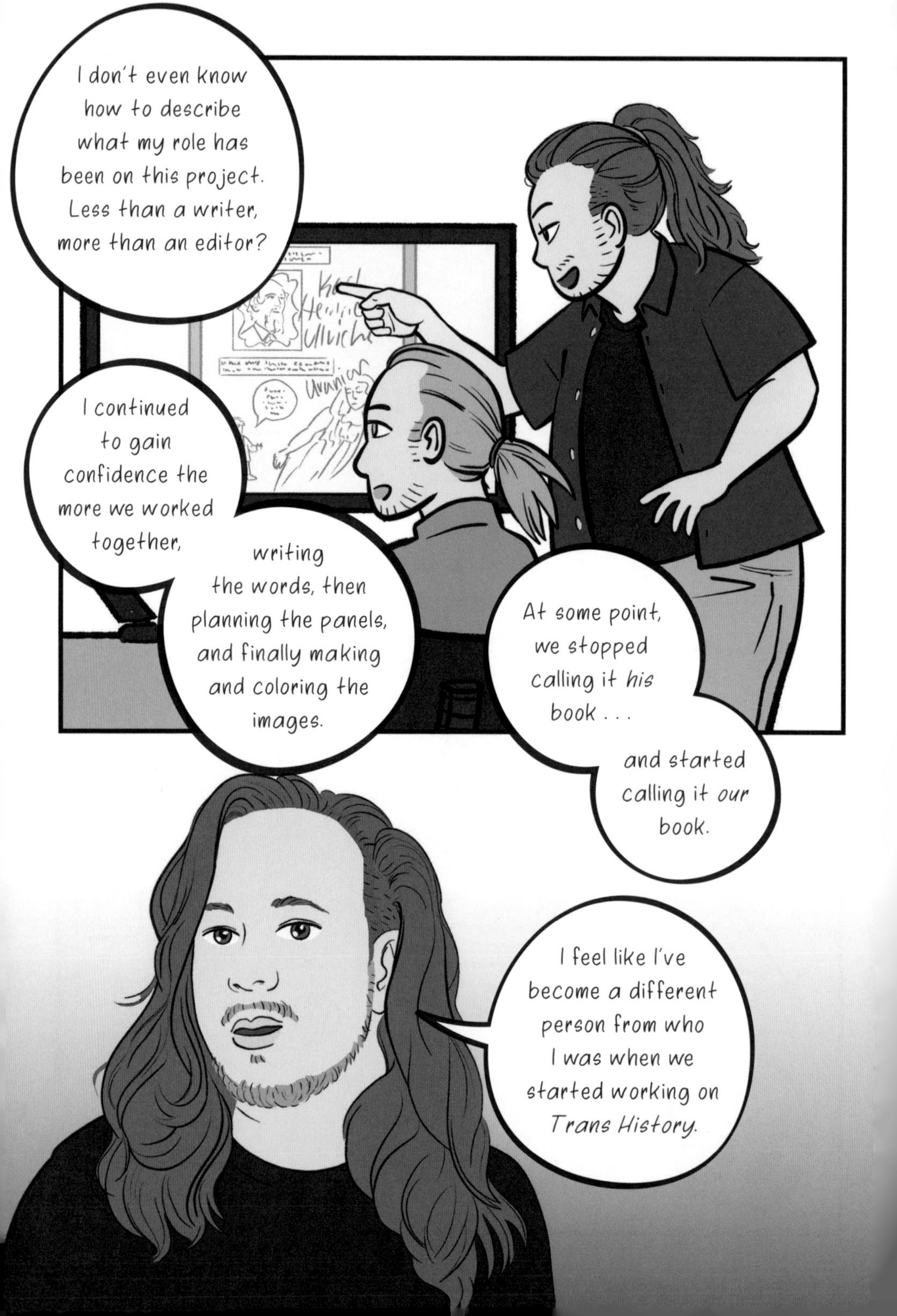
I don't even know how to describe what my role has been on this project. Less than a writer, more than an editor?
I continued to gain confidence the more we worked together,
writing the words, then planning the panels, and finally making and coloring the images.
At some point, we stopped calling it *his* book . . .
and started calling it *our* book.
I feel like I've become a different person from who I was when we started working on *Trans History*.

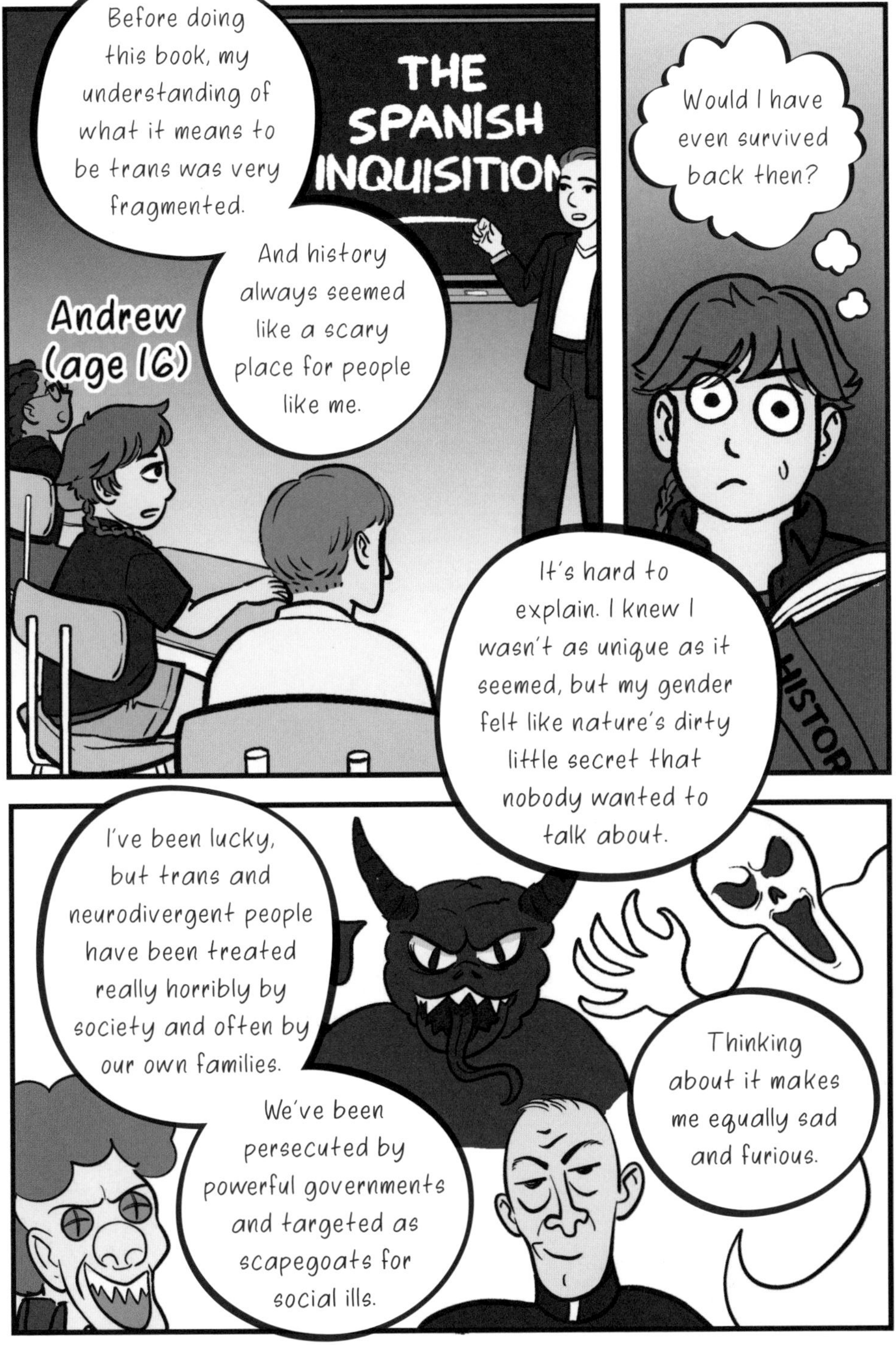
THE SPANISH INQUISITION
Before doing this book, my understanding of what it means to be trans was very fragmented.
And history always seemed like a scary place for people like me.
Andrew (age 16)
Would I have even survived back then?
HISTOR
It's hard to explain. I knew I wasn't as unique as it seemed, but my gender felt like nature's dirty little secret that nobody wanted to talk about.
I've been lucky, but trans and neurodivergent people have been treated really horribly by society and often by our own families.
We've been persecuted by powerful governments and targeted as scapegoats for social ills.
Thinking about it makes me equally sad and furious.

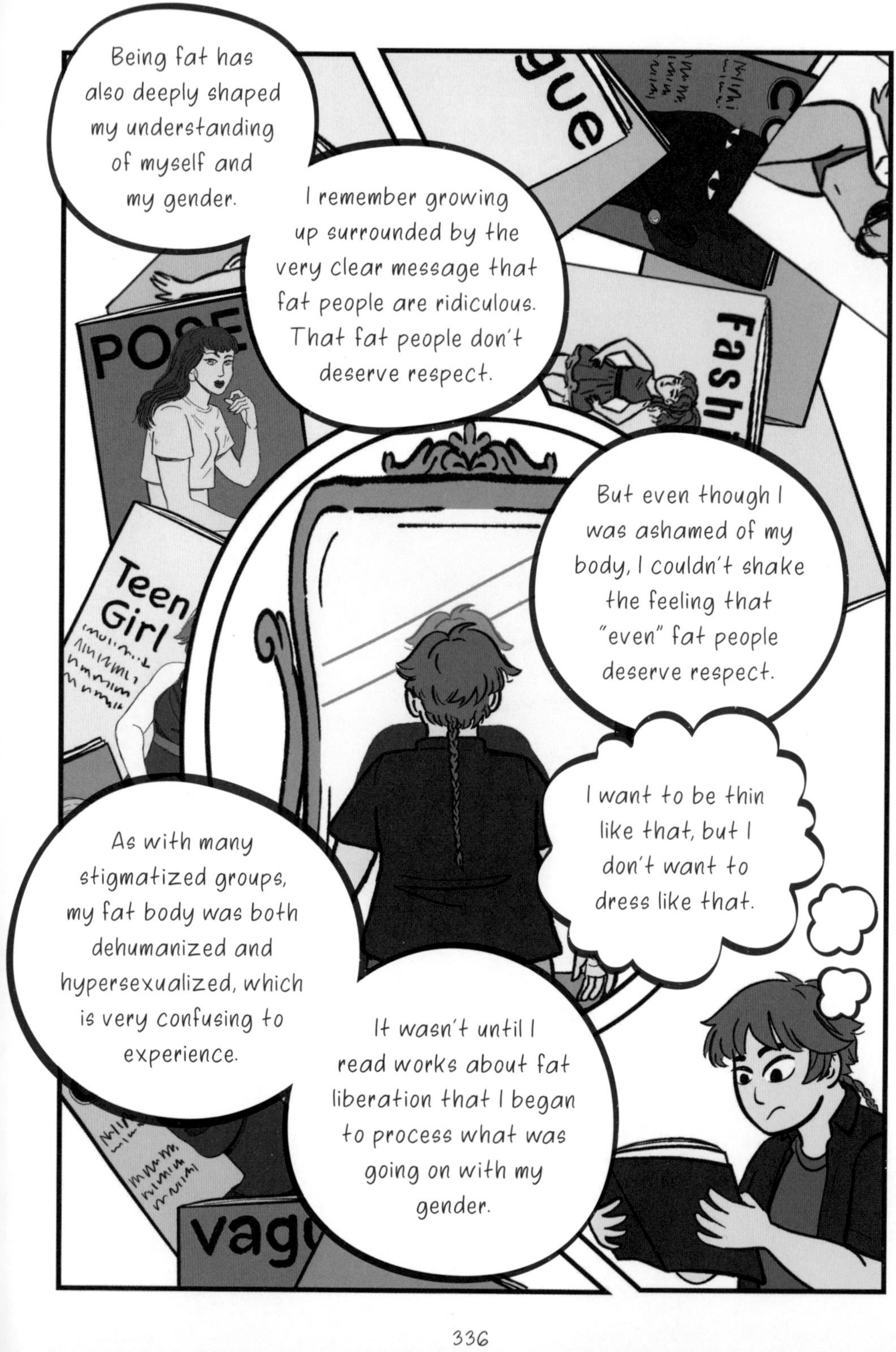

Being fat has also deeply shaped my understanding of myself and my gender.
I remember growing up surrounded by the very clear message that fat people are ridiculous. That fat people don't deserve respect.
POSE
Teen Girl
But even though I was ashamed of my body, I couldn't shake the feeling that "even" fat people deserve respect.
I want to be thin like that, but I don't want to dress like that.
As with many stigmatized groups, my fat body was both dehumanized and hypersexualized, which is very confusing to experience.
It wasn't until I read works about fat liberation that I began to process what was going on with my gender.

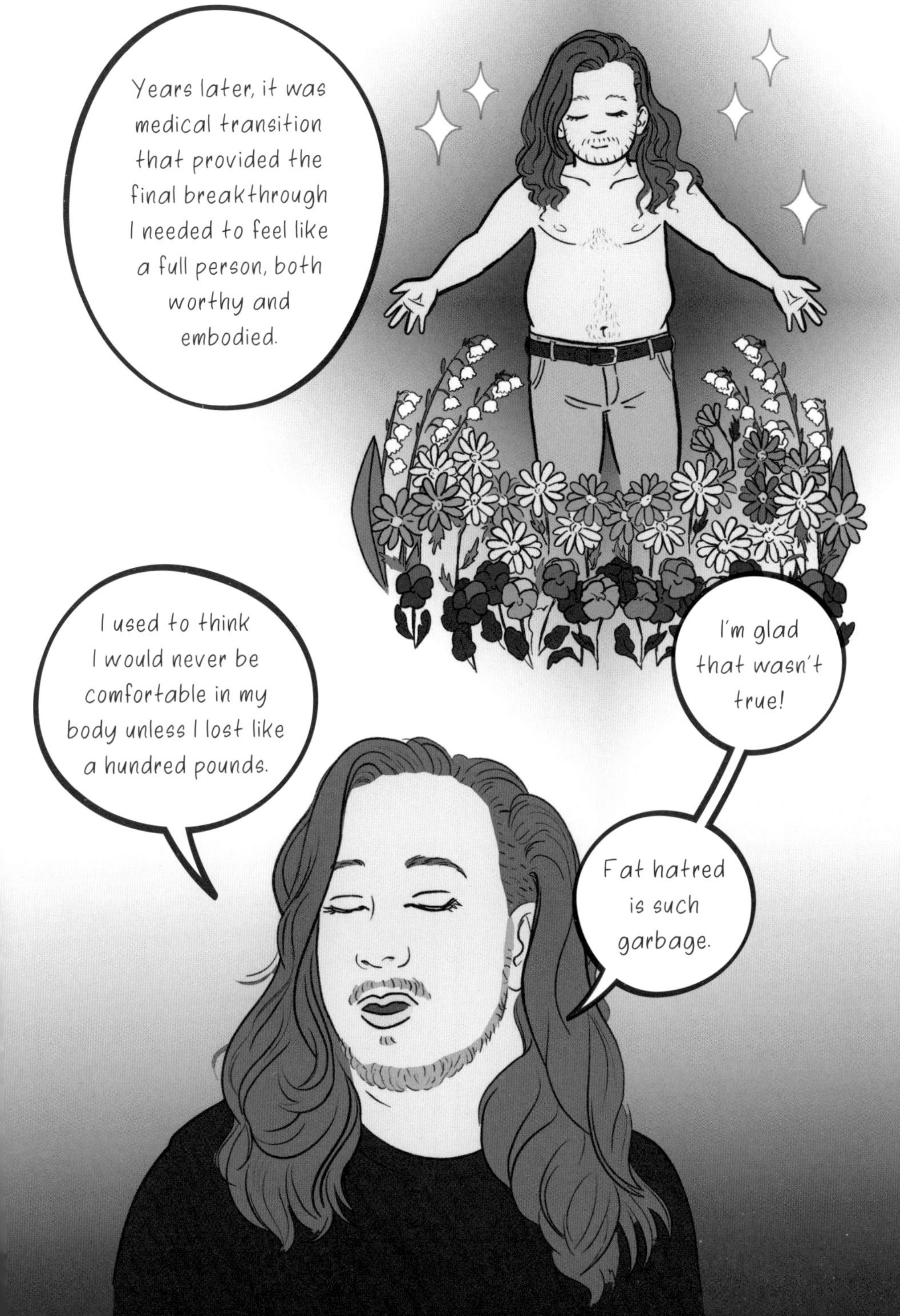
Years later, it was medical transition that provided the final breakthrough I needed to feel like a full person, both worthy and embodied.
I used to think I would never be comfortable in my body unless I lost like a hundred pounds.
I'm glad that wasn't true!
Fat hatred is such garbage.

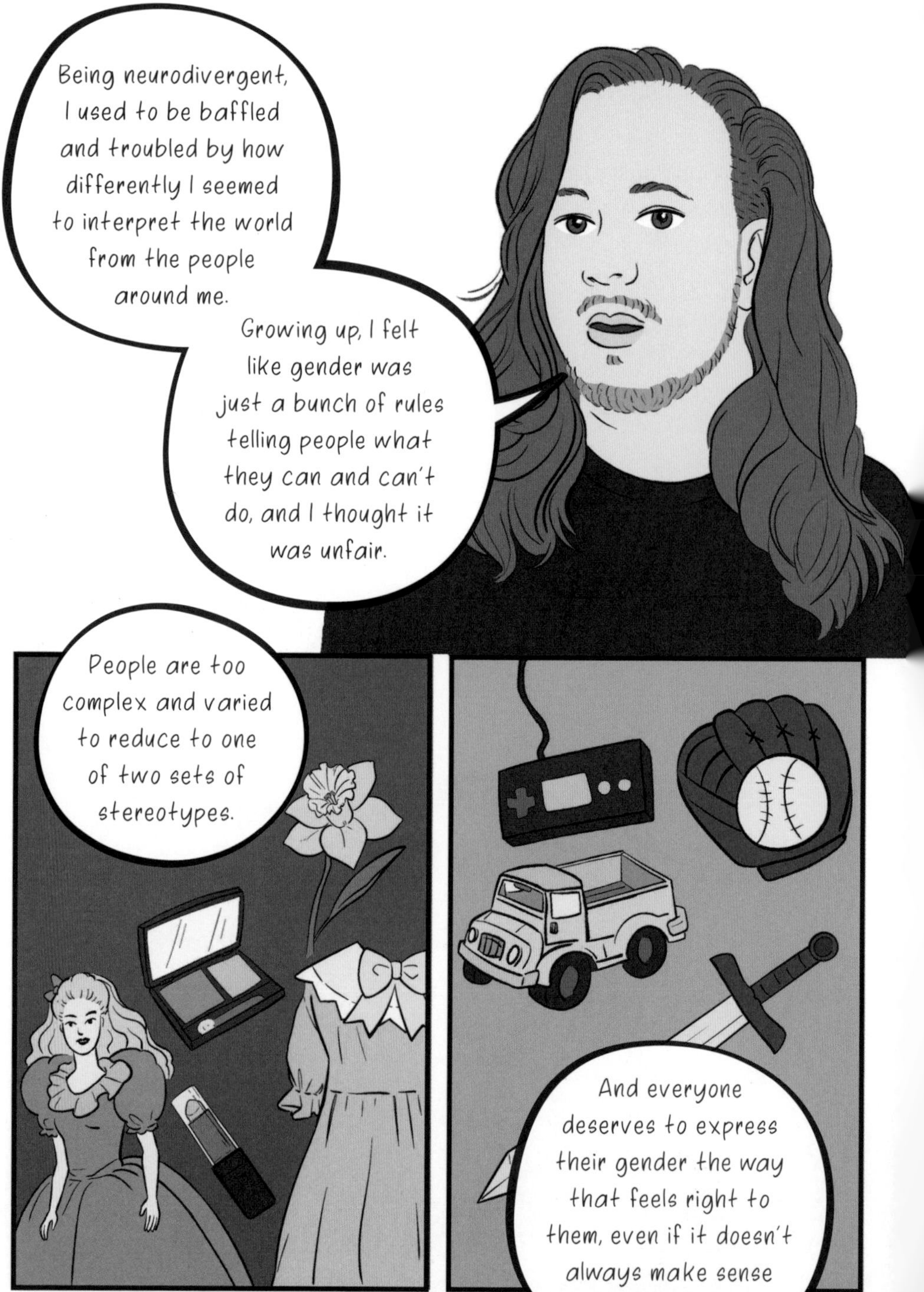
Being neurodivergent, I used to be baffled and troubled by how differently I seemed to interpret the world from the people around me.
Growing up, I felt like gender was just a bunch of rules telling people what they can and can't do, and I thought it was unfair.
People are too complex and varied to reduce to one of two sets of stereotypes.
And everyone deserves to express their gender the way that feels right to them, even if it doesn't always make sense to other people.

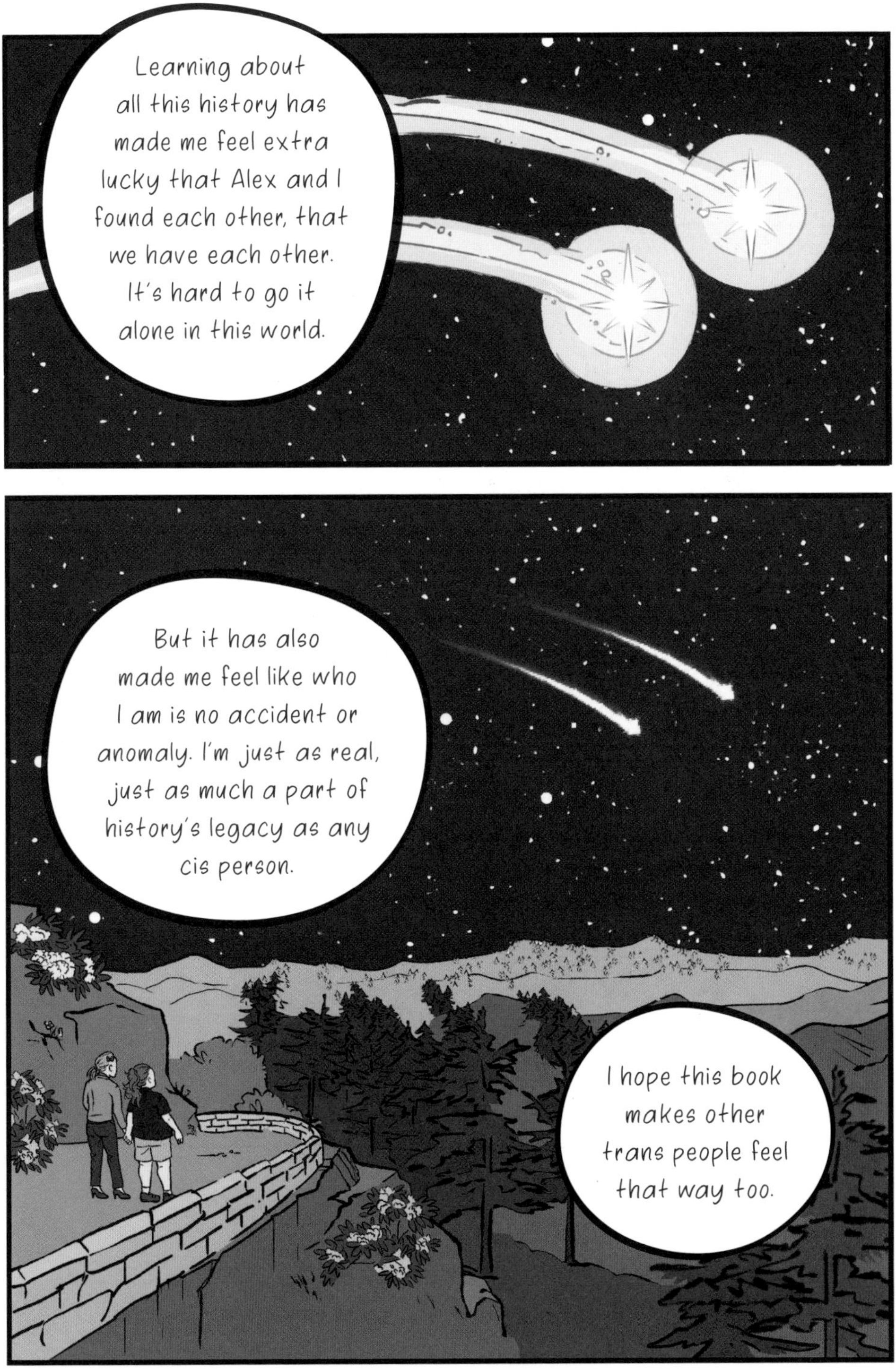
Learning about all this history has made me feel extra lucky that Alex and I found each other, that we have each other. It's hard to go it alone in this world.
But it has also made me feel like who I am is no accident or anomaly. I'm just as real, just as much a part of history's legacy as any cis person.
I hope this book makes other trans people feel that way too.

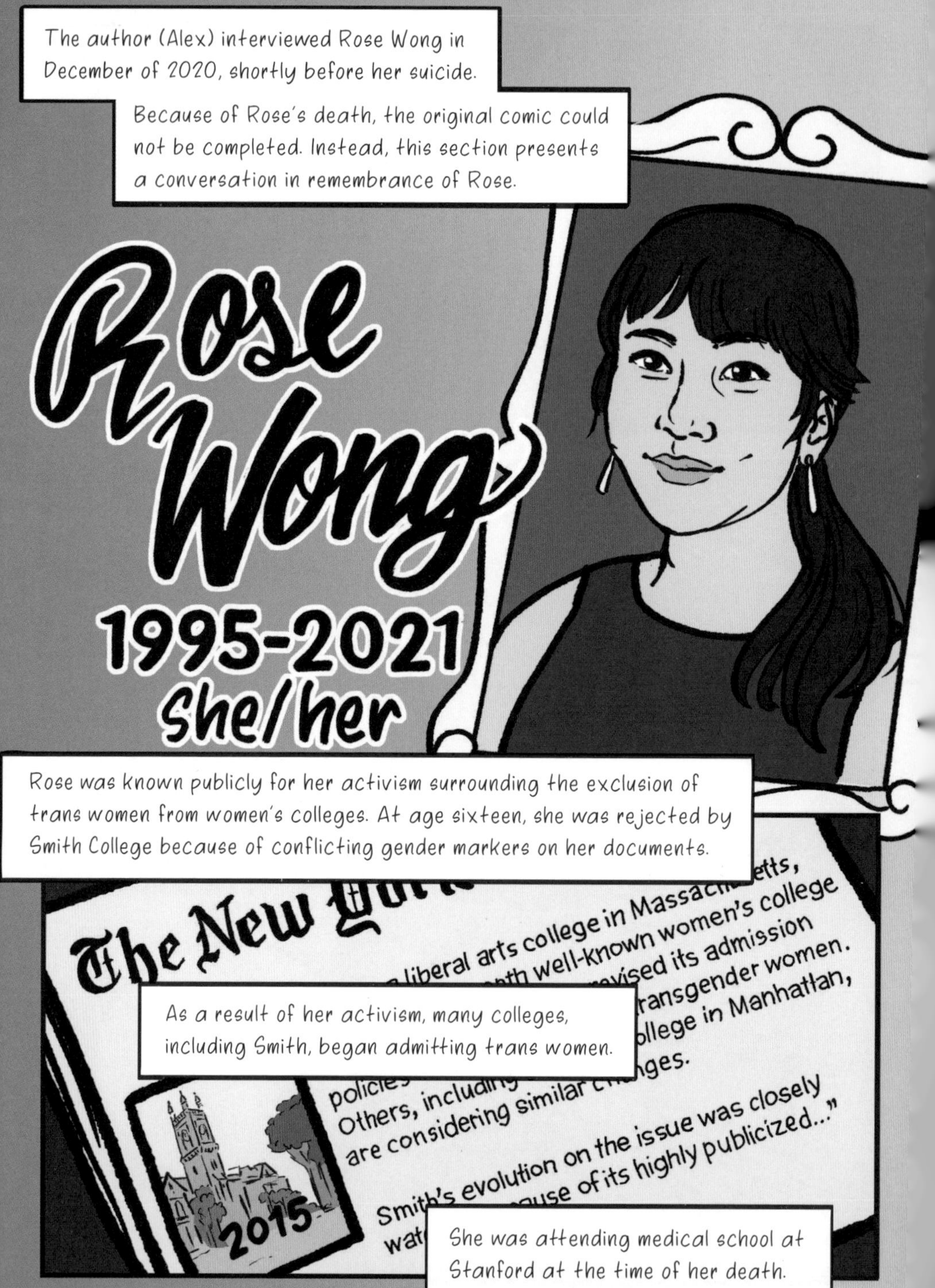
The author (Alex) interviewed Rose Wong in December of 2020, shortly before her suicide.
Because of Rose's death, the original comic could not be completed. Instead, this section presents a conversation in remembrance of Rose.
Rose Wong
1995-2021
she/her
Rose was known publicly for her activism surrounding the exclusion of trans women from women's colleges. At age sixteen, she was rejected by Smith College because of conflicting gender markers on her documents.
The New
liberal arts college in Massac
etts,
nth well-known women's college
vised its admission
ransgender women.
ollege in Manhattan,
ges.
policie
Others, includin
are considering similar c
Smith's evolution on the issue was closely
use of its highly publicized..."
wat
2015
As a result of her activism, many colleges, including Smith, began admitting trans women.
She was attending medical school at Stanford at the time of her death.

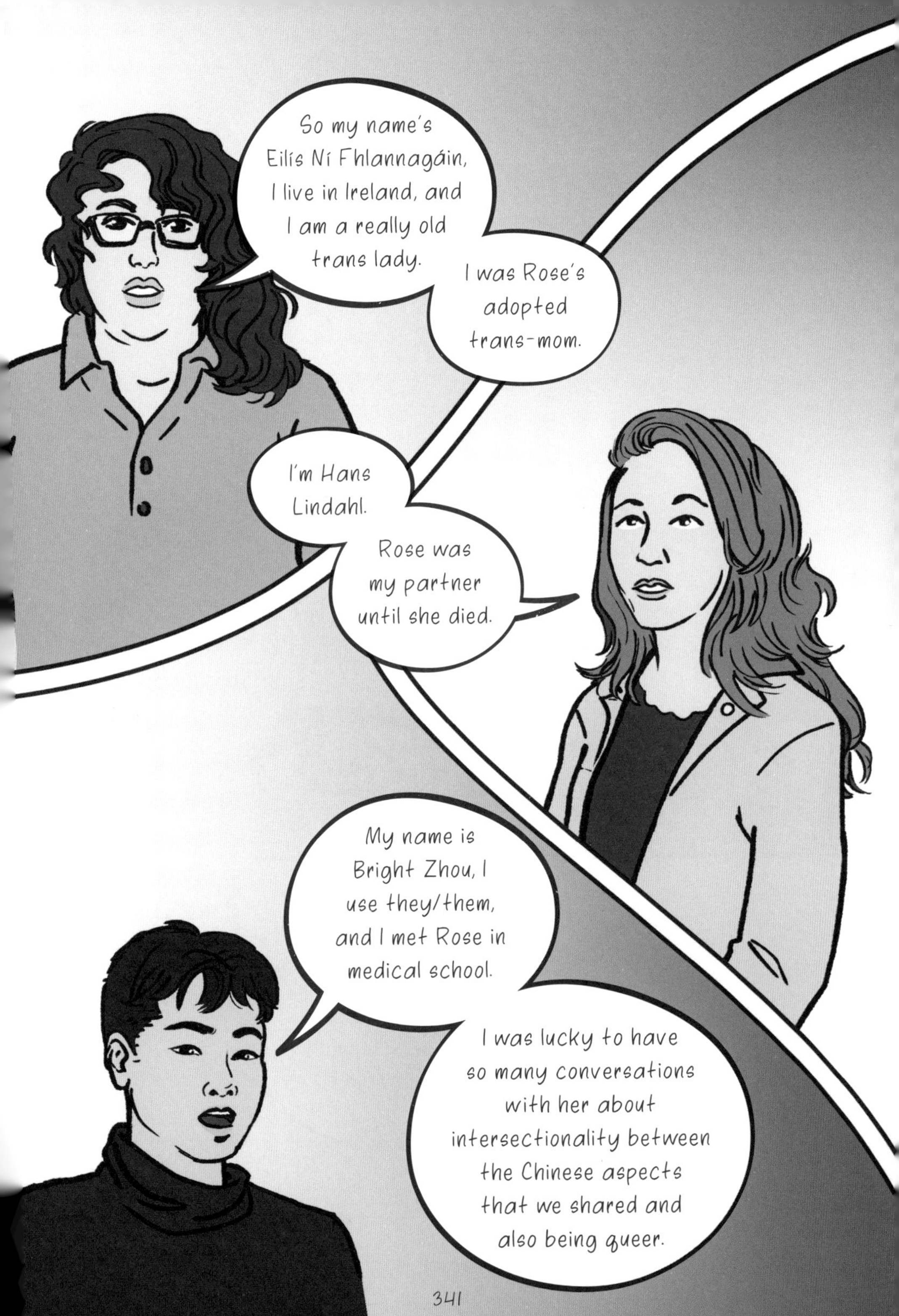
So my name's Eilís Ní Fhlannagáin, I live in Ireland, and I am a really old trans lady.
I was Rose's adopted trans-mom.
I'm Hans Lindahl.
Rose was my partner until she died.
My name is Bright Zhou, I use they/them, and I met Rose in medical school.
I was lucky to have so many conversations with her about intersectionality between the Chinese aspects that we shared and also being queer.

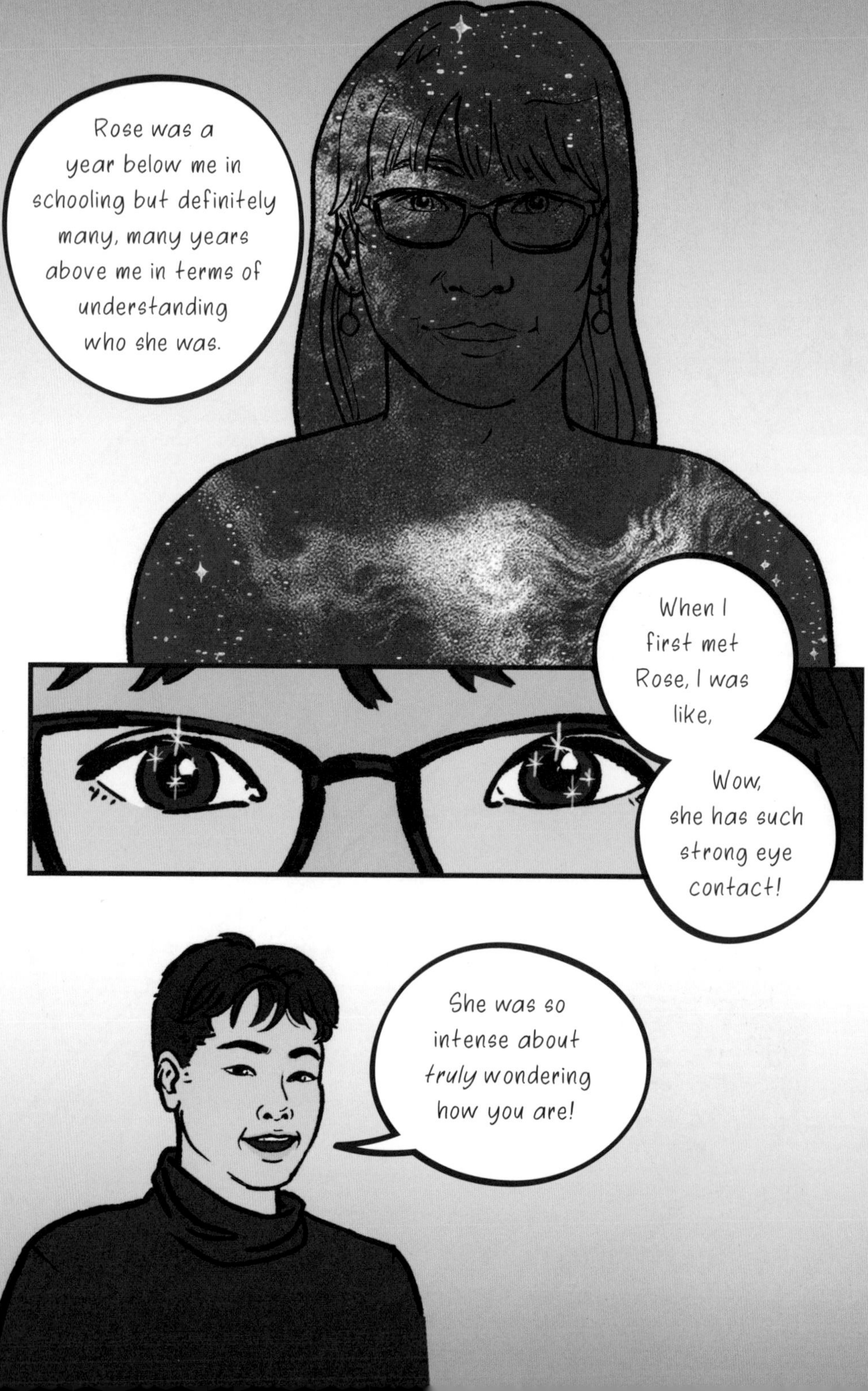
Rose was a year below me in schooling but definitely many, many years above me in terms of understanding who she was.
When I first met Rose, I was like,
Wow, she has such strong eye contact!
She was so intense about *truly* wondering how you are!

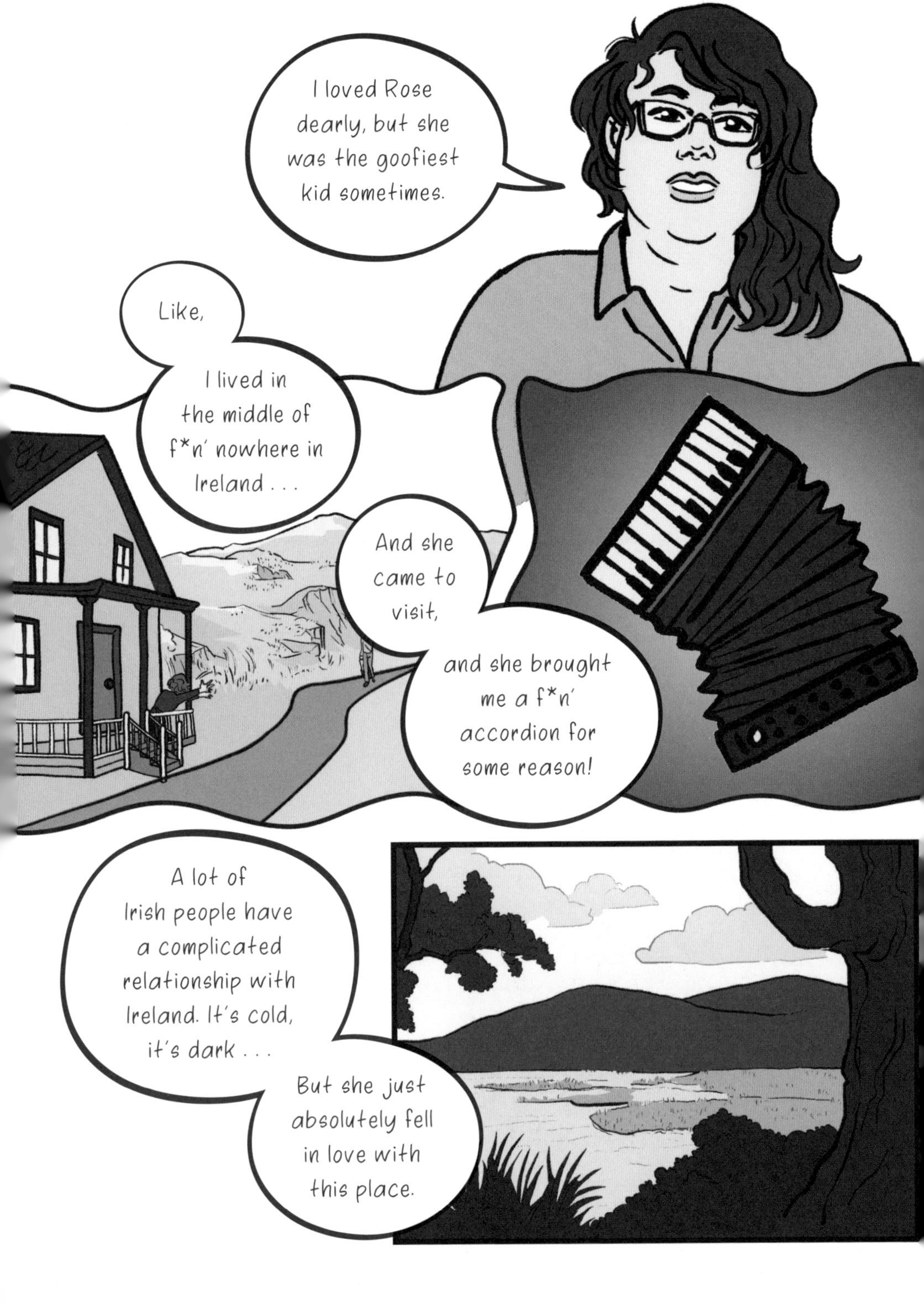
I loved Rose dearly, but she was the goofiest kid sometimes.
Like,
I lived in the middle of f*n' nowhere in Ireland . . .
And she came to visit,
and she brought me a f*n' accordion for some reason!
A lot of Irish people have a complicated relationship with Ireland. It's cold, it's dark . . .
But she just absolutely fell in love with this place.

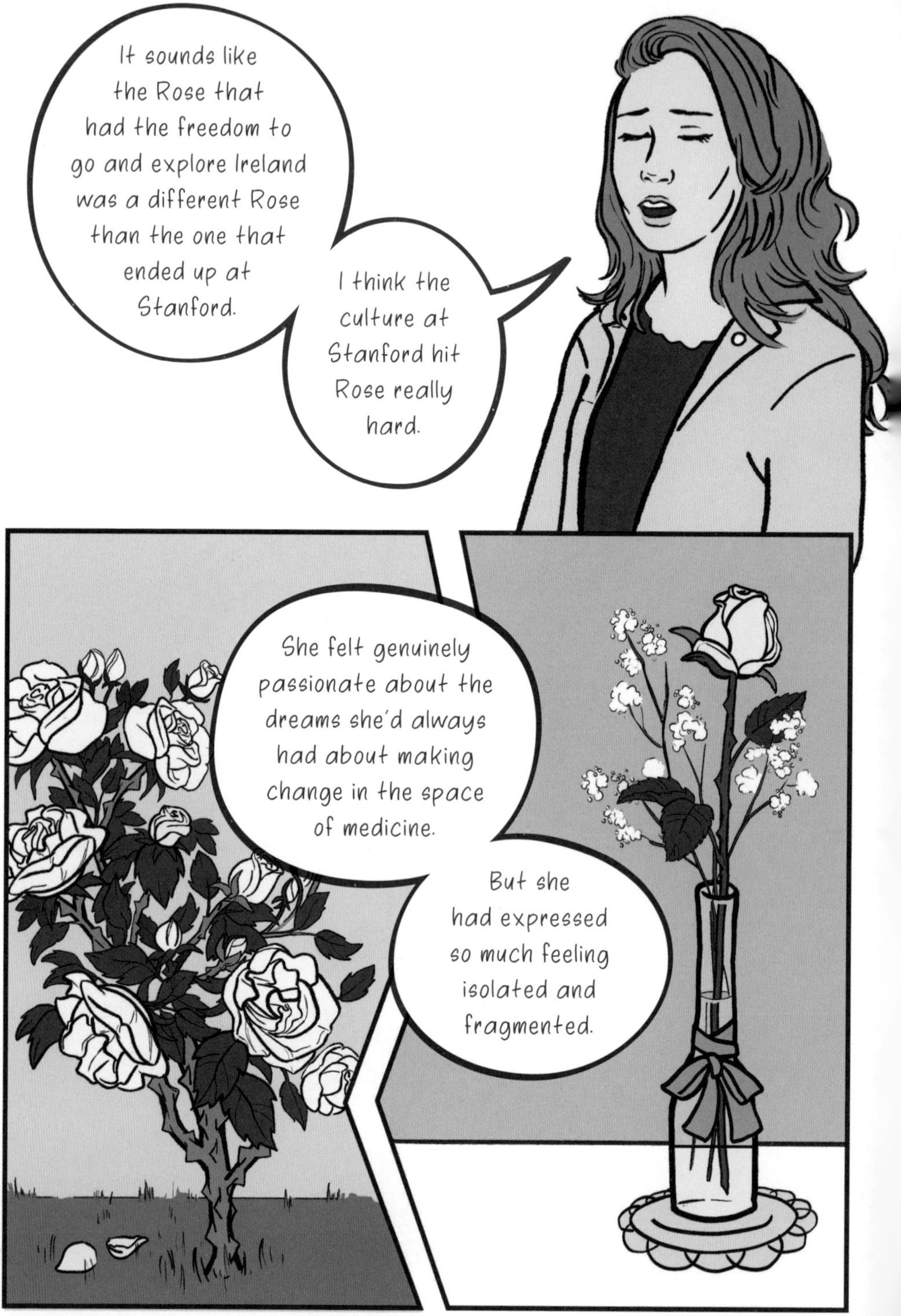
It sounds like the Rose that had the freedom to go and explore Ireland was a different Rose than the one that ended up at Stanford.
I think the culture at Stanford hit Rose really hard.
She felt genuinely passionate about the dreams she'd always had about making change in the space of medicine.
But she had expressed so much feeling isolated and fragmented.

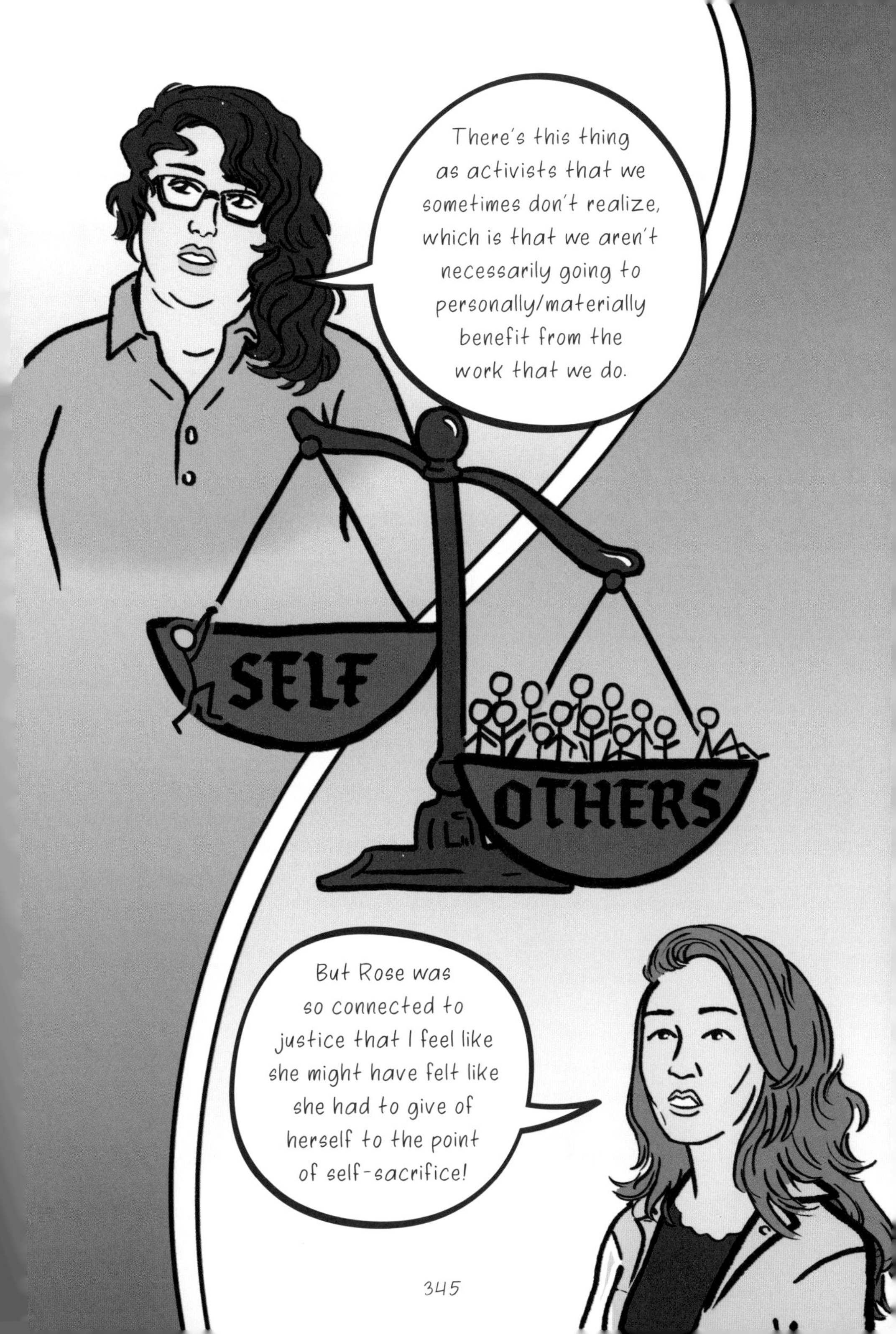
There's this thing as activists that we sometimes don't realize, which is that we aren't necessarily going to personally/materially benefit from the work that we do.
SELF
OTHERS
But Rose was so connected to justice that I feel like she might have felt like she had to give of herself to the point of self-sacrifice!

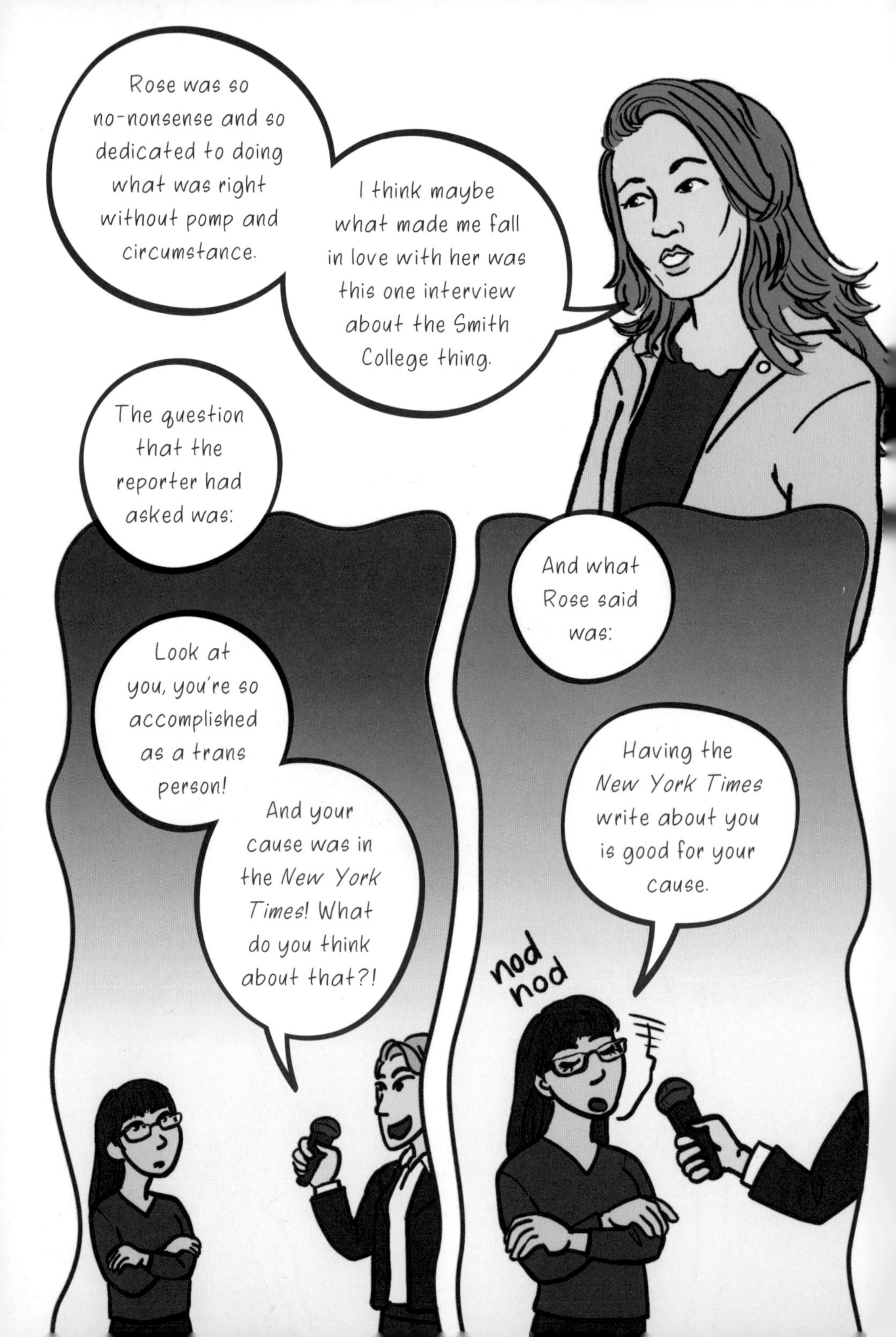
Rose was so no-nonsense and so dedicated to doing what was right without pomp and circumstance.
I think maybe what made me fall in love with her was this one interview about the Smith College thing.
The question that the reporter had asked was:
Look at you, you're so accomplished as a trans person!
And your cause was in the *New York Times*! What do you think about that?!
And what Rose said was:
Having the *New York Times* write about you is good for your cause.
nod nod

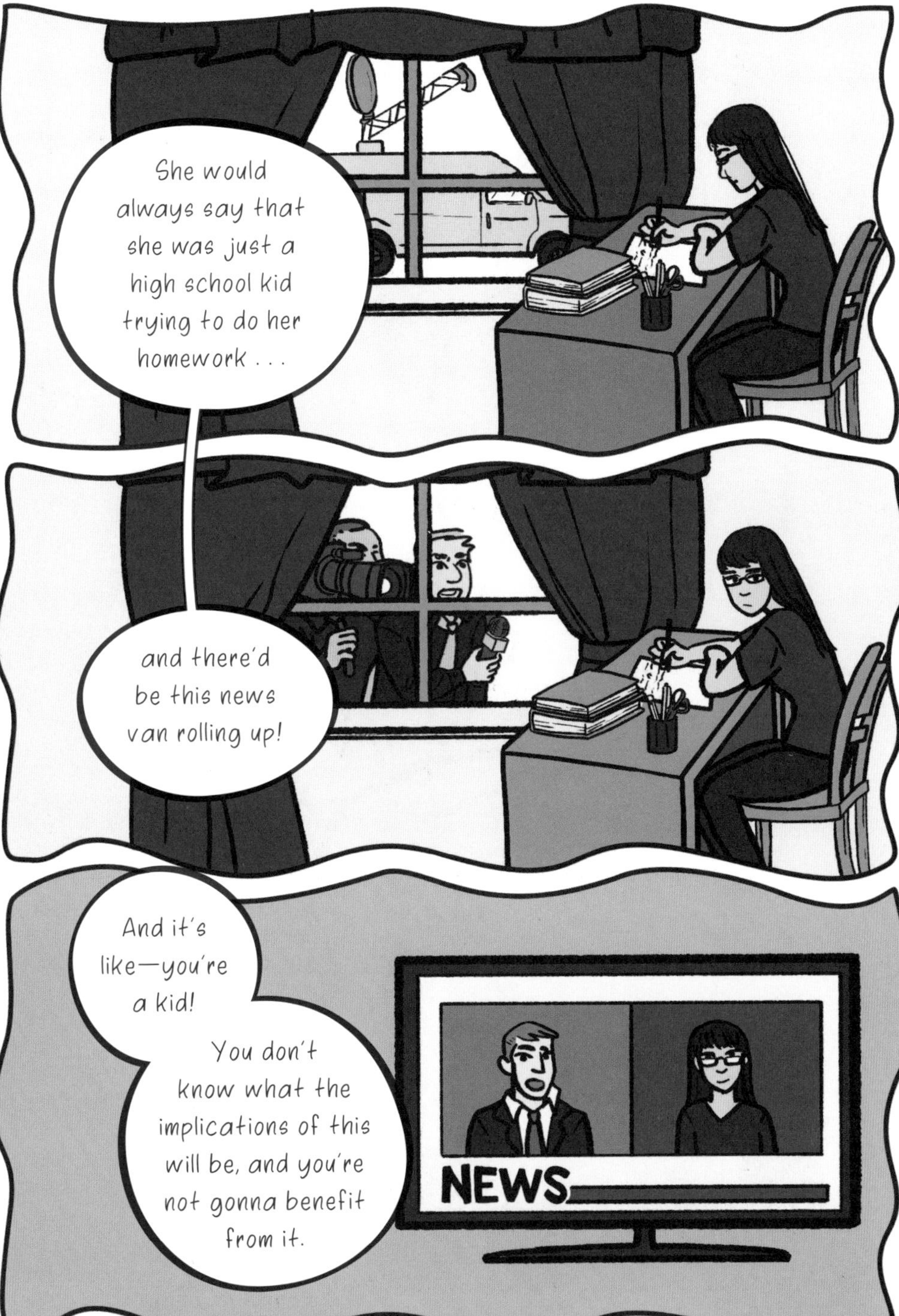
She would always say that she was just a high school kid trying to do her homework . . .
and there'd be this news van rolling up!
And it's like—you're a kid!
You don't know what the implications of this will be, and you're not gonna benefit from it.
NEWS

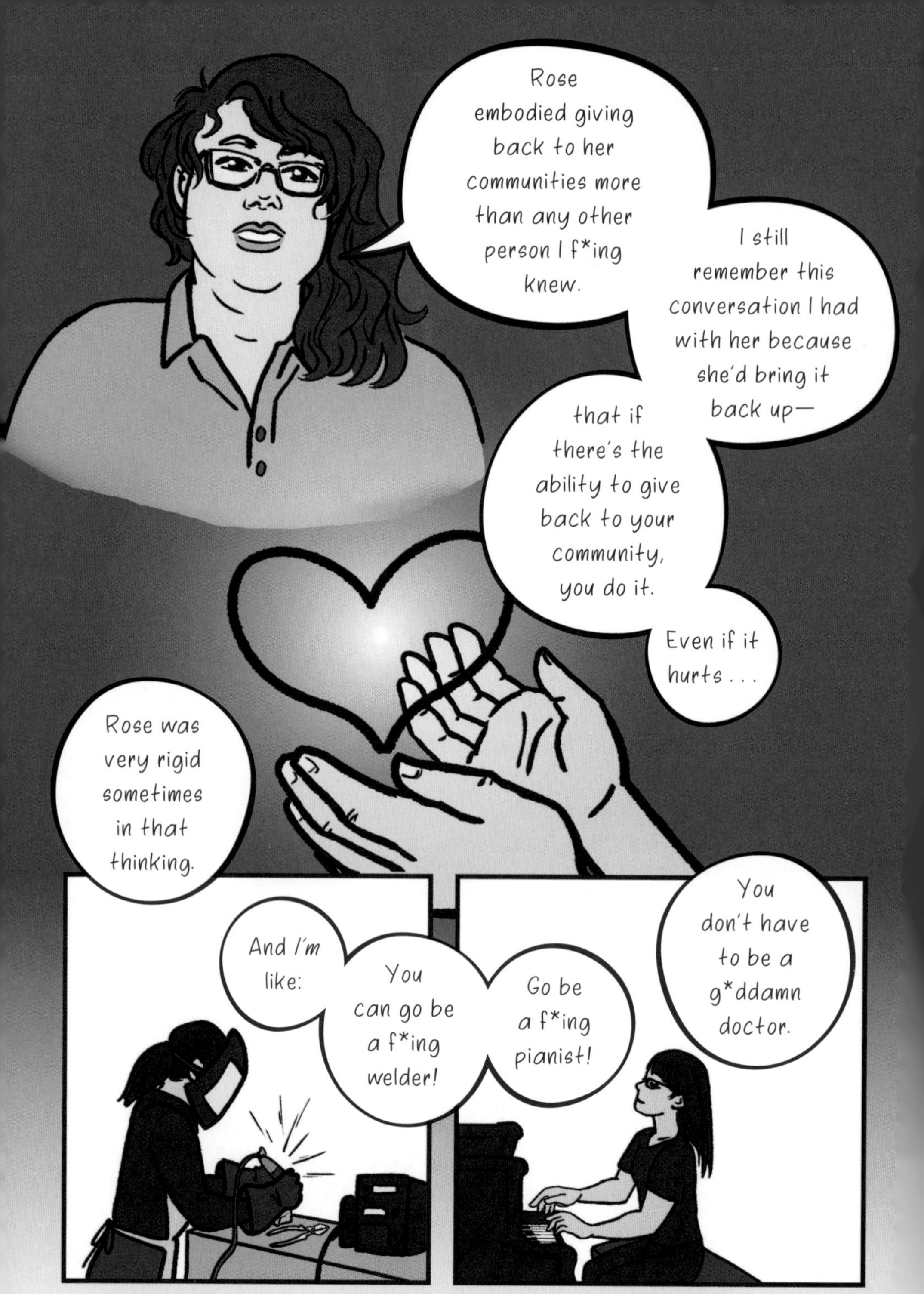
Rose embodied giving back to her communities more than any other person I f*ing knew.
I still remember this conversation I had with her because she'd bring it back up—
that if there's the ability to give back to your community, you do it.
Even if it hurts . . .
Rose was very rigid sometimes in that thinking.
And I'm like:
You can go be a f*ing welder!
Go be a f*ing pianist!
You don't have to be a g*ddamn doctor.

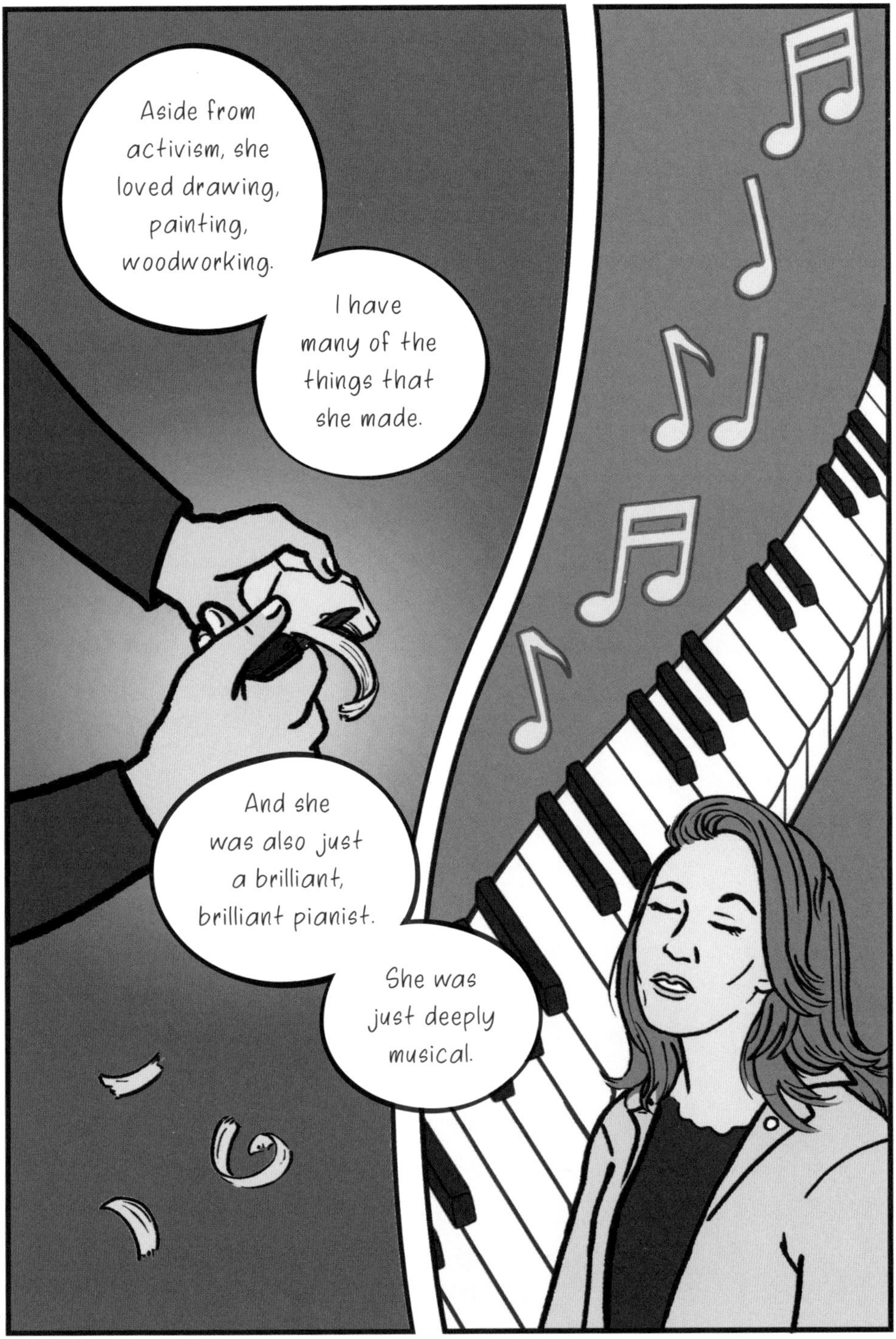
Aside from activism, she loved drawing, painting, woodworking.
I have many of the things that she made.
And she was also just a brilliant, brilliant pianist.
She was just deeply musical.

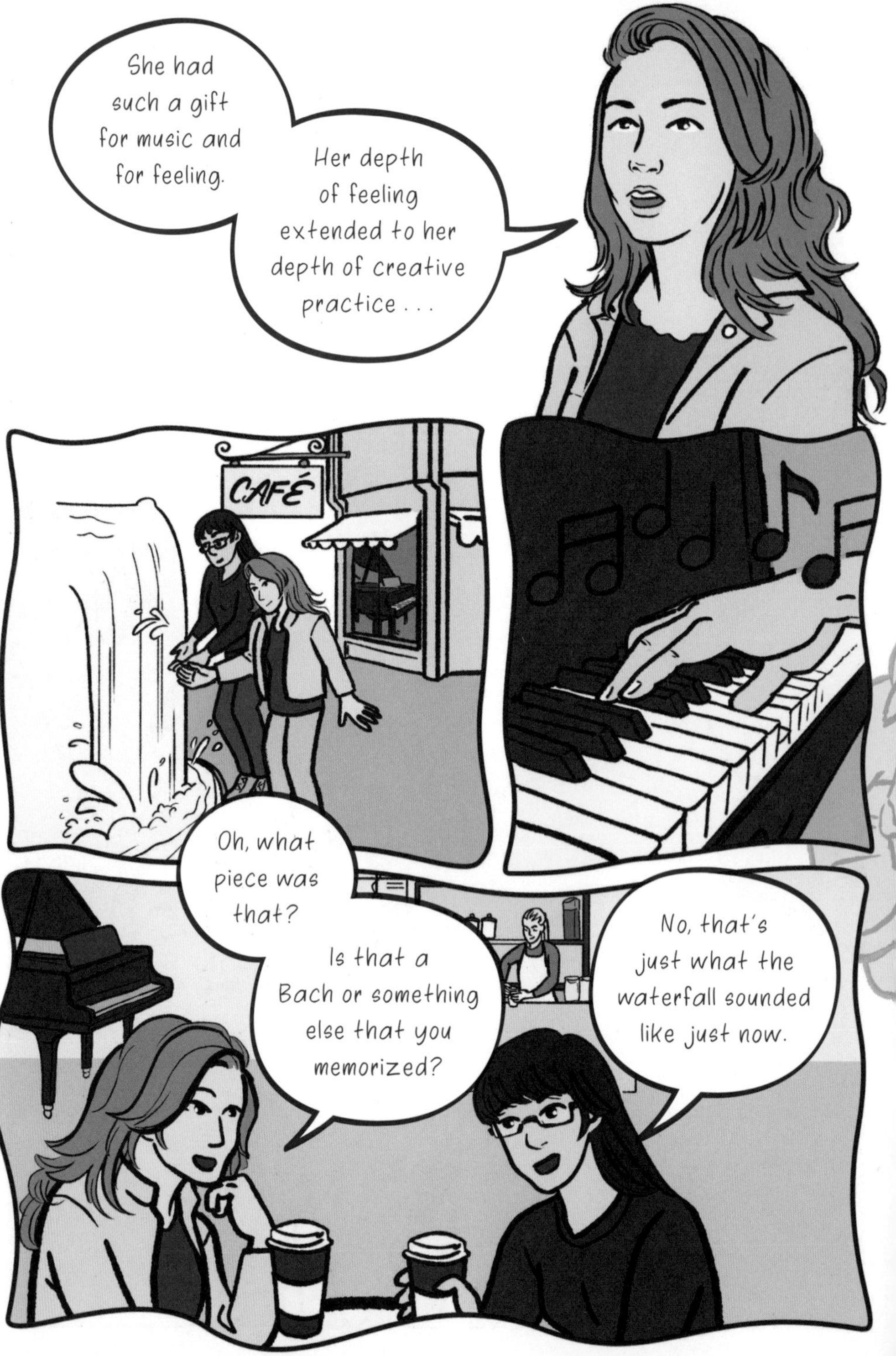
She had such a gift for music and for feeling.
Her depth of feeling extended to her depth of creative practice . . .
CAFÉ
Oh, what piece was that?
Is that a Bach or something else that you memorized?
No, that's just what the waterfall sounded like just now.

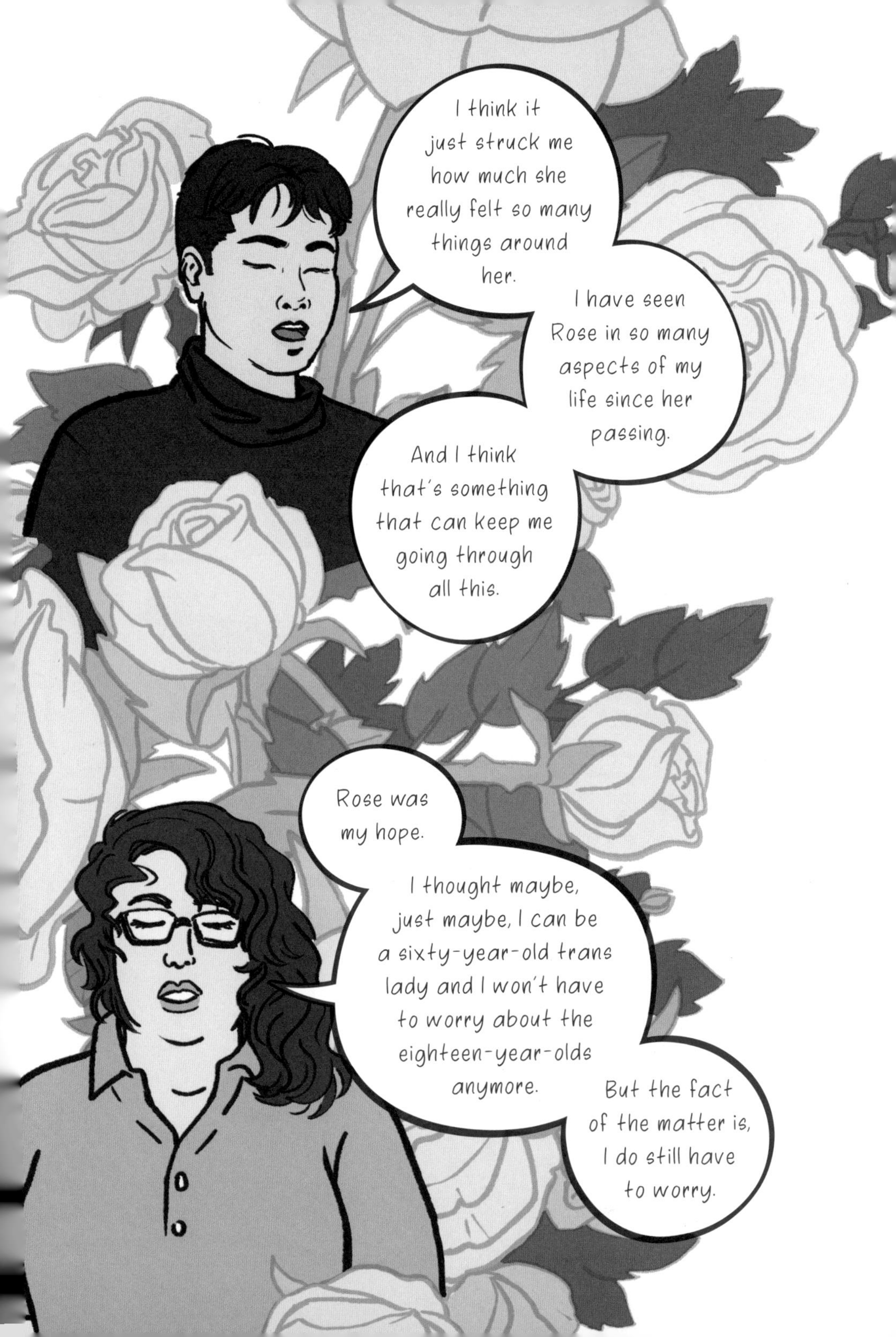
I think it just struck me how much she really felt so many things around her.
I have seen Rose in so many aspects of my life since her passing.
And I think that's something that can keep me going through all this.
Rose was my hope.
I thought maybe, just maybe, I can be a sixty-year-old trans lady and I won't have to worry about the eighteen-year-olds anymore.
But the fact of the matter is, I do still have to worry.

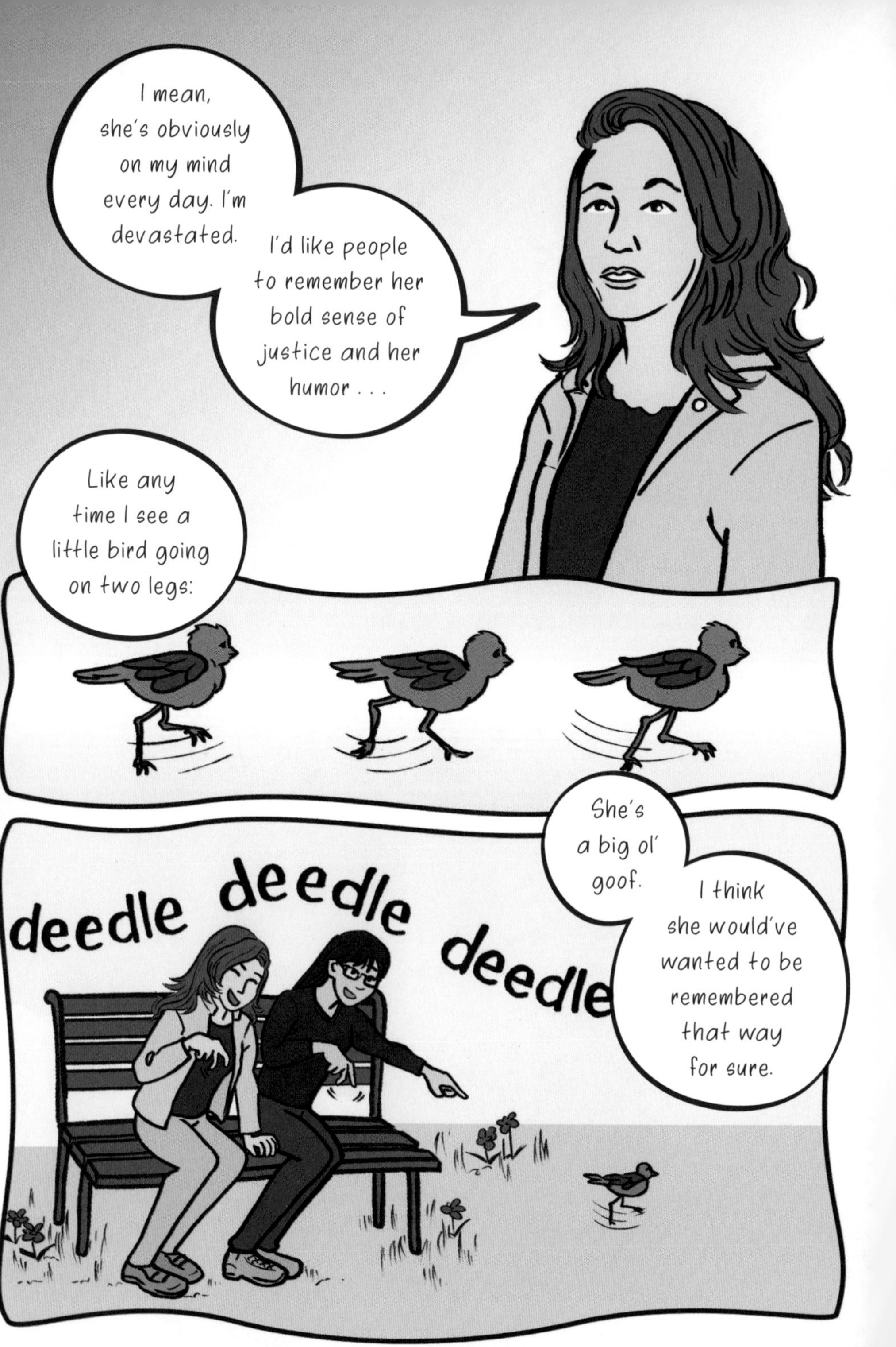
I mean, she's obviously on my mind every day. I'm devastated.
I'd like people to remember her bold sense of justice and her humor . . .
Like any time I see a little bird going on two legs:
She's a big ol' goof.
deedle deedle deedle
I think she would've wanted to be remembered that way for sure.

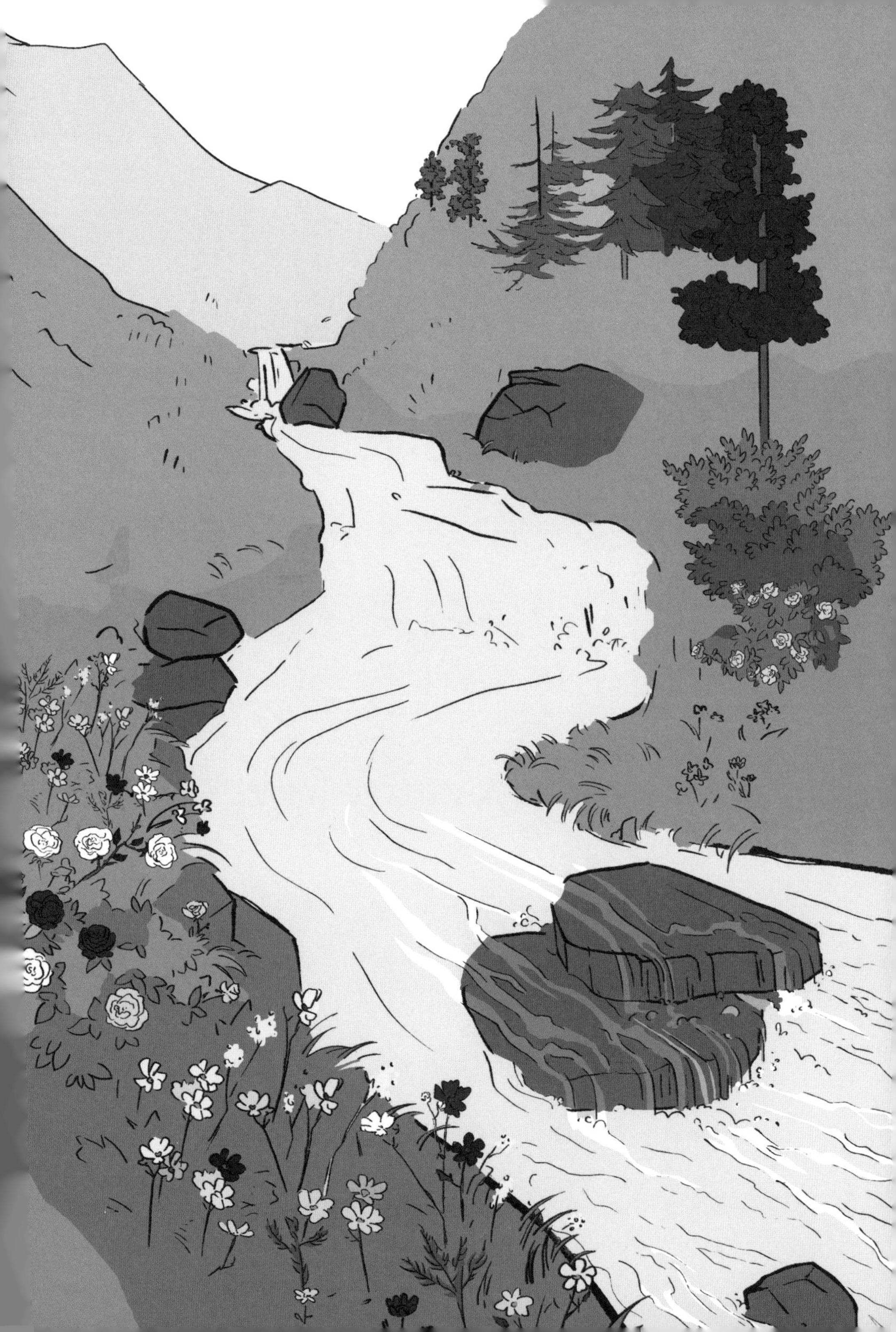

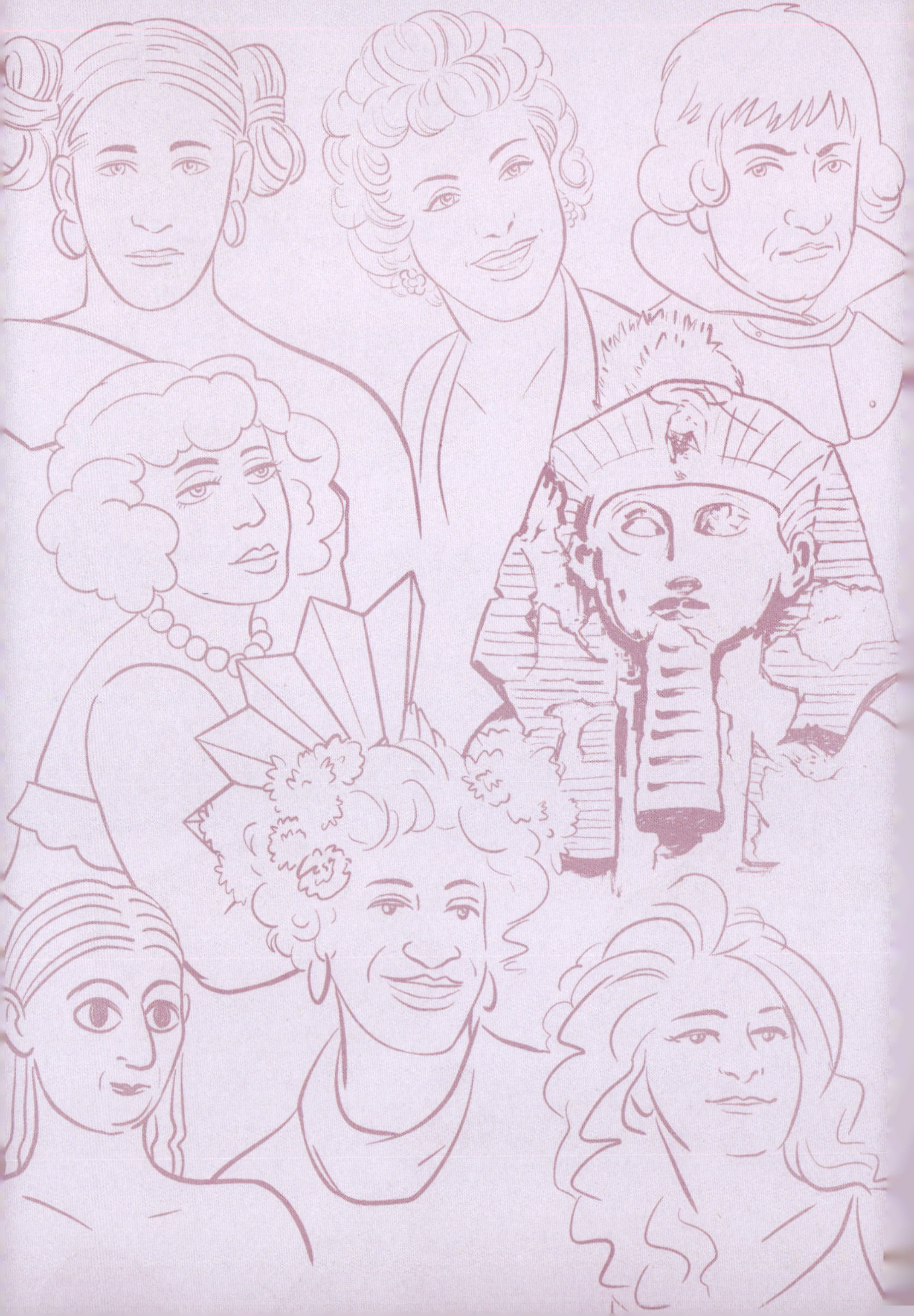

ACKNOWLEDGMENTS

FROM ALEX L. COMBS

Thank you to my agent, Zabé Ellor, who took a chance on me to represent my first graphic novel, and to my editor, Andrea Tompa, and the team at Candlewick, who believed in me and supported me through the process of creating this book.

A huge thank-you to the following people who took the time to have conversations with me, advise me in detail on the relevant sections, and provide insightful quotations:

Cheryl Morgan (ancient history, Michael Dillon), Dr. María Fernanda Ugalde Mora (ancient Ecuador), Dr. Hilary Rhodes (Eleanor Rykener, medieval Europe), Dr. Louie Dean Valencia (Antonio de Erauso, European colonialism), Bogi Takács (Herculine Barbin), Mason Jairo Olaya-Smith (Lucy Hicks Anderson, Michael Dillon, drag), Jaye C. Watts (Reed Erickson), Tyler Albertario (Stonewall, STAR).

A very special thank-you to those who agreed to be featured in the Community Voices section:

Ben Power, for answering all my archive-related questions, talking about your friendship with Lou Sullivan and Leslie Feinberg, and for your dedication to keeping the Sexual Minority Archives running and expanding.

Dee Dee Watters, for talking about your friendship with Monica Roberts and also about some very difficult parts of contemporary trans history. Thank you for your commitment to preserving and growing TransGriot.com and keeping it accessible.

Dr. Ardel Haefele-Thomas, for your enthusiasm when I first reached out for advice on writing a book about trans history, for being one of the first to agree to be in the comic, and for writing *Introduction to Transgender Studies*, which was the perfect starting point for my research.

Sulique Waqa, for being willing to talk to this kooky American and be featured in my comic book to share your knowledge of trans history, perspectives on non-Western gender identities, and your advocacy in Fiji and internationally.

Dr. Ajuan Mance, for being an out academic and comics nerd who inspired me when I was a grad student. Thank you for sharing your personal and professional knowledge about trans history.

Marie Angel Venarsian Pink Moon Midnight Blue, for advising me on handling multiple sensitive aspects of this material, for sharing your wisdom, and for introducing me to some of your brilliant friends.

Lilac Maldonado, for stopping to do a zine trade with me at LA Zine Fest all those years ago—and then it turned out you're also a trans historian! Thank you for sharing your knowledge with me and the readers.

Jahni Leggett, for being an ambassador with all the advocacy work you do in spite of the many pressures put upon you from doing so, and thank you for sharing your insight and authenticity.

Ms. Billie Cooper, for all your encouragement and for being my friend, in addition to sharing your knowledge as a trans elder, and for giving me the opportunity to draw a superhero comic as part of this graphic novel!

Rani (Bishakh) Som, for sharing your stories with me, for your enthusiasm about the project, and for being a supportive peer and friend in our small queer comics world.

Hans Lindahl, for being a part of the project from the beginning, advising me on researching and writing about intersex material, and for coming together with Rose Wong's friends Bright Zhou and Eilís Ní Fhlannagáin at the last minute to create a comic about Rose. I want to honor the trust you have all placed in me and the difficulty of going through the process of creating the comic.

Andrew Eakett, for supporting me through every single step of making this book; I could NOT have done it without you. I'm so glad that your wisdom, which I've been selfishly keeping to myself all these years, will finally be shared with a wider audience.

Finally, thank you to:

Dr. Lucy Barnhouse for helping me with the Latin translations and connecting me with some of your brilliant colleagues, Tina Danner-Groves for helping me gather some of my initial research material, the sensitivity readers for their thoughtful feedback, Diana Jo Davies for generously allowing me to draw from her many photographs, and to the many other photographers, archivists, and museum curators who gave me permission to draw from their collections.

FROM ANDREW EAKETT

Zabé, thank you for going for it and being Alex's agent. I really appreciate your professionalism and effectiveness.

Andrea, thank you for being the kindest and most patient first editor we could have asked for (while also getting the job done!).

Thank you to Lisa, Juan, and the rest of the Candlewick team for all your enthusiasm and great work surrounding this project.

Thank you to everyone who spoke with Alex, both those who are in the book and those who aren't. Your wisdom and vulnerability are cherished.

And Alex, thank you for being a co-creator with me. I can't wait to do this again!

SOURCE NOTES

INTRODUCTION TO TRANS HISTORY

p. 5: "*Transgender* is a word . . . under construction": Susan Stryker, *Transgender History: The Roots of Today's Revolution*, 2nd ed. (Berkeley: Seal Press, 2017), 1.

CHAPTER 1: A LONG, LONG TIME AGO: THE ANCIENT WORLD

p. 10: "whose maleness . . . awe of the people": quoted in Cheryl Morgan, "Evidence for Trans Lives in Sumer," *Notches* (blog), May 2, 2017, http://notchesblog.com/2017/05/02/evidence-for-trans-lives-in-sumer.

p. 11: "The British Museum's . . . 'person-man-woman'": ibid.

p. 14: "I could see . . . transgender people": María Fernanda Ugalde Mora, "What Ancient Gender Fluidity Taught Me About Modern Patriarchy," *SAPIENS*, July 9, 2020, https://www.sapiens.org/archaeology/archaeology-biases/.

p. 15: "Chorrera style . . . male attribute)," "Tolita style . . . and skirt," and "Guangala style . . . male clothes)": María Fernanda Ugalde Mora, email correspondence with the author, June 2021.

p. 17: "I prefer to leave . . . big cities": María Fernanda Ugalde Mora, interview with the author, 2021.

p. 22: "strange androgyny": Kara Cooney, *The Woman Who Would Be King: Hatshepsut's Rise to Power in Ancient Egypt* (New York: Crown, 2014), 149.

p. 22: "shocking . . . femininity": ibid.

p. 22: "deeply schizophrenic": Toby Wilkinson, *The Rise and Fall of Ancient Egypt* (New York: Random House, 2010), 210.

p. 23: The Living Horus . . . Khenemet-Amun: adapted from Miriam Lichtheim, *Ancient Egyptian Literature: The New Kingdom*, vol. 2 (Berkeley: University of California Press, 1978), 26.

p. 25: "Go, to make her . . . are in me": quoted in James Henry Breasted, *Ancient Records of Egypt: Historical Documents from the Earliest Times to the Persian Conquest*, vol. 2 (Chicago: University of Chicago Press, 1906), 81.

p. 26: "[Amun-Ra] . . . form of a god": ibid., 80.

p. 27: "I have given to thee . . . has commanded": ibid., 82.

p. 27: "the bodily son": quoted in Dimitri Laboury, "How and Why Did Hatshepsut Invent the Image of Her Royal Power?," in *Creativity and Innovation in the Reign of Hatshepsut*, eds. José M. Galán, Betsy M. Bryan, and Peter Dorman (Chicago: Oriental Institute of the University of Chicago, 2010), 90.

p. 28: "Keep from saying . . . really happened": quoted in Luc Gabolde, "Hatshepsut at Karnak: A Woman under God's Commands," in *Creativity and Innovation in the Reign of Hatshepsut*, eds. José M. Galán, Betsy M. Bryan, and Peter Dorman (Chicago: Oriental Institute of the University of Chicago, 2010), 46–47.

p. 29: "Now my heart . . . I have done": quoted in Miriam Lichtheim, *Ancient Egyptian Literature: The New Kingdom*, vol. 2 (Berkeley: University of California Press, 1978), 27.

p. 32: "Next day . . . the flute": *Apuleius: The Golden Ass*, trans. A. S. Kline, 2013, book 8, 26–28, https://www.poetryintranslation.com/PITBR/Latin/TheGoldenAssVIII.php.

p. 34: "For there are some eunuchs . . . heaven's sake": *Webster Bible Translation*, Bible Hub: Online Bible Study Suite, https://biblehub.com/wbt/matthew/19.htm.

p. 35: "Modern definitions . . . eunuchs themselves": Howard Chiang, "How China Became a 'Castrated Civilization' and Eunuchs a 'Third Sex,'" in *Transgender China*, ed. Howard Chiang (New York: Palgrave Macmillan, 2012), 24.

p. 41: "When trying someone . . . his voice": Cassius Dio, *Roman History*, vol. 9, trans. Earnest Cary and Herbert B. Foster (Cambridge, MA: Harvard University Press, 1927), 465.

p. 41: "He asked the physicians . . . an incision": ibid., 471.

p. 43: "slaying boys," "barbaric chants," "using charms," "unholy rites," and "innumerable amulets": ibid., 461.

p. 43: "actually shutting up . . . human genitals": ibid.

p. 45: "godlike children": ibid., 459.

CHAPTER 2: EUROPEANS BEHAVING BADLY: FROM THE OLD WORLD TO THE "NEW" WORLD

p. 52: "For a man to be linked . . . elegant coupling": quoted in John Boswell, *Christianity, Social Tolerance, and Homosexuality: Gay People in Western Europe from the Beginning of the Christian Era to the Fourteenth Century* (Chicago: University of Chicago Press, 1980), 385.

p. 53: "The world teems . . . abound in them": Bernard de Cluny, "The Scorn of the World," trans. Henry Preble, in *The American Journal of Theology* 10, no. 3, ed. Samuel Macauley Jackson (Chicago: University of Chicago Press, 1906), 500–501.

p. 56: "John Rykener . . . ignominious vice": quoted in David Lorenzo Boyd and Ruth Mazo Karras, "The Interrogation of a Male Transvestite Prostitute in Fourteenth-Century London," *GLQ: A Journal of Lesbian and Gay Studies* 1, no. 4 (October 1995), 462.

p. 57: "Who had taught . . . what persons?": ibid., 463.

p. 58: "The name Eleanor . . . as playful": Dr. Hilary Rhodes, interview with the author, 2021.

p. 65: "Many times people . . . able to marry": quoted in Israel Burshatin, "Elena Alias Eleno: Genders, Sexualities, and 'Race' in the Mirror of Natural History in Sixteenth-Century Spain," in *Gender Reversals and Gender Cultures: Anthropological and Historical Perspectives*, ed. Sabrina Petra Ramet (London: Routledge, 2004), 112.

p. 67: "At present I have . . . fifteen days": quoted in Christof Rolker, "'I am and have been a hermaphrodite': Elena/Eleno de Céspedes and the Spanish Inquisition," *Männlich-weiblich-zwischen* (blog), April 4, 2016, https://intersex.hypotheses.org/2720.

p. 73: "We shall powerfully . . . damage that we can": Council of Castile, "Requerimiento," National Humanities Center Toolbox Library: Primary Resources in U.S. History & Literature, https://nationalhumanitiescenter.org/pds/amerbegin/contact/text7/requirement.pdf.

p. 75: "He found the home . . . feminine clothing": from Peter Martyr d'Anghiera, *De Orbo Novo*, translated by Dr. Lucy Barnhouse for the author, 2021.

p. 75: "[He] ordered . . . by dogs": Peter Martyr d'Anghiera, *De Orbo Novo*, trans. Francis Augustus MacNutt, vol. 1 (New York: Putnam, 1912), https://www.gutenberg.org/ebooks/12425.

p. 76: "I have submitted . . . great esteem": quoted in Clark A. Pomerleau, "Norms in Colonial America through the Civil War," in "U.S. LGBTQ History," *LGBTQ+ Studies: An Open Textbook*, https://courses.lumenlearning.com/suny-lgbtq-studies/chapter/norms-in-colonial-america-through-the-civil-war/.

p. 79: "Like many queer . . . toxic masculinity": Dr. Louie Dean Valencia, interview with the author, 2021.

pp. 80–82: For this monologue, we used a combination of two translations: Doña Catalina de Erauso, *The Nun Ensign*, trans. James Fitzmaurice-Kelly (London: T. Fisher Unwin, 1908) (TNE) and Catalina de Erauso, *Lieutenant Nun: Memoir of a Basque Transvestite in the New World*, trans. Michele Stepto and Gabriel Stepto (Boston: Beacon Press, 1996) (LN). "One Sunday . . . cut off my view": TNE, 18; "I asked him . . . the same": LN, 12; "Then he told me . . . my face": TNE, 19; "The next morning . . . do you want?'": LN, 12; "'I'll show you . . . slashed!'": TNE, 19; "I gave him . . . free to go": LN, 12–13.

p. 84: "My case . . . entertained by princes": Doña Catalina de Erauso, *The Nun Ensign*, trans. James Fitzmaurice-Kelly (London: T. Fisher Unwin, 1908), 140.

p. 86: "Our manifest . . . multiplying millions": John O'Sullivan, "Annexation," *United States Magazine and Democratic Review* 17, no. 1 (1845), 5.

p. 88: "A Zuni Princess . . . Strange People": "A Zuni Princess: Interesting Facts Concerning a Strange People," *National Tribune* (Washington, DC), May 20, 1886, 2, *Chronicling America: Historic American Newspapers*, Library of Congress, https://chroniclingamerica.loc.gov/lccn/sn82016187/1886-05-20/ed-1/seq-2/.

p. 88: "A Zuni Princess . . . Child of Nature": "A Zuni Princess in Washington: Among Pale-Faced Society Ladies—An Eccentric Child of Nature," *Bismarck (ND) Weekly Tribune*, May 28, 1886, 2, *Chronicling America: Historic American Newspapers*, Library of Congress, https://chroniclingamerica.loc.gov/lccn/sn85042588/1886-05-28/ed-1/seq-2/.

p. 90: "Yet this Zuñian . . . of culture": Matilda Coxe Stevenson, "The Zuñi Indians: Their Mythology, Esoteric Fraternities, and Ceremonies," in *Twenty-Third Annual Report of the Bureau of American Ethnology to the Secretary of the Smithsonian Institution 1901–1902*, J. W. Powell, director (Washington, DC: Government Printing Office, 1904), 130.

CHAPTER 3: SEX AND GENDER UNDER THE MICROSCOPE: SEXOLOGY

p. 98: "Barbin's voice . . . heartfelt": Bogi Takács, correspondence with the author, 2022.

p. 98: "What I felt . . . adored her!": Herculine Barbin, *Herculine Barbin: Being the Recently Discovered Memoirs of a Nineteenth-Century Hermaphrodite*, intro. Michel Foucault and trans. Richard McDougal (New York: Pantheon, 1980), 48.

p. 99: "Destined to live . . . to each other!!!": ibid., 51.

p. 100: "I, who had been . . . behind me": ibid., 89.

p. 100: "Barbin uses . . . transitioning": Bogi Takács, correspondence with the author, 2022.

p. 102: "Many people . . . overwhelmed me!!!": Herculine Barbin, *Herculine Barbin: Being the Recently Discovered Memoirs of a Nineteenth-Century Hermaphrodite*, intro. Michel Foucault and trans. Richard McDougal (New York: Pantheon, 1980), 85.

p. 105: "a female soul . . . male body": Gert Hekma, "A Female Soul in a Male Body: Sexual Inversion as Gender Inversion in Nineteenth-Century Sexology," in *Third Sex, Third Gender: Beyond Sexual Dimorphism in Culture and History*, ed. Gilbert Herdt (New York: Zone Books, 1993), 219.

p. 106: "We Urnings . . . hermaphrodites": Karl Heinrich Ulrichs, *The Riddle of "Man-Manly" Love: The Pioneering Work on Male Homosexuality*, vol. 1, trans. Michael A. Lombardi-Nash (New York: Prometheus, 1994), 36.

p. 108: "A male who commits . . . punished by imprisonment": quoted in Craig Kaczorowski, "Paragraph 175," glbtq Archives, 2004, 2, www.glbtqarchive.com/ssh/paragraph_175_S.pdf.

p. 108: "The Urning, too, is . . . nature gave them": Karl Heinrich Ulrichs, "Araxes: a Call to Free the Nature of the Urning from Penal Law," quoted in Michael Bronski, *A Queer History of the United States* (Boston: Beacon Press, 2011), 79.

p. 113: "I. Degree . . . transformation of sex": R. von Krafft-Ebing, *Psychopathia Sexualis: With Especial Reference to the Antipathic Sexual Instinct; A Medico-Forensic Study*, trans. Charles Gilbert Chaddock (Philadelphia: F. A. Davis, 1894), 191, 197, 202, 216.

p. 117: "Eugenic Certificate . . . the race": "Eugenic Certificate," circa 1924, Disability Museum, https://www.disabilitymuseum.org/dhm/lib/catcard.html?id=2925.

p. 119: "More marked . . . savage societies": Havelock Ellis, *Man and Woman: A Study of Human Secondary Sexual Characters*, 2nd ed. (London: Walter Scott, 1897), 13.

p. 119: "It . . . this anomaly": Havelock Ellis, "Studies in the Psychology of Sex, Volume VII: Eonism," in *Sexology Uncensored: The Documents of Sexual Science*, eds. Lucy Bland and Laura Doan (Chicago: University of Chicago Press, 1998), 258.

p. 120: "One disadvantage . . . internal is limitless": Magnus Hirschfeld, "Transvestites," in *Sexology Uncensored: The Documents of Sexual Science*, eds. Lucy Bland and Laura Doan (Chicago: University of Chicago Press, 1998), 104.

p. 121: "Every conceivable . . . intermediary types": Magnus Hirschfeld, *The Homosexuality of Men and Women*, trans. Michael Lombardi-Nash (New York: Prometheus, 2000), 419.

p. 124: "If you . . . Esquimaux Village": "1893 World's Fair Chicago," Human Zoos, https://humanzoos.net/?page_id=99.

p. 124: "The differences . . . same channels": Magnus Hirschfeld, *The Homosexuality of Men and Women*, trans. Michael Lombardi-Nash (New York: Prometheus, 2000), 598.

p. 128: "If children . . . risky venture": ibid., 451.

p. 129: "the world's most dangerous Jew": quoted in Leslie Katz, "Life of Gay German Jewish Sexologist Honored in S.F.," *The Jewish News of Northern California*, June 6, 1997, https://jweekly.com/1997/06/06/life-of-gay-german-jewish-sexologist-honored-in-s-f/.

p. 131: "Only ignorance . . . to humanity": "A Visit to a Sexologist—Clip from *Different from the Others*" (Germany, 1919), 4:05, https://www.youtube.com/watch?v=mmoSJonRlVs.

p. 132: "Love is . . people are": quoted in Edward Ross Dickinson, *Sex, Freedom, and Power in Imperial Germany, 1880-1914* (New York: Cambridge University Press, 2014), 159.

p. 135: "but where were you hiding yesterday?": Lili Elbe, *Man Into Woman: A Comparative Scholarly Edition*, eds. Pamela L. Caughie and Sabine Meyer (London: Bloomsbury Academic, 2020), 89.

p. 135: "[Einar] has voluntarily . . . that is me": "An Existence Through Two Lives—A Past as a Man and a Future as a Woman—Lili Elbe Talks About the Painter Einar Wegener and Herself," *Politiken*, February 28, 1931, trans. Lili Elbe Digital Archive, http://lilielbe.org/context/periodicals/1931-02-28_Politiken.html.

p. 137: "Excellent French . . . to their wish": "The Man Who Became a Woman: An interview with Professor von Warnekros: Lili Elbe Came into Being by Means of a Procedure Unique in the Annals of Medical Science," *Ekstra Bladet*, February 28, 1931, trans. Lili Elbe Digital Archive, http://lilielbe.org/context/periodicals/1931-02-28_EkstraBladet.html.

p. 138: "Now Lili was . . . higher Power": Lili Elbe, *Man Into Woman: A Comparative Scholarly Edition*, eds. Pamela L. Caughie and Sabine Meyer (London: Bloomsbury Academic, 2020), 147.

p. 139: "It may be said . . . human life": ibid., 198.

p. 140: "It may be asked . . . same experience": Michael Dillon/Lobzang Jivaka, *Out of the Ordinary: A Life of Gender and Spiritual Transitions*, eds. Jacob Lau and Cameron Partridge (New York: Fordham University Press, 2017), 88.

p. 141: "see what [these pills] can do": ibid., 90.

p. 142: "Four miserable years": ibid., 91.

p. 145: "One must not . . . children": ibid., 125.

p. 145: "Some people are . . . uncommonly used": Michael Dillon, *Self: A Study in Ethics and Endocrinology* (London: William Heinemann Medical Books, 1946), 9.

p. 146: "it's easier to . . . a mind": quoted in Matthew Bell, "'It's Easier to Change a Body than to Change a Mind': The Extraordinary Life and Lonely Death of Roberta Cowell," *Independent* (London), October 26, 2013, https://www.independent.co.uk/news/people/profiles/it-s-easier-to-change-a-body-than-to-change-a-mind-the-extraordinary-life-and-lonely-death-of-roberta-cowell-8899823.html.

p. 149: "Never before . . . the bed": Michael Dillon/Lobzang Jivaka, *Out of the Ordinary: A Life of Gender and Spiritual Transitions*, eds. Jacob Lau and Cameron Partridge (New York: Fordham University Press, 2017), 143.

p. 150: "Do you intend to . . . *The Daily Express*": ibid., 214.

p. 150: "At that moment . . . 'change their sex'": ibid., 29.

p. 151: "I could never . . . more be waiting?": ibid., 216.

p. 151: "A Change of Heir": "Britain: A Change of Heir," *Time*, May 26, 1958, https://content.time.com/time/subscriber/article/0,33009,936913,00.html.

CHAPTER 4: PROGRESS AND BACKLASH: TRANS IN THE USA

p. 157: "To understand . . . sexism": Susan Stryker, *Transgender History: The Roots of Today's Revolution*, 2nd ed. (Berkeley: Seal Press, 2017), 51.

p. 158: "You is no gentlemen!": quoted in "2019 Creative Nonfiction Grantee

Channing Gerard Joseph," Whiting Foundation website, https://www.whiting.org/content/channing-gerard-joseph#/.

p. 159: "'Who could this . . . in history": Channing Gerard Joseph, "My Discovery of the First Drag Queen," Channing Gerard Joseph website, http://www.channingjoseph.com/elements/discoveries.html.

p. 160: "Certainly many scholars . . . and straight": Charles H. Rowell, "An Interview with Henry Louis Gates, Jr.," *Callaloo: A Journal of African Diaspora Arts* 14, no. 2 (Spring 1991), 453.

p. 162: "masculine-garbed . . . entertainer": quoted in Regina V. Jones, "How Does a Bulldagger Get Out of the Footnote? or Gladys Bentley's Blues," *ninepatch: A Creative Journal for Women and Gender Studies* 1, no. 1 (July 2012), 5.

p. 165: "I have violated . . . way of living": Gladys Bentley, "I Am a Woman Again," *Ebony* (August 1952), 93, Queer Music Heritage website, https://www.queermusicheritage.com/bentley6.html.

p. 165: "For many years . . . inconceivable": ibid.

p. 168: "The way Lucy's . . . social norms": Mason Jairo Olaya-Smith, interview with the author, 2022.

p. 174: "It's only petty . . . much better": quoted in "Lucy Hicks Says: 'I Will Die a Woman,'" *Oxnard (CA) Press-Courier*, November 24, 1945, 2.

p. 176: "Night Life . . . Case": "Night Life Queen Guilty of Perjury in Sex Case," *Afro American* (Baltimore, MD), December 15, 1945, 1, https://news.google.com/newspapers/p/afro?nid=UBnQDr5gPskC&dat=19451215&printsec=frontpage&hl=en.

p. 177: "I have lived . . . die a woman": quoted in "Lucy Hicks Says: 'I Will Die a Woman,'" *Oxnard (CA) Press-Courier*, November 24, 1945, 2.

p. 179: "[My sister] . . . feeling of belonging": Christine Jorgensen, *Christine Jorgensen: A Personal Autobiography* (San Francisco: Cleis Press, 1967), 5.

p. 180: "sheer force of will": ibid., 36.

p. 180: "I didn't measure . . . young male": ibid., 14.

p. 181: "I was twenty-three . . . despair": ibid., 73.

p. 183: "Nature made . . . your daughter": ibid., 114.

p. 183: "Letter . . . Mom and Dad": ibid., 117.

p. 184: "I thank . . . too much!": "Ex-G.I., Now a Woman, Returns to U.S.," Warner-Pathe News, February 1, 1953, https://www.gettyimages.com/detail/video/ex-g-i-now-a-woman-returns-to-u-s-superimposed-over-news-footage/500738698.

p. 184: "Hormones, Surgery Changes 26-Year Man into Woman," *Nome Nugget*, December 1, 1952.

p. 184: "Ex-GI Becomes Blonde Beauty: Operations Transform Bronx Youth," *Daily News* (New York), December 1, 1952.

p. 184: "Ex-GI Is Happy as Doctors in Denmark Change His Sex," *Evening Star* (Washington, DC), December 1, 1952.

p. 185: "It was like . . . about me": Christine Jorgensen, interview with Ron Niles at Ron's in Laguna (Alron Productions), 1986, 28:49, https://www.youtube.com/watch?v=_BZpnTyRrD4.

p. 185: "They got . . . the car?": ibid.

p. 186: "Tonight my guest . . . the world": ibid.

p. 187: "BARS MARRIAGE . . . being a female": *New York Times*, April 4, 1959, 20, https://timesmachine.nytimes.com/timesmachine/1959/04/04/issue.html.

p. 188: "A lot of . . . notoriety" and "If making . . . suppose I did": Christine Jorgensen, interview by the BBC, 1970, in Chloe Hadjimatheou, "Christine Jorgensen: 60 Years of Sex Change Ops," *BBC News*, November 30, 2012, https://www.bbc.com/news/magazine-20544095.

p. 188: "It was the sexual . . . kick in the pants": Christine Jorgensen, interview by Richard Beene, "Christine Jorgensen Is Fighting a New Battle," *Los Angeles Times*, September 3, 1988, https://www.latimes.com/archives/la-xpm-1988-09-03-me-3079-story.html.

p. 189: "I was getting . . . Harry Benjamin": Christine Jorgensen, at 1987 memorial service for Harry Benjamin, in *Harry Benjamin, M.D.*, dir. Mark Schoen (2007), https://sexsmartfilms.com/premium/film/763/.

p. 191: "Transsexuals . . . adjustment": David O. Cauldwell, "Questions and Answers on the Sex Life and Sexual Problems of Trans-sexuals," *International Journal of Transgenderism* 5, no. 2 (April–June 2001; reprint of original column from 1950), https://cdn.atria.nl/ezines/web/IJT/97-03/numbers/symposion/cauldwell_04.htm.

p. 191: "It seems . . . could be effected": R. E. L. Masters, "Appendix D: Transsexuals' Lives," in Harry Benjamin, MD, *The Transsexual Phenomenon* (New York: Julian Press, 1966), 104.

p. 193: "He shook . . . someone in need": Renée Richards in *Harry Benjamin, M.D.*, dir. Mark Schoen (2007), https://sexsmartfilms.com/premium/film/763/.

p. 194: "TYPE I . . . Intensity": "The Benjamin Sex Orientation Scale," Digital Transgender Archive, https://www.digitaltransgenderarchive.net/files/5d86p0399.

p. 194: "exclusively heterosexual" and "exclusively homosexual"; the Kinsey Scale: The Kinsey Institute, https://kinseyinstitute.org/research/publications/kinsey-scale.php.

p. 200: "Reed Erickson's . . . be imagined": Jaye C. Watts, correspondence with the author, 2022.

p. 202: "probably . . . have happened": quoted in Christine Jorgensen, *Christine Jorgensen: A Personal Autobiography* (San Francisco: Cleis Press, 1967), xiv.

p. 205: "One is not born . . . woman": Simone de Beauvoir, *The Second Sex*, trans. Constance Borde and Sheila Malovany-Chevallier (New York: Knopf, 2010), 283.

p. 205: "gender identity gate": John Money and Patricia Tucker, *Sexual Signatures: On Being a Man or a Woman* (Boston: Little, Brown, 1975), 88, https://archive.org/details/sexualsignatures0000mone.

p. 207: "Their purpose . . . psychiatric abuse": Zoë Playdon, *The Hidden Case of Ewan Forbes: The Transgender Trial That Threatened to Upend the British Establishment* (New York: Scribner, 2021), 233.

p. 210: "A. A marked . . . significant distress": Kenneth J. Zucker, "The DSM-5 Diagnostic Criteria for Gender Dysphoria," in *Management of Gender Dysphoria: A Multidisciplinary Approach*, eds. Carlo Trombetta, Giovanni Liguori, and Michele Bertolotto (Milan, Italy: Springer, 2015), 33–37.

p. 213: "The period when . . . political urgency": Susan Stryker, *Transgender History: The Roots of Today's Revolution*, 2nd ed. (Berkeley: Seal Press, 2017), 119.

p. 215: "femmiphile" and "love of the feminine": Virginia Prince, "An Introduction to the Subject of Transvestism or Femmiphilia (Cross Dressing)," Foundation for Full Personality Expression, 1960, https://dspace.library.uvic.ca/handle/1828/4513.

p. 215: "homosexuals . . . disturbed people": quoted in Deborah Heller Feinbloom, *Transvestites & Transsexuals: Mixed Views* (New York: Delacorte, 1976), 62, https://archive.org/details/transvestitestra0000unse.

p. 215: "Be the LADY . . . a clerk": quoted in Richard Ekins and Dave King, eds., *Virginia Prince: Pioneer of Transgendering* (Binghamton, NY: Haworth Medical Press, 2005), 11.

p. 216: "dedicated . . . express it": Virginia Prince, "Purpose of *Transvestia*," *Transvestia* 11, no. 61 (1970).

p. 217: "I, at least . . . not the former": quoted in Richard Ekins and Dave King, eds., *Virginia Prince: Pioneer of Transgendering* (Binghamton, NY: Haworth Medical Press, 2005), 11.

p. 226: "The shows will . . . transsexualism": "Transsex," *Berkeley Barb*, February 1970, https://www.digitaltransgenderarchive.net/files/6w924c10d.

p. 227: "The Erickson . . . stuff like that": Elliot Blackstone, interview by Susan Stryker, 1996, http://docs.glbthistory.org/oh/Blackstone_Elliot11-6-1996_web.pdf.

p. 232: "Stonewall . . . group like STAR": Tyler Albertario, interview with the author, 2021.

p. 232: "You people . . . until we get them": 1970 leaflet by Street Transvestites Action Revolutionaries (STAR), quoted in Arthur Bell, *Dancing the Gay Lib Blues: A Year in the Homosexual Liberation Movement* (New York: Simon and Schuster, 1971), 120.

p. 233: "The oppression . . . the system": STAR, "Statement of STAR's political platform," ca. 1970, reproduced in *Trap Door: Trans Cultural Production and the Politics of Visibility*, ed. Reina Gossett, Eric A. Stanley, and Johanna Burton (Cambridge, MA: MIT Press, 2017), 76.

p. 235: "We [STAR] died . . . wearing makeup": Sylvia Rivera, "Queens in Exile, The Forgotten Ones," in *Street Transvestite Action Revolutionaries: Survival, Revolt, and Queer Antagonist Struggle* (n.p.: Untorelli Press, 2013), 53.

p. 247: "When people have . . . difference": Katy Steinmetz, "The Transgender Tipping Point," *Time*, May 29, 2014, https://time.com/magazine/us/135460/june-9th-2014-vol-183-no-22-u-s/.

p. 248: "Trump administration . . . transgender students": Ariane de Vogue et al., *CNN*, February 23, 2017, https://www.cnn.com/2017/02/22/politics/doj-withdraws-federal-protections-on-transgender-bathrooms-in-schools/index.html.

p. 248: "'Transgender' could . . . Trump administration": Erica L. Green et al., *The New York Times*, October 21, 2018, https://www.nytimes.com/2018/10/21/us/politics/transgender-trump-administration-sex-definition.html.

p. 248: "Trump says . . . the country": Reuters, *NBC News*, October 23, 2018, https://www.nbcnews.com/feature/nbc-out/trump-says-transgender-policy-seeks-protect-country-n923266.

p. 248: "US Supreme Court . . . transgender ban": *BBC News*, January 22, 2019, https://www.bbc.com/news/world-us-canada-46963426.

p. 248: "Transgender Health . . . Trump Administration": Selena Simmons-Duffin, *NPR*, June 12, 2020, https://www.npr.org/sections/health-shots/2020/06/12/868073068/transgender-health-protections-reversed-by-trump-administration.

p. 250: "It was . . . fringes": Imara Jones, "Transphobia in a Suit," *The Anti-Trans Hate Machine: A Plot Against Equality* (podcast), episode 3 (July 2021), TransLash Media, audio file, 36:47, https://translash.org/antitranshatemachine/.

p. 252: "turns the idea . . . discriminate": ibid.

p. 253: 2021 UCLA study: "Transgender People over Four Times More Likely Than Cisgender People to Be Victims of Violent Crime," UCLA School of Law, Williams Institute, press release, March 23, 2021, https://williamsinstitute.law.ucla.edu/press/ncvs-trans-press-release/.

p. 253: deadliest year on record: Orion Rummler, "2021 Set to Become Deadliest Year on Record for Trans Americans," *Axios*, June 12, 2021, https://www.axios.com/2021/06/12/trans-killings-america-deadliest.

p. 253: Texas, the state where . . . have taken place: Orion Rummler, "Texas Is Pushing the Most Anti-Trans Bills in the Country. Advocates Fear Deadly Consequences," *PBS News Hour*, September 13, 2021, https://www.pbs.org/newshour/nation/texas-is-pushing-the-most-anti-trans-bills-in-the-country-advocates-fear-deadly-consequences.

CHAPTER 5: THE PRESENT MOMENT: COMMUNITY VOICES

p. 265: "The TransGriot blog's . . . the Diaspora": Monica Roberts, "TransGriot Blog Mission Statement," *TransGriot* (blog), https://transgriot.blogspot.com/.

p. 280: five nanomoles per liter: Jeré Longman, "Caster Semenya Will Challenge Testosterone Rule in Court," *New York Times*, June 18, 2018, https://www.nytimes.com/2018/06/18/sports/caster-semenya-iaaf-lawsuit.html.

p. 281: "New rules . . . some races": "New Rules to Limit Testosterone Levels Could Keep Caster Semenya Out of Some Races," Associated Press, *USA Today*, April 26, 2018, https://www.usatoday.com/story/sports/olympics/2018/04/26/new-rules-limit-testosterone-levels-could-keep-caster-semenya-out/554333002/.

p. 281: "I just want to run . . . am fast": quoted in Jeré Longman, "Caster Semenya Will Challenge Testosterone Rule in Court," *New York Times*, June 18, 2018, https://www.nytimes.com/2018/06/18/sports/caster-semenya-iaaf-lawsuit.html.

p. 284: "175: Any person . . . a felony": Fiji Penal Code of 1945, Equipo Nizkor database, https://www.derechos.org/intlaw/doc/fji3.html.

p. 297: "NORTH AMERICAN . . . campsite": Albert McLeod, "Itinerary for the North American Native Gay and Lesbian Gathering," July 17, 1990, https://cdm15931.contentdm.oclc.org/digital/collection/two-spirit/id/24/rec/7.

p. 298: 2.5x more likely: "The Facts on Violence Against American Indian/Alaskan Native Women," Futures Without Violence, 2, https://www.futureswithoutviolence.org/userfiles/file/Violence%20Against%20AI%20AN%20Women%20Fact%20Sheet.pdf.

p. 298: 10x the national average: "Murdered & Missing Indigenous Women," Native Women's Wilderness, https://www.nativewomenswilderness.org/mmiw.

p. 340: "Smith, a liberal arts college . . . publicized": Editorial, "Transgender Students at Women's Colleges," *New York Times*, May 5, 2015, https://www.nytimes.com/2015/05/05/opinion/transgender-students-at-womens-colleges.html.

p. 346: "Having the *New York Times* . . . your cause": quoted in Lisa Stiepock "Student Perspective: Calliope Wong '16," *UConn Today*, March 9, 2016, https://today.uconn.edu/2016/03/student-perspective-calliope-wong-16/.

INDEX

activism, 157–159, 212–237, 242–243, 286–287, 290, 340, 348–349
Ahmose, 26
AIDS, 240–241
Albertario, Tyler, 232
Americas, the, 14–17, 72–77, 86–91, 297, 298–299. *See also* South America; United States
Amun-Ra, 25–27
Anderson, Lucy Hicks, 167–177
anti-trans laws, 100, 163, 248, 250–253, 284
   anti-crossdressing, 61, 84, 156–159, 162, 221
   Paragraph 175, 108, 126, 131–132
Aquilia Severa, 45
archiving, 131–132, 256–258, 260–263, 264–265. *See also* historical records
Assyria, 10, 19
athletics, 251, 279–281
autobiographies, 78–82, 97–102, 136–139, 152–153, 164–165, 179

Baer, Karl M., 127
Barbin, Herculine/Adélaïde/Alexina/Camille, 97–103
Barry, James, 278
Barton, Crawford, 235
Beauvoir, Simone de, 205
Benavides, Hugo, 16

Benjamin, Harry, 189–196, 198, 201–202, 206, 227
Bentley, Gladys, 161–165
Berlin, 122, 125, 126, 226
Blackstone, Elliot, 227
bodily modification, 12, 34–35, 36, 41, 125, 137–138, 144–146, 182–184
Bornstein, Kate, 243
Bubbles (Bubbles Rose Lee), 232

California, 76, 169–177, 219–227, 235, 312, 344
Carle, Luis, 235
Cassius Dio, 40–41, 43, 45
Catholicism. *See* religion: Christianity; *see also* Inquisitions
Cauldwell, David Oliver, 191
Céspedes, Eleno de, 62–71
Chiang, Howard, 35
Chicago, 122–124, 231
China, 35
Christianity. *See under* religion; *see also* Inquisitions
colonialism, 14, 16–17, 72–92, 123–124, 149, 282–287, 292–295
Combs, Alex, 255–258, 332–334, 339, 340
community organizing. *See* activism
Compton's Cafeteria uprising, 219–226

Cooper, Mme. Ms. Billie, 310–317
Cowell, Roberta, 146–148, 151, 189
Cox, Laverne, 246–247
Cuerauáperi, 299
Cunningham, Phillipe, 249
Cybele, 31, 33

Davies, Diana Jo, 231, 232, 237
Deir el-Bahari, 29
Denmark, 182–184
d'Éon, Chevalier, 119
Dillon, Michael. *See* Lobzang Jivaka
drag balls, 157–158

Eakett, Andrew, 332–339
Ecuador, 14–17
Edward II, 59
Elagabal (deity), 39
Elagabalus (emperor), 37–49
Elbe, Lili, 133–139
Ellis, Havelock, 119
enchaquirados, 16–17
England, 56–59, 140–149, 151, 218
Erauso, Antonio de, 78–85, 278
Erickson, Reed, 196–203, 227
eugenics, 116–118, 128
eunuchs, 34–35, 64
Europe
  "Age of Discovery," 72–85 (*see also* colonialism)
  ancient, 18–22
  early modern, 60–85
  medieval, 52–59
  See also specific countries

Feinberg, Leslie, 243, 262–263
Fiji, 6, 282–287
Finkel, Irving, 10
Forbes, Ewan, 207
Fox, Fallon, 246
France, 97–103

gala, 10–12
galli, 30–34
Gates, Henry Louis Jr., 160
Germany, 122–131, 190, 226
Gillies, Harold, 144
gods/goddesses, 10, 25–27, 33, 39
Griffin-Gracy, Miss Major, 245

Haefele-Thomas, Ardel, 276–281
Hamburger, Christian, 183
Hatshepsut Maatkare, 20–29
Hierocles, 44, 48
hijra, 319–325
Hirschfeld, Magnus, 120–132, 190
historical records
  arrest records, 54–59, 61–62, 174–176, 216
  artifacts, 10, 34, 37
  destroyed, 40, 77, 130–131, 283
  statues, 11–15, 21–22, 24, 31, 33
  written records, 16, 18, 21, 23, 25–27, 283 (*see also* autobiographies)
Honduras, 292–295

identification documents, 126–127, 136, 147, 150, 220–221, 226
Inanna/Ishtar, 10–11

372

India, 6, 152–153, 319–325
Indigenous Americans, 14–17, 72–75, 77, 83, 85, 86
  Chumash, 76
  Maya, 294
  Purépecha, 296–301
  Tolupan, 292–295
  Zuni, 87–91
Indigenous Pacific Islanders, 282–287
Inquisitions, 60–71
intersectionality
  Asian, 35, 318–325, 340–352
  Black, 62–71, 158–177, 264–275, 280–281, 288–291, 292–295, 302–309, 310–313
  Chicanx/Latinx, 296–301
  disabled, 296–301, 332–339
  fat, 302–309, 332–339
  Indigenous, 14–17, 75–77, 83, 85, 86–91, 282–287, 292–295, 296–301 (*see also* Indigenous Americans; Indigenous Pacific Islanders)
intersex, 95–103, 104, 146–147, 151, 191, 205, 279, 302–309, 326–331
  intersex defense, 164–165, 175
Ireland, 341, 343
Iwatomo, Kim Coco, 245

Jairo Olaya-Smith, Mason, 168
Jenkins, Andrea, 249
Johnson, Marsha P., 230–237
Jones, Imara, 250, 252
Jorgensen, Christine, 151, 178–189, 311

Joseph, Channing Gerard, 158–159
joyas, 76
Julia Maesa, 47

Khnum, 25–27
Kinsey, Alfred, 194
Krafft-Ebing, Richard von, 110–113
Kruif, Paul de, 181

Lavender Scare, 163, 198
Leggett, Jahni, 302–309
lhamana, 87–91
Lindahl, Hans, 326–331, 341–352
Lobzang Jivaka, 140–153, 189
Los Angeles, 132, 162, 176–177, 296

Maldonado, Lilac, 296–301
Mance, Ajuan, 288–291
marriage, 44–45, 63–70, 127–128, 133–136, 148, 169, 172–176, 187
Massachusetts, 340
McCarthy, Joseph, 163
media coverage, 101, 151, 176, 226, 269–272, 281, 346–347
  at the beginning of the twenty-first century, 244–247
  Christine Jorgensen and, 184–188
  Gladys Bentley and, 162, 164–165
  medical establishment abuse and, 137–138, 189, 204–209, 329–330

examinations, 64–67, 99, 102–103, 173
gender-affirming(-ish) care, 3, 140–142, 144–147, 181–183, 190–195, 198, 203, 206–207, 218, 304–305,
hormone therapy, 125, 141–142, 146, 181–182, 217, 251
medical theories of transness, 68–69, 95–96, 110–116, 119, 121, 194–195, 210–211
surgery, 116, 125, 127, 128, 137–138, 144, 146, 183, 217 (*see also* bodily modification)
trans doctors, 62–71, 130–132, 140–143, 280, 340–348
memoirs. *See* autobiographies
Mesopotamia, 10–12, 19
Mexico, 6, 85, 299
Minton, Bobbie. *See* Bentley, Gladys
Money, John, 205–206
Morgan, Cheryl, 11

New York, 151, 160–162, 179, 228, 230–237, 319
Ní Fhlannagáin, Ellis, 341–352
North Carolina, 252

Pacific Islands, 282–287
Pakistan, 6, 319
Philadelphia, 310
Philip IV of Spain, 84
Pink Moon Midnight Blue. *See* Venarsian, Marie Angel
Playdon, Zoë, 207

Pope Urban VIII, 84
Portugal, 72
Power, Ben, 260–263
Prince, Virginia, 214–218

religion
ancient, 10, 25–29, 30–34, 38–39, 43, 45
Buddhism, 152–153
Christianity, 34, 60–71, 73, 83–84, 99–100, 109, 165, 169, 283–284
Indigenous American, 16, 292–295, 299–300, 304–305
Rhodes, Hilary, 58
Richard II, 59
Richards, Renée, 193
Richter, Dora, 125
Rivera, Sylvia, 230–237
Roberts, Monica, 245, 264–275
Roem, Danica, 249
Rome, ancient, 31–34, 36–49
Rykener, Eleanor, 56–59

San Francisco, 219–227, 235, 312
Semenya, Caster, 280–281
Severus Alexander, 40, 47–48
sexologists, 95–96, 104–154, 189–196. *See also* medical establishment
sexual orientation, 107, 128, 163
categorization of, 107, 112–113, 119, 193–195
in medieval Europe, 52–54

Silimabzuta, 10
Som, Bishakh, 318–325
South America, 6, 14–17, 78–83
South Asia, 319–325
Spain, 61–71, 72, 74
Stevenson, Matilda Coxe, 87–91
Stonewall uprising, 228–235
Stryker, Susan, 5, 157, 213
Sullivan, Lou, 242, 262
Swann, William Dorsey, 158–159
Syria, 38

Takács, Bogi, 98–100
terminology
   culturally specific identities, 6, 17, 35, 282, 296–297, 300, 319
   difficulty finding the right terms, 261, 296, 318, 326–327
   historical terms, 105, 107, 112, 119, 120–121, 202, 205, 262, 311, 326–327
   meanings of *trans*, 4–6
   usage of *transgender*, 217, 294, 311
Texas, 197, 199, 253
Thutmose I, 26
trials, 64–71, 174–177. *See also* anti-trans laws; historical records: arrest records
Trump, Donald, 248, 250
two-spirit, 292–295, 296–301

Ugalde Mora, María Fernanda, 14–17
Ulrichs, Karl Heinrich, 105–108, 121

United States, 86–91, 122–124, 151, 156–254, 310, 327
Ur-Nanshe, 12

vakasalewalewa, 282–287
Valencia, Louie Dean, 79
Venarsian, Marie Angel, 264–275, 292–295
Victoria, BC, Canada, 89
violence against trans people, 129, 234, 236, 252–253, 267–270, 312
   in ancient times, 38, 48
   in Indigenous communities, 75
   by police, 126, 158, 219, 223–225, 228
   and suicide, 102, 340
   See also Inquisitions; medical establishment: abuse and

Waqa, Sulique, 282–287
Warnekros, Kurt, 137–139
Washington, DC, 87–91
Watters, Dee Dee, 264–275
Watts, Jaye C., 200
We'wha, 87–91
Wegener, Gerda Gottlieb, 133–135, 139
Wong, Rose, 340–352

Zhou, Bright, 341–352

Dedicated to the archivists, historians, researchers, journalists, photographers, writers, and artists who have kept trans history alive

Copyright © 2025 by Alex L. Combs and Andrew Eakett
Lettering by Tif Bucknor

All rights reserved. No part of this book may be reproduced, transmitted, or stored in an information retrieval system in any form or by any means, graphic, electronic, or mechanical, including photocopying, taping, and recording, without prior written permission from the publisher.

First edition 2025

Library of Congress Catalog Card Number pending
ISBN 978-1-5362-1923-4 (hardcover)
ISBN 978-1-5362-4417-5 (paperback)

25 26 27 28 29 30 TTP 10 9 8 7 6 5 4 3 2 1

Printed in Huizhou, Guangdong, China

This book was typeset in Alex Font.
The illustrations were created using traditional and digital methods.

Candlewick Press
99 Dover Street
Somerville, Massachusetts 02144

www.candlewick.com

EU Authorized Representative: HackettFlynn Ltd., 36 Cloch Choirneal, Balrothery, Co. Dublin, K32 C942, Ireland. EU@walkerpublishinggroup.com